ROADWATCH

Wherever you're driving, call AA Roadwatch for the latest reports on roadworks and weather. Information is regularly updated throughout the day and night. Save yourself time and frustration— phone before you go . . .

NATIONAL ROADWORKS AND WEATHER

National motorways		0836-401-110
1.	West Country	0836-401-111
2.	Wales	0836-401-112
3.	Midlands	0836-401-113
4.	East Anglia	0836-401-114
5.	North-west England	0836-401-115
6.	North-east England	0836-401-116
7.	Scotland	0836-401-117
8.	Northern Ireland	0836-401-118
9.	South-east England	see below

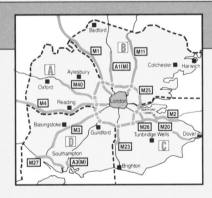

LONDON AND THE SOUTH-EAST— TRAFFIC, ROADWORKS AND WEATHER

	Central London (inside North/South Circulars)	0836-401-122
A.	Motorways/roads between M4 and M1	0836-401-123
B.	Motorways/roads between M1 and Dartford Tunnel	0836-401-124
C.	Motorways/roads between Dartford Tunnel and M23	0836-401-125
D.	Motorways/roads between M23 and M4	0836-401-126
	M25 London Orbital only	0836-401-127
	London special events (certain weekends only)	0836-401-128

ROADWATCH

Messages are charged at a rate of 25p per minute cheap rate, 38p per minute at all other times.
Callers pay only for the time they use.

FOR YOUR FREE COPY OF THE FULL AA DIRECTORY OF RECORDED INFORMATION WRITE TO
AA INFORMATION SERVICES (DEPT BRA) CWI, FANUM HOUSE, BASINGSTOKE, HANTS RG21 2EA.

AA

COMPLETE ATLAS OF BRITAIN

12th edition October 1989
11th edition October 1988
10th edition October 1987
9th edition October 1986
Reprinted March 1987
8th edition October 1985
7th edition October 1984
Reprinted May 1985
6th edition March 1984
5th edition January 1983
4th edition October 1981
3rd edition January 1981
2nd edition January 1980
1st edition April 1979

Published by The Automobile Association, Fanum House, Basingstoke, Hampshire RG21 2EA.
ISBN 07495 0001 8

Printed in Spain by Artes Gráficas Toledo, S.A.
D.L.TO:996–1989

The contents of this book are believed correct at the time of printing. Nevertheless, the publisher can accept no responsibility for errors or omissions, or for changes in the details given.

Mapping produced by the Cartographic Department of The Automobile Association. This atlas has been compiled and produced from the Automaps database utilising electronic and computer technology.

The London section is based on Ordnance Survey maps with the permission of the Controller of Her Majesty's Stationery Office. Crown copyright.

Every effort has been made to ensure that the contents of our new database are correct. However, if there are any errors or omissions, please write to the Cartographic Editor, Publishing Division, The Automobile Association, Fanum House, Basingstoke, Hampshire RG21 2EA.

A CIP catalogue record for this book is available from the British Library.

Contents

U*sing* *this atlas*

Whether you wish to trace the route of the M4 from London to South Wales, find the most direct route from Ipswich to Liverpool, pick your way round Coventry, or need to solve any other journey planning problem the Complete Atlas of Britain is an essential guide.

ROUTE PLANNING
Specially designed route planning maps, showing a basic road network of motorways, primary routes and most A roads, help you plan long distance journeys quickly and easily.

ATLAS
Clear, easy-to-read mapping helps you to plan more detailed journeys, and provides a wealth of information for the motorist. All motorways, primary, A and B roads and unclassified roads are shown. The atlas also identifies those roads outside urban areas which are under construction. Additional features include rivers, lakes and reservoirs, railway lines, interesting places to visit, picnic sites and Tourist Information Centres, and to assist you in estimating journey length, distances are shown in miles between blue marker symbols.

Motorway   Primary routes
A road
Oakham
LEICESTER
NCKLEY
TON   Uppingham
Market
Harborough
RY   KETTERING
CORBY
NORTHAMPT

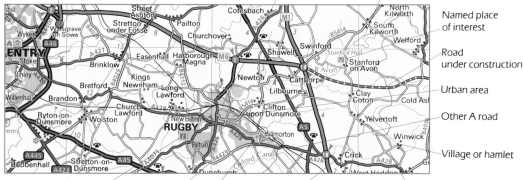

Motorways and junctions   Primary route   Railway   Reservoir or large water feature
Named place of interest
Road under construction
Urban area
Other A road
Village or hamlet
Tourist Information Centre   B road   Mileage   River   Unclassified road

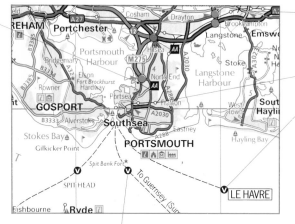

AA Port Service Centre
Level crossing
Railway station
Continental ferry routes

FERRY AND RAIL ROUTES
Coastal stretches of mapping provide basic off-shore information including ferry routes within Great Britain and to the Continent, to assist you in planning journeys overseas. Throughout the atlas, railway lines with stations and level crossings are shown, to assist with general navigation or rail travel requirements.

Local ferry route

MOTORWAYS
The principal motorway maps, arranged in easy-to-follow strip form, highlight junctions, exit signs, service areas, and access on and off the motorway.

Tourist attraction within urban area
Long distance footpath marked
Place of interest located and named

TOURISM AND LEISURE
Red pictorial symbols and red type, highlight numerous places of interest, catering for every taste. Red symbols within yellow boxes show tourist attractions in towns. Use them to plan days out or places to visit on holiday. Remember to check opening times before you visit to avoid disappointment.

AA viewpoint

Tourist Information Centre

Restricted junction
Motorway service area
Numbered junction (unrestricted access)
Access roads on and off the motorway
Junction layout
Signposts as seen from the motorway

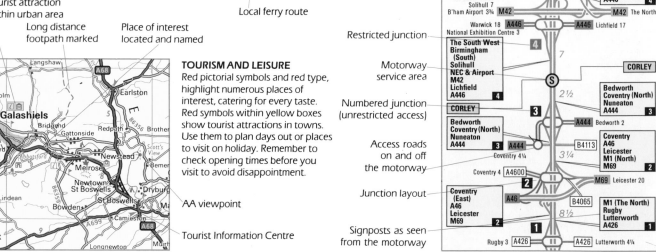

PORTS AND AIRPORTS

Maps show the major Channel and east coast ports, plus detailed maps of the main airports in Britain, giving approach roads as well as car parking facilities, and information about garages, hotels and public transport services. The map on page 119 locates *all* British ports and airports.

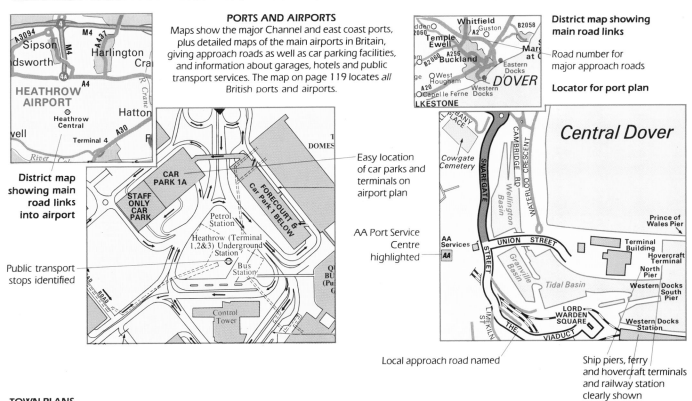

District map showing main road links into airport

Public transport stops identified

Easy location of car parks and terminals on airport plan

AA Port Service Centre highlighted

District map showing main road links

Road number for major approach roads

Locator for port plan

Local approach road named

Ship piers, ferry and hovercraft terminals and railway station clearly shown

TOWN PLANS

Up-to-date, fully-indexed town plans show AA recommended roads and other practical information such as one way streets, car parks and restricted roads, making navigation much easier. Area plans show major road networks into and out of the region.

Area map showing main road links and neighbouring towns

Locator for town plan

AA recommended throughroutes clearly identified

Town parking facilities

Major buildings and places of interest highlighted and named

Street index with every plan

Aberdeen

Abbotsford Lane	C2-D2
Academy Street	C4-D4
Advocates Road	E8
Affleck Street	D3
Albert Quay	E3-F3
Albert Place	A5-A6
Albert Street	A4-A5
Albert Terrace	A4-A5
Albury Place	B2-C2
Albury Road	B2-C2-C3
Albyn Grove	A4

Churches located

Pedestrian areas located

One way streets shown

LONDON

Easy-to-read, fully-indexed street maps of Inner London, including a map of Theatreland, provide a simple guide to finding your way around the city.

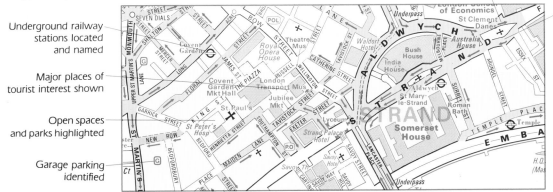

Underground railway stations located and named

Major places of tourist interest shown

Open spaces and parks highlighted

Garage parking identified

One way systems clearly shown

AA recommended routes for easier navigation

Alphabetical street index

Tudor St EC4	184	M
Tufton St SW1	188	H
Turk's Row SW3	187	K
Turnmill St EC1	184	F
Turpentine Ln SW1	187	L
Turquand St SE17	200	G
Tyers St SE11	188	M
Tyer's Ter SE11	188	M
Tysoe St EC1	184	B
Udall St SW1	188	G
Ufford St SE1	189	E
Ulster Pl NW1	182	F
Union St SE1	189	D
University St WC1	183	D

Signs and symbols

To assist you in journey planning and making the most of the comprehensive information contained in this atlas, it helps if you understand the signs on the roads and the symbols used on the maps. The principal benefit of the Department of Transport road signs is that the primary road signs (green) indicate the most straightforward route between one town and another. They do not necessarily indicate the most *direct* route, but it should be remembered that direct routes may not be the quickest, or the easiest to follow.

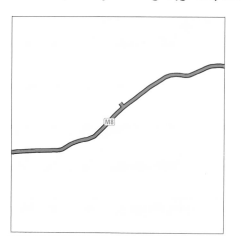

MOTORWAYS

On the map – all motorways are blue. Motorway signposts have white lettering on a blue background. Advance direction signs approaching an interchange generally include the junction number in a black box. On the map, the junction number appears in white on a solid *blue* circle.

A white number on a solid *red* circle indicates restricted access on or off the motorway at that point.

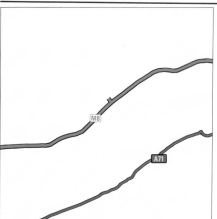

PRIMARY ROUTES

On the map – all the primary routes are green. The signposts on primary roads are also green, with white lettering and yellow numbers. Apart from the motorways, primary routes are the most important traffic routes in both urban and rural areas. They form a network of throughroutes connecting 'primary towns', which are generally places of traffic importance. Primary routes are usually along A roads.

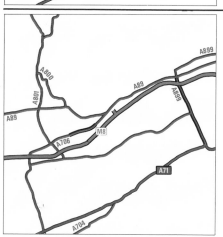

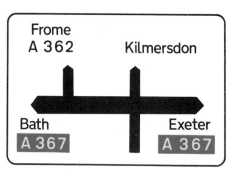

A ROADS

On the map – all A roads are shown in red, unless part of the primary network when they are green. The signposts along these roads have black lettering on a white background. At a junction with a primary route, the primary road number appears yellow in a green box.

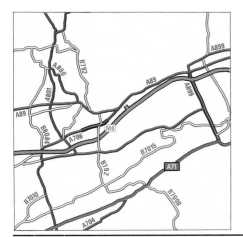

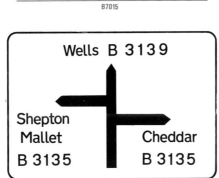

B ROADS
On the map – all B roads not in the primary network are represented in yellow. The signs on B roads are black lettering on a white background, the same as for A roads.

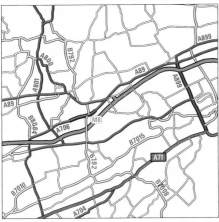

UNCLASSIFIED ROADS
On the map – all unclassified (unnumbered) roads are white. New signposts along unclassified roads are usually of the 'local direction' type. These have black lettering on a white background with a blue border. Many minor roads still have pre-World War II 'finger' post signs.

PLACE NAMES
Throughout the atlas, the size of lettering and its style is an indication of the size and importance of a place or location. This is generally related to population. All places with over 3,000 inhabitants are shown, plus there is a selection of smaller locations which are useful navigation points or possible destinations in some of the more isolated rural areas.

The section of map below highlights the various population categories and explains the difference in the size and style of lettering. The name London is a special category as it has a population in excess of 8 million.

Stourbridge
Places with this style and size of lettering include major towns and cities with populations between 50,000 and 200,000.

Chaddesley Corbett
This style and size of lettering is used to show villages and hamlets with less than 3,000 inhabitants. In isolated rural areas in the north a selection of crossroads and farms are shown in slightly smaller lettering – Auchnotteroch

Bromsgrove
Metropolitan Districts, larger market and developing towns with populations between 10,000 and 50,000 are indicated by this size and style of lettering.

Birmingham
Places using this style and size of lettering indicate cities and very large towns with populations between 200,000 and 500,000.

King's Norton
This style and size of lettering is used to show suburban locations within large urban areas. Their population size is included within the 200,000 and 500,000 category.

Alvechurch
Locations shown in this style and size of lettering are generally small market towns or developing communities situated on the fringes of large urban areas. Their populations vary between 3,000 and 10,000 inhabitants.

Journey planning

Whether you are planning a journey for business or for pleasure, the Complete Atlas will make it much easier. A little preparation can save valuable time.

Alertness

If you are planning a long journey, or just going out for the day, it is essential you set out feeling alert and confident. Tired, frustrated drivers are a potential danger to themselves, to their passengers and to other road users. You will feel more capable of dealing with unexpected situations, and have a more comfortable journey if you plan ahead.

CHECK LIST

On long journeys, in particular, it pays to make a check list of thing to do, even down to cancelling the milk and papers, taking the dog to the kennels, making sandwiches and a thermos, checking the roof rack and locking the door. We all forget something at some time or other! Have you never set off without having to stop just a few miles from home to wonder if you had remembered to turn the gas off?

PREPARATION
How to get there

The special route planning maps will help you to plan a basic route, and the atlas will enable you to make a more detailed one. (Taking a note of road numbers, towns and directions is useful, as this reduces the need to consult the atlas on the way.)

Distance and time

One of the fundamental considerations to be taken into account when planning any journey is how far it is. The mileage chart on the inside back cover will help you estimate the distance and this in turn can help you calculate your journey time. On the atlas, distances between places are indicated as blue numbers between blue arrowheads eg. ◀ 12 ▶ Do not forget to allow extra time for peak hours and holiday weekends.

Motorways

Despite ever-increasing traffic, motorways are still the quickest and most efficient means of travelling across the country. The map on page 108 gives an overall picture of the system, while pages 109 to 118 show the principal motorways.

A Roads

London is the hub for the spokes of roads numbered A1 to A6, and Edinburgh is the hub for the A7, A8 and A9.

Starting with the A1 running north from London, the roads radiate clockwise: the A2 runs generally east, the A3 south-west etc. This system has made the numbering of other roads very simple. Generally, the lower the subsequent number, the closer the road's starting point to London – similarly to Edinburgh.

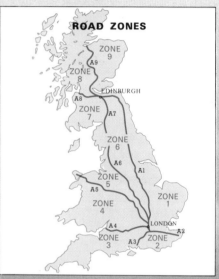

ROAD ZONES

DELAYS AND HOLD-UPS
Radio
Frequent radio bulletins are issued by the BBC and Independent Local radio stations on road conditions, possible hold-ups etc, and these can be of great assistance. By tuning in to the local stations as you pass through the area, you can avoid delays, and prepare yourself to make changes to your route. However, local radio does not yet cover the entire country. For radio frequencies consult the map on the inside back cover.

AA Roadwatch
However, if you require this information *before* setting out, you can call AA Roadwatch. This service provides information (updated every 15 minutes) on major roadworks and weather conditions for the whole country, and can be used as part of your basic journey planning. (See inside front cover.)

Getting the most out of the maps
The mapping contains a wide range of practical information for the motorist. Not only does it show the existing road network, but it also shows new roads which are due to be opened shortly or within approximately the next 12 months. It even indicates where A and B roads are very narrow in the Scottish Highlands. Passing bays are usually provided on these roads at regular intervals.

In addition you can use the atlas to plan trips and days out. Look for the special red tourist symbols and red names. The attractions highlighted in this way range from the cultural and historic – abbeys, museums, stately homes, to the sporting – cricket, golf, gliding, horseracing, and include Tourist Information Centres and AA viewpoints.

You can find any place listed in the index by using the National Grid, which is explained in simple terms below.

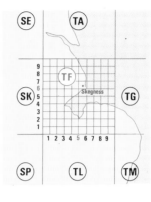

FINDING YOUR PLACE
One of the unique features of AA mapping is the use of the National Grid system.

It covers Britain with an imaginary network of squares, using blue horizontal lines called northings and vertical lines called eastings.

On the atlas pages these lines are numbered along the bottom and up the left hand side.

Each entry in the index is followed by a page number, two letters denoting an area on the map and a 4-figure grid reference. You will not need to use the two letters for simple navigation, but they come in useful if you want to use your map in relation to the rest of the country and other map series.

For quick reference, the 4 figures of the grid reference in the index are arranged so that the 1st and 3rd are larger in size than the 2nd and 4th.

The 1st figure shows which number along the bottom to locate, and the 3rd figure, which number up the left hand side. These will indicate the square in which you will find the place name. However, to pinpoint a place more accurately, you use the 2nd and 4th numbers also. The 2nd will tell you how many imaginary tenths along the bottom line to go from the 1st number, and the 4th will tell you how many tenths up the line to go from the 3rd number.

Where these two lines intersect, you will locate your place. Eg Skegness 51 TF 5663. Skegness is located on page 51, within grid square 56, in National Grid square TF. Its exact location is 5663.

If you find you get the numbers confused, it might help if you can imagine entering a house, walking in the door and along a corridor first, and then going up the stairs, then you will remember how to get them in the correct order.

Routeplanner

The Complete Atlas of Britain combines superb mapping with accurate and practical routefinding information which are designed to help you complete a journey as quickly and easily as possible.

PLANNING YOUR ROUTE

The route planning maps on the following pages are an invaluable guide when deciding on a *general route*.

These maps show the principal routes throughout the country and you can use them to plan a *basic route*.

Look for the name of your destination in the index section at the back of the book. The entry is followed by an atlas page number and a National Grid reference.

Turn to the atlas page indicated and use the grid reference to pinpoint the place (see page   for an explanation of how to use the reference).

When you have located it, find the nearest place to it shown on the routeplanner maps.

In the same way, by locating the nearest place to your start point, you can plot the route between the two.

A more detailed route can be worked out from studying the main atlas.

Remember to take a note of road numbers and directions, then you will not need to stop to use the atlas while on the journey.

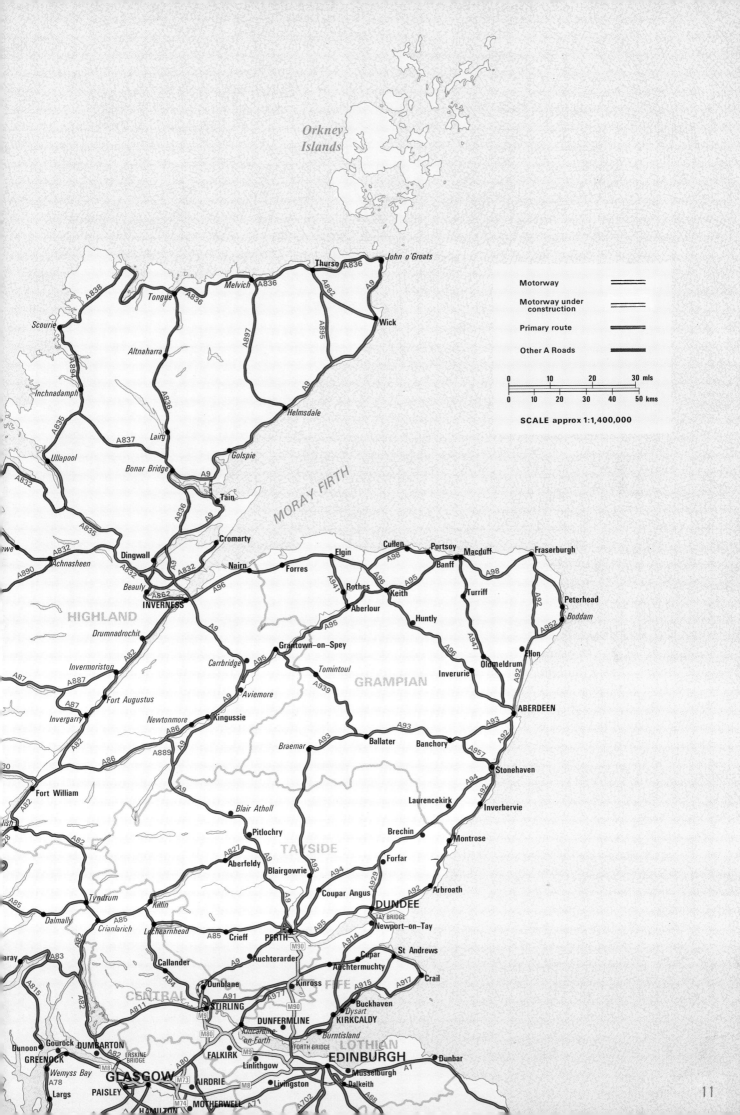

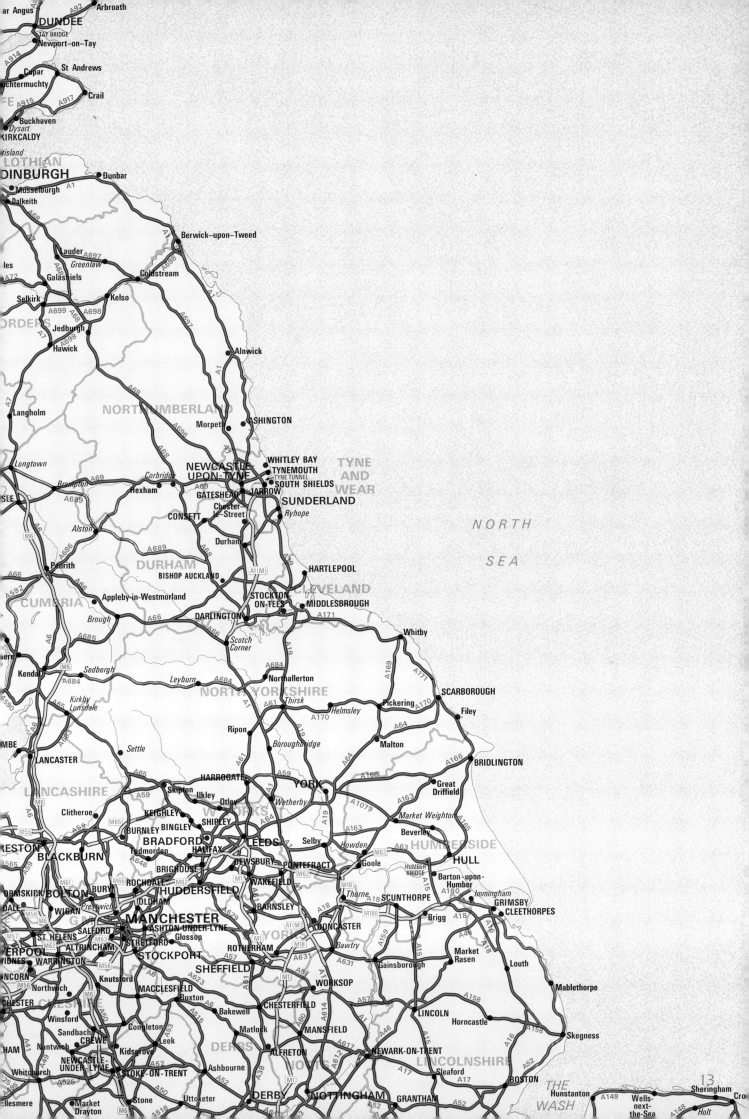

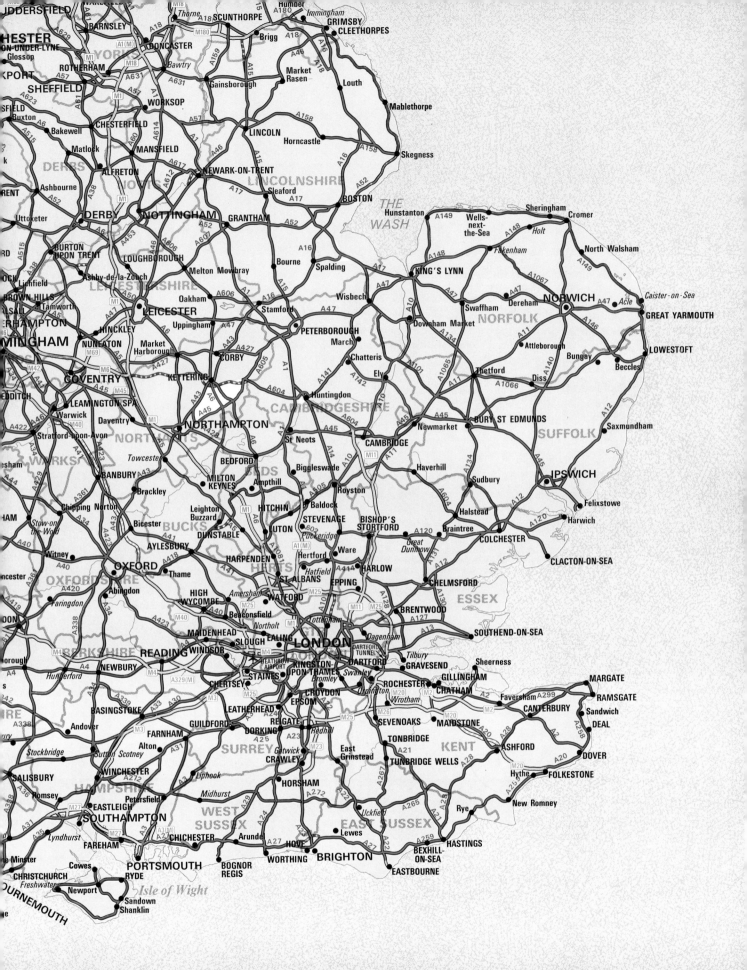

Map symbols

MOTORING INFORMATION : VERKEHRSINFORMATIONEN : INFORMATIONS ROUTIERES		TOURIST INFORMATION : FREMDENVERKEHR : RENSEIGNEMENTS TOURISTIQUES	
M4 Motorway with number / Autobahn mit Nummer / Autoroute avec numéro	**V** Vehicle ferry – Great Britain / Autofähre – Inland / Bac pour automobiles en Grande Bretagne	Tourist Information Centre / Informationsbüro / Syndicat d'initiative	Hill fort / Prähistorische Festungsanlage / Colline fortifiée
Motorway junction with and without number / Anschlußstelle mit/ohne Nummer / Echangeur avec/sans numéro	**CHERBOURG V** Vehicle ferry – Continental / Autofähre – Ausland / Bac pour automobile – à l'étranger	Tourist Information Centre (summer only) / Informationsbüro (nur im Sommer) / Syndicat d'initiative (seulement en été)	Roman antiquity / Überreste aus der Römerzeit / Antiquités romaines
3 Motorway junction with limited access / Anschlußstelle mit beschränkter Auf- bzw. Abfahrt / Echangeur partiel	**H** Hovercraft ferry / Luftkissenfähre / Aéroglisseur	Abbey, cathedral or priory / Abtei, Dom, Kloster / Abbaye, cathédrale, prieuré	Prehistoric monument / Prähistorisches Monument / Monument préhistorique
S Motorway service area / Tanken und Rasten / Aire de Service	Airport / Flughafen / Aéroport	Ruined abbey, cathedral or priory / Abtei-, Dom-, Klosterruine / Abbaye, cathédrale, prieuré en ruines	Battle site with year / Schlachtfeld mit Datum / Champ de bataille et Date
Motorway and junction under construction / Autobahn und Anschlußstelle im Bau / Autoroute et échangeur en construction	**H** Heliport / Hubschrauberlandungsplatz / Héliport	Castle / Schloss/Burg / Château	Preserved railway/steam centre / Museumbahn/Dampflokomotivmuseum / Chemin de fer touristique/musée de la vapeur
A4 Primary route single/dual carriageway / Hauptverbindungsstraße 1 Fahrspur/2 Fahrspuren / Route principale 1 voie/2 voies	Railway line/in tunnel / Bahnlinie/im Tunnel / Voie ferrée/sous tunnel	Historic house / Historisches Gebäude / Edifice d'intérêt historique	Cave / Höhle / Grotte
A1123 Other A road single/dual carriageway / Andere Straße der Klasse A 1 Fahrspur/2 Fahrspuren / Autre route catégorie A 1 voie/2 voies	Railway station and level crossing / Bahnhof und Bahnübergang / Gare et passage à niveau	Museum or art gallery / Museum/Kunstgalerie / Musée/galerie d'art	Windmill / Windmühle / Moulin à vent
B2070 B road single/dual carriageway / Straße der Klasse B 1 Fahrspur/2 Fahrspuren / Route catégorie B 1 voie/2 voies	**AA** AA Centre – full services / AA-Hauptdienststelle / Centre AA principal	Industrial interest / Von industriellem Interesse / De l'intérêt industriel	AA viewpoint / AA-Aussichtspunkt / AA-Panorama
Unclassified road, single/dual carriageway / Nicht klassifizierte Straße 1 Fahrspur/2 Fahrspuren / Route non classifiée 1 voie/2 voies	**AA** AA Road Service Centre – limited services / AA-Straßendienststelle – beschränkte Dienstleistungen / Centre-service routier auxiliare	Garden / Gartenanlage / Jardin	Picnic site / Picknickplatz / Lieu pour pique-nique
Road under construction / Straße im Bau / Route en construction	**AA** AA Port Services – open as season demands / AA-Hafendienststelle – Öffnungszeiten von Jahreszeit abhängig / AA Centre-service de port – heures d'ouvertures varient selon la saison	Arboretum / Arboretum / Arboretum	Golf course / Golfplatz / Golf
Narrow primary, other A or B road with passing places (Scotland) / enge Hauptverbindungsstraße, 'A' bzw. 'B' Straße mit Ausweichstellen (in Schottland) / Route principale étroite/autre route catégorie A ou B étroite avec places d'évitement (en Ecosse)	AA and RAC telephones / AA bzw. RAC-Telefon / Téléphone AA et RAC	Country park / Park auf dem Lande / Parc promenade	County cricket ground / wichtiger Kricketspielplatz / Terrain de cricket important
Road tunnel / Straßentunnel / Tunnel routier	BT telephone in isolated places / Öffentliche Telefonzelle in abgelegenen Gebieten / Téléphone PTT aux endroits isolés	Theme park / Freizeitpark / Parc d'attractions	Horse racing / Pferderennbahn / Hippodrome
Steep gradient (arrows point downhill) / Steigung/Gefälle (Pfeile weisen bergab) / Montée/Descente (à la flèche dirigée vers le bas)	Urban area/village / Stadtgebiet/Dorf / Agglomération/Village	Zoo / Tiergarten / Zoo	Show jumping/equestrian circuit / Reit-und Springturnier / Saut d'obstacles/circuit equestre
Toll Road toll / Straße mit Gebühr / Route à péage	628 ▲ Spot height in metres / Höhenangabe in Meters / Altitude en mètres	Wildlife collection – mammals / Tierpark – Säugetiere / Réserve d'animaux sauvages/mammifères	Motor racing circuit / Autorennen / Courses automobiles
5 Distance in miles between symbols / Entfernungen in Meilen zwischen Zeichen / Distance en milles entre symboles	River, canal, lake / Fluss, Kanal, See / Fleuve, canal, lac	Wildlife collection – birds / Tierpark – Vögel / Réserve Ornithologique	Gliding centre / Segelflugplatz / Centre de vol à voile
	Sandy beach / Sandstrand / Plage de sable	Aquarium / Aquarium / Aquarium	Coastal launching site / Slipanlage für Boote / Air de mise à l'eau
	National boundary / Landesgrenze / Frontière nationale	Nature reserve / Naturschutzgebiet / Réserve naturelle	Ski slope – natural / Skigelände / Piste de ski
	88 Page overlap and number / Hinweiszahlen für die Anschlußkarten / Suite à la page indiquée	Nature trail / Naturlehrpfad / Sentier de découverte de la nature	Ski slope – artificial / Skigelände – künstlich / Piste de ski artificielle
		Forest drive / Waldstraße / Route forestière	Other places of interest / ★ Weitere Sehenswürdigkeiten / Autres curiosités
		Long distance footpath / Fernwanderweg / Sentier de grande randonnée	Boxed symbols indicate attractions within urban areas / Das Einrahmen eines Zeichens bedeutet: die Sehenswürdigkeit befindet sich in einem Stadtgebiet / Dans le cas où le symbole est dans une case, la curiosité se trouve dans une localité

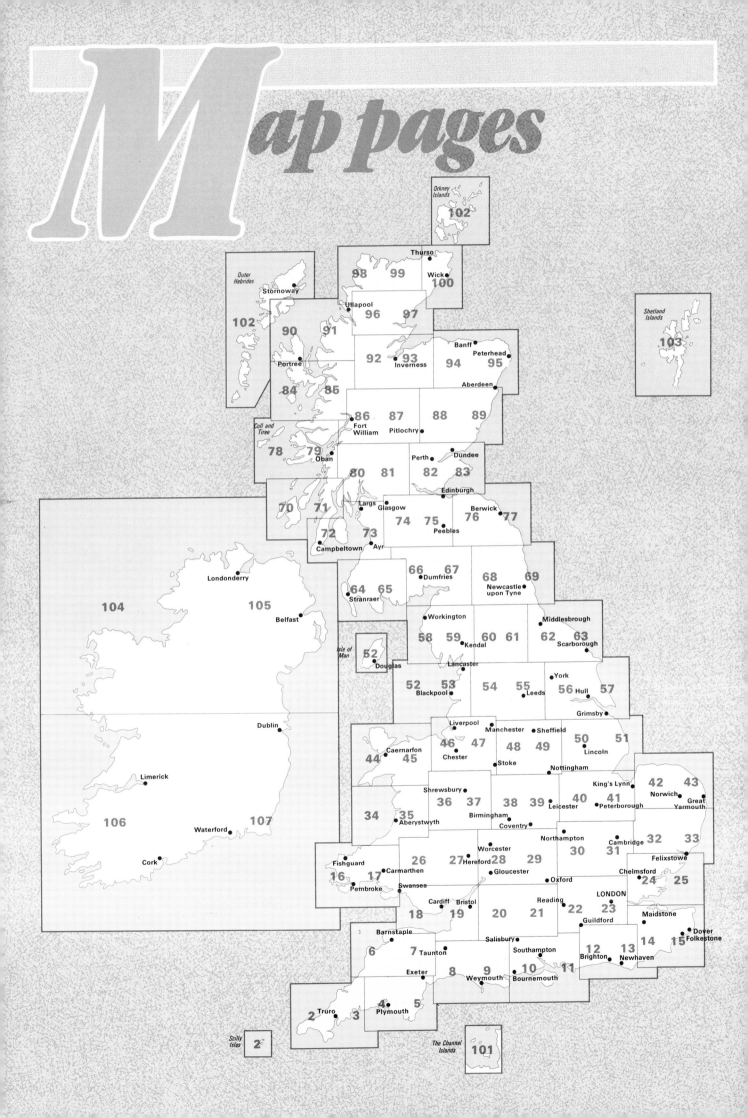

Map pages

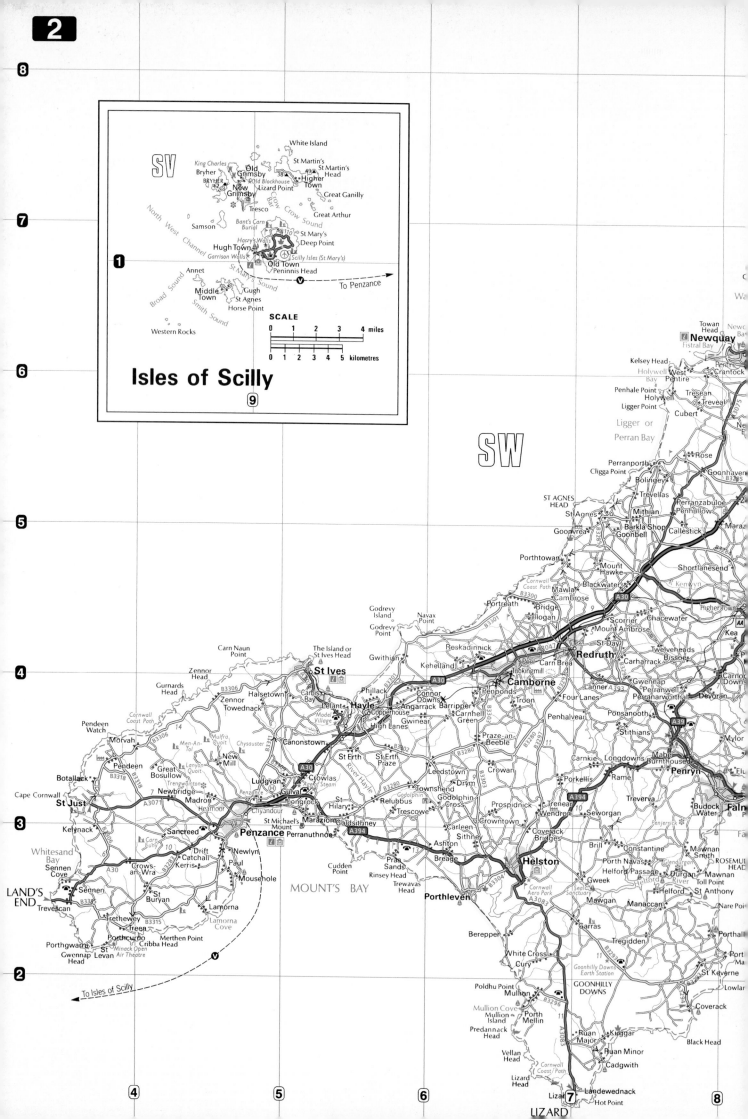

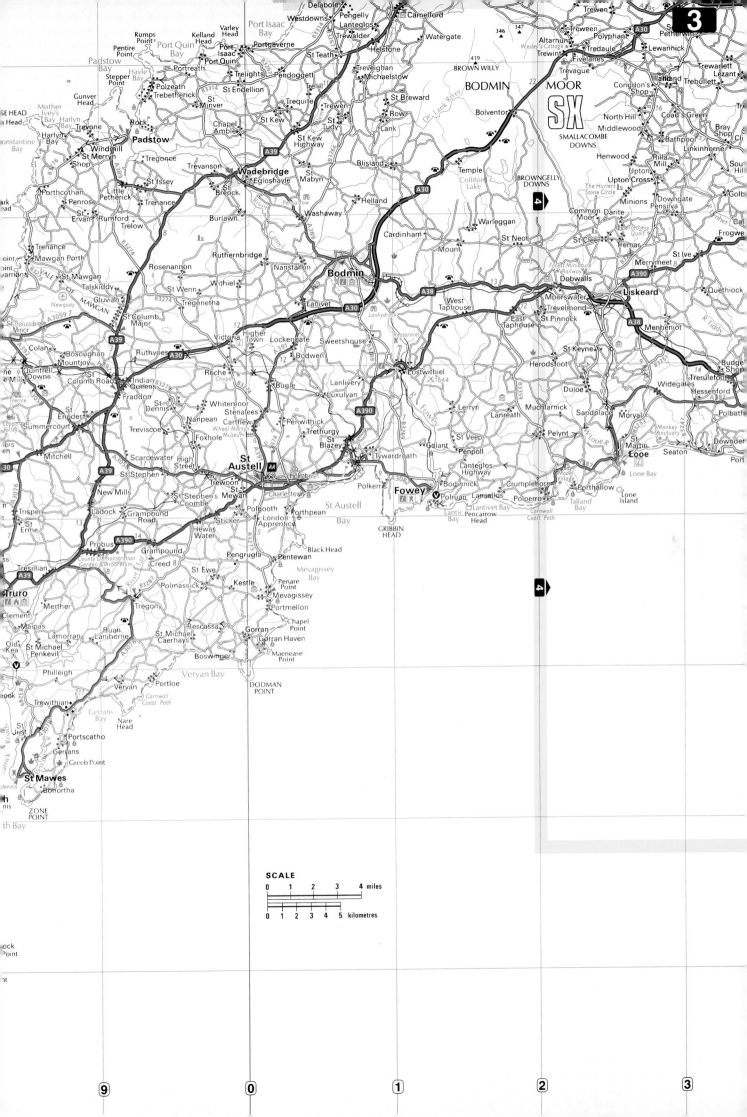

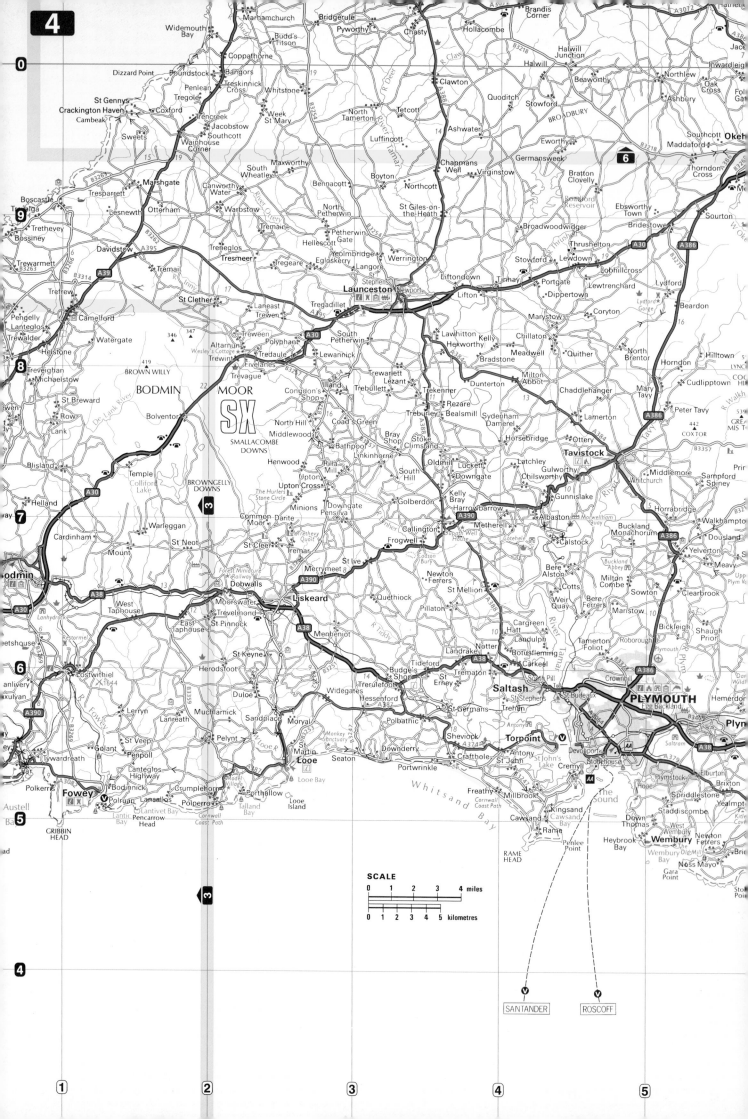

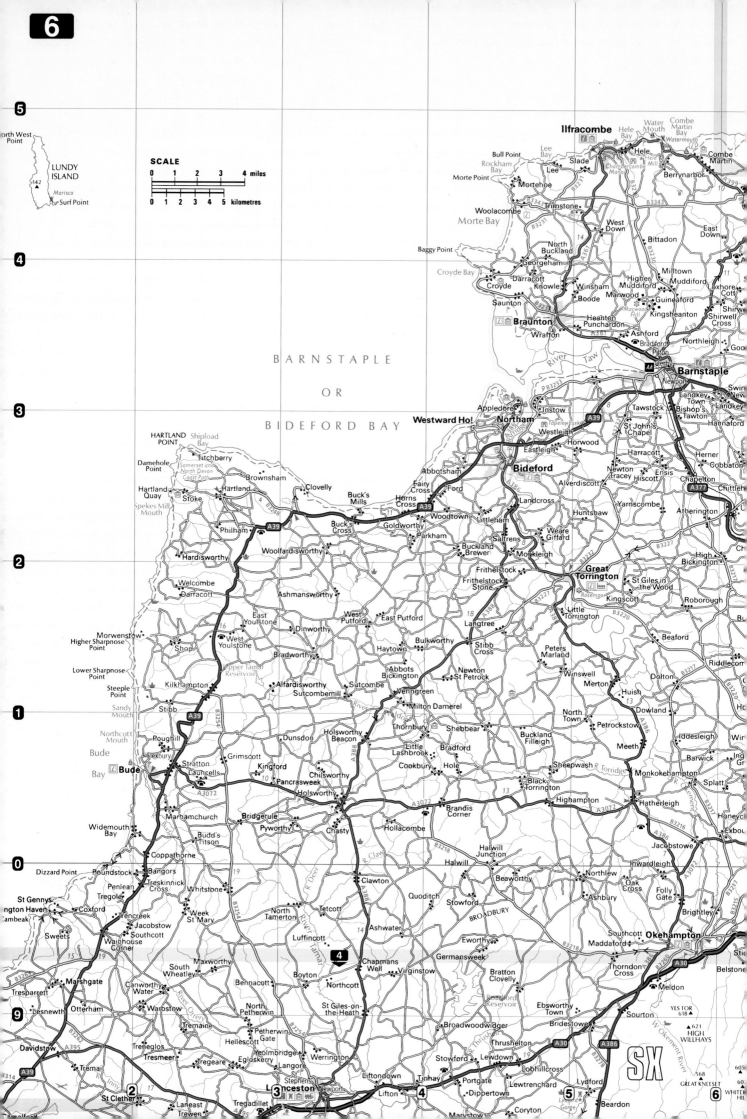

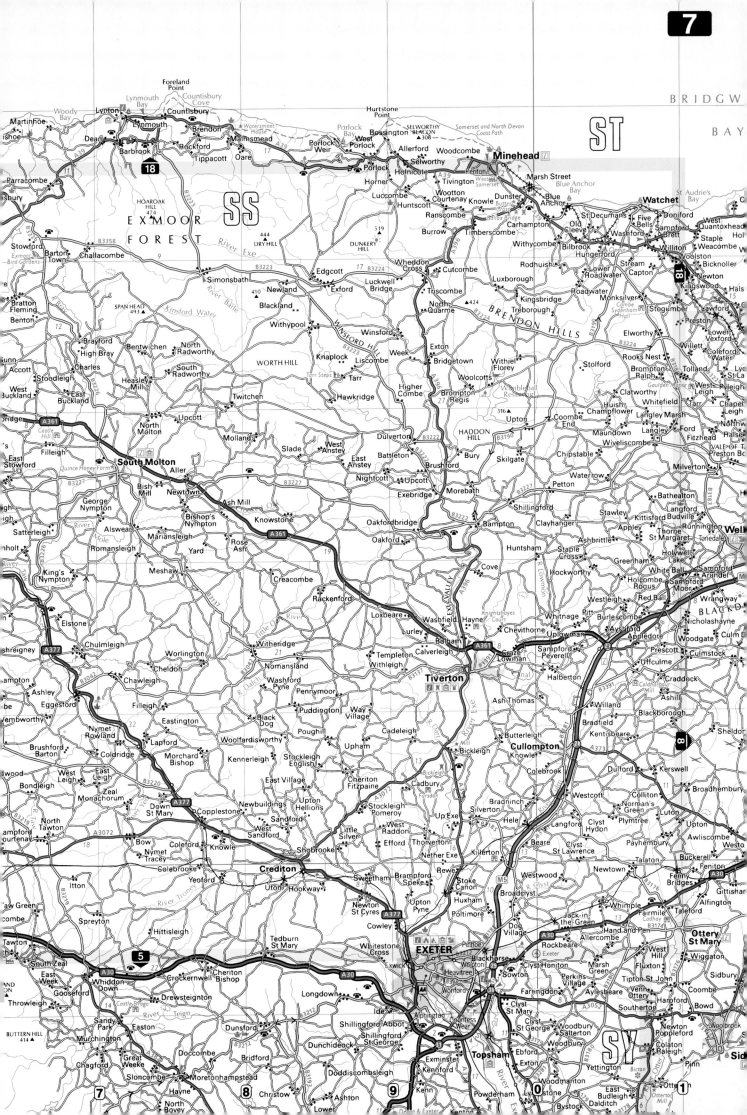

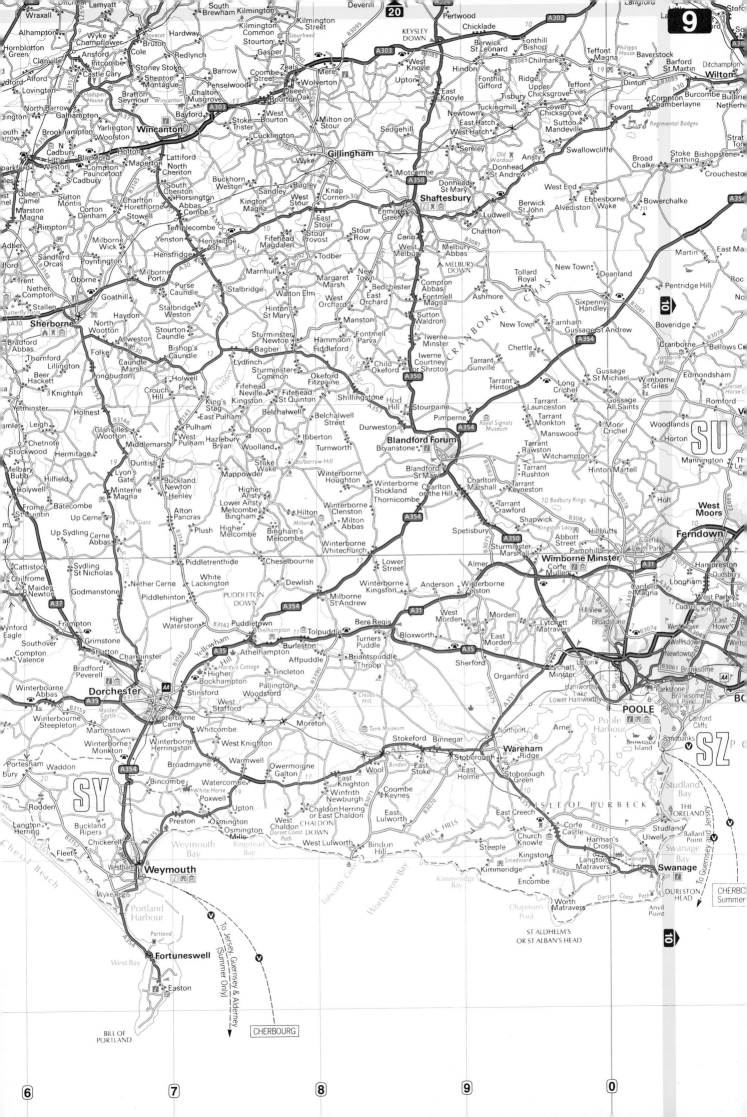

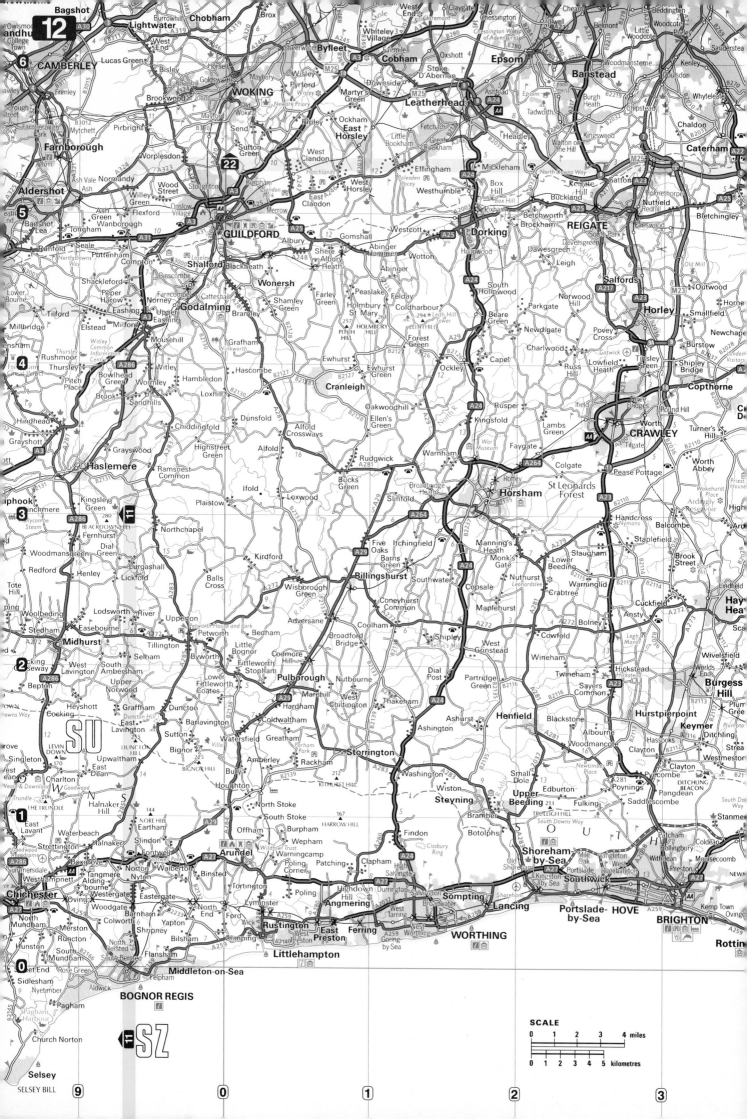

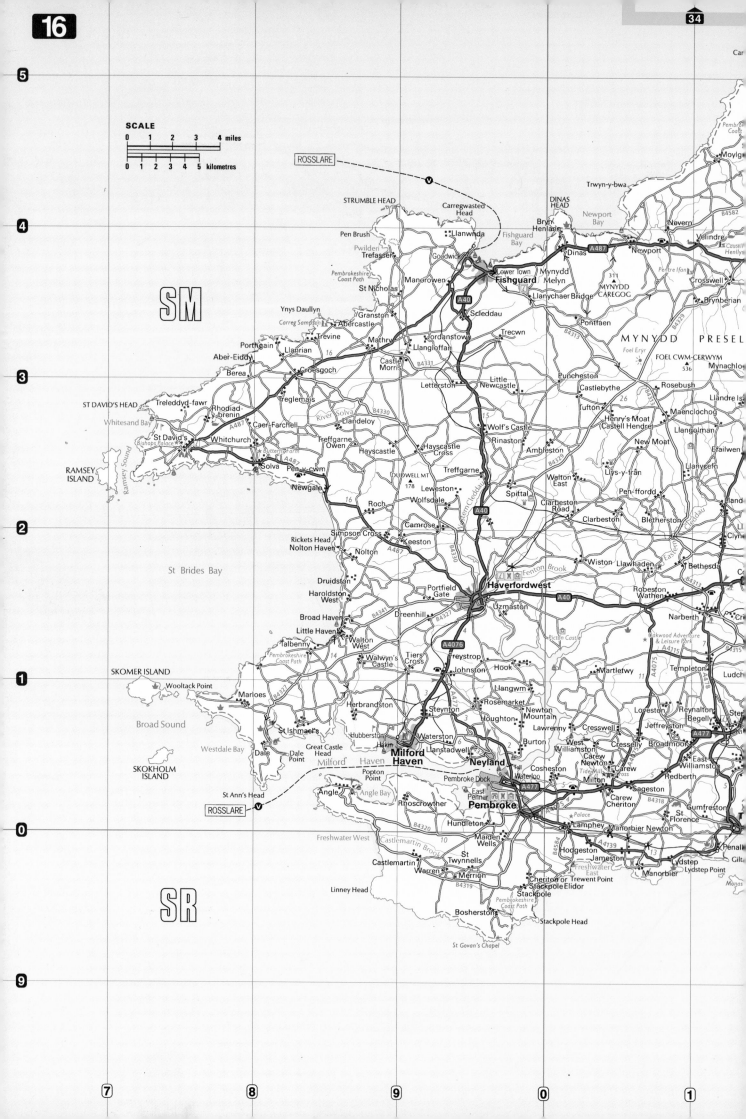

SCALE
0   1   2   3   4 miles
0 1 2 3 4 5 kilometres

SM

SR

ROSSLARE

STRUMBLE HEAD
Carregwasted Head
DINAS HEAD
Newport Bay
Trwyn-y-bwa

Pen Brush
Llanwnda
Fishguard Bay
Bryn Henllan
Dinas
A487
Newport
Nevern
Velindre
Moylg

Pwilderi
Trefasser
Goodwick
Lower Town
Mynydd Melyn
Crosswell

Manorowen
Fishguard
Llanychaer Bridge
MYNYDD CAREGOG
Pentre Ifan
Brynberian

St Nicholas
Scleddau
311
Pembrokeshire Coast Path

Ynys Daullyn
Granston
Jordanstown
Trecwn
Foel Eryr
MYNYDD PRESEL

Carreg Sampson
Abercastle
Mathry
Llangloffan
FOEL CWM-CERWYM
Mynachlo

Trevine
Castle Morris
536

Porthgain
Llanrian
16
B4331
Letterston
Little Newcastle
Puncheston
Castlebythe
Rosebush
Llàndre Is

Aber-Eiddy
Treglemais
Croesgoch
B4330
Tufton
26
B4313
Maenclochog

Berea
Wolf's Castle
Henry's Moat (Castell Hendre)
Llangolman

ST DAVID'S HEAD
Treleddyd-fawr
Rhodiad-y-brenin
River Solva
Llandeloy
15
Rinaston
Ambleston
New Moat
Efailwen

Whitesand Bay
Caer-Farchell
Treffgarne Owen
Hayscastle
Hayscastle Cross
B4329
Llanycefn

St David's
Whitchurch
Treffgarne
Walton East
Llys-y-frân
Llancland

RAMSEY ISLAND
Bishops Palace
Solva
Pen-y-cwm
DUDWELL MT
178
Lewiston
Spittal
Clarbeston Road
Pen-ffordd

Newgale
Roch
Wolfsdale
A40
Clarbeston
Bletherston

St David's Head
16
Camrose
Clyn

St Brides Bay
Simpson Cross
Keeston
B4330
Wiston
Llawhaden
Bethesda

Rickets Head
Nolton Haven
Nolton
A487
Fenton Brook
Robeston Wathen

Druidston
Haverfordwest
A40
Narberth
Cr

Haroldston West
Portfield Gate
Uzmaston
Picton Castle
Oakwood Adventure & Leisure Park
A4075
A4115

Broad Haven
Dreenhill
B4327
A4076
Freystrop
Martletwy
Templeton
Ludch

SKOMER ISLAND
Wooltack Point
Little Haven
Walton West
Walwyn's Castle
Tiers Cross
Johnston
Hook
Llangwm
Loveston
Reynalton
Begelly

Marloes
Talbenny
B4327
14
Llangwm
Rosemarket
Newton Mountain
Cresswell
Jeffreyston
Broadmoor

Broad Sound
Herbrandston
Steynton
Houghton
Lawrenny
West Williamston
Cresselly
East Williamston

St Ishmael's
Hubberston
Waterston
Burton
Carew Newton
Carew
Redberth

Westdale Bay
Dale
Dale Point
Hakin
Llanstadwell
Coshestqn
Carew Cheriton
Sageston
Gumfreston

SKOKHOLM ISLAND
Great Castle Head
Milford Haven
Milford HAVEN
Neyland
Toll
Waterloo
Milton
Tide Mill
St Florence

St Ann's Head
Popton Point
Pembroke Dock
East Pennar
A477
Palace
Penal

ROSSLARE
Angle
Angle Bay
Rhoscrowther
Pembroke
Hundleton
Lamphey
Manorbier Newton
Gilt

Freshwater West
Castlemartin Brook
Maiden Wells
B4584
Hodgeston
Jameson
Lydstep

Castlemartin
Warren
St Twynnells
Merrion
Cheriton or Trewent Point
Stackpole Elidor
Stackpole
Manorbier
Lydstep Point
Monas

Linney Head
B4319
Bosherston
Pembrokeshire Coast Path
Stackpole Head

St Govan's Chapel

5
4
3
2
1
0
9

7   8   9   0   1

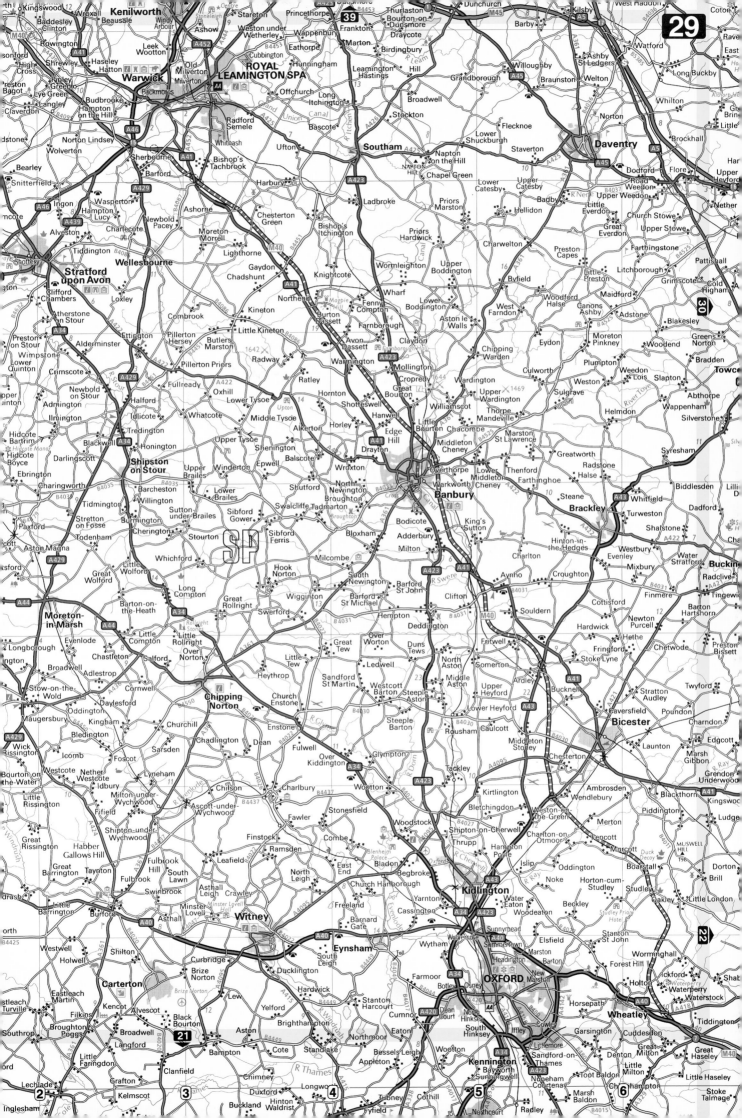

Bardsey Sound

St Mary's

BARDSEY ISLAND

Aberdaron Bay

Porth Ysgo

Porth Ceiriad

Neigwl

Bwlchtocyn

St Tudwal's Island East

St Tudwal's Island West

Moes Artro Tourist Village

Dyffryn Arddudwy

Llanddwyw

Barmouth Bay

SCALE

| 0 | 1 | 2 | 3 | 4 miles |

| 0 | 1 | 2 | 3 | 4 | 5 kilometres |

SH

Lla

Rho

Aber Dysynni

Tywyn

C A R D I G A N

B A Y

Clarach Bay

Aberystwyth

SN

Blaenplwyf

A487

Llanddeinio

16

Llanrhystud

Llansantffraid

Llanon

Joppa

Nebo

Aberarth

Aberaeron

A487

Cilcennin

New Quay

Llanina

Maen-y-groes

Gilfachrheda

Llwyncelyn

Oakford

Afon Aeron

Bw

Nanternis

Cross Inn

Llanarth

Trefilan

Ynys-Lochtyn

Llwyndafydd

Caerwedros

A487

Dihewyd

Ystrad Aeron

Talsarn

Llwyndafydd

Llan nog

Mydroilyn

Temple Bar

Pontgarreg

Plwm

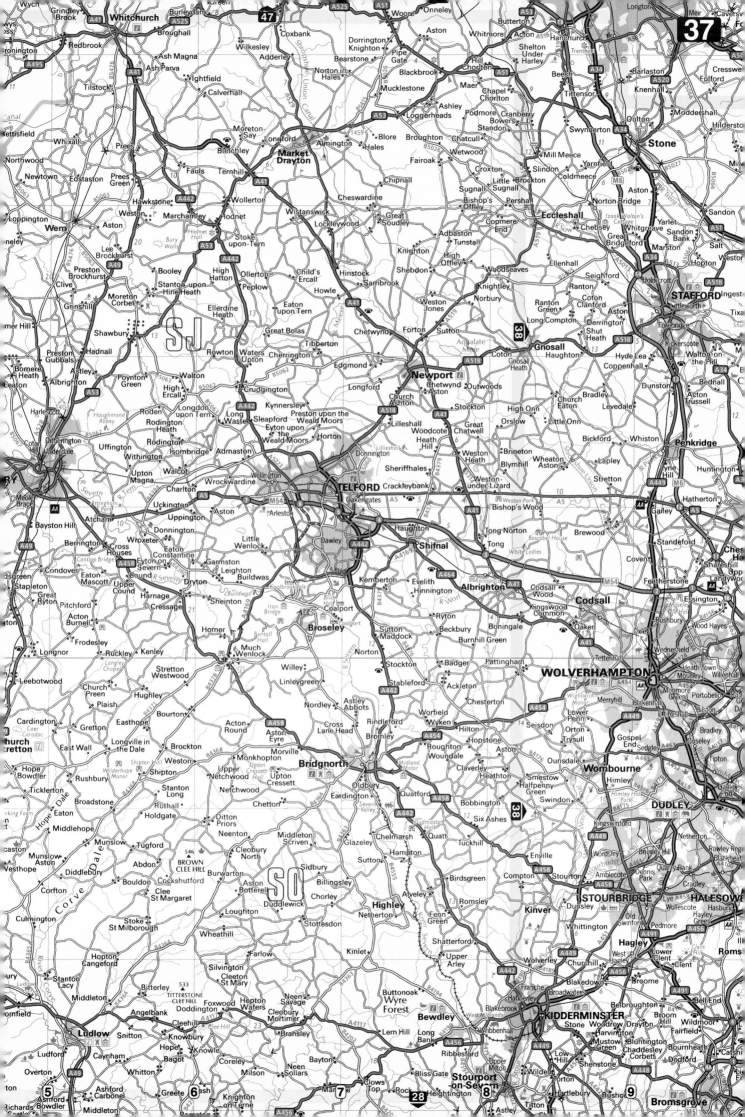

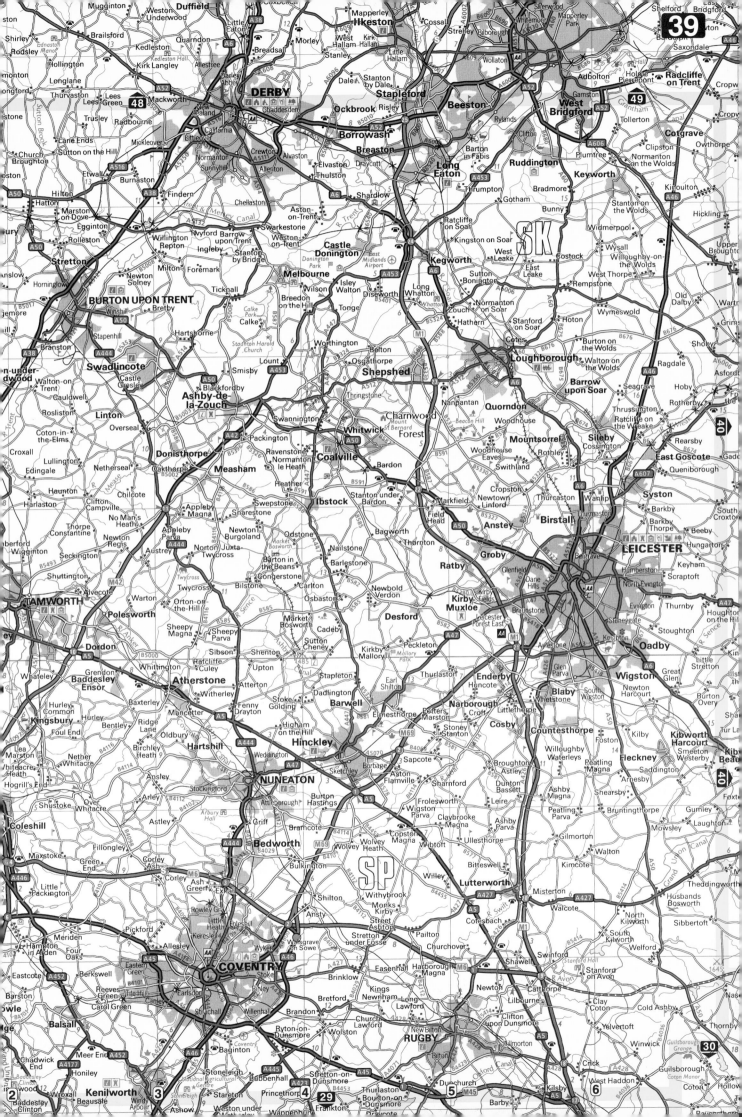

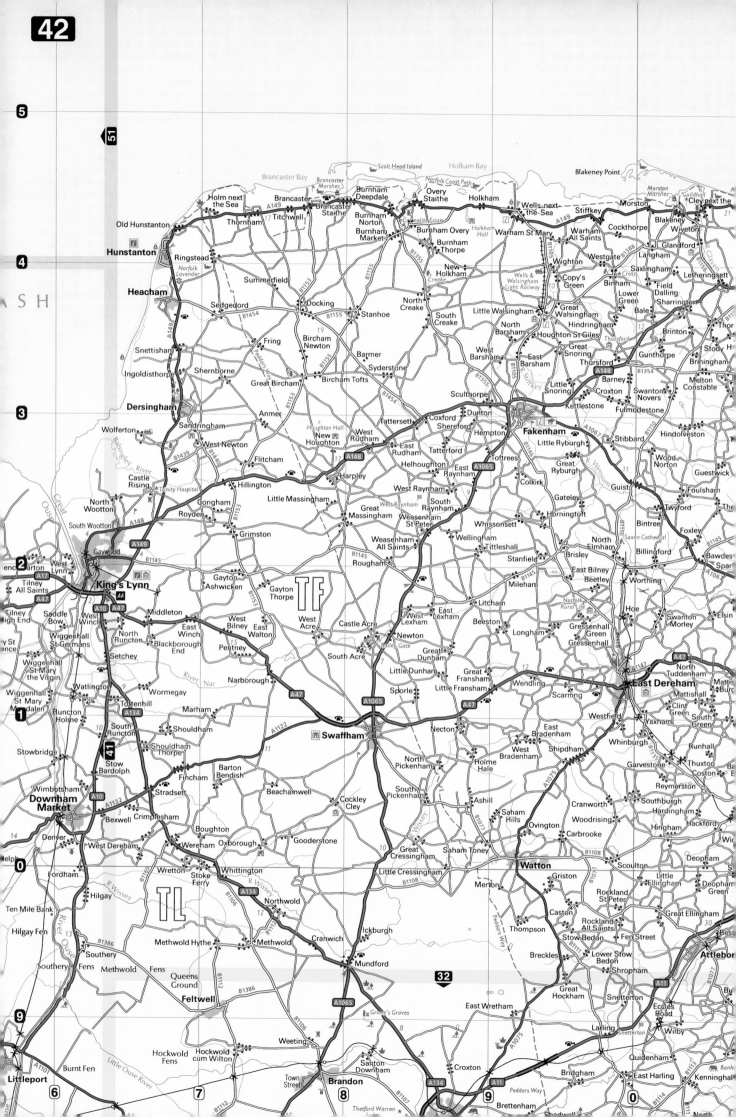

SCALE

0 1 2 3 4 miles

0 1 2 3 4 5 kilometres

Sheringham West Runton East Runton **Cromer** Overstrand Sidestrand

Weybourne Upper Sheringham Beeston Regis Felbrigg Hall Northrepps Trimingham

Kelling Bodham Street Aylmerton East Beckham Felbrigg Crossdale Street Southrepps Gimingham Mundesley

West Beckham Gresham Metton Hanworth Roughton Thorpe Market Lower Street Crunch Knapton Paston Bacton

Baconsthorpe Sustead Bradfield Suffield Antingham Edingthorpe Walcott

Edgefield Green Matlaske Aldborough Wickmere Erpingham Colby Swafield Edingthorpe Green Witton Ridlington Happisburgh

Little Barningham Calthorpe Banningham Colby **North Walsham** Meeting House Hill Whimpwell Green

Saxthorpe Itteringham Ingworth Blickling Felmingham Honing Happisburgh Common Hempstead

Oulton Oulton Street **Aylsham** Burgh next Aylsham Tuttington Briggate East Ruston Lessingham Ingham Corner Waxham

Heydon Marsham Swanton Abbot Worstead Dilham Stalham Ingham Sea Palling

Cawston Reepham Eastgate Brandiston Buxton Heath Brampton Oxnead Lamas Market Street Tunstead Smallburgh Sutton Hickling Hickling Green Horsey

Whitwell Street Buxton Stratton Strawless Neatishead Wood Street Catfield Barton Broad Hickling Broad Horsey Windpump

Alderford Swannington Hevingham Horstead Coltishall Irstead Ludham Potter Heigham Martham Winterton-on-Sea

Felthorpe Upgate Hainford Frettenham Belaugh Hoveton Horning Bastwick Repps **Hemsby** Hemsby Hole

Morton Attlebridge St Helena Newton St Faith Wroxham Upper Street Thurne Clippesby Ormesby St Michael Scratby

Weston Longville Horsford Crostwick Woodbastwick Upper Street Ranworth Rollesby Burgh St Margaret California

Ringland Costessey Drayton Taverham Horsham St Faith Spixworth Rackheath Salhouse Pilson Green Cargate Green Ormesby St Margaret **Caister-on-Sea**

Honingham Easton Hellesdon New Costessey New Rackheath Panxworth South Walsham Upton Billockby Thrigby Filby Mautby West End

Colton Marlingford Eaton Thorpe End Little Plumstead Great Plumstead Hemblington Burlingham Green Acle Stokesby West Caister Runham

Barford Bawburgh Colney **NORWICH** Witton Lingwood Blofield Beighton Moulton St Mary Damgate **GREAT YARMOUTH**

Framlingham High Green Little Melton Cringleford Thorpe St Andrew **Brundall** Postwick Strumpshaw South Burlingham Tunstall Halvergate Southtown

Carleton Forehoe Lynch Green Keswick Caistor St Edmund Trowse Newton Kirby Bedon Surlingham Buckenham Freethorpe Wickhampton Burgh Castle Gorleston on Sea

Hethersett Ketteringham Arminghall Framingham Earl Bramerton Hassingham Cantley Freethorpe Common Berney Arms Bradwell

Swardeston Dunston Hellington Rockland St Mary Claxton Carleton St Peter Limpenhoe **Belton**

East Carleton Mulbarton Swainsthorpe Upper Stoke Stoke Holy Cross Framingham Pigot Yelverton Ashby St Mary Langley Street Reedham Pettitts Crafts

Wymondham Bracon Ash Newton Flotman Hawe's Green Howe Bergh Apton Thurton Hardley Street Fritton Hopton on Sea

Silfield Wreningham Toprow Flordon Saxlingham Thorpe Saxlingham Nethergate Brooke Mundham Chedgrave Norton Subcourse St Olaves Lound Herringfleet Blundeston Corton

Ashwellthorpe Hapton Low Tharston Tasburgh Saxlingham Green Seething Kirstead Green Loddon Hales Thurlton Haddiscoe Somerleyton

Spooner Row Fundenhall Tacolneston Tharston Upper Tasburgh Thwaite St Mary Woodton Kirby Cane Raveningham Maypole Green Toft Monks Wheatacre Oulton **LOWESTOFT** Kirkley

Bunwell Street Forncett St Mary Stratton St Michael Hempnall Woodton Stockton Aldeby Burgh St Peter Pleasurewood Hills

Forncett End Forncett St Peter Morningthorpe Fritton Hempnall Green Topcroft Ellingham Kirby Row Gillingham Oulton Broad Pakefield

New Buckenham Wacton Long Stratton Shelton Topcroft Street Ditchingham Broome Geldeston Shipmeadow Worlingham Barnby

Aslacton Great Moulton Hardwick **Bungay** Mettingham Barsham North Cove Carlton Colville Gisleham

Tibenham High Green Colegate End Denton Ringsfield Corner **Beccles** Mutford Black Street

New Buckenham Tivetshall St Margaret Pulham Market Alburgh Earsham The Otter Trust Flixton Ilketshall St Margaret Ringsfield Rushmere **Kessingland**

Gissing Tivetshall St Mary Pulham St Mary Starston Homersfield Aviation Museum Ilketshall St Andrew Sotterly Hulver Street Henstead

Garlic Street Wortwell St Margaret South Elmham St Michael Redisham Shadingfield Wrentham

Benacre Benacre Ness

1 2 3 4 5

A148 A140 A149 A47 A143 A146 A12 A1064 A1062 A1151 A1151 A1135

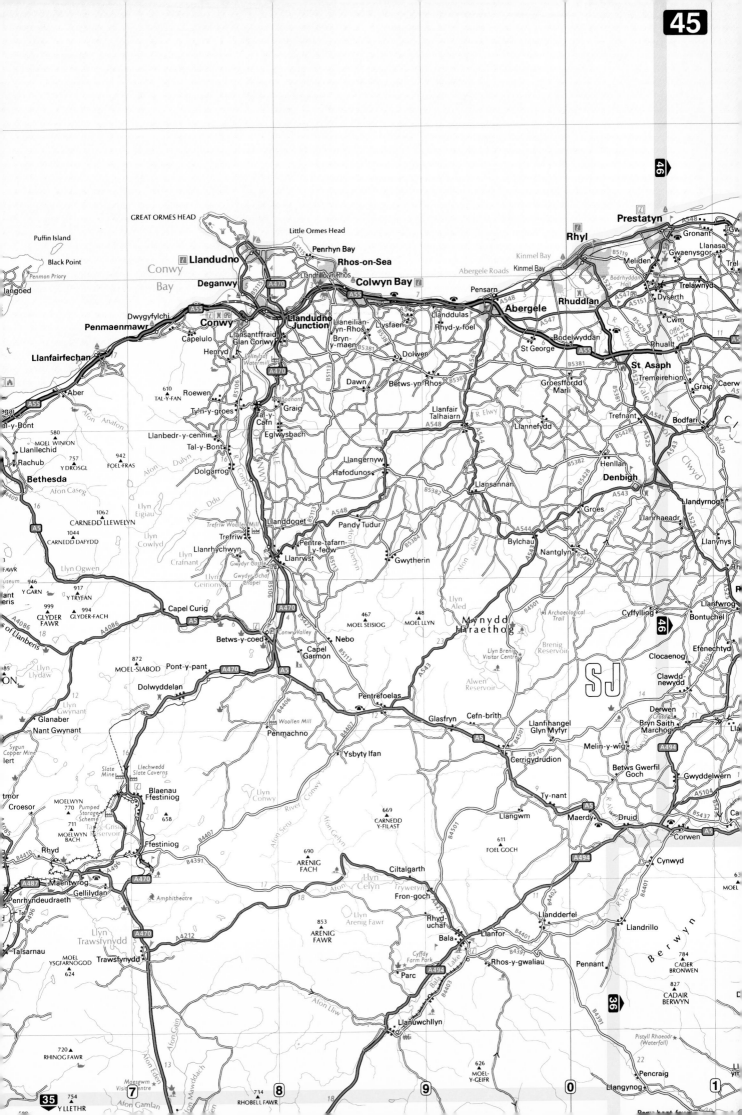

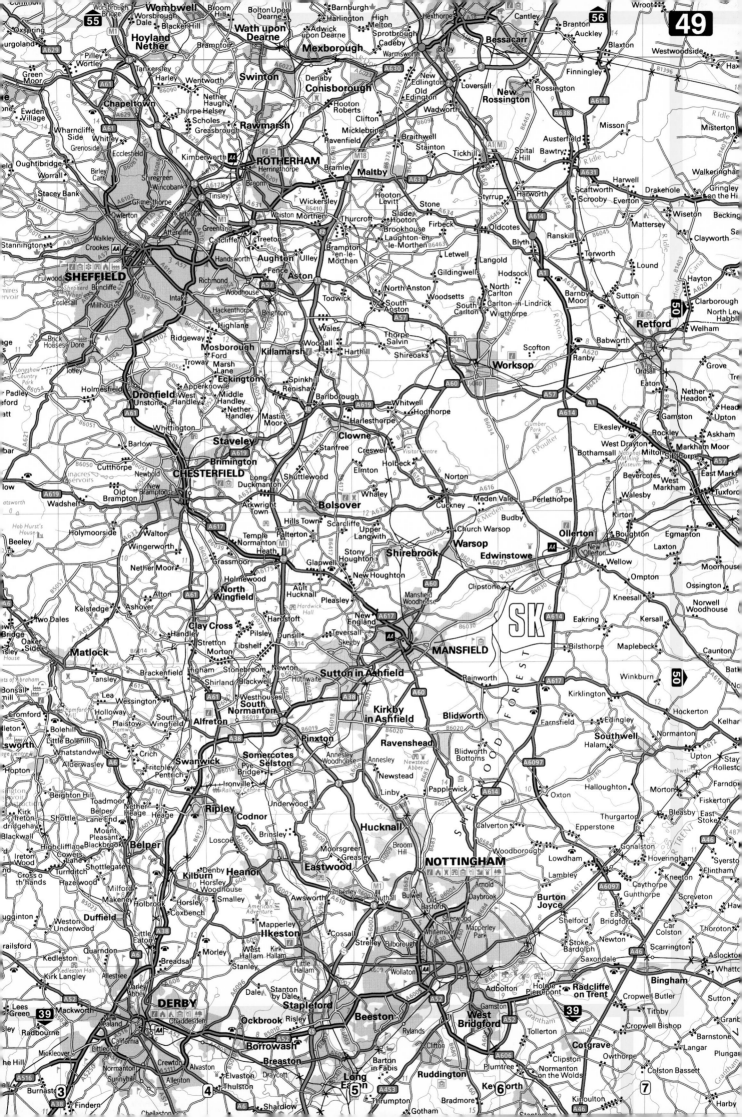

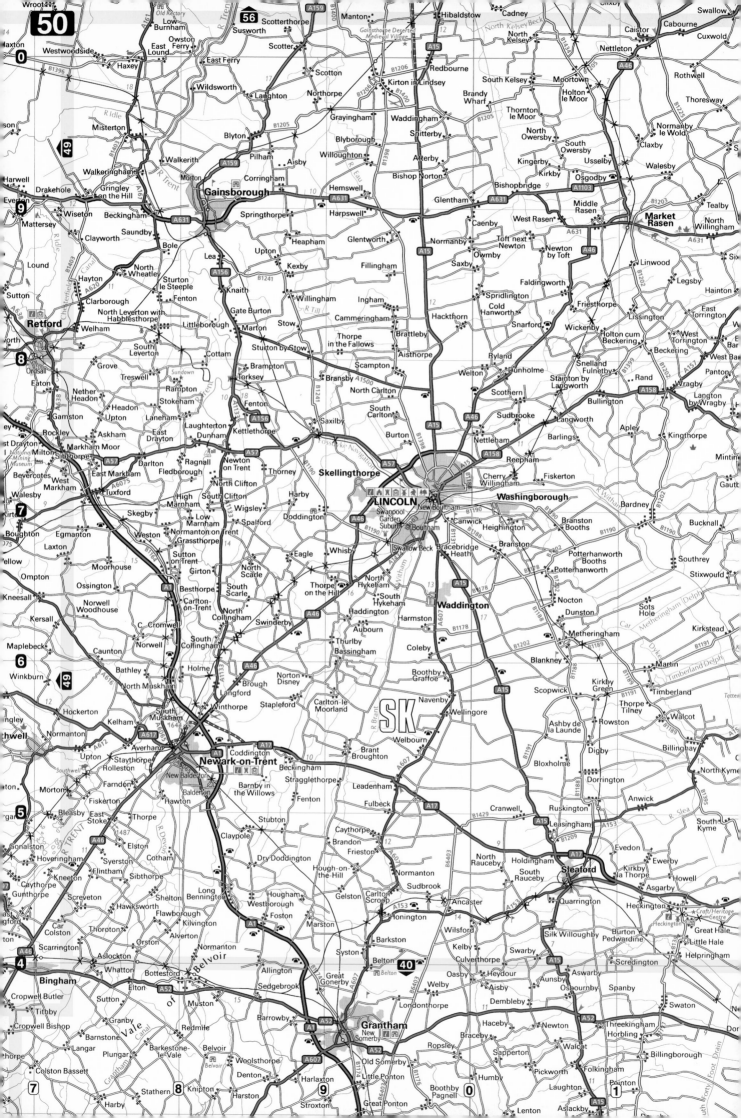

Isle of Man

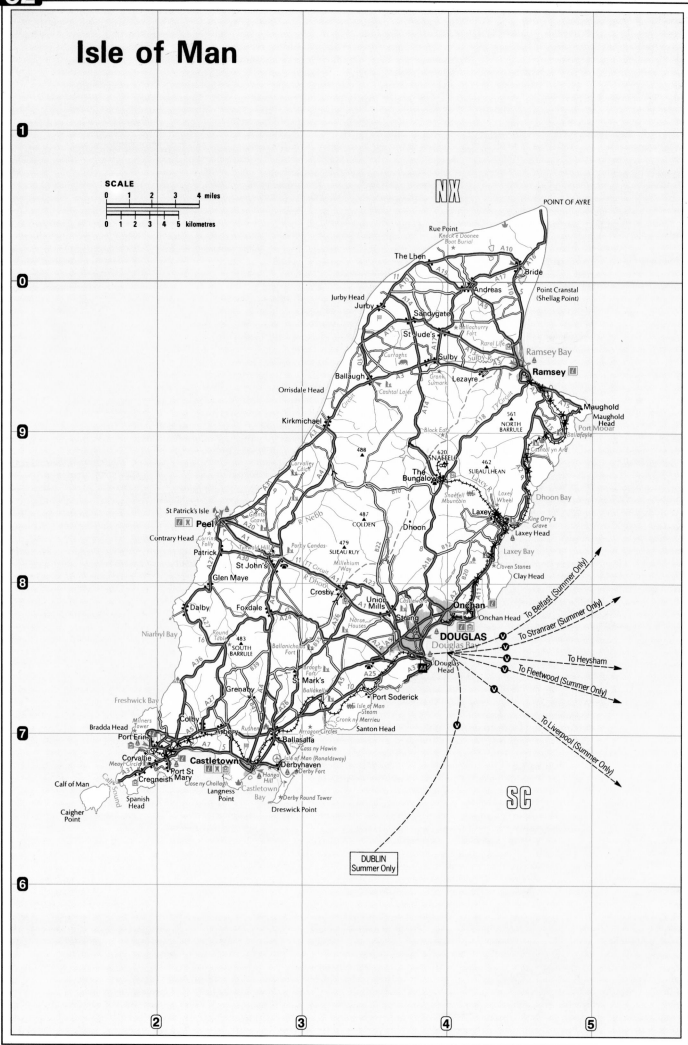

NX

POINT OF AYRE

Rue Point
Knock e Doonee
Boat Burial
The Lhen
Bride
Point Cranstal
(Shellag Point)
Andreas
Jurby Head
Jurby
Sandygate
St Jude's
Ballachurry
Fort
Rural Life
Ramsey Bay
Curraghs
Sulby
Sulby R.
Ramsey
Ballaugh
Gronk
Sumark
Lezayre
Maughold
Orrisdale Head
Cashtal Lajer
Maughold
Head
Port Mooar
TT Circuit
561
Block Eary
NORTH
BARRULE
Ballafayle
Kirkmichael
Cashtal yn Ard
488
620
SNAEFELL
462
SLIEAU LHEAN
St Patrick's Isle
Corvalley
Cliff
The Bungalow
Laxey R.
Laxey
Wheel
Dhoon Bay
Peel
487
COLDEN
Snaefell
Mountain
Laxey
Contrary Head
Giant's
Grave
Dhoon
King Orry's
Grave
Patrick
Corrins
Folly
Tynwald Hill
Ballig
R. Neb
Poorty Candas
479
SLIEAU RUY
Laxey Head
Laxey Bay
St John's
TT Circuit
Millennium
Way
Cloven Stones
Glen Maye
R. Dhoo
Crosby
Clay Head
Dalby
Foxdale
Union
Mills
Castleward
Onchan
Norse
Houses
Strang
Onchan Head
To Belfast (Summer Only)
Niarbyl Bay
Round
Table
483
SOUTH
BARRULE
Ballanicholas
Fort
DOUGLAS
To Stranraer (Summer Only)
Douglas Bay
To Heysham
Ardoghy
Fort
To Fleetwood (Summer Only)
St Mark's
Ballakelly
Douglas
Head
Grenaby
Port Soderick
To Liverpool (Summer Only)
Freshwick Bay
Milners
Tower
Colby
Arbory
Rushen
Arragon
Circles
Isle of Man
Steam
Railway
Santon Head
Bradda Head
Port Erin
Ballasalla
Cronk ny Merriu
Corvalie
Meayl Circle
A7
Castletown
Cass ny Hawin
Derbyhaven
Cregneish
Port St
Mary
Isle of Man (Ronaldsway)
Derby Fort
Langness
Point
Close ny Chollagh
Hango
Hill
Castletown
Bay
Derby Round Tower
SC
Calf of Man
Spanish
Head
Dreswick Point
Caigher
Point

DUBLIN
Summer Only

SCALE
0   1   2   3   4 miles
0 1 2 3 4 5 kilometres

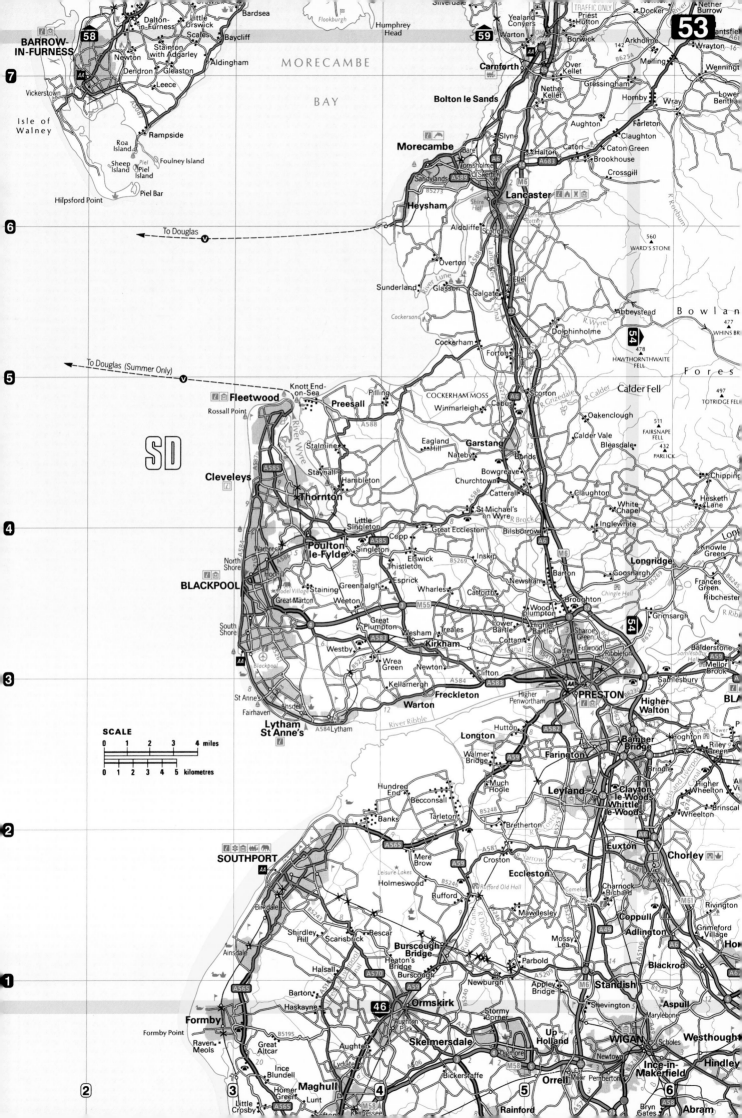

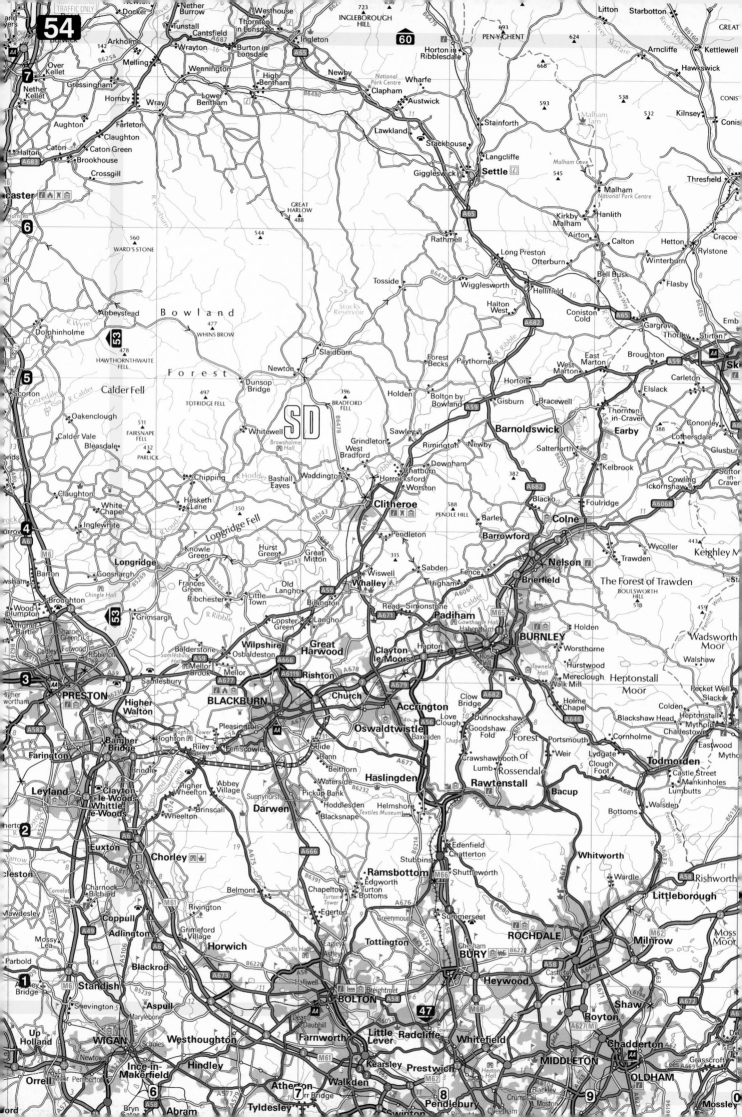

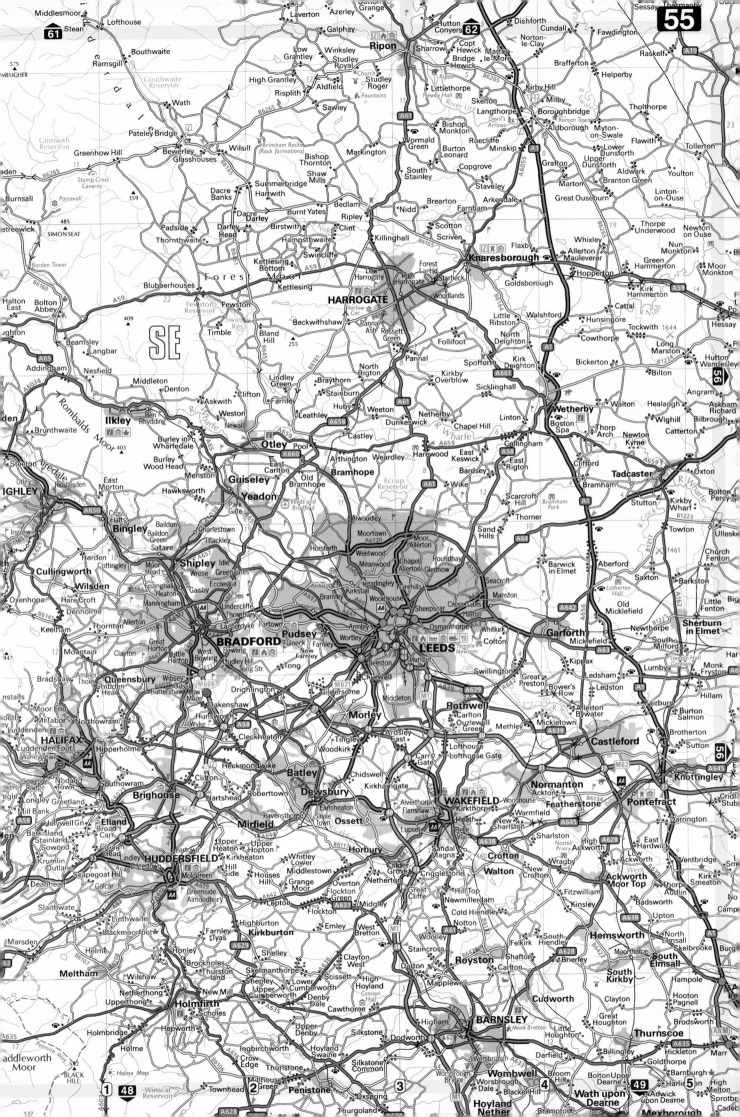

Wold Newton
Speeton
Thornwick Bay
Buckton
Bempton
Burton Fleming
Grindale
Thwing
Selwicks Bay
FLAMBOROUGH HEAD
Flamborough
Boynton
B1253
Rudston
Monolith
Sewerby
Bessingby
Carnaby
Bridlington
Haisthorpe
Hilderthorpe
A165
Kilham
Burton Agnes
Thornholme
Carnaby
BRIDLINGTON
BAY
Parva
Norman Manor House
Harpham
Fraisthorpe
Lowthorpe
Nafferton
Gransmoor
Great Kelk
Lisset
Barmston
Gembling
Ulrome
B1249
Wansford
Foston on the Wolds
16
Beeford
Skipsea
Skerne
B1249
15
Brigham
North Frodingham
B1249
A165
Dunnington
Atwick
Bewholme
Nunkeeling
Hornsea Mere
Hornsea
Brandesburton
Seaton
Hornsea Pottery
Leven
Catwick
Sigglesthorne
Rolston
B1244
Goxhill
Little Hatfield
Mappleton
Mappleton Sands
Aike
Long Riston
Rise
Great Hatfield
Great Cowden
Routh
A1035
Arnold
Withernwick
Tickton
New Ellerby
Beverley
Weel
North Skirlaugh
Marton
West Newton
Aldbrough
Woodmansey
South Skirlaugh
17
Wawne
Old Ellerby
B1242
Thearne
Swine
Flinton
Garton
Dunswell
Coniston
Burton Constable Hall
Ganstead
Sproatley
Humbleton
Hilston
Wyton
B1238
Bilton
B1240
Lelley
Owstwick
Elstronwick
B1239
Tunstall
Newland
A1165
Sutton on Hull
Stoneferry
Preston
Burton Pidsea
Roos
B1233
Marfleet
Rimswell
Owthorne
KINGSTON UPON HULL
A1033
Hedon
Burstwick
B1362
Halsham
Withernsea
A63
Thorngumbald
Paull
Keyingham
Hollym
East Ella
16
Winestead
A1033
B1231
Ottringham
Holmpton
A1033
New Holland
Patrington
Barrow Haven
B1445
Goxhill
Welwick
East Halton
Weeton
Easington
Skeffling
w-upon-mber
A1077
14
Thornton Abbey
North Killingholme
Kilnsea
Thornton Curtis
South Killingholme
A160
Immingham Dock
Wootton
Ulceby Skitter
10
RIVER HUMBER
Ulceby
B1211
Habrough
15
B1211
Immingham
A180
Kirmington
Brocklesby
Stallingborough
GRIMSBY
Croxton
Keelby
Healing
West Marsh
Melton Ross
A18
Great Limber
Great Coates
Old Clee
Cleethorpes
Humberside
Riby
Aylesby
Lincolnshire Coast
Barnetby le Wold
Nunsthorpe
Thrunscoe
Bigby
Bradley
Scartho
Humberston
merby
Searby
Laceby
New Waltham
Owmby
Irby upon Humber
Waltham
Grasby
Clixby
Swallow
Barnoldby le Beck
Holton le Clay
SPURN HEAD

ROTTERDAM (EUROPOORT)
ZEEBRUGGE

Caistor
Cabourne
Beelsby
Brigsley
Cuxwold
Ashby cum

SCALE
0   1   2   3   4 miles
0 1 2 3 4 5 kilometres

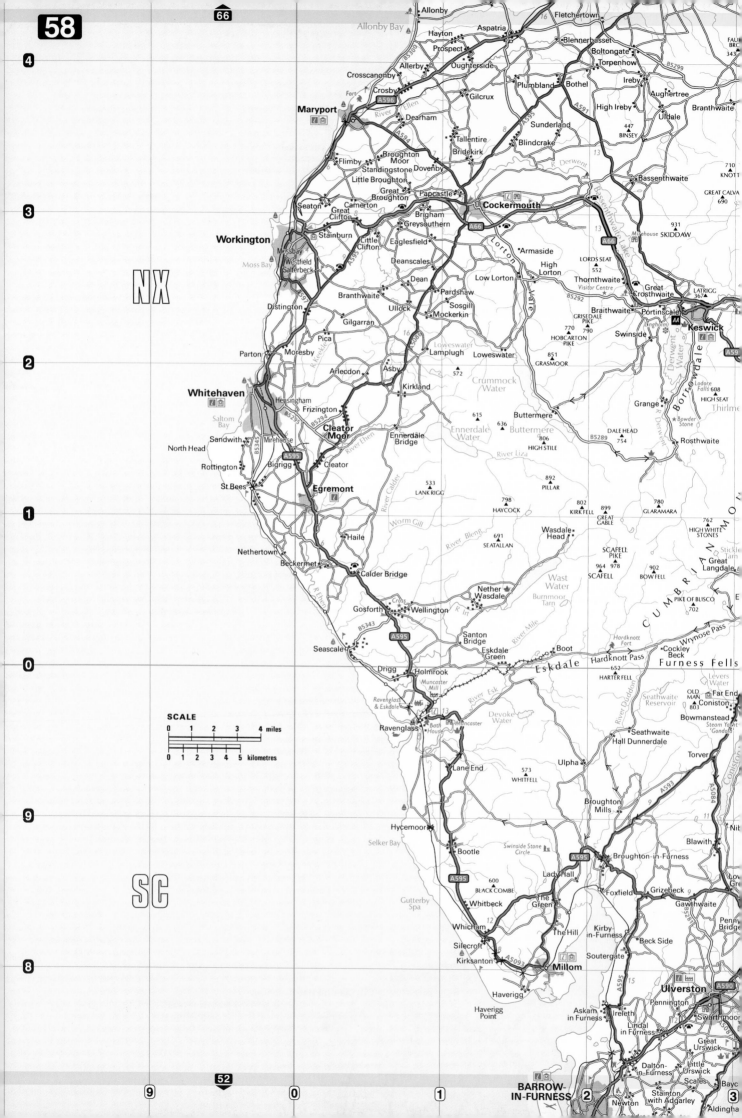

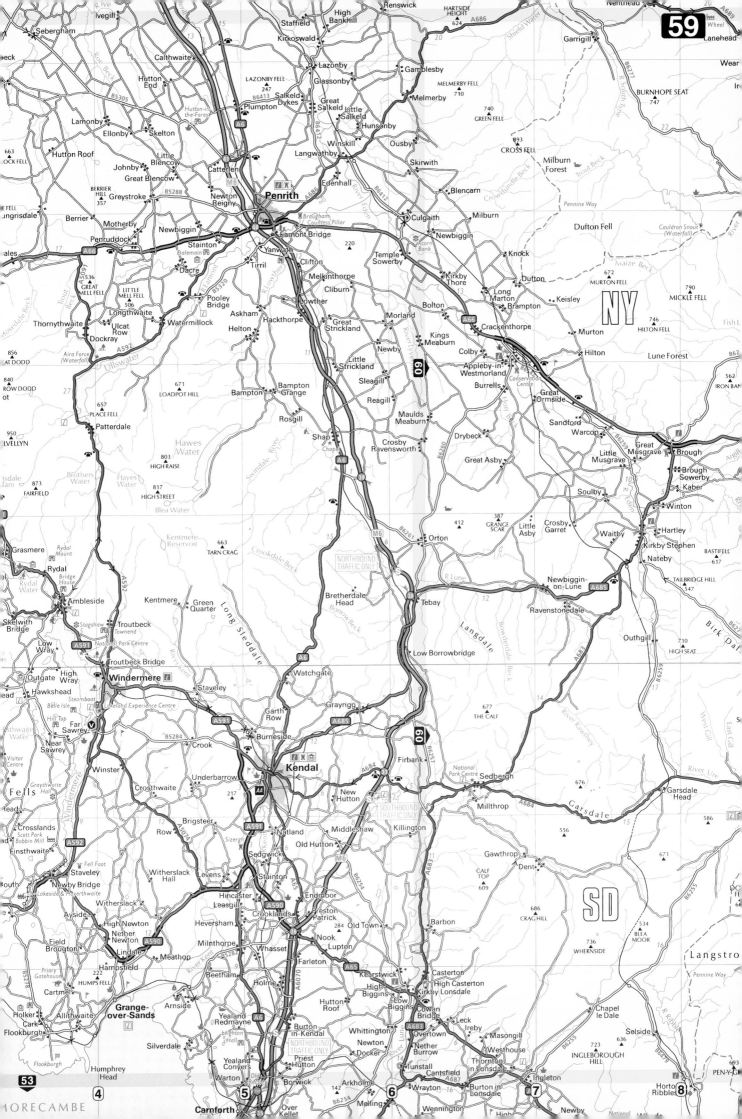

SCALE

0   1   2   3   4 miles

0 1 2 3 4 5 kilometres

Hummersea Scar

Loftus
Easington
Staithes
Hinderwell
Runswick
Runswick Bay
Goldsborough
Ellerby
Scaling
B1266
Lythe
Overdale Wyke
Mickleby
A174
Sandsend
West Barnby
East Barnby
Sandsend Wyke
Whitby
Dunsley
Newholm
Saltwick Bay
Ugthorpe
Ruswarp
Aislaby
Briggswath
Stainsacre
Sneaton
High Hawsker
Lealholm
A171
Sleights
Ugglebarnby
Ness Point or North Cheek
Iburndale
Robin Hood's Bay
Grosmont
Robin Hood's Bay
Glaisdale
Egton
Fylingthorpe
Egton Bridge
Old Peak or South Cheek
326
PIKE HILL
Goathland
369
292
A171
Staintondale
Hayburn Wyke
FORK MOORS
Wheeldale Roman Road
Harwood Dale
Cloughton Wyke
Rosedale Abbey
290
Cloughton
Stape
20
Burniston
Cromer Point
Cleveland Way
Bridestones (Rock formations)
Bickley
Silpho
Levisham
Broxa
Lockton
Langdale End
Hackness
Suffield
Scalby
239
astingham
Newton Dale
Scarborough
Cropton
Bee Dale
Falsgrave
Oliver's Mount
Wrelton
A170
Aislaby
Middleton
Sawdon
West Ayton
East Ayton
A170
Sinnington
North Yorkshire Moors
Hutton Buscel
Osgodby
Cayton Bay
TA
Wilton
Ruston
Irton
The Wyke
Pickering
Ebberston
Wykeham
Seamer
Cayton
B1261
Lebberston
Normanby
Thornton Dale
Allerston
A170
Brompton
Gristhorpe
Filey Brigg
Kirby Misperton
Snainton
A64
Folkton
Muston
Filey
Salton
Flamingo Land
Yedingham
Willerby
A1039
Staxton
Flixton
Filey Bay
Great Barugh
Sherburn
Ganton
Hunmanby
A165
Knapton
East Heslerton
Potter Brompton
Barton-le-Street
Amotherby
West Knapton
West Heslerton
Fordon
Reighton
Broughton
Scampston
A64
Wold Newton
Speeton
pleton-Street
Rillington
Wintringham
Foxholes
Burton Fleming
57
Buckton
Swinton
Old Malton
A64
56
Thorpe Bassett
Butterwick
Bempton
neysthorpe
Malton
Norton
8
Scagglethorpe
Weaverthorpe
Grindale
9
Wolds Way
0
1
2

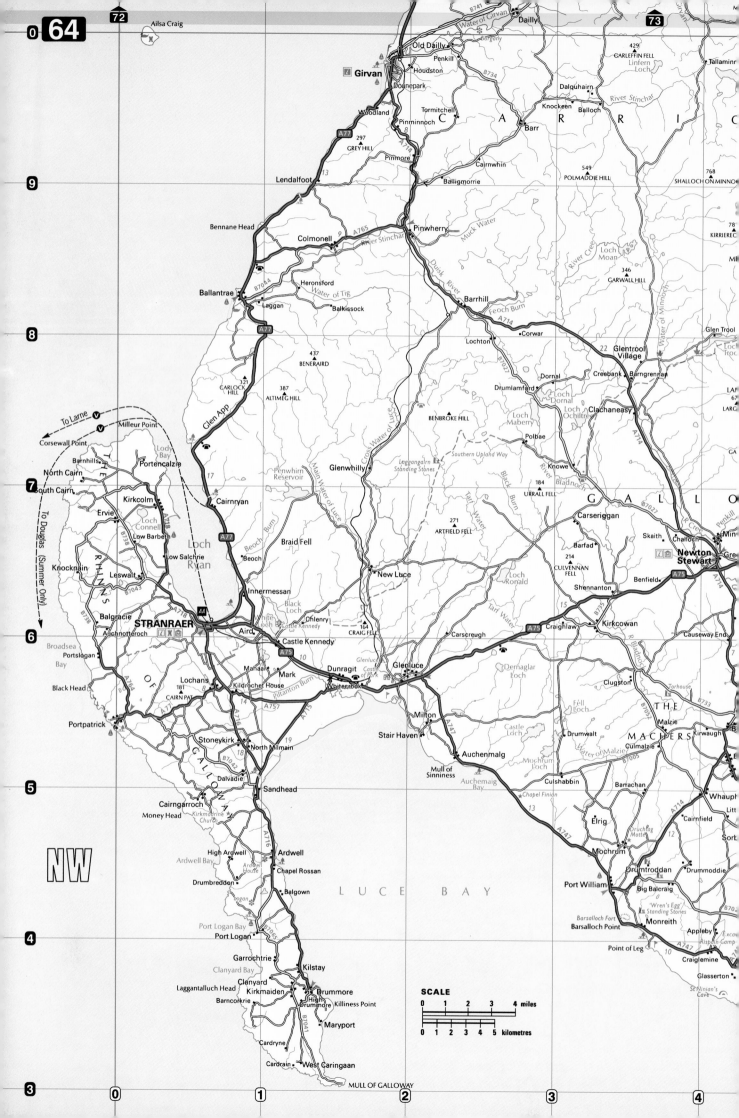

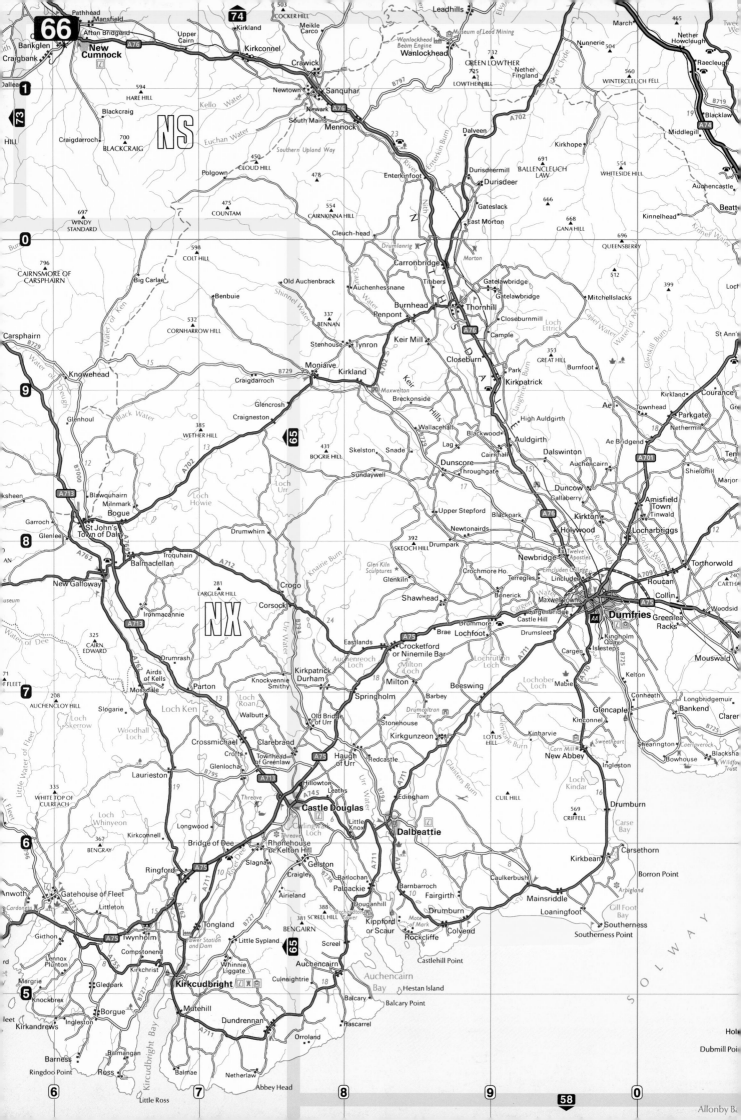

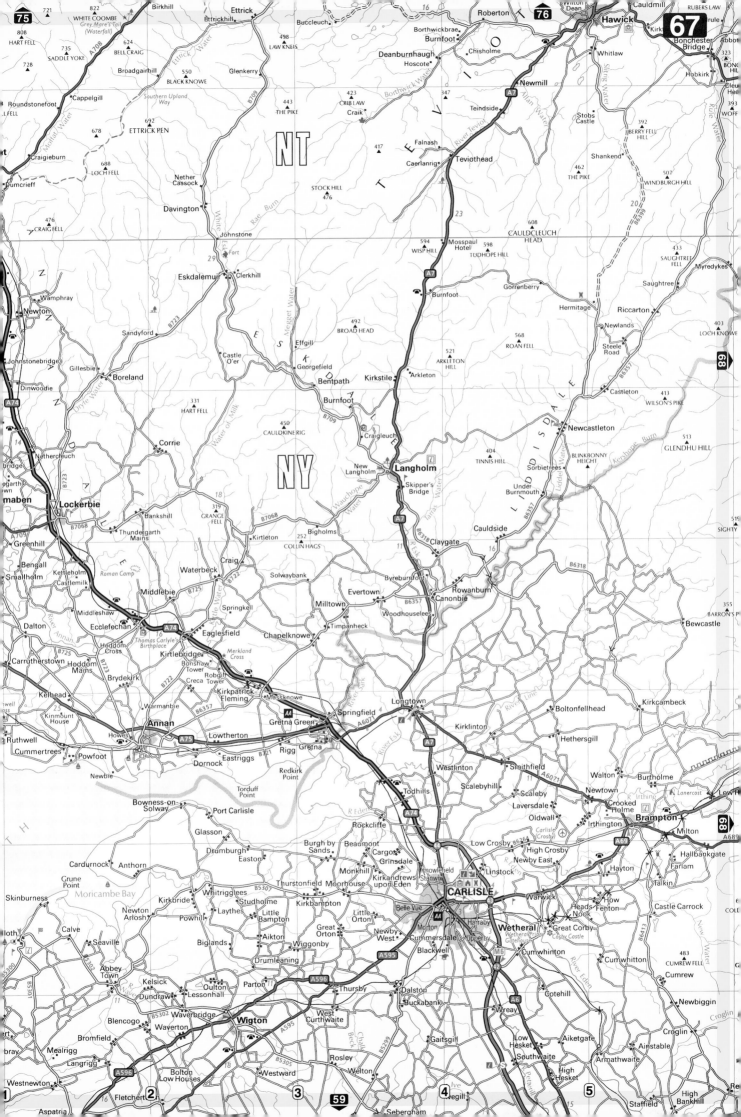

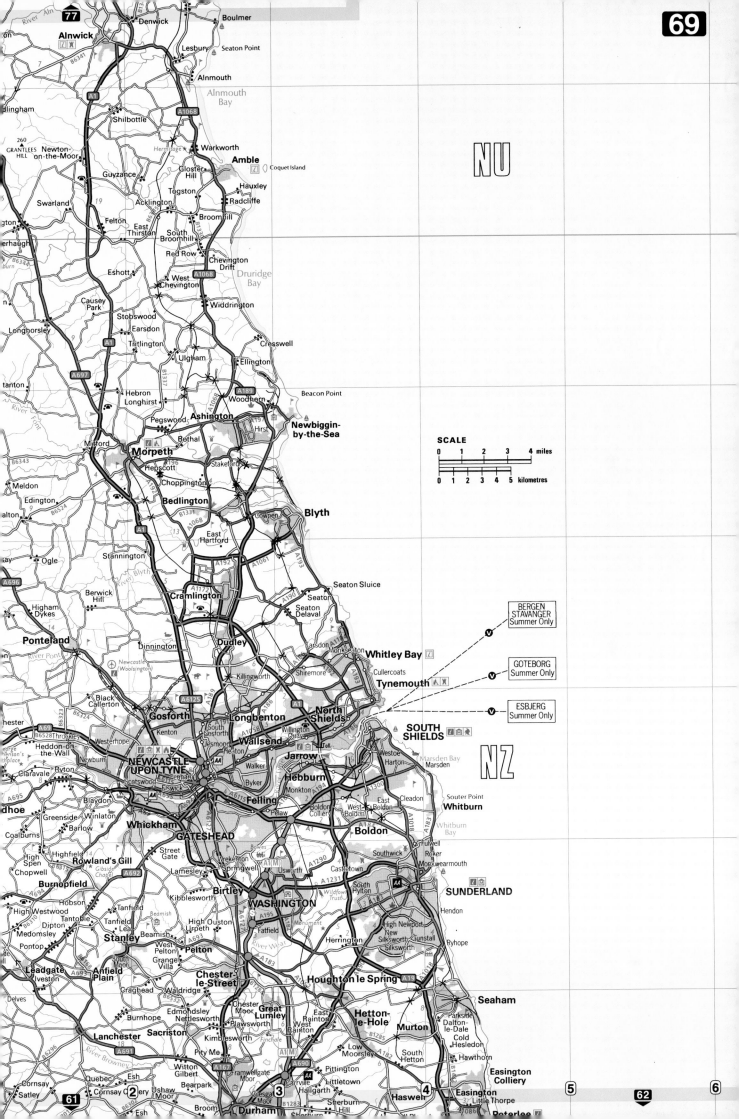

Eilean Dubh
Rudh'a'Geodha
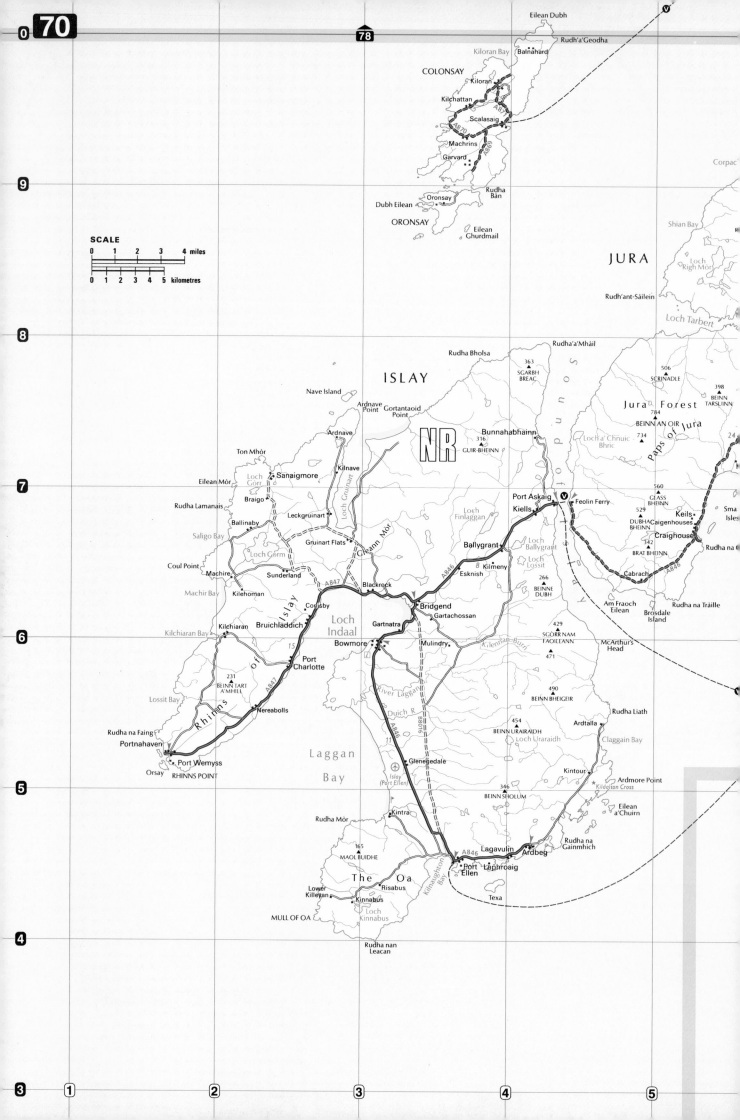

Kiloran Bay
Balnahard

COLONSAY
Kiloran
Kilchattan
A870
Scalasaig
A869
Machrins
Garvard

Corpac

9

Dubh Eilean
Oronsay
Rudha
Bàn

ORONSAY
Eilean
Ghurdmail

Shian Bay

JURA
Loch
Righ Mòr

SCALE
0 1 2 3   4 miles
0 1 2 3 4 5 kilometres

Rudh'ant-Sàilein

Loch Tarbert

8

Rudha Bholsa

Rudha'a'Mhàil

363
SGARBH
BREAC

506
SCRINADLE

398
BEINN
TARSUINN

ISLAY

Nave Island

Ardnave
Point

Gortantaoid
Point

NR

Bunnahabhainn

316
GUIR-BHEINN

Jura Forest

784
BEINN AN OIR

Paps of Jura

24

Ardnave

Ton Mhòr

Kilnave

Loch'a' Chnuic
Bhric

734

Eilean Mòr

Loch
Gorr

Sanaigmore

560

7

Braigo

Rudha Lamanais

Leckgruinart

Loch Gruinart

Port Askaig
Kiells

Feolin Ferry

529
GLASS
BHEINN

DUBHA
Caigenhouses
BHEINN

Keils

Sma
Isles

Ballinaby

Saligo Bay

Gleann Mòr

Loch
Finlaggan

Ballygrant

Loch
Ballygrant

Craighouse

342
BRAT BHEINN

Rudha na

Gruinart Flats

8

Loch Gorm

Coul Point

Machire

Sunderland

A847

Blackrock

Bridgend
Gartachossan

Kilmeny

Esknish

266
BEINNE
DUBH

Loch
Lossit

Cabrach

A846

Machir Bay

Kilchoman

Kilehoman

Conisby

Rhinns of Islay

Loch
Indaal

Gartnatra

Am Fraoch
Eilean

Rudha na Tràille

Brosdale
Island

6

Kilchiaran Bay

Kilchiaran

Bruichladdich

Port
Charlotte

15

Bowmore

Mulindry

Kilennan Burn

429
SGÒRR NAM
FAOILEANN

471

McArthur's
Head

231
BEINN TART
A'MHILL

A847

River Laggan

Duich R

B8016

A846

490
BEINN BHEIGEIR

Rudha Liath

Ardtalla

Claggain Bay

Lossit Bay

Nereabolls

454
BEINN URARAIDH

Loch Uraraidh

Rudha na Faing

Portnahaven

Laggan

11

Glenegedale

Kintour

Ardmore Point
Kildalton Cross

Port Wemyss

Orsay
RHINNS POINT

5

Bay

Islay
(Port Ellen)

346
BEINN SHOLUM

Eilean
a'Chuirn

Kintra

Rudha Mòr

Rudha na
Gainmhich

165
MAOL BUIDHE

Risabus

The   Oa

Lagavulin
A846
Laphroaig

Ardbeg

Lower
Killeyan

Kinnabus

Port
Ellen

MULL OF OA

Loch
Kinnabus

Texa

4

Rudha nan
Leacan

3

1   2   3   4   5

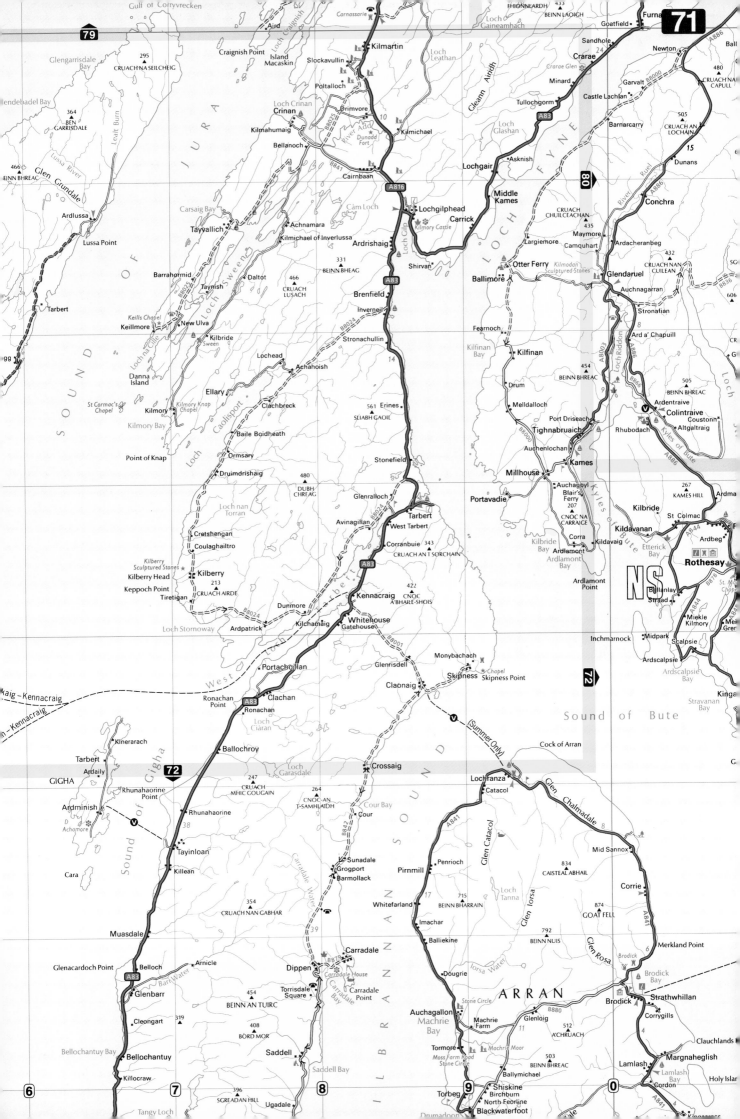

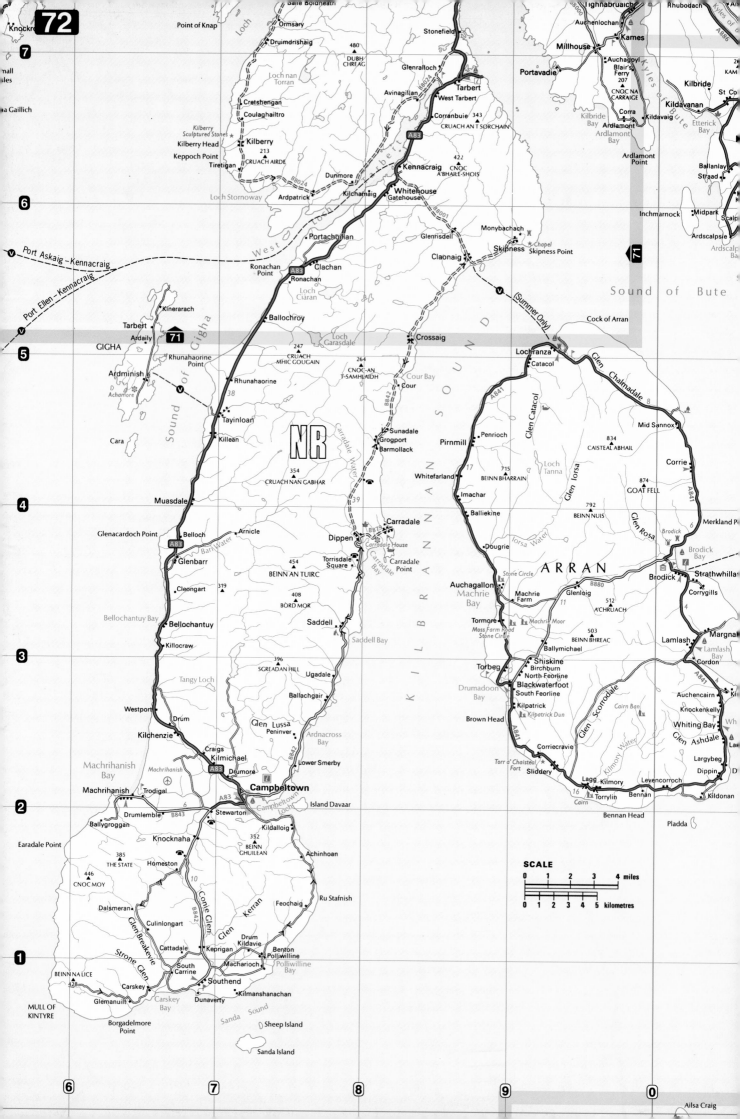

SCALE

0   1   2   3   4 miles

0 1 2 3 4 5 kilometres

NU

Fast Castle Head

196
BROWN RIG

ST ABB'S HEAD

Northfield   St Abbs

Coldingham   Coldingham Bay

21   22

Houndwood

Heugh Head   Cairncross   Eyemouth

262
ELEY HILL

Reston   Ayton   Burnmouth

Auchencrow

Lamberton

East
Blanerne   Chirnside   Edington
Foulden   Marshall Meadows Bay

Chirnsidebridge

Broadhaugh   Whiteadder   Tithe Barn

Allanton   Water   1333

Hutton   Paxton   Barracks
Town Ramparts

Blackadder   Sunwick   Tweedmouth   **Berwick-upon-Tweed**

Whitsome   Hilton   East Ord   Spittal
Fishwick

Simprim   Horncliffe   Huds Head

Horndean   Murton

Ladykirk   Thornton

Swinton   Norham   Scremerston

Upsettlington   Cheswick

Ladykirk
Ho.

Ancroft   Haggerston

Lennel   Duddo   Beal

Cornhill-on-
Tweed   Bowsden

Etal   Lowick   East
Kyloe   Fenwick

Crookham   Heatherslaw
Mill   Buckton

Branxton   The Lady
Waterford Hall   Ford

1513   St Cuthbert's
Cave

Howtel   Fenton
Town   Belford

Milfield

Thornington   Nesbit   Doddington

Lanton

Coupland   River Till   Lucker

Yeavering   Kirknewton   Warenford

Akeld

Hethpool   Wooler   Chatton   Newstead

Ros Castle   Ellingham

Newtown   Chillingham

North
Charlton

Preston Hill   267   CATERAN HILL   Falloden

Ilderton   Old Bewick   Ditchburn   South
Charlton

THE CHEVIOT   New
Bewick   Eglingham   Rock

567
DUNMOOR HILL   River Breamish   Beanley   Rennington

Hartside   Branxton   Powburn

Ingram   Fawdon   Glanton   River Aln

WINDYGATE HILL

CAUSEWAY
FLOODED
AT HIGH TIDE

HOLY ISLAND

Holy
Island

Lindisfarne
Priory   Lindisfarne

Castle Point

Guile Point

Budle
Bay

Staple
Sound   FARNE
ISLANDS

Inner
Sound

Bamburgh

Seahouses

North
Sunderland   Beadnell

Swinhoe   Beadnell Bay

Chathill   Tughall

Preston   High Newton
by-the-Sea

Brunton

Christon
Bank   Embleton

Embleton
Bay   Dunstanburgh

Dunstan   Craster

Stamford   Howick
Hall

Cullernose Point

Howick

Longhoughton

Denwick   Boulmer

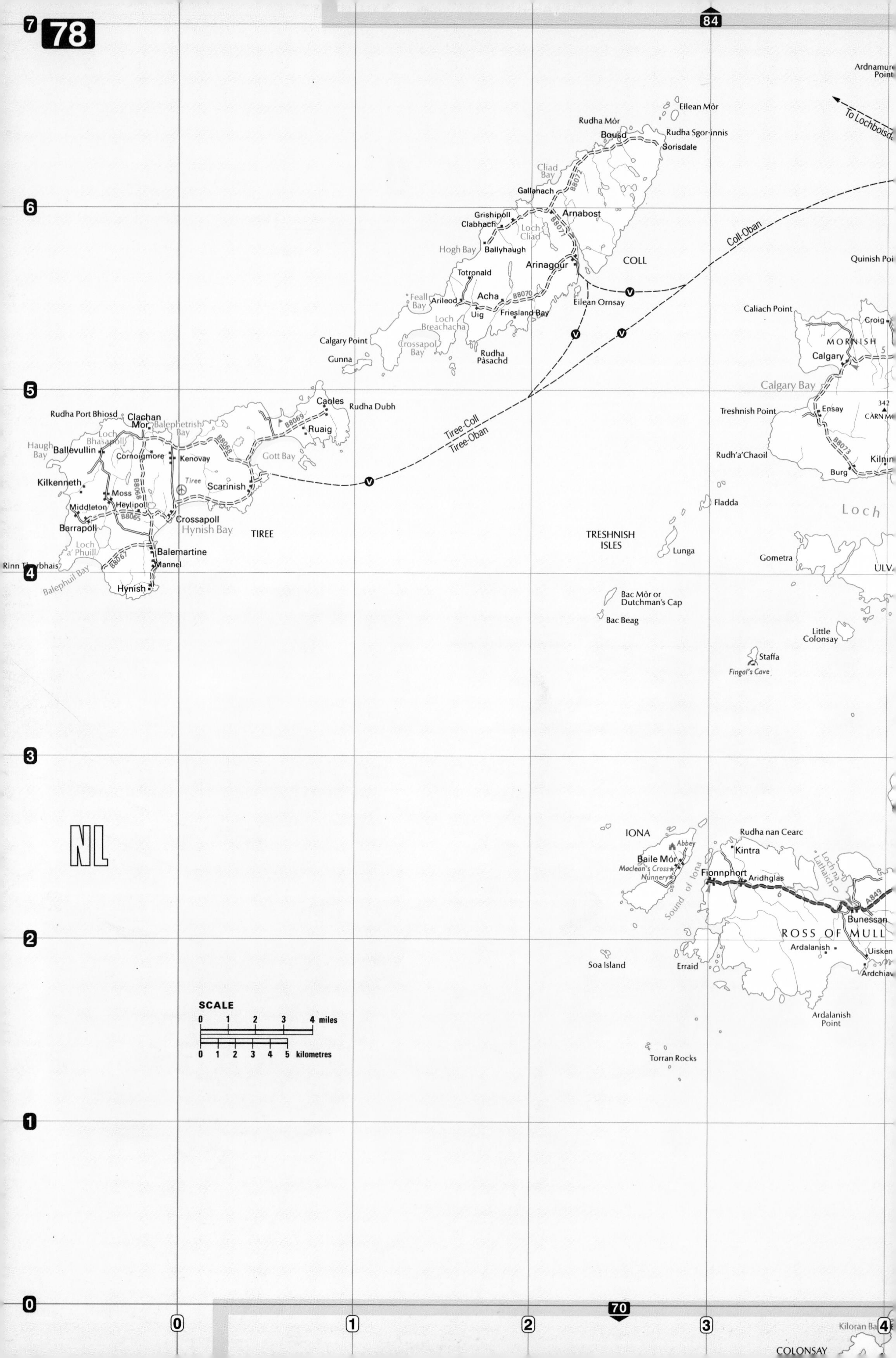

Ardnamurchan Point

To Lochboisda

Eilean Mòr
Rudha Mòr
Bousd
Rudha Sgor-innis
Sorisdale

Cliad
Bay
Gallanach

6

Grishipoll
Clabhach
Loch
Cliad
Arnabost

Coll-Oban

COLL

Quinish Poi

Hogh Bay
Ballyhaugh

Totronald
Arinagour

Calgary Point

MORNISH
Caliach Point
Croig

Feall
Bay
Arileod
Acha
B8070
Uig
Friesland Bay
Eilean Ornsay

Calgary

V

Calgary Point
Loch
Breachacha
Crossapol
Bay
Rudha Pàsachd

V

V

342
Treshnish Point
Ensay
CÀRN M

Gunna

5

Rudha Port Bhiosd
Clachan
Mor
Balephetrish
Bay
Caoles
Rudha Dubh

B8069
Ruaig

Tiree-Coll
Tiree-Oban

Rudh'a'Chaoil
Burg
Kilnin

Haugh
Bay
Loch
Bhasapoll
Ballevullin
Cornaigmore
Kenovay
Gott Bay

B8068

V

Fladda
Loch

Kilkenneth
Moss
Tiree
Scarinish

TRESHNISH
ISLES

Lunga

Gometra
ULV

Middleton
Heylipoll

Barrapoll
B8065
Crossapoll
Hynish Bay

TIREE

4

Rinn Thorbhais
Mannel
Balemartine

B8067

Loch
a' Phuill

Balephuil Bay
Hynish

Bac Mòr or
Dutchman's Cap

Bac Beag

Little
Colonsay

Staffa
Fingal's Cave

3

NL

IONA

Rudha nan Cearc

Abbey
Baile Mòr
Maclean's Cross
Nunnery
Fionnphort
Aridhglas

Kintra

Loch na
Lathaich

B8849

Bunessan

ROSS OF MULL

2

Soa Island
Erraid

Ardalanish
Uisken
Ardchia

SCALE

0 1 2 3 4 miles

0 1 2 3 4 5 kilometres

Ardalanish
Point

Torran Rocks

1

0

0   1   2   3   4

Kiloran Ba

COLONSAY

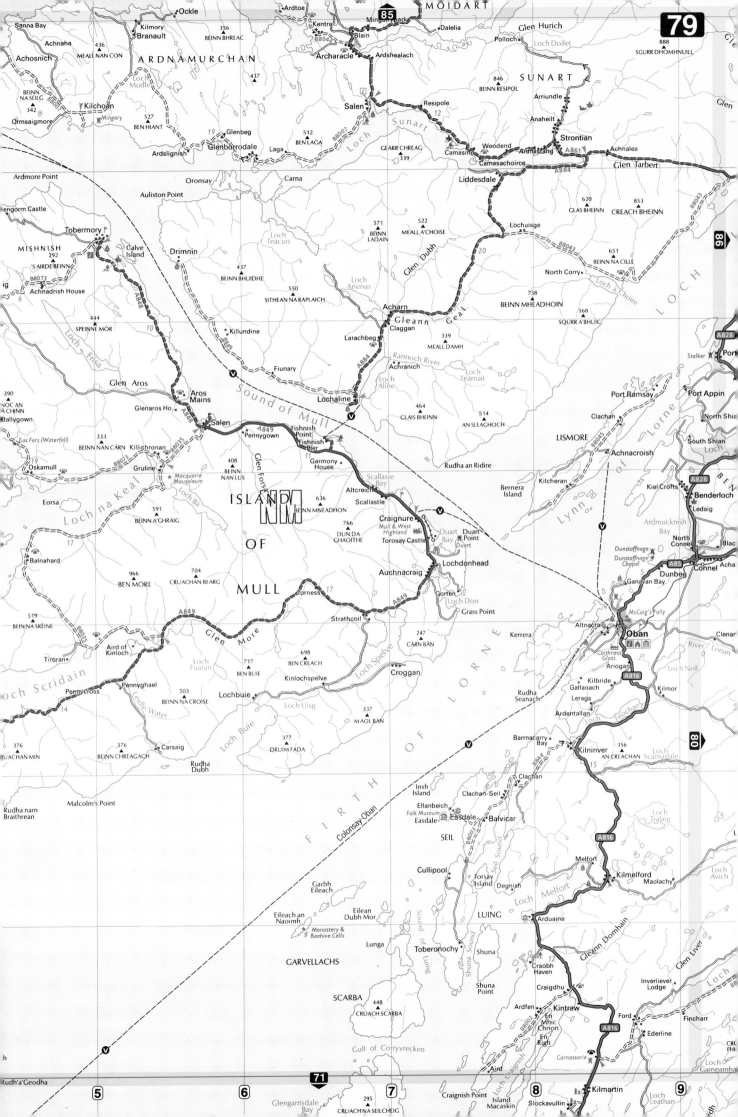

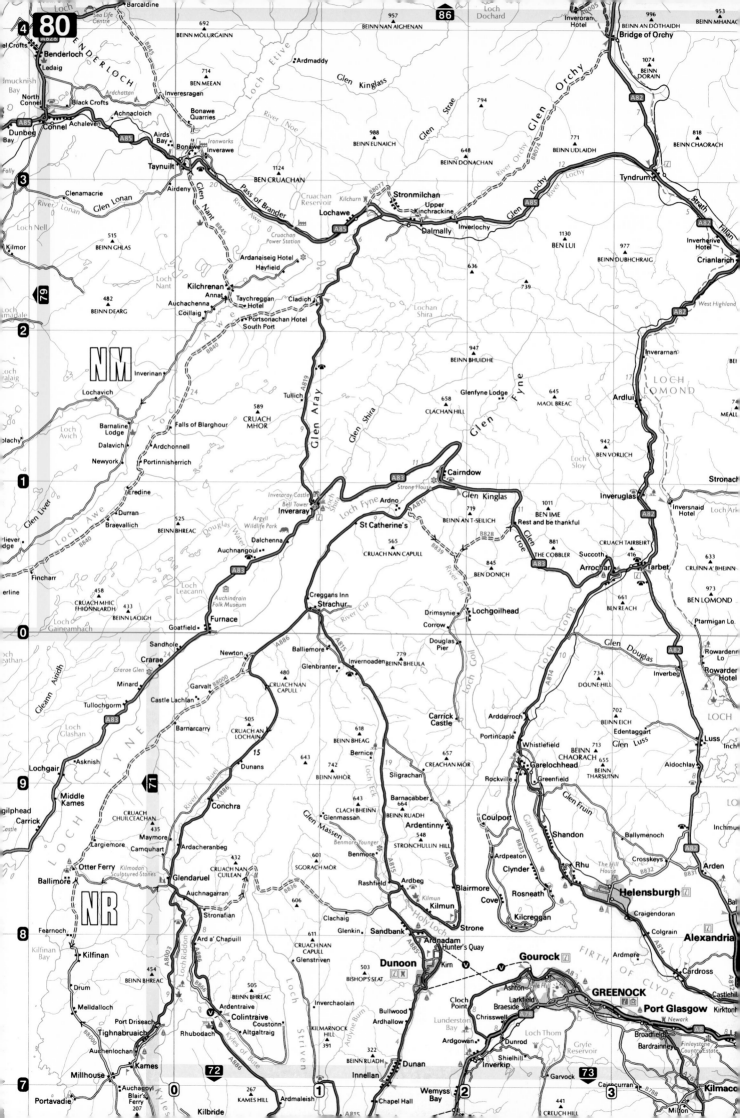

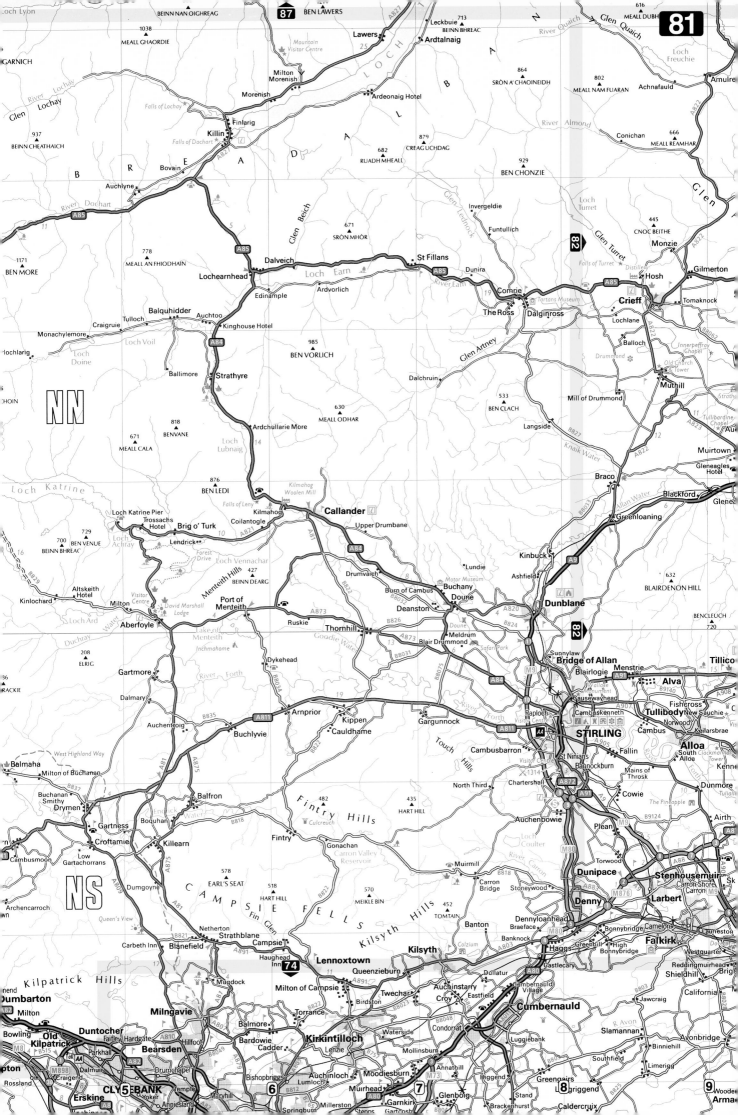

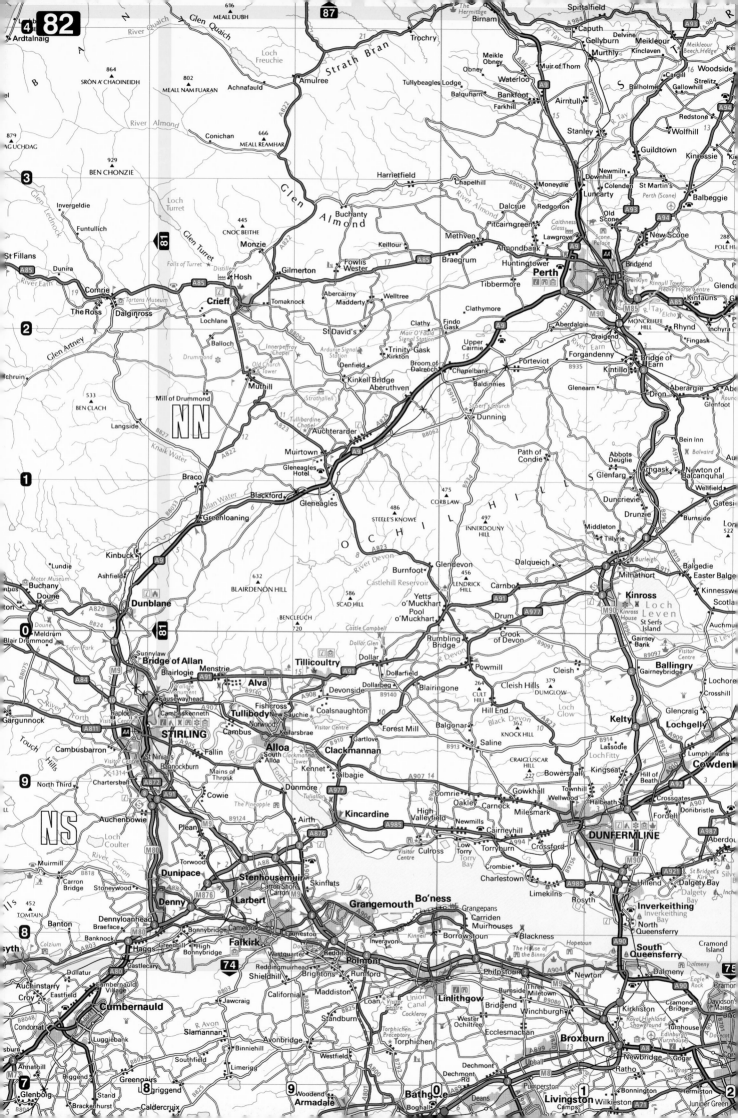

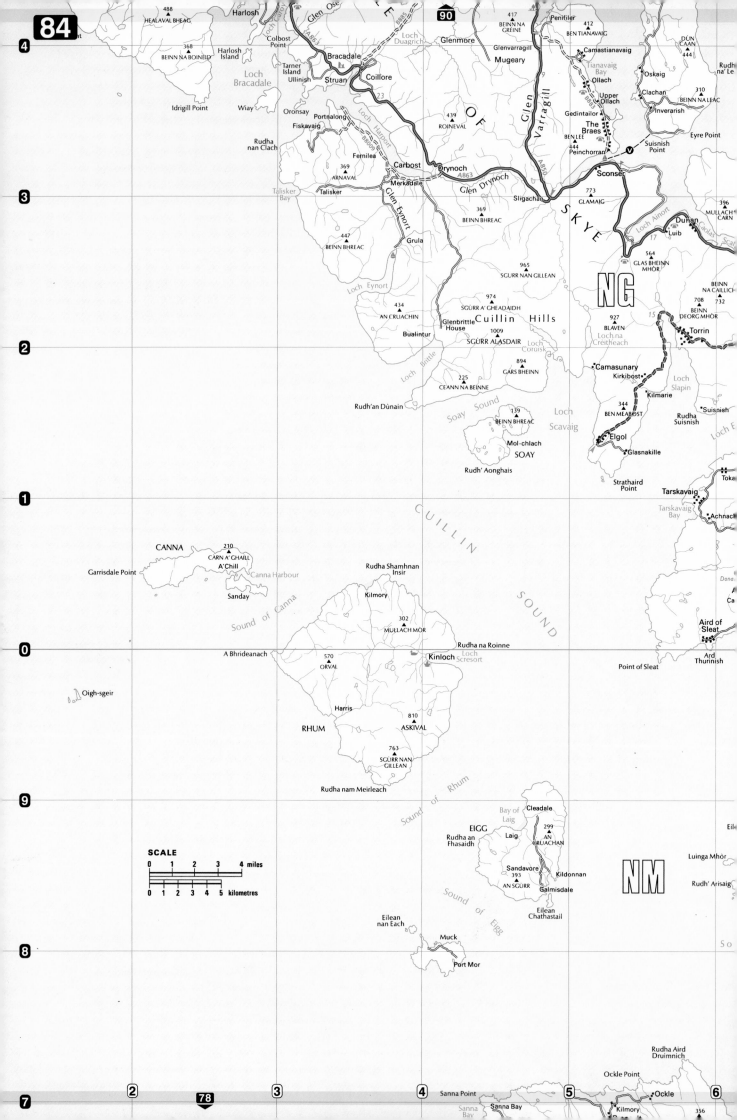

90

SCALE
0 1 2 3 4 miles
0 1 2 3 4 5 kilometres

CANNA

Garrisdale Point
CÀRN A' GHAILL 210
A'Chill
Canna Harbour
Sanday
Sound of Canna

Oigh-sgeir

A Bhrideanach
ORVAL 570
Harris
RHUM
ASKIVAL 810
SGÙRR NAN 763
GILLEAN
Rudha nam Meirleach

Rudha Shamhnan
Insir
Kilmory
MULLACH MÒR 302
Rudha na Roinne
Kinloch
Loch
Scresort

CUILLIN SOUND

EIGG
Rudha an
Fhasaidh
Bay of
Laig
Cleadale
Laig
AN 299
CRUACHAN
Sandavore
AN SGÙRR 393
Kildonnan
Galmisdale
Eilean
Chathastail

NM

Luinga Mhòr
Rudh' Arisaig

Sound of Rhum

Sound of Eigg

Eilean
nan Each
Muck
Port Mor

Aird of
Sleat
Ard
Thurinish
Point of Sleat

Rudha Aird
Druimnich
Ockle Point
Ockle
Kilmory
356

HEALAVAL BHEAG 488
Harlosh
Glen Ose
Colbost
Point
Bracadale
Coillore
BEINN NA BOINÈID 368
Harlosh
Island
Tarner
Island
Ullinish
Struan
Loch
Bracadale
Idrigill Point
Wiay
Oronsay
Fiskavaig
Portnalong
Rudha
nan Clach
Fernilea
Carbost
Talisker
Bay
ARNAVAL 369
Talisker
Merkadale
Drynoch
A863
BEINN BHREAC 447
Grula
Glen Eynort
Loch Eynort
Loch Harport
B8009
AN CRUACHIN 434
Bualintur
Glenbrittle
House
Loch Brittle
Rudh'an Dùnain
CEANN NA BEINNE 225
Soay Sound
BEINN BHREAC 139
Mol-chlach
SOAY
Rudh' Aonghais
Loch
Scavaig

Glenmore
Mugeary
Glen
Varragill
ROINEVAL 439
Drynoch
Glen Drynoch
Sligachan
SGÙRR NAN GILLEAN 965
SGÙRR A' GHEADAIDH 974
Cuillin Hills
SGÙRR ALASDAIR 1009
Loch
Coruisk
GARS BHEINN 894
Loch
Brittle
OF
SKYE
BEINN BHREAC 369
GLAMAIG 773
GLAS BHEINN 564
MHÒR
BLAVEN 927
Loch na
Crèitheach
Camasunary
Kirkibost
BEN MEABOST 344
Elgol
Glasnakille
Strathaird
Point

BEINN NA GRÈINE 417
Penifiler
BEINN TIANAVAIG 412
Camastianavaig
DÙN CAAN 444
Glenvarragill
Tianavaig
Bay
Ollach
Upper
Ollach
Gedintailor
The Braes
BEN LEE
444
Peinchorran
Sconser
Oskaig
Clachan
Inverarish
BEINN NA LEAC 310
Eyre Point
Suisnish
Point
Loch Ainort
Dunan
Luib
MULLACH 396
CARN
BEINN 708
DEORG MHÒR
BEINN 732
NA CAILLICH
Torrin
Camasunary
Loch
Slapin
Kilmarie
Rudha
Suisnish
Suisnish
Tarskavaig
Tarskavaig
Bay
Achnac
Toka

NG

Rudh'
na' Le

Sanna Point
Sanna Bay
Sanna
Bay

So

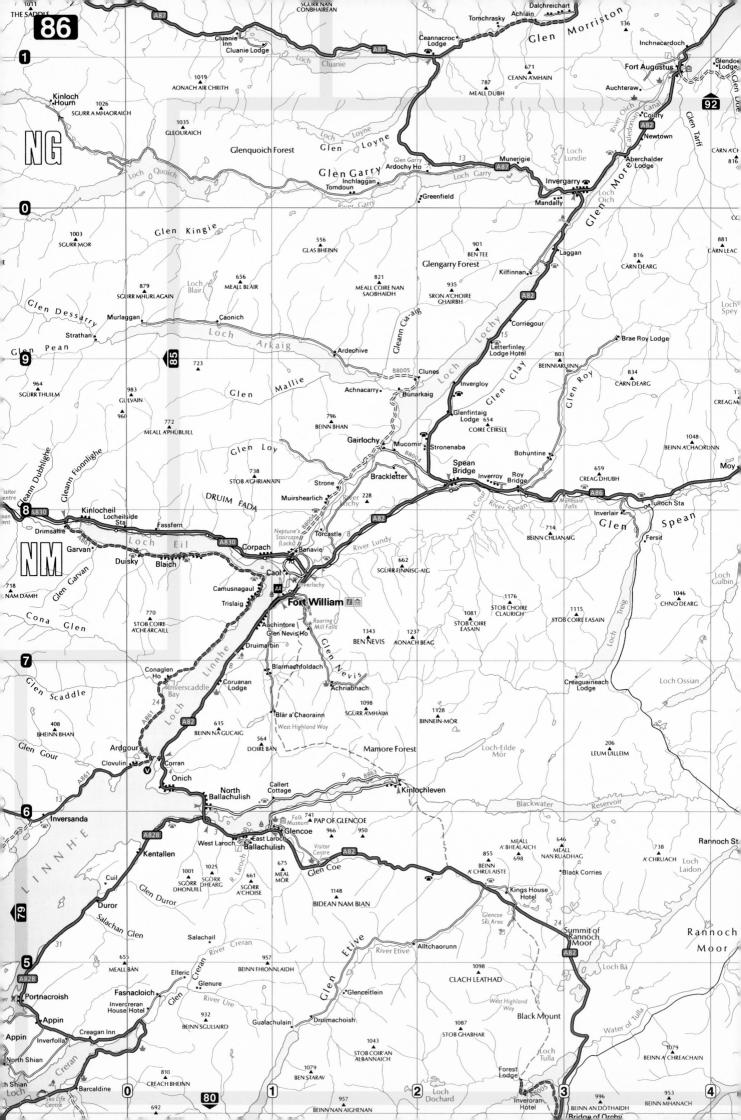

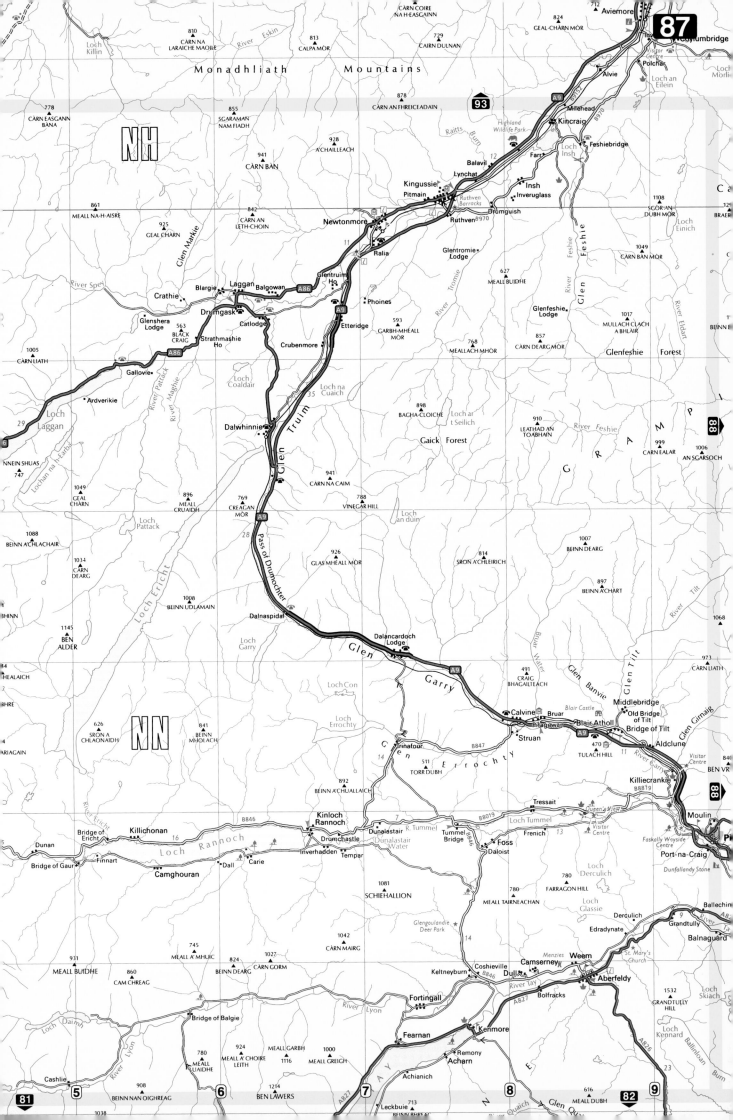

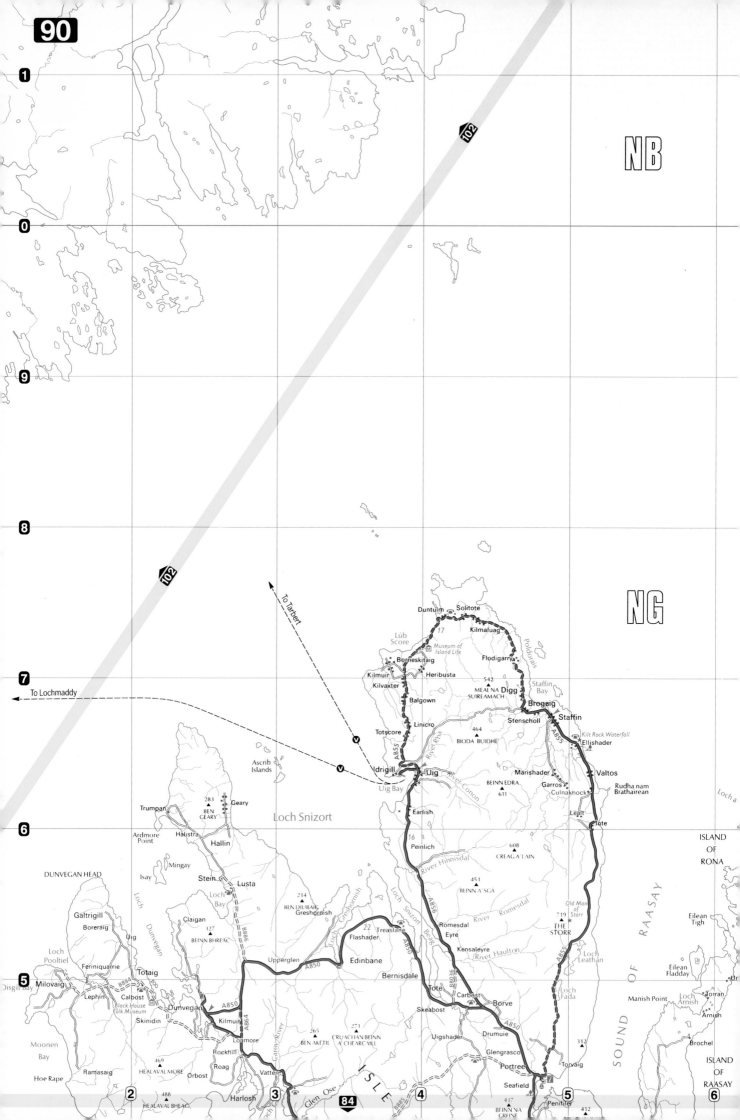

NB

NG

1

0

9

8

7

6

5

Duntulm Solitote

Kilmaluag

17

Borneskitaig Flodigarry

Museum of Island Life

Kilmuir Heribusta

Kilvaxter

542

MEAL NA Digg

Balgown SUIREAMACH

Brogaig

Staffin Bay

Staffin

Linicro Stenscholl

Totscore 464

BIODA BUIDHE Kilt Rock Waterfall

Ellishader

Idrigill Valtos

Uig Marishader

Uig Bay Garros Rudha nam

BEINN EDRA Brathairean

Earlish 611 Culnaknock

Lealt

Tote

Loch Snizort 16

Peinlich 608

CREAG A'LAIN

Trumpan 283 Geary

BEN River Hinnisdal

GEARY 451

Ardmore Halistra BEINN A'SGA

Point Hallin ISLAND

OF

Mingay RONA

Isay Stein Lusta Romesdal River Romesdal Eilean

214 Eyre 719 Tigh

DUNVEGAN HEAD BEN DIUBAIG Old Man

Greshornish Kensaleyre of Storr

Galtrigill THE STORR

Boreraig Claigan 427 22 Treaslane

BEINN BHREAC Flashader

Uig Upperglen Edinbane

Loch Bernisdale Eilean

Pooltiel Fladday

Feriniquarrie Tote

Milovaig Totaig Carbost Loch Manish Point

Disgill bay Borve Fada Loch

Lephin Skeabost Arnish

Black House Dunvegan Arnish

Folk Museum Kilmuir Drumuie

Skinidin Uigshader 312

Lonmore Glengrasco

Moonen 265 271 Portree ISLAND

Bay Rockhill BEN AKETIL CRUACHAN BEINN Seafield OF

Roag A' CHEARCAILL RAASAY

469 Vatten Torvaig

Hoe Rape Ramasaig HEALAVAL MORE 417 Penifiler

Orbost BEINN NA

Harlosh GRENE 412

488

HEALAVAL BHEAG

To Tarbert

To Lochmaddy

SOUND OF RAASAY

Loch Snizort Beag

A855

A856

A87

A850

A863

A864

B884

B886

B885

B8036

102

84

2 3 4 5 6

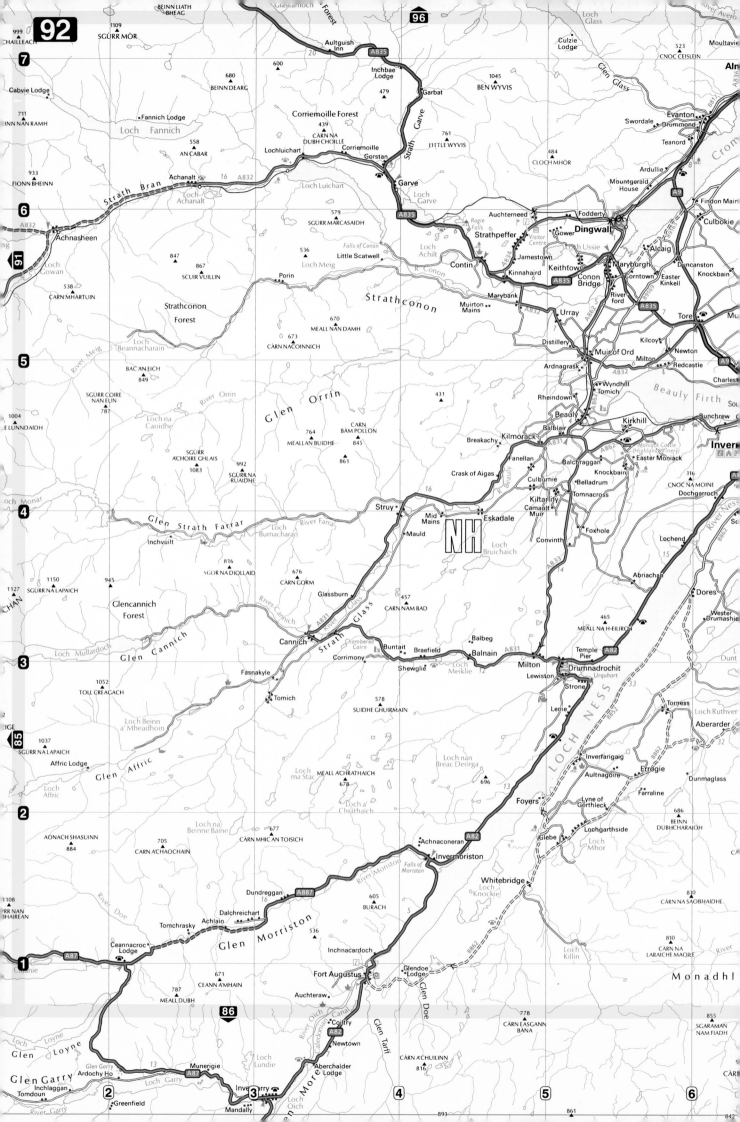

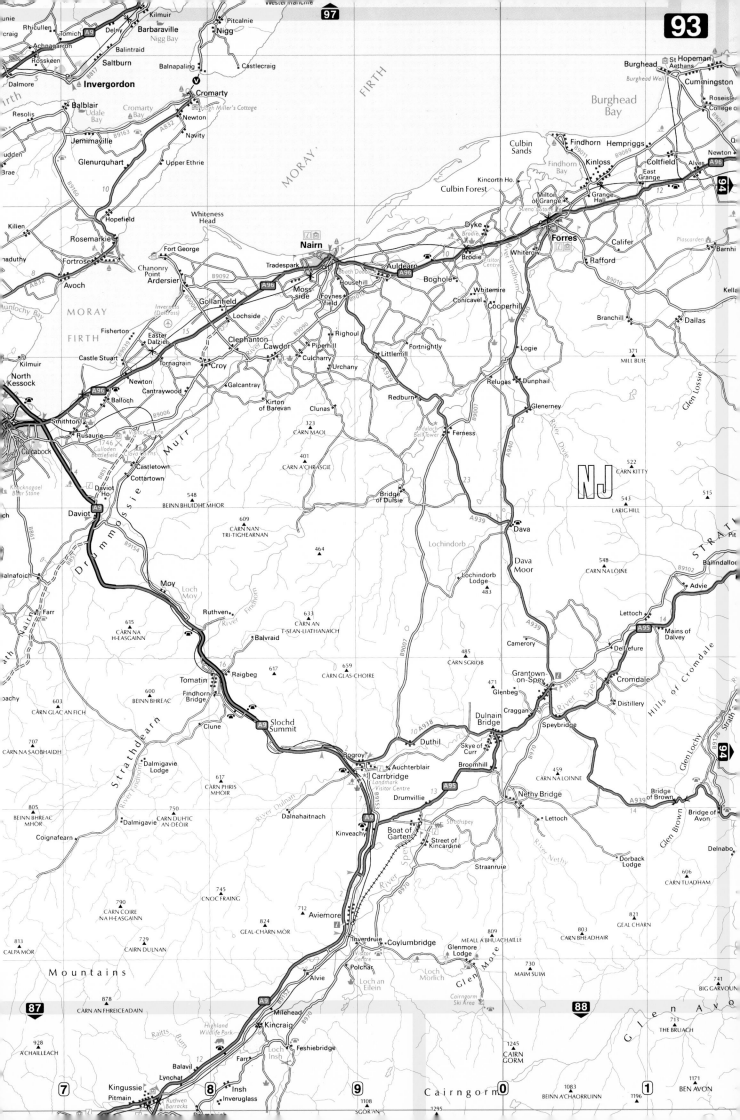

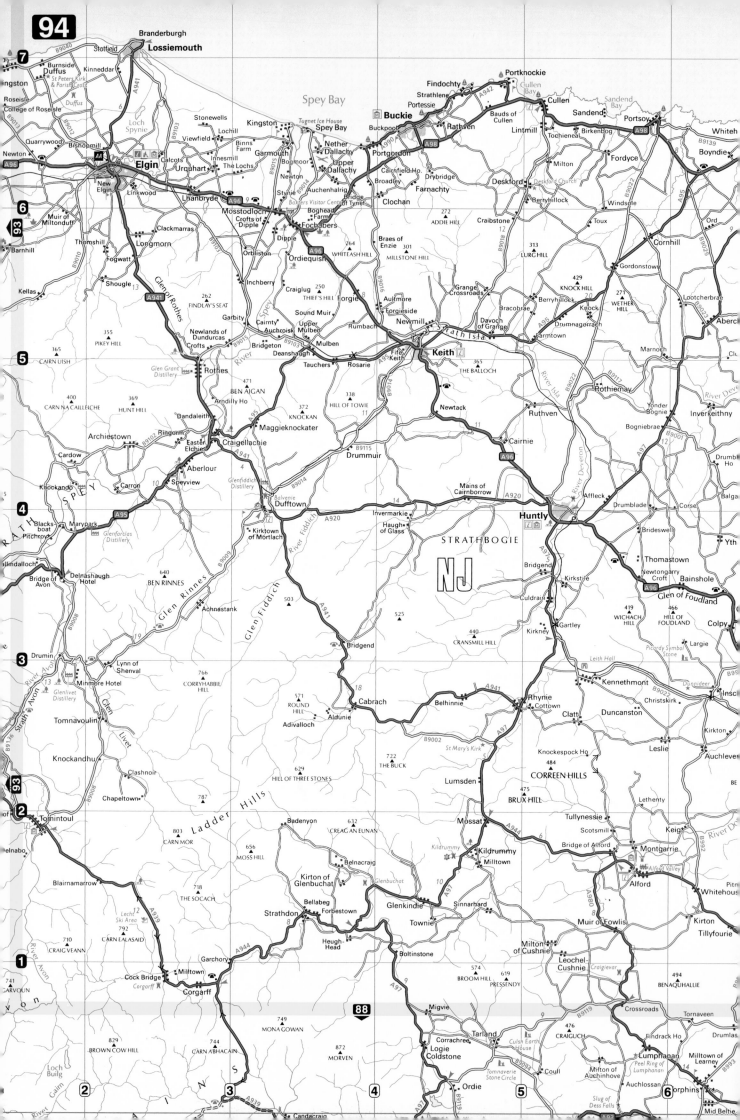

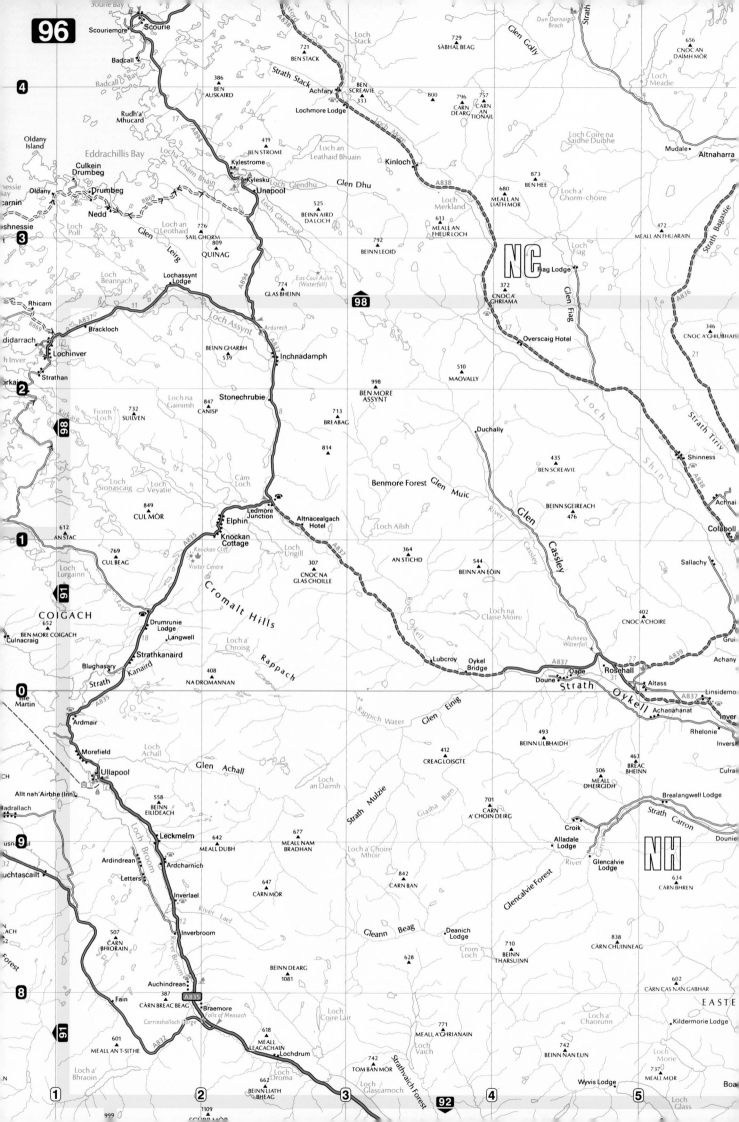

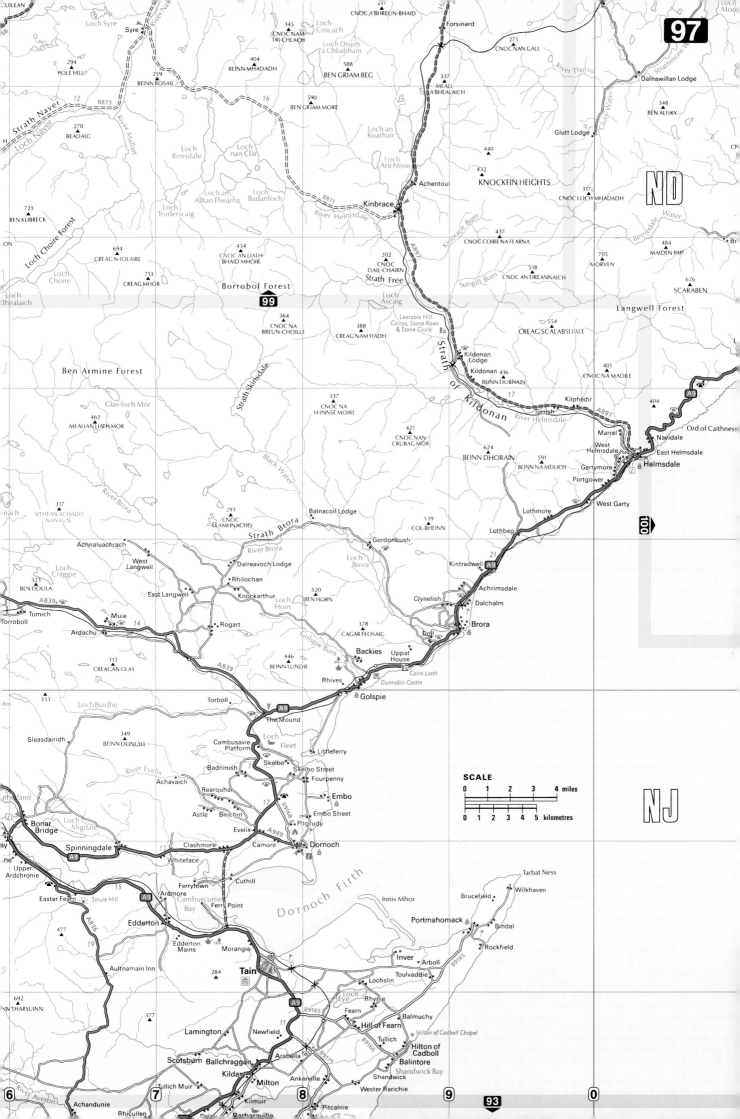

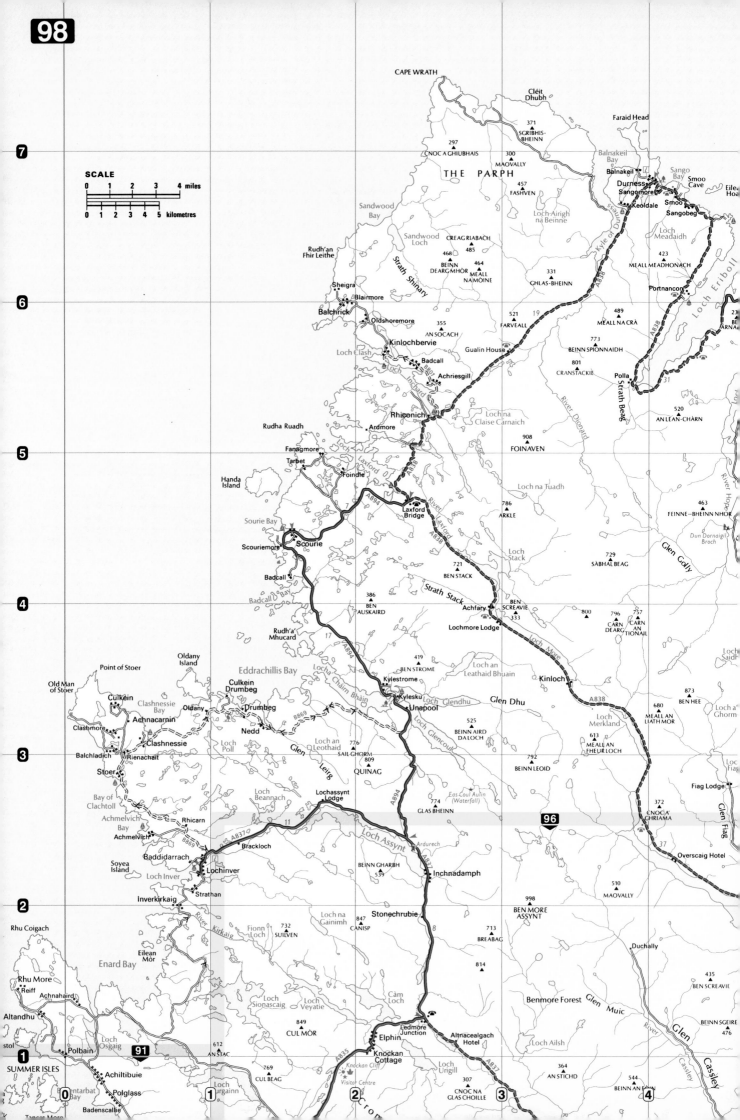

SCALE

0   1   2   3   4 miles

0 1 2 3 4 5 kilometres

CAPE WRATH

Cléit
Dhubh

Faraid Head

371
SCRIBHIS-
BHEINN

297
CNOC A GHIUBHAIS

300
MAOVALLY

THE PARPH

Balnakeil
Bay

Balnakeil

Sango
Bay

457
FASHVEN

Durness
Sangomore

Smoo
Cave

Eilea
Hoa

Loch Airigh
na Beinne

Keoldale

Smoo

Sangobeg

Sandwood
Bay

Sandwood
Loch

485
CREAG RIABACH

Loch
Meadaidh

Rudh'an
Fhir Leithe

468
BEINN
DEARG MHÓR

464
MEALL
NA MÒINE

423
MEALL MEADHONACH

331
GHLAS-BHEINN

Portnancon

Loch Eriboll

Sheigra

Blairmore

521
FARVEALL

19

489
MEALL NA CRÀ

23
BI
ARNA

Balchrick

Oldshoremore

355
AN SOCACH

773
BEINN SPIONNAIDH

31

Kinlochbervie

Gualin House

801
CRANSTACKIE

Polla

520
AN LEAN-CHÀRN

Loch Clash

Badcall

Strath Beag

Achriesgill

Loch na
Claise Carnaich

Rhiconich

908
FOINAVEN

Rudha Ruadh

Ardmore

Fanagmore

463
FEINNE-BHEINN NHOR

Tarbet

Foindle

786
ARKLE

Dun Dornaigil
Broch

Handa
Island

Loch na Tuadh

Laxford
Bridge

729
SÀBHAL BEAG

Glen Golly

Sourie Bay

7

A894

Scouriemore   Scourie

Loch
Stack

721
BEN STACK

Badcall

386
BEN
AUSKAIRD

Strath Stack

Achfary

BEN
SCREAVIE
333

800

796
CARN
DEARG

757
CARN
AN
TIONAIL

Badcall Bay

Lochmore Lodge

Loch
Saidh

Rudh'a'
Mhucard

17

Loch More

Point of Stoer

Oldany
Island

Eddrachillis Bay

419
BEN STROME

Loch an
Leathaid Bhuain

Kinloch

A838

873
BEN HEE

Loch a'
Ghorm

Old Man
of Stoer

Culkein

Culkein
Drumbeg

Kylestrome

680
MEALL AN
LIATH MÒR

Clashnessie
Bay

Drumbeg

Kylesku

Loch Glendhu

Glen Dhu

Achnacarnin

Oldany

Loch Merkland

Clashmore

Nedd

Unapool

525
BEINN AIRD
DA LOCH

613
MEALL AN
FHEUR LOCH

Clashnessie

BB69

Loch
Poll

776
SAIL GHORM

Loch Glencoul

Balchladich

Rienachait

Glen
Leirg

Loch an
t-Leothaid

809
QUINAG

792
BEINN LEOID

Stoer

Bay of
Clachtoll

Loch
Beannach

Lochassynt
Lodge

Eas Coul Aulin
(Waterfall)

774
GLAS BHEINN

Fiag Lodge

Achmelvich
Bay

Rhicarn

11

372
CNOC A'
GHRIAMA

Glen Fiag

Soyea
Island

A869

A837

Bracloch

Loch Assynt

Ardvreck

96

37

Baddidarrach

BEINN GHARBH
539

A837

Overscaig Hotel

Loch Inver

Lochinver

Inchnadamph

Inverkirkaig

Strathan

Stonechrubie

510
MAOVALLY

Rhu Coigach

River Kirkaig

Fionn
Loch

732
SUILVEN

847
CANISP

998
BEN MORE
ASSYNT

713
BREABAG

Duchally

Eilean
Mòr

Loch na
Gainimh

814

435
BEN SCREAVIE

Enard Bay

Loch
Veyatie

Rhu More

Reiff

Achnahaird

Càm
Loch

Benmore Forest

Glen Muic

BEINN SGEIRE
476

Loch
Sionascaig

Altandhu

849
CUL MÓR

Ledmore
Junction

Altnacealgach
Hotel

Loch Ailsh

Glen

stol

Loch
Osgaig

91

612
AN STAC

Elphin

A835

A837

364
AN STICHD

Polbain

SUMMER ISLES

Knockan
Cottage

Loch
Urigill

307
CNOC NA
GLAS CHOILLE

544
BEINN AN EOIN

Achiltibuie

769
CUL BEAG

Knockan Cliff

Visitor Centre

2

3

4

River Cassley

Glen
Cassley

Polglass

Badenscallie

1

Loch
Urgainn

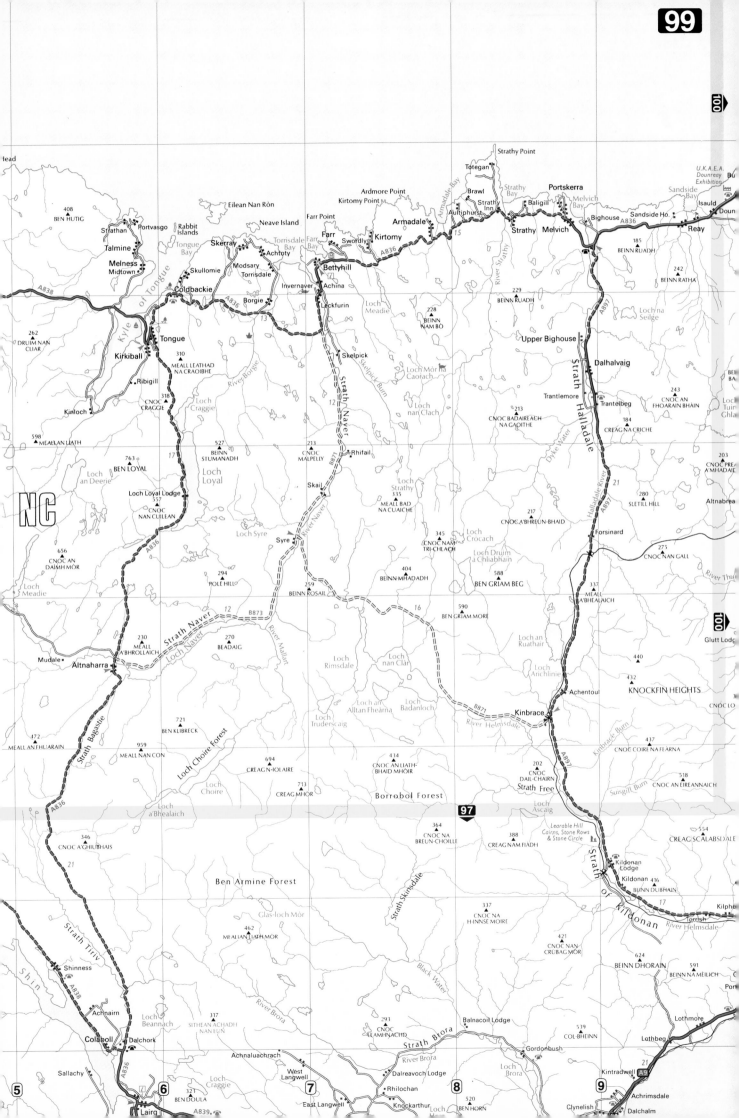

100

Head

408
BEN HUTIG

Portvasgo
Strathan
Talmine
Melness
Midtown

Rabbit
Islands
Eilean Nan Ròn

Skerray
Achtoty

Modsary
Torrisdale

Neave Island

Farr Point
Kirtomy Point
Ardmore Point

Armadale
Aultiphurst

Strathy
Inn
Brawl

Strathy Point

Strathy
Bay

Baligill

Portskerra

Melvich
Bay

Sandside
Bay

Isauld

U.K.A.E.A.
Dounreay
Exhibition

Doun

A838

Kyle of Tongue

Tongue
Bay

Coldbackie

Kirkiball

Tongue

Skullomie

A836

Borgie

Torrisdale
Bay

Farr
Bay

Farr
Swordly

Kirtomy

A836

Bettyhill
Invernaver
Achina

Leckfurin

15

A836

Strathy
Melvich
Bighouse

A836

Reay

185
BEINN RUADH

242
BEINN RATHA

River Strathy

229
BEINN RUADH

Loch
Meadie

228
BEINN
NAM BÒ

Upper Bighouse

Dalhalvaig

Trantlemore
Trantlebeg

A897

243
CNOC AN
FHOARAIN BHAIN

Loch na
Seilge

BE
BA

Loch
Tui
Gha

262
DRUIM NAN
CLIAR

Ribigill

13

318
CNOC
CRAGGIE

310
MEALL LEATHAD
NA CRAOIBHE

River Borgie

Loch
Craggie

Skelpick

Skelpick Burn

Strath Naver

12

Loch Mòr na
Caorach

Loch
nan Clach

213
CNOC BADAIREACH
NA GADITHE

Strath Halladale

203
CNOC PRE
A'MHADAI

Kinloch

598
MEALLAN LIATH

17

763
BEN LOYAL

Loch
an Deerie

527
BEINN
STUMANADH

Loch
Loyal

213
CNOC
MALPELLY

B871
Rhifail

Skail

Loch
Strathy

335
MEALL BAD
NA CUAICHE

217
CNOC A'BHREUN-BHAID

184
CREAG NA CRICHE

280
SLETILL HILL

Altnabrea

NC

Loch Loyal Lodge

557
CNOC
NAN CUILEAN

Loch Syre

Syre

River Naver

345
CNOC NAM
TRI-CHLACH

Loch
Crocach

Loch Druim
a'Chliabhain

Forsinard

Halladale River

21

275
CNOC NAN GALL

River Thu

656
CNOC AN
DAIMH MÒR

Loch
Meadie

294
POLE HILL

259
BEINN ROSAIL

404
BEINN MHADADH

588
BEN GRIAM BEG

337
MEALL
A'BHEALAICH

100

Glutt Lodg

12
B873

Strath Naver

230
MEALL
A'BHROLLAICH

270
BEADAIG

River Mallart

16

590
BEN GRIAM MORE

Loch an
Ruathair

440

432

KNOCKFIN HEIGHTS

CNÓC LO

Mudale
Altnaharra

Loch Naver

Loch
Rimsdale

Loch
nan Clàr

Loch
Arichlinie

Achentoul

472
MEALL AN FHUARAIN

721
BEN KLIBRECK

959
MEALL NAN CON

Strath Bagastie

Loch
Truderscaig

Loch an
Alltan Fhearna

Loch
Badanloch

B871

Kinbrace

River Helmsdale

Kinbrace Burn

437
CNOC COIRE NA FÉARNA

Loch Choire Forest

694
CREAG N-IOLAIRE

414
CNOC AN LIATH-
BHAID MHÒIR

202
CNOC
DAIL-CHAIRN

518
CNOC AN EIREANNAICH

Suisgill Burn

713
CREAG MHOR

Loch
Choire

Borrobol Forest

Strath Free

A897

97

Loch
a'Bhealaich

346
CNOC A'GHIUBHAIS

364
CNOC NA
BREUN-CHOILLE

388
CREAG NAM FIADH

Loch
Ascaig

Learable Hill
Cairns, Stone Rows
& Stone Circle

Strath of Kildonan

554
CREAG SCALABSDALE

A836

21

Ben Armine Forest

Kildonan
Lodge

Kildonan

416
BEINN DUBHAIN

Strath Skinsdale

Glas-loch Mòr

462
MEALL AN LIATH MÒR

337
CNOC NA
H-INNSE MOIRE

421
CNOC NAN
CRUBAG MÒR

17

Kilph

River Helmsdale

Torrish

Shin

Strath Tirry

Shinness

A838

624
BEINN DHORAIN

591
BEINN NA MEILICH

Por

Achnairn

Loch
Beannach

317
SITHEAN ACHADH
NAN EUN

River Brora

293
CNOC
LEAMHNACHD

Balnacoil Lodge

Strath Brora

539
COL-BHEINN

Lothmore

Colaboll
Dalchork

Sallachy

321
BEN DOULA

Achnaluachrach

West
Langwell

Dalreavoch Lodge

Gordonbush

Loch
Brora

Kintradwell

Lothbeg

21

A9

Lairg

A839

East Langwell

Rhilochan

Knockarthur

520
BEN HORN

Clynelish

Achrimsdale

Dalchalm

5   6   7   8   9

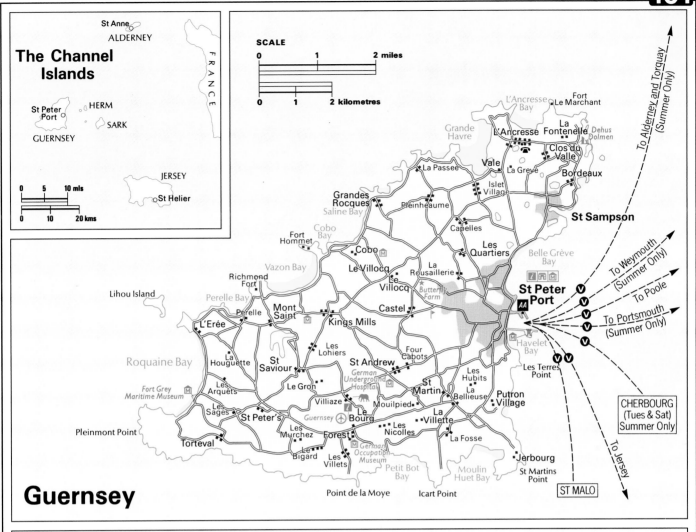

Guernsey

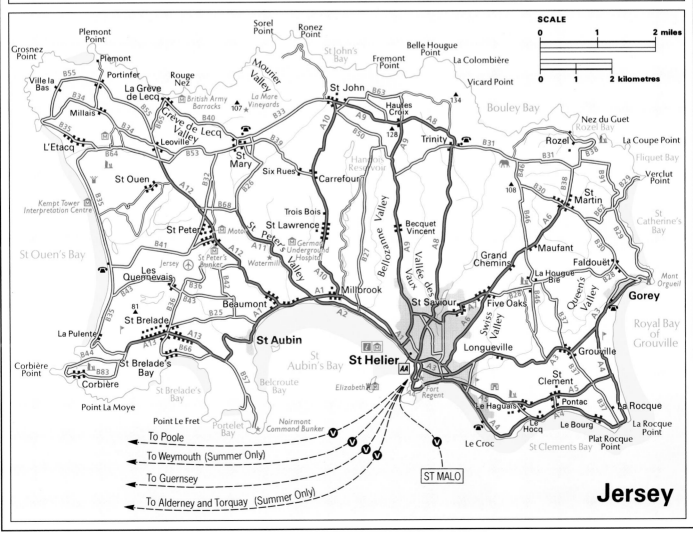

Jersey

Outer Hebrides

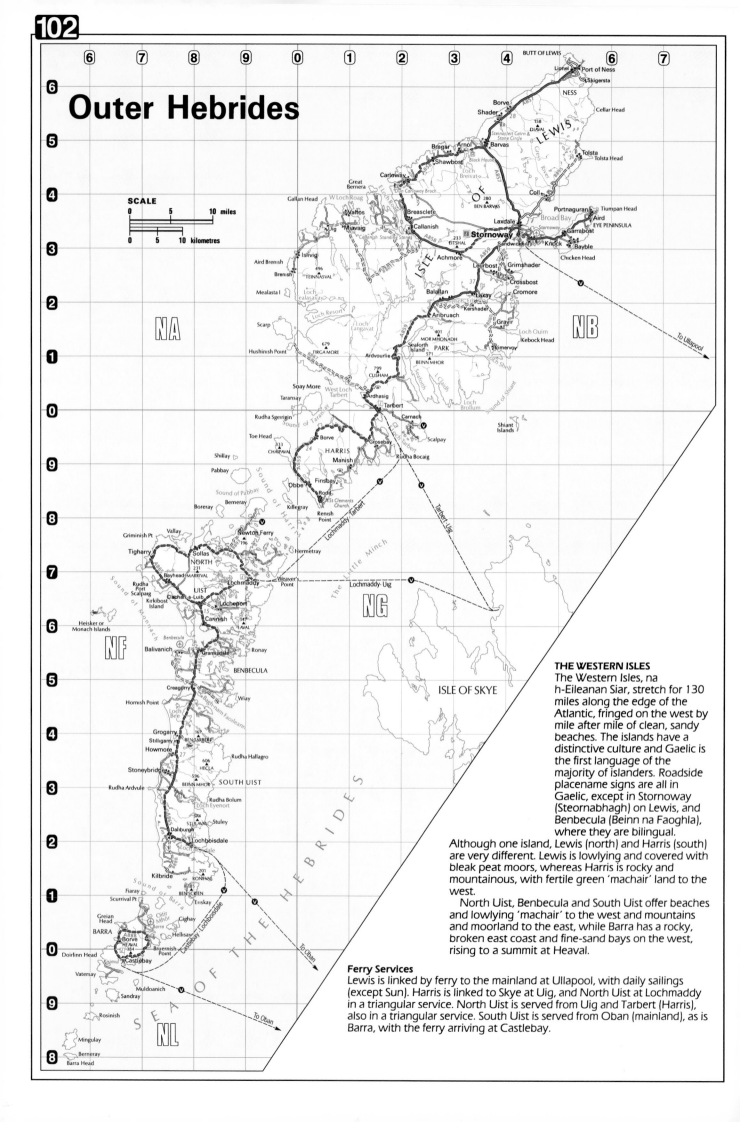

SCALE

0 — 5 — 10 miles

0 — 5 — 10 kilometres

BUTT OF LEWIS

NA

NB

NG

NF

NL

ISLE OF SKYE

THE WESTERN ISLES

The Western Isles, na h-Eileanan Siar, stretch for 130 miles along the edge of the Atlantic, fringed on the west by mile after mile of clean, sandy beaches. The islands have a distinctive culture and Gaelic is the first language of the majority of islanders. Roadside placename signs are all in Gaelic, except in Stornoway (Steornabhagh) on Lewis, and Benbecula (Beinn na Faoghla), where they are bilingual.

Although one island, Lewis (north) and Harris (south) are very different. Lewis is lowlying and covered with bleak peat moors, whereas Harris is rocky and mountainous, with fertile green 'machair' land to the west.

North Uist, Benbecula and South Uist offer beaches and lowlying 'machair' to the west and mountains and moorland to the east, while Barra has a rocky, broken east coast and fine-sand bays on the west, rising to a summit at Heaval.

Ferry Services

Lewis is linked by ferry to the mainland at Ullapool, with daily sailings (except Sun). Harris is linked to Skye at Uig, and North Uist at Lochmaddy in a triangular service. North Uist is served from Uig and Tarbert (Harris), also in a triangular service. South Uist is served from Oban (mainland), as is Barra, with the ferry arriving at Castlebay.

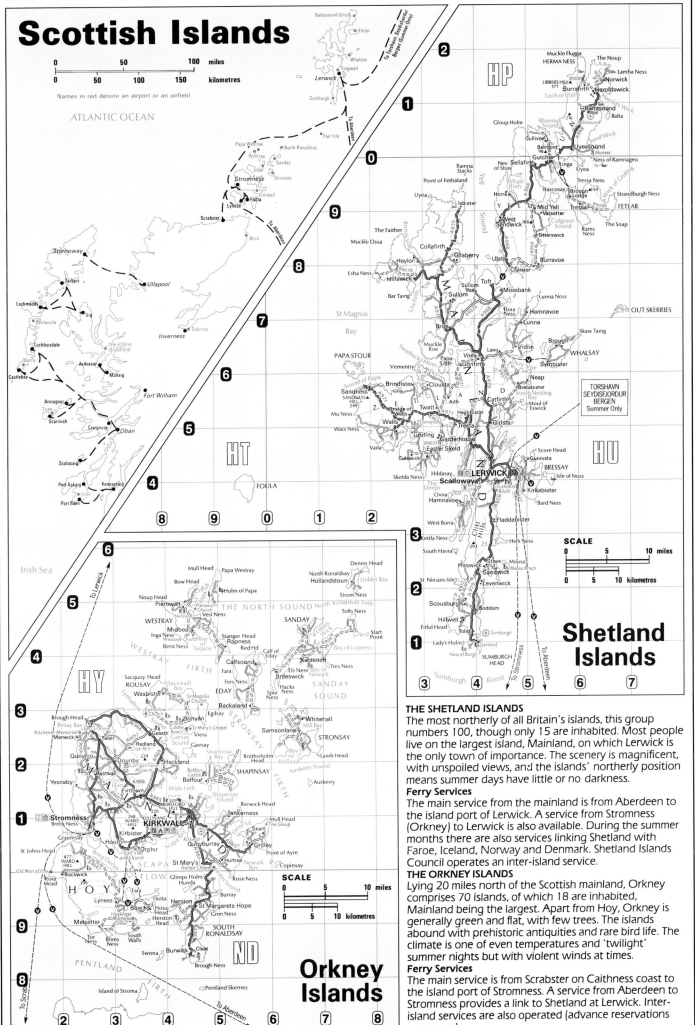

Scottish Islands

0 50 100 miles
0 50 100 150 kilometres

Names in red denote an airport or an airfield

ATLANTIC OCEAN

Irish Sea

Shetland Islands

SCALE
0   5   10 miles
0   5   10 kilometres

Orkney Islands

SCALE
0   5   10 miles
0   5   10 kilometres

THE SHETLAND ISLANDS
The most northerly of all Britain's islands, this group numbers 100, though only 15 are inhabited. Most people live on the largest island, Mainland, on which Lerwick is the only town of importance. The scenery is magnificent, with unspoiled views, and the islands' northerly position means summer days have little or no darkness.

Ferry Services
The main service from the mainland is from Aberdeen to the island port of Lerwick. A service from Stromness (Orkney) to Lerwick is also available. During the summer months there are also services linking Shetland with Faroe, Iceland, Norway and Denmark. Shetland Islands Council operates an inter-island service.

THE ORKNEY ISLANDS
Lying 20 miles north of the Scottish mainland, Orkney comprises 70 islands, of which 18 are inhabited, Mainland being the largest. Apart from Hoy, Orkney is generally green and flat, with few trees. The islands abound with prehistoric antiquities and rare bird life. The climate is one of even temperatures and 'twilight' summer nights but with violent winds at times.

Ferry Services
The main service is from Scrabster on Caithness coast to the island port of Stromness. A service from Aberdeen to Stromness provides a link to Shetland at Lerwick. Inter-island services are also operated (advance reservations necessary).

Ireland

Abbeydorney G2
Abbeyfeale G2
Abbeyleix G4
Adamstown G4
Adare G2
Adrigole H2
Ahascragh F3
Ahoghill D5
Allihies H1
Anascaul H1
Annalong E5
Annestown H4
Antrim D5
Ardagh G2
Ardara D3
Ardcath F5
Ardee E4
Ardfert G2
Ardfinnan G3
Ardglass E5
Ardgroom H1
Arklow G5
Arless G4
Armagh D4
Armoy C5
Arthurstown H4
Arvagh E4
Ashbourne F4
Ashford F5
Askeaton G2
Athboy E4
Athea G2
Athenry F3
Athleague F3
Athlone F3
Athy F4
Augher D4
Aughnacloy D4
Aughrim G5
Avoca G5

Bailieborough E4
Balbriggan F5
Balla E2
Ballacolla G4
Ballaghaderreen E3
Ballina G3
Ballina E2
Ballinafad E3
Ballinagh E4
Ballinakill G4
Ballinalee E3
Ballinamallard D4
Ballinamore F3
Ballinamore E3
Ballinascarty H2
Ballinasloe F3
Ballindine E2
Ballineen H2
Ballingarry G3
Ballingarry G2
Ballingeary H2
(Beal Atha an Ghaorfthaidh)
Ballinhassig H3
Ballinlough E3
Ballinrobe E2
Ballinspittle H2
Ballintober E3
Ballintra D3
Ballivor F4
Ballon G4
Ballybaun F3
Ballybay E4
Ballybofey D3
Ballybunion G2
Ballycanew G5
Ballycarry D5
Ballycastle D2
Ballycastle C5
Ballyclare D5
Ballyconneely F1
Ballycotton H3
Ballycumber F3
Ballydehob J2
Ballydesmond H2
Ballyduff H3
Ballyduff G2
Ballyfarnan E3
Ballygalley D5
Ballygar F3
Ballygawley D4
Ballygowan D5
Ballyhaise E4
Ballyhale G4
Ballyhaunis E3
Ballyhean E2
Ballyheige G1
Ballyjamesduff E4
Ballykeeran F3
Ballylanders G3
Ballylongford G2
Ballylooby G3
Ballylynan G4
Ballymahon F3
Ballymakeery H2
Ballymaloe H3
Ballymena D5
Ballymoe E3
Ballymoney C4
Ballymore F3
Ballymore Eustace F4
Ballymote E3
Ballynahinch D5
Ballynure D5

Ballyragget G4
Ballyroan G4
Ballyronan D4
Ballysadare E3
Ballyshannon D3
Ballyvaughan F2
Ballywalter D5
Balrothery F5
Baltimore J2
Baltinglass G4
Banagher F3
Banbridge D5
Bandon H2
Bangor D5
Bangor Erris E2
Bansha G3
Banteer H2
Bantry H2
Barryporeen H3
Beaufort H2
Belcoo D3
Belfast D5
Belgooly H3
Bellaghy D4
Belleek D3
Belmullet D2
(Beal an Mhuirhead)
Belturbet E4
Benburb D4
Bennetsbridge G4
Beragh D4
Birr F3
Blacklion D3
Blackwater G5
Blarney H3
Blessington F4
Boherbue H2
Borris G4
Borris-in-Ossory G3
Borrisokane F3
Borrisoleigh G3
Boyle E3
Bracknagh F4
Bray F5
Bridgetown H4
Brittas F4
Broadford G3
Broadford G2
Broughshane D5
Bruff G3
Bruree G3
Bunclody G4
Buncrana C4
Bundoran D3
Bunnahowen D2
Bunnyconnellan E2
Bushmills C4
Butler's Bridge E4
Buttevant H2

Cadamstown F3
Caherconlish G3
Caherdaniel H1
Cahir G3
Cahirciveen H1
Caledon D4
Callan G4
Caltra F3
Camolin G4
Camp G1
Cappagh White G3
Cappamore G3
Cappoquin H3
Carlanstown E4
Carlingford E5
Carlow G4
Carndonagh C4
Carnew G4
Carnlough C5
Carracastle E3
Carrick D3
(An Charraig)
Carrickfergus D5
Carrickmacross E4
Carrickmore D4
Carrick-on-Shannon E3
Carrick -on-Suir G4
Carrigahorig F3
Carrigaline H3
Carrigallen E3
Carriganimmy H2
Carrigans C4
Carrigtohill H3
Carrowkeel C4
Carryduff D5
Cashel G3
Castlebar E2
Castlebellingham E5
Castleblayney E4
Castlebridge G4
Castlecomer G4
Castle Cove H1
Castlederg D4
Castledermot G4
Castleisland G2
Castlemaine H2
Castlemartyr H3
Castleplunkett E3
Castlepollard E4
Castlerea E3
Castlerock C4
Castleshane E4
Castletown F4
Castletownbere H1

Castletownroche H3
Castletownshend J2
Castlewellan E5
Causeway G2
Cavan E4
Ceanannus Mor (Kells) E4
Celbridge F4
Charlestown E3
Clady D4
Clane F4
Clara F3
Clarecastle G2
Claremorris E2
Clarinbridge F2
Clashmore H3
Claudy C4
Cliffony D3
Clogan F3
Clogh G4
Clogheen H3
Clogher D4
Clohamon G4
Clonakilty H2
Clonard F4
Clonaslee F4
Clonbulloge F4
Clonbur (An Fhairche) E2
Clondalkin F4
Clones E4
Clonmany C4
Clonmel G3
Clonmellon E4
Clonmore G3
Clonony F3
Clonoulty G3
Clonroche G4
Clontibret E4
Cloonbannin H2
Cloondara E3
Cloonkeen H2
Cloonlara G3
Clough D5
Cloughjordan F3
Cloyne H3
Coagh D4
Coalisland D4
Cobh H3
Coleraine C4
Collinstown E4
Collon E4
Collooney E3
Comber D5
Conna H3
Cookstown D4
Coole E4
Cooraclare G2
Cootehill E4
Cork H3
Cork Airport H3
Cornamona F2
Corofin F2
Courtmacsherry H2
Courtown Harbour G5
Craigavon D5
Craughwell F3
Creggs E3
Cresslough C3
Croagh G2
Crolly (Croithli) C3
Crookedwood E4
Crookhaven J1
Crookstown H2
Croom G2
Crossakeel E4
Cross Barry H2
Crosshaven H3
Crossmaglen E4
Crossmolina E2
Crumlin D5
Crusheen F2
Culdaff C4
Culleybackey D5
Curracloe G4
Curraghboy F3
Curry E3

Daingean F4
Delvin E4
Derrygonnelly D3
Derrylin E4
Dervock C4
Dingle (An Daingean) H1
Doagh D5
Donaghadee D5
Donaghmore G3
Donegal D3
Doneraile H3
Doonbeg G2
Douglad H3
Downpatrick D5
Dowra E3
Draperstown D4
Drimoleague H2
Dripsey H2
Drogheda E5
Droichead Nua F4
(Newbridge)
Dromahair D3
Dromcolliher G2
Dromore D5

Dromore D4
Dromore West D2
Drum E4
Drumconrath E4
Drumkeeran E3
Drumlish E3
Drumod E3
Drumquin D4
Drumshanbo E3
Drumsna E3
Duagh G2
Dublin F5
Duleek E4
Dunboyne F4
Duncormick H4
Dundalk E5
Dunderrow H2
Dundrum E5
Dunfanaghy C3
Dungannon D4
Dungarvan H3
Dungarvan G4
Dungiven C4
Dungloe C3
Dungourney H3
Dunkineely D3
Dun Laoghaire F5
Dunlavin F4
Dunleer E4
Dunloy C5
Dunmanway H2
Dunmore E3
Dunmore East H4
Dunmurry D5
Dunshaughlin F4
Durrow G4
Durrus H2

Eaky D2
Edenderry F4
Edgeworthstown E3
Eglinton C4
Elphin E3
Emyvale D4
Enfield F4
Ennis G2
Enniscorthy G4
Enniscrone D2
Enniskean H2
Enniskillen D4
Ennistymon F2
Eyrecourt F3

Farnaght E3
Farranfore H2
Feakle F3
Fenagh E3
Fermoy H3
Ferns G4
Fethard H4
Fethard G3
Finnea E4
Fintona D4
Fivemiletown D4
Fontstown F4
Foulkesmills G4
Foxford E2
Foynes G2
Freemount G2
Frenchpark E3
Freshford G4
Fuerty E3

Galbally G3
Galway F2
Garrison D3
Garvagh C4
Geashill F4
Gilford D5
Glandore J2
Glanmire H3
Glanworth H3
Glaslough D4
Glassan F3
Glenamaddy E3
Glenarm C5
Glenavy D5
Glenbeigh H1
Glencolumbkille D3
(Gleann Cholm Cille)
Glendalough F5
Glenealy G5
Glenfarne D3
Glengarriff H2
Glenmore G4
Glenties D3
Glenville H3
Glin G2
Glinsk F2
(Glinsce)
Golden G3
Goleen J1
Goresbridge G4
Gorey G5

Gort F2
Gortin D4
Gowran G4
Graiguenamanagh G4
Grallagh E3
Granard E4
Grange D3
Greencastle E5
Greyabbey D5
Greystones F5
Gulladuff D4

Hacketstown G4
Headford F2
Herbertstown G3
Hillsborough D5
Hilltown E5
Hospital G3
Holycross G3
Holywood D5
Howth F5

Inch H1
Inchigeelagh H2
Inishannon H2

Johnstown G3

Kanturk H2
Keadue E3
Keady E4
Keel E1
Keenagh E3
Kells D5
Kenmare H2
Kesh D3
Kilbeggan F4
Kilberry E4
Kilbrittain H2
Kilcar D3
(Cill Charthaigh)
Kilcock F4
Kilcolgan F2
Kilconnell F3
Kilconnell F2
Kilcoole F5
Kilcormac F3
Kilcullen F4
Kilcurry E4
Kildare F4
Kildavin G4
Kildorrery H3
Kildress D4
Kilfenora F2
Kilfinnane G3
Kilgarvan H2
Kilkee G2
Kilkeel E5
Kilkelly E2
Kilkenny G4
Kilkieran F2
(Cill Ciarain)
Kilkinlea G2
Kill H4
Killadysert G2
Killala D2
Killaloe G3
Killarney H2
Killashandra E4
Killashee E3
Killeagh H3
Killeigh F4
Killenaule G3
Killimer G2
Killimor F3
Killiney F5
Killinick H4
Killorglin H1
Killough E5
Killucan F4
Killybegs D3
Killyleagh D5
Kilmacanoge F5
Kilmacrenan C3
Kilmacthomas H4
Kilmaganny G4
Kilmaine E2
Kilmallock G3
Kilmanagh G4
Kilmanahan G3
Kilmeaden H4
Kilmeage F4
Kilmeedy G2
Kilmichael H2
Kilmore Quay H4
Kilnaleck E4
Kilrea C4
Kilrush G2
Kilsheelan G3
Kiltealy G4
Kiltegan G4
Kiltimagh E2
Kiltoom F3
Kingscourt E4

Kinlough D3
Kinnegad F4
Kinnitty F3
Kinsale H3
Kinvarra F2
Kircubbin D5
Knock E2
Knockcroghery E3
Knocklofty G3
Knockmahon H4
Knocktopher G4

Lahinch F2
Lanesborough E3
Laragh F5
Lauragh H1
Laurencetown F3
Leap J2
Leenene E2
Leighlinbridge G4
Leitrim E3
Leixlip F4
Lemybrien H3
Letterfrack E2
Letterkenny C3
Lifford D4
Limavady C4
Limerick G3
Lisbellaw D4
Lisburn D5
Liscarroll G2
Lisdoonvarna F2
Lismore H3
Lisnaskea D4
Lisryan E4
Listowel G2
Loghill G2
Londonderry C4
Longford E3
Loughbrickland D5
Loughgall D4
Loughglinn E3
Loughrea F3
Louisburgh E2
Lucan F4
Lurgan D5
Lusk F5

Macroom H2
Maghera E5
Maghera D4
Magherafelt D4
Maguiresbridge D4
Malahide F5
Malin C4
Malin More D3
Mallow H2
Manorhamilton D3
Markethill D4
Maynooth F4
Maze D5
Middletown D4
Midleton H3
Milford C4
Millstreet H2
Milltown H2
Milltown Malbay G2
Mitchelstown H3
Moate F3
Mohill E3
Molls Cap H2
Monaghan E4
Monasterevin F4
Moneygall G3
Moneymore D4
Monivea F3
Mooncoin H4
Moorfields D5
Mount Bellew F3
Mount Charles D3
Mountmellick F4
Mountrath F4
Mountshannon F3
Mourne Abbey H3
Moville C4
Moy D4
Moylett E4
Moynalty E4
Moyvore F3
Muckross H2
Muff C4
Muine Bheag G4
Mullabohy E4
Mullagh F4
Mullinavat G4
Mullingar F4
Myshall G4

Naas F4
Nad H2
Naul F5
Navan E4
Neale E2
Nenagh G3

Newbliss E4
Newcastle E5
Newcastle West G2
Newinn G3
Newmarket H2
Newmarket-on-Fergus G2
Newport G3
Newport E2
New Ross G4
Newry E5
Newtown G4
Newtownabbey D5
Newtownards D5
Newtown Butler E4
Newtown Forbes E3
Newtownhamilton E4
Newtown Mount Kennedy F5
Newtownstewart D4
Nobber E4

Oilgate G4
Oldcastle E4
Omagh D4
Omeath E5
Oola G3
Oranmore F2
Oughterard F2
Ovens H2

Pallasgreen G3
Parknasilla H1
Partry E2
Passage East H4
Passage West H3
Patrickswell G2
Paulstown G4
Pettigo D3
Plumbridge D4
Pomeroy D4
Portadown D4
Portaferry D5
Portarlington F4
Portavogie D5
Portglenone D4
Port Laoise F4
Portmarnock F5
Portrane F5
Portroe G3
Portrush C4
Portstewart C4
Portumna F3
Poyntzpass D5

Raharney F4
Randalstown D5
Rasharkin C4
Rathangen F4
Rathcoole F4
Rathcormack H3
Rathdowney G3
Rathdrum G5
Rathfriland E5
Rathkeale G2
Rath Luric G2
(Charleville)
Rathmelton C4
Rathmolyon F4
Rathmore H2
Rathmullan C4
Rathnew F5
Rathowen E4
Rathvilly G4
Ratoath F4
Ray C4
Ring H3
(An Rinn)
Ringaskiddy H3
Riverstown F3
Rockcorry E4
Rooskey E3
Rosapenna C3
Rosbercon G4
Roscommon E3
Roscrea F3
Ross Carbery J2
Rosscor D3
Rosses Point D3
Rosslare Harbour H4
Rosslea E4
Rostrevor E5
Roundstone F2
Roundwood F5
Rush F5

St Johnstown C4
Saintfield D5
Sallins F4
Scarriff G3
Scartaglen H2
Scarva D5
Schull J2
Scramoge E3
Scribbagh D3
Seskinore D4
Shanagolden G2
Shannon Airport G2
Shannonbridge F3
Shercock E4
Shillelagh G4
Shinrone F3
Shrule F2
Silvermines G3
Sion Mills D4
Sixmilebridge G2
Skerries F5
Skibbereen J2
Slane E4
Sligo D3
Smithborough E4
Sneem H1
Spiddal F2
(An Spideal)
Sporthouse Cross Roads H4
Stewartstown D4
Stonyford G4
Strabane D4
Stradbally F4
Stradone E4
Strandhill D3
Strangford D5
Stranorlar D3
Stratford F4
Strokestown E3
Summerhill F4
Swanlinbar E3
Swatragh D4
Swinford E2
Swords F5

Taghmon G4
Tagoat H4
Tahilla H1
Tallaght F5
Tallow H3
Tallowbridge H3
Tandragee D5
Tang F3
Tarbert G2
Templemore G3
Templepatrick D5
Templetouhy G3
Termonfeckin E5
Thomas Street F3
Thomastown G4
Thurles G3

Timahoe F4
Timoleague H2
Tinahely G4
Tipperary G3
Tobercurry E3
Tobermore D4
Togher F3
Toomyvara G3
Toormore J1
Tralee G2
Tramore H4
Trim F4
Tuam F2
Tuamgraney G3
Tulla G2
Tullamore F4
Tullow G4
Tulsk E3
Turlough E2
Tyholland D4
Tyrrellspass F4

Urlingford G3

Virginia E4
Waddington H4
Warrenpoint E5
Waterford H4
Watergrasshill H3
Waterville H1
Westport E2
Wexford G4
Whitegate H3
Whitehead D5
Wicklow F5
Woodenbridge G5
Woodford F3

Youghal H3

Aran Island
Rossan Point
Malin More
Glencolumbkille
(Gleann Cholm Cille)
Glencolumbkille Folk Museum
Carrick
SLIEVE LEAGUE
Kilcar
(Cill Charthaigh)
St John's Poi
Inishmurray

C
D
E

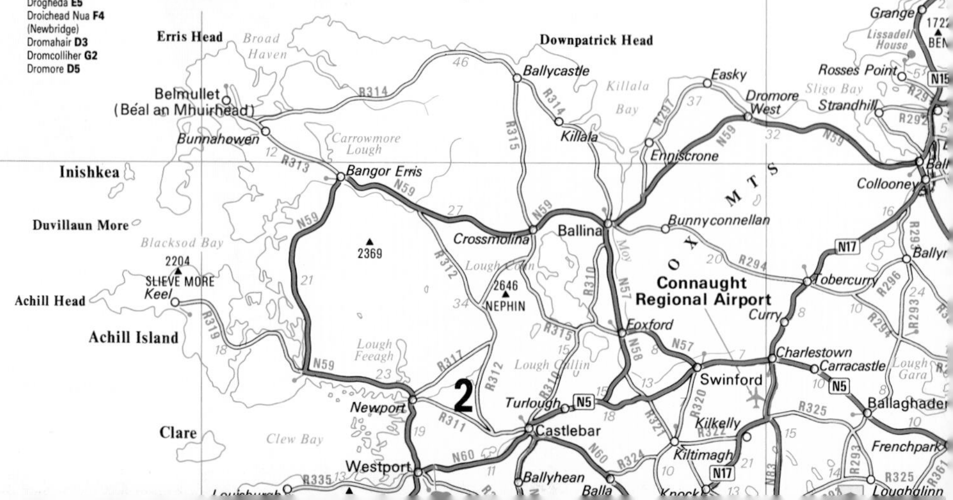
Erris Head
Broad Haven
Downpatrick Head
Ballycastle
Killala Bay
Killala
Easky
Dromore West
Belmullet
(Béal an Mhuirhead)
Bunnahowen
Carrowmore Lough
Enniscrone
Inishkea
Bangor Erris
Duvillaun More
Blacksod Bay
Crossmolina
Ballina
Bunnyconnellan
SLIEVE MORE
Keel
Achill Head
Achill Island
NEPHIN
Connaught Regional Airport
Foxford
Curry
Tobercurry
Charlestown
Carracastle
Swinford
Newport
Turlough
Castlebar
Kilkelly
Kiltimagh
Ballaghaderreen
Frenchpark
Clare
Clew Bay
Westport
Ballyhean
Grange
Rosses Point
Strandhill
Collooney
1
2

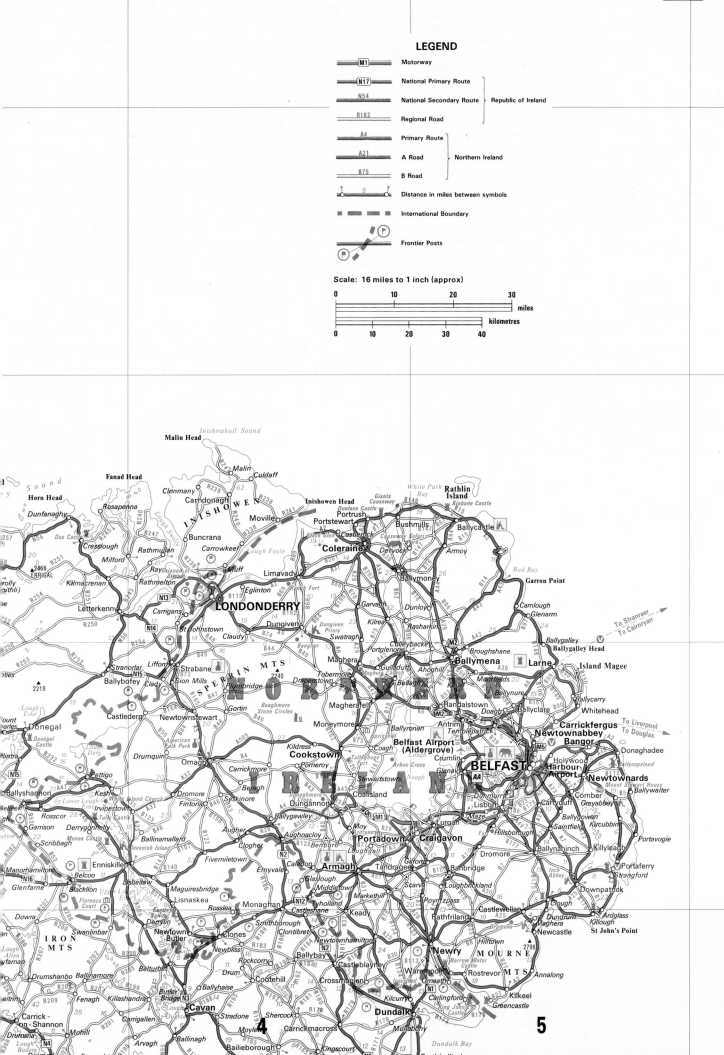

LEGEND

M1	Motorway
N17	National Primary Route
N54	National Secondary Route — Republic of Ireland
R182	Regional Road
A4	Primary Route
A21	A Road — Northern Ireland
B75	B Road
5	Distance in miles between symbols
	International Boundary
	Frontier Posts

Scale: 16 miles to 1 inch (approx)

0   10   20   30   miles

0   10   20   30   40   kilometres

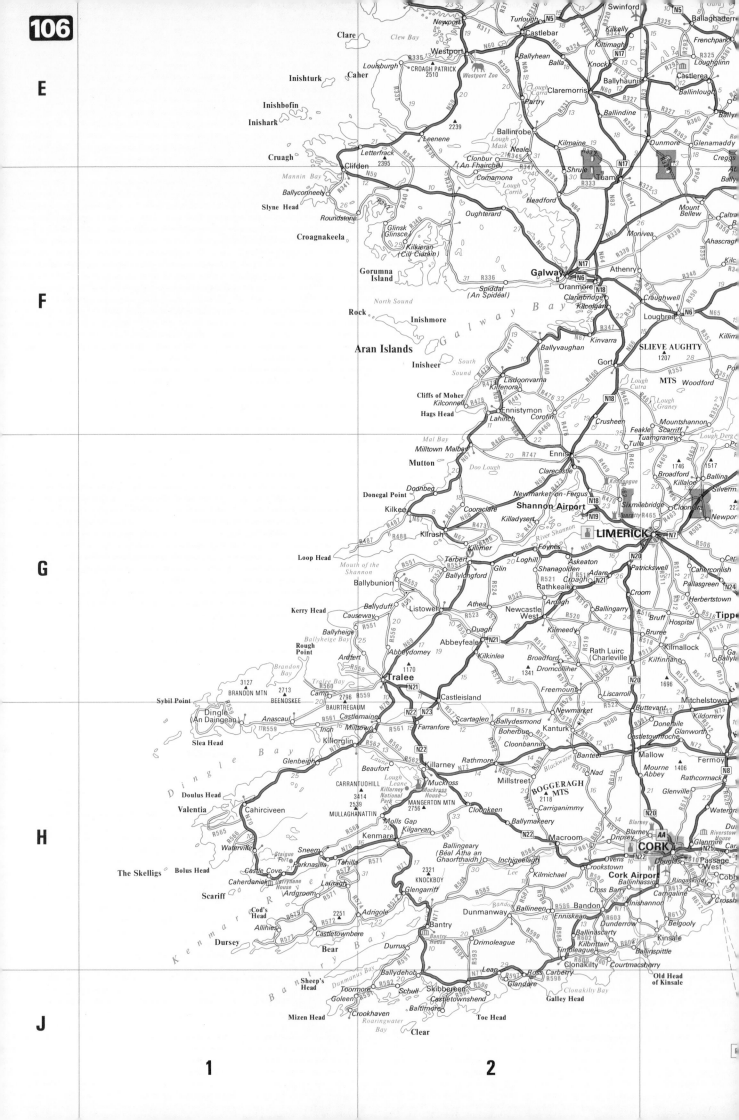

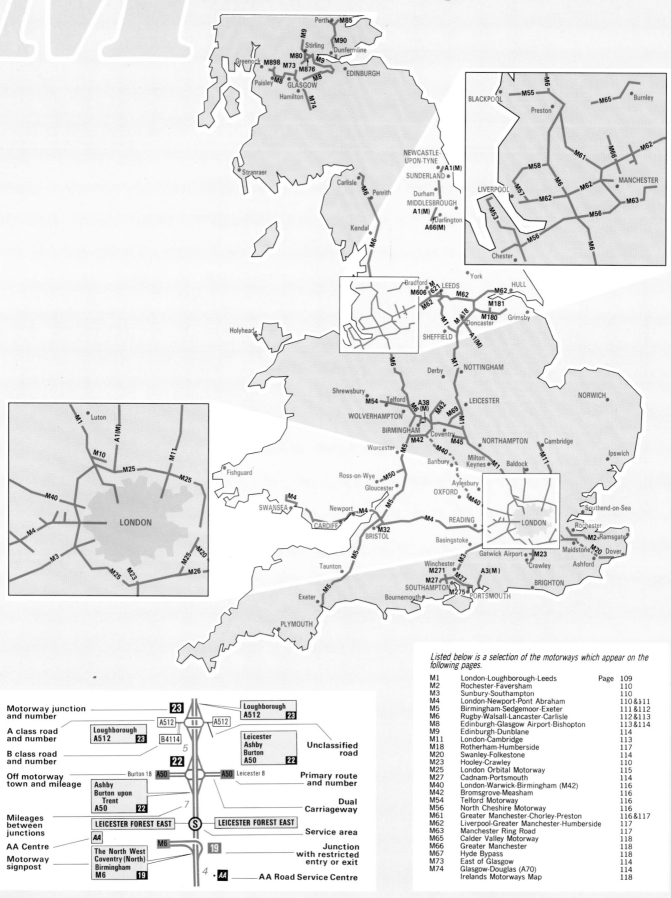

Motorways

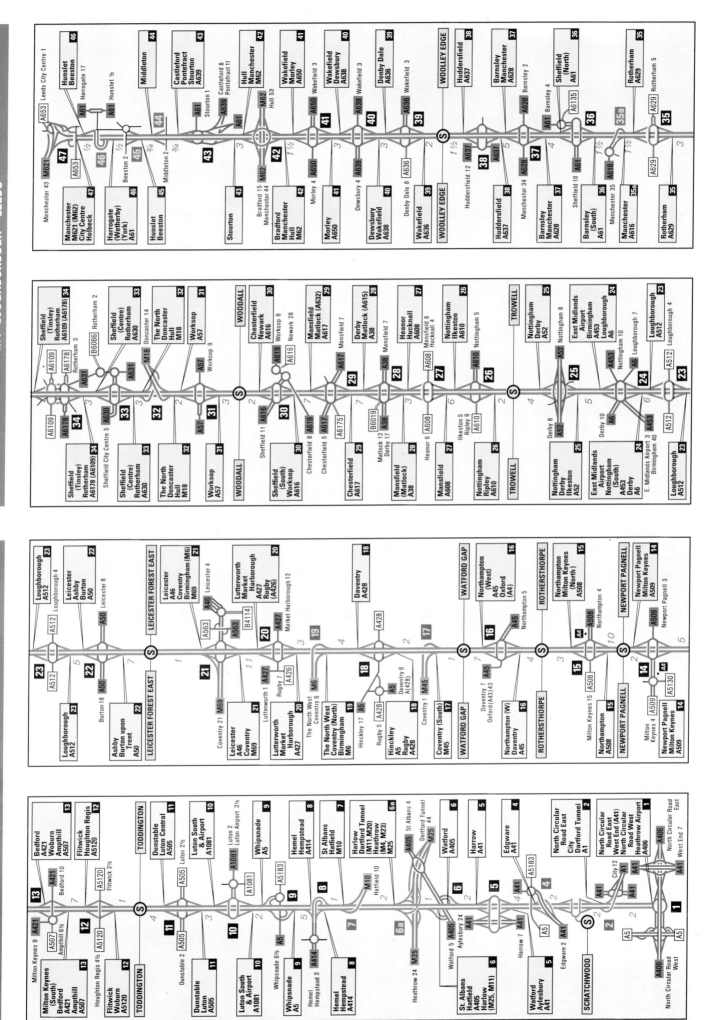

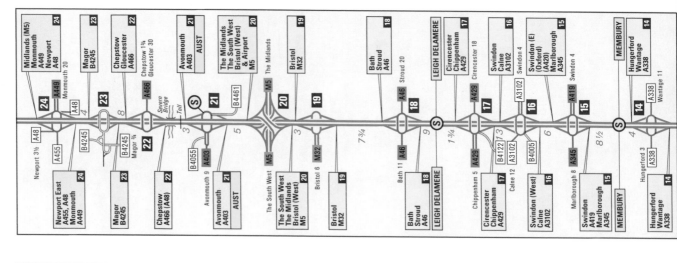

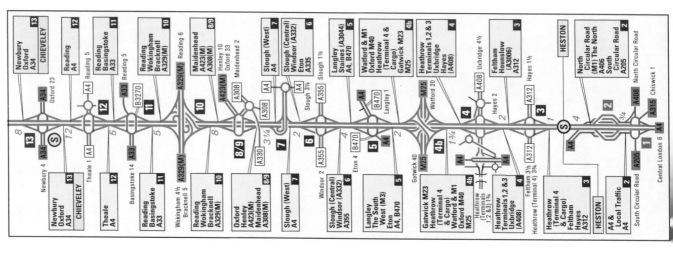

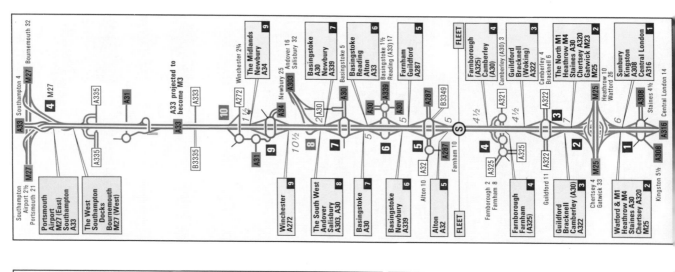

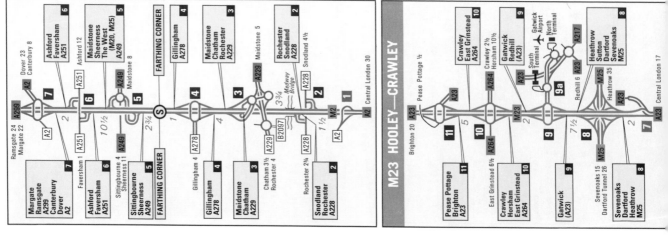

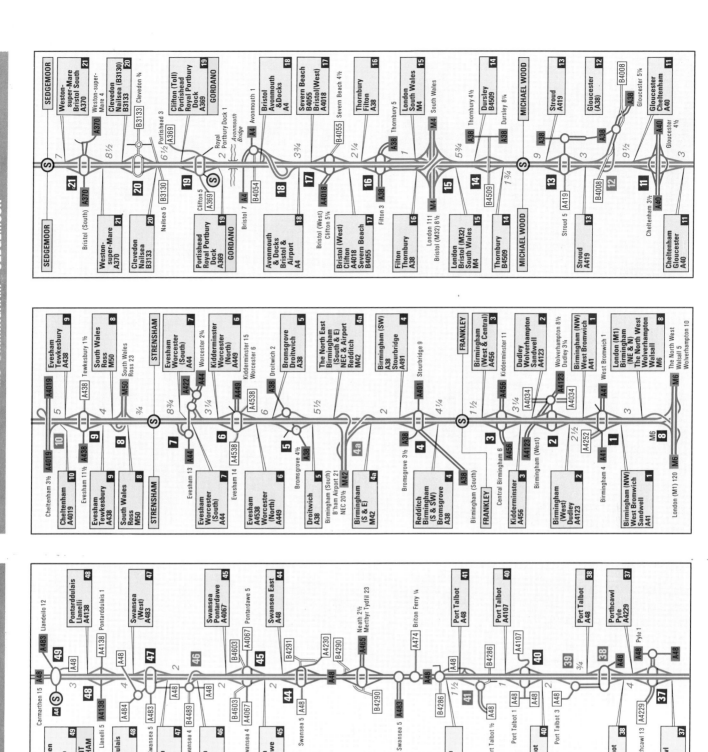

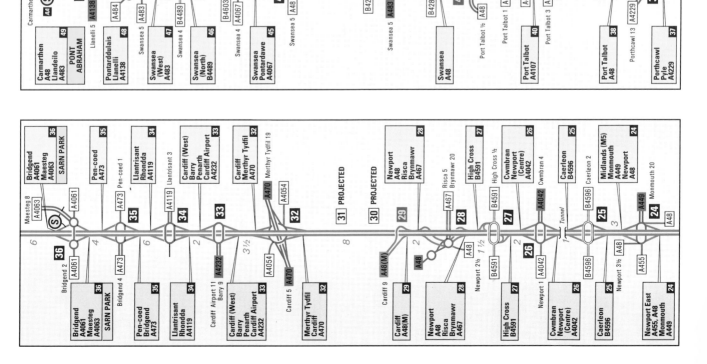

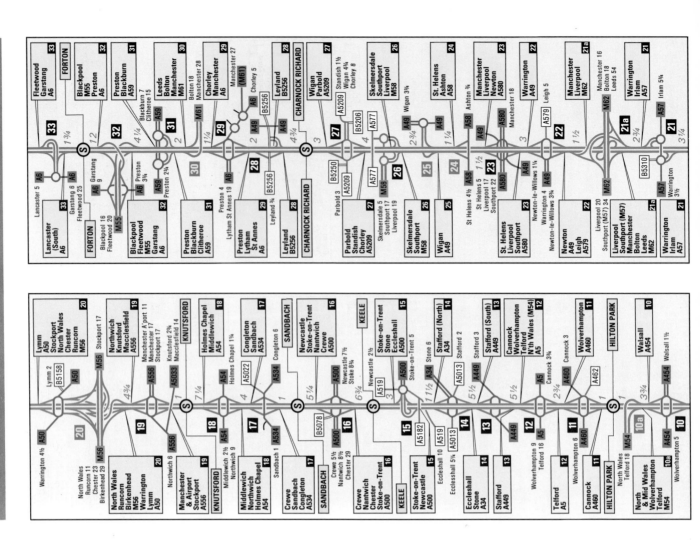

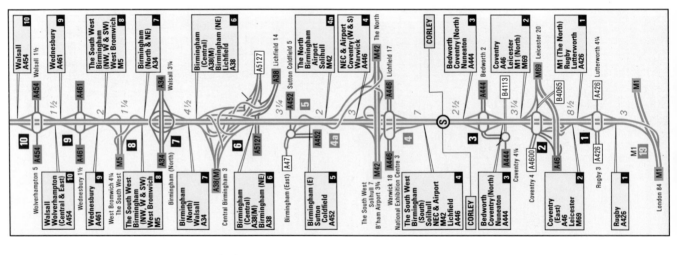

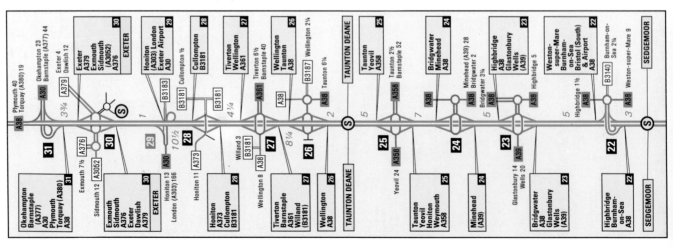

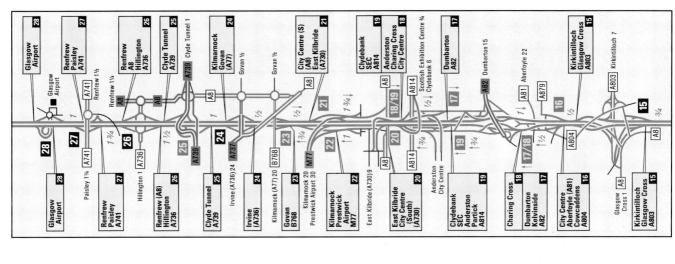

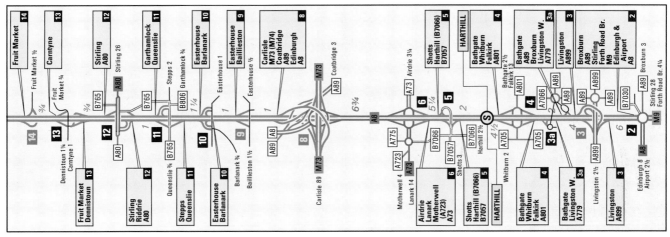

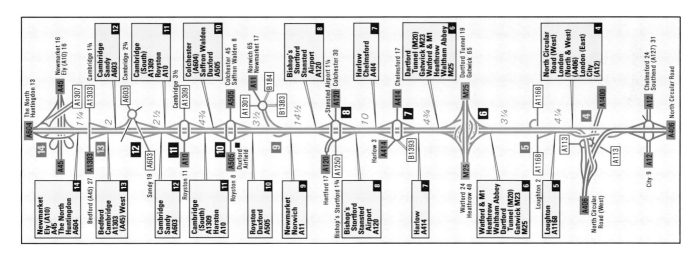

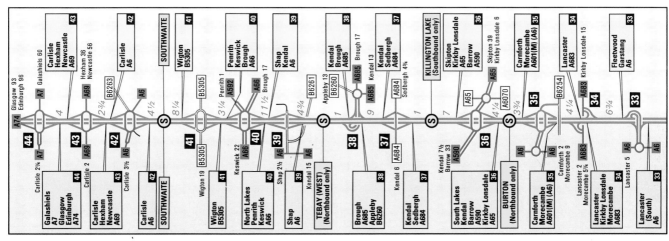

113

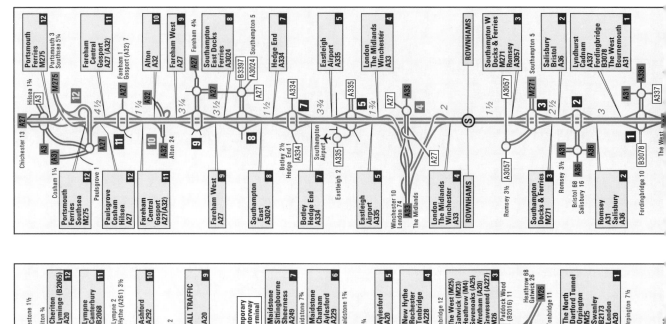

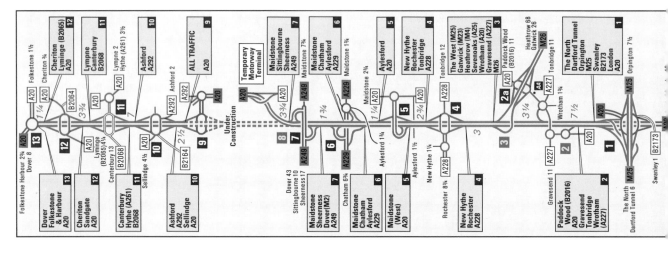

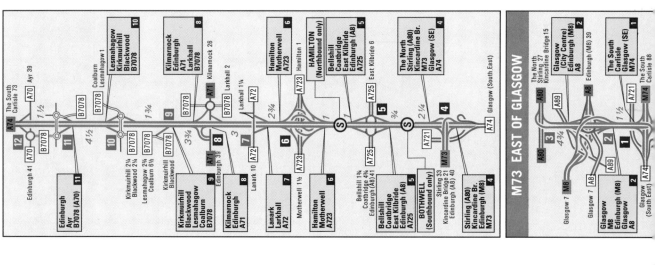

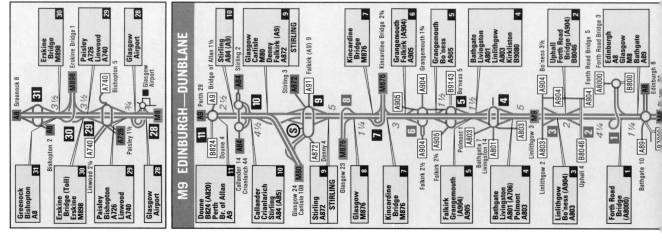

114

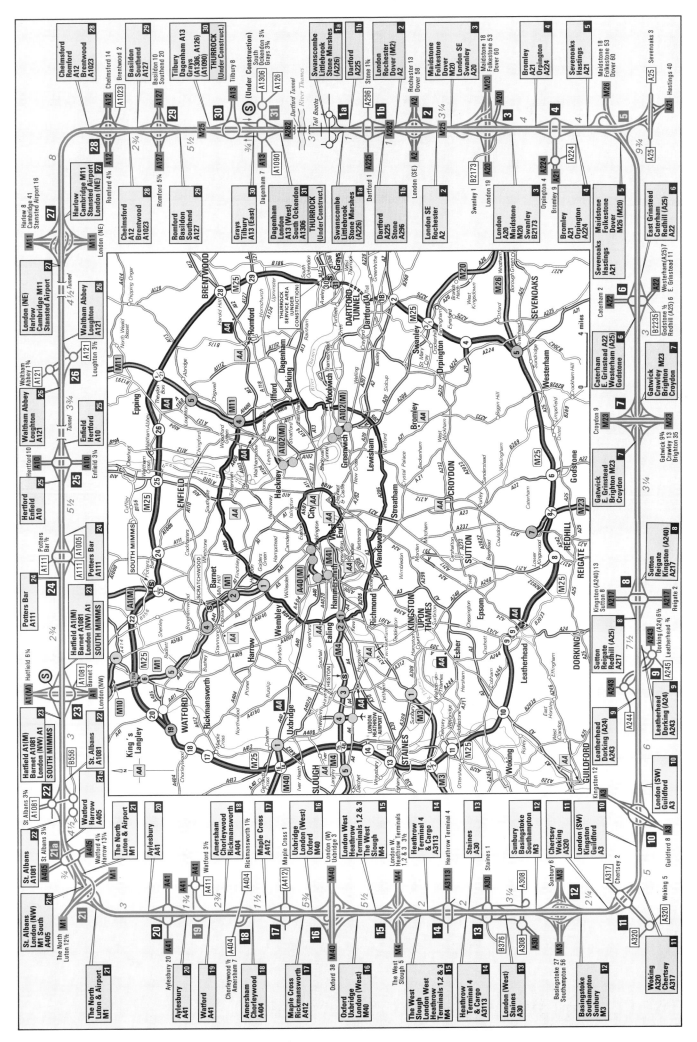

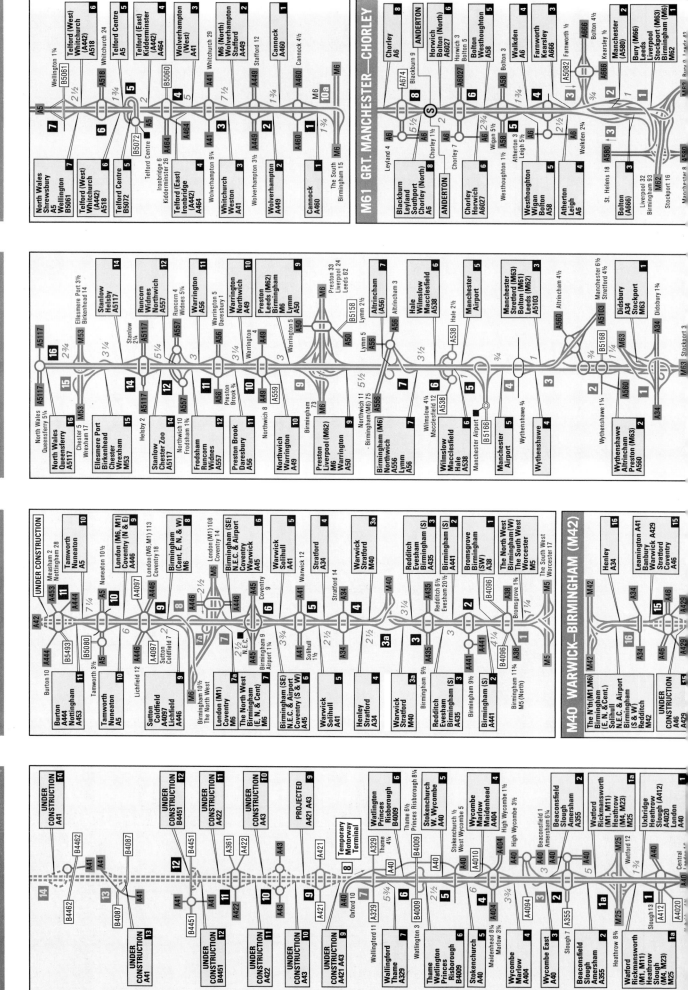

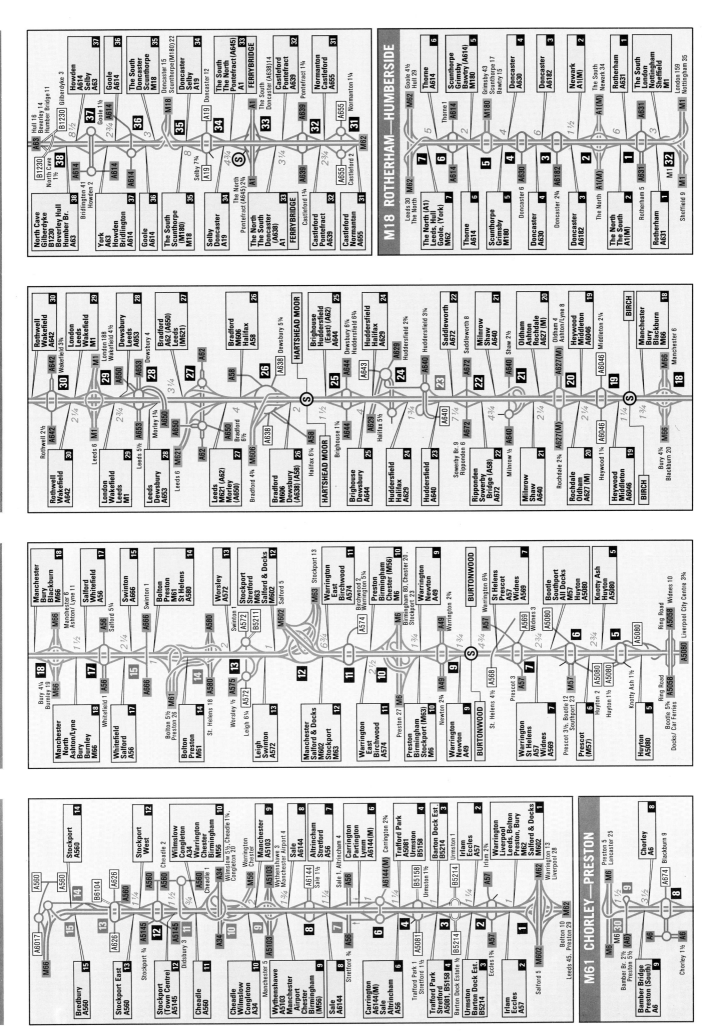

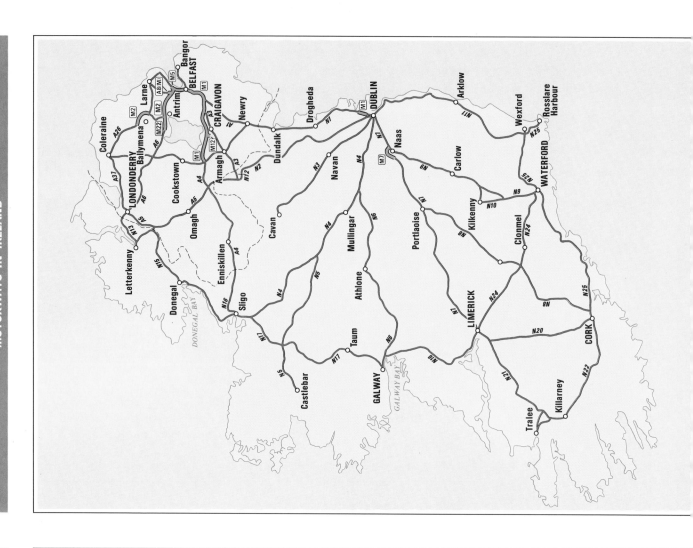

MOTORWAYS IN IRELAND

M66 GREATER MANCHESTER

M67 HYDE BYPASS

M65 CALDER VALLEY MOTORWAY

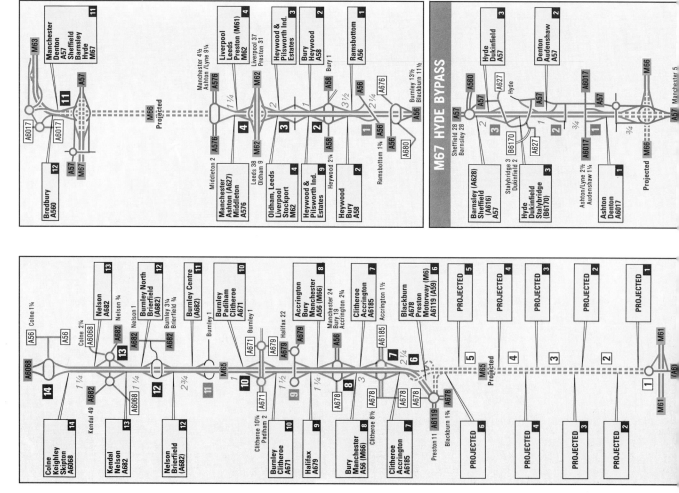

Ports and airports

MANCHESTER	International airports
LUTON	Airports with regular scheduled services abroad
Lydd	Other airports and airfields
DOVER	Major ports
Weymouth	Ports with summer services only

Detailed location plans are included on the following pages for those ports and airports named with capital letters on this map

Military airfields are not shown on this map. Ports and airports on the Channel Islands and the Scottish Islands are located within the main atlas section.

Map labels:

Wick
Stornoway
Benbecula
Barra
Isle of Skye
Tiree
Inverness
Aberdeen
Aberdeen
Dundee
Islay
GLASGOW
EDINBURGH
Machrihanish
Prestwick
Newcastle-upon-Tyne
Newcastle-upon-Tyne
Londonderry
Stranraer
Cairnryan
Carlisle
Larne
Belfast
Belfast
Belfast Harbour
Teesside
Isle of Man
Barrow-in-Furness
Heysham
Fleetwood
Blackpool
Leeds/Bradford
HULL
Dublin
Dublin
Liverpool
Liverpool
MANCHESTER
Humberside
Holyhead
Dun Laoghaire
East Midlands
Norwich
Rosslare
BIRMINGHAM
Cambridge
Ipswich
Fishguard
Cranfield
LUTON
London Stansted
FELIXSTOWE
Pembroke Dock
Hatfield
HARWICH
Cardiff
London-City
Southend
Bristol
Sheerness
LONDON HEATHROW
Ramsgate
Biggin Hill
DOVER
LONDON GATWICK
Lydd
FOLKESTONE
Exeter
Southampton
Shoreham
St Mawgan
Bournemouth
Poole
Portsmouth
NEWHAVEN
Plymouth
Torquay
Weymouth
Plymouth
Penzance (Heliport)

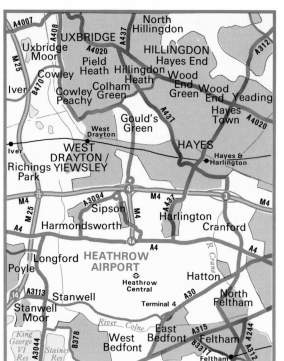

HEATHROW AIRPORT Tel: 01-759 4321 (Airport Information)

Heathrow, one of the world's busiest international airports, lies sixteen miles west of London. The airport is situated on the Piccadilly Underground line at Heathrow Central station. It is also served by local bus and long distance coach services. For short-term parking, multi-storey car parks are sited at each of the passenger terminals Tel: 01-745 7160 (terminals 1, 2, 3) & 01-759 4931 (terminal 4). Charges for the long-term car parks on the northern perimeter road are designed to encourage their use for a stay in excess of four hours. A free coach takes passengers to and from the terminals. Commercial garages offering long-term parking facilities within easy reach of the airport include: Airways Garage Ltd. Tel: 01-759 9661/4; Quo-Vadis Airport Parking Tel: 01-759 2778;

Cranford Parking Tel: 01-759 9661; Flyaway Car Storage Tel: 01-759 1567 or 2020; Kenning Car Hire Tel: 01-759 9701; and National Car Parks Tel: 01-759 9878. Car Hire: Avis Rent-A-Car Tel: 01-897 9321; Budget Rent-A-Car Tel: 01-759 2216; Godfrey Davis Europcar Tel: 01-897 0811/5; Guy Salmon Tel: 01-897 0541; Hertz Rent-A-Car Tel: 01-897 3347; and Kenning Car Hire Tel: 01-759 9701. The 4-star hotels in the area are The Excelsior Tel: 01-759 6611; the Heathrow Penta Tel: 01-897 6363; the Holiday Inn Tel: (0895) 445555 and the Sheraton-Heathrow Tel: 01-759 2424. The 3-star hotels are the Berkeley Arms Tel: 01-897 2121; the Ariel Tel: 01-759 2552; the Post House Tel: 01-759 2323; and the Skyway Tel: 01-759 6311.

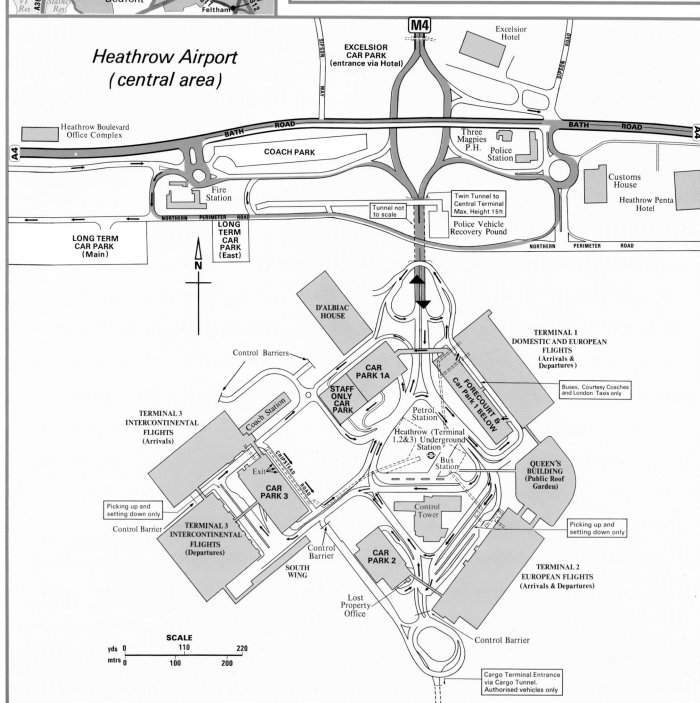

Heathrow Airport (central area)

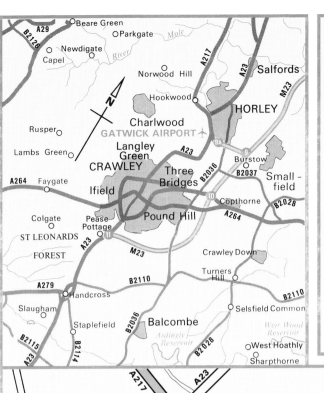

GATWICK AIRPORT Tel: (0293) 28822 or 01-668 4211. London's second airport is served by regular bus and coach services. There is direct covered access by escalator and lift to the South Terminal concourse from the adjacent airport railway station where fast 15-minute frequency services link London (Victoria) with Gatwick 24 hours a day. Parking: ample multi-storey and open-air car parking is available. Tel: Gatwick (0293) 28822 or 01-668 4211. South Terminal ext 2395, North Terminal ext 2747 for information.

MANCHESTER AIRPORT Tel: 061-489 3000. Situated nine miles south of the city, Manchester Airport provides regular scheduled services for many of the leading airlines. A spacious concourse, restaurants and parking facilities are available for passengers. For parking inquiries Tel: 061-489 3723 or 061-489 3000 ext 4635 or 2021.

LUTON AIRPORT Tel: (0582) 405100. Used mainly for package holiday tour operators, the airport has ample open-air car parking. Covered garage space is available from Central Car Storage Tel: (0582) 26189 or (0582) 20957 for a booking form. Allow five weeks.

BIRMINGHAM AIRPORT Tel: 021-767 5511. A three-storey terminal building gives access from the first floor to the Maglev transit system which offers a 90 second shuttle service to Birmingham International Railway Station. Multi-storey parking for 800 cars, and surface parking is available Tel: 021-767 7861.

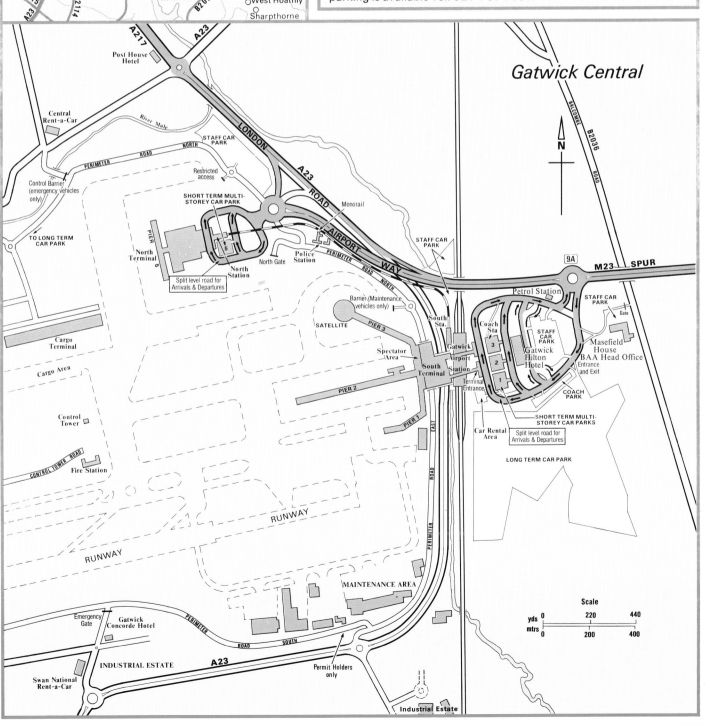

Gatwick Central

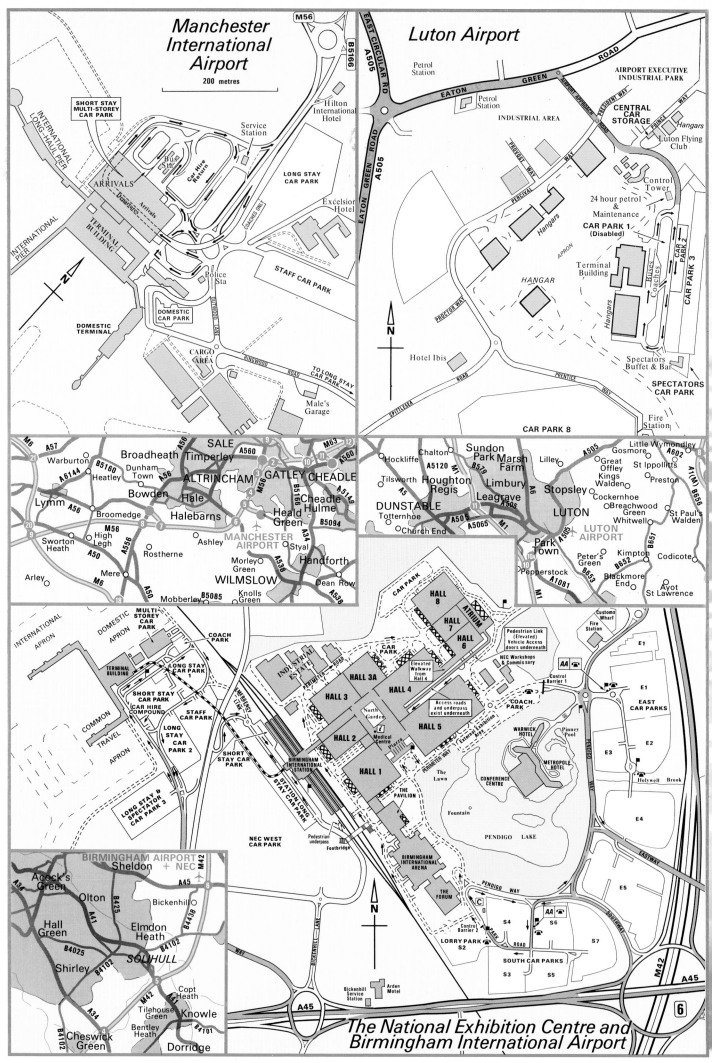

Manchester International Airport

200 metres

SHORT STAY MULTI-STOREY CAR PARK

INTERNATIONAL LONG-HAUL PIER

Hilton International Hotel

Service Station

Bus Stn

Car Hire Return

ARRIVALS

Departures

Arrivals

TERMINAL BUILDING

INTERNATIONAL PIER

Police Sta

COACHES ONLY

LONG STAY CAR PARK

Excelsior Hotel

DOMESTIC CAR PARK

STAFF CAR PARK

DOMESTIC TERMINAL

N

CARGO AREA

OUTWOOD LANE

RINGWOOD ROAD

TO LONG STAY CAR PARK

Male's Garage

Luton Airport

M56

B5166

EAST CIRCULAR RD

A505

EATON

GREEN

ROAD

AIRPORT APPROACH ROAD

Petrol Station

Petrol Station

INDUSTRIAL AREA

PRESIDENT WAY

AIRPORT EXECUTIVE INDUSTRIAL PARK

PRINCE WAY

WAY

CENTRAL CAR STORAGE

Hangars

Luton Flying Club

PERCIVAL

WAY

Hangars

PROCTOR WAY

APRON

HANGAR

Control Tower

24 hour petrol & Maintenance

CAR PARK 1 (Disabled)

Terminal Building

Buses Coaches

CAR PARK 2

CAR PARK 3

Hangars

N

Hotel Ibis

SPITTLESEA ROAD

PRENTICE WAY

Spectators Buffet & Bar

SPECTATORS CAR PARK

Fire Station

CAR PARK 8

M6 A57
A21 Warburton
Lymm A56
B5160 Dunham Town
Heatley
A6144
Bowden
Broomedge
Mere
M56 High Legh
Sworton Heath
A50 A556
Arley
M6
Mobberley B5085

SALE
Broadheath Timperley
ALTRINCHAM
Hale
Halebarns
Ashley
Rostherne
Morley Green
WILMSLOW

A560 M63
A56 A560
GATLEY CHEADLE
M56
Cheadle Hulme
Heald Green
Styal
MANCHESTER AIRPORT
A34
B5094
Handforth
A538
Knolls Green
Dean Row
A538

Hockliffe
Chalton
Sundon Park
Tilsworth
A5120 Houghton Regis
DUNSTABLE
Totternhoe
Church End
A505
B579
Marsh Farm
Limbury
Leagrave
A5065
M1

Little Wymondley
Gosmore
A602
Lilley A505 Great Offley St Ippollitts
Kings Walden Preston
Stopsley
Cockernhoe
LUTON
Breachwood Green
Whitwell St Paul's Walden
B651
Park Town
A505
A1(M) B656
B657
LUTON AIRPORT
Pepperstock
A1081
Peter's Green
Kimpton
B652 Codicote
B653 Blackmore End
Ayot St Lawrence

INTERNATIONAL APRON

DOMESTIC APRON

MULTI-STOREY CAR PARK

COACH PARK

TERMINAL BUILDING

LONG CAR PARK

SHORT STAY CAR PARK

CAR HIRE COMPOUND

STAFF CAR PARK

LONG STAY CAR PARK 2

SHORT STAY CAR PARK

EMERGENCY LINK

BIRMINGHAM INTERNATIONAL STATION

STATION LONG STAY CAR PARK

LONG STAY & SPECTATOR CAR PARK 3

COMMON TRAVEL APRON

NEC WEST CAR PARK

Pedestrian underpass

Footbridge

INDUSTRIAL ESTATE

PERIMETER ROAD

HALL 3

HALL 3A

HALL 2

North Garden

HALL 1

Medical Centre

THE PAVILION

Plaza

HALL 8

HALL 7

HALL 6

ATRIUM

CAR PARK

HALL 4

HALL 5

Access roads and underpass exist underneath

PERIMETER WAY

External Exhibition Area

The Lawn

Fountain

CAR PARK

Pedestrian Link (Elevated) Vehicle Access doors underneath

Elevated Walkway from Hall 4

NEC Workshops & Commissary

AA

COACH PARK

WARWICK HOTEL

Pinney Pool

CONFERENCE CENTRE

METROPOLE HOTEL

PENDIGO LAKE

BIRMINGHAM INTERNATIONAL ARENA

THE FORUM

PENDIGO WAY

C

Control Barrier 2

LORRY PARK S2

S4

AA

S6

S7

S3

SOUTH CAR PARKS

S5

Control Barrier 1

Customs Wharf

Fire Station

E1

E1

EAST CAR PARKS

E2

E3

E2

Holywell Brook

E4

PENDIGO WAY

EASTWAY

E5

SOUTHWAY

M42

A45

N

BICKENHILL LANE

Bickenhill Service Station

Arden Motel

A45

6

BIRMINGHAM AIRPORT + NEC

Acock's Green
Olton
Hall Green
Shirley
Cheswick Green

Sheldon
A45
Bickenhill
Elmdon Heath
SOLIHULL
Tilehouse Green
Bentley Heath
Dorridge
Knowle
Copt Heath

A34 A41 B425 B4438 B4102 B4025 B4101 M42

The National Exhibition Centre and Birmingham International Airport

122

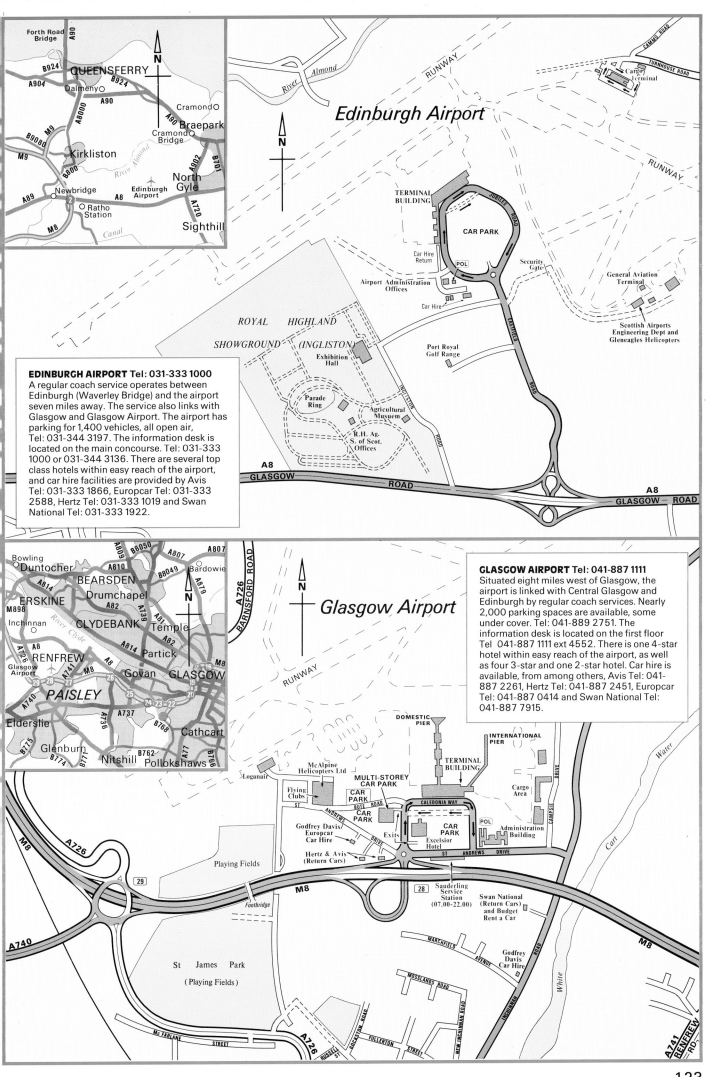

Edinburgh Airport

EDINBURGH AIRPORT Tel: 031-333 1000
A regular coach service operates between Edinburgh (Waverley Bridge) and the airport seven miles away. The service also links with Glasgow and Glasgow Airport. The airport has parking for 1,400 vehicles, all open air, Tel: 031-344 3197. The information desk is located on the main concourse. Tel: 031-333 1000 or 031-344 3136. There are several top class hotels within easy reach of the airport, and car hire facilities are provided by Avis Tel: 031-333 1866, Europcar Tel: 031-333 2588, Hertz Tel: 031-333 1019 and Swan National Tel: 031-333 1922.

Glasgow Airport

GLASGOW AIRPORT Tel: 041-887 1111
Situated eight miles west of Glasgow, the airport is linked with Central Glasgow and Edinburgh by regular coach services. Nearly 2,000 parking spaces are available, some under cover. Tel: 041-889 2751. The information desk is located on the first floor Tel: 041-887 1111 ext 4552. There is one 4-star hotel within easy reach of the airport, as well as four 3-star and one 2-star hotel. Car hire is available, from among others, Avis Tel: 041-887 2261, Hertz Tel: 041-887 2451, Europcar Tel: 041-887 0414 and Swan National Tel: 041-887 7915.

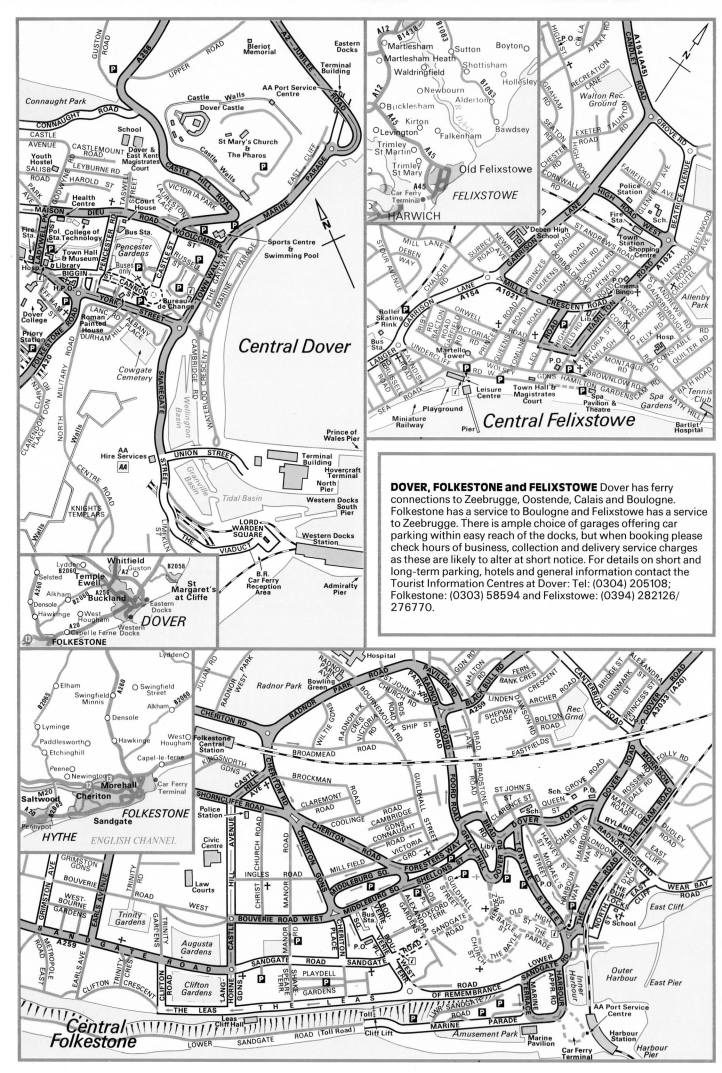

Central Dover

Connaught Park

Prince of Wales Pier

Terminal Building

Hovercraft Terminal

North Pier

Western Docks South Pier

Western Docks Station

B.R. Car Ferry Reception Area

Admiralty Pier

LORD WARDEN SQUARE

Tidal Basin

Granville Basin

Wellington Basin

Cowgate Cemetery

KNIGHT'S TEMPLARS

DOVER

Whitfield
Temple Ewell
Buckland
St Margaret's at Cliffe
Eastern Docks
Western Docks
Capel le Ferne

FOLKESTONE

FELIXSTOWE

Martlesham
Martlesham Heath
Waldringfield
Newbourn
Bucklesham
Kirton
Levington
Trimley St Martin
Trimley St Mary
Old Felixstowe
Car Ferry Terminal

HARWICH

Sutton
Boyton
Shottisham
Hollesley
Alderton
Falkenham
Bawdsey

Central Felixstowe

Walton Rec. Ground
Police Station
Fire Sta.
Town Station Shopping Centre
Allenby Park
Roller Skating Rink
Bus Sta.
Martello Tower
Leisure Centre
Playground
Miniature Railway
Pier
Town Hall & Magistrates Court
Spa Pavilion & Theatre
Spa Gardens
Tennis Club
Bartlet Hospital

DOVER, FOLKESTONE and FELIXSTOWE Dover has ferry connections to Zeebrugge, Oostende, Calais and Boulogne. Folkestone has a service to Boulogne and Felixstowe has a service to Zeebrugge. There is ample choice of garages offering car parking within easy reach of the docks, but when booking please check hours of business, collection and delivery service charges as these are likely to alter at short notice. For details on short and long-term parking, hotels and general information contact the Tourist Information Centres at Dover: Tel: (0304) 205108; Folkestone: (0303) 58594 and Felixstowe: (0394) 282126/276770.

Central Folkestone

Radnor Park
Bowling Green
Folkestone Central Station
Rec. Grnd
Police Station
Civic Centre
Law Courts
Trinity Gardens
Augusta Gardens
Clifton Gardens
Leas Cliff Hall
Cliff Lift
Amusement Park
Marine Pavilion
Outer Harbour
East Pier
Inner Harbour
AA Port Service Centre
Harbour Station
Car Ferry Terminal
Harbour Pier
East Cliff

HYTHE
ENGLISH CHANNEL
Saltwood
Cheriton
Morehall
Sandgate
FOLKESTONE
Lydden
Elham
Swingfield Street
Swingfield Minnis
Alkham
Lyminge
Densole
Paddlesworth
Etchinghill
Hawkinge
West Hougham
Peene
Newington
Capel-le-ferne

THE LEAS

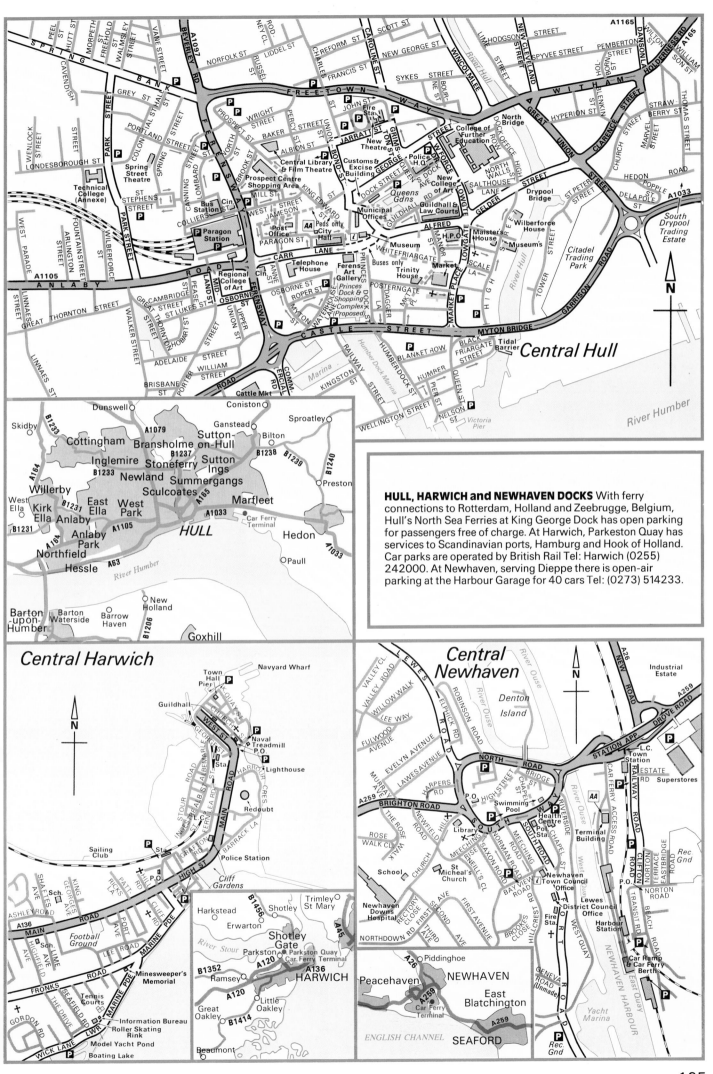

Central Hull

HULL, HARWICH and NEWHAVEN DOCKS With ferry connections to Rotterdam, Holland and Zeebrugge, Belgium, Hull's North Sea Ferries at King George Dock has open parking for passengers free of charge. At Harwich, Parkeston Quay has services to Scandinavian ports, Hamburg and Hook of Holland. Car parks are operated by British Rail Tel: Harwich (0255) 242000. At Newhaven, serving Dieppe there is open-air parking at the Harbour Garage for 40 cars Tel: (0273) 514233.

Central Harwich

Central Newhaven

Town plans

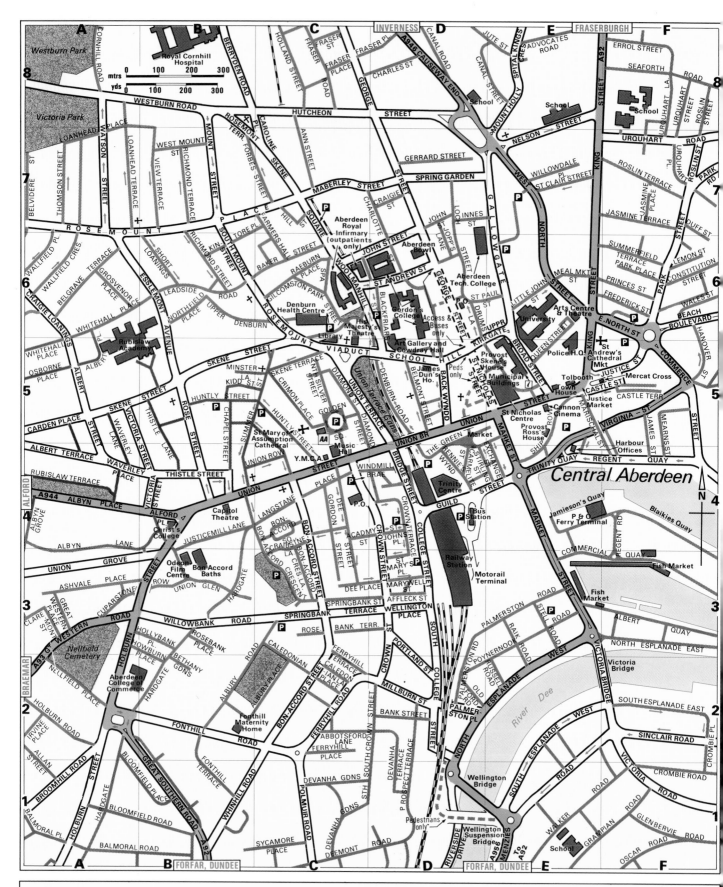

Aberdeen

Granite gives Aberdeen its especial character; but this is not to say that the city is a grim or a grey place, the granites used are of many hues – white, blue, pink and grey. Although the most imposing buildings date from the 19th century, granite has been used to dramatic effect since at least as early as the 15th century. From that time dates St Machar's Cathedral, originally founded in AD580,

but rebuilt several times, especially after a devasting fire started on the orders of Edward III of England in 1336. St Machar's is in Old Aberdeen, traditionally the ecclesiastical and educational hub of the city, while 'New' Aberdeen (actually no newer) has always been the commercial centre. Even that definition is deceptive, for although Old Aberdeen has King's College, founded in 1494, New Aberdeen has Marischal College, founded almost exactly a century later (but rebuilt in 1844)

and every bit as distinguished as a seat of learning. Both establishments functioned as independent universities until they were merged in 1860 to form Aberdeen University. The North Sea oil boom has brought many changes to the city, some of which threatened its character. But even though high-rise buildings are now common, the stately façades, towers and pillars of granite still reign supreme and Union Street remains one of the best thoroughfares in Britain.

128

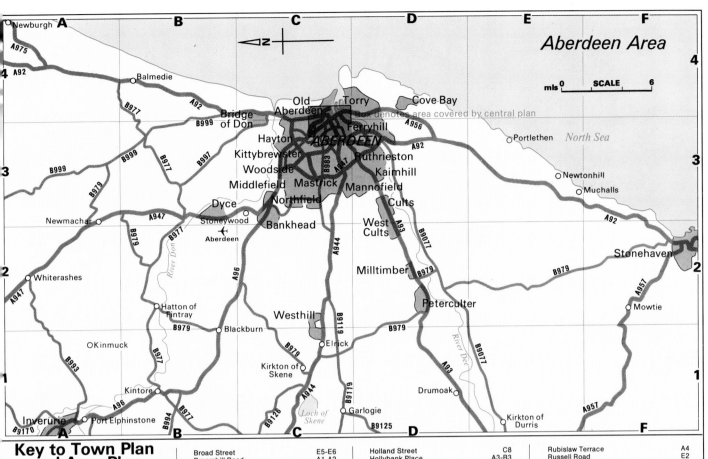
Aberdeen Area

mls 0 SCALE 6

North Sea

Box denotes area covered by central plan

Key to Town Plan and Area Plan

Town Plan
A A Recommended roads
Other roads
Restricted roads
Buildings of interest   Cinema
Car Parks
Parks and open spaces
One Way Streets
Churches

Area Plan
A roads
B roads
Locations   Hattoncrook O
Urban area

Street Index with Grid Reference

Aberdeen

129

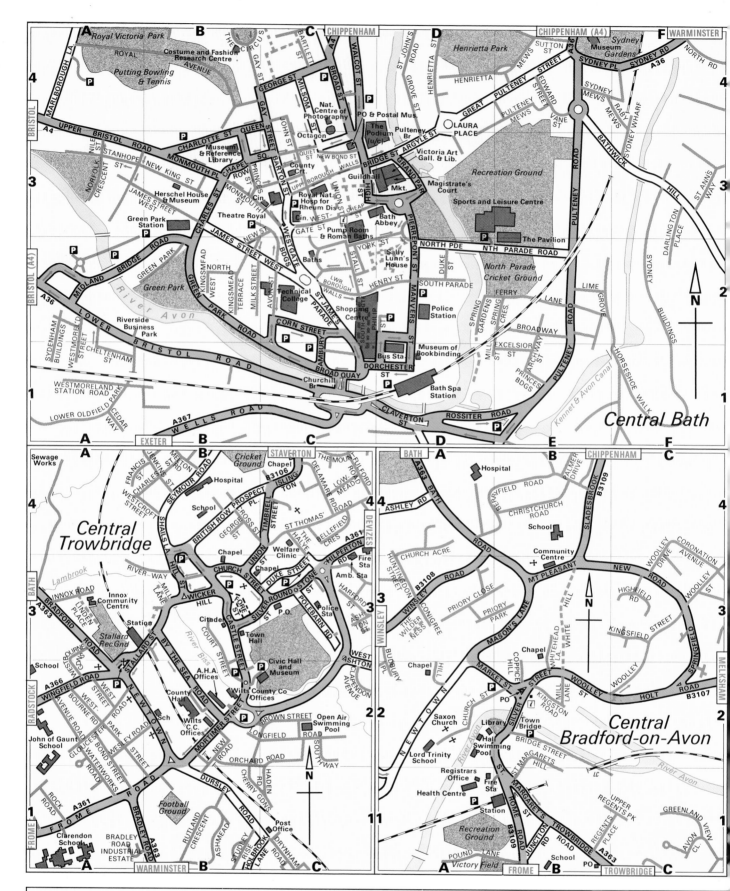

Bath

This unique city combines Britain's most impressive collection of Roman relics with the country's finest Georgian townscape. Its attraction to Romans and fashionable 18th-century society alike was its mineral springs, which are still seen by thousands of tourists who visit the Roman Baths every year. They are now the centre-piece of a Roman museum, where exhibits give a vivid impression of life 2000 years ago. The adjacent Pump Room to which the waters were piped for drinking was a focal point of social life in 18th- and 19th-century Bath.

The Georgian age of elegance also saw the building of Bath's perfectly proportioned streets, terraces and crescents. The finest examples are Queen Square, the Circus, and Royal Crescent, all built of golden local stone. Overlooking the Avon from the west is the great tower of Bath Abbey – sometimes called the "Lantern of the West" because of its large and numerous windows.

Bath has much to delight the museum-lover. Near the abbey, in York Street, is the Burrows Toy Museum – a treasure-trove of playthings spanning two centuries.

The Assembly Rooms in Bennett Street, very much a part of the social scene in Georgian Bath, are now the home of the Museum of Costume with displays illustrating fashion through the ages.

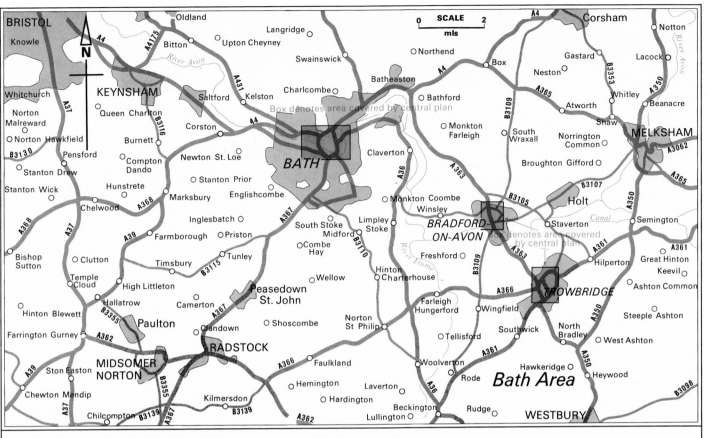

Key to Town Plan and Area Plan

Town Plan

- A A Recommended roads
- Other roads
- Restricted roads
- Buildings of interest   **Library**
- Car Parks   **P**
- Parks and open spaces
- Churches   †

Area Plan

- A roads
- B roads
- Locations   Box ○
- Urban Area

Street Index with Grid Reference

Central Bath

Ambury	C1-C2
Archway Street	E1-E2
Argyle Street	D3-D4
Avon Street	C2
Bartlett Street	C4
Barton Street	C3
Bathwick Hill	E3-F3
Bridge Street	C3-D3
Broadway	E2
Broad Street	C3-C4
Broad Quay	C1
Chapel Row	D3
Charles Street	B2-B3
Charlotte Street	B3-B4
Cheap Street	C3
Cheltenham Street	A1
Claverton Street	C1-D1
Corn Street	C2
Darlington Place	F2-F3
Dorchester Street	C1-D1
Duke Street	D2
Edward Street	E4
Excelsior Street	E1
Ferry Lane	D2-E2
Gay Street	B4-C4-C3
George Street	B4-C4
Grand Parade	D3
Great Pulteney Street	D4-E4
Green Park	A2-B2
Green Park Road	B1-B2-C2-C1
Grove Street	D3-D4
Henrietta Mews	D4-E4
Henrietta Street	D4
Henry Street	C2-D2
High Street	C3
Horseshoe Walk	F1
James Street West	A3-B3-B2-C2
John Street	C3-C4
Kingsmead North	B2
Kingsmead Terrace	B2
Kingsmead West	B2
Laura Place	D3-D4
Lime Grove	E2-F2-F1
Lower Bristol Road	A2-A1-B1-C1
Lower Borough Walls	C2
Lower Oldfield Park	A1
Manvers Street	D1-D2
Marlborough Lane	A4
Midland Bridge Road	A2-B2-B3
Milk Street	B2
Mill Street	D1
Milsom Street	C3-C4
Monmouth Place	B3
Monmouth Street	B3-C3
New Street	B2-B3-C2
New Bond Street	C3
New King Street	A3-B3
Nile Street	A3
Norfolk Crescent	A3
North Parade	D2
North Parade Road	D2-E2
North Road	F4
Philip Street	C1-C2-D2
Pierrepont Street	E1
Princes Buildings	E1
Princes Street	B3
Pulteney Mews	E4
Pulteney Road	E1-E2-E3-E4
Queen Square	B3-B4-C4-C3
Quiet Street	C3
Raby Mews	E4-F4
Rossiter Road	D1-E1
Royal Avenue	A4-B4
St Ann's Way	F3
St Jame's Parade	C2
St John's Road	D4r
Southgate	C1-C2
South Parade	D2
Spring Crescent	E2
Spring Gardens	D2
Stall Street	C2-C3
Stanhope Street	A3
Sutton Street	E4
Sydenham Buildings	A1-A2
Sydney Buildings	F1-F2-F3
Sydney Mews	E4-F4
Sydney Place	E4-F4
Sydney Road	F4
Sydney Wharf	F3-F4
The Circus	B4
Union Street	C3
Upper Borough Walls	C3
Upper Bristol Road	A4-A3-B3

Vane Street	E4
Walcot Street	C3-C4
Wells Road	A1-B1-C1
Westgate Buildings	C2-C3
Westgate Street	C3
Westmoreland Station Road	A1
Westmoreland Street	A1
York Street	C2-D2-D3

Trowbridge

Ashmead	D1
Ashton Street	C3
Avenue Road	A2
Bellefield Crescent	C4
Bond Street	A1-A2
Bradford Road	A2-A3
Bradley Road	A1-B1
British Row	B4
Brown Street	B2-C2
Bythesea Road	B2-B3
Castle Street	B2-B3
Charles Street	A4-B4
Cherry Gardens	B1-C1
Church Street	B3-C3
Clapendon Avenue	C2
Court Street	B2-B3
Cross Street	B4-C4
Delamare Road	C4
Dynham Road	C1
Duke Street	C3-C4
Dursley Road	B1-C1
Fore Street	B3
Francis Street	A4-B4
Frome Road	A1-B1
Fulford Road	C4
George Street	B4
Gloucester Road	A2
Haden Road	C1
Harford Street	C3
Hill Street	B3
Hilperton Road	C3-C4
Holbrook Lane	B1-C1
Innox Road	A3
Islington	C4
Jenkins Street	A4-B4
Linden Place	A3
Longfield Road	B2-C2
Lowmead	C4
Melton Road	B4
Mill Lane	B3
Mortimer Street	B2
New Road	B1-B2
Newtown	åA2-B2
Orchard Road	B1-B2-C2-C1
Park Street	A2-A1-B1
Polebarn Road	C3
Prospect Place	D4-C4
River Way	A3-B3
Rock Road	A1
Roundstone Street	C3
Rutland Crescent	B1
St Thomas' Road	C4
Seymour Road	B3-B4
Shails Lane	B3-B4
Silver Street	B3-C3

Southway	C2
Stallard Street	A2-A3-B3
Studley Rise	B1
The Hayle	C4
The Mount	C4
Timbrell Street	C4
Union Street	B3-B4-C4-C3
Waterworks Road	A1-A2
Wesley Road	A2-B2
West Street	A2
West Ashton	C2-C3
Westbourne Gardens	A2-A3
Westbourne Road	A2
Westcroft Street	A4-B4
Wicker Hill	B3
Wingfield Road	A2

Bradford-upon-Avon

Ashley Road	A4
Avon Close	C1
Bath Road	A3-A4-B4-B3
Berryfield Road	A4-B4
Bridge Street	B2
Christchurch Road	B4
Christchurch Road	B4
Church Acre	A4
Church Street	A2-B2
Church Street	A2-A3
Conigre Hill	B2-B3
Coppice Hill	C3-C4
Coronation Avenue	C1
Greenland View	C1
Highfield Road	C3
Holt Road	B2-C2
Huntingdon Street	A3
Kingston Road	B2
Junction Road	B1
Market Street	A2-B2
Masons Lane	A3-B3
Mill Lane	B2
Mount Pleasant	B2
Newtown	A1-A2-A3
New Road	B3-C3
Palmer Drive	B4
Pound Lane	A1-B1
Priory Close	A3-B3
Priory Park	A3-B3
Regents Place	B1-C1
Rome Road	B1
St Margaret's Place	B1-B2
St Margaret's Street	B1-C2
Silver Street	B2
Sladesbrook	B3-B4
Springfield	C2-C3
The Wilderness	A3
Trowbridge Road	B1
Upper Regents Park	B1-C1
White Hill	B2-B3
Whitehead Lane	B2-B3
Winsley Road	A3-A4
Woolley Drive	C3-C4
Woolley Street	C2-C3

HTT

131

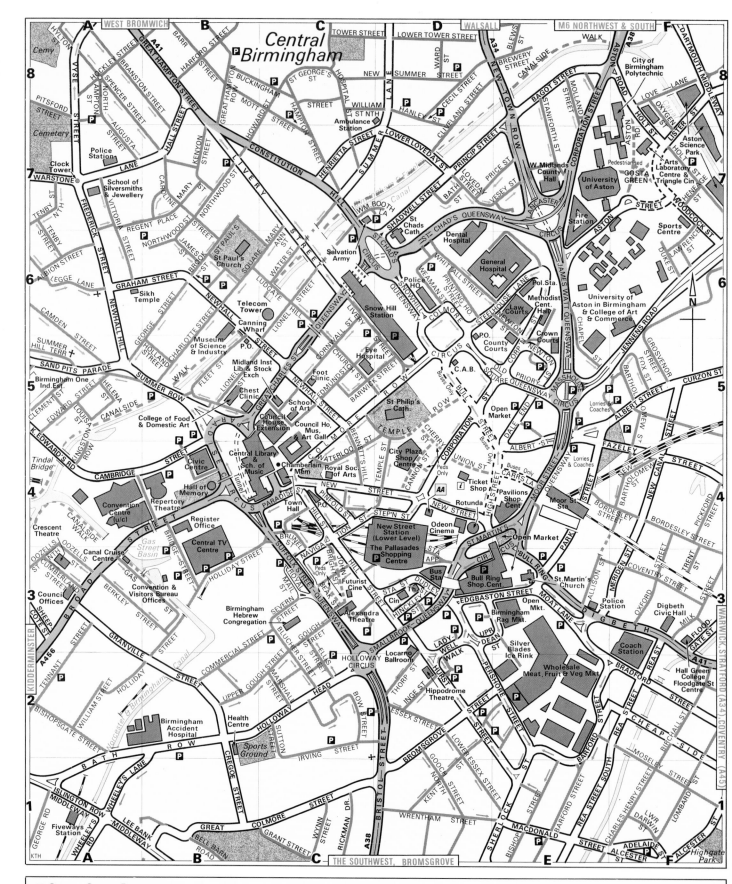

Birmingham

It is very difficult to visualise Birmingham as it was before it began the growth which eventually made it the second-largest city in England. When the Romans were in Britain it was little more than a staging post on Icknield Street. Throughout medieval times it was a sleepy agricultural centre in the middle of a heavily-forested region. Timbered houses clustered together round a green that was

eventually to be called the Bull Ring. But by the 16th century, although still a tiny and unimportant village by today's standards, it had begun to gain a reputation as a manufacturing centre. Tens of thousands of sword blades were made here during the Civil War. Throughout the 18th century more and more land was built on. In 1770 the Birmingham Canal was completed, making trade very much easier and increasing the town's development dramatically. All of that pales into near

insignificance compared with what happened in the 19th century. Birmingham was not represented in Parliament until 1832 and had no town council until 1838. Yet by 1889 it had already been made a city, and after only another 20 years it had become the second largest city in England. Many of Birmingham's most imposing public buildings date from the 19th century, when the city was growing so rapidly. Surprisingly, the city has more miles of waterway than Venice.

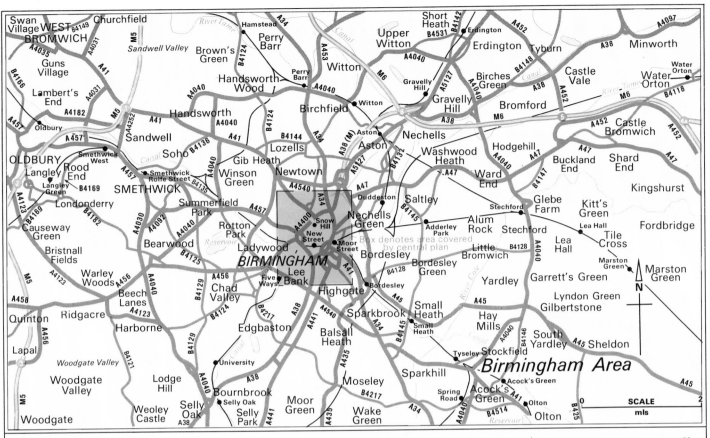

Key to Town Plan and Area Plan

Town Plan

AA Recommended roads	
Restricted roads	
Other roads	
Buildings of interest	Station ▣
One Way Streets	
Car Parks	ℙ
Parks and open spaces	
Churches	†

Area Plan

A roads	
B roads	
Locations	Meer End ○
Urban area	

Street Index with Grid Reference

Birmingham

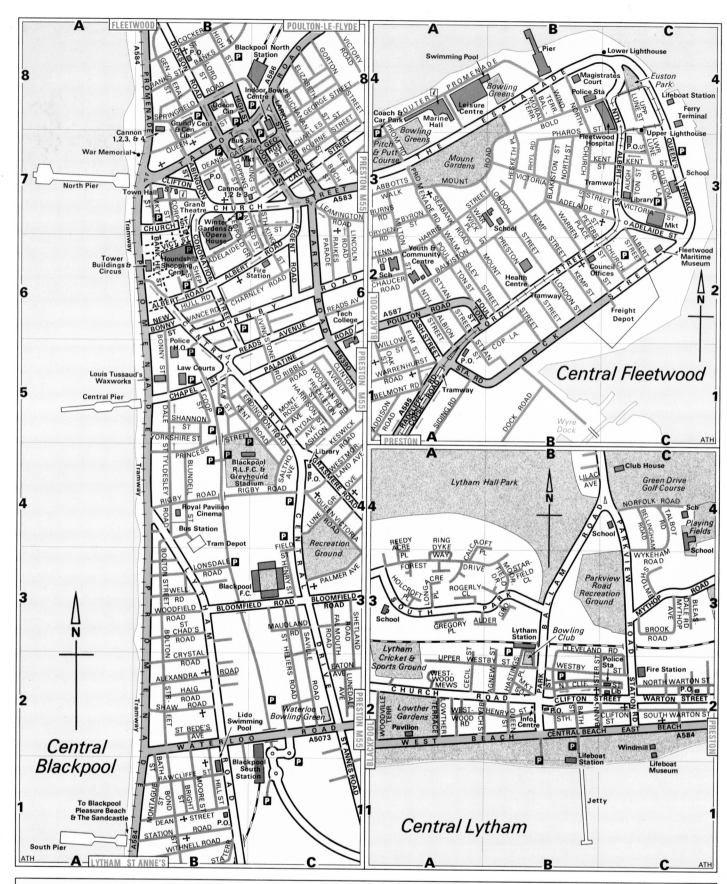

Blackpool

No seaside resort is regarded with greater affection than Blackpool. It is still the place where millions of North Country folk spend their holidays; its famous illuminations draw visitors from all over the world. It provides every conceivable kind of traditional holiday entertainment, and in greater abundance than any other seaside resort in Britain. The famous tower – built in the 1890s as a replica of the Eiffel Tower – the three piers, seven miles of promenade, five miles of illuminations, countless guesthouses, huge numbers of pubs, shops, restaurants and cafes play host to eight million visitors a year.

At the base of the tower is a huge entertainment complex that includes a ballroom, a circus and an aquarium. Other 19th-century landmarks are North Pier and Central Pier, the great Winter Gardens and Opera House and the famous trams that still run along the promenade – the only electric trams still operating in Britain. The most glittering part of modern Blackpool is the famous Golden Mile, packed with amusements, novelty shops and snack stalls. Every autumn it becomes part of the country's most extravagant light show – the illuminations – when the promenade is ablaze with neon representations of anything and everything from moon rockets to the Muppets. Autumn is also the time when Blackpool is a traditional venue for political party conferences.

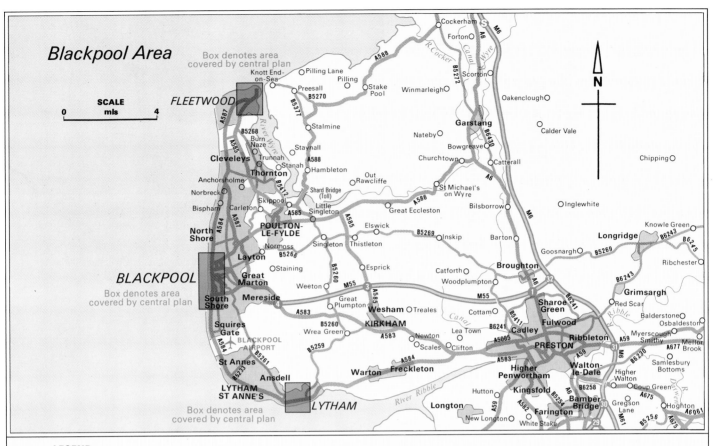

Blackpool Area

SCALE
mls
0 ——— 4

FLEETWOOD

Box denotes area covered by central plan

BLACKPOOL

Box denotes area covered by central plan

N

Box denotes area covered by central plan

LYTHAM

LEGEND

Town Plan
AA Recommended roads
Restricted roads
Other roads
Buildings of interest — Hall
Car parks — P
Parks and open spaces

Area Plan
A roads
B roads
Locations — Trunnah ○
Urban area

Street Index with Grid Reference

Blackpool

Abingdon Street	B7
Adelaide Street	B6-B7-C7
Albert Road	B6-C6
Alexandra Road	B2
Alfred Street	B7-C7-C6
Ashton Road	C4-C5
Bank Hey Street	B6-B7
Banks Street	B8
Bath Street	B1-B2
Bloomfield Road	B3-C3
Blundell Street	B4
Bolton Street	B2-B3-B4
Bond Street	B1-B2
Bonny Street	B5-B6
Bright Street	B1
Buchanan Street	C7-C8
Caunce Street	C7-C8
Central Drive	B6-B5-C5-C4-C3-C2
Chapel Street	B5
Charles Street	C7-C8
Charnley Road	B6-C6
Church Street	B7-C7
Clifton Street	B7
Clinton Avenue	C5
Cocker Street	B8
Cookson Street	B8-B7-C7
Coop Street	B5
Coronation Street	B5-B6-B7
Corporation Street	B7
Crystal Road	B2

Dale Street	B4-B5
Deansgate	B7-C7
Dean Street	B1
Dickson Road	B7-B8
Eaton Avenue	C2
Erdington Road	B5-C5-C4
Elizabeth Street	C7-C8
Falmouth Road	C2-C3
Field Street	C3
Freckleton Street	C5
General Street	B8
George Street	C7-C8
Gorton Street	C8
Grasmere Road	C4
Grosvenor Street	C7
Haig Road	B2
Harrison Street	C5
Henry Street	C3
High Street	B8
Hill Street	B1
Hornby Road	B6-C6
Hull Road	B6
Kay Street	B5
Kent Road	B5-C5-C4
Keswick Road	C4-C5
King Street	C7
Larkhill Street	C8
Leamington Road	C7
Leopold Grove	B7-B6-C6
Lincoln Road	C6-C7
Livingstone Road	C5-C6
Lonsdale Road	B3
Lord Street	B8
Lune Grove	C2
Lunedale Avenue	C2
Lytham Road	B1-B2-B3-B4
Market Street	B7
Maudland Road	B3-C3
Milbourne Street	C7-C8
Montague Street	B1
Montrose Avenue	B5-C5
Moore Street	B1
New Bonny Street	B5-B6
Palatine Road	B5-C5-C6
Palmer Avenue	C3
Park Road	C5-C6-C7
Princes Street	B4-B5-C5
Promenade	B1-B2-B3-B4-B5-B6-A6-A7-B7-B8
Queen Street	B7-B8
Queen Victoria Road	C3-C4
Raikes Parade	C6-C7
Rawcliffe Street	B1
Reads Avenue	B5-C5-C6
Regent Road	C6-C7
Ribble Road	C5
Rigby Road	B4-C4
Rydal Avenue	C5
St Annes Road	C1-C2
St Bede's Avenue	B2
St Chad's Road	B3
St Heliers Road	C2-C3
Salthouse Avenue	C4
Saville Road	C2-C3
Shannon Street	B5
Shaw Road	B2
Sheppard Street	B6
Shetland Road	C2-C3
South King Street	C6-C7
Springfield Road	B8

Station Road	B1
Station Terrace	B1
Talbot Road	B7-B8-C8
Topping Street	B7
Tyldesley Road	B4
Vance Road	B6
Victoria Street	B6
Victory Road	C8
Waterloo Road	B2-C2
Wellington Road	B3
Westmorland Avenue	C4
Withnell Road	B1
Woodfield Road	B3
Woolman Road	C5
Yorkshire Street	B5

Fleetwood

Abbots Walk	A3
Adelaide Street	B3-C3-C2
Addison Road	A1
Albert Street	C2-C3
Ash Street	A1-A2
Aughton Street	C3
Balmoral Terrace	B4
Belmont Road	A1
Blakiston Street	A2-B2-B3
Bold Street	B4-C4
Burns Road	A3
Byron Street	A3
Chaucer Road	A2
Church Street	C2
Cop Lane	A1-B1-B2
Copse Road	A1
Custom House Lane	C3
Dock Road	B1
Dock Street	B1-B2-C2
Dryden Road	A2-A3
Elm Street	A1-A2
Harris Street	A2-A3-B3
Hesketh Place	B3
Kemp Street	B2-B3
Kent Street	B3-C3
London Street	B2-B3
Lord Street	A1-A2-B2-C2-C3
Lower Lune Street	C3
Milton Street	A2-A3
Mount Road	A3-B3
Mount Street	A2-B2
North Albert Street	C3-C4
North Albion Street	A1-A2
North Church Street	B3-B4
North Street	B3
Oak Street	A1
Outer Promenade	A4-B4
Pharos Street	B3-C3-C4
Poulton Road	A2
Poulton Street	A2
Preston Street	B2
Promenade Road	A3-A4
Queen's Terrace	C3-C4
Radcliffe Road	A1
Rhyl Street	B3
St Peters Place	B2-B3
Seabank Road	A2-A3

Siding Road	A1
Station Road	A1
Styan Street	A2-A1-B1
Tennyson Road	A2
The Esplanade	A3-A4-B4
Upper Lune Street	C4
Victoria Street	B3-C3
Walmsley Street	A3-A2-B2
Warrenhurst Road	A1
Warren Street	B3-B2-C2
Warwick Place	A3
Willow Street	A1
Windsor Terrace	B4

Lytham

Agnew Street	B2-B3
Alder Grove	A3-B3
Ballam Road	B2-B3-B4-C4
Bath Street	B2
Beach Street	B2
Bellingham Road	C4
Bleasdale Road	C3
Brook Road	C3
Calcroft Place	A3-B4
Cecil Street	A2-A3
Central Beach	B2-C2
Church Road	A2-B2
Cleveland Road	B3-C3
Clifton Street	B2-C2
East Beach	C2
Forest Drive	A3-B3
Gregory Place	A3
Hastings Place	B2-B3
Henry Street	B2
Holcroft Place	A3
Lilac Avenue	B4
Longacre Place	A3
Lowther Terrace	A2
Market Square	B2
Moorfield Drive	B3
Mythop Avenue	C3
Mythop Road	C3
Norfolk Road	C4
North Clifton Street	B2-C2
North Warton Street	C2
Park Street	B2
Parkview Road	C2-C3-C4
Queen Street	B2
Reedy Acre Place	A3-A4
Ring Dyke Way	A3
Rogerly Close	A3
South Clifton Street	B2-C2
South-Holme	C3
South Park	A3-B3
South Warton Street	C2
Starfield Close	B3
Station Road	C2
Talbot Road	C2
Upper Westby Street	A2-B2
Warton Street	C2
West Beach	A2-B2
Westby Street	B2-C2
Westwood Mews	A2
Westwood Road	A2

Woodville Terrace	A2
Wykeham Road	C3-C4

ATH

Street Index with Grid Reference

Bournemouth

Albert Road	C3-D3
Avenue Road	B3-C3
Bath Road	D2-E2-E3-E4-F4
Beacon Road	C1
Bodorgan Road	C4
Bourne Avenue	B3-C3
Bradbourne Road	B3
Braidley Road	B3-B4
Branksome Wood Gardens	A4
Branksome Wood Road	A4
Cambridge Road	A2-A3
Central Drive	B4
Chine Crescent	A1
Chine Crescent Road	A1-A2
Christchurch Road	F4
Commercial Road	B2
Cotlands Road	F4
Cranborne Road	B2-C2
Crescent Road	A3-B3
Cumnor Road	E4
Dean Park Crescent	C4-D4
Dean Park Road	C4
Durley Chine Road	A1-A2
Durley Chine Road South	A1
Durley Gardens	A1-A2
Durley Road	A1-A2-B1
Durrant Road	B4
East Overcliff Drive	E2-F2-F3
Exeter Crescent	C2
Exeter Park Road	C2-D2
Exeter Road	C2-D2
Fir Vale Road	D3-D4
Gervis Place	C3-D3
Gervis Road	E3-F3
Glenfern Road	D3-E3-E4
Grove Road	E3-F3
Hahnemann Road	A1-B1-B2
Hinton Road	D2-D3-E2
Holdenhurst Road	F4
Kensington Drive	A4
Kerley Road	C1
Lansdowne Road	E4-F4
Lorne Park Road	E4
Madeira Road	D4-E4
Marlborough Road	A2
Meyrick Road	F3-F4
Norwich Avenue	A2
Norwich Avenue West	A3
Norwich Road	A2-B2
Old Christchurch Road	D3-D4-E4-F4-F4
Orchard Street	C2-C3
Parsonage Road	D3-E3
Poole Hill	A2-B2
Poole Road	A2
Post Office Road	C3
Priory Road	C1-C2
Purbeck Road	B2
Richmond Gardens	C4
Richmond Hill	C3-C4
Richmond Hill Drive	C4
Russell Cotes Road	E2
Somerville Road	A2
St Michael's Road	B2-B1-C1
St Peter's Road	D3-E3
St Stephen's Road	B3-B4-C4-C3
St Stephen's Way	C4
Stafford Road	E4
Suffolk Road	A3-B3
Surrey Road	A3
Terrace Road	B2-C2
The Triangle	B2-B3
Tregonwell Road	B2-C2-C1
Trinity Road	E4
Undercliffe Drive	D1-D2-E1-E2-F2
Upper Hinton Road	D2-D3-E2
Upper Norwich Road	A2-B2
Upper Terrace Road	B2-C2
Wessex Way	A3-A4-B4-C4-D4-E4
West Cliff Gardens	B1
West Cliff Promenade	B1-C1-D1-C1
West Cliff Road	A1-B1
Westhill Road	A2-B2-B1
Westover Road	D2-D3
West Promenade	C1-D1
Wimborne Road	C4
Wootton Gardens	E3-E4
Wootton Mount	E4
Yelverton Road	C3-D3

Christchurch

Albion Road	A4
Arcadia Road	A4
Arthur Road	B3
Avenue Road	A3-B3-B4
Avon Road West	A3-A4-B4
Bargates	B2-B3
Barrack Road	A4-A3-B2-B3

Beaconsfield Road	B2-B3
Bridge Street	C2
Bronte Avenue	B4
Canberra Road	A4
Castle Street	B2-C2
Christchurch By-Pass	B2-C2-C3
Clarendon Road	A3-B3
Douglas Avenue	A2-B2
Endfield Road	A4
Fairfield	B3
Fairfield Drive	A2
Fairmile Road	A4-B4-B3
Flambard Avenue	A4
Gardner Road	A3-A4
Gleadows Avenue	A2-B2
Grove Road East	A3-B3
Grove Road West	A3
High Street	B2
Iford Lane	A1
Jumpers Avenue	A4
Jumpers Road	A3-A4-B4
Kings Avenue	A2-B2
Manor Road	B2
Milhams Street	B2-C2
Mill Road	B3-B4
Portfield Road	A3-B3
Queens Avenue	B1
Quay Road	B1
River Lea Road	B2
Soapers Lane	B2
Saxonbury Road	A1
St John's Road	A2
St Margarets Avenue	B1
Sopers Lane	B1-B2
South View Road	A1-B1
Stony Lane	C4-C3-C2
Stour Road	B3-B2-A1-A2
Stourbank Road	B2
The Grove	A4
Tuckton Road	A1
Twynham Avenue	B2-B3
Walcott Avenue	A4-B4
Waterloo Place	C2
Wickfield Avenue	B1-B2
Wick Lane	A1-B1-B2
Willow Drive	A1-B1
Willow Way	A1-B1
Windsor Road	A3

Poole

Ballard Road	B1-C1
Church Street	A1
Dear Hay Lane	A2-B2
Denmark Road	C3
East Quay Road	B1
East Street	B1
Elizabeth Road	C3
Emerson Road	B1-B2
Esplanade	B3
Garland Road	C4
Green Road	B2-B1-C1
Heckford Road	C3-C4
High Street	A1-B1-B2
Hill Street	B2
Johns Road	C3-C4
Jolliffe Road	C4
Kingland Road	B2-C2
Kingston Road	C3-C4
Lagland Street	B1-B2
Longfleet Road	C3
Maple Road	C3-C4
Mount Pleasant Road	C2-C3
Newfoundland Drive	C1
New Orchard	A1-A2
North Street	B2
Old Orchard	B1
Parkstone Road	C1-C2
Perry Gardens	B1
Poole Bridge	A1
Sandbourne Road	C4
St Mary's Road	C3
Seldown Lane	C2-C3
Shaftesbury Road	C3
Skinner Street	B1
South Road	B2
Stanley Road	B1
Sterte Avenue	A4-B4
Sterte Road	B2-B3-B4
Stokes Avenue	B4-C4
Strand Street	A1-B1
Tatnam Road	B4-C4
The Quay	A1-B1
Towngate Bridge	B2-B3
West Quay Road	A1-A2-B2
West Street	A1-A2-B2
Wimborne Road	B3-C3-C4

Swanage

Argyle Road	A2
Atlantic Road	A1-B1
Battlemead	B4
Beach Gardens	B4

Bon Accord Road	B1
Broad Road	C1
Cauldron Avenue	B4
Cauldron Barn Road	A4-B4
Cauldron Crescent	A4
Church Hill	A2
Clifton Road	B4
Cluny Crescent	B1-C1
Court Hill	A2
Court Road	A2
Cowlease	A1-A2
Cranborne Road	B2
De Moulham Road	B3-B4
D'uberville Drive	A4-B4
Eldon Terrace	B2
Encombe Road	C1
Exeter Road	B1-C1
Gannets Park	B3
Gilbert Road	A2-B2
Gordon Road	B1
Grosvenor Road	C1
Hanbury Road	A2
High Street	A2-B3
Ilminster Road	B2-B3
Institute Road	B2-B2
Kings Road	A2-B2
Kings Road East	B2
Kings Road West	A2
Locarno Road	A2
Manor Road	B1-C1
Manwell Drive	A1
Manwell Road	A1
Mariners Drive	A1
Marshall Rqw	C1
Mount Pleasant Lane	B1-B2
Mountscar	A1
Newton Road	B1
Northbrook Road	A2-A3-B3-B4
Osborne Road	A1
Park Road	A2
Princess Road	A2
Prospect Crescent	A3
Peveril Heights	C1
Peveril Point Road	C1
Priests Road	C1
Queens Mead	B1
Queens Road	A1-B1-C1
Rabling Road	A3-B3
Rempstone Road	B2-B3
Richmond Road	B1
St Vast's Road	B1
Sentry Road	C1
Seymer Road	C1
Shore Road	B3-B4

Springfield Road	B2
Stafford Road	B1-B2
Station Road	B2
Sunridge Close	B1
Taunton Road	C1
The Parade	C2
Townsend Road	A1
Ulwell Road	B4
Victoria Avenue	A3-B3
Vivian Park	B4
Walrond Road	A3-B3

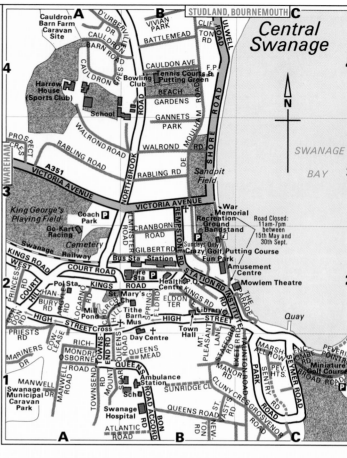

LEGEND

AA Recommended roads	
Other roads	
Restricted roads	
Buildings of interest	Sta
AA Centre	AA
Churches	+
Car parks	P
One Way streets	
Parks and open spaces	

STT

Bournemouth

Until the beginning of the 19th-century the landscape was open heath. Bournemouth's rise began in Victorian times when the idea of seaside holidays was very new. In the next 50 years it had become a major resort. Holidaymakers today enjoy miles of sandy beaches, a mild climate and beautiful setting, along with a tremendous variety of amenities, including some of the best shopping in the south. Entertainments range from variety shows, cinemas, opera and the world famous Bournemouth Symphony Orchestra.

Christchurch is situated at the confluence of the rivers Avon and Stour which flow into Christchurch Harbour at Mudeford. The Priory Church dominates the town with its many attractive walks and old buildings.

Poole is famous for the large natural harbour and Poole Quay with its unique historical interest.

The Maritime Museum illustrates the town's associations with the sea since prehistoric times and the famous Poole Pottery offers guided tours of its workshops with exhibits of pottery past and present.

Swanage is one of Dorset's most popular holiday resorts that has still retained much of its Victorian influence. Dramatic coastal scenery with cliff top walks and many places of interest are within easy reach.

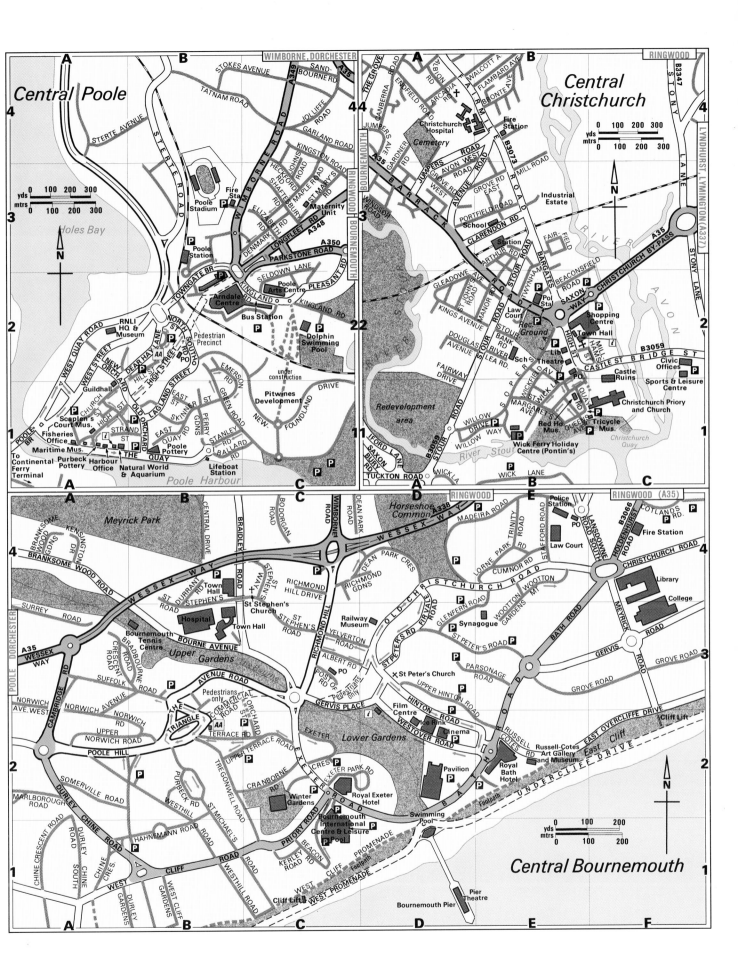

BOURNEMOUTH

The pier, safe sea-bathing, golden sands facing south and sheltered by steep cliffs, and plenty of amenities for the holiday maker make Bournemouth one of the most popular resorts on the south coast of England.

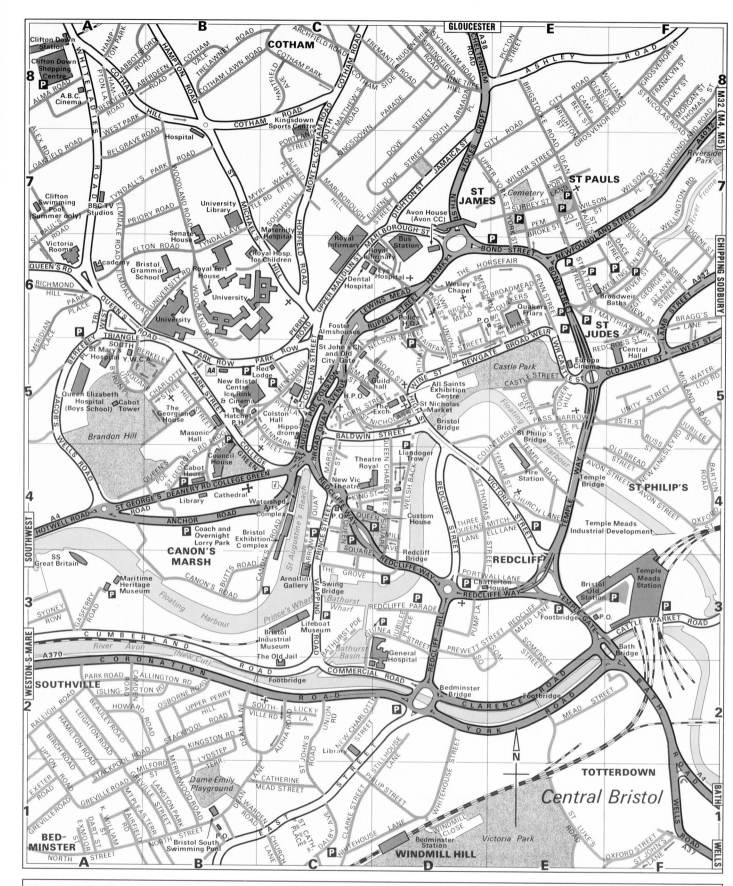

Bristol

One of Britain's most historic seaports, Bristol retains many of its visible links with the past, despite terrible damage inflicted during bombing raids in World War II. Most imposing is the cathedral, founded as an abbey church in 1140. Perhaps even more famous than the cathedral is the Church of St Mary Redcliffe. Ranking among the finest churches in the country, it owes much of its splendour to 14th- and 15th-century merchants who bestowed huge sums of money on it.

The merchant families brought wealth to the whole of Bristol, and their trading links with the world are continued in today's modern aerospace and technological industries. Much of the best of Bristol can be seen in the area of the Floating Harbour – an arm of the Avon. Several of the old warehouses have been converted into museums, galleries and exhibition centres. Among them are genuinely picturesque old pubs, the best-known of which is the Llandoger Trow. It is a timbered 17th-century house, the finest of its kind in Bristol. Further up the same street – King Street – is the Theatre Royal, built in 1766 and the oldest theatre in the country. In Corn Street, the heart of the business area, is a magnificent 18th-century corn exchange. In front of it are the four pillars known as the 'nails', on which merchants used to make cash transactions, hence 'to pay on the nail'.

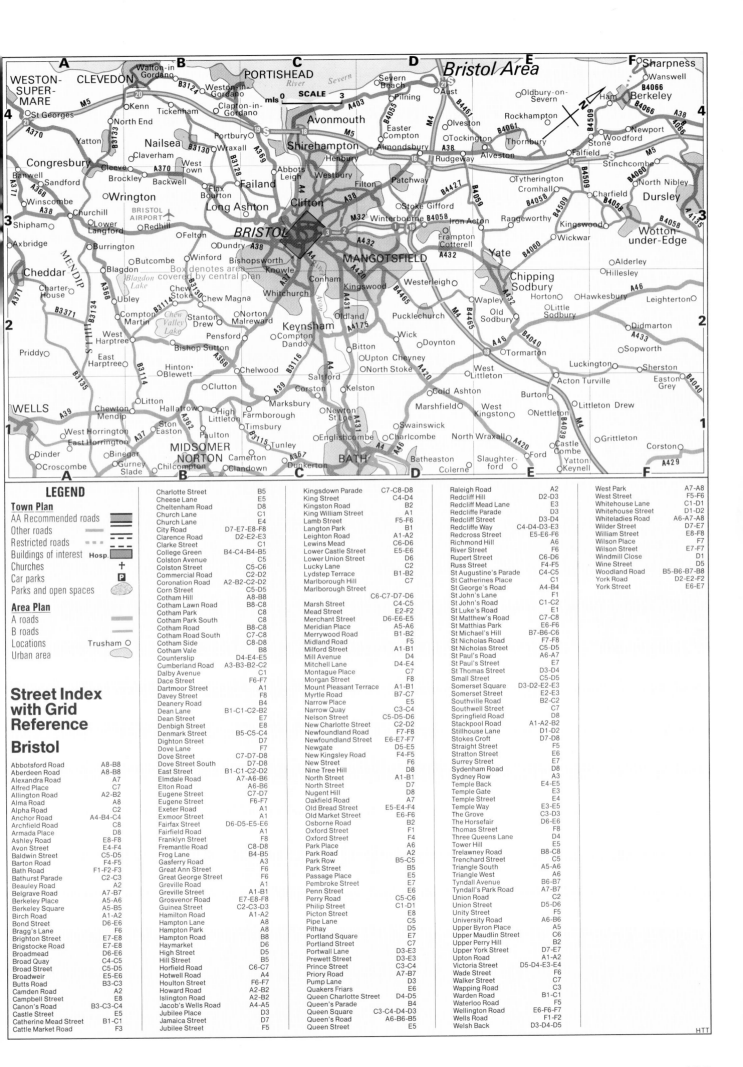

LEGEND

Town Plan

AA Recommended roads	
Other roads	
Restricted roads	
Buildings of interest	Hosp.
Churches	†
Car parks	P
Parks and open spaces	

Area Plan

A roads	
B roads	
Locations	Trusham ○
Urban area	

Street Index with Grid Reference

Bristol

Abbotsford Road	A8-B8
Aberdeen Road	A8-B8
Alexandra Road	A7
Alfred Place	C7
Allington Road	A2-B2
Alma Road	A8
Alpha Road	C2
Anchor Road	A4-B4-C4
Archfield Road	C8
Armada Place	D8
Ashley Road	E8-F8
Avon Street	E4-F4
Baldwin Street	C5-D5
Barton Road	F4-F5
Bath Road	F1-F2-F3
Bathurst Parade	C2-C3
Beauley Road	A2
Belgrave Road	A7-B7
Berkeley Place	A5-A6
Berkeley Square	A5-B5
Birch Road	A1-A2
Bond Street	D6-E6
Bragg's Lane	F6
Brighton Street	E7-E8
Brigstocke Road	E7-E8
Broadmead	D6-E6
Broad Quay	C4-C5
Broad Street	C5-D5
Broadweir	E5-E6
Butts Road	B3-C3
Camden Road	A2
Campbell Street	E8
Canon's Road	B3-C3-C4
Castle Street	E5
Catherine Mead Street	B1-C1
Cattle Market Road	F3
Charlotte Street	B5
Cheese Lane	E5
Cheltenham Road	D8
Church Lane	C1
Church Lane	E4
City Road	D7-E7-E8-F8
Clarence Road	D2-E2-E3
Clarke Street	C1
College Green	B4-C4-B4-B5
Colston Avenue	C5
Colston Street	C5-C6
Commercial Road	C2-D2
Coronation Road	A2-B2-B2-C2
Corn Street	C5-D5
Cotham Hill	A8-B8
Cotham Lawn Road	B8-C8
Cotham Park	C8
Cotham Park South	C8
Cotham Road	B8-C8
Cotham Road South	C7-C8
Cotham Side	C8-D8
Cotham Vale	B8
Countership	D4-E4-E5
Cumberland Road	A3-B3-B2-C2
Dalby Avenue	C1
Dace Lane	F6-F7
Dartmoor Street	A1
Davey Street	F8
Deanery Road	B4
Dean Lane	B1-C1-C2-B2
Dean Street	E7
Denbigh Street	E8
Denmark Street	B5-C5-C4
Dighton Street	D7
Dove Lane	F7
Dove Street	C7-D7-D8
Dove Street South	D7-D8
East Street	B1-C1-C2-D2
Elmdale Road	A7-A6-B6
Elton Road	A6-B6
Eugene Street	C7-D7
Eugene Street	F6-F7
Exeter Road	A1
Exmoor Street	A1
Fairfax Street	D6-D5-E5-E6
Fairfield Road	A1
Franklyn Street	F8
Fremantle Road	C8-D8
Frog Lane	B4-B5
Gasferry Road	A3
Great Ann Street	F6
Great George Street	F6
Greville Road	A1
Greville Street	A1-B1
Grosvenor Road	E7-E8-F8
Guinea Street	C2-C3-D3
Hamilton Road	A1-A2
Hampton Lane	A8
Hampton Park	A8
Hampton Road	B8
Haymarket	D6
High Street	D5
Hill Street	B5
Horfield Road	C6-C7
Hotwell Road	A4
Houlton Street	F6-F7
Howard Road	A2-B2
Islington Road	A2-B2
Jacob's Wells Road	A4-A5
Jubilee Place	D3
Jamaica Street	D7
Jubilee Street	F5
Kingsdown Parade	C7-C8-D8
King Street	C4-D4
Kingston Road	B2
King William Street	A1
Lamb Street	F5-F6
Langton Park	B1
Leighton Road	A1-A2
Lewins Mead	C6-D6
Lower Castle Street	E5-E6
Lower Union Street	D6
Lucky Lane	C2
Lydstep Terrace	B1-B2
Marlborough Hill	C7
Marlborough Street	C6-C7-D7-D6
Marsh Street	C4-C5
Mead Street	E2-F2
Merchant Street	D6-E6-E5
Meridian Place	A5-A6
Merrywood Road	B1-B2
Midland Road	F5
Milford Street	A1-B1
Mill Avenue	D4
Mitchell Lane	D4-E4
Montague Place	C7
Morgan Street	F8
Mount Pleasant Terrace	A1-B1
Myrtle Road	B7-C7
Narrow Place	E5
Narrow Quay	C3-C4
Nelson Street	C5-D5-D6
New Charlotte Street	C2-D2
Newfoundland Road	F7-F8
Newfoundland Street	E6-E7-F7
Newgate	D5-E5
New Kingsley Road	F4-F5
New Street	F6
Nine Tree Hill	D8
North Street	A1-B1
North Street	D7
Nugent Hill	D8
Oakfield Road	A7
Old Bread Street	E5-E4-F4
Old Market Street	E6-F6
Osborne Road	B2
Oxford Street	F1
Oxford Street	F4
Park Place	A6
Park Road	A2
Park Row	B5-C5
Park Street	B5
Passage Place	E5
Pembroke Street	E7
Penn Street	E6
Perry Road	C5-C6
Philip Street	C1-D1
Picton Street	E8
Pipe Lane	C5
Pithay	D5
Portland Square	E7
Portland Street	C7
Portwall Lane	D3-E3
Prewett Street	D3-E3
Prince Street	C3-C4
Priory Road	A7-B7
Pump Lane	D3
Quakers Friars	E6
Queen Charlotte Street	D4-D5
Queen's Parade	B4
Queen Square	C3-C4-D4-D3
Queen's Road	A6-B6-B5
Queen Street	E5
Raleigh Road	A2
Redcliff Hill	D2-D3
Redcliff Mead Lane	E3
Redcliffe Parade	D3
Redcliff Street	D3-D4
Redcliffe Way	C4-D4-D3-E3
Redcross Street	E5-E6-F6
Richmond Hill	A6
River Street	F6
Rupert Street	C6-D6
Russ Street	F4-F5
St Augustine's Parade	C4-C5
St Catherines Place	C1
St George's Road	A4-B4
St John's Lane	F1
St John's Road	C1-C2
St Luke's Road	E1
St Matthew's Road	C7-C8
St Matthias Park	E6-F6
St Michael's Hill	B7-B6-C6
St Nicholas Road	F7-F8
St Nicholas Street	C5-D5
St Paul's Road	A6-A7
St Paul's Street	E7
St Thomas Street	D3-D4
Small Street	C5-D5
Somerset Square	D3-D2-E2-E3
Somerset Street	E2-E3
Southville Road	B2-C2
Southwell Street	C7
Springfield Road	D8
Stackpool Road	A1-A2-B2
Stillhouse Lane	D1-D2
Stokes Croft	D7-D8
Straight Street	F5
Stratton Street	E6
Surrey Street	E7
Sydenham Road	D8
Sydney Row	A3
Temple Back	E4-E5
Temple Gate	E3
Temple Street	E4
Temple Way	E3-E5
The Grove	C3-D3
The Horsefair	D6-E6
Thomas Street	F8
Three Queens Lane	D4
Tower Hill	E5
Trelawney Road	B8-C8
Trenchard Street	C5
Triangle South	A5-A6
Triangle West	A6
Tyndall Avenue	B6-B7
Tyndall's Park Road	A7-B7
Union Road	C2
Union Street	D5-D6
Unity Street	F5
University Road	A6-B6
Upper Byron Place	A5
Upper Maudlin Street	C6
Upper Perry Hill	B2
Upper York Street	D7-E7
Upton Road	A1-A2
Victoria Street	D5-D4-E3-E4
Wade Street	F6
Walker Street	C7
Wapping Road	C3
Warden Road	B1-C1
Waterloo Road	F5
Wellington Road	E6-F6-F7
Wells Road	F1-F2
Welsh Back	D3-D4-D5
West Park	A7-A8
West Street	F5-F6
Whitehouse Lane	C1-D1
Whitehouse Street	D1-D2
Whiteladies Road	A6-A7-A8
Wilder Street	D7-E7
William Street	E8-F8
Wilson Place	F7
Wilson Street	E7-F7
Windmill Close	D1
Wine Street	D5
Woodland Road	B5-B6-B7-B8
York Road	D2-E2-F2
York Street	E6-E7

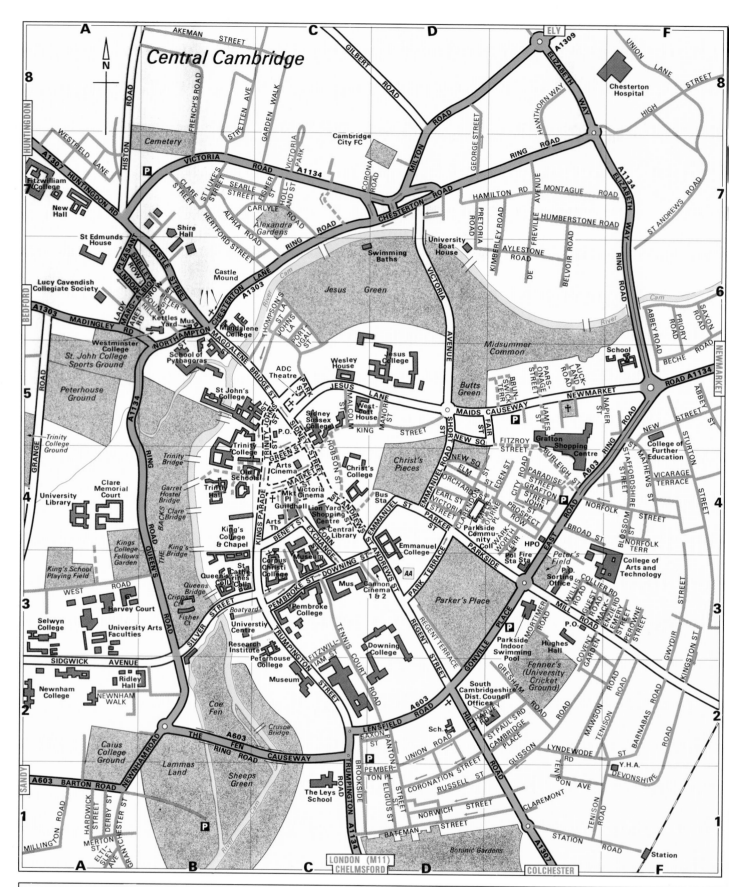

Cambridge

Few views in England, perhaps even in Europe, are as memorable as that from Cambridge's Backs towards the colleges. Dominating the scene, in every sense, is King's College Chapel. One of the finest Gothic buildings anywhere, it was built in three stages from 1446 to 1515.

No one would dispute that the chapel is Cambridge's masterpiece, but there are dozens of buildings here that would be the finest in any other town or city. Most are colleges, or are attached to colleges, and it is the university which permeates every aspect of Cambridge's landscape and life. In all there are 33 university colleges in the city, and nearly all have buildings and features of great interest. Guided tours of the colleges are available.

Cambridge can provide a complete history of English architecture. The oldest surviving building is the tower of St Benet's Church dating back to before the Norman Conquest, and its most famous church is the Church of the Holy Sepulchre, one of only four round churches of its kind.

Of the many notable museums in Cambridge, the Fitzwilliam Museum contains some of the best collections of ceramics, paintings, coins, medals and Egyptian, Greek and Roman antiquities outside London.

Huntingdon and Ely are both within easy driving distance of Cambridge.

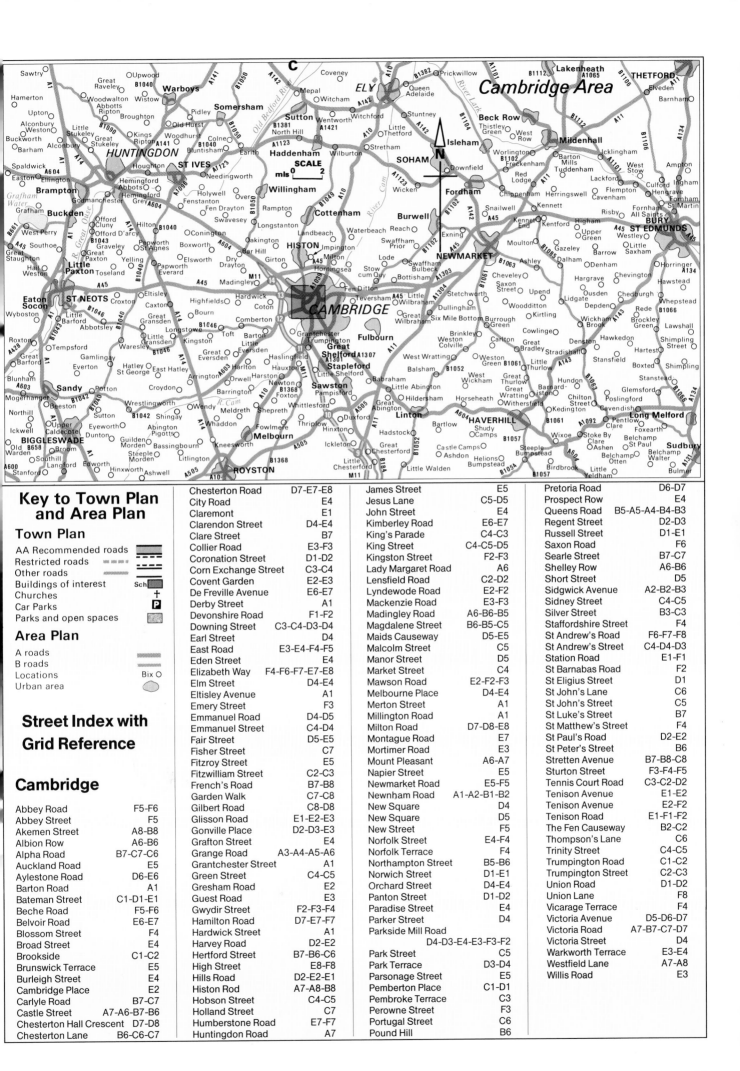

Cambridge Area

Key to Town Plan and Area Plan

Town Plan

AA Recommended roads
Restricted roads
Other roads
Buildings of interest — Sch
Churches — †
Car Parks — P
Parks and open spaces

Area Plan

A roads
B roads
Locations — Bix ○
Urban area

Street Index with Grid Reference

Cambridge

Abbey Road	F5-F6
Abbey Street	F5
Akemen Street	A8-B8
Albion Row	A6-B6
Alpha Road	B7-C7-C6
Auckland Road	E5
Aylestone Road	D6-E6
Barton Road	A1
Bateman Street	C1-D1-E1
Beche Road	F5-F6
Belvoir Road	E6-E7
Blossom Street	F4
Broad Street	E4
Brookside	C1-C2
Brunswick Terrace	E5
Burleigh Street	E4
Cambridge Place	E2
Carlyle Road	B7-C7
Castle Street	A7-A6-B7-B6
Chesterton Hall Crescent	D7-D8
Chesterton Lane	B6-C6-C7
Chesterton Road	D7-E7-E8
City Road	E4
Claremont	E1
Clarendon Street	D4-E4
Clare Street	B7
Collier Road	E3-F3
Coronation Street	D1-D2
Corn Exchange Street	C3-C4
Covent Garden	E2-E3
De Freville Avenue	E6-E7
Derby Street	A1
Devonshire Road	F1-F2
Downing Street	C3-C4-D3-D4
Earl Street	D4
East Road	E3-E4-F4-F5
Eden Street	E4
Elizabeth Way	F4-F6-F7-E7-E8
Elm Street	D4-E4
Eltisley Avenue	A1
Emery Street	F3
Emmanuel Road	D4-D5
Emmanuel Street	C4-D4
Fair Street	D5-E5
Fisher Street	C7
Fitzroy Street	E5
Fitzwilliam Street	C2-C3
French's Road	B7-B8
Garden Walk	C7-C8
Gilbert Road	C8-D8
Glisson Road	E1-E2-E3
Gonville Place	D2-D3-E3
Grafton Street	E4
Grange Road	A3-A4-A5-A6
Grantchester Street	A1
Green Street	C4-C5
Gresham Road	E2
Guest Road	E3
Gwydir Street	F2-F3-F4
Hamilton Road	D7-E7-F7
Hardwick Street	A1
Harvey Road	D2-E2
Hertford Street	B7-B6-C6
High Street	E8-F8
Hills Road	D2-E2-E1
Histon Rod	A7-A8-B8
Hobson Street	C4-C5
Holland Street	C7
Humberstone Road	E7-F7
Huntingdon Road	A7
James Street	E5
Jesus Lane	C5-D5
John Street	E4
Kimberley Road	E6-E7
King's Parade	C4-C3
King Street	C4-C5-D5
Kingston Street	F2-F3
Lady Margaret Road	A6
Lensfield Road	C2-D2
Lyndewode Road	E2-F2
Mackenzie Road	E3-F3
Madingley Road	A6-B6-B5
Magdalene Street	B6-B5-C5
Maids Causeway	D5-E5
Malcolm Street	C5
Manor Street	D5
Market Street	C4
Mawson Road	E2-F2-F3
Melbourne Place	D4-E4
Merton Street	A1
Millington Road	A1
Milton Road	D7-D8-E8
Montague Road	E7
Mortimer Road	E3
Mount Pleasant	A6-A7
Napier Street	E5
Newmarket Road	E5-F5
Newnham Road	A1-A2-B1-B2
New Square	D4
New Square	D5
New Street	F5
Norfolk Street	E4-F4
Norfolk Terrace	F4
Northampton Street	B5-B6
Norwich Street	D1-E1
Orchard Street	D4-E4
Panton Street	D1-D2
Paradise Street	E4
Parker Street	D4
Parkside Mill Road	D4-D3-E4-E3-F3-F2
Park Street	C5
Park Terrace	D3-D4
Parsonage Street	E5
Pemberton Place	C1-D1
Pembroke Terrace	C3
Perowne Street	F3
Portugal Street	C6
Pound Hill	B6
Pretoria Road	D6-D7
Prospect Row	E4
Queens Road	B5-A5-A4-B4-B3
Regent Street	D2-D3
Russell Street	D1-E1
Saxon Road	F6
Searle Street	B7-C7
Shelley Row	A6-B6
Short Street	D5
Sidgwick Avenue	A2-B2-B3
Sidney Street	C4-C5
Silver Street	B3-C3
Staffordshire Street	F4
St Andrew's Road	F6-F7-F8
St Andrew's Street	C4-D4-D3
Station Road	E1-F1
St Barnabas Road	F2
St Eligius Street	D1
St John's Lane	C6
St John's Street	C5
St Luke's Street	B7
St Matthew's Street	F4
St Paul's Road	D2-E2
St Peter's Street	B6
Stretten Avenue	B7-B8-C8
Sturton Street	F3-F4-F5
Tennis Court Road	C3-C2-D2
Tenison Avenue	E1-E2
Tenison Avenue	E2-F2
Tenison Road	E1-F1-F2
The Fen Causeway	B2-C2
Thompson's Lane	C6
Trinity Street	C4-C5
Trumpington Road	C1-C2
Trumpington Street	C2-C3
Union Road	D1-D2
Union Lane	F8
Vicarage Terrace	F4
Victoria Avenue	D5-D6-D7
Victoria Road	A7-B7-C7-D7
Victoria Street	D4
Warkworth Terrace	E3-E4
Westfield Lane	A7-A8
Willis Road	E3

141

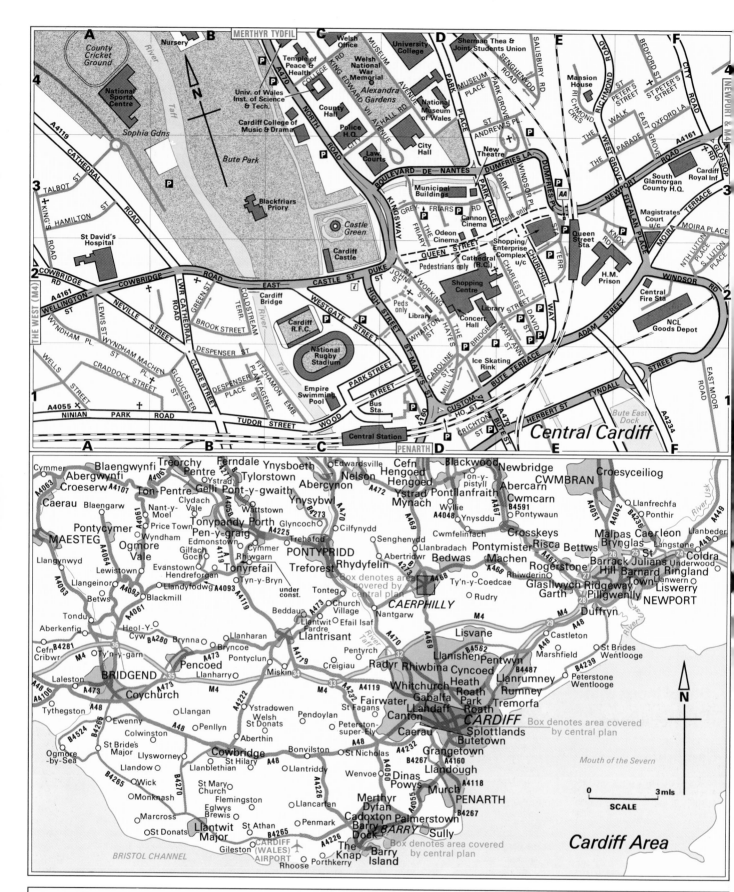

MERTHYR TYDFIL

County Cricket Ground · Nursery · River Taff · National Sports Centre · Sophia Gdns · Cathedral Road · A4119 · A4055 · Talbot St · King's · Hamilton · St David's Hospital · Wellington St · Wyndham Pl · Wyndham Machen · Lewis St · Neville Street · Craddock Street · Gloucester Street · Clare Street · Coldstream Terr · Brook Street · Despenser St · Despenser Place · Fitzhamon Emb · Plantagenet St · Tudor Street · Ninian Park Road · Wells Street · A4161 · Cowbridge Rd · Cowbridge Road East · Castle St · Green St · Lwr Cathedral Road · Cardiff Bridge · Cardiff R.F.C. · Westgate Street · National Rugby Stadium · Empire Swimming Pool · Park Street · Wood Street · Bute Park · Blackfriars Priory · Castle Green · Cardiff Castle · Temple of Peace & Health · Univ. of Wales Inst. of Science & Tech. · Cardiff College of Music & Drama · North Road · County Hall · King Edward VII Avenue · Welsh Office · Museum · University College · Welsh National War Memorial · Alexandra Gardens · National Museum of Wales · Police H.Q. · City Hall · Law Courts · Boulevard de Nantes · Kingsway · Municipal Buildings · Duke St · High Street · St Mary's St · Queen Street · Working St · Odeon Cinema · Cannon Cinema · Cathedral (R.C.) · Pedestrians only · Shopping Enterprise Complex u/c · Library · Hayes · Bridge · St David's · The Friary · Wharton St · Caroline St · Mill La · Ice Skating Rink · Bus Sta. · Central Station · Custom Ho. St · Crichton St · Herbert St · Bute Terrace · Adam Street · Tyndall Street · Bute East Dock · A4234 · A470 · East Moor Road · East Grove · Windsor Rd · Fitzalan Place · Moira Place · Moira Terrace · Nth Luton Pl · S. Luton Pl · H.M. Prison · Central Fire Sta · NCL Goods Depot · Sherman Thea & Joint Students Union · Salisbury Rd · Senghenydd Rd · Mansion House · Richmond Cres · Peter's Street · St Peter's Street · Walk · West Parade · West Grove · The Parade · The Walk · Richmond Road · City Road · A4161 · Newport Road · Glossop Rd · South Glamorgan County H.Q. · Cardiff Royal Inf · Magistrates Court u/c · Queen Street Sta. · Churchill Way · David Street · Knox Rd · Park Grove · Park Place · Dumfries La · Windsor Pl · New Theatre · Concert Hall · Grey Friars Rd · Windsor Place · Charles Street · Mary Ann St · Library Street · St Andrews Pl · Dumfries Pl · AA · Sandringham · The West (M4) · Newport & M4

Central Cardiff

PENARTH

Cymmer · Abergwynfi · Blaengwynfi · Treorchy · Pentre · Ferndale · Ynysboeth · Edwardsville · Hengoed · Cefn Hengoed · Blackwood · Newbridge · Croesyceiliog · Croeserw · Ton-Pentre · Gelli · Pont-y-gwaith · Tylorstown · Abercynon · Nelson · Ystrad Mynach · Pontllanfraith · Abercarn · CWMBRAN · Caerau · Blaengarw · Nant-y-Moel · Clydach Vale · Wattstown · Ynysybwl · Cilfynydd · Wyllie · Ynysddu · Pontywaun · Cwmcarn · Llanfrechfa · Ponthir · Pontycymer · Wyndham · Price Town · Pen-y-graig · Tonypandy · Porth · Glyncoch · A470 · Cwmfelinfach · Crosskeys · Risca · Bettws · Malpas · Caerleon · Langstone · Llanbeder · MAESTEG · Ogmore Vale · Edmonstown · Gilfach Goch · Rhiwgarn · Trehafod · Senghenydd · Llanbradach · Pontymister · Machen · Rogerstone · Barrack Julians · Bryn glas · St Julians · Coldra · Llangynwyd · Lewistown · Evanstown · Hendreforgan · Tonyrefail · Treforest · PONTYPRIDD · Rhydyfelin · Abertridwr · Bedwas · Rhiwderin · Glasllwch · Garth · Ridgeway · Barnard Town · Underwood · Ringland · Llangeinor · Betws · Llandyfodwg · Tyn-y-Bryn · under const. · Tonteg · Box denotes area covered by central plan · Ty'n-y-Coedcae · Pillgwenlly · Lisswerry · NEWPORT · Tondu · Aberkenfig · Blackmill · Heol-Y-Cyw · Brynna · Beddau · Llantwit Fardre · Church Village · Efail Isaf · Nantgarw · Rudry · CAERPHILLY · Duffryn · Cefn Cribwr · Ty'n-y-garn · Brynna · Llanharan · Llantrisant · Pentyrch · River Taff · Lisvane · Castleton · St Brides Wentlooge · Laleston · Bryncoe · Pontyclun · Creigiau · Radyr · Rhiwbina · Llanishen · Pentwyn · Marshfield · Peterstone Wentlooge · BRIDGEND · Pencoed · Llanharry · Miskin · Cyncoed · Llanrumney · St Brides Wentlooge · A239 · Coychurch · Fairwater · Whitchurch · Heath · Roath · Rumney · Tythegston · Ystradowen · Pendoylan · St Fagans · Gabalfa · Roath Park · Tremorfa · Llangan · Welsh St Donats · Peterston-super-Ely · Llandaff · CARDIFF · Ewenny · Penllyn · Canton · Caerau · Splottlands · Box denotes area covered by central plan · Colwinston · St Nicholas · Butetown · Ogmore-by-Sea · St Bride's Major · Bonvilston · Grangetown · Llysworney · Llandow · COWBRIDGE · St Hilary · Llanblethian · Llantriddy · Wenvoe · Dinas Powys · Llandough · Mouth of the Severn · Wick · St Mary Church · Flemingston · Eglwys Brewis · Llancarfan · Murch · A4118 · PENARTH · Monknash · Marcross · St Athan · Penmark · Merthyr Dyfan · Cadoxton · Palmerstown · B4267 · St Donats · Llantwit Major · Gileston · Barry Dock · BARRY · Sully · CARDIFF (WALES) AIRPORT · Rhoose · Porthkerry · The Knap · Barry Island · Box denotes area covered by central plan · BRISTOL CHANNEL

Cardiff Area

SCALE 0 ———— 3 mls

N

Cardiff

Strategically important to both the Romans and the Normans, Cardiff slipped from prominence in medieval times and remained a quiet market town in a remote area until it was transformed – almost overnight – by the effects of the Industrial Revolution. The valleys of South Wales were a principal source of iron and coal – raw materials which helped to change the shape and course of

the 19th-century world. Cardiff became a teeming export centre; by the end of the 19th century it was the largest coal-exporting city in the world.

Close to the castle – an exciting place with features from Roman times to the 19th century – is the city's civic centre – a fine concourse of buildings dating largely from the early part of the 20th century. Among them is the National Museum of Wales – a superb collection of art and antiquities from Wales and around the world.

Barry has sandy beaches, landscaped gardens and parks, entertainment arcades and funfairs. Like Cardiff it grew as a result of the demand for coal and steel, but now its dock complex is involved in the petrochemical and oil industries.

Caerphilly is famous for two things – a castle and cheese. The cheese is no longer made here, but the 13th-century castle, slighted by Cromwell, still looms above its moat. No castle in Britain – except Windsor – is larger.

142

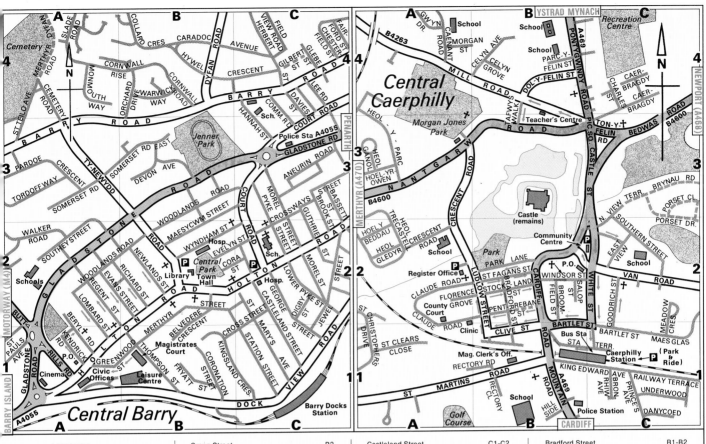

Central Barry — *Central Caerphilly*

LEGEND

Town Plan

AA recommended route	
Restricted roads	
Other roads	
Buildings of interest	Cinema ■
Car parks	P
Parks and open spaces	▲
One way streets	↳

Area Plan

A roads	
B roads	
Locations	Glyncoch ○
Urban area	

Street Index with Grid Reference

Cardiff

Adam Street	E1-E2-F2
Bedford Street	F4
Boulevard de Nantes	C3-D3
Bridge Street	D1-D2-E2
Brook Street	B2
Bute Street	D1-E1
Bute Terrace	D1-E1
Caroline Street	D1
Castle Street	C2
Cathedral Street	A4-A3-B3-B2-A2
Charles Street	D2-E2
Churchill Way	E2-E3
City Hall Road	C3-C4-D4
City Road	F4
Clare Street	B1
Coldstream Terrace	B2
College Road	C4
Cowbridge Road	A2
Cowbridge Road East	A2-B2-C2
Craddock Street	A1-B1
Crichton Street	D1
Customhouse Street	D1
David Street	E2
Despenser Place	B1
Despenser Street	B1
Duke Street	C2-D2
Dumfries Lane	D3-E3
Dumfries Place	E3
East Grove	F4-F3
East Moor Road	F1
Fitzalan Place	F3-F2
Fitzhamon Embankment	B1-C1
Glossop Road	F3
Gloucester Street	B1
Green Street	B2
Greyfriars Road	D3
Hamilton Street	A3
Herbert Street	E1
High Street	C2-D2
King Edward VII Avenue	C4-D4-D3-C3
King's Road	A2-A3
Kingsway	C3-D3-D2
Knox Road	E3-F3-F2
Lewis Street	A2
Lower Cathedral Road	B1-B2
Machen Place	A1-B1
Mary Ann Street	E1-E2
Mill Lane	D1
Moira Place	F3
Moira Terrace	F2-F3
Museum Avenue	C4-D4
Museum Place	D4
Neville Street	A2-B2-B1
Newport Road	E3-F3-F4
Ninian Park Road	A1-B1
North Luton Place	F2-F3
North Road	B4-C4-C3
Oxford Lane	F4
Park Grove	D4-E4
Park Lane	D3-E3
Park Place	D4-D3-E3
Park Street	C1-D1
Plantagenet Street	B1-C1
Queen Street	D2-D3
Richmond Crescent	E4
Richmond Road	E4
St Andrew's Place	D4-E4
St John Street	D2
St Mary's Street	D1-D2
St Peter's Street	E4-F4
Salisbury Road	E4
Senghenydd Road	D4-E4
South Luton Place	F2-F3
Station Terrace	E2-E3
The Friary	D2-D3
The Hayes	D1-D2
The Parade	E3-F3-F4
The Walk	E3-E4-F4
Talbot Street	A3
Tudor Street	B1-C1
Tyndall Street	E1-F1
Wellington Street	A2-B2
Wells Street	A1
Westgate Street	C2-D2-D1
West Grove	E4-E3-F3
Wharton Street	D1-D2
Windsor Place	E3
Windsor Road	F2
Wood Street	C1-D1
Working Street	D2
Wyndham Place	A2
Wyndham Street	A1-A2

Barry

Aneurin Road	C3
Barry Road	A3-A4-B3-B4-C4
Bassett Street	C2-C3
Belvedere Crescent	B1-B2
Beryl Road	A1-A2
Brook Street	C2-C3
Buttrills Road	A1-A2
Caradoc Avenue	B4-C4

Castleland Street	C1-C2
Cemetery Road	A3-A4
Chesterfield Street	C4
Collard Crescent	C3-C4
Commercial Road	C4
Cora Street	B2-C2
Cornwall Rise	A3-A4
Cornwall Road	B4
Coronation Street	B1
Cross Street	B1-C1-C2
Crossways Street	C2-C3
Court Road	C2-C3-C4
Davies Street	C3-C4
Devon Avenue	B3
Digby Street	C2
Dock View Road	B1-C1-C2
Dyfan Road	B4
Evans Street	A2-B2
Evelyn Street	B2-C2
Fairford Street	C4
Field View Road	C4
Fryatt Street	B1
George Street	C1-C2
Gilbert Street	C4
Gladstone Road	A1-A2-B2-B3-C3
Glebe Street	C4
Greenwood Street	A1-B1
Guthrie Street	C3-C2
Hannah Street	C4-C3
Herbert Street	C4
Holton Road	A1-B1-B2-C2
Hywell Crescent	B4-C4
Jewel Street	C1-C2
Kendrick Road	A1
Kingsland Crescent	B1-C1
Lee Road	C4
Lombard Street	A1-A2
Lower Pyke Street	C2
Maesycwm Street	B2-B3-C3
Merthyr Dyfan Road	A4
Merthyr Street	B1-B2-C2
Monmouth Way	A4
Morel Street	C2-C3
Newlands Street	B2
Orchard Drive	B3-B4
Pardoe Crescent	A3
Pyke Street	C3-C2
Regent Street	A2-B2
Richard Street	A2-B2
St Mary's Avenue	C1-C2
St Pauls Avenue	A1
St Teilo Avenue	A3-A4
Slade Road	A4
Somerset Road	A3
Somerset Road East	A3-B3
Southey Street	A2-A3
Station Street	C1
Thompson Street	B1
Tordoff Way	A3
Ty-Newydd Road	A3-B3-B2
Walker Road	A2
Warwick Way	B4
Woodlands Road	A2-B2-B3-C3
Wyndham Street	B2-C2

Caerphilly

Bartlet Street	B2-B1-C1
Bedwas Road	C3-C4
Bradford Street	B1-B2
Broomfield Street	B2
Bronrhiw Avenue	C1
Brynau Road	C3
Caenant Road	A4
Caer Bragdy	C4
Cardiff Road	B1-B2
Castle Street	C3
Celyn Avenue	B4
Celyn Grove	B4
Charles Street	C4
Claude Road	A1-A2-B2
Clive Street	B1-B2
Crescent Rod	A2-A3-B3
Danycoed	C1
Dol-y-Felen Street	B4
East View	C2
Florence Grove	A2-B2
Goodrich Street	C1-C2
Gwyn Drive	A4
Heol Ganol	A3
Heol Gledyr	A2
Heol Trecastell	A2-A3
Hillside	B1
Heol y Beddau	A2
Heol-yr-Owen	A3
King Edward Avenue	B1-C1
Ludlow Street	A2-B2-B1
Maes Glas	C1
Meadow Crescent	C1-C2
Mill Road	A4-B4-B3
Morgan Street	A4-B4
Mountain Road	B1
Nantgarw Road	A3-B3
North View Terrace	C2-C3
Parc-y-Felin Street	B4
Park Lane	B2
Pentrebone Street	B2
Piccadilly Square	C3
Pontygwindy Road	B4-C4
Porset Close	C3
Porset Drive	C2-C3
Prince's Avenue	C1
Railway Terrace	C1
Rectory Road	A1-B1
Rectory Close	B1
St Christopher's Drive	A1-A2
St Clears Close	A1
St Fagans Street	B2
St Martins Road	A1-B1
Salop Street	B2
Southern Street	C2-C3
Station Terrace	B1-C1
Stockland Street	B2
Tafwy Walk	B3-B4
Ton-y-Felin Road	C3
Underwood	C1
Van Road	C2
White Street	C2
Windsor Street	B2

143

LTH

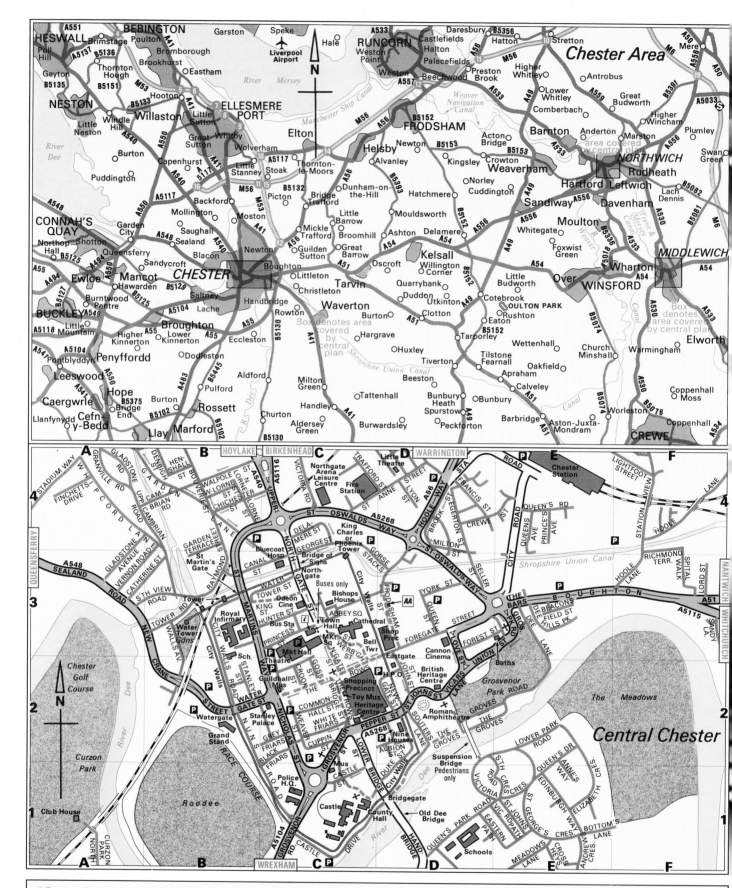

Chester

Chester is the only English city to have preserved the complete circuit of its Roman and medieval walls. On the west side, the top of the walls is now at pavement level, but on the other three sides the walk along the ramparts is remarkable. Two of the old watchtowers contain small museums: the Water Tower, built to protect the old river port, displays relics of medieval Chester; King Charles's

Tower, from which Charles I watched the defeat of the Royalist army at the Battle of Rowton Moor in 1645, portrays Chester's role in the Civil War.

Looking down from the top of the Eastgate, crowned with the ornate and gaily-coloured Jubilee Clock erected in 1897, the view down the main street, the old Roman *Via Principalis*, reveals a dazzling display of the black-and-white timbered buildings for which Chester is famous. One of these, Providence House, bears the inscription

'God's Providence is Mine Inheritance', carved in thanks for sparing the survivors of the plague of 1647 that ravaged the city.

On either side of Eastgate, Watergate and Bridge Street are the Rows, a feature unique to Chester, and dating back at least to the 13th century. These covered galleries of shops, raised up at first-floor level, protected pedestrians from weather and traffic. Chester's magnificent cathedral has beautifully carved choir stalls.

144

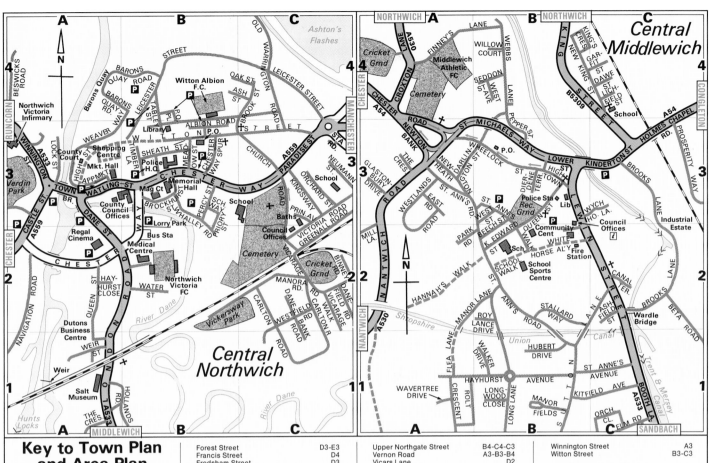

Key to Town Plan and Area Plan

Town Plan

AA Recommended roads
Other roads
Restricted roads
Buildings of interest   College
AA Service Centre   AA
Car Parks   P
Parks and open spaces
Churches   †

Area Plan

A roads
B roads
Locations   Duddon○
Urban area
Locks

Street Index with Grid Reference

Chester

Abbey Square	C3
Albion Street	D2
Andrews Crescent	E1
Anne's Way	E2-E1
Beaconsfield Street	E3
Black Friars	C1-C2
Bottom's Lane	E1-F1
Boughton	E3-F3
Bouverie Street	B4
Bridge Street	C2
Brook Street	D4
Cambrian Road	A4-B4
Canal Street	B3-C3
Castle Drive	C1
Castle Street	C1
Catherine Street	A3-B3
Chichester Street	B4-C4
City Road	E3-E4
City Walls Road	B3-B2
Commonhall Street	C2
Crewe Street	D4-E4
Crook Street	C2
Cross Heys	E1
Cuppin Street	C2
Curzon Park North	A1
Dee Hills Park	E3
Dee Lane	E3
Delamere Street	C4
Denbigh Street	B4
Duke Street	D1-D2
Eastern Path	D1-E1
Edinburgh Way	E1
Egerton Street	D4
Elizabeth Crescent	E1-E2
Finchetts Drive	A4
Foregate Street	D3
Forest Street	D3-E3
Francis Street	D4
Frodsham Street	D3
Garden Lane	A4-B4
Garden Terrace	B3-B4
George Street	C3-C4
Gladstone Avenue	A3-A4
Gladstone Road	A4
Gorse Stacks	C4-C3-D3
Goss Street	C2
Granville Road	A4
Grey Friars	C2
Grosvenor Park Road	E3
Grosvenor Road	C1
Grosvenor Street	C1-C2
Groves Road	D2-E2
Handbridge	D1
Henshall Street	B4
Hoole Lane	F3-F4
Hoole Way	D4
Hunter Street	B3-C3
King Street	B3-C3
Lightfoot Street	E4-F4
Lord Street	F3
Lorne Street	B4
Lower Bridge Street	C2-C1-D1
Lower Park Road	D2-E2
Love Street	D3
Lyon Street	D4
Meadows Lane	E1
Milton Street	D4
New Crane Street	A3-B3-B2
Newgate Street	D2
Nicholas Street	C2-C1
Northgate Street	C3-C2
North Lorne Street	B4
Nuns Road	B2-B1-C1
Pepper Street	C2-D2
Princess Street	C3
Prince's Avenue	E4
Queens Avenue	E4
Queen's Drive	E1-E2
Queen's Park Road	D1-E1
Queen's Road	E4
Queen Street	D3
Raymond Street	B3-B4
Richmond Terrace	F4
St Anne Street	C4-D4
St Georges Crescent	E1
St Johns Road	E1
St Johns Street	D2
St John Street	D3-D2
St Martins Way	B4-B3-C3-B2-C2
St Oswalds Way	C4-D4-D3
St Werburgh Street	C3
Sealand Road	A3
Sellier Street	D3
Souters Lane	D2
South Crescent Road	D2-E2-E1
South View Road	A3-B3
Spittal Walk	F4-F3
Stadium Way	A4
Stanley Street	B2
Station Road	D4-E4
Station View	F4
The Bars	E3
The Groves	D2-E2
The Rows	C2
Tower Road	B3
Trafford Street	C4-D4
Union Street	D2-D3-E3
Upper Cambrian Road	A4-B4-B3
Upper Northgate Street	B4-C4-C3
Vernon Road	A3-B3-B4
Vicars Lane	D2
Victoria Crescent	D1-E1
Victoria Path	D1-E1
Victoria's Road	C4
Walls Avenue	B3-B2
Walpole Street	B4
Watergate Street	B2-C2
Water Tower Street	B3-C3
Weaver Street	C2
West Lorne Street	B4
White Friars	C2
Whipcord Lane	A4-B4
York Street	D3

Northwich

Albion Road	B3
Apple Market	A3
Ash Street	B4-C4
Barons Quay Road	A4-B4
Beswicks Road	A4
Binney Road	C2
Brockhurst Street	B3
Brook Street	B3-C3-C4
Carlton Road	C2-C1
Castle Street	A2-A3
Chester Way	A2-B2-B3-C3
Chester Way Spur	B3
Church Road	C3
Danebank Road	C2-C1
Danefield Road	C2
Dane Street	A3-A2
Greenall Road	C2-C3
Hayhurst Close	A2
High Street	A3
Hollands Road	A1-B1
Kingsway	C3
Leicester Street	B3-B4
Lock Street	A3
London Road	A1-A2-B2
Manora Road	C2
Meadow Street	B3
Navigation Road	A1-A2
Neumann Street	C3
Oak Street	B4-C4
Old Warrington Road	C4-C3
Orchard Street	C3
Paradise Street	C3
Percy Street	B3
Post Office Place	B4-B3
Princes Avenue	C3
Priory Street	B2-B3
Queen Street	A2
School Way	B3
Sheath Street	B3
Station Road	C3
The Crescent	A1
Tabley Street	B4-B3
Timber Lane	B3
Town Bridge	A3
Vicarage Road	C2
Vicarage Walk	C2
Victoria Road	C2-C3
Water Street	B2
Watling Street	A3
Weaver Way	A3-B3-B4
Weir Street	A1
Wesley Place	C3
Westfield Road	C2
Whalley Road	B3-B2
Winnington Street	A3
Witton Street	B3-C3

Middlewich

Ashfield Street	C2
Beech Street	B2-B3
Beta Road	C2-C1
Booth Lane	C1
Brooks Lane	C3-C2
Canal Terrace	C2
Chester Road	A4-A3
Croxton Lane	A4
Darlington Street	A3-B3
Dawe Street	C4
Dierdene Terrace	B3
East Road	A3
Elm Road	C1
Finney's Lane	A4-B4
Flea Lane	A1
Garfit Street	B4-C4
Glastonbury Drive	A3
Hannah's Walk	A2-B2
Hauhurst Avenue	A1-B1
High Town	B3
Holmes Chapel Road	C3-C4
Hubert Drive	B1
Kinderton Street	B3-C3
King Edward Street	B2
King's Crescent	B4-C4
King Street	B4-C4-C3
Kittfield Avenue	B1-C1
Lewin Street	B3-B2-C2-C1
Lichfield Street	C4
Long Lane	B1
Longwood Close	B2
Lower Street	B3
Manor Fields	B3
Manor Lane	A2-B2
Mill Lane	A2
Nantwich Road	A1-A2-A3
New King Street	B4-C4
Newton Bank	A4-A3
Newton Heath	A3
Orchard Close	C1
Park Road	A2-B2
Pepper Street	B4-B3
Prosperity Way	C3
Queen Street	B2-B3
Rolt Crescent	A1-B1
Roy Lance Drive	B2
St Anne's Avenue	B1-C1
St Ann's Road	A3-B3-B2-B1
St Ann's Walk	B2-B3
St Michaels Way	A3-B3
School Walk	B2
Seddon Street	B4
Southway	B3
Stallard Way	B2
Sutton Lane	B1-B2-C2
The Crescent	A3
Walker Drive	B1
Wavertree Drive	A1
Webbs Lane	B4
West Avenue	B4
Westlands Road	A3-A2
West Street	B3
Wheelock Street	A3-B3
White Horse Alley	B2
Willow Court	B4
Wych House Lane	B3-C3

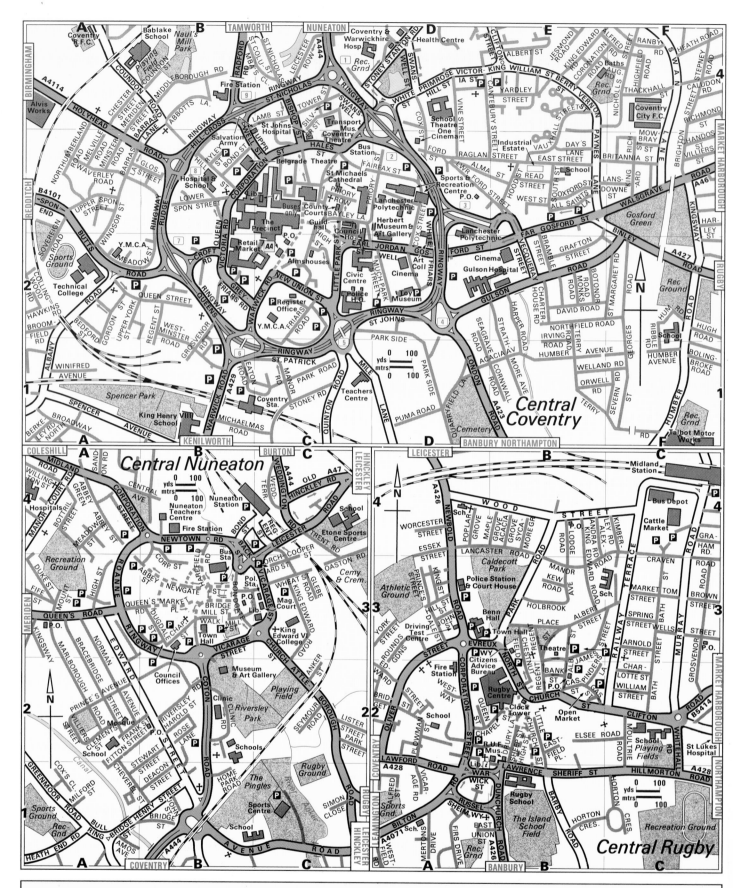

Coventry

Few British towns were as battered by the Blitz as Coventry. A raid in November 1940 flattened most of the city and left the lovely cathedral church a gaunt shell with only the tower and spire still standing. Rebuilding started almost immediately. Symbolising the creation of the new from the ashes of the old is Sir Basil Spence's cathedral, completed in 1962 beside the bombed ruins.

A few medieval buildings have survived intact in the city. St Mary's Guildhall is a finely restored 14th-century building with an attractive minstrels' gallery. Whitefriars Monastery now serves as a local museum. The Herbert Art Gallery and Museum has several collections. Coventry is an important manufacturing centre – most notably for cars – and it is also a university city with the fine campus of the University of Warwick some four miles from the centre.

Nuneaton is an industrial town to the north of Coventry with two distinguished old churches – St Nicholas' and St Mary's. Like Coventry it was badly damaged in the war and its centre has been rebuilt.

Rugby was no more than a sleepy market town until the arrival of the railway. Of course it did have the famous Rugby School, founded in 1567 and one of the country's foremost educational establishments. The railway brought industry – still the town's mainstay.

146

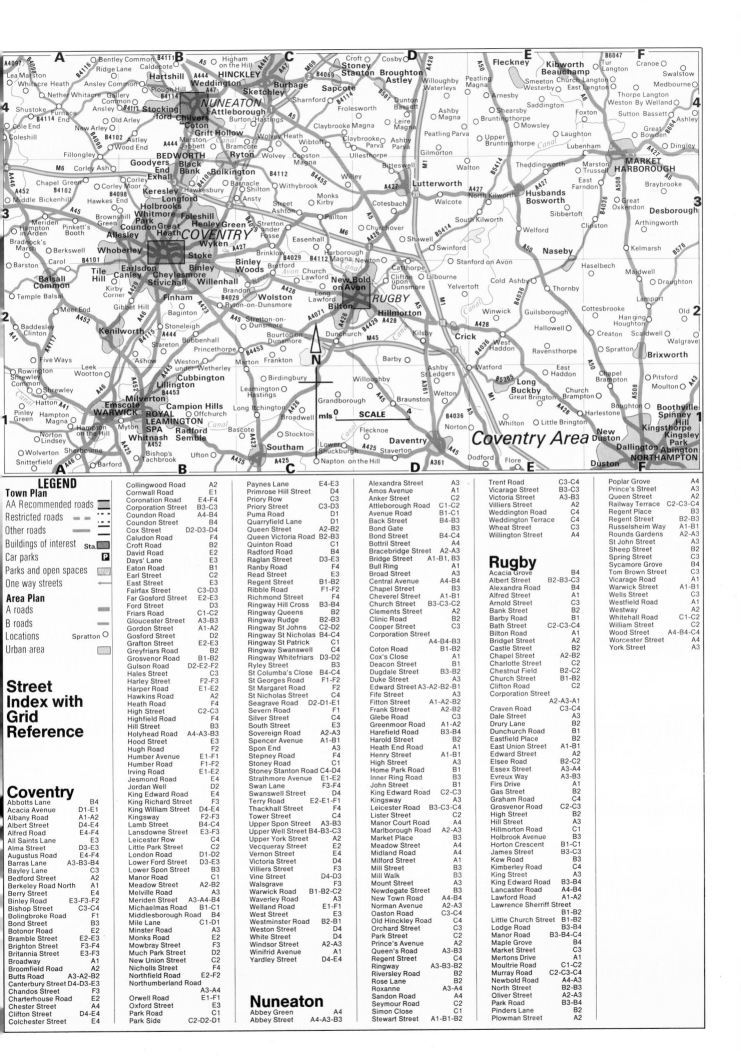

LEGEND

Town Plan
- AA Recommended roads
- Restricted roads
- Other roads
- Buildings of interest — Sta.
- Car parks — P
- Parks and open spaces
- One way streets

Area Plan
- A roads
- B roads
- Locations — Spratton ○
- Urban area

Street Index with Grid Reference

Coventry

Abbotts Lane	B4
Acacia Avenue	D1-E1
Albany Road	A1-A2
Albert Street	D4-E4
Alfred Road	E4-F4
All Saints Lane	E3
Alma Street	D3-E3
Augustus Road	E4-F4
Barras Lane	A3-B3-B4
Bayley Lane	C3
Bedford Street	A2
Berkeley Road North	A1
Berry Street	E4
Binley Road	E3-F3-F2
Bishop Street	C3-C4
Bolingbroke Road	F1
Bond Street	B3
Botoner Road	E2
Bramble Street	E2-E3
Brighton Street	F3-F4
Britannia Street	E3-F3
Broadway	A1
Broomfield Road	A2
Butts Road	A3-A2-B2
Canterbury Road	D4-D3-E3
Chandos Street	F3
Charterhouse Road	E2
Chester Street	A4
Clifton Street	D4-E4
Colchester Street	E4
Collingwood Road	A2
Cornwall Road	E1
Coronation Road	E4-F4
Corporation Street	B3-C3
Coundon Road	A4-B4
Coundon Street	B4
Cox Street	D2-D3-D4
Caludon Road	F4
Croft Road	B2
David Road	E2
Days' Lane	E3
Eaton Road	B1
Earl Street	C2
East Street	E3
Fairfax Street	C3-D3
Far Gosford Street	E2-E3
Ford Street	D3
Friars Road	C1-C2
Gloucester Street	A3-B3
Gordon Street	A1-A2
Gosford Street	D2
Grafton Street	E2-E3
Greyfriars Road	B2
Grosvenor Road	B1-B2
Gulson Road	D2-E2-F2
Hales Street	C3
Harley Street	F2-F3
Harper Road	E1-E2
Hawkins Road	A2
Heath Road	F4
High Street	C2-C3
Highfield Road	F4
Hill Street	B3
Holyhead Road	A4-A3-B3
Hood Street	E3
Hugh Road	F2
Humber Avenue	E1-F1
Humber Road	F1-F2
Irving Road	E1-E2
Jesmond Road	E4
Jordan Well	D2
King Edward Road	E4
King Richard Street	F3
King William Street	D4-E4
Kingsway	F2-F3
Lamb Street	B4-C4
Lansdowne Street	E3-F3
Leicester Row	C4
Little Park Street	C2
London Road	D1-D2
Lower Ford Street	D3-E3
Lower Spon Street	B3
Manor Road	C1
Meadow Street	A2-B2
Melville Road	A3
Meriden Street	A3-A4-B4
Michaelmas Road	B1-C1
Middlesborough Road	B4
Mile Lane	C1-D1
Minster Road	A3
Monks Road	E2
Mowbray Street	F3
Much Park Street	D2
New Union Street	C2
Nicholls Street	D4
Northfield Road	E2-F2
Northumberland Road	A3-A4
Orwell Road	E1-F1
Oxford Street	E3
Park Road	C1
Park Side	C2-D2-D1
Paynes Lane	E4-E3
Primrose Hill Street	D4
Priory Row	C3
Priory Street	C3-D3
Puma Road	D1
Quarryfield Lane	D1
Queen Street	A2-B2
Queen Victoria Road	B2-B3
Quinton Road	C1
Radford Road	B4
Raglan Street	D3-E3
Ranby Road	F4
Read Street	E3
Regent Street	B1-B2
Ribble Road	F1-F2
Richmond Street	F4
Ringway Hill Cross	B3-B4
Ringway Queens	B2
Ringway Rudge	B2-B3
Ringway St Johns	C2-D2
Ringway St Nicholas	B4-C4
Ringway St Patrick	C1
Ringway Swanswell	C4
Ringway Whitefriars	D3-D2
Ryley Street	B3
St Columba's Close	B4-C4
St Georges Road	F1-F2
St Margaret Road	F2
St Nicholas Street	C4
Seagrave Road	D2-D1-E1
Severn Road	F1
Silver Street	C4
South Street	E3
Sovereign Road	A2-A3
Spencer Avenue	A1-B1
Spon End	A3
Stepney Road	F4
Stoney Road	C1
Stoney Stanton Road	C4-D4
Strathmore Avenue	E1-E2
Swan Lane	F3-F4
Swanswell Street	D4
Terry Road	E2-E1-F1
Thackhall Street	F4
Tower Street	C4
Upper Spon Street	A3-B3
Upper Well Street	B4-B3-C3
Upper York Street	A2
Vecqueray Street	E2
Vernon Street	E4
Victoria Street	D4
Villiers Street	F3
Vine Street	D4-D3
Walsgrave	A3
Warwick Road	B1-B2-C2
Waverley Road	A3-A4
Welland Road	E1-F1
West Street	E3
Westminster Road	B2-B1
Weston Street	D4
White Street	D4
Windsor Street	A2-A3
Winifrid Avenue	A1
Yardley Street	D4-E4

Nuneaton

Abbey Green	A4
Abbey Street	A4-A3-B3
Alexandra Street	A3
Amos Avenue	A1
Anker Street	C2
Attleborough Road	C1-C2
Avenue Road	B1-C1
Back Street	B4-B3
Bond Gate	B3
Bond Street	B4-C4
Bottril Street	A4
Bracebridge Street	A2-A3
Bridge Street	A1-B1, B3
Bull Ring	A3
Broad Street	A3
Central Avenue	A4-B4
Chapel Street	B3
Cheverel Street	A1-B1
Church Street	B3-C3-C2
Clements Street	A2
Clinic Road	B2
Cooper Street	C3
Corporation Street	A4-B4-B3
Coton Road	B1-B2
Cox's Close	A1
Deacon Street	B1
Dugdale Street	B3-B2
Duke Street	A3
Edward Street	A3-A2-B2-B1
Fife Street	A3
Fitton Street	A1-A2-B2
Frank Street	A2-B2
Glebe Road	C3
Greenmoor Road	A1-A2
Harefield Road	B3-B4
Harold Street	B2
Heath End Road	A1
Henry Street	A1-B1
High Street	A3
Home Park Road	B1
Inner Ring Road	B3
John Street	B1
King Edward Road	C2-C3
Kingsway	A3
Leicester Road	B3-C3-C4
Lister Street	A3
Manor Court Road	A4
Marlborough Road	A2-A3
Market Place	B3
Meadow Street	A4
Midland Road	A4
Milford Street	A1
Mill Street	B3
Mill Walk	B3
Mount Street	A3
Newdegate Street	B3
New Town Road	A4-B4
Norman Avenue	A2-A3
Oaston Road	C3-C4
Old Hinckley Road	C4
Orchard Street	C3
Park Street	C2
Prince's Avenue	A2
Queen's Road	A3-B3
Regent Street	C4
Ringway	A3-B3-B4
Riversley Road	B2
Rose Lane	A3
Roxanne	A3-A4
Sandon Road	A4
Seymour Road	C2
Simon Close	C1
Stewart Street	A1-B1-B2
Trent Road	C3-C4
Vicarage Street	B3-C3
Victoria Street	A3-B3
Villiers Street	A2
Weddington Road	C4
Weddington Terrace	C4
Wheat Street	C3
Willington Street	A4

Rugby

Acacia Grove	B4
Albert Street	B2-B3-C3
Alexandra Road	B4
Alfred Street	A1
Arnold Street	C3
Bank Street	B2
Barby Road	B1
Bath Street	C2-C3-C4
Bilton Road	A1
Bridget Street	A2
Castle Street	B2
Chapel Street	A2-B2
Charlotte Street	A1
Chestnut Field	B2-C2
Church Street	B1-B2
Clifton Road	C2
Corporation Street	A2-A3-A1
Craven Road	C3-C4
Dale Street	A3
Drury Lane	B2
Dunchurch Road	B1
Eastfield Place	B2
East Union Street	A1-B1
Edward Street	A2
Elsee Road	B2-C2
Essex Street	A3-A4
Evreux Way	A3-B3
Firs Drive	A1
Gas Street	B2
Graham Road	A3
Grosvenor Road	C2-C3
High Street	B2
Hill Street	A3
Hillmorton Road	C1
Holbrook Avenue	B3
Horton Crescent	B1-C1
James Street	B3-C3
Kew Road	B3
Kimberley Road	C4
King Street	A3
King Edward Road	B3-B4
Lancaster Road	A4-B4
Lawford Road	A1-A2
Lawrence Sheriff Street	B1-B2
Little Church Street	B1-B2
Lodge Road	B4
Manor Road	B3-B4-C4
Maple Grove	B4
Market Place	C3
Mertons Drive	A3
Moultrie Road	C1-C2
Murray Road	C2-C3-C4
Newbold Road	A4-A3
North Street	B2-B3
Oliver Street	A2-A3
Park Road	B3-B4
Pinders Lane	B2
Plowman Street	A2
Poplar Grove	A4
Prince's Street	A3
Queen Street	A2
Railway Terrace	C2-C3-C4
Regent Place	B3
Regent Street	B2-B3
Russelsheim Way	A1-B1
Rounds Gardens	A2-A3
St John Street	A3
Sheep Street	B2
Spring Street	C3
Sycamore Grove	B4
Tom Brown Street	C3
Vicarage Road	A1
Warwick Street	A1-B1
Wells Street	C3
Westfield Road	A1
Westway	A2
Whitehall Road	C1-C2
William Street	C2
Wood Street	A4-B4-C4
Worcester Street	A4
York Street	A3

147

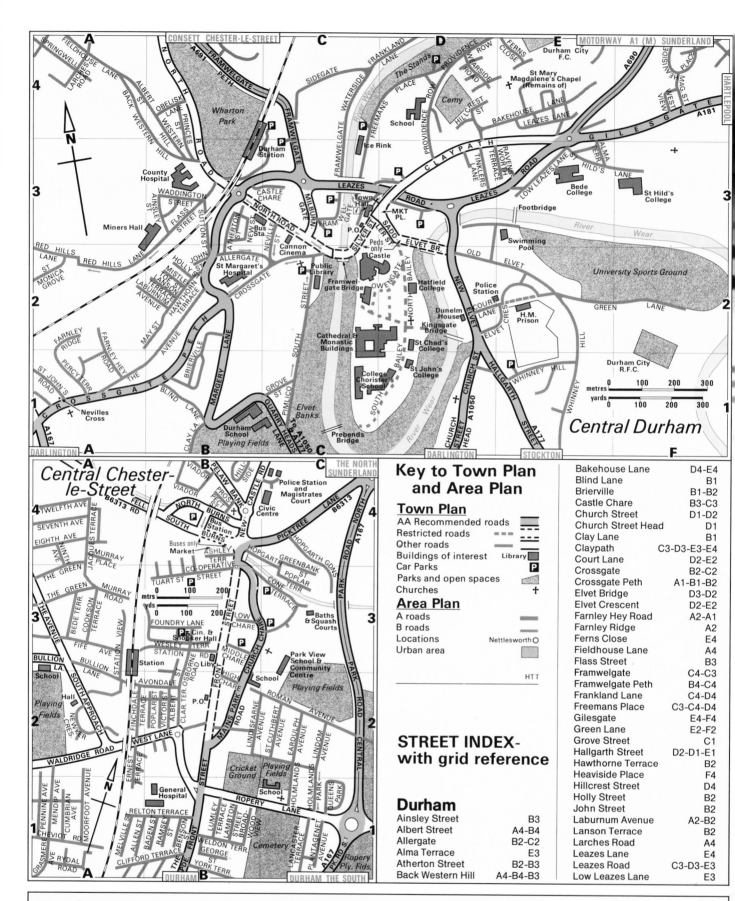

Key to Town Plan and Area Plan

Town Plan
AA Recommended roads	
Restricted roads	
Other roads	
Buildings of interest	Library
Car Parks	P
Parks and open spaces	
Churches	†

Area Plan
A roads	
B roads	
Locations	Nettlesworth ○
Urban area	

HTT

STREET INDEX- with grid reference

Durham
Ainsley Street	B3
Albert Street	A4-B4
Allergate	B2-C2
Alma Terrace	E3
Atherton Street	B2-B3
Back Western Hill	A4-B4-B3

Bakehouse Lane	D4-E4
Blind Lane	B1
Brierville	B1-B2
Castle Chare	B3-C3
Church Street	D1-D2
Church Street Head	D1
Clay Lane	B1
Claypath	C3-D3-E3-E4
Court Lane	D2-E2
Crossgate	B2-C2
Crossgate Peth	A1-B1-B2
Elvet Bridge	D3-D2
Elvet Crescent	D2-E2
Farnley Hey Road	A2-A1
Farnley Ridge	A2
Ferns Close	E4
Fieldhouse Lane	A4
Flass Street	B3
Framwelgate	C4-C3
Framwelgate Peth	B4-C4
Frankland Lane	C4-D4
Freemans Place	C3-C4-D4
Gilesgate	E4-F4
Green Lane	E2-F2
Grove Street	C1
Hallgarth Street	D2-D1-E1
Hawthorne Terrace	B2
Heaviside Place	F4
Hillcrest Street	D4
Holly Street	B2
John Street	B2
Laburnum Avenue	A2-B2
Lanson Terrace	B2
Larches Road	A4
Leazes Lane	E4
Leazes Road	C3-D3-E3
Low Leazes Lane	E3

Durham

The castle and the cathedral stand side by side high above the city like sentinels, dramatically symbolising the military and religious power Durham wielded in the past. Its origins date from about 995 when the remains of St Cuthbert arrived from Lindisfarne and his shrine was a popular centre of pilgrimage. Soon after that early fortifications were built, later replaced by a stone castle which became the residence of the Prince-Bishops of Durham – powerful feudal rulers appointed by the King. Today the city's university, the oldest in England after Oxford and Cambridge, occupies the castle and most of the buildings around peaceful, secluded Palace Green. The splendid Norman cathedral, sited on the other side of the Green, is considered to be one of the finest in Europe. Its combination of strength and size, tempered with grace and beauty, is awe-inspiring.

Under the shadow of these giants the old city streets, known as vennels, ramble down the bluff past the 17th-century Bishop Cosin's House and the old grammar school, to the thickly-wooded banks of the Wear. Here three historic bridges link the city's heart with the pleasant Georgian suburbs on the other side of the river.

Although Durham is not an industrial city, it has become the venue for the North-East miners' annual Gala Day in July.

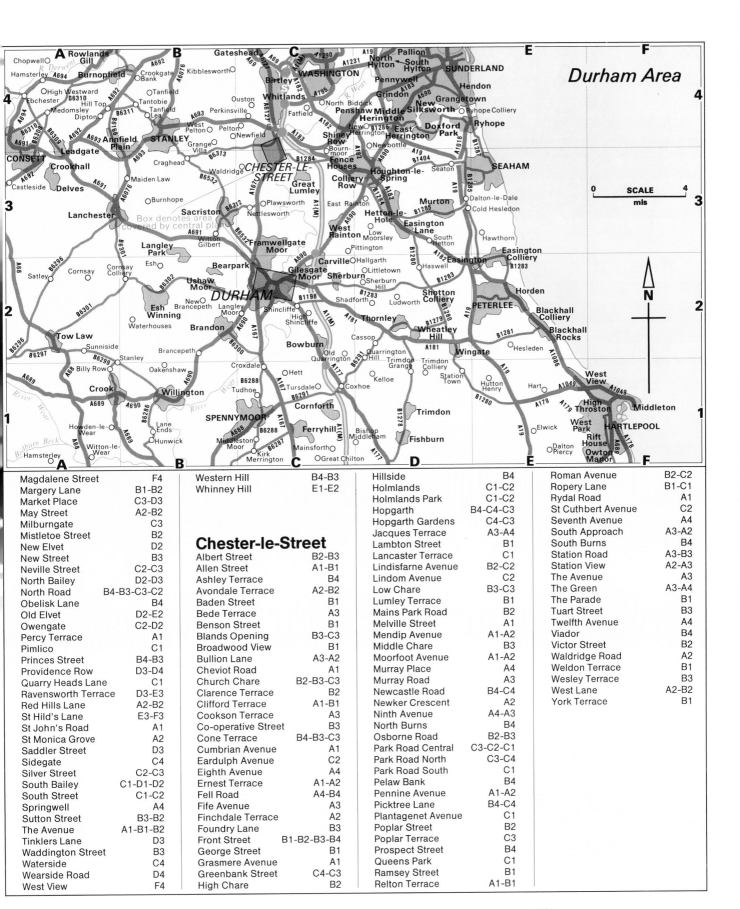

Durham Area

SCALE
0 — 4
mls

N

Magdalene Street	F4	Western Hill	B4-B3
Margery Lane	B1-B2	Whinney Hill	E1-E2
Market Place	C3-D3		
May Street	A2-B2		
Milburngate	C3		
Mistletoe Street	B2		
New Elvet	D2		
New Street	B3	**Chester-le-Street**	
Neville Street	C2-C3	Albert Street	B2-B3
North Bailey	D2-D3	Allen Street	A1-B1
North Road	B4-B3-C3-C2	Ashley Terrace	B4
Obelisk Lane	B4	Avondale Terrace	A2-B2
Old Elvet	D2-E2	Baden Street	B1
Owengate	C2-D2	Bede Terrace	A3
Percy Terrace	A1	Benson Street	B1
Pimlico	C1	Blands Opening	B3-C3
Princes Street	B4-B3	Broadwood View	B1
Providence Row	D3-D4	Bullion Lane	A3-A2
Quarry Heads Lane	C1	Cheviot Road	A1
Ravensworth Terrace	D3-E3	Church Chare	B2-B3-C3
Red Hills Lane	A2-B2	Clarence Terrace	B2
St Hild's Lane	E3-F3	Clifford Terrace	A1-B1
St John's Road	A1	Cookson Terrace	A3
St Monica Grove	A2	Co-operative Street	B3
Saddler Street	D3	Cone Terrace	B4-B3-C3
Sidegate	C4	Cumbrian Avenue	A1
Silver Street	C2-C3	Eardulph Avenue	C2
South Bailey	C1-D1-D2	Eighth Avenue	A4
South Street	C1-C2	Ernest Terrace	A1-A2
Springwell	A4	Fell Road	A4-B4
Sutton Street	B3-B2	Fife Avenue	A3
The Avenue	A1-B1-B2	Finchdale Terrace	A2
Tinklers Lane	D3	Foundry Lane	B3
Waddington Street	B3	Front Street	B1-B2-B3-B4
Waterside	C4	George Street	B1
Wearside Road	D4	Grasmere Avenue	A1
West View	F4	Greenbank Street	C4-C3
		High Chare	B2

Hillside	B4	Roman Avenue	B2-C2
Holmlands	C1-C2	Ropery Lane	B1-C1
Holmlands Park	C1-C2	Rydal Road	A1
Hopgarth	B4-C4-C3	St Cuthbert Avenue	C2
Hopgarth Gardens	C4-C3	Seventh Avenue	A4
Jacques Terrace	A3-A4	South Approach	A3-A2
Lambton Street	B1	South Burns	B4
Lancaster Terrace	C1	Station Road	A3-B3
Lindisfarne Avenue	B2-C2	Station View	A2-A3
Lindom Avenue	C2	The Avenue	A3
Low Chare	B3-C3	The Green	A3-A4
Lumley Terrace	B1	The Parade	B1
Mains Park Road	B2	Tuart Street	B3
Melville Street	A1	Twelfth Avenue	A4
Mendip Avenue	A1-A2	Viador	B4
Middle Chare	B3	Victor Street	B2
Moorfoot Avenue	A1-A2	Waldridge Road	A2
Murray Place	A4	Weldon Terrace	B1
Murray Road	A3	Wesley Terrace	B3
Newcastle Road	B4-C4	West Lane	A2-B2
Newker Crescent	A2	York Terrace	B1
Ninth Avenue	A4-A3		
North Burns	B4		
Osborne Road	B2-B3		
Park Road Central	C3-C2-C1		
Park Road North	C3-C4		
Park Road South	C1		
Pelaw Bank	B4		
Pennine Avenue	A1-A2		
Picktree Lane	B4-C4		
Plantagenet Avenue	C1		
Poplar Street	B2		
Poplar Terrace	C3		
Prospect Street	B4		
Queens Park	C1		
Ramsey Street	B1		
Relton Terrace	A1-B1		

DURHAM
High above the wooded banks of the River Wear, Durham's castle and cathedral crown the steep hill on which the city is built. They share the site with several of the university's attractive old buildings.

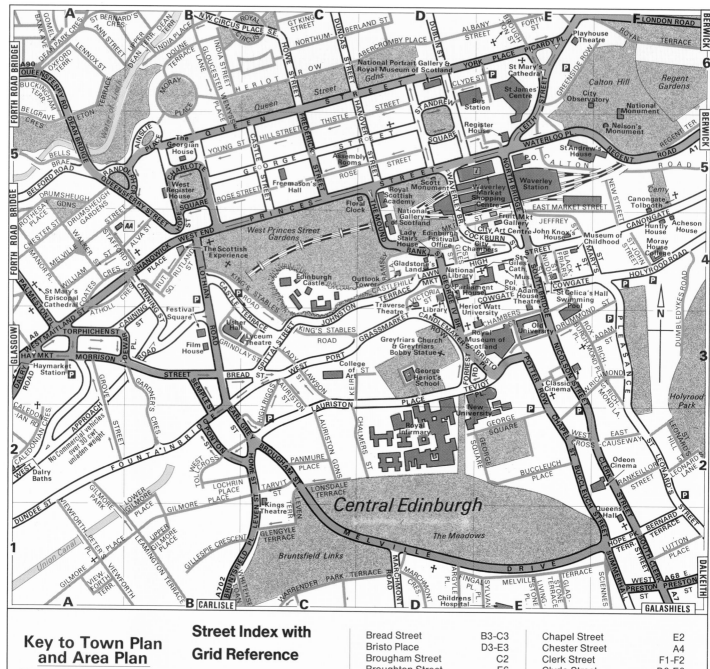

Key to Town Plan and Area Plan

Town Plan
A A Recommended roads
Other roads
Restricted roads
Buildings of intrest   Gallery
Car Parks   P
Parks and open spaces
A A Service Centre   AA
Churches   †

Area Plan
A roads
B roads
Locations   Newcraighall ○
Urban area

Street Index with Grid Reference

Edinburgh

Edinburgh

Scotland's ancient capital, dubbed the "Athens of the North", is one of the most splendid cities in the whole of Europe. Its buildings, its history and its cultural life give it an international importance which is celebrated every year in its world-famous festival. The whole city is overshadowed by the craggy castle which seems to grow out of the rock itself. There has been a fortress here since the 7th century and most of the great figures of Scottish history have been associated with it. The old town grew up around the base of Castle Rock within the boundaries of the defensive King's Wall and, unable to spread outwards, grew upwards in a maze of tenements. However, during the 18th century new prosperity from the shipping trade resulted in the building of the New Town and the regular, spacious layout of the Georgian development makes a striking contrast with the old

hotch-potch of streets. Princes Street is the main east-west thoroughfare with excellent shops on one side and Princes Street Gardens with their famous floral clock on the south side.

As befits such a splendid capital city there are numerous museums and art galleries packed with priceless treasures. Among these are the famous picture gallery in 16th-century Holyroodhouse, the present Royal Palace, and the fascinating and unusual Museum of Childhood.

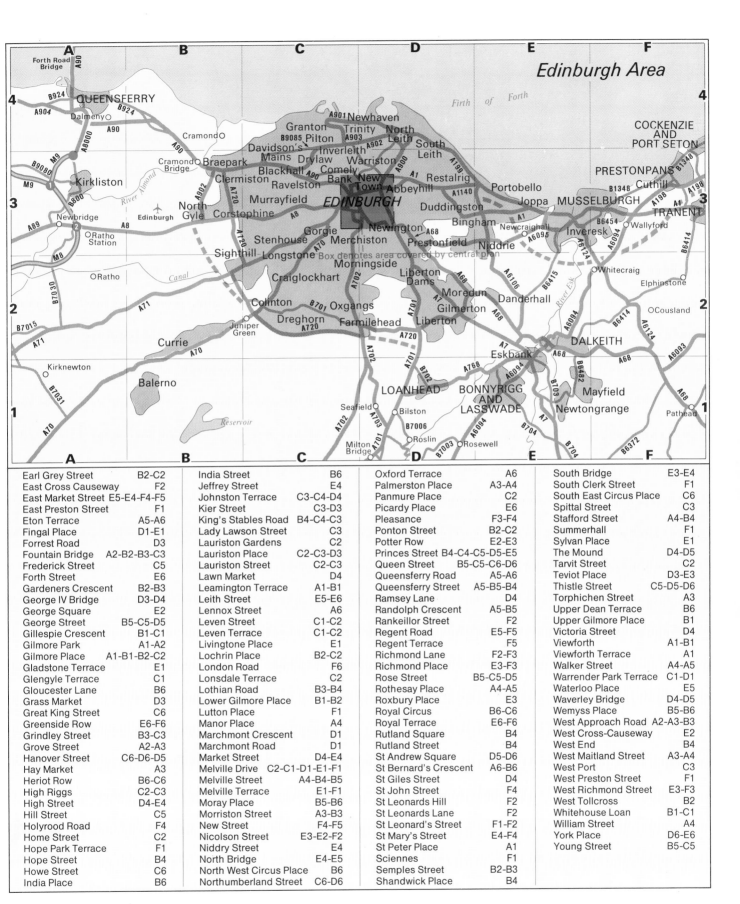

Edinburgh Area

Earl Grey Street	B2-C2	India Street	B6
East Cross Causeway	F2	Jeffrey Street	E4
East Market Street	E5-E4-F4-F5	Johnston Terrace	C3-C4-D4
East Preston Street	F1	Kier Street	C3-D3
Eton Terrace	A5-A6	King's Stables Road	B4-C4-C3
Fingal Place	D1-E1	Lady Lawson Street	C3
Forrest Road	D3	Lauriston Gardens	C2
Fountain Bridge	A2-B2-B3-C3	Lauriston Place	C2-C3-D3
Frederick Street	C5	Lauriston Street	C2-C3
Forth Street	E6	Lawn Market	D4
Gardeners Crescent	B2-B3	Leamington Terrace	A1-B1
George IV Bridge	D3-D4	Leith Street	E5-E6
George Square	E2	Lennox Street	A6
George Street	B5-C5-D5	Leven Street	C1-C2
Gillespie Crescent	B1-C1	Leven Terrace	C1-C2
Gilmore Park	A1-A2	Livingtone Place	E1
Gilmore Place	A1-B1-B2-C2	Lochrin Place	B2-C2
Gladstone Terrace	E1	London Road	F6
Glengyle Terrace	C1	Lonsdale Terrace	C2
Gloucester Lane	B6	Lothian Road	B3-B4
Grass Market	D3	Lower Gilmore Place	B1-B2
Great King Street	C6	Lutton Place	F1
Greenside Row	E6-F6	Manor Place	A4
Grindley Street	B3-C3	Marchmont Crescent	D1
Grove Street	A2-A3	Marchmont Road	D1
Hanover Street	C6-D6-D5	Market Street	D4-E4
Hay Market	A3	Melville Drive	C2-C1-D1-E1-F1
Heriot Row	B6-C6	Melville Street	A4-B4-B5
High Riggs	C2-C3	Melville Terrace	E1-F1
High Street	D4-E4	Moray Place	B5-B6
Hill Street	C5	Morriston Street	A3-B3
Holyrood Road	F4	New Street	F4-F5
Home Street	C2	Nicolson Street	E3-E2-F2
Hope Park Terrace	F1	Niddry Street	E4
Hope Street	B4	North Bridge	E4-E5
Howe Street	C6	North West Circus Place	B6
India Place	B6	Northumberland Street	C6-D6

Oxford Terrace	A6	South Bridge	E3-E4
Palmerston Place	A3-A4	South Clerk Street	F1
Panmure Place	C2	South East Circus Place	C6
Picardy Place	E6	Spittal Street	C3
Pleasance	F3-F4	Stafford Street	A4-B4
Ponton Street	B2-C2	Summerhall	F1
Potter Row	E2-E3	Sylvan Place	E1
Princes Street	B4-C4-C5-D5-E5	The Mound	D4-D5
Queen Street	B5-C5-C6-D6	Tarvit Street	C2
Queensferry Road	A5-A6	Teviot Place	D3-E3
Queensferry Street	A5-B5-B4	Thistle Street	C5-D5-D6
Ramsey Lane	D4	Torphichen Street	A3
Randolph Crescent	A5-B5	Upper Dean Terrace	B6
Rankeillor Street	F2	Upper Gilmore Place	B1
Regent Road	E5-F5	Victoria Street	D4
Regent Terrace	F5	Viewforth	A1-B1
Richmond Lane	F2-F3	Viewforth Terrace	A1
Richmond Place	E3-F3	Walker Street	A4-A5
Rose Street	B5-C5-D5	Warrender Park Terrace	C1-D1
Rothesay Place	A4-A5	Waterloo Place	E5
Roxbury Place	E3	Waverley Bridge	D4-D5
Royal Circus	B6-C6	Wemyss Place	B5-B6
Royal Terrace	E6-F6	West Approach Road	A2-A3-B3
Rutland Square	B4	West Cross-Causeway	E2
Rutland Street	B4	West End	B4
St Andrew Square	D5-D6	West Maitland Street	A3-A4
St Bernard's Crescent	A6-B6	West Port	C3
St Giles Street	D4	West Preston Street	F1
St John Street	F4	West Richmond Street	E3-F3
St Leonards Hill	F2	West Tollcross	B2
St Leonards Lane	F2	Whitehouse Loan	B1-C1
St Leonard's Street	F1-F2	William Street	A4
St Mary's Street	E4-F4	York Place	D6-E6
St Peter Place	A1	Young Street	B5-C5
Sciennes	F1		
Semples Street	B2-B3		
Shandwick Place	B4		

EDINBURGH
Holyrood Palace orginated as a guest house for the Abbey of Holyrood in the 16th century, but most of the present building was built for Charles II. Mary Queen of Scots was one of its most famous inhabitants.

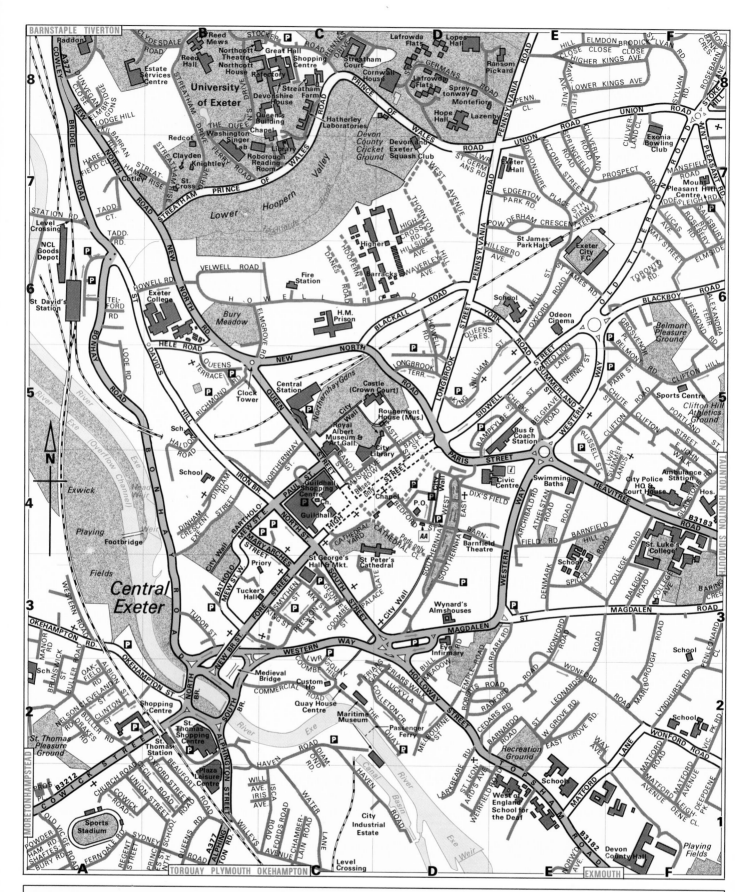

Exeter

The cathedral is Exeter's greatest treasure. Founded in 1050, but rebuilt by the Normans during the 12th century and again at the end of the 13th century, it has many beautiful and outstanding features – especially the exquisite rib-vaulting of the nave. Most remarkable, perhaps, is the fact that it still stood after virtually everything around it was flattened during the bombing raids in World War II.

There are still plenty of reminders of Old Exeter; Roman and medieval walls encircle parts of the city; 14th-century underground passages can be explored; the Guildhall is 15th-century; and Sir Francis Drake is said to have met his explorer companions at Mol's Coffee House. Of the city's ancient churches, the most interesting are St Mary Steps, St Mary Arches and St Martin's. The extensive Maritime Museum has over 100 boats from all over the world. Other museums include the

Rougemont House, the Devonshire Regiment and the Royal Albert Memorial Museum and Art Gallery.

Exmouth has a near-perfect position at the mouth of the Exe estuary. On one side it has expanses of sandy beach, on another a wide estuary alive with wildfowl and small boats, while inland is beautiful Devon countryside.

Honiton is famous for traditional hand-made lace and pottery which can still be bought in the busy town.

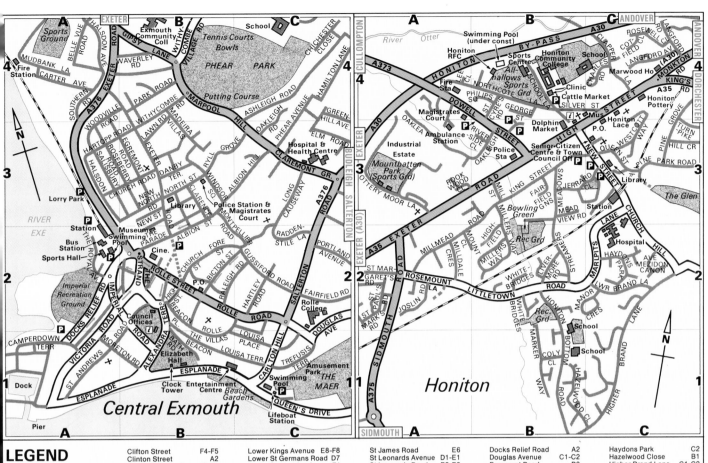

Central Exmouth

Honiton

LEGEND

AA Recommended roads
Other roads
Restricted roads
Buildings of interest
Churches †
Car parks P
Parks, open spaces
One way streets

Street Index with Grid Reference

Exeter

Albion Street	A2
Alexandra Terrace	F6
Alphington Road	B1
Alphington Street	B1-B2
Archibald Road	E4
Athelstan Road	E4
Bailey Street	D5
Bampfylde Street	D4-D5-E5
Baring Crescent	F3
Barnado Road	E2
Barnfield Hill	E4-F4
Barnfield Road	D4-E4
Bartholomew Street East	B4-C4
Bartholomew Street West	B3
Bedford Street	D4
Belgrave Road	E5
Belmont Road	F6-F5
Blackall Road	C6-D6
Blackboy Road	F6
Bonhay Road	A5-B4-B3
Brodick Close	F8
Brunswick Street	A2
Buller Road	A2-A3
Bull Meadow Road	D2
Castle Street	D5
Cathedral Close	D4
Cathedral Yard	C4
Cecil Road	A1-B1
Cedars Road	E2
Chamberlain Road	C1
Cheeke Street	E5
Church Road	A1-A2-B2
Chute Street	E5-F5
Clevedon Road	A2
Clifton Hill	F5
Clifton Road	E5-F5
Clifton Street	F4-F5
Clinton Street	A2
Clydesdale Road	A8-B8
College Avenue	F3
College Road	F3-F4
Colleton Crescent	C2-D2
Commercial Road	B2-C2
Coombe Street	C3
Cowick Road	A1
Cowick Street	A1-A2-B2
Cowley Bridge Road	A6-A7-A8
Culverland Close	F7-F8
Culverland Road	E7-E8
Danes Road	C6
Deepdene Park	F1
Denmark Road	F3-F4
Devonshire Place	F1
Diamond Road	C2-C1
Dineham Crescent	B4
Dinham Road	B4
Dix's Field	D4
Drakes Road	A2
East John Walk	F4-F5
Dunvegan Close	A8
East Grove Road	E2
Edgerton Park Road	E7
Elmbridge Gardens	A8
Elmdon Close	E8-F8
Elmgrove Road	B6-C6-B5
Elmside	F6
Exe Street	B4
Fairpark Road	E2-E3
Ferndale Road	A1
Fords Road	C1
Fore Street	B3-C3
Friars Gate	C2-D2
Friars Walk	D2
Gandy Street	C4
George Street	C3
Gladstone Road	F4
Grosvenor Place	F3
Haldon Road	B4-B5
Harefield Close	A7
Haven Road	C1-C2-D1
Heavitree Road	E4-F4
Hele Road	B6-B5
Highcross Road	D7
Higher Kings Avenue	E8-F8
High Street	C4-D4-D5
Hill Close	E8
Hillsborough Avenue	D6-E6
Hillside Avenue	D6
Holloway Street	D2
Hoopern Street	C6-C7
Howell Road	A6-D6
Iddesleigh Road	F7
Iris Avenue	B1-C1
Iron Bridge	B4-C4
Isca Road	C1
Jesmond Road	F6-F5-F6
Kilbarran Rise	A7-A8
King Street	C3
King William Street	D5-E5-E6
Larkbeare Road	D1-D2
Leighdene Close	F1
Lodge Hill	A8
Longbrook Street	D5-D6
Longbrook Terrace	E5
Looe Road	A5-A6
Lower Coombe Street	C2

Lower Kings Avenue	E8-F8
Lower St Germans Road	D7
Lower Summerlands	F4
Lucas Avenue	F7
Lucky Lane	D2
Lyndhurst Road	F2
Magdalen Road	E3-F3
Magdalen Street	D3-E3
Manor Road	A3
Mansfield Road	F7
Market Street	C3
Marlborough Road	F2-F3
Mary Arches Street	B4-C3
Maryfield Avenue	E8
Matford Avenue	F2-F1-F2
Matford Lane	E1-F1-F2
Matford Road	F1-F2
May Street	F7-F6
Melbourne Street	D2
Mount Pleasant Road	F8-F7
Musgrave Row	C4-C5
Nelson Road	A3
New Bridge Street	B2-B3
New North Road	A7-B6-C6-D5
North Bridge	B2
Northernhay Street	C4-C5
North Street	C4
Norwood Avenue	E1
Oakfield Road	A2
Oakhampton Street	A2-B2
Okehampton Road	A3-A2-B2
Old Tiverton Road	E6-F7
Old Vicarage Road	A1
Oxford Road	E6
Oxford Street	B1-B2
Palace Gate	C3-D3
Paris Street	D5-D4-E4
Parr Street	F5
Paul Street	C4
Penleonard Close	F3
Pennsylvania Close	E8
Pennsylvania Road	D6-E8
Perry Road	B7
Portland Street	F5
Powderham Crescent	D7-E7
Powderham Road	A1
Preston Street	C3
Prince of Wales Road	B7-C8-D7
Princes Street North	B3
Prospect Park	E7-F7
Prospect Place	A1
Quay Hill	C2
Queens Crescent	D6
Queens Road	B1
Queen Street	B5-C5-C4
Queens Terrace	C5
Radford Road	D2-E2
Raleigh Road	F3
Red Lion Lane	E5
Regent Street	E5
Rennes Drive	C8
Richmond Road	B5
Roberts Road	D2-E2
Rosebank Crescent	F8
Rosebarn Lane	F8
Rosebery Road	F6-F7
Russell Street	E5
St David's Hill	A6-B5
St Germans Road	D8-E8

St James Road	E6
St Leonards Avenue	D1-E1
St Leonards Road	E2-E3
Salisbury Road	F7-F6
School Road	B1
Shaftesbury Road	A1
Sidwell Street	D5-E5-E6
Smythen Street	C3
South Bridge	B2
Southernhay East	D3-D4
Southernhay West	D3-D4
South Street	D3
South View Terrace	E7
Spicer Road	E3-E4-F4
Springfield Road	E8-E7
Station Road	A7
Stocker Road	B8-C8
Stoke Hill	F8
Streatham Drive	B7-B8
Streatham Rise	A7-B7
Summerland Street	E5
Sydney Road	A1-B1
Sylvan Road	F8
Taddiforde Court	A7
Taddiforde Road	A6-A7
Telford Road	A6
Temple Road	D2-D3
The Quay	C2-D2
The Queen's Drive	B8
Thornton Hill	D7-D6
Topsham Road	E2-E1-F1
Toronto Road	F6
Tudor Street	B3
Union Road	E7-E8-F8
Union Street	A1-B1
Velwell Road	B6-C6
Verney Street	E5
Victoria Park Road	F2
Victoria Street	E7
Water Lane	C1
Waverley Avenue	C6
Way Avenue	C2
Weirfield Road	D1-E1
Well Street	E6
West Avenue	D7
Western Road	A3
Western Way	E3-E5, C3
West Grove Road	E2
Willeys Avenue	B1-C1
Williams Avenue	B1-C1
Wonford Road	E3-E2-E2
York Road	D6-E6-E5

Exmouth

Albion Hill	B3-C3
Albion Street	B2-B3
Alexandra Terrace	B1-B2
Ashleigh Road	C4
Bath Road	B1-B2
Beacon Place	B2
Belle View Road	A4
Bicton Street	B2-C2
Camperdown Terrace	A1
Carter Avenue	A4
Carlton Hill	C1-C2
Chichester Close	C4
Church Road	A3-B3
Claremont Grove	C3
Clarence Road	B3
Danby Terrace	B3

Docks Relief Road	A2
Douglas Avenue	C1-C2
Egremont Road	B3
Elm Road	C3
Esplanade	A1-B1-C1
Exeter Road	B3-A4
Fairfield Road	C2
Fore Street	B2-C2
Gipsy Lane	A4-B4
Green Hill Avenue	C3-C4
Gussiford Road	C2
Halsdon Avenue	A4
Hamilton Lane	C4
Hartley Road	C2
Hartopp Road	A3-B3
Halsdon Road	A3
High Street	B2
Imperial Road	A2-B1
Lawn Road	B3
Long Causeway	C3
Louisa Place	B1-C1
Louisa Terrace	B1-C1
Lyndhurst Road	A4-B4
Madeira Villas	B3-B4
Marpool Hill	B4-C3
Montpellier Road	B3-B2-C2
Moreton Road	A1-B1
Mudbank Lane	A4
New North Road	B3
New Street	B3
North Street	B3
Oakleigh Road	C3-C4
Park Road	B4
Phear Avenue	C3-C4
Portland Avenue	C2
Queens Drive	C1
Raddenstile Lane	C2
Raleigh Road	B2-C2
Rolle Road	B2-C2
Rolle Street	B2
Rolle Villas	B1-B2
Roseberry Road	B3-C3
Ryll Grove	B4
St Andrews Road	A1-B1-B2
Salisbury Road	A3-B3
Salterton Road	C2-C3
Southern Road	A4
The Beacon	B1-B2
The Parade	B2
The Strand	B2
The Royal Avenue	A2
Trefusis Terrace	C1
Victoria Road	A1-A2-B2
Waverley Road	B4
Windsor Square	B3
Withycombe Road	B3-B4
Withycombe Village Road	B4
Woodville Road	A3-A4-B4

Honiton

Avenue Mezidon-Canon	C2
Charles Road	C4
Church Hill	C2-C3
Clapper Lane	C4
Coly Close	B1
Cotfield Close	C4
Dowell Street	A4-B3
Exeter Road	A2-B3
Fairfield Gardens	B3
George Street	B4

Haydons Park	C2
Hazelwood Close	B1
Higher Brand Lane	C1-C2
Highfield	C3
High Street	B3-C4
Hill Crescent	C3
Honiton Bottom Road	B1-B2
Honiton By-Pass	A4-B4
Jerrard Close	B3-C3
Jerrard Crescent	C3
Joslin Road	A2
King's Road	C4
Kings Road	B3
Langford Avenue	C4
Langford Road	C4
Lee Close	A4
Littledown Road	A2
Livermore Road	B2
Lower Brand Lane	C2
Manor Crescent	B2-C2
Marker Way	B1
Marlpits Lane	C2
Mead View Road	B3
Milldale Crescent	A2
Millers Way	B2-B3
Millmead Road	A2-B3
Mill Street	B3
Monkton Road	C4
Mount Close	A2
New Street	C3
Northcote Lane	B4
Oaklea	A3
Oakleigh	B3
Ottery Moor Lane	A3
Philips Square	B4
Pine Grove	C3-C3
Pine Park Road	C3
Queen Street	C3
Riverside Close	B3
Rookwood Close	A3
Rosemount Lane	A2
Rosewell Close	C4
St Cyre's Road	B4
St Margaret's Road	A2
St Mark's Road	A2
St Paul's Road	A2
School Lane	B4
Sidmouth Road	A1-A2
Silver Street	B4-C4
Streamers Meadows	B2-B3
Turnpike	C3
Westcott Way	C3
Whitebridges	B2

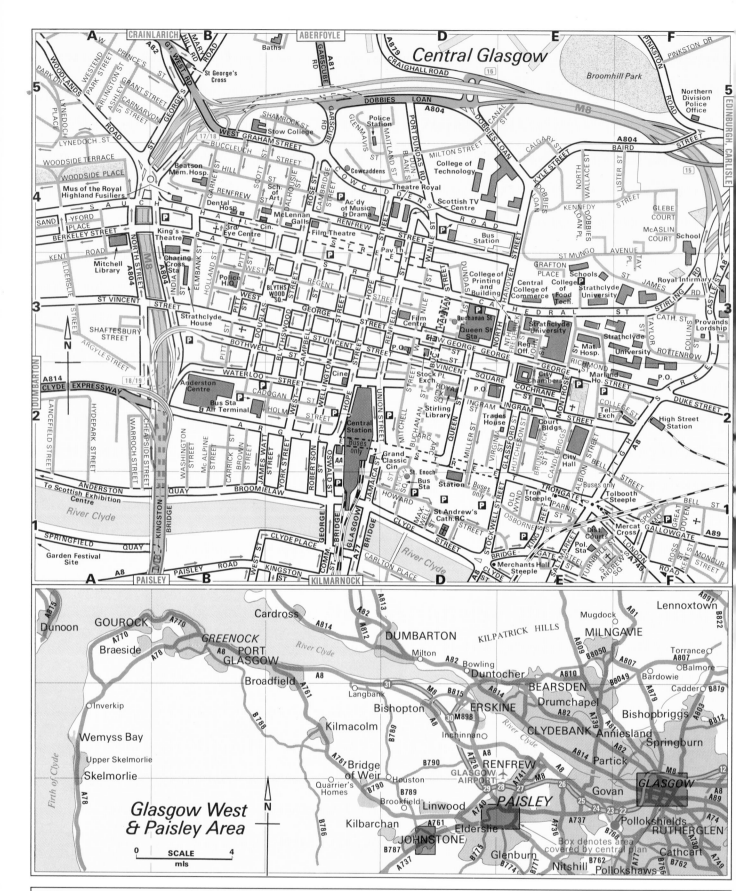

Glasgow

Although much of Glasgow is distinctly Victorian in character, its roots go back very many centuries. Best link with the past is the cathedral; founded in the 6th century, it has features from many succeeding centuries, including an exceptional 13th-century crypt. Nearby is Provand's Lordship, the city's oldest house. It dates from 1471 and is now a museum. Two much larger museums are to be found a little out of the centre – the Art Gallery and Museum contains one of the finest collections of paintings in Britain, while the Hunterian Museum, attached to the University, covers geology, archaeology, ethnography and more general subjects. On Glasgow Green is People's Palace – a museum of city life. Most imposing of the Victorian buildings are the City Chambers and City Hall which was built in 1841 as a concert hall but now houses the Scottish National Orchestra.

Paisley is famous for the lovely fabric pattern to which it gives its name. It was taken from fabrics brought from the Near East in the early 19th century, and its manufacture, along with the production of thread, is still important. Coats Observatory is one of the best-equipped in the country.

Johnstone grew rapidly as a planned industrial town in the 19th century, but suffered from the effects of the Industrial Revolution. Today, engineering is the main industry.

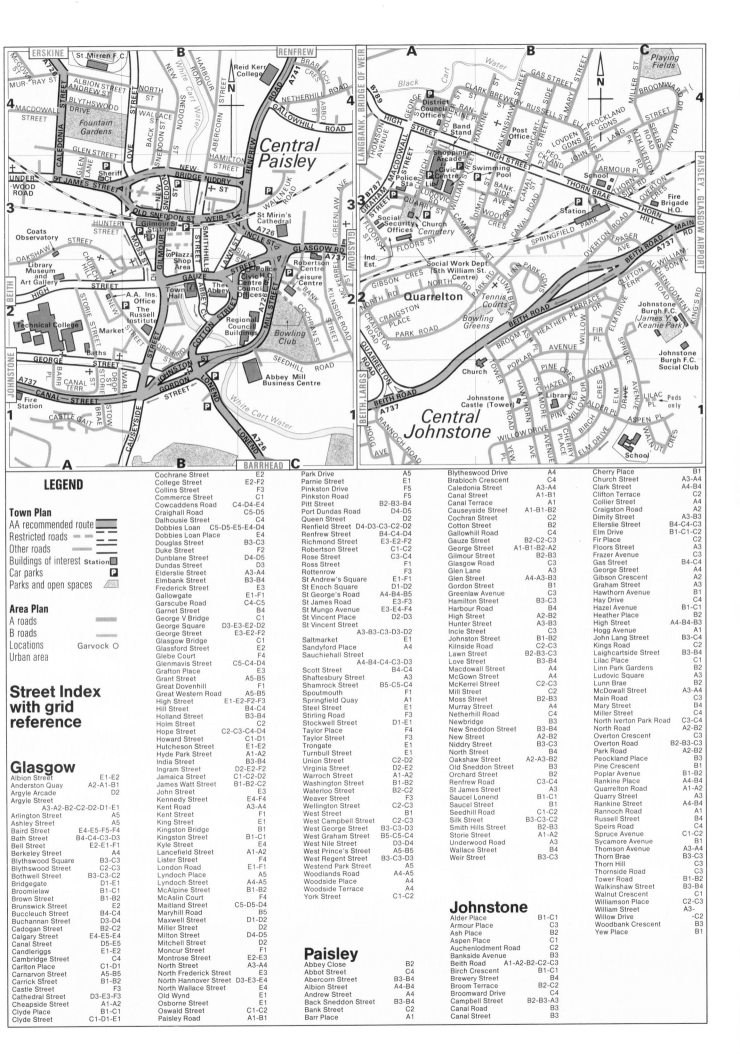

ERSKINE · RENFREW · Central Paisley · BARRHEAD · LANGBANK, BRIDGE OF WEIR · MOSS-WOOD · PAISLEY, GLASGOW AIRPORT · Central Johnstone · BEITH-LARGS

LEGEND

Town Plan

AA recommended route
Restricted roads
Other roads
Buildings of interest   Station
Car parks   P
Parks and open spaces

Area Plan

A roads
B roads
Locations   Garvock O
Urban area

Street Index with grid reference

Glasgow

Albion Street	E1-E2
Anderston Quay	A2-A1-B1
Argyle Arcade	D2
Argyle Street	A3-A2-B2-C2-D2-D1-E1
Arlington Street	A5
Ashley Street	A5
Baird Street	E4-E5-F5-F4
Bath Street	B4-C4-C3-D3
Bell Street	E2-E1-F1
Berkeley Street	A4
Blythswood Square	B3-C3
Blythswood Street	C2-C3
Bothwell Street	B3-C3-C2
Bridgegate	D1-E1
Broomielaw	B1-C1
Brown Street	B1-B2
Brunswick Street	E2
Buccleuch Street	B4-C4
Buchanan Street	D3-D4
Cadogan Street	B2-C2
Calgary Street	E4-E5-E4
Canal Street	D5-E5
Candleriggs	E1-E2
Cambridge Street	C4
Carlton Place	C1-D1
Carnarvon Street	A5-B5
Carrick Street	B1-B2
Castle Street	F3
Cathedral Street	D3-E3-F3
Cheapside Street	A1-A2
Clyde Place	B1-C1
Clyde Street	C1-D1-E1
Cochrane Street	E2
College Street	E2-F2
Collins Street	F3
Commerce Street	C1
Cowcaddens Road	C4-D4-E4
Craighall Road	C5-D5
Dalhousie Street	C4
Dobbies Loan	C5-D5-E5-E4-D4
Dobbies Loan Place	E4
Douglas Street	B3-C3
Duke Street	F2
Dunblane Street	D4-D5
Dundas Street	D3
Elderslie Street	A3-A4
Elmbank Street	B3-B4
Frederick Street	E3
Gallowgate	E1-F1
Garscube Road	C4-C5
Garnet Street	B4
George V Bridge	C1
George Square	D3-E3-E2-D2
George Street	E3-E2-F2
Glasgow Bridge	C1
Glassford Street	E2
Glebe Court	F4
Glenmavis Street	C5-C4-D4
Grafton Place	E3
Grant Street	A5-B5
Great Dovenhill	F1
Great Western Road	A5-B5
High Street	E1-E2-F2-F3
Hill Street	B4-C4
Holland Street	B3-B4
Holm Street	C2
Hope Street	C2-C3-C4-D4
Howard Street	C1-D1
Hutcheson Street	E1-E2
Hyde Park Street	A1-A2
India Street	B3-B4
Ingram Street	D2-E2-F2
Jamaica Street	C1-C2-D2
James Watt Street	B1-B2-C2
John Street	E3
Kennedy Street	E4-F4
Kent Road	A3-A4
Kent Street	F1
King Street	E1
Kingston Bridge	B1
Kingston Street	B1-C1
Kyle Street	E4
Lancefield Street	A1-A2
Lister Street	F4
London Road	E1-F1
Lyndoch Place	A5
Lyndoch Street	A4-A5
McAlpine Street	B1-B2
McAslin Court	F4
Maitland Street	C5-D5-D4
Maryhill Road	B5
Maxwell Street	D1-D2
Miller Street	D2
Milton Street	D4-D5
Mitchell Street	D2
Moncur Street	F1
Montrose Street	E2-E3
North Street	A3-A4
North Frederick Street	E3
North Hannover Street	D3-E3-E4
North Wallace Street	E4
Old Wynd	E1
Osborne Street	E1
Oswald Street	C1-C2
Paisley Road	A1-B1

Park Drive	A5
Parnie Street	E1
Pinkston Drive	F5
Pinkston Road	F5
Pitt Street	B2-B3-B4
Port Dundas Road	D4-D5
Queen Street	D2
Renfield Street	D4-D3-C3-C2-D2
Richmond Street	E3-E2-F2
Robertson Street	C1-C2
Rose Street	C3-C4
Ross Street	F1
Rottenrow	F3
St Andrew's Square	E1-F1
St Enoch Square	D1-D2
St George's Road	A4-B4-B5
St James Road	E3-F3
St Mungo Avenue	E3-E4-F4
St Vincent Place	D2-D3
St Vincent Street	A3-B3-C3-D3-D2
Saltmarket	E1
Sandyford Place	A4
Sauchiehall Street	A4-B4-C4-C3-D3
Scott Street	B4-C4
Shaftesbury Street	A3
Shamrock Street	B5-C5-C4
Spoutmouth	F1
Springfield Quay	A1
Steel Street	E1
Stirling Road	F3
Stockwell Street	D1-E1
Taylor Place	F4
Taylor Street	F3
Trongate	E1
Turnbull Street	E1
Union Street	C2-D2
Virginia Street	D2-E2
Warroch Street	A1-A2
Washington Street	B1-B2
Waterloo Street	B2-C2
Weaver Street	F3
Wellington Street	C2-C3
West Street	B1
West Campbell Street	C2-C3
West George Street	B3-C3-D3
West Graham Street	B5-C5-C4
West Nile Street	D3-D4
West Prince's Street	A5-B5
West Regent Street	B3-C3-D3
Westend Park Street	A4-A5
Woodlands Road	A4-A5
Woodside Place	A4
Woodside Terrace	A4
York Street	C1-C2

Paisley

Abbey Close	B2
Abbot Street	C4
Abercorn Street	B3-B4
Albion Street	A4-B4
Andrew Street	A4
Back Sneddon Street	B3-B4
Bank Street	C2
Barr Place	A1
Blytheswood Drive	A4
Brabloch Crescent	C4
Caledonia Street	A3-A4
Canal Street	A1-B1
Canal Terrace	A1
Causeyside Street	A1-B1-B2
Cochran Street	C2
Cotton Street	B2
Gauze Street	B2-C2-C3
George Street	A1-B1-B2-A2
Gilmour Street	B2-B3
Glasgow Road	C3
Glen Lane	A3
Glen Street	A4-A3-B3
Gordon Street	B1
Greenlaw Avenue	C3
Hamilton Street	B3-C3
Harbour Road	B4
High Street	A2-B2
Hunter Street	A3-B3
Incle Street	C3
Johnston Street	B1-B2
Kilnside Road	C2-C3
Lawn Street	B2-B3
Love Street	B3-B4
Macdowall Street	A4
McGown Street	A4
McKerrel Street	C2-C3
Mill Street	C2
Moss Street	B2-B3
Murray Street	A4
Netherhill Road	C4
Newbridge	B3
New Sneddon Street	B3-B4
New Street	A2-B2
Niddry Street	B3-C3
North Street	B4
Oakshaw Street	A2-A3-B2
Old Sneddon Street	B3
Orchard Street	B2
Renfrew Road	C3-C4
St James Street	A3
Saucel Lonend	B1-C1
Saucel Street	B1
Seedhill Road	C1-C2
Silk Street	B3-C3-C2
Smith Hills Street	B2-B3
Storie Street	A1-A2
Underwood Road	A3
Wallace Street	B4
Weir Street	B3-C3

Johnstone

Alder Place	B1-C1
Armour Place	C3
Ash Place	B2
Aspen Place	C1
Auchenlodment Road	C2
Bankside Avenue	B3
Beith Road	A1-A2-B2-C2-C3
Birch Crescent	B1-C1
Brewery Street	B4
Broom Terrace	B2-C2
Broomward Drive	C4
Campbell Street	B2-B3-A3
Canal Road	B3
Canal Street	B3
Cherry Place	B1
Church Street	A3-A4
Clark Street	A4-B4
Clifton Terrace	C2
Collier Street	A4
Craigston Road	A2
Dimity Street	A3-B3
Ellerslie Street	B4-C4-C3
Elm Drive	B1-C1-C2
Fir Place	C2
Floors Street	A3
Frazer Avenue	C3
Gas Street	B4-C4
George Street	A4
Gibson Crescent	A2
Graham Street	A3
Hawthorn Avenue	B1
Hay Drive	B2
Hazel Avenue	B1-C1
Heather Place	B2
High Street	A4-B4-B2
Hogg Avenue	A1
John Lang Street	B3-C4
Kings Road	C2
Laighcartside Street	B3-B4
Lilac Place	C1
Linn Park Gardens	B2
Ludovic Square	A3
Lunn Brae	B2
McDowall Street	A3-A4
Main Road	C3
Mary Street	B4
Miller Street	C4
North Iverton Park Road	C3-C4
North Road	A2-B2
Overton Crescent	C3
Overton Road	B2-B3-C3
Park Road	A2-B2
Peockland Place	B3
Pine Crescent	B1
Poplar Avenue	B1-B2
Rankine Place	A4-B4
Quarrelton Road	A1-A2
Quarry Street	A3
Rankine Street	A4-B4
Rannoch Road	A1
Russell Street	B4
Speirs Road	C4
Spruce Avenue	C1-C2
Sycamore Avenue	B1
Thomson Avenue	A3-A4
Thorn Brae	B3-C3
Thorn Hill	C3
Thornside Road	C3
Tower Road	B1-B2
Walkinshaw Street	B3-B4
Walnut Crescent	C1
Williamson Place	C2-C3
William Street	A3-
Willow Drive	-C2
Woodbank Crescent	B3
Yew Place	B1

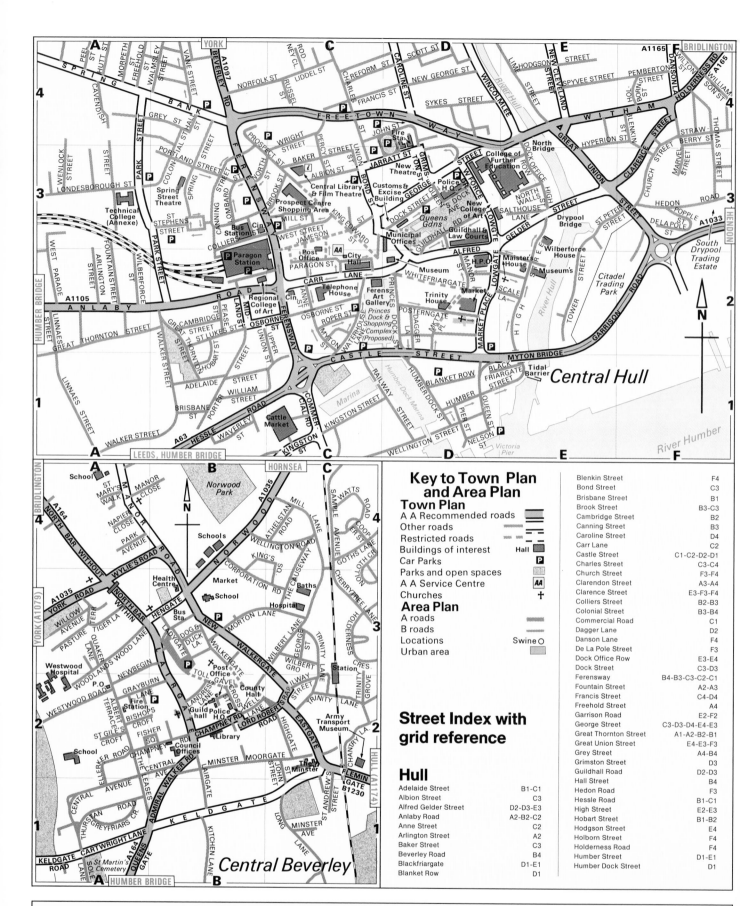

Hull

Officially Kingston-upon-Hull, this ancient port was specially laid out with new docks in 1293, on the decree of Edward I, and echoes of the town's past can be seen in the Town Docks Museum. The docks and the fishing industry are synonymous with Hull — it has Britain's busiest deep-sea fishing port — although flour-milling, vegetable oil extraction and petrochemical production are also important. The centre of Hull consists of broad streets and spacious squares and parks, such as Queen's Gardens, laid out on the site of what used to be Queen's Dock. The older part of the town which lies south-east of here is full between the docks and the River Hull is full of character, with a number of Georgian buildings and places of interest.

Beverley is one of England's most distinguished towns. Between its two principal buildings — the famous Minster and St Mary's Church — are medieval streets and pleasing market squares graced by redbrick Georgian houses built by the landed gentry of the East Riding during the town's heyday as a fashionable resort. The Minster's twin towers soar above the rooftops of the town as a constant reminder that here is one of the most beautiful pieces of Gothic architecture in Europe. The wealth of beauty and detail throughout is immense, but carving in both stone and wood is one of its most outstanding features.

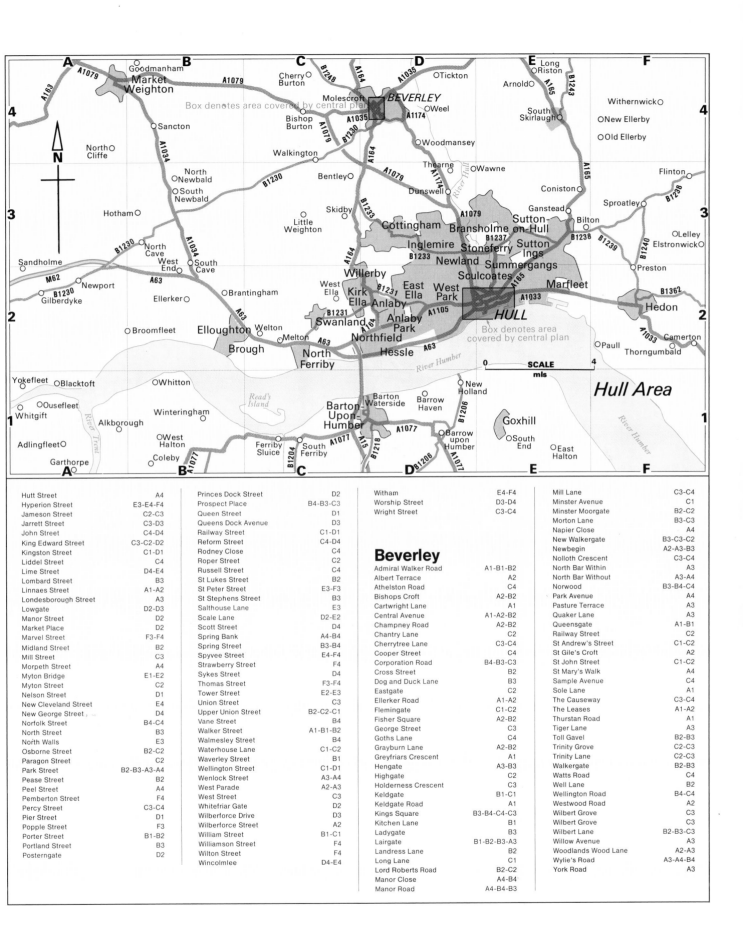

Hull Area

Box denotes area covered by central plan

SCALE 0 — 4 mls

HULL
Schemes to cross the Humber estuary were first discussed over 100 years ago, but it was not until 1981 that the mammoth project was sucessfully completed. At 4626ft, the Humber Bridge has the longest main span in the world.

157

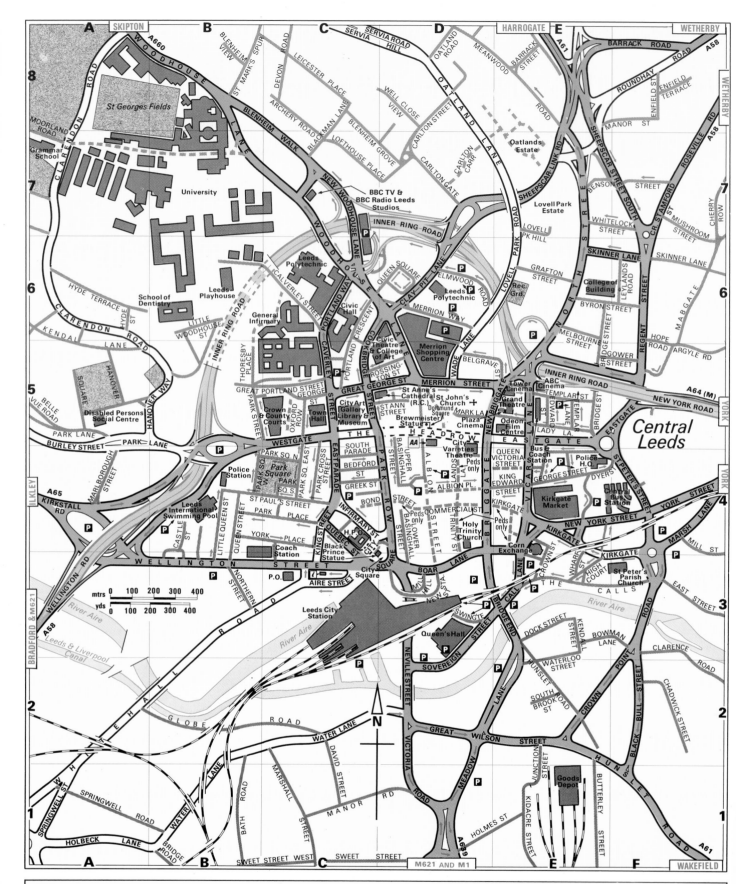

Leeds

In the centre of Leeds is its town hall – a monumental piece of architecture with a 225ft clock-tower. It was opened by Queen Victoria in 1858, and has been a kind of mascot for the city ever since. It exudes civic pride; such buildings could only have been created in the heyday of Victorian prosperity and confidence. Leeds' staple industry has always been the wool trade, but it only became a boom town towards the end of the 18th century, when textile mills were introduced. Today, the wool trade and ready-made clothing (Mr Hepworth and Mr Burton began their work here) are still important, though industries like paper, leather, furniture and electrical equipment are prominent.

Across Calverley Street from the town hall is the City Art Gallery, Library and Museum. Its collections include sculpture by Henry Moore, who was a student at Leeds School of Art. Nearby is the Headrow, Leeds' foremost shopping thoroughfare. On it is the City Varieties Theatre, venue for many years of the famous television programme 'The Good Old Days'. Off the Headrow are several shopping arcades, of which Leeds has many handsome examples. Leeds has a good number of interesting churches; perhaps the finest is St John's, unusual in that it dates from 1634, a time when few churches were built.

158

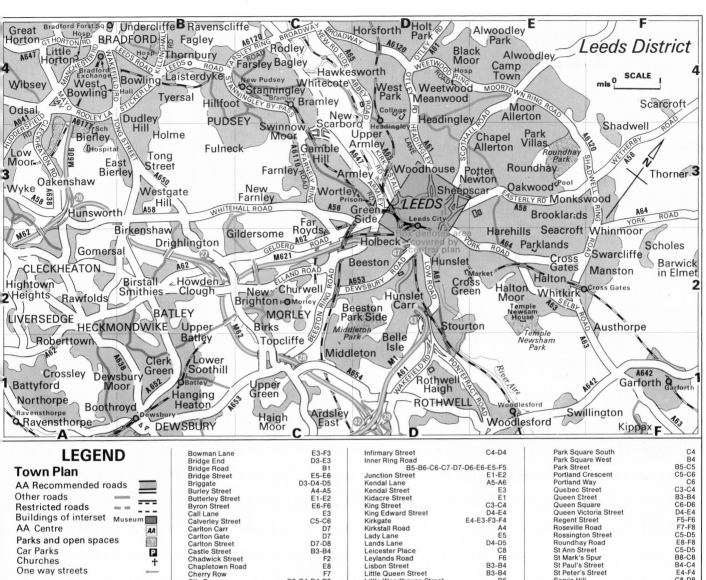

Leeds District

SCALE

LEGEND

Town Plan
AA Recommended roads	
Other roads	
Restricted roads	
Buildings of interset	Museum
AA Centre	AA
Parks and open spaces	
Car Parks	P
Churches	†
One way streets	←

District Plan
A roads	
B roads	
Stations	Kirkgate ○
Urban area	
Buildings of interest	Hospital

Street Index with Grid Reference

Leeds

Aire Street	C3
Albion Place	D4
Albion Street	D3-D4-D5
Archery Road	C7-C8
Argyle Road	F5
Barrack Road	E8-F8
Barrack Street	E8
Bath Road	B1-B2
Bedford Street	C4
Belgrave Street	D5-E5
Belle Vue Road	A5
Benson Street	E7-F7
Black Bull Street	F1-F2-F3
Blackman Lane	C7-C8
Blenheim Grove	C8-C7-D7
Blenheim View	B8
Blenheim Walk	B8-C8-C7
Boar Lane	D3-D4
Bond Street	C4-D4

Bowman Lane	E3-F3
Bridge End	D3-E3
Bridge Road	B1
Bridge Street	E5-E6
Briggate	D3-D4-D5
Burley Street	A4-A5
Butterley Street	E1-E2
Byron Street	E6-F6
Call Lane	E3
Calverley Street	C5-C6
Carlton Carr	D7
Carlton Gate	D7
Carlton Street	D7-D8
Castle Street	B3-B4
Chadwick Street	F2
Chapeltown Road	E8
Cherry Row	F7
City Square	C3-C4-D4-D3
Clarence Road	F2-F3
Clarendon Road	A8-A7-A6-A5-B5
Clay Pit Lane	D6
Commercial Street	D4
Cookridge Street	C5-C6-D6
Cross Stamford Street	F6-F7
Crown Street	E3-E4
Crown Point Road	E2-F2-F3
David Street	C1-C2
Devon Road	C8
Dock Street	E3
Dyer Street	E4-F4
East Parade	C4-C5
East Street	F3
Eastgate	E5-F5
Edward Street	E5
Elmwood Road	D6
Enfield Street	F8
Enfield Terrace	F8
George Street	C5
George Street	E4
Globe Road	A2-B2-C2
Gower Street	E5-F5
Grafton Street	E6
Great George Street	C5-D5
Great Portland Street	B5-C5
Great Wilson Street	D2-E2
Greek Street	C4-D4
Hanover Square	A5
Hanover Way	A5-B5
High Court	E4
Holbeck Lare	A1-B1
Holmes Street	D1-E1
Hope Road	F5-F6
Hunslett Road	E3-E2-E1-F1-F2
Hyde Street	A6
Hyde Terrace	A6

Infirmary Street	C4-D4
Inner Ring Road	B5-B6-C6-C7-D7-D6-E6-E5-F5
Junction Street	E1-E2
Kendal Lane	A5-A6
Kendal Street	E3
Kidacre Street	E1
King Street	C3-C4
King Edward Street	D4-E4
Kirkgate	E4-E3-F3-F4
Kirkstall Road	A4
Lady Lane	E5
Lands Lane	D4-D5
Leicester Place	C8
Leylands Road	F6
Lisbon Street	B3-B4
Little Queen Street	B3-B4
Little Woodhouse Street	B6
Lofthouse Place	C7-D7
Lovell Park Hill	E7
Lovell Park Road	D6-E6-E7
Lower Basinghall Street	D3-D4
Mabgate	F6
Manor Road	C1-D1
Manor Street	E8-F8
Mark Lane	D5
Marlborough Street	A4
Marsh Lane	F4
Marshall Street	C1-C2
Meadow Lane	D1-D2-E2-E1
Meanwood Road	D8-E8
Melbourne Street	E6
Merrion Street	D5-E5
Merrion Way	D6
Mill Hill	D3
Mill Street	F4
Moorland Road	A7-A8
Mushroom Street	F6-F7
Neville Street	D2-D3
New Briggate	D5-E5
New Station Street	D3
New Woodhouse Lane	C6-C7
New York Road	F5
New York Street	E4-F4
North Street	E5-E6-E7
Northern Street	B3
Oatland Lane	D8-D7-E7
Oatland Road	D8
Oxford Row	C5
Park Cross Street	C4-C5
Park Lane	A5-B5-B4
Park Place	B4-C4
Park Row	C4-C5-D5-D4
Park Square East	C4
Park Square North	B4-C4

Park Square South	C4
Park Square West	B4
Park Street	B5-C5
Portland Crescent	C5-C6
Portland Way	C6
Quebec Street	C3-C4
Queen Street	B3-B4
Queen Square	C6-D6
Queen Victoria Street	D4-E4
Regent Street	F5-F6
Roseville Road	F7-F8
Rossington Street	C5-D5
Roundhay Road	E8-F8
St Ann Street	C5-D5
St Mark's Spur	B8-C8
St Paul's Street	B4-C4
St Peter's Street	E4-F4
Servia Hill	C8-D8
Servia Road	C8-D8
Sheepscar Link Road	E7-E8
Sheepscar Street North	E8
Sheepscar Street South	E8-E7-F7
Skinner Lane	E6-F6
South Brook Street	E2
South Parade	C4
Sovereign Street	D2-D3-E3
Springwell Road	A1-B1
Springwell Street	A1
Sweet Street	C1-D1
Sweet Street West	B1-C1
Swinegate	D3
The Calls	E3-F3
The Headrow	C5-D5
Templar Lane	E5
Templar Street	E5
Thoresby Place	B5-B6
Trinity Street	D4
Upper Basinghall Street	D4-D5
Vicar Lane	E4-E5
Victoria Road	D1-D2
Wade Lane	D5-D6
Water Lane	B1-B2-C2-D2
Waterloo Street	E2-E3
Well Close View	D8
Wellington Road	A3
Wellington Street	A3-B3-C3
Westgate	B4-B5-C5-C4
Wharf Street	E3-E4
Whitehall Road	A1-A2-B2-B3-C3
Whitelock Street	E7-F7
Woodhouse Lane	A8-B8-B7-C7-C6-D6-D5
York Place	B4-C4
York Street	F4

LEEDS
Offices now occupy the handsome twin-towered Civic Hall which stands in Calverley Street in front of the new buildings of Leeds Polytechnic. This area of the city – the commercial centre – has been extensively redeveloped

159

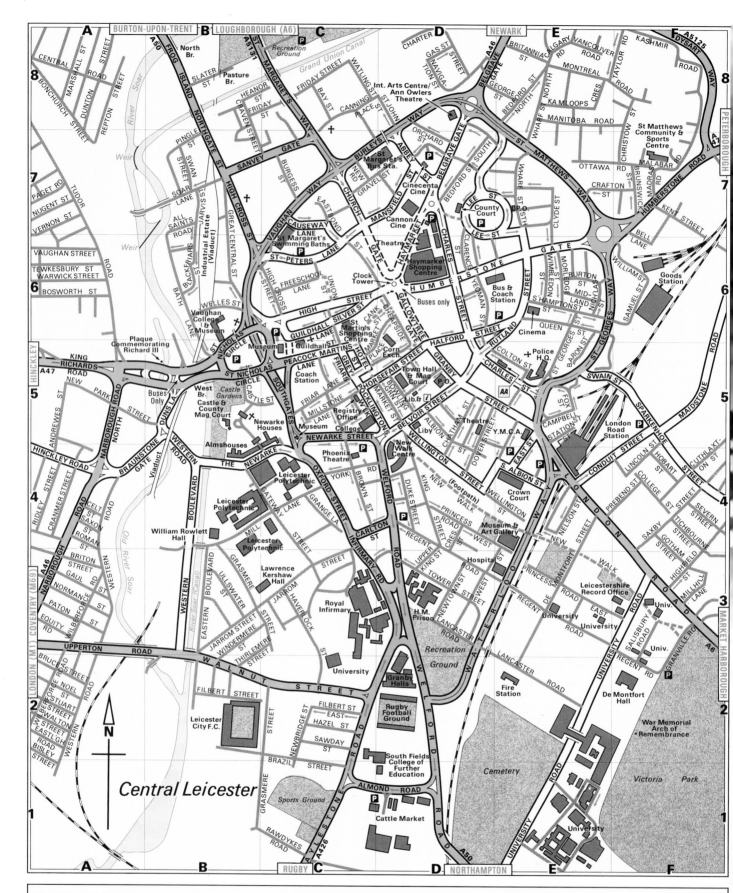

Leicester

A regional capital in Roman times, Leicester has retained many buildings from its eventful and distinguished past. Today the city is a thriving modern place, a centre for industry and commerce, serving much of the Midlands. Among the most outstanding monuments from the past is the Jewry Wall, a great bastion of Roman masonry. Close by are remains of the Roman baths and

several other contemporary buildings. Attached is a museum covering all periods from prehistoric times to 1500. Numerous other museums include the Wygston's House Museum of Costume, with displays covering the period 1769 to 1924; Newarke House, with collections showing changing social conditions in Leicester through four hundred years; and Leicestershire Museum and Art Gallery, with collections of drawings, paintings, ceramics, geology and natural history.

The medieval Guildhall has many features of interest, including a great hall, library and police cells. Leicester's castle, although remodelled in the 17th century, retains a 12th-century great hall. The Church of St Mary de Castro, across the road from the castle, has features going back at least as far as Norman times; while St Nicholas's Church is even older, with Roman and Saxon foundations. St Martin's Cathedral dates mainly from the 13th to 15th centuries and has a notable Bishop's throne.

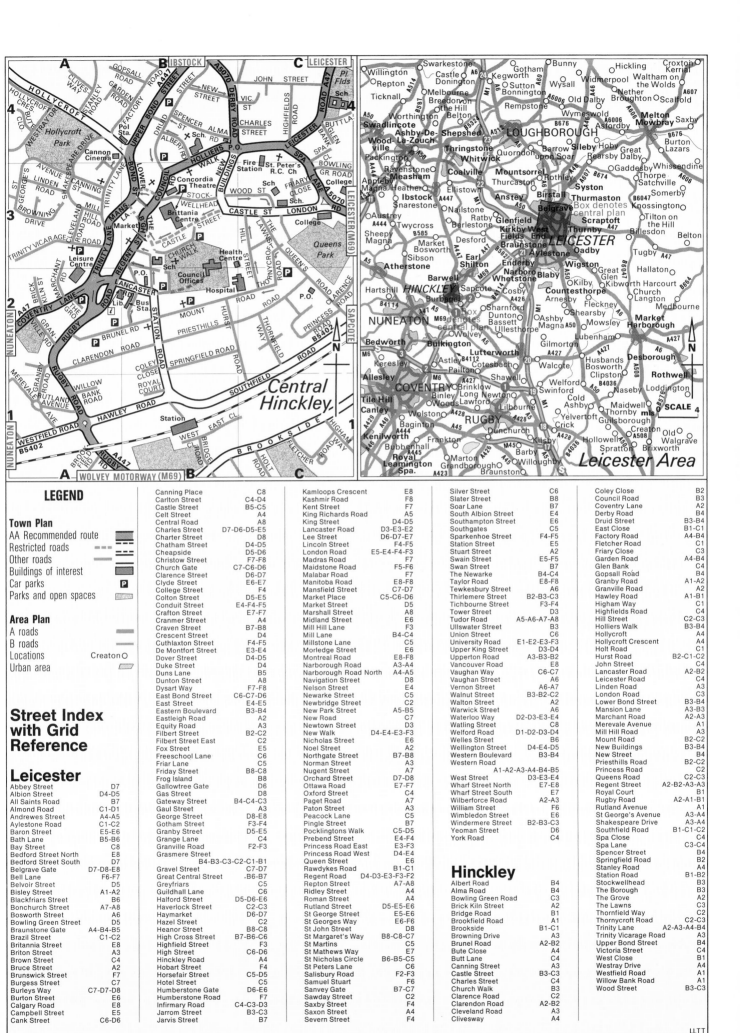

LEGEND

Town Plan

AA Recommended route
Restricted roads
Other roads
Buildings of interest
Car parks   P
Parks and open spaces

Area Plan

A roads
B roads
Locations   Creaton ○
Urban area

Street Index with Grid Reference

Leicester

Abbey Street	D7
Albion Street	D4-D5
All Saints Road	B7
Almond Road	C1-D1
Andrewes Street	A4-A5
Aylestone Road	C1-C2
Baron Street	E5-E6
Bath Lane	B5-B6
Bay Street	C8
Bedford Street North	E8
Bedford Street South	D7
Belgrave Gate	D7-D8-E8
Bell Lane	F6-F7
Belvoir Street	D5
Bisley Street	A1-A2
Blackfriars Street	B6
Bonchurch Street	A7-A8
Bosworth Street	A6
Bowling Green Street	D5
Braunstone Gate	A4-B4-B5
Brazil Street	C1-C2
Britannia Street	E8
Briton Street	A3
Brown Street	C4
Bruce Street	A2
Brunswick Street	F7
Burgess Street	C7
Burleys Way	C7-D7-D8
Burton Street	E6
Calgary Road	E8
Campbell Street	E5
Cank Street	C6-D6

Canning Place	C8
Carlton Street	C4-D4
Castle Street	B5-C5
Celt Street	A4
Central Road	A8
Charles Street	D7-D6-D5-E5
Charter Street	D8
Chatham Street	D5
Cheapside	D5-D6
Christow Street	F7-F8
Church Gate	C7-C6-D6
Clarence Street	D6-D7
Clyde Street	E6-E7
College Street	F4
Colton Street	D5-E5
Conduit Street	E4-F4-F5
Crafton Street	E7-F7
Cranmer Street	A4
Craven Street	B7-B8
Crescent Street	D4
Cuthlaxton Street	F4-F5
De Montfort Street	E3-E4
Dover Street	D4-D5
Duke Street	D4
Duns Lane	B5
Dunton Street	A8
Dysart Way	F7-F8
East Bond Street	C6-C7-D6
East Street	E4-E5
Eastern Boulevard	B3-B4
Eastleigh Road	A2
Equity Road	A3
Filbert Street	B2-C2
Filbert Street East	C2
Fox Street	E5
Freeschool Lane	C6
Friar Lane	C5
Friday Street	B8-C8
Frog Island	B8
Gallowtree Gate	D6
Gas Street	D8
Gateway Street	B4-C4-C3
Gaul Street	A3
George Street	D8-E8
Gotham Street	F3-F4
Granby Street	D5-E5
Grange Lane	C4
Granville Road	F2-F3
Grasmere Street	B4-B3-C3-C2-C1-B1
Gravel Street	C7-D7
Great Central Street	B6-B7
Greyfriars	C5
Guildhall Lane	C6
Halford Street	D5-D6-E6
Haverlock Street	C2-C3
Haymarket	D6-D7
Hazel Street	C2
Heanor Street	B8-C8
High Cross Street	B7-B6-C6
Highfield Street	F3
High Street	C6-D6
Hinckley Road	A4
Hobart Street	F4
Horsefair Street	C5-D5
Hotel Street	C5
Humberstone Gate	D6-E6
Humberstone Road	F7
Infirmary Road	C4-C3-D3
Jarrom Street	B3-C3
Jarvis Street	B7

Kamloops Crescent	E8
Kashmir Road	F8
Kent Street	F7
King Richards Road	A5
King Street	D4-D5
Lancaster Road	D3-E3-E2
Lee Street	D6-D7-E7
Lincoln Street	F4-F5
London Road	E5-E4-F4-F3
Madras Road	F7
Maidstone Road	F5-F6
Malabar Road	F7
Manitoba Road	E8-F8
Mansfield Street	C7-D7
Market Place	C5-C6-D6
Market Street	D5
Marshall Street	A8
Midland Street	E6
Mill Hill Lane	F3
Mill Lane	B4-C4
Millstone Lane	C5
Morledge Street	E6
Montreal Road	E8-F8
Narborough Road	A3-A4
Narborough Road North	A4-A5
Navigation Street	D8
Nelson Street	E4
Newarke Street	C5
Newbridge Street	C2
New Park Street	A5-B5
New Road	C7
Newtown Street	D3
New Walk	D4-E4-E3-F3
Nicholas Street	E6
Noel Street	A2
Northgate Street	B7-B8
Norman Street	A7
Nugent Street	A7
Orchard Street	D7-D8
Ottawa Road	E7-F7
Oxford Street	C4
Paget Road	A7
Paton Street	A3
Peacock Lane	C5
Pingle Street	B7
Pocklingtons Walk	C5-D5
Prebend Street	E4-F4
Princess Road East	E3-F3
Princess Road West	D4-E4
Queen Street	E6
Rawdykes Road	B1-C1
Regent Road	D4-D3-E3-F3-F2
Repton Street	A7-A8
Ridley Street	A4
Roman Street	A4
Rutland Street	D5-E5-E6
St George Street	E5-E6
St Georges Way	E6-F6
St John Street	D8
St Margaret's Way	B8-C8-C7
St Martins	C5
St Mathews Way	E7
St Nicholas Circle	B6-B5-C5
St Peters Lane	C6
Salisbury Road	F2-F3
Samuel Stuart	F6
Sanvey Gate	B7-C7
Sawday Street	C2
Saxby Street	F4
Saxon Street	A4
Severn Street	F4

Silver Street	C6
Slater Street	B8
Soar Lane	B7
South Albion Street	E4
Southampton Street	E6
Southgates	C5
Sparkenhoe Street	F4-F5
Station Street	E5
Stuart Street	A2
Swain Street	E5-F5
Swan Street	B7
The Newarke	B4-C4
Taylor Road	E8-F8
Tewkesbury Street	A6
Thirlemere Street	B2-B3-C3
Tichbourne Street	F3-F4
Tower Street	D3
Tudor Road	A5-A6-A7-A8
Ullswater Street	B3
Union Street	C6
University Road	E1-E2-E3-F3
Upper King Street	D3-D4
Upperton Road	A3-B3-B2
Vancouver Road	E8
Vaughan Way	C6-C7
Vaughan Street	A6
Vernon Street	A6-A7
Walnut Street	B3-B2-C2
Walton Street	A2
Warwick Street	A6
Waterloo Way	D2-D3-E3-E4
Watling Street	C8
Welford Road	D1-D2-D3-D4
Welles Street	B6
Wellington Street	D4-E4-D5
Western Boulevard	B3-B4
Western Road	A1-A2-A3-A4-B4-B5
West Street	D3-E3-E4
Wharf Street North	E7-E8
Wharf Street South	E7
Wilberforce Road	A2-A3
William Street	F6
Wimbledon Street	E6
Windermere Street	B2-B3-C3
Yeoman Street	D6
York Road	C4

Coley Close	B2
Council Road	B3
Coventry Lane	A2
Derby Road	B3-B4
Druid Street	B4
East Close	B1-C1
Factory Road	A4-B4
Fletcher Road	C1
Friary Close	C3
Garden Road	A4-B4
Glen Bank	C4
Gopsall Road	B4
Granby Road	A1-A2
Granville Road	A2
Hawley Road	A1-B1
Higher Way	C1
Highfields Road	C2-C3
Hill Street	C2-C3
Holliers Walk	B3-B4
Hollycroft	A4
Hollycroft Crescent	A4
Holt Road	C1
Hurst Road	B2-C1-C2
John Street	C4
Lancaster Road	A2-B2
Leicester Road	C4
Linden Road	A3
London Road	C3
Lower Bond Street	B3-B4
Mansion Lane	A3-B3
Marchant Road	A2-A3
Merevale Avenue	A1
Mill Hill Road	A3
Mount Road	B2-C2
New Buildings	B3-B4
New Street	B4
Priesthills Road	B2-C2
Princess Road	C2
Queens Road	C2-C3
Regent Street	A2-B2-A3-A3
Royal Court	B1
Rugby Road	A2-A1-B1
Rutland Avenue	A1
St George's Avenue	A3-A4
Shakespeare Drive	A3-A4
Southfield Road	B1-C1-C2
Spa Close	C4
Spa Lane	C3-C4
Spencer Street	B4
Springfield Road	B2
Stanley Road	A4
Station Road	B1-B2
Stockwellhead	B3
The Borough	B3
The Grove	A2
The Lawns	C3
Thornfield Way	C2
Thornycroft Road	C2-C3
Trinity Lane	A2-A3-A4-B4
Trinity Vicarage Road	A3
Upper Bond Street	B4
Victoria Street	C4
West Close	B1
Westray Drive	A4
Westfield Road	A1
Willow Bank Road	A1
Wood Street	B3-C3

Hinckley

Albert Road	B4
Alma Road	B4
Bowling Green Road	C3
Brick Kiln Street	A2
Bridge Road	B1
Brookfield Road	A1
Brookside	B1-C1
Browning Drive	A3
Brunel Road	A2-B2
Bute Close	A4
Butt Lane	C4
Canning Street	A3
Castle Street	B3-C3
Charles Street	C4
Church Walk	B3
Clarence Road	C2
Clarendon Road	A2-B2
Cleveland Road	A3
Clivesway	A4

161

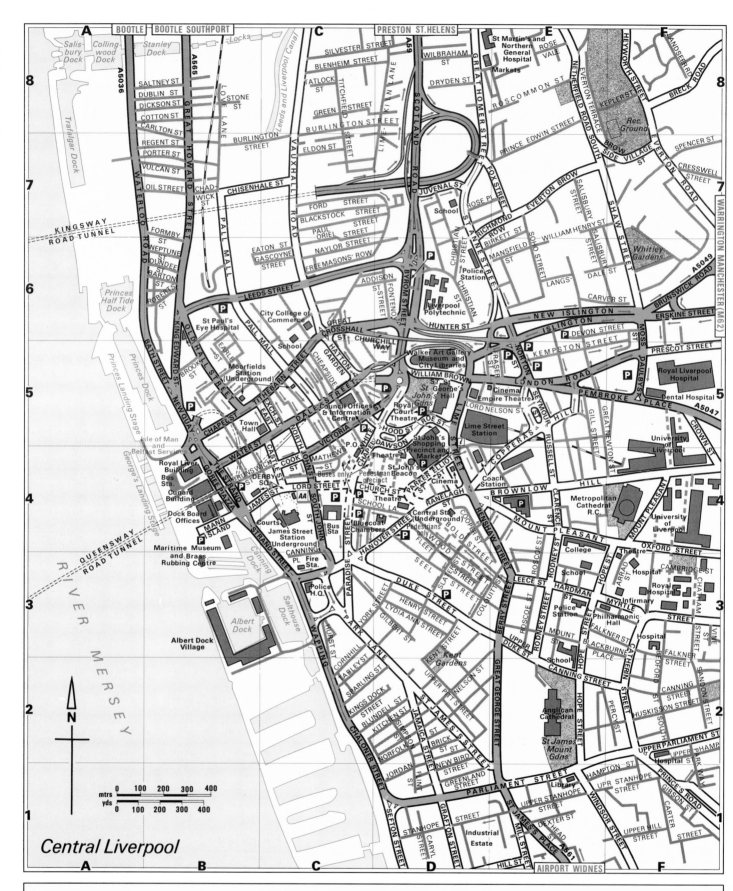

Liverpool

Although its dock area has been much reduced, Liverpool was at one time second only to London in pre-eminence as a port. Formerly the centrepiece of the docks area are three monumental buildings – the Dock Board Offices, built in 1907 with a huge copper-covered dome; the Cunard Building, dating from 1912 and decorated with an abundance of ornamental carving; and best-known of all, the world-famous Royal Liver Building, with the two 'liver birds' crowning its twin cupolas.

Some of the city's best industrial buildings have fallen into disuse in recent years, and have been preserved as monuments of the industrial age. One has become a maritime museum housing full-sized craft and a workshop where maritime crafts are demonstrated. Other museums and galleries include the Walker Art Gallery, with excellent collections of European painting and sculpture; Liverpool City Libraries, one of the oldest and largest public libraries in Britain, with a vast collection of books and manuscripts; and Bluecoat Chambers, a Queen Anne building now used as a gallery and concert hall. Liverpool has two outstanding cathedrals: the Roman Catholic, completed in 1967 in an uncompromising controversial style; and the Protestant, constructed in the great tradition of Gothic architecture, but begun in 1904 and only recently completed.

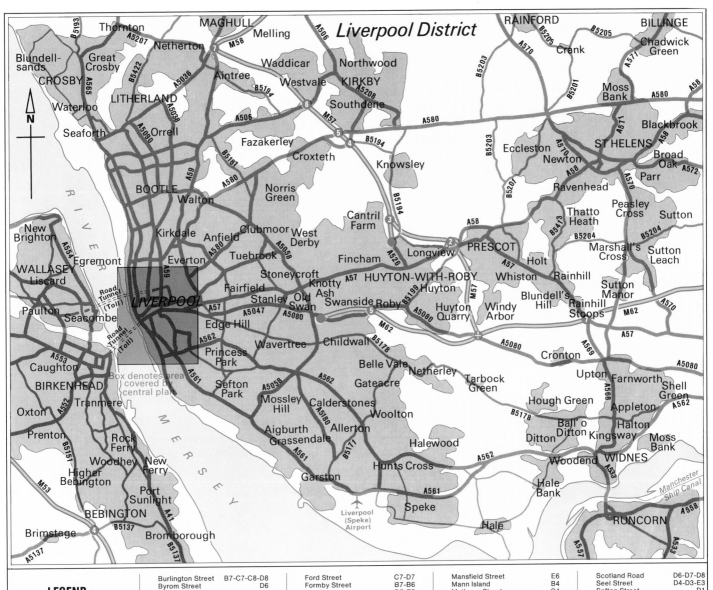

Liverpool District

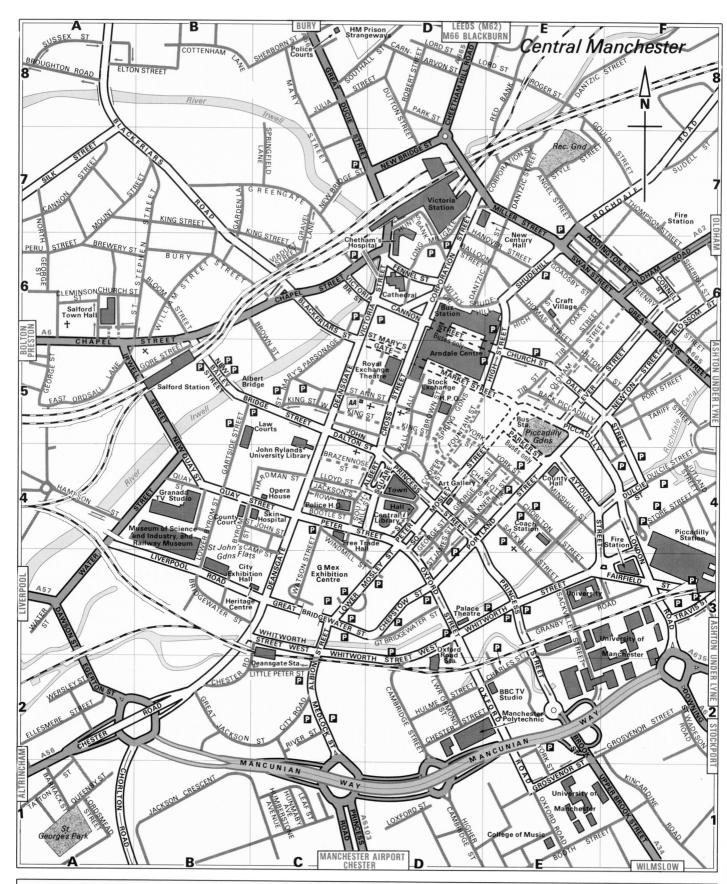

Manchester

The gigantic conurbation called Greater Manchester covers a staggering 60 square miles, reinforcing Manchester's claim to be Britain's second city. Commerce and industry are vital aspects of the city's character, but it is also an important cultural centre – the Halle Orchestra has its home at the Free Trade Hall (a venue for many concerts besides classical music), there are several theatres, a library (the John Rylands) which houses one of the most important collections of books in the world, and a number of museums and galleries, including the Whitworth Gallery with its lovely watercolours.

Like many great cities it suffered badly during the bombing raids of World War II, but some older buildings remain, including the town hall, a huge building designed in Gothic style by Alfred Waterhouse and opened in 1877. Manchester Cathedral dates mainly from the 15th century and is noted for its fine tower and outstanding carved woodwork. Nearby is Chetham's Hospital, also 15th-century and now housing a music school. Much new development has taken place, and more is planned. Shopping precincts cater for the vast population, and huge hotels have provided services up to international standards. On the edge of the city is the Belle Vue centre, a large entertainments complex including concert and exhibition facilities, and a speedway stadium.

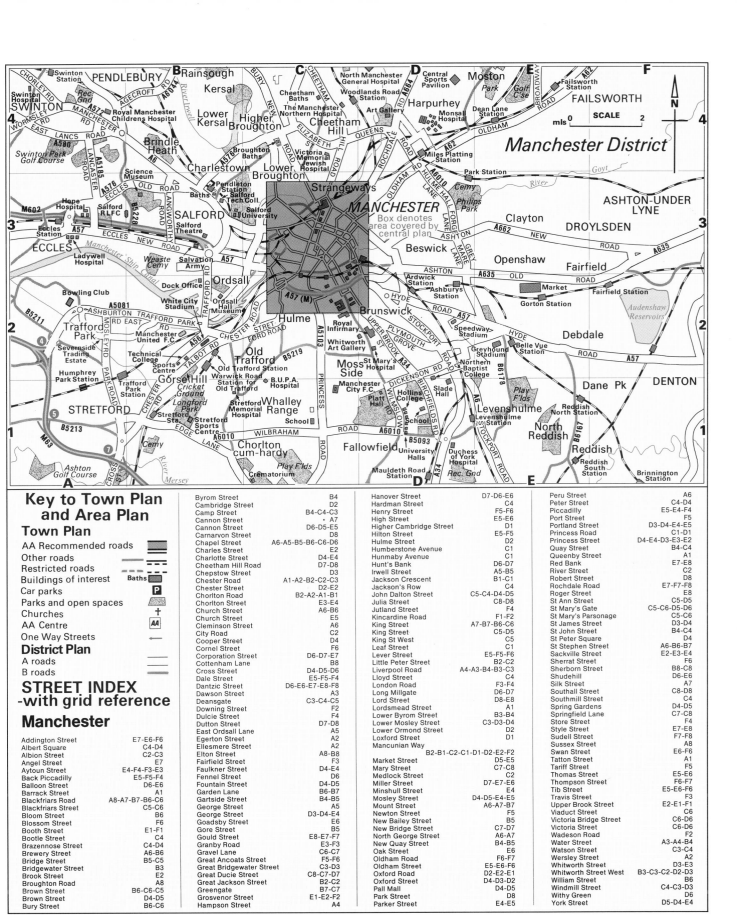

Manchester District

SCALE mls 0 ___ 2

MANCHESTER
The Barton Swing Bridge carries the Bridgewater Canal over the Manchester Ship Canal, which links Manchester with the sea nearly 40 miles away. Completed in 1894, the canal is navigable by vessels up to 15,000 tons.

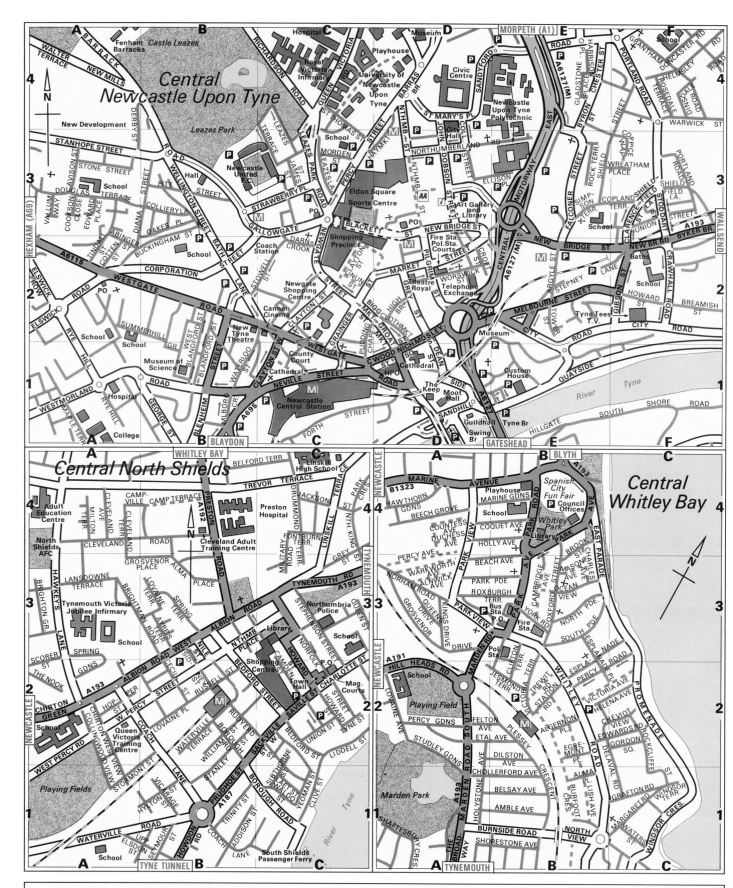

Newcastle

Six bridges span the Tyne at Newcastle; they all help to create a striking scene, but the most impressive is the High Level Bridge, built by Robert Stephenson in 1845-49 and consisting of two levels, one for the railway and one for the road. It is from the river that some of the best views of the city can be obtained. Grey Street is Newcastle's most handsome thoroughfare. It dates from the time, between 1835 and 1840, when much of this part of the city was replanned and rebuilt. Elegant façades curve up to Grey's Monument. Close to the Monument is the Eldon Centre, combining sports facilities and shopping centre to form an integrated complex which is one of the largest of its kind in Europe. Newcastle has many museums. The industrial background of the city is traced in the Museum of Science and Engineering, while the Laing Art Gallery and Museum covers painting, costumes and local domestic history. The Hancock Museum has an exceptional natural history collection and the John George Joicey Museum has period displays in a 17th-century almshouse. In Black Gate is one of Britain's most unusual museums – a collection of over 100 sets of bagpipes. Within the University precincts are three further museums. Of the city's open spaces, Town Moor is the largest. At nearly 1,000 acres it is big enough to feel genuinely wild.

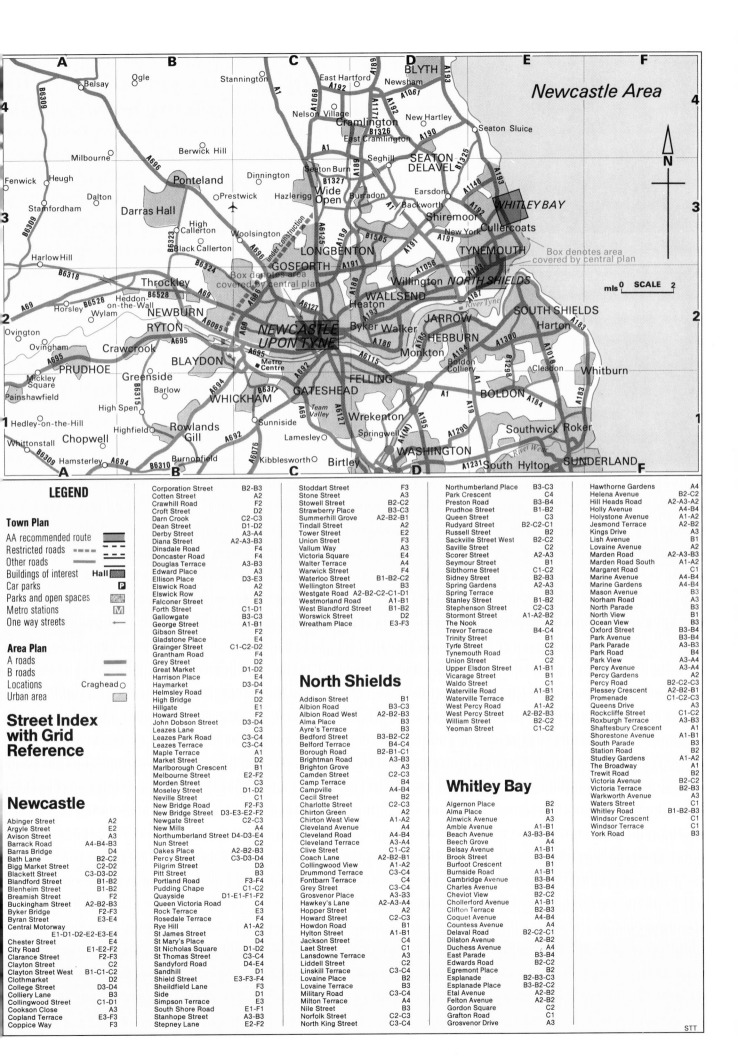

Newcastle Area

mls 0 SCALE 2

LEGEND

Town Plan

AA recommended route	
Restricted roads	-----
Other roads	
Buildings of interest	Hall
Car parks	P
Parks and open spaces	
Metro stations	M
One way streets	←

Area Plan

A roads	
B roads	
Locations	Craghead ○
Urban area	

Street Index with Grid Reference

Newcastle

Abinger Street	A2
Argyle Street	E2
Avison Street	A3
Barrack Road	A4-B4-B3
Barras Bridge	D4
Bath Lane	B2-C2
Bigg Market Street	C2-D2
Blackett Street	C3-D3-D2
Blandford Street	B1-B2
Blenheim Street	B1-B2
Breamish Street	F2
Buckingham Street	A2-B2-B3
Byker Bridge	F2-F3
Byran Street	E3-E4
Central Motorway	E1-D1-D2-E2-E3-E4
Chester Street	E4
City Road	E1-E2-F2
Clarance Street	F2-F3
Clayton Street	C2
Clayton Street West	B1-C1-C2
Clothmarket	D2
College Street	D3-D4
Colliery Lane	B3
Collingwood Street	C1-D1
Cookson Close	A3
Copland Terrace	E3-F3
Coppice Way	F3
Corporation Street	B2-B3
Cotten Street	A2
Crawhill Road	F2
Croft Street	D2
Darn Crook	C2-C3
Dean Street	D1-D2
Derby Street	A3-A4
Diana Street	A2-A3-B3
Dinsdale Road	F4
Doncaster Road	F4
Douglas Terrace	A3-B3
Edward Place	A3
Ellison Place	D3-E3
Elswick Road	A2
Elswick Row	A2
Falconer Street	E3
Forth Street	C1-D1
Gallowgate	B3-C3
George Street	A1-B1
Gibson Street	F2
Gladstone Place	E4
Grainger Street	C1-C2-D2
Grantham Road	F4
Grey Street	D2
Great Market	D1-D2
Harrison Place	E4
Haymarket	D3-D4
Helmsley Road	F4
High Bridge	D2
Hillgate	E1
Howard Street	F2
John Dobson Street	D3-D4
Leazes Lane	C3
Leazes Park Road	C3-C4
Leazes Terrace	C3-C4
Maple Terrace	A1
Market Street	D2
Marlborough Crescent	B1
Melbourne Street	E2-F2
Morden Street	C3
Moseley Street	D1-D2
Neville Street	C1
New Bridge Road	F2-F3
New Bridge Street	D3-E3-E2-F2
Newgate Street	C2-C3
New Mills	A4
Northumberland Street	D4-D3-E4
Nun Street	C2
Oakes Place	A2-B2-B3
Percy Street	C3-D3-D4
Pilgrim Street	D2
Pitt Street	B3
Portland Road	F3-F4
Pudding Chape	E1-C2
Quayside	D1-E1-F1-F2
Queen Victoria Road	C4
Rock Terrace	E3
Rosedale Terrace	E3
Rye Hill	A1-A2
St James Street	C3
St Mary's Place	D4
St Nicholas Square	D1-D2
St Thomas Street	C3-C4
Sandyford Road	D4-E4
Sandhill	D1
Shield Street	E3-F3-F4
Sheildfield Lane	F3
Side	D1
Simpson Terrace	E3
South Shore Road	E1-F1
Stanhope Street	A3-B3
Stepney Lane	E2-F2
Stoddart Street	F3
Stone Street	A3
Stowell Street	B2-C2
Strawberry Place	B3-C3
Summerhill Grove	A2-B2-B1
Tindall Street	A2
Tower Street	E2
Union Street	F3
Vallum Way	A3
Victoria Square	E4
Walter Terrace	A4
Warwick Street	F4
Waterloo Street	B1-B2-C2
Wellington Street	B3
Westgate Road	A2-B2-C2-C1-D1
Westmorland Road	A1-B1
West Blandford Street	B1-B2
Worswick Street	D2
Wreatham Place	E3-F3

North Shields

Addison Street	B1
Albion Road	B3-C3
Albion Road West	A2-B2-B3
Alma Place	B3
Ayre's Terrace	B3
Bedford Street	B3-B2-C2
Belford Terrace	B4-C4
Borough Road	B2-B1-C1
Brightman Road	A3-B3
Brighton Grove	A3
Camden Street	C2-C3
Camp Terrace	B4
Campville	A4-B4
Cecil Street	B2
Charlotte Street	C2-C3
Chirton Green	A2
Chirton West View	A1-A2
Cleveland Avenue	A4
Cleveland Road	A4-B4
Cleveland Terrace	A3-A4
Clive Street	C1-C2
Coach Lane	A2-B2-B1
Collingwood View	A1-A2
Drummond Terrace	C3-C4
Fontbarn Terrace	C4
Grey Street	C3-C4
Grosvenor Place	A3-B3
Hawkey's Lane	A2-A3-A4
Hopper Street	A2
Howard Street	C2-C3
Howdon Road	B1
Hylton Street	A1-B1
Jackson Street	C4
Laet Street	C1
Lansdowne Terrace	A3
Liddell Street	C2
Linskill Terrace	C3-C4
Lovaine Place	B2
Lovaine Terrace	B3
Military Road	C3-C4
Milton Terrace	A4
Nile Street	B3
Norfolk Street	C2-C3
North King Street	C3-C4
Northumberland Place	B3-C3
Park Crescent	C4
Preston Road	B3-B4
Prudhoe Street	B1-B2
Queen Street	C3
Rudyard Street	B2-C2-C1
Russell Street	B2
Sackville Street West	B2-C2
Saville Street	C2
Scorer Street	A2-A3
Seymour Street	B1
Sibthorpe Street	C1-C2
Sidney Street	B2-B3
Spring Gardens	A2-A3
Spring Terrace	B3
Stanley Street	B1-B2
Stephenson Street	C2-C3
Stormont Street	A1-A2-B2
The Nook	A2
Trevor Terrace	B4-C4
Trinity Street	B1
Tyrie Street	C2
Tynemouth Road	C3
Union Street	C2
Upper Elsdon Street	A1-B1
Vicarage Street	B1
Waldo Street	C1
Waterville Road	A1-B1
Waterville Terrace	B2
West Percy Road	A1-A2
West Percy Street	A2-B2-B3
William Street	B2-C2
Yeoman Street	C1-C2

Whitley Bay

Algernon Place	B2
Alma Place	B1
Alnwick Avenue	A3
Amble Avenue	A1-B1
Beach Avenue	A3-B3-B4
Beech Grove	A4
Belsay Avenue	A1-B1
Brook Street	B3-B4
Burfoot Crescent	B1
Burnside Road	A1-B1
Cambridge Avenue	B3-B4
Charles Avenue	B3-B4
Cheviot View	B2-C2
Chollerford Avenue	A1-B1
Clifton Terrace	B2-B3
Coquet Avenue	A4-B4
Countess Avenue	A4
Delaval Road	B2-C2-C1
Dilston Avenue	A2-B2
Duchess Avenue	A4
East Parade	B3-B4
Edwards Road	B2-C2
Egremont Place	B2
Esplanade	B2-B3-C3
Esplanade Place	B3-B2-C1
Etal Avenue	A2-B2
Felton Avenue	A2-B2
Gordon Square	C2
Grafton Road	C1
Grosvenor Drive	A3
Hawthorne Gardens	A4
Helena Avenue	B2-C2
Hill Heads Road	A2-A3-A2
Holly Avenue	A4-B4
Holystone Avenue	A1-A2
Jesmond Terrace	A2-B2
Kings Drive	A3
Lish Avenue	B1
Lovaine Avenue	A2
Marden Road	A2-A3-B3
Marden Road South	A1-A2
Margaret Road	C1
Marine Avenue	A4-B4
Marine Gardens	A4-B4
Mason Avenue	B3
Norham Road	A3
North Parade	B3
North View	B1
Ocean View	B3
Oxford Street	B3-B4
Park Avenue	B3-B4
Park Parade	A3-B3
Park Road	B4
Park View	A3-A4
Percy Avenue	A3-A4
Percy Gardens	A2
Percy Road	B2-C2-C3
Plessey Crescent	A2-B2-B1
Promenade	C1-C2-C3
Queens Drive	A3
Rockcliffe Street	C1-C2
Roxburgh Terrace	A3-B3
Shaftesbury Crescent	A1
Shorestone Avenue	A1-B1
South Parade	B3
Station Road	B2
Studley Gardens	A1-A2
The Broadway	A1
Trewit Road	B2
Victoria Avenue	B2-C2
Victoria Terrace	B2-B3
Warkworth Avenue	A3
Waters Street	C1
Whitley Road	B1-B2-B3
Windsor Crescent	C1
Windsor Terrace	C1
York Road	B3

STT

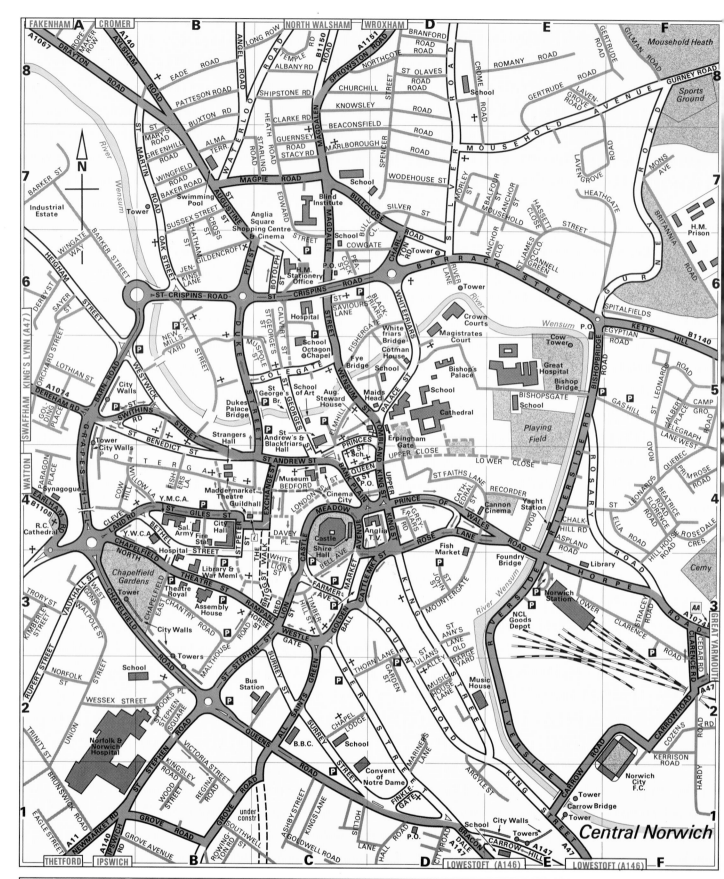

Norwich

Fortunately the heart has not been ripped out of Norwich to make way for some bland precinct, so its ancient character has been preserved. Narrow alleys run between the streets – sometimes opening out into quiet courtyards, sometimes into thoroughfares packed with people, sometimes into lanes which seem quite deserted. It is a unique place, with something of interest on every corner.

The cathedral was founded in 1096 by the city's first bishop, Herbert de Losinga. Among its most notable features are the nave, with its huge pillars, the bishop's throne (a Saxon survival unique in Europe) and the cloisters with their matchless collection of roof bosses. Across the city is the great stone keep of the castle, set on a mound and dominating all around it. It dates from Norman times, but was refaced in 1834. The keep now forms part of Norwich Castle Museum – an extensive and

fascinating collection. Other museums are Bridewell Museum – collections relating to local crafts and industries within a 14th-century building – and Strangers' Hall, a genuinely 'old world' house, rambling and full of surprises, both in its tumble of rooms and in the things which they contain. Especially picturesque parts of the city are Elm Hill – a street of ancient houses; Tombland – with two gateways into the Cathedral Close; and Pull's Ferry – a watergate by the river.

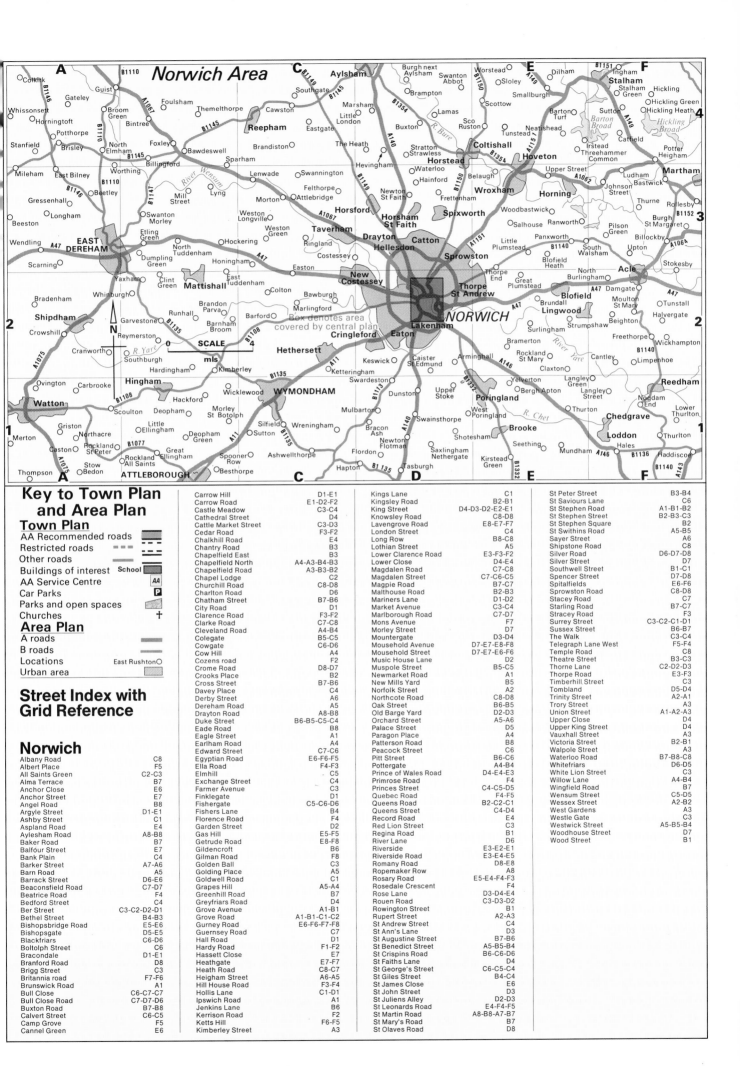

Key to Town Plan and Area Plan

Town Plan
AA Recommended roads
Restricted roads
Other roads
Buildings of interest   School
AA Service Centre   AA
Car Parks   P
Parks and open spaces
Churches   †

Area Plan
A roads
B roads
Locations   East Rushton ○
Urban area

Street Index with Grid Reference

Norwich

Albany Road	C8
Albert Place	F5
All Saints Green	C2-C3
Alma Terrace	B7
Anchor Close	E6
Anchor Street	E7
Angel Road	B8
Argyle Street	D1-E1
Ashby Street	C1
Aspland Road	E4
Aylesham Road	A8-B8
Baker Road	B7
Balfour Street	E7
Bank Plain	C4
Barker Street	A7-A6
Barn Road	B4
Barrack Street	D6-E6
Beaconsfield Road	C7-D7
Beatrice Road	F4
Bedford Street	C4
Ber Street	C3-C2-D2-D1
Bethel Street	B4-B3
Bishopsbridge Road	E5-E6
Bishopsgate	D5-E5
Blackfriars	C6-D6
Boltolph Street	C6
Bracondale	D1-E1
Branford Road	D8
Brigg Street	C3
Britannia road	F7-F6
Brunswick Road	A1
Bull Close	C6-C7-C7
Bull Close Road	C7-D7-D6
Buxton Road	B7-B8
Calvert Street	C6-C5
Camp Grove	F5
Cannel Green	E6

Carrow Hill	D1-E1
Carrow Road	E1-D2-F2
Castle Meadow	C3-C4
Cathedral Street	D4
Cattle Market Street	C3-D3
Cedar Road	F3-F2
Chalkhill Road	E4
Chantry Road	B3
Chapelfield East	B3
Chapelfield North	A4-A3-B4-B3
Chapelfield Road	A3-B3-B2
Chapel Lodge	C2
Churchill Road	C8-D8
Charlton Road	D6
Chatham Street	B7-B6
City Road	D1
Clarence Road	F3-F2
Clarke Road	C7-C8
Cleveland Road	A4-B4
Colegate	B5-C5
Cowgate	C6-D6
Cow Hill	A4
Cozens road	F2
Crome Road	D8-D7
Crooks Place	B2
Cross Street	B7-B6
Davey Place	C3
Derby Street	A6
Dereham Road	A5
Drayton Road	A8-B8
Duke Street	B6-B5-C5-C4
Eade Road	B8
Eagle Street	A1
Earlham Road	B8
Edward Street	C7-C6
Egyptian Road	E6-F6-F5
Ella Road	F4-F3
Elmhill	C5
Exchange Street	C4
Farmer Avenue	C3
Finkelgate	D1
Fishergate	C5-C6-D6
Fishers Lane	B4
Florence Road	F4
Garden Street	D2
Gas Hill	E5-F5
Getrude Road	E8-F8
Gildencroft	B6
Gilman Road	F8
Golden Ball	C3
Golding Place	A5
Goldwell Road	C1
Grapes Hill	A5-A4
Greenhill Road	B7
Greyfriars Road	D4
Grove Avenue	A1-B1
Grove Road	A1-B1-C1-C2
Gurney Road	E6-F6-F7-F8
Guernsey Road	C7
Hall Road	D1
Hardy Road	F1-F2
Hassett Close	E7
Heathgate	E7-F7
Heath Road	C8-C7
Heigham Street	A6-A5
Hill House Road	F3-F4
Hollis Lane	C1-D1
Ipswich Road	A1
Jenkins Lane	B6
Kerrison Road	F2
Ketts Hill	F6-F5
Kimberley Street	A3

Kings Lane	C1
Kingsley Road	B2-B1
King Street	D4-D3-D2-E2-E1
Knowsley Road	C8-D8
Lavengrove Road	E8-E7-F7
London Street	C4
Long Row	B8-C8
Lothian Street	B7
Lower Clarence Road	E3-F3-F2
Lower Close	D4-E4
Magdalen Road	C7-C8
Magdalen Street	C7-C6-C5
Magpie Road	B7-C7
Malthouse Road	B2-B3
Mariners Lane	D1-D2
Market Avenue	C3-C4
Marlborough Road	C7-D7
Mons Avenue	F7
Morley Street	D7
Mountergate	D3-D4
Mousehold Avenue	D7-E7-E8-F8
Mousehold Street	D7-E7-E6-F6
Music House Lane	D2
Muspole Street	B5-C5
Newmarket Road	A1
New Mills Yard	B5
Norfolk Street	A2
Northcote Road	C8-D8
Oak Street	B6-B5
Old Barge Yard	D2-D3
Orchard Street	A5-A6
Palace Street	D5
Paragon Place	A4
Patterson Road	B8
Peacock Street	C6
Pitt Street	B6-C6
Pottergate	A4-B4
Prince of Wales Road	D4-E4-E3
Primrose Road	F4
Princes Street	C4-C5-D5
Quebec Road	F4-F5
Queens Road	B2-C2-C1
Queens Street	C4-D4
Record Road	E4
Red Lion Street	C3
Regina Road	B1
River Lane	D6
Riverside	E3-E2-E1
Riverside Road	E3-E4-E5
Romany Road	D8-E8
Ropemaker Row	A8
Rosary Road	E5-E4-F4-F3
Rosedale Crescent	F4
Rose Lane	D3-D4-E4
Rouen Road	C3-D3-D2
Rowington Street	B1
Rupert Street	A2-A3
St Andrew Street	C4
St Ann's Lane	D3
St Augustine Street	B7-B6
St Benedict Street	A5-B5-B4
St Crispins Road	B6-C6-D6
St Faiths Lane	D4
St George's Street	C6-C5-C4
St Giles Street	B4-C4
St James Close	E6
St John Street	D3
St Juliens Alley	D2-D3
St Leonards Road	E4-F4-F5
St Martin Road	A8-B8-A7-B7
St Mary's Road	B7
St Olaves Road	D8

St Peter Street	B3-B4
St Saviours Lane	C6
St Stephen Road	A1-B1-B2
St Stephen Street	B2-B3-C3
St Stephen Square	B2
St Swithins Road	A5-B5
Sayer Street	A6
Shipstone Road	C8
Silver Road	D6-D7-D8
Silver Street	D7
Southwell Street	B1-C1
Spencer Street	D7-D8
Spitalfields	E6-F6
Sprowston Road	C8-D8
Stacey Road	C7
Starling Road	B7-C7
Stracey Road	F3
Surrey Street	C3-C2-C1-D1
Sussex Street	B6-B7
The Walk	C3-C4
Telegraph Lane West	F5-F4
Temple Road	C8
Theatre Street	B3-C3
Thorne Lane	C2-D2-D3
Thorpe Road	E3-F3
Timberhill Street	C3
Tombland	D5-D4
Trinity Street	A2-A1
Trory Street	A3
Union Street	A1-A2-A3
Upper Close	D4
Upper King Street	D4
Vauxhall Street	A3
Victoria Street	B2-B1
Walpole Street	A3
Waterloo Road	B7-B8-C8
Whitefriars	D6-D5
White Lion Street	C3
Willow Lane	A4-B4
Wingfield Road	B7
Wensum Street	C5-D5
Wessex Street	A2-B2
West Gardens	A3
Westle Gate	C3
Westwick Street	A5-B5-B4
Woodhouse Street	D7
Wood Street	B1

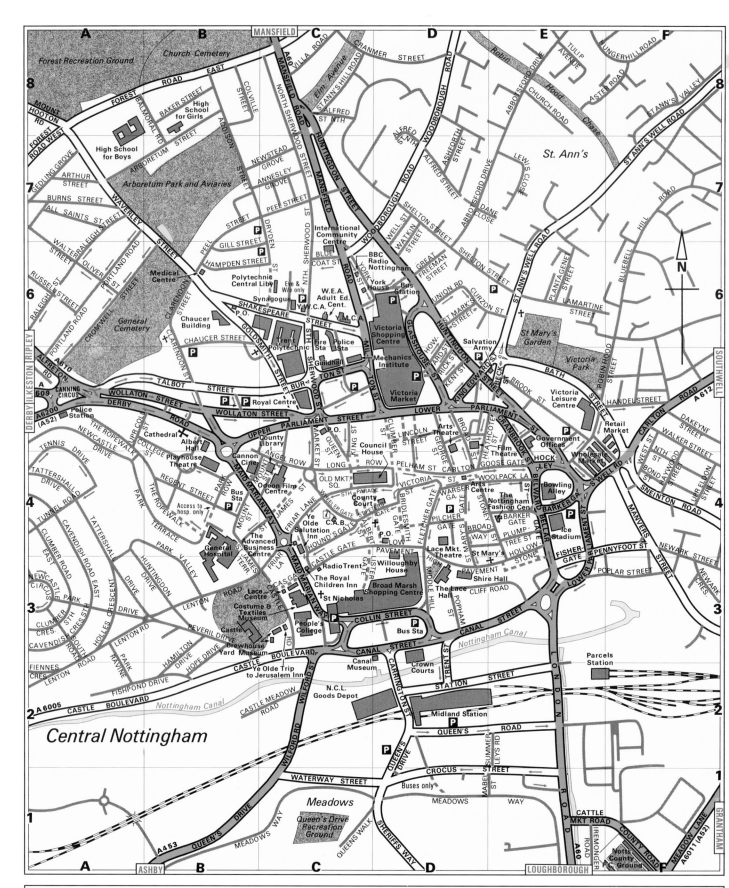

Nottingham

Hosiery and lace were the foundations upon which Nottingham's prosperity was built. The stockings came first – a knitting machine for these had been invented by a Nottinghamshire man as early as 1589 – but a machine called a 'tickler', which enabled simple patterns to be created in the stocking fabric, prompted the development of machine-made lace. The earliest fabric was produced in 1768, and an example from not much later than that is kept in the city's Castlegate Costume and Textile Museum. In fact, the entire history of lacemaking is beautifully explained in this converted row of Georgian terraces. The Industrial Museum at Wollaton Park has many other machines and exhibits tracing the development of the knitting industry, as well as displays on the other industries which have brought wealth to the city – tobacco, pharmaceuticals, engineering and printing. At Wollaton Hall is a natural history museum, while nearer the centre are the Canal Museum and the Brewhouse Yard Museum, a marvellous collection which shows items from daily life in the city up to the present day. Nottingham is not complete without mention of Robin Hood, the partly mythical figure whose statue is in the castle grounds. Although the castle itself has Norman foundations, the present structure is largely Victorian. It is now a museum.

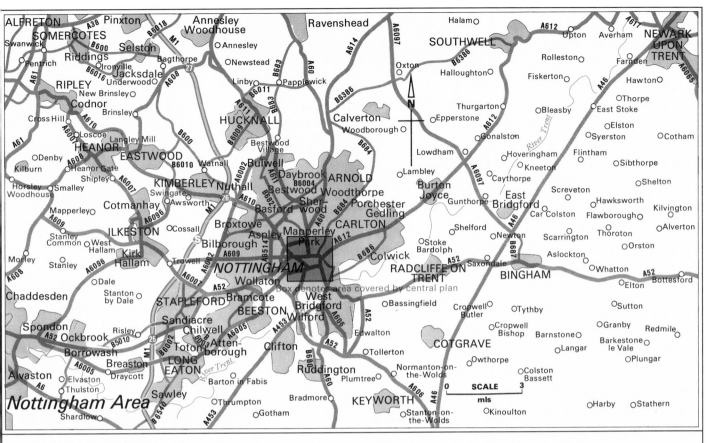

Nottingham Area

Box denotes area covered by central plan

SCALE

0   3

mls

Key to Town Plan and Area Plan

Town Plan

AA Recommended roads
Restricted roads
Other roads
Buildings of interest   Theatre ▣
Car Parks   P
Parks and open spaces ▨
Churches   †
One Way Streets →

Area Plan

A roads
B roads
Locations   Bagthorpe○
Urban area ▨

Street Index with Grid Reference

Nottingham

Abbotsford Drive	D6-D7-D7-E7-E8
Addison Street	B8-B7
Albert Street	C4
Alfred Street	D7
Alfred Street North	C8, D7-D8
Alfreton Road	A5-A6
All Saints Street	A7
Angel Row	B5-B4-C4
Annesley Grove	B7-C7
Ashforth Street	D7-D8
Aster Road	E8-F8
Arboretum Street	A7-B7-B8
Arthur Street	A7
Baker Street	B8
Balmoral Road	A8-B8-B7
Barker Gate	E4
Bath Street	E5-F5
Beck Street	E5
Bellar Gate	E4
Belward Street	E4
Bluebell Hill Road	F6-F7
Bluecoat Street	C6
Bond Street	F4
Bridlesmith Gate	D4
Broad Street	D4-D5
Broadway	D4-E4
Brook Street	E5
Burns Street	A7

Burton Street	C5
Canal Street	C3-D3-E3
Canning Circus	A5
Carlton Road	F5
Carlton Street	D4
Carrington Street	D2-D3
Castle Boulevard	A2-B2-B3-C3
Castle Gate	C3-C4
Castle Meadow Road	B2-C2
Castle Road	C3
Cattle Market Road	E1-F1
Cavendish Crescent South	A3
Cavendish Road East	A3-A4
Chaucer Street	B5-B6
Church Road	E8
Clarendon Street	B5-B6
Cliff Road	D3-E3
Clumber Crescent South	A3
Clumber Road East	A3-A4
Clumber Street	D4-D5
College Street	A5-B5-B4
Collin Street	C3-D3
Colville Street	B8
County Road	F1
Cranbrook Street	E4-E5
Cranmer Street	C8-D8
Crocus Street	D1-E1
Cromwell Street	A5-A6-B6
Curzon Street	D6-E6
Dane Close	D7-E7
Dakeyne Street	F5
Derby Road	A5-B5
Dryden Street	C6-C7
Fienness Crescent	A2
Fishergate	E3-E4
Fishpond Drive	A2-B2
Fletcher Gate	D4
Forest Road East	A8-B8-C8
Forest Road West	A7-A8
Friar Lane	C3-C4
Gedling Grove	A7
George Street	D4-D5
Gill Street	B6-C6
Glasshouse Street	D5-D6
Goldsmith Street	B6-C6-C5
Goose Gate	D4-E4
Great Freeman Street	D6
Hamilton Drive	B2-B3
Hampden Street	B6-C6
Handel Street	E5-F5
Haywood Street	F4-F5
Heathcote Street	D4-D5-E5
High Pavement	D4-D3-E3
Hockley	E4
Holles Crescent	A3
Hollowstone	E3-E4

Hope Drive	B2-B3
Hound's Gate	C4
Howard Street	D5-D6
Hungerhill Road	E8-F8
Huntingdon Drive	A4-A3-B3
Huntingdon Street	C8-D7-D6-E5
Iremonger Road	E1
Kent Street	D5
King Edward Street	D5-E5
King Street	C4-C5
Lamartine Street	E6-F6
Lenton Road	A2-A3-B3
Lewis Close	E7
Lincoln Street	D5
Lister Gate	C3-C4
London Road	E1-E2-E3
Long Row	C4-D4
Lower Parliament Street	D5-E4-E3
Low Pavement	C4-D4
Mabel Street	E1
Maid Marian Way	B4-C4-C3
Mansfield Road	C6-C7-C8
Manvers Street	F3-F4
Market Street	C4-C5
Meadow Lane	F1
Meadows Way	B1-C1-D1-E1
Middle Hill	D3-D4
Milton Street	C6-C5-D5
Mount Hooton Road	A8
Mount Street	B4-C4
Newark Crescent	F3
Newark Street	F3-F4
Newcastle Circus	A3
Newcastle Drive	A4-A5
Newstead Grove	B7-C7
North Street	F4-F5
North Sherwood Street	C6-C7-C8
Old Market Square	C4
Oliver Street	A6
Park Drive	A3-B3
Park Ravine	A2-A3
Park Row	B4
Park Terrace	A4-B4
Park Valley	A4-B4-B3
Peel Street	B6-B7-C7
Pelham Street	D4
Pennyfoot Street	E4-F4
Peveril Drive	B3
Pilcher Gate	D4
Plantagenet Street	E6
Plumptree Street	E4
Popham Street	D3
Poplar Street	E3-F3
Portland Road	A5-A6-A7
Queen's Drive	B1-C1, D1-D2
Queen's Road	D2-E2

Queen Street	C4-C5
Queen's Walk	C1
Raleigh Street	A6-A7
Regent Street	B4
Rick Street	D5
Robin Hood Street	E5-F5-F6
Russell Street	A6
St Ann's Hill Road	C8
St Ann's Valley	F7-F8
St Ann's Well Road	E5-E6-E7-F7-F8
St James Street	C4
St James Terrace	B4-B3-C3
St Mark's Street	D6
St Mary's Gate	D3-D4
St Peters Gate	C4-D4
Shakespeare Street	B6-C6
Shelton Street	D7-D6-E6
Sheriff's Way	D1
Sneinton Road	F4
South Parade	C4-D4
South Road	A3
South Sherwood Street	C5-C6
Southwell Road	E4-F4
Station Street	D2-E2
Stony Street	D4-E4
Summer Leys Road	E1
Talbot Street	A5-B5-C5
Tattershall Drive	A4-A3-B3
Tennis Drive	A4-A5-A4
The Ropewalk	A5-A4-B4
Trent Street	D2-D3
Tulip Avenue	E8
Tunnel Road	A4
Union Road	D6
Upper College Street	A5-B5
Upper Eldon Street	F4
Upper Parliament Street	B5-C5-D5
Victoria Street	D4
Villa Road	C8
Walker Street	F4-F5
Walter Street	A6-A7
Warser Gate	D4
Waterway Street	C1-D1
Watkin Street	D6-D7
Waverely Street	A8-A7-B7-B6
Wellington Street	D6-D7
West Street	F4-F5
Wheeler Gate	C4
Wilford Road	C1-C2
Wilford Street	C2-C3
Wollaton Street	A5-B5-C5
Woodborough Road	C6-C7-D7-D8
Woolpack Lane	D4-E4
York Street	C6-D6

LBTT

171

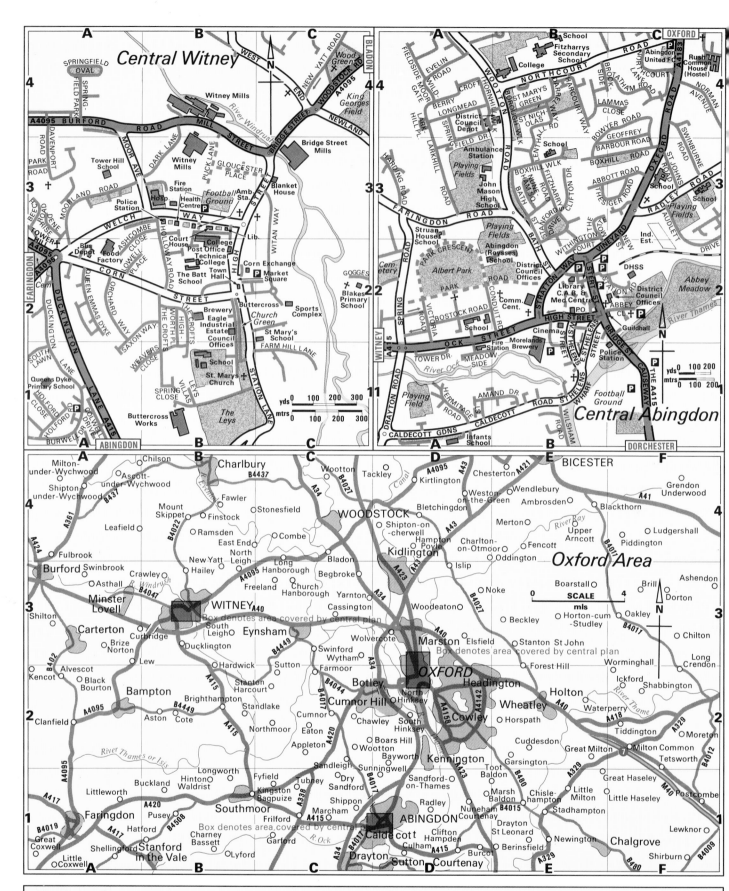

Oxford

From Carfax (at the centre of the city) round to Magdalen Bridge stretches High Street, one of England's best and most interesting thoroughfares. Shops rub shoulders with churches and colleges, alleyways lead to ancient inns and to a large covered market, and little streets lead to views of some of the finest architecture to be seen anywhere. Catte Street, beside St Mary's Church (whose lovely tower gives a panoramic view of Oxford), opens out into Radcliffe Square, dominated by the Radcliffe Camera, a great round structure built in 1749. Close by is the Bodleian Library, one of the finest collections of books and manuscripts in the world. All around are ancient college buildings. Close to Magdalen Bridge is Magdalen College, founded in 1448 and certainly not to be missed. Across the High Street are the Botanical Gardens, founded in 1621 and the oldest such foundation in England. Footpaths lead through Christ Church Meadow to Christ Church College and the cathedral. Tom Tower is the college's most notable feature; the cathedral is actually its chapel and is the smallest cathedral in England. Among much else not to be missed in Oxford is the Ashmolean Museum, whose vast collections of precious and beautiful objects from all over the world repay many hours of study; perhaps the loveliest treasure is the 9th-century Alfred Jewel.

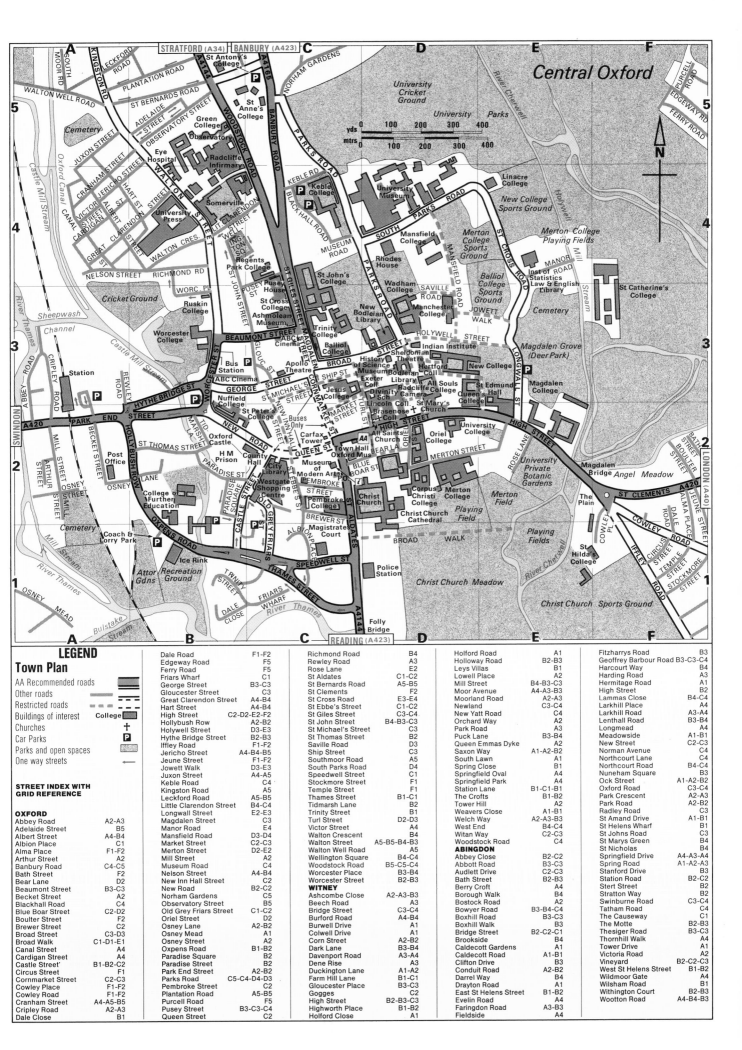

LEGEND

Town Plan

AA Recommended roads
Other roads
Restricted roads
Buildings of interest   College
Churches   +
Car Parks   P
Parks and open spaces
One way streets   ←

STREET INDEX WITH GRID REFERENCE

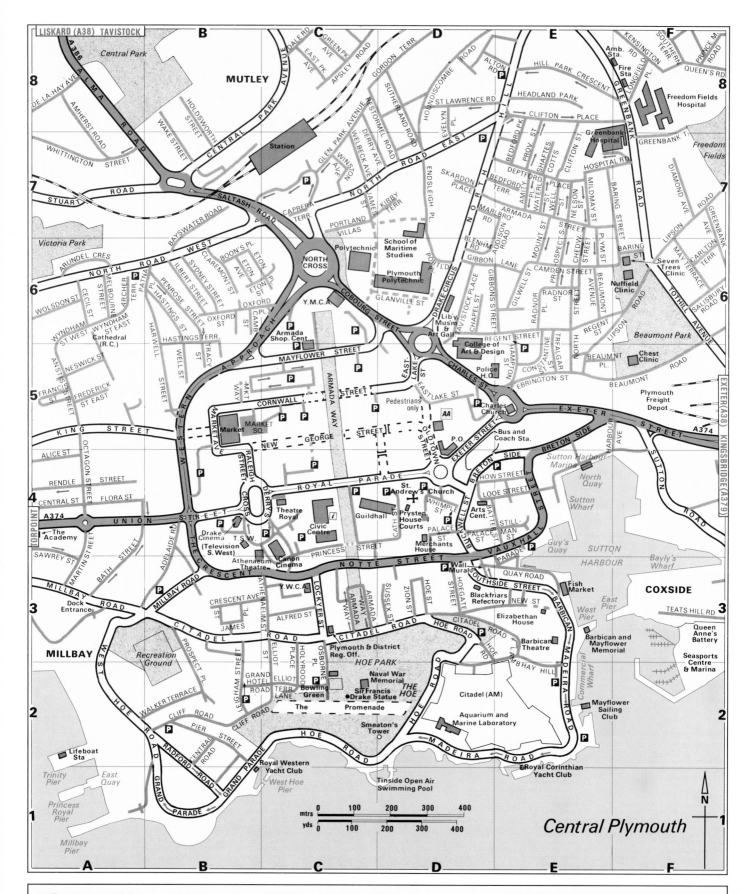

Plymouth

Ships, sailors and the sea permeate every aspect of Plymouth's life and history. Its superb natural harbour – Plymouth Sound – has ensured its importance as a port, yachting centre and naval base (latterly at Devonport) over many centuries. Sir Francis Drake is undoubtedly the city's most famous sailor. His statue stands on the Hoe – where he really did play bowls before tackling the

Spanish Armada. Also on the Hoe are Smeaton's Tower, which once formed the upper part of the third Eddystone Lighthouse, and the impressive Royal Naval War Memorial. Just east of the Hoe is the Royal Citadel, an imposing fortress built in 1666 by order of Charles II. North is Sutton Harbour, perhaps the most atmospheric part of Plymouth. Here fishing boats bob up and down in a harbour whose quays are lined with attractive old houses, inns and warehouses. One of the memorials on

Mayflower Quay just outside the harbour commemorates the sailing of the *Mayflower* from here in 1620. Plymouth's shopping centre is one of the finest of its kind, and was built after the old centre was badly damaged in World War II. Nearby is the 200ft-high tower of the impressive modern Civic Centre. Some buildings escaped destruction, including the Elizabethan House and the 500-year-old Prysten House. Next door is St Andrew's Church, with stained glass by John Piper.

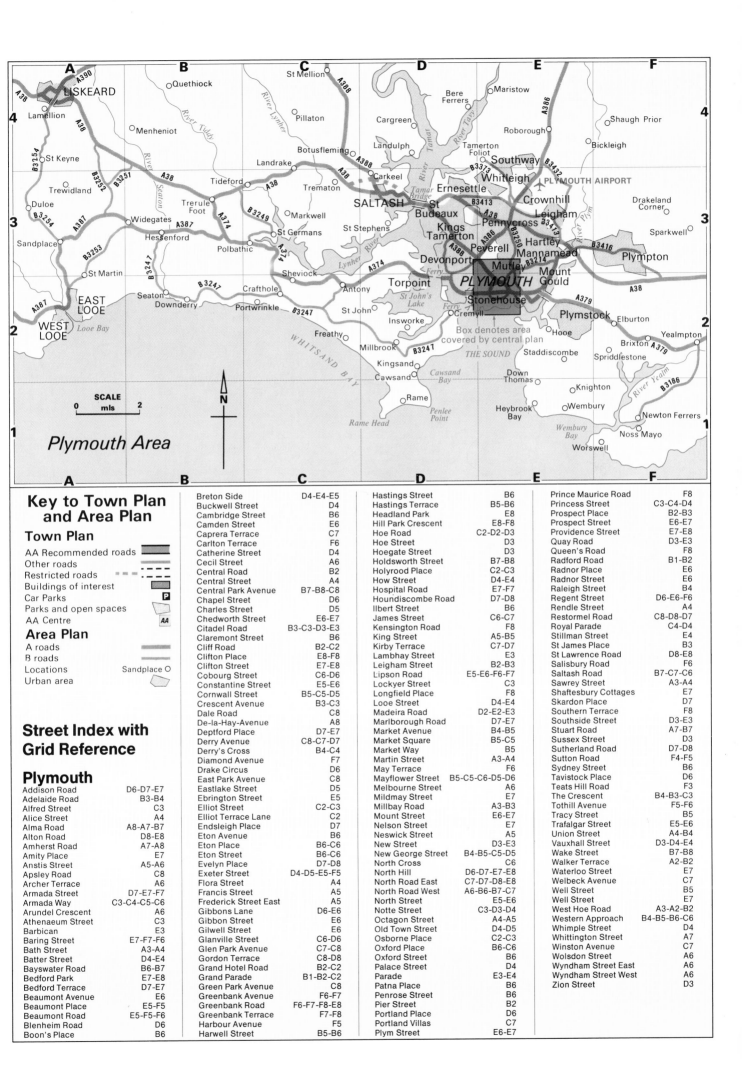

Plymouth Area

SCALE
0 — mls — 2

N

Key to Town Plan and Area Plan

Town Plan
AA Recommended roads
Other roads
Restricted roads
Buildings of interest
Car Parks — P
Parks and open spaces
AA Centre — AA

Area Plan
A roads
B roads
Locations — Sandplace O
Urban area

Street Index with Grid Reference

Plymouth

Street	Grid Ref
Addison Road	D6-D7-E7
Adelaide Road	B3-B4
Alfred Street	C3
Alice Street	A4
Alma Road	A8-A7-B7
Alton Road	D8-E8
Amherst Road	A7-A8
Amity Place	E7
Anstis Street	A5-A6
Apsley Road	C8
Archer Terrace	A6
Armada Street	D7-E7-F7
Armada Way	C3-C4-C5-C6
Arundel Crescent	A6
Athenaeum Street	C3
Barbican	E3
Baring Street	E7-F7-F6
Bath Street	A3-A4
Batter Street	D4-E4
Bayswater Road	B6-B7
Bedford Park	E7-E8
Bedford Terrace	D7-E7
Beaumont Avenue	E6
Beaumont Place	E5-F5
Beaumont Road	E5-F5-F6
Blenheim Road	D6
Boon's Place	B6
Breton Side	D4-E4-E5
Buckwell Street	D4
Cambridge Street	B6
Camden Street	E6
Caprera Terrace	C7
Carlton Terrace	F6
Catherine Street	D4
Cecil Street	A6
Central Road	B2
Central Street	A4
Central Park Avenue	B7-B8-C8
Chapel Street	D6
Charles Street	D5
Chedworth Street	E6-E7
Citadel Road	B3-C3-D3-E3
Claremont Street	B6
Cliff Road	B2-C2
Clifton Place	E8-F8
Clifton Street	E7-E8
Cobourg Street	C6-D6
Constantine Street	E5-E6
Cornwall Street	B5-C5-D5
Crescent Avenue	B3-C3
Dale Road	C8
De-la-Hay-Avenue	A8
Deptford Place	D7-E7
Derry Avenue	C8-C7-D7
Derry's Cross	B4-C4
Diamond Avenue	F7
Drake Circus	D6
East Park Avenue	C8
Eastlake Street	D5
Ebrington Street	E5
Elliot Street	C2-C3
Elliot Terrace Lane	C2
Endsleigh Place	D7
Eton Avenue	B6
Eton Place	B6-C6
Eton Street	B6-C6
Evelyn Place	D7-D8
Exeter Street	D4-D5-E5-F5
Flora Street	A4
Francis Street	A5
Frederick Street East	A5
Gibbons Lane	D6-E6
Gibbon Street	E6
Gilwell Street	E6
Glanville Street	C6-D6
Glen Park Avenue	C7-C8
Gordon Terrace	C8-D8
Grand Hotel Road	B2-C2
Grand Parade	B1-B2-C2
Green Park Avenue	C8
Greenbank Avenue	F6-F7
Greenbank Road	F6-F7-F8-E8
Greenbank Terrace	F7-F8
Harbour Avenue	F5
Harwell Street	B5-B6
Hastings Street	B6
Hastings Terrace	B5-B6
Headland Park	E8
Hill Park Crescent	E8-F8
Hoe Road	C2-D2-D3
Hoe Street	D3
Hoegate Street	D3
Holdsworth Street	B7-B8
Holyrood Place	C2-C3
How Street	D4-E4
Hospital Road	E7-F7
Houndiscombe Road	D7-D8
Ilbert Street	B6
James Street	C6-C7
Kensington Road	F8
King Street	A5-B5
Kirby Terrace	C7-D7
Lambhay Street	E3
Leigham Street	B2-B3
Lipson Road	E5-E6-F6-F7
Lockyer Street	C3
Longfield Place	F8
Looe Street	D4-E4
Madeira Road	D2-E2-E3
Marlborough Road	D7-E7
Market Avenue	B4-B5
Market Square	B5-C5
Market Way	B5
Martin Street	A3-A4
May Terrace	F6
Mayflower Street	B5-C5-C6-D5-D6
Melbourne Street	A6
Mildmay Street	E7
Millbay Road	A3-B3
Mount Street	E6-E7
Nelson Street	E7
Neswick Street	A5
New Street	D3-E3
New George Street	B4-B5-C5-D5
North Cross	C6
North Hill	D6-D7-E7-E8
North Road East	C7-D7-D8-E8
North Road West	A6-B6-B7-C7
North Street	E5-E6
Notte Street	C3-D3-D4
Octagon Street	A4-A5
Old Town Street	D4-D5
Osborne Place	C2-C3
Oxford Place	B6-C6
Oxford Street	B6
Palace Street	D4
Parade	E3-E4
Patna Place	B6
Penrose Street	B6
Pier Street	B2
Portland Place	D6
Portland Villas	C7
Plym Street	E6-E7
Prince Maurice Road	F8
Princess Street	C3-C4-D4
Prospect Place	B2-B3
Prospect Street	E6-E7
Providence Street	E7-E8
Quay Road	D3-E3
Queen's Road	F8
Radford Road	B1-B2
Radnor Place	E6
Radnor Street	E6
Raleigh Street	B4
Regent Street	D6-E6-F6
Rendle Street	A4
Restormel Road	C8-D8-D7
Royal Parade	C4-D4
Stillman Street	E4
St James Place	B3
St Lawrence Road	D8-E8
Salisbury Road	F6
Saltash Road	B7-C7-C6
Sawrey Street	A3-A4
Shaftesbury Cottages	E7
Skardon Place	D7
Southern Terrace	F8
Southside Street	D3-E3
Stuart Road	A7-B7
Sussex Street	D3
Sutherland Road	D7-D8
Sutton Road	F4-F5
Sydney Street	B6
Tavistock Place	D6
Teats Hill Road	F3
The Crescent	B4-B3-C3
Tothill Avenue	F5-F6
Tracy Street	B5
Trafalgar Street	E5-E6
Union Street	A4-B4
Vauxhall Street	D3-D4-E4
Wake Street	B7-B8
Walker Terrace	A2-B2
Waterloo Street	E7
Welbeck Avenue	C7
Well Street	B5
Well Street	B5
West Hoe Road	A3-A2-B2
Western Approach	B4-B5-B6-C6
Whimple Street	D4
Whittington Street	A7
Winston Avenue	C7
Wolsdon Street	A6
Wyndham Street East	A6
Wyndham Street West	A6
Zion Street	D3

175

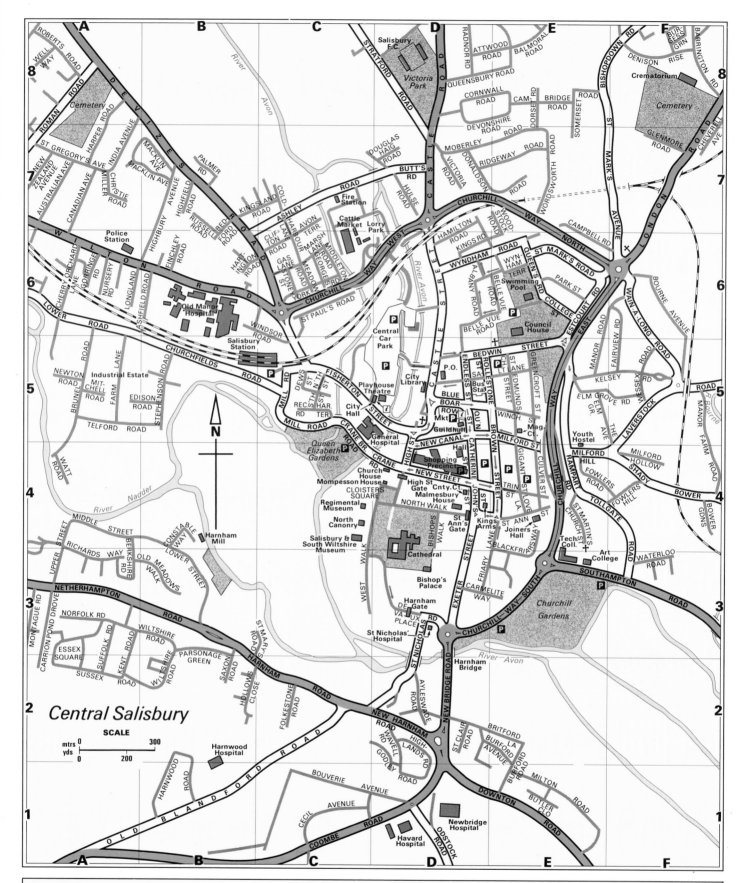

Salisbury

Its attractive site where the waters of the Avon and Nadder meet, its beautiful cathedral and its unspoilt centre put Salisbury among England's finest cities. In 1220 the people of the original settlement at Old Sarum, two miles to the north, moved down to the plain and laid the first stone of the cathedral. Within 38 years its was completed and the result is a superb example of Early English architecture.

The cloisters are the largest in England and the spire the tallest in Britain. All the houses within the Cathedral Close were built for cathedral functionaries, and although many have Georgian façades, most date back to the 13th century. Mompesson House is one of the handsome mansions here and as it belongs to the National Trust, its equally fine interior can be seen. Another building houses the Museum of the Duke of Edinburgh's Royal Regiment. At one time, relations

between the clergy and the citizens of Salisbury were not always harmonious, so the former built a protective wall around the Close.

The streets of the modern city follow the medieval grid pattern of squares, or 'chequers', and the tightly-packed houses provide a very pleasing townscape. Salisbury was granted its first charter in 1227 and flourished as a market and wool centre; there is still a twice-weekly market in the spacious square.

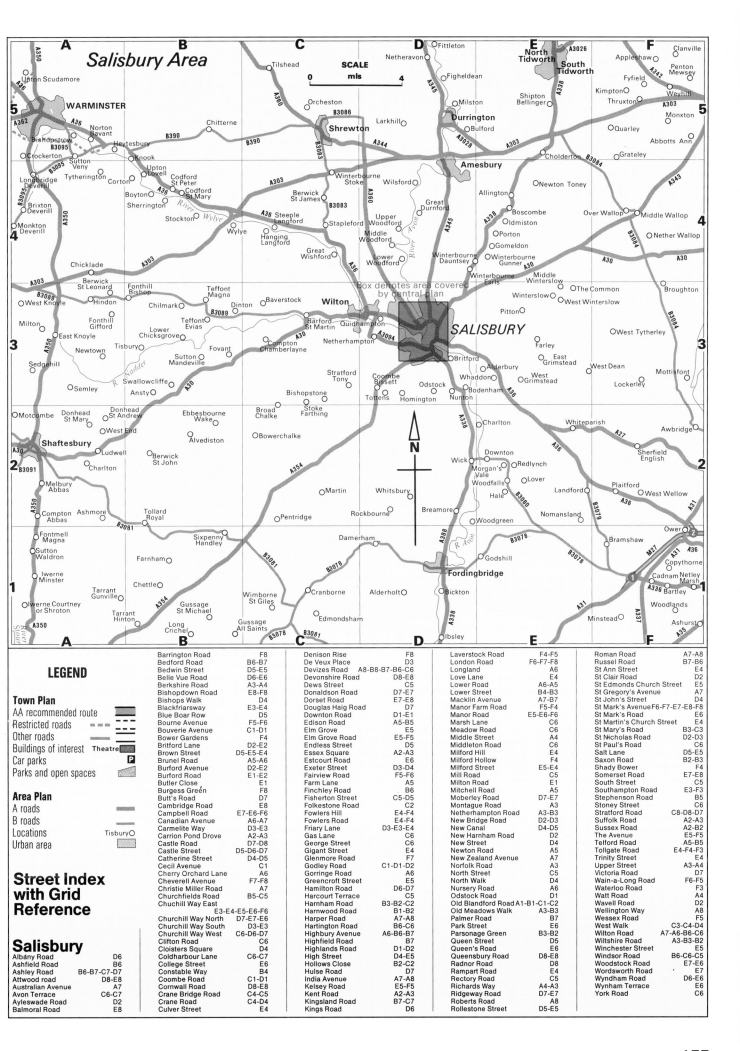

Salisbury Area

SCALE
0 — mls — 4

Box denotes area covered by central plan

SALISBURY

LEGEND

Town Plan
- AA recommended route
- Restricted roads
- Other roads
- Buildings of interest — Theatre
- Car parks — P
- Parks and open spaces

Area Plan
- A roads
- B roads
- Locations — Tisbury○
- Urban area

Street Index with Grid Reference

Salisbury

Albany Road	D6
Ashfield Road	B6
Ashley Road	B6-B7-C7-D7
Attwood road	D8-E8
Australian Avenue	A7
Avon Terrace	C6-C7
Ayleswade Road	D2
Balmoral Road	E8

Barrington Road	F8
Bedford Road	B6-B7
Bedwin Street	D5-E5
Belle Vue Road	D6-E6
Berkshire Road	A3-A4
Bishopdown Road	E8-F8
Bishops Walk	D4
Blackfriarsway	E3-E4
Blue Boar Row	D5
Bourne Avenue	F5-F6
Bouverie Avenue	C1-D1
Bower Gardens	F4
Britford Lane	D2-E2
Brown Street	D5-E5-E4
Brunel Road	A5-A6
Burford Avenue	D2-E2
Burford Road	E1-E2
Butler Close	E1
Burgess Green	F8
Butt's Road	D7
Cambridge Road	E8
Campbell Road	E7-E6-F6
Canadian Avenue	A6-A7
Carmelite Way	D3-E3
Carrion Pond Drove	A2-A3
Castle Road	D7-D8
Castle Street	D5-D6-D7
Catherine Street	D4-D5
Cecil Avenue	C1
Cherry Orchard Lane	A6
Cheverell Avenue	F7-F8
Christie Miller Road	A7
Churchfields Road	B5-C5
Chuchill Way East	E3-E4-E5-E6-F6
Churchill Way North	D7-E7-E6
Churchill Way South	D3-E3
Churchill Way West	C6-D6-D7
Clifton Road	C6
Cloisters Square	D4
Coldharbour Lane	C6-C7
College Street	E6
Constable Way	B4
Coombe Road	C1-D1
Cornwall Road	D8-E8
Crane Bridge Road	C4-C5
Crane Road	C4-D4
Culver Street	E4

Denison Rise	F8
De Veux Place	D3
Devizes Road	A8-B8-B7-B6-C6
Devonshire Road	D8-E8
Dews Street	C5
Donaldson Road	D7-E7
Dorset Road	E7-E8
Douglas Haig Road	D7
Downton Road	D1-E1
Edison Road	A5-B5
Elm Grove	E5
Elm Grove Road	E5-F5
Endless Street	D5
Essex Square	A2-A3
Estcourt Road	E6
Exeter Street	D3-D4
Fairview Road	F5-F6
Farm Lane	A5
Finchley Road	B6
Fisherton Street	C5-D5
Folkestone Road	C2
Fowlers Hill	E4-F4
Fowlers Road	E4-F4
Friary Lane	D3-E3-E4
Gas Lane	C6
George Street	C6
Gigant Street	E4
Glenmore Road	F7
Godley Road	C1-D1-D2
Gorringe Road	A6
Greencroft Street	E5
Hamilton Road	D6-D7
Harcourt Terrace	C5
Harnham Road	B3-B2-C2
Harnwood Road	B1-B2
Harper Road	A7-A8
Hartington Road	B6-C6
Highbury Avenue	A6-B6-B7
Highfield Road	B7
Highlands Road	D1-D2
High Street	D4-E5
Hollows Close	B2-C2
Hulse Road	D7
India Avenue	A7-A8
Kelsey Road	E5-F5
Kent Road	A2-A3
Kingsland Road	B7-C7
Kings Road	D6

Laverstock Road	F4-F5
London Road	F6-F7-F8
Longland	A6
Love Lane	E4
Lower Road	A6-A5
Lower Street	B4-B3
Macklin Avenue	A7-B7
Manor Farm Road	F5-F4
Manor Road	E5-E6-F6
Marsh Lane	C6
Meadow Road	C6
Middle Street	A4
Middleton Road	C6
Milford Hill	E4
Milford Hollow	F4
Milford Street	E5-E4
Mill Road	C5
Milton Road	E1
Mitchell Road	A5
Moberley Road	D7-E7
Montague Road	A3
Netherhampton Road	A3-B3
New Bridge Road	D2-D3
New Canal	D4-D5
New Harnham Road	D2
New Street	D4
Newton Road	A5
New Zealand Avenue	A7
Norfolk Road	A3
North Street	C5
North Walk	D4
Nursery Road	A6
Odstock Road	D1
Old Blandford Road	A1-B1-C1-C2
Old Meadows Walk	A3-B3
Palmer Road	B7
Park Street	E6
Parsonage Green	B3-B2
Queen Street	D5
Queen's Road	E6
Queensbury Road	D8-E8
Radnor Road	D8
Rampart Road	E4
Rectory Road	C5
Richards Way	A4-A3
Ridgeway Road	D7-E7
Roberts Road	A8
Rollestone Street	D5-E5

Roman Road	A7-A8
Russel Road	B7-B6
St Ann Street	E4
St Clair Road	D2
St Edmonds Church Street	E5
St Gregory's Avenue	A7
St John's Street	D4
St Mark's Avenue	F6-F7-E7-E8-F8
St Mark's Road	E6
St Martin's Church Street	E4
St Mary's Road	B3-C3
St Nicholas Road	D2-D3
St Paul's Road	C6
Salt Lane	D5-E5
Saxon Road	B2-B3
Shady Bower	F4
Somerset Road	E7-E8
South Street	C5
Southampton Road	E3-F3
Stephenson Road	B5
Stoney Street	C6
Stratford Road	C8-D8-D7
Suffolk Road	A2-A3
Sussex Road	A2-B2
The Avenue	E5-F5
Telford Road	A5-B5
Tollgate Road	E4-F4-F3
Trinity Street	E4
Upper Street	A3-A4
Victoria Road	D7
Wain-a-Long Road	F6-F5
Waterloo Road	F3
Watt Road	A4
Wavell Road	D2
Wellington Way	A8
Wessex Road	F5
West Walk	C3-C4-D4
Wilton Road	A7-A6-B6-C6
Wiltshire Road	A3-B3-B2
Winchester Street	E5
Windsor Road	B6-C6-C5
Woodstock Road	E7-E6
Wordsworth Road	E4
Wyndham Road	D6-E6
Wynham Terrace	E6
York Road	C6

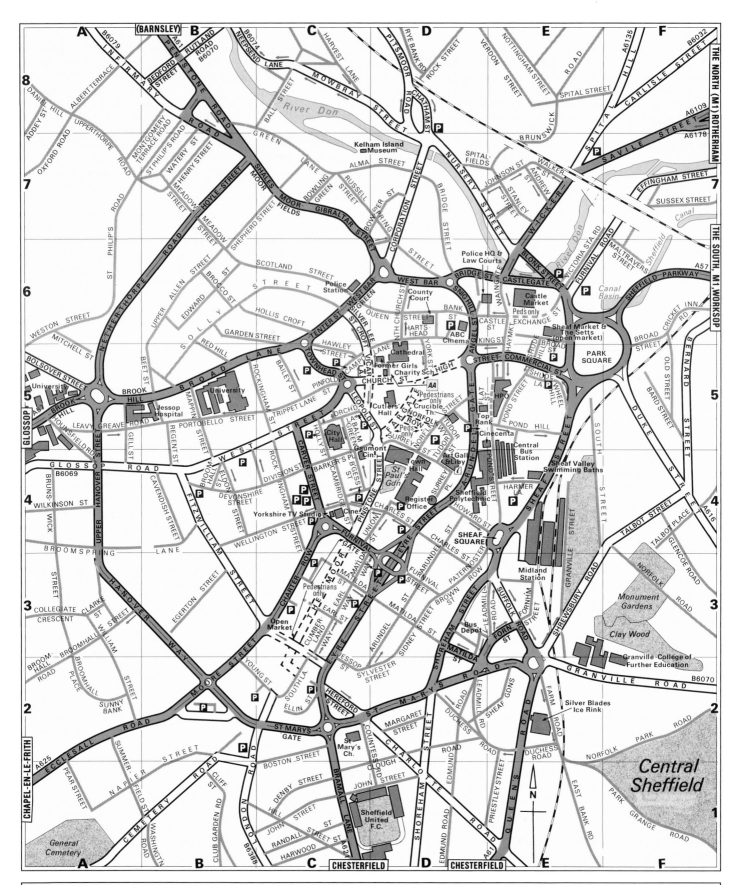

Sheffield

Cutlery – which has made the name of Sheffield famous throughout the world – has been manufactured here since at least as early as the time of Chaucer. The god of blacksmiths, Vulcan, is the symbol of the city's industry, and he crowns the town hall, which was opened in 1897 by Queen Victoria. At the centre of the industry, however, is Cutlers' Hall, the headquarters of the Company of Cutlers. This society was founded in 1624 and has the right to grant trade marks to articles of a sufficiently high standard. In the hall is the company's collection of silver, with examples of craftsmanship dating back every year to 1773. A really large collection of cutlery is kept in the city museum. Steel production, a vital component of the industry, was greatly improved when the crucible process was invented here in 1740. At Abbeydale Industrial Hamlet, 3½ miles south-west of the city centre, is a complete restored site open as a museum and showing 18th-century methods of steel production. Sheffield's centre, transformed since World War II, is one of the finest and most modern in Europe. There are no soot-grimed industrial eyesores here, for the city has stringent pollution controls and its buildings are carefully planned and set within excellent landscaping projects. Many parks are set in and around the city, and the Pennines are within easy reach.

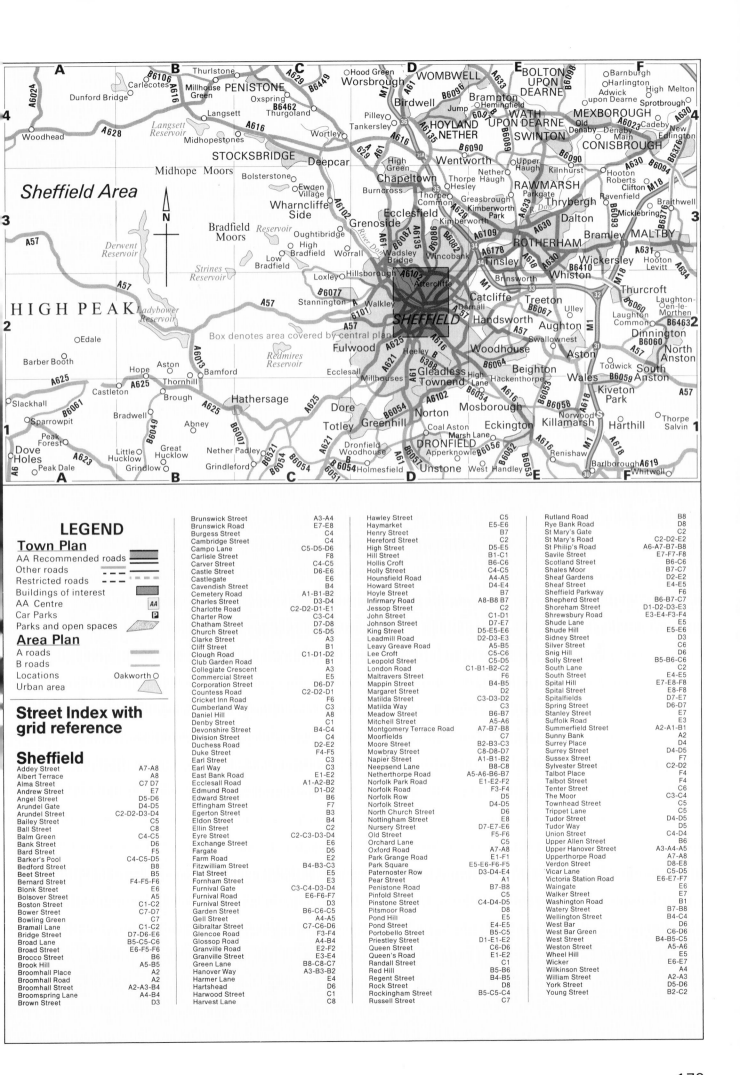

LEGEND

Town Plan

AA Recommended roads
Other roads
Restricted roads
Buildings of interest
AA Centre — AA
Car Parks — P
Parks and open spaces

Area Plan

A roads
B roads
Locations — Oakworth ○
Urban area

Street Index with grid reference

Sheffield

Addey Street	A7-A8
Albert Terrace	A8
Alma Street	C7 D7
Andrew Street	E7
Angel Street	D5-D6
Arundel Gate	D4-D5
Arundel Street	C2-D2-D3-D4
Bailey Street	C5
Ball Street	C8
Balm Green	C4-C5
Bank Street	D6
Bard Street	F5
Barker's Pool	C4-C5-D5
Bedford Street	B8
Beet Street	B5
Bernard Street	F4-F5-F6
Blonk Street	E6
Bolsover Street	A5
Boston Street	C1-C2
Bower Street	C7-D7
Bowling Green	C7
Bramall Lane	C1-C2
Bridge Street	D7-D6-E6
Broad Lane	B5-C5-C6
Broad Street	E6-F5-F6
Brocco Street	B5
Brook Hill	A5-B5
Broomhall Place	A2
Broomhall Road	A2
Broomhall Street	A2-A3-B4
Broomspring Lane	A4-B4
Brown Street	D3
Brunswick Street	A3-A4
Brunswick Road	E7-E8
Burgess Street	C4
Cambridge Street	C4
Campo Lane	C5-D5-D6
Carlisle Street	F8
Carver Street	C4-C5
Castle Street	D6-E6
Castlegate	E6
Cavendish Street	B4
Cemetery Road	A1-B1-B2
Charles Street	D3-D4
Charlotte Road	C2-D2-D1-E1
Charter Row	C3-C4
Chatham Street	D7-D8
Church Street	C5-D5
Clarke Street	A3
Cliff Street	B1
Clough Road	C1-D1-D2
Club Garden Road	B1
Collegiate Crescent	A3
Commercial Street	E5
Corporation Street	D6-D7
Countess Road	C2-D2-D1
Cricket Inn Road	F6
Cumberland Way	C3
Daniel Hill	A8
Denby Street	C1
Devonshire Street	B4-C4
Division Street	C4
Duchess Road	D2-E2
Duke Street	F4-F5
Earl Street	C3
Earl Way	C3
East Bank Road	E1-E2
Ecclesall Road	A1-A2-B2
Edmund Road	D1-D2
Edward Street	B6
Effingham Street	F7
Egerton Street	B3
Eldon Street	B4
Ellin Street	C2
Eyre Street	C2-C3-D3-D4
Exchange Street	E6
Fargate	D5
Farm Road	E2
Fitzwilliam Street	B4-B3-C3
Flat Street	E5
Fornham Street	E3
Furnival Gate	C3-C4-D3-D4
Furnival Road	E6-F6-F7
Furnival Street	D3
Garden Street	B6-C6-C5
Gell Street	A4-A5
Gibraltar Street	C7-C6-D6
Glencoe Road	F3-F4
Glossop Road	A4-B4
Granville Road	E2-F2
Granville Street	E3-E4
Green Lane	B8-C8-C7
Hanover Way	A3-B3-B2
Harmer Lane	E4
Hartshead	D6
Harwood Street	C1
Harvest Lane	C8

Hawley Street	C5
Haymarket	E5-E6
Henry Street	B7
Hereford Street	C2
High Street	D5-E5
Hill Street	B1-C1
Hollis Croft	B6-C6
Holly Street	C4-C5
Hounsfield Road	A4-A5
Howard Street	D4-E4
Hoyle Street	B7
Infirmary Road	A8-B8 B7
Jessop Street	C2
John Street	C1-D1
Johnson Street	D7-E7
King Street	D5-E5-E6
Leadmill Road	D2-D3-E3
Leavy Greave Road	A5-B5
Lee Croft	C5-C6
Leopold Street	C5-D5
London Road	C1-B1-B2-C2
Maltravers Street	F6
Mappin Street	B4-B5
Margaret Street	D2
Matilda Street	C3-D3-D2
Matilda Way	C3
Meadow Street	B6-B7
Mitchell Street	A5-A6
Montgomery Terrace Road	A7-B7-B8
Moorfields	C7
Moore Street	B2-B3-C3
Mowbray Street	C8-D8-D7
Napier Street	A1-B1-B2
Neepsend Lane	B8-C8
Netherthorpe Road	A5-A6-B6-B7
Norfolk Park Road	E1-E2-F2
Norfolk Road	F3-F4
Norfolk Row	D5
Norfolk Street	D4-D5
North Church Street	D6
Nottingham Street	E8
Nursery Street	D7-E7-E6
Old Street	F5-F6
Orchard Lane	C5
Oxford Road	A7-A8
Park Grange Road	E1-F1
Park Square	E5-E6-F6-F5
Paternoster Row	D3-D4-E4
Pear Street	A1
Penistone Road	B7-B8
Pinfold Street	C5
Pinstone Street	C4-D4-D5
Pitsmoor Road	D8
Pond Hill	E5
Pond Street	E4-E5
Portobello Street	B5-C5
Priestley Street	D1-E1-E2
Queen Street	C6-D6
Queen's Road	E1-E2
Randall Street	C1
Red Hill	B5-B6
Regent Street	B4-B5
Rock Street	D8
Rockingham Street	B5-C5-C4
Russell Street	C7

Rutland Road	B8
Rye Bank Road	D8
St Mary's Gate	C2
St Mary's Road	C2-D2-E2
St Philip's Road	A6-A7-B7-B8
Savile Street	E7-F7-F8
Scotland Street	B6-C6
Shales Moor	B7-C7
Sheaf Gardens	D2-E2
Sheaf Street	E4-E5
Sheffield Parkway	F6
Shepherd Street	B6-B7-C7
Shoreham Street	D1-D2-D3-E3
Shrewsbury Road	E3-E4-F3-F4
Shude Lane	E5
Shude Hill	E5-E6
Sidney Street	D3
Silver Street	C6
Snig Hill	D6
Solly Street	B5-B6-C6
South Lane	C2
South Street	E4-E5
Spital Hill	E7-E8-F8
Spital Street	E8-F8
Spitalfields	D7-E7
Spring Street	D6-D7
Stanley Street	E7
Suffolk Road	E3
Summerfield Street	A2-A1-B1
Sunny Bank	A2
Surrey Place	D4
Surrey Street	D4-D5
Sussex Street	F7
Sylvester Street	C2-D2
Talbot Place	F4
Talbot Street	F4
Tenter Street	C6
The Moor	C3-C4
Townhead Street	C5
Trippet Lane	C5
Tudor Street	D4-D5
Tudor Way	D5
Union Street	C4-D4
Upper Allen Street	B6
Upper Hanover Street	A3-A4-A5
Upperthorpe Road	A7-A8
Verdon Street	D8-E8
Vicar Lane	C5-D5
Victoria Station Road	E6-E7-F7
Waingate	E6
Walker Street	E7
Washington Road	B1
Watery Street	B7-B8
Wellington Street	B4-C4
West Bar	D6
West Bar Green	C6-D6
West Street	B4-B5-C5
Weston Street	A5-A6
Wheel Hill	E5
Wicker	E6-E7
Wilkinson Street	A4
William Street	A2-A3
York Street	D5-D6
Young Street	B2-C2

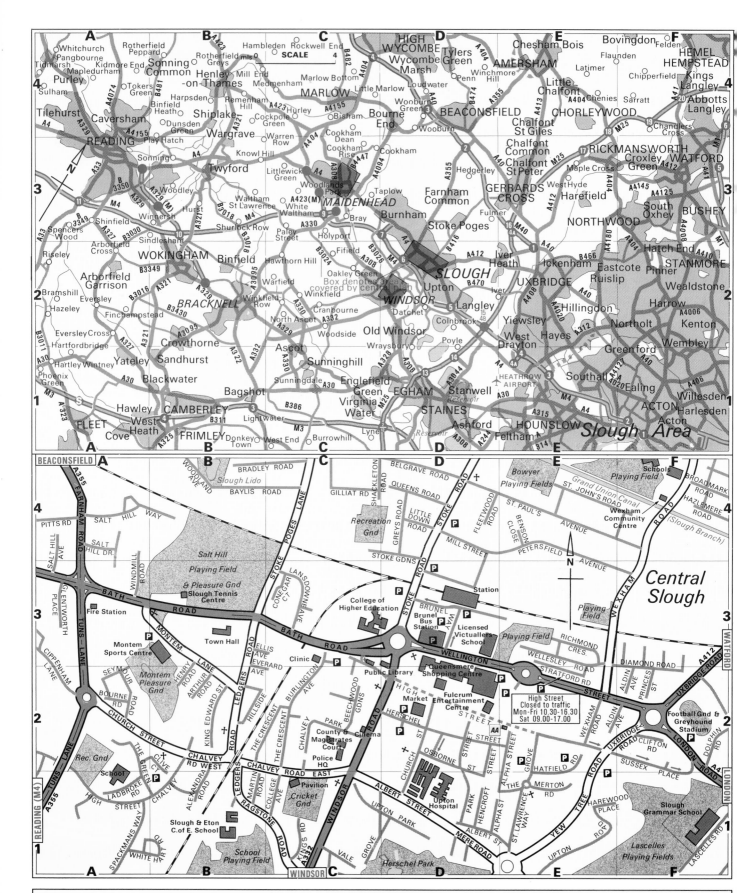

Slough

The town is something of a non-starter as far as architectural beauty or historical interest is concerned. However, it is a good shopping centre and has plenty of sports and leisure facilities.

Windsor The distinctive outline of the castle's towers and battlements above the Thames completely dominates the town. First built by the Normans to guard the approaches to London, it has been altered and added to at different times by various kings, but Henry III and Edward III contributed most to its present haphazard shape. The State Apartments are magnificent, as is St George's Chapel, with its superb fan-vaulted ceiling. Queen Mary's Dolls House is an exquisite model house of the 1920s, complete down to the last detail. The town itself, squeezed between the castle walls and the river, has several attractive streets graced with fine buildings. One 17th-century colonnaded building by Sir Christopher Wren contains a small museum of local interest, and a fairly new attraction is the Madame Tussaud's Royalty and Railways Exhibition.

Maidenhead used to be an important stage-post on the London to Bath road and is now a prosperous Thameside residential town. Oldfield House, near the ancient bridge designed by Brunel, contains the Henry Reitlinger Bequest Museum, specialising in glass and ceramics.

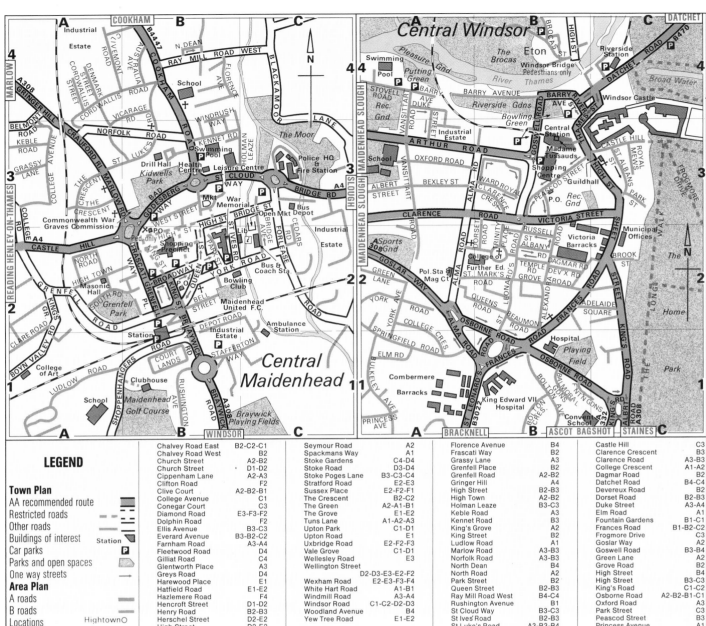

LEGEND

Town Plan

AA recommended route	
Restricted roads	
Other roads	
Buildings of interest	Station
Car parks	P
Parks and open spaces	
One way streets	→

Area Plan

A roads	
B roads	
Locations	HightownO
Urban area	

Street Index with Grid Reference

Slough

Albert Street	C1-D1-E1
Aldin Avenue	E2-F2
Alexandra Road	B1-B2
Alpha Street	D1-E1-E2
Arthur Road	B2
Bath Road	A3-B3-C3
Baylis Road	B4-C4
Beechwood Gardens	C2
Belgrave Road	D4
Benson Close	E4
Bourne Road	A2
Bradley Road	B4-C4
Broadmark Road	F4
Brunel Way	D3
Burlington Avenue	C2-C3
Chalvey Park	C2
Chalvey Road East	B2-C2-C1
Chalvey Road West	B2
Church Street	A2-B2
Church Street	D1-D2
Cippenham Lane	A2-A3
Clifton Road	F2
Clive Court	A2-B2-B1
College Avenue	C1
Conegar Court	C3
Diamond Road	E3-F3-F2
Dolphin Road	F2
Ellis Avenue	B3-C3
Everard Avenue	B3-B2-C2
Farnham Road	A3-A4
Fleetwood Road	D4
Gilliat Road	C4
Glentworth Place	A3
Greys Road	D4
Harewood Place	E1
Hatfield Road	E1-E2
Hazlemere Road	F4
Hencroft Street	D1-D2
Henry Road	B2-B3
Herschel Street	D2-E2
High Street	D2-E2
High Street Chalvey	A2-A1-B1-B2
Hillside	B2
King Edward Street	B2
Kings Road	C1
Ladbroke Road	A1
Landsowne Avenue	C3
Lascelles Road	F1
Ledgers Road	B1-B2-B3
Little Down Road	D4
London Road	F1-F2
Martin Road	B1
Mere Road	D1
Merton Road	E1
Mill Street	D4
Montem Lane	A3-B3-B2
Osborne Street	D1-D2
Park Street	D1-D2
Petersfield Avenue	E4-E3-F3
Pitts Road	A4
Princes Street	F2
Queens Road	D4
Ragstone Road	B1-C1
Richmond Crescent	E3
St John's Road	E4-F4
St Lawrence Way	E1
St Paul's Avenue	D4-E4-F4
Salt Hill Avenue	A3-A4
Salt Hill Drive	A4
Salt Hill Way	A4-B4
Shackleton Road	C4

Seymour Road	A2
Spackmans Way	A1
Stoke Gardens	C4-D4
Stoke Road	D3-D4
Stoke Poges Lane	B3-C3-C4
Stratford Road	E2-E3
Sussex Place	E2-F2-F1
The Crescent	B2-C2
The Green	A2-A1-B1
The Grove	E1-E2
Tuns Lane	A1-A2-A3
Upton Park	C1-D1
Upton Road	E1
Uxbridge Road	E2-F2-F3
Vale Grove	C1-D1
Wellesley Road	E3
Wellington Street	D2-D3-E3-E2-F2
Wexham Road	E2-E3-F3-F4
White Hart Road	A1-B1
Windmill Road	A3-A4
Windsor Road	C1-C2-D2-D3
Woodland Avenue	B4
Yew Tree Road	E1-E2

Maidenhead

Australia Avenue	B4
Bad Godesberg Way	B3
Bell Street	B2
Belmont Road	A3-A4
Blackamoor Lane	C3-C4
Boyn Valley Road	A1-A2
Braywick Road	B1-B2
Bridge Avenue	C2-C3
Bridge Road	C3
Bridge Street	B3-C3
Broadway	B2
Castle Hill	A2
Cedars Road	C2-C3
Clare Road	A1-A2
Clivemont Road	A4-B4
College Avenue	A3
College Road	A2-A3
Cookham Road	B3-B4
Cordwallis Road	A3-A4-B4
Cordwallis Street	A4
Court Lands	B1
Crauford Rise	A3
Denmark Street	A4
Depot Road	B1-B2-C2
Forlease Road	C2-C3

Florence Avenue	B4
Frascati Way	B2
Grassy Lane	A3
Grenfell Place	B2
Grenfell Road	A2-B2
Gringer Hill	A4
High Street	B2-B3
High Town	A2-B2
Holman Leaze	B3-C3
Keble Road	A3
Kennet Road	B3
King's Grove	A2
King Street	B2
Ludlow Road	A1
Marlow Road	A3-B3
Norfolk Road	A3-B3
North Dean	B4
North Road	A2
Park Street	B2
Queen Street	B2-B3
Ray Mill Road West	B4-C4
Rushington Avenue	B1
St Cloud Way	B3-C3
St Ives' Road	B2-B3
St Luke's Road	A3-B3-B4
Shoppenhangers Road	A1-B1
South Road	A2-B2
Stafferton Way	B1-C1
The Crescent	A3
Vicarage Road	A3-A4-B4
West Street	B3
Windrush Way	B3-B4
York Road	B2-C2

Windsor

Adelaide Square	B2-C2
Albany Road	B2
Albert Road	C1
Albert Street	A3
Alexandra Road	B2-B3
Alma Road	B3-A3-A2-A1-B1
Arthur Road	A3-B3
Balmoral Gardens	B1
Barry Avenue	A4-B4
Beaumont Road	B2
Bexley Street	A3
Bolton Avenue	B1
Bolton Crescent	B1
Brocas Street	B4
Brook Street	C2
Bulkeley Avenue	A1

Castle Hill	C3
Clarence Crescent	B3
Clarence Road	A3-B3
College Crescent	A1-A2
Dagmar Road	B2
Datchet Road	B4-C4
Devereux Road	B2
Dorset Road	B2-B3
Duke Street	A3-A4
Elm Road	A1
Fountain Gardens	B1-C1
Frances Road	B1-B2-C2
Frogmore Drive	C3
Goslar Way	A2
Goswell Road	B3-B4
Green Lane	A2
Grove Road	B2
High Street	B4
High Street	B3-C3
King's Road	C1-C2
Osborne Road	A2-B2-B1-C1
Oxford Road	A3
Park Street	C3
Peascod Street	B3
Princess Avenue	A1
Queens Road	A2-B2
River Street	B4
Royal Mews	C3
Russell Street	B2
St Albans Street	C3
St Leonard's Road	A1-B1-B2
St Mark's Road	A2-B2
Sheet Street	C2-C3
Springfield Road	A1-A2
Stovell Road	A4
Temple Road	B2
Thames Street	B3-B4-C4
The Long Walk	C1-C2-C3
Trinity Place	B2-B3
Vansittart Road	A2-A3-A4
Victoria Street	B3-C3
Ward Royal	B3
York Avenue	A1-A2
York Road	A2

SLOUGH
Salt Hill Park in the centre of Slough features a bowling green, tennis courts and a children's play area, as well as pleasant walks through landscaped gardens. This is one of several recreational areas scattered throughout the town.

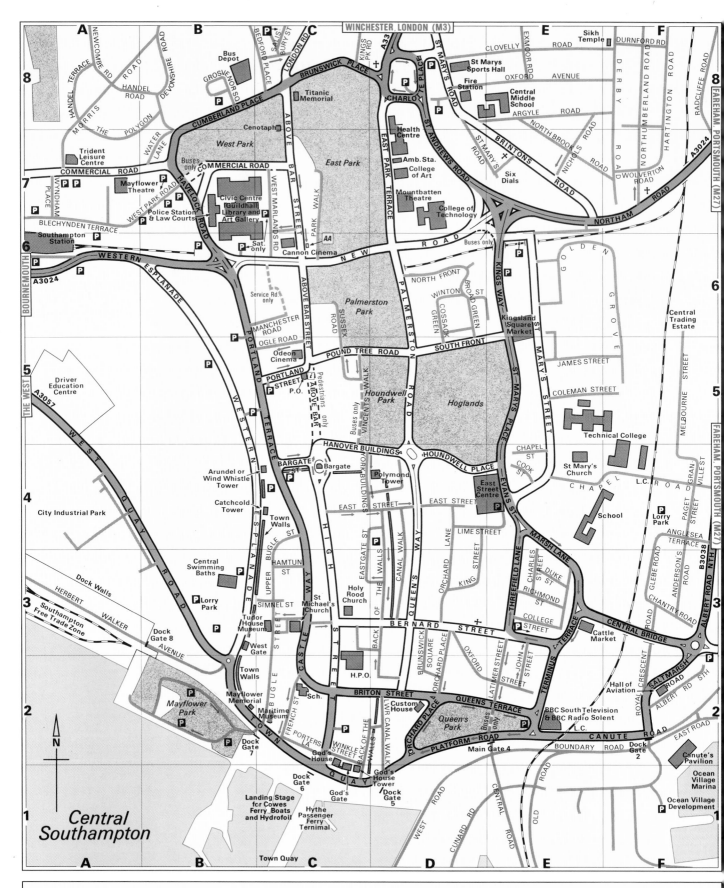

Southampton

In the days of the great ocean-going liners, Southampton was Britain's premier passenger port. Today container traffic is more important, but cruise liners still berth there. A unique double tide caused by the Solent waters, and protection from the open sea by the Isle of Wight, has meant that Southampton has always been a superb and important port. Like many great cities it was devastated by bombing raids during World War II. However, enough survives to make the city a fascinating place to explore. Outstanding are the town walls, which stand to their original height in some places, especially along Western Esplanade. The main landward entrance to the walled town was the Bargate – a superb medieval gateway with a Guildhall (now a museum) on its upper floor. The best place to appreciate old Southampton is in and around St Michael's Square. Here is St Michael's Church, oldest in the city and founded in 1070. Opposite is Tudor House Museum, a lovely gabled building housing much of interest. Down Bugle Street are old houses, with the town walls, pierced by the 13th-century West Gate, away to the right. At the corner of Bugle Street is the Wool House Maritime Museum, contained in a 14th-century warehouse. On the quayside is God's House Tower, part of the town's defences and now an archaeological museum.

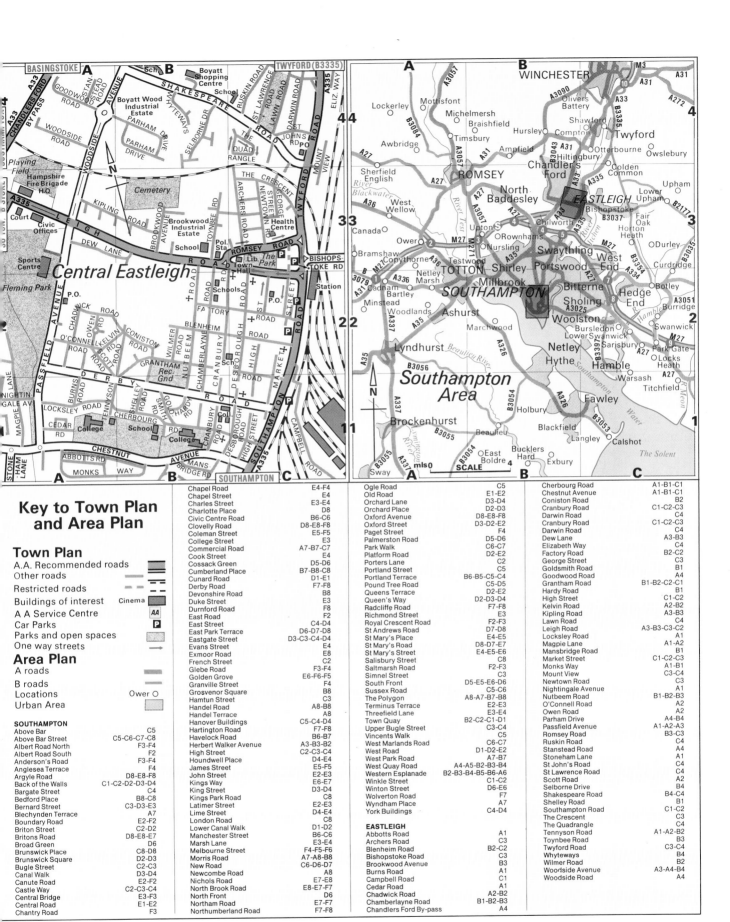

Key to Town Plan and Area Plan

Town Plan

A.A. Recommended roads	
Other roads	
Restricted roads	
Buildings of interest	Cinema
A A Service Centre	AA
Car Parks	P
Parks and open spaces	
One way streets	→

Area Plan

A roads	
B roads	
Locations	Ower ○
Urban Area	

SOUTHAMPTON

Above Bar	C5
Above Bar Street	C5-C6-C7-C8
Albert Road North	F3-F4
Albert Road South	F2
Anderson's Road	F3-F4
Anglesea Terrace	F4
Argyle Road	D8-E8-F8
Back of the Walls	C1-C2-D2-D3-D4
Bargate Street	C4
Bedford Place	B8-C8
Bernard Street	C3-D3-E3
Blechynden Terrace	A7
Boundary Road	E2-F2
Briton Street	C2-D2
Britons Road	D8-E8-E7
Broad Green	D6
Brunswick Place	C8-D8
Brunswick Square	D2-D3
Bugle Street	C2-C3
Canal Walk	D3-D4
Canute Road	E2-F2
Castle Way	C2-C3-C4
Central Bridge	E3-F3
Central Road	E1-E2
Chantry Road	F3

Chapel Road	E4-F4
Chapel Street	E4
Charles Street	E3-E4
Charlotte Place	D8
Civic Centre Road	B6-C6
Clovelly Road	D8-E8-F8
Coleman Street	E5-F5
College Street	E3
Commercial Road	A7-B7-C7
Cook Street	E4
Cossack Green	D5-D6
Cumberland Place	B7-B8-C8
Cunard Road	D1-E1
Derby Road	F7-F8
Devonshire Road	B8
Duke Street	E3
Durnford Road	F8
East Road	C4-D4
East Street	C4-D4
East Park Terrace	D6-D7-D8
Eastgate Street	D3-C3-C4-D4
Evans Street	E4
Exmoor Road	E8
French Street	C2
Glebe Road	F3-F4
Golden Grove	E6-F6-F5
Granville Street	F4
Grosvenor Square	B8
Hamtun Street	C3
Handel Road	A8-B8
Handel Terrace	A8
Hanover Buildings	C5-C4-D4
Hartington Road	F7-F8
Havelock Road	B6-B7
Herbert Walker Avenue	A3-B3-B2
High Street	C2-C3-C4
Houndwell Place	D4-E4
James Street	E5-F5
John Street	E2-E3
Kings Way	E6-E7
King Street	D3-D4
Kings Park Road	C8
Latimer Street	E2-E3
Lime Street	D4-E4
London Road	C8
Lower Canal Walk	D1-D2
Manchester Street	B6-C6
Marsh Lane	E3-E4
Melbourne Street	F4-F5-F6
Morris Road	A7-A8-B8
New Road	C6-D6-D7
Newcombe Road	A8
Nichols Road	E7-E8
North Brook Road	E8-E7-F7
North Front	D6
Northam Road	E7-F7
Northumberland Road	F7-F8

Ogle Road	C5
Old Road	E1-E2
Orchard Lane	D3-D4
Orchard Place	D2-D3
Oxford Avenue	D8-E8-F8
Oxford Street	D3-D2-E2
Paget Street	F4
Palmerston Road	D5-D6
Park Walk	C6-C7
Platform Road	D2-E2
Porters Lane	C2
Portland Street	C5
Portland Terrace	B6-B5-C5-C4
Pound Tree Road	C5-D5
Queens Terrace	D2-E2
Queen's Way	D2-D3-D4
Radcliffe Road	F7-F8
Richmond Street	E3
Royal Crescent Road	F2-F3
St Andrews Road	D7-D8
St Mary's Place	E4-E5
St Mary's Road	D8-D7-E7
St Mary's Street	E4-E5-E6
Salisbury Street	C8
Saltmarsh Road	E2-F3
Simnel Street	C3
South Front	D5-E5-E6-D6
Sussex Road	C5-C6
The Polygon	A8-A7-B7-B8
Terminus Terrace	E2-E3
Threefield Lane	E3-E4
Town Quay	B2-C2-C1-D1
Upper Bugle Street	C3-C4
Vincents Walk	C5
West Marlands Road	D1-D2-E2
West Road	A7-B7
West Park Road	A7-B7
West Quay Road	A4-A5-B2-B3-B4
Western Esplanade	B2-B3-B4-B5-B6-A6
Winkle Street	C1-C2
Winton Street	D6-E6
Wolverton Road	F7
Wyndham Place	A7
York Buildings	C4-D4

EASTLEIGH

Abbotts Road	A1
Archers Road	C3
Blenheim Road	B2-C2
Bishopstoke Road	C3
Brookwood Avenue	B3
Burns Road	A1
Campbell Road	C1
Cedar Road	A1
Chadwick Road	A2-B2
Chamberlayne Road	B1-B2-B3
Chandlers Ford By-pass	A4

Cherbourg Road	A1-B1-C1
Chestnut Avenue	A1-B1-C1
Coniston Road	B2
Cranbury Road	C1-C2-C3
Darwin Road	C4
Cranbury Road	C1-C2-C3
Darwin Road	C4
Dew Lane	A3-B3
Elizabeth Way	C4
Factory Road	B2-C2
George Street	C3
Goldsmith Road	B1
Goodwood Road	A4
Grantham Road	B1-B2-C2-C1
Hardy Road	B1
High Street	C1-C2
Kelvin Road	A2-B2
Kipling Road	A3-B3
Lawn Road	C4
Leigh Road	A3-B3-C3-C2
Locksley Road	A1
Magpie Lane	A1-A2
Mansbridge Road	B1
Market Street	C1-C2-C3
Monks Way	A1-B1
Mount View	C3-C4
Newtown Road	C3
Nightingale Avenue	A1
Nutbeem Road	B1-B2-B3
O'Connell Road	A2
Owen Road	A2
Parham Drive	A4-B4
Passfield Avenue	A1-A2-A3
Romsey Road	B3-C3
Ruskin Road	A4
Stanstead Road	A4
Stoneham Lane	A1
St John's Road	C4
St Lawrence Road	C4
Scott Road	A2
Selborne Drive	B4
Shakespeare Road	B4-C4
Shelley Road	B1
Southampton Road	C1-C2
The Crescent	C3
The Quadrangle	C4
Tennyson Road	A1-A2-B2
Toynbee Road	B3
Twyford Road	C3-C4
Whyteways	B4
Wilmer Road	B2
Woodside Avenue	A3-A4-B4
Woodside Road	A4

SOUTHAMPTON
Although liners still use Southampton's docks which handled all the great ocean-going passenger ships before the age of air travel replaced sea travel, the port is chiefly used by commercial traffic today.

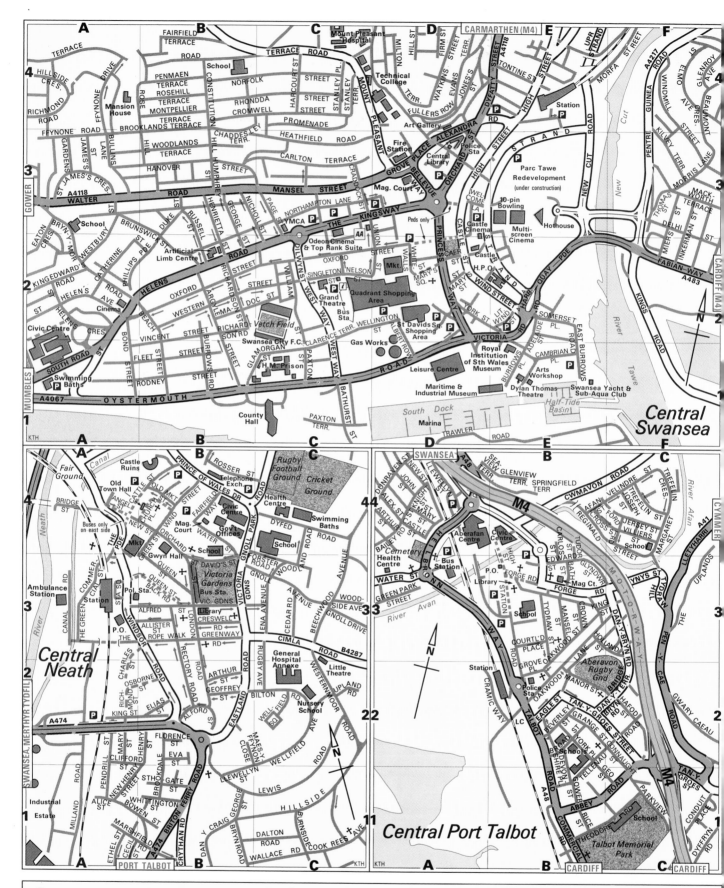

Swansea

Like nearly all the towns in the valleys and along the coast of Glamorgan, Swansea grew at an amazing speed during the Industrial Revolution. Ironworks, non-ferrous metal smelting works and mills and factories of every kind were built to produce the goods which were exported from the city's docks. There had been a settlement here from very early times – the city's name is derived from Sweyn's Ea – Ea means island, and Sweyn was a Viking pirate who had a base here. Heavy industry is still pre-eminent in the area, but commerce is of increasing importance and the university exerts a strong influence. Hundreds of acres of parkland and open space lie in and around the city, and just to the west is the Gower, one of the most beautiful areas of Wales. The history of Swansea is traced in the Maritime, Industrial and Royal Institution of South Wales Museums, while

the Glynn Vivian Art Gallery contains notable paintings and porcelain.

Neath and **Port Talbot** are, like Swansea, dominated by heavy industry. Neath was once a Roman station, and later had a castle and an abbey, ruins of which can still be seen. Port Talbot has been an industrial centre since 1770, when a copper-smelting works was built. Steelworks and petrochemical works stretch for miles around Swansea Bay.

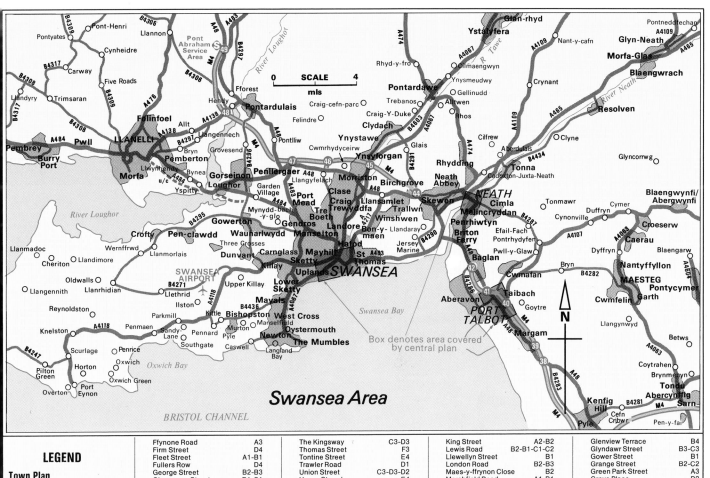

Swansea Area

BRISTOL CHANNEL

LEGEND

Town Plan
- AA Recommended roads
- Other roads
- Restricted roads
- Buildings of interest
- Car parks — P
- Parks and open spaces
- One way streets

Area Plan
- A roads
- B roads
- Locations — Bishopston ○
- Urban area

Street Index with Grid Reference

Swansea

Adelaide Street	E1-E2
Albert Row	D1-D2
Alexandra Road	D3-D4-E4
Argyle Street	B1-B2
Bathurst Street	C1
Beach Street	A2-B2-B1
Beaumont Crescent	F3-F4
Bellevue Way	D3
Bond Street	A1-A2
Brooklands Terrace	A3-B3-B4
Brunswick Street	A3-B3-B2
Bryn-y-mor Road	A2-A3
Bullins Lane	A3
Burrows Place	E1
Burrows Road	B1-B2
Caer Street	D2
Cambrian Place	E1
Carlton Terrace	B3-C3
Castle Street	D2-D3
Catherine Street	A2-B2
Chaddesley Terrace	B3-B4
Clarence Terrace	C1-C2
Constitution Hill	B3-B4
Craddock Street	C3
Cromwell Street	B4-C4
Delhi Street	F2-F3
Dilwyn Street	C2
Duke Street	B2-B3
Dyfatty Street	D4-E4
East Burrows Road	E1-E2
Eaton Crescent	A2-A3
Evans Terrace	D4
Fabian Way	E2-E3-F3-F2
Fairfield Terrace	B4
Ffynone Drive	A3-A4
Ffynone Road	A3
Firm Street	D4
Fleet Street	A1-B1
Fullers Row	D4
George Street	B2-B3
Glamorgan Street	B1-C1
Glenroy Avenue	F4
Grove Place	D3
Hanover Street	A3-B3-C3
Harbour Road	E2
Harcourt Street	C4
Heathfield Road	C3
Henrietta Street	B2-B3
High Street	D3-E3-E4
Hill Street	D4
Hillside Crescent	A4
Humphrey Street	B3
Inkerman Street	F2-F3
Jones's Street	D4
Kilvey Terrace	F3-F4
King Edward's Road	A2
Kings Road	F1-F2
Little Wind Street	E2
Mackworth Terrace	F3
Madoc Street	B2-C2
Mansel Street	B3-C3-D3
Miers Street	F2-F3
Milton Terrace	D4
Montpellier Terrace	B4
Morfa Street	E4-F4
Morris Lane	F3
Mount Pleasant	C4-D4-D3
Nelson Street	C2
New Cut Road	E3-E4
Nicholl Street	B3-C3-C2
Norfolk Street	B4-C4
Northampton Lane	C3-D3
Orchard Street	D3-D4
Oxford Street	A2-B2-C2-D2
Oystermouth Road	A1-B1-C1-D1-D2
Page Street	C3
Paxton Street	C1
Paxton Terrace	C1
Penmaen Terrace	B4
Pentre Guinea Road	F2-F3-F4
Phillips Parade	A2-B2
Princess Way	D2-D3
Promenade	C4
Quay Parade	E2
Rhondda Street	B4-C4
Richardson Road	B2
Richardson Street	B2
Richmond Road	A4
Rodney Street	A1-B1
Rose Hill	A4-B4-B3
Rosehill Terrace	B4
Russell Street	B2-B3
St Elmo Avenue	F4
St Helen's Avenue	A2
St Helens Crescent	A2
St Helens Road	A1-A2-B2-C2
St James's Crescent	A3
St James's Gardens	A3
St Mary's Square	D2
St Mary's Street	D2
Singleton Street	C2
Somerset Place	E2
South Road	A1
Stanley Place	C4
Stanley Terrace	C4
Strand	E2-D2-D3-E3-E4
Terrace Road	A4-B4-C4
The Kingsway	C3-D3
Thomas Street	F3
Tontine Street	E4
Trawler Road	D1
Union Street	C3-D3-D2
Upper Strand	E4
Victoria Road	D2-E2
Vincent Street	A1-B1-B2
Walter Road	A3-B3
Watkins Street	D4
Welcome Lane	D3
Wellington Street	D3
West Way	C1-C2
Westbury Street	A2-A3
Western Street	B2-C2
Whitewalls	D2
William Street	C2
Wind Street	D2-E2
Windmill Terrace	F3-F4
Woodlands Terrace	A3-B3
York Street	D2-E2

Neath

Alford Street	B2
Alfred Street	A3-B3
Alice Street	A1
Allister Street	A3-B3
Angel Street	A4
Arthur Street	B2
Beechwood Avenue	C3-C4
Bilton Road	B2-C2
Bowen Street	A1-B1
Bridge Street	A4
Briton Ferry Road	B1-B2
Brookdale Street	B1-B2
Bryn Road	B1
Burnside	C1
Canal Road	A3-A4
Cattle Street	A4-B4
Cecil Street	A1
Cedar Road	C3
Charles Street	A2-A3-B3
Church Place	A4-B4
Cimla Road	B3-C3-C2
Clifford Street	A2-B2
Commercial Street	A3
Cook Ness Avenue	C1
Creswell Road	B3
Croft Road	A4
Crytham Road	B1
Dalton Road	B1-C1
Dan Y Craig	B1
Dyfed Road	C4
Eastland Road	B2-B3
Elias Street	B2
Ena Avenue	C3
Ethel Street	A1
Eva Street	B2
Fairfield Way	B4
Florence Street	B2
Forster Road	B4-C4-C3
Geoffrey Street	B2
George Street	B1
Gnoll Street	B3-C3
Gnoll Drive	C3
Gnoll Park Road	B4-C4
Green Street	A3-B3-B4
Greenway Road	B3
Henry Street	B2
Hillside	B1-C1-C2

Port Talbot

Abbey Road	B1-C1-C2
Afan Street	B4
Alexander Street	A4
Arthur Street	A4
Bailey Road	A4
Bath Street	B3
Beverley Street	B4
Bridge Terrace	C2
Broad Street	B2
Carlos Street	B3-B4
Castle Street	A4
Commercial Road	B1
Conduit Place	C1
Connaught Street	C1-C2
Courtland Place	B3
Cramic Way	B1-B2
Cross Street	B4-C4
Crown Street	B3
Cwmavon Road	B4-C4
Dan-y-Bryn Road	B2-C2-C3
Devonshire Place	B1-B2
Dunraven Street	A4
Dyffryn Road	C1
Eagle Street	B2
Edward Street	B3
Ford Road	B4-C4
Forge Road	B3
George Street	B2-B1-C1

King Street	A2-B2
Lewis Road	B2-B1-C1-C2
Llewellyn Street	B1
London Road	B2-B3
Maes-y-ffrynon Close	B2
Marshfield Road	A1-B1
Mary Street	A2
Milland Road	A1
New Street	A4-B4
New Henry Street	A1-B1
Old Market Street	B4
Orchard Street	B3-B4
Osborne Street	A2-B2
Pendrill Street	A1-A2
Prince of Wales Drive	B4
Queen Street	B3
Queen Street Back Road	A3-B3
Rectory Road	B2-B3
Richmond Street	A2
Rosser Street	B4-C4
Rugby Avenue	C2-C3
Russell Street	A4-B4
St Davids Street	B3
Southgate Street	B1
Station Square	A3
The Green	A3
The Parade	A4
The Rope Walk	A3-B3
Upland Road	C2
Victoria Gardens	B3
Wallace Road	B1-C1
Water Street	B3-B4
Wellfield Avenue	C1-C2
Wellfield Square	C2
Westernmoor Road	C2-C3
Whittington Street	B1
Windsor Road	A3-B3-B2
Wind Street	B4
Woodland Road	C3-C4
Woodside Avenue	C3

Glenview Terrace	B4
Glyndawr Street	B3-C3
Gower Street	B1
Grange Street	B2-C2
Green Park Street	A3
Grove Place	B2
Gwary Caeau	C2
Hafod Street	C2
Heilbronn Way	A4-A3-B3-B2
High Street	B3-B4
Holland Street	B3-C3
Jersey Street	C4
John Street	A4
Joseph Street	C4
King Street	B3-C3
Lletyharri	C3-C4
Llewellyn Street	A4
Manor Street	B2-C2
Mansel Street	B3
Margaret Street	C4
New Street	A4
Oakwood Lane	B2-B3
Oakwood Street	B2-B3
Parkview	C1
Pen-y-cae Road	C1-C2-C3
Reginald Street	B4-C4-C3
Rice Street	B1
St Mary Street	A4
St Knight Street	A4
Seaview Terrace	A4-B4
Springfield Terrace	A4-B4
Station Road	B2-B3
Talbot Road	B1-B2
Tan-y-groes Street	B2-C2-C1
Tellenau Road	B1-B2-C1
The Uplands	C3-C4
Theodore Road	B1-C1
Trefelin Crescent	C4
Trefelin Street	C4
Tudor Street	B3-B4
Tyndraw Hill	C3
Tyndraw Street	B3
Velindre Street	B4-C4
Villiers Street	C4
Water Street	A3
Ynys Street	C3
York Place	B2

185

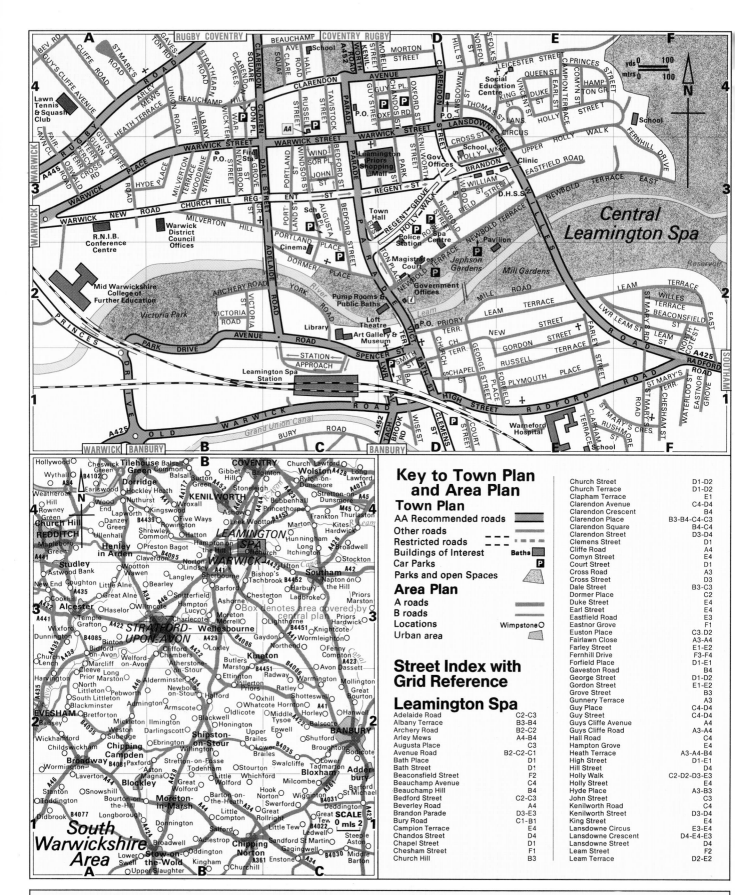

Warwick

The old county town of the shire, Warwick lies in the shadow of its massive, historic castle which occupies the rocky ridge above the River Avon. Thomas Beauchamp and his son built the huge towers and curtain walls in the 14th century, but it was the Jacobean holders of the earldom, the Grevilles, who transformed the medieval stronghold into a nobleman's residence. In 1694, the heart of the town was almost completely destroyed by fire and the few medieval buildings that survived lie on the outskirts of the present 18th-century centre. Of these Oken House, now a doll museum, and Lord Leycester's Hospital, almshouses dating back to the 14th century, are particularly striking.

Stratford-upon-Avon, as the birthplace of William Shakespeare, England's most famous poet and playwright, is second only to London as a tourist attraction. This charming old market town is a living memorial to him; his plays are performed in the Royal Shakespeare Theatre which dominates the river bank, a waxwork museum specialises in scenes from his works, and his childhood home in Henley Street is a museum.

Leamington Spa, an inland spa on the River Leam, gained the prefix 'Royal' after Queen Victoria had visited it in 1838, and the town has been a fashionable health resort ever since.

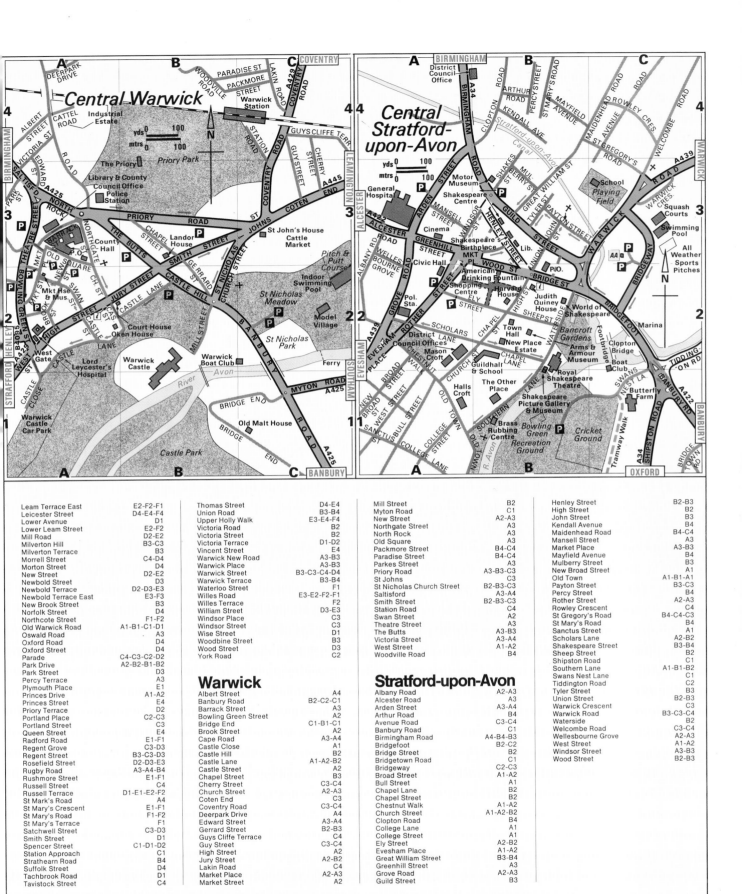

Central Warwick

Central Stratford-upon-Avon

Leam Terrace East	E2-F2-F1
Leicester Street	D4-E4-F4
Lower Avenue	D1
Lower Leam Street	E2-F2
Mill Road	D2-E2
Milverton Hill	B3-C3
Milverton Terrace	B3
Morrell Street	C4-D4
Morton Street	D4
New Street	D2-E2
Newbold Street	D3
Newbold Terrace	D2-D3-E3
Newbold Terrace East	E3-F3
New Brook Street	B3
Norfolk Street	D4
Northcote Street	F1-F2
Old Warwick Road	A1-B1-C1-D1
Oswald Road	A3
Oxford Road	D4
Oxford Street	D4
Parade	C4-C3-C2-D2
Park Drive	A2-B2-B1-B2
Park Street	D3
Percy Terrace	A3
Plymouth Place	E1
Princes Drive	A1-A2
Princes Street	E4
Priory Terrace	D2
Portland Place	C2-C3
Portland Street	C3
Queen Street	E4
Radford Road	E1-F1
Regent Grove	C3-D3
Regent Street	B3-C3-D3
Rosefield Street	D2-D3-E3
Rugby Road	A3-A4-B4
Rushmore Street	E1-F1
Russell Street	C4
Russell Terrace	D1-E1-E2-F2
St Mark's Road	A4
St Mary's Crescent	E1-F1
St Mary's Road	F1-F2
St Mary's Terrace	F1
Satchwell Street	C3-D3
Smith Street	D1
Spencer Street	C1-D1-D2
Station Approach	C1
Strathearn Road	B4
Suffolk Street	D4
Tachbrook Road	D1
Tavistock Street	C4

Thomas Street	D4-E4
Union Road	B3-B4
Upper Holly Walk	E3-E4-F4
Victoria Road	B2
Victoria Street	B2
Victoria Terrace	D1-D2
Vincent Street	E4
Warwick New Road	A3-B3
Warwick Place	A3-B3
Warwick Street	B3-C3-C4-D4
Warwick Terrace	B3-B4
Waterloo Street	F1
Willes Road	E3-E2-F2-F1
Willes Terrace	F2
William Street	D3-E3
Windsor Place	C3
Windsor Street	C3
Wise Street	D1
Woodbine Street	B3
Wood Street	D3
York Road	C2

Warwick

Albert Street	A4
Banbury Road	B2-C2-C1
Barrack Street	A3
Bowling Green Street	A2
Bridge End	C1-B1-C1
Brook Street	A2
Cape Road	A3-A4
Castle Close	A1
Castle Hill	B2
Castle Lane	A1-A2-B2
Castle Street	A2
Chapel Street	B3
Cherry Street	C3-C4
Church Street	A2-A3
Coten End	C3
Coventry Road	C3-C4
Deerpark Drive	A4
Edward Street	A3-A4
Gerrard Street	B2-B3
Guys Cliffe Terrace	C4
Guy Street	C3-C4
High Street	A2
Jury Street	A2-B2
Lakin Road	C4
Market Place	A2-A3
Market Street	A2

Mill Street	B2
Myton Road	C1
New Street	A2-A3
Northgate Street	A3
North Rock	A3
Old Square	A3
Packmore Street	B4-C4
Paradise Street	B4-C4
Parkes Street	A3
Priory Road	A3-B3-C3
St Johns	C3
St Nicholas Church Street	B2-B3-C3
Saltisford	A3-A4
Smith Street	B2-B3-C3
Station Road	C4
Swan Street	A2
Theatre Street	A3
The Butts	A3-B3
Victoria Street	A3-A4
West Street	A1-A2
Woodville Road	B4

Stratford-upon-Avon

Albany Road	A2-A3
Alcester Road	A3
Arden Street	A3-A4
Arthur Road	B4
Avenue Road	C3-C4
Banbury Road	C1
Birmingham Road	A4-B4-B3
Bridgefoot	B2-C2
Bridge Street	B2
Bridgetown Road	C1
Bridgeway	C2-C3
Broad Street	A1-A2
Bull Street	A1
Chapel Lane	B2
Chapel Street	B2
Chestnut Walk	A1-A2
Church Street	A1-A2-B2
Clopton Road	B4
College Lane	A1
College Street	A1
Ely Street	A2-B2
Evesham Place	A1-A2
Great William Street	B3-B4
Greenhill Street	A3
Grove Road	A2-A3
Guild Street	B3

Henley Street	B2-B3
High Street	B2
John Street	B3
Kendall Avenue	B4
Maidenhead Road	B4-C4
Mansell Street	A3
Market Place	A3-B3
Mayfield Avenue	B4
Mulberry Street	B3
New Broad Street	A1
Old Town	A1-B1-A1
Payton Street	B3-C3
Percy Street	B4
Rother Street	A2-A3
Rowley Crescent	C4
St Gregory's Road	B4-C4-C3
St Mary's Road	B4
Sanctus Street	A1
Scholars Lane	A2-B2
Shakespeare Street	B3-B4
Sheep Street	B2
Shipston Road	C1
Southern Lane	A1-B1-B2
Swans Nest Lane	C1
Tiddington Road	C2
Tyler Street	B3
Union Street	B2-B3
Warwick Crescent	C3
Warwick Road	B3-C3-C4
Waterside	B2
Welcombe Road	C3-C4
Wellesbourne Grove	A2-A3
West Street	A1-A2
Windsor Street	A3-B3
Wood Street	B2-B3

WARWICK
These pretty brick and timbered cottages standing in the shadow of the great medieval towers of Warwick Castle are among the few buildings in the town that survived a devastating fire in the late 17th century.

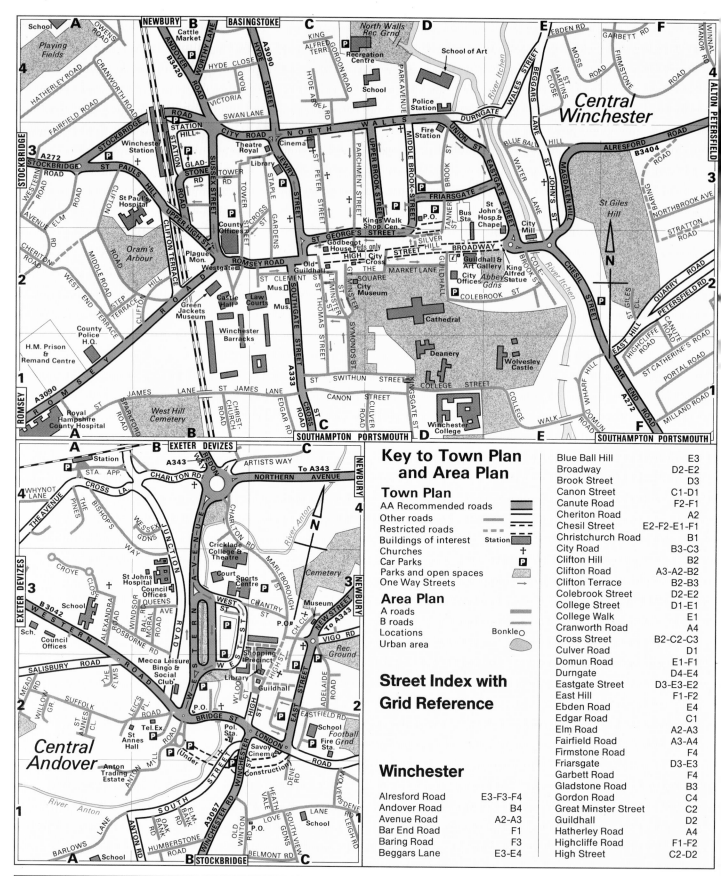

Key to Town Plan and Area Plan

Town Plan

AA Recommended roads	
Other roads	
Restricted roads	
Buildings of interest	Station
Churches	†
Car Parks	P
Parks and open spaces	
One Way Streets	→

Area Plan

A roads	
B roads	
Locations	Bonkle ○
Urban area	

Street Index with Grid Reference

Winchester

Winchester

King Alfred designated Winchester capital of England, a stutus it retained until after the Norman Conquest. Although gradually eclipsed by London, the city maintained close links with the Crown until the reign of Charles II.

Tucked away unobtrusively in the heart of Winchester is the impressive cathedral which encompasses Norman, and all the later Gothic styles of architecture. William of Wykeham was a bishop here in the 14th century and it was he who founded Winchester College, one of the oldest and most famous public schools in England. The buildings lie just outside the peaceful, shady Close where Pilgrims' Hall can be visited. Nearby are the Bishop's Palace and remains of Wolvesley Castle, one of Winchester's two Norman castles. Of the other, only the Great Hall, just outside the Westgate, survives. Here hangs the 14th-century Round Table associated with the legend of King Arthur.

The streets of the city, which cover a remarkably small area, are lined with many charming old buildings of different periods. A walk along the pedestrianised High Street takes you past the former Guildhall – now a bank – and the old Butter Cross, into the Broadway where a statue of King Alfred stands near the River Itchen. A delightful path follows the river alongside the remnants of the old city walls.

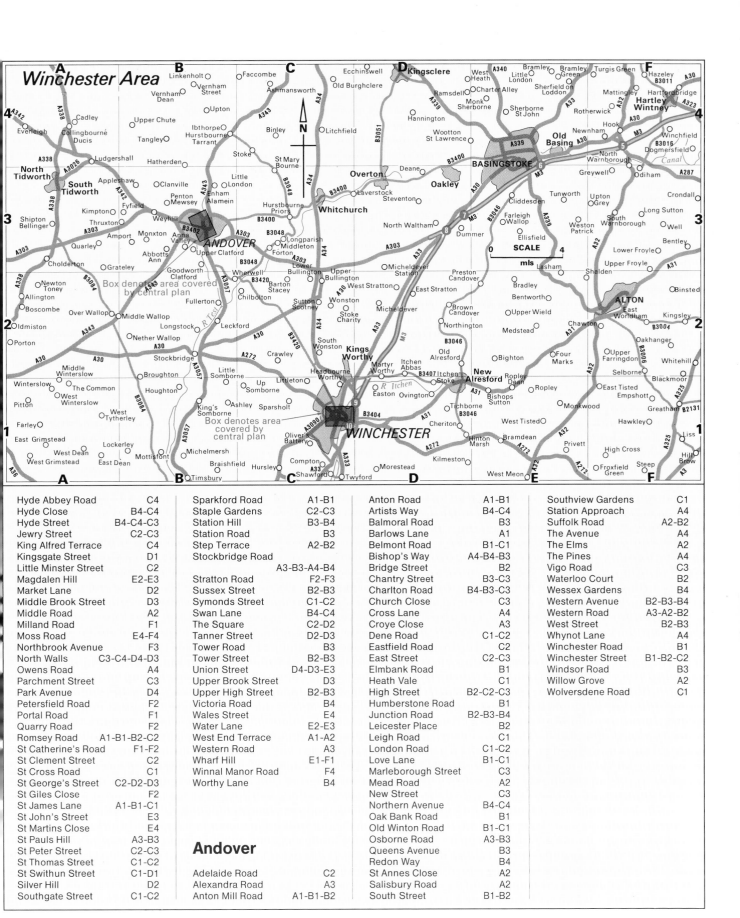

Winchester Area

Hyde Abbey Road	C4
Hyde Close	B4-C4
Hyde Street	B4-C4-C3
Jewry Street	C2-C3
King Alfred Terrace	C4
Kingsgate Street	D1
Little Minster Street	C2
Magdalen Hill	E2-E3
Market Lane	D2
Middle Brook Street	D3
Middle Road	A2
Milland Road	F1
Moss Road	E4-F4
Northbrook Avenue	F3
North Walls	C3-C4-D4-D3
Owens Road	A4
Parchment Street	C3
Park Avenue	D4
Petersfield Road	F2
Portal Road	F1
Quarry Road	F2
Romsey Road	A1-B1-B2-C2
St Catherine's Road	F1-F2
St Clement Street	C2
St Cross Road	C1
St George's Street	C2-D2-D3
St Giles Close	F2
St James Lane	A1-B1-C1
St John's Street	E3
St Martins Close	E4
St Pauls Hill	A3-B3
St Peter Street	C2-C3
St Thomas Street	C1-C2
St Swithun Street	C1-D1
Silver Hill	D2
Southgate Street	C1-C2

Sparkford Road	A1-B1
Staple Gardens	C2-C3
Station Hill	B3-B4
Station Road	B3
Step Terrace	A2-B2
Stockbridge Road	A3-B3-A4-B4
Stratton Road	F2-F3
Sussex Street	B2-B3
Symonds Street	C1-C2
Swan Lane	B4-C4
The Square	C2-D2
Tanner Street	D2-D3
Tower Road	B3
Tower Street	B2-B3
Union Street	D4-D3-E3
Upper Brook Street	D3
Upper High Street	B2-B3
Victoria Road	B4
Wales Street	E4
Water Lane	E2-E3
West End Terrace	A1-A2
Western Road	A3
Wharf Hill	E1-F1
Winnal Manor Road	F4
Worthy Lane	B4

Andover

Adelaide Road	C2
Alexandra Road	A3
Anton Mill Road	A1-B1-B2

Anton Road	A1-B1
Artists Way	B4-C4
Balmoral Road	B3
Barlows Lane	A1
Belmont Road	B1-C1
Bishop's Way	A4-B4-B3
Bridge Street	B2
Chantry Street	B3-C3
Charlton Road	B4-B3-C3
Church Close	C3
Cross Lane	A4
Croye Close	A3
Dene Road	C1-C2
Eastfield Road	C2
East Street	C2-C3
Elmbank Road	B1
Heath Vale	C1
High Street	B2-C2-C3
Humberstone Road	B1
Junction Road	B2-B3-B4
Leicester Place	B2
Leigh Road	C1
London Road	C1-C2
Love Lane	B1-C1
Marleborough Street	C3
Mead Road	A2
New Street	C3
Northern Avenue	B4-C4
Oak Bank Road	B1
Old Winton Road	B1-C1
Osborne Road	A3-B3
Queens Avenue	B3
Redon Way	B4
St Annes Close	A2
Salisbury Road	A2
South Street	B1-B2

Southview Gardens	C1
Station Approach	A4
Suffolk Road	A2-B2
The Avenue	A4
The Elms	A2
The Pines	A4
Vigo Road	C3
Waterloo Court	B2
Wessex Gardens	B4
Western Avenue	B2-B3-B4
Western Road	A3-A2-B2
West Street	B2-B3
Whynot Lane	A4
Winchester Road	B1
Winchester Street	B1-B2-C2
Windsor Road	B3
Willow Grove	A2
Wolversdene Road	C1

WINCHESTER
Standing on the site of the old Hall of Court in the Broadway is the city's Guildhall. Built in 1873, its style was influenced by Northampton Town Hall. It is now a centre for culture and the arts.

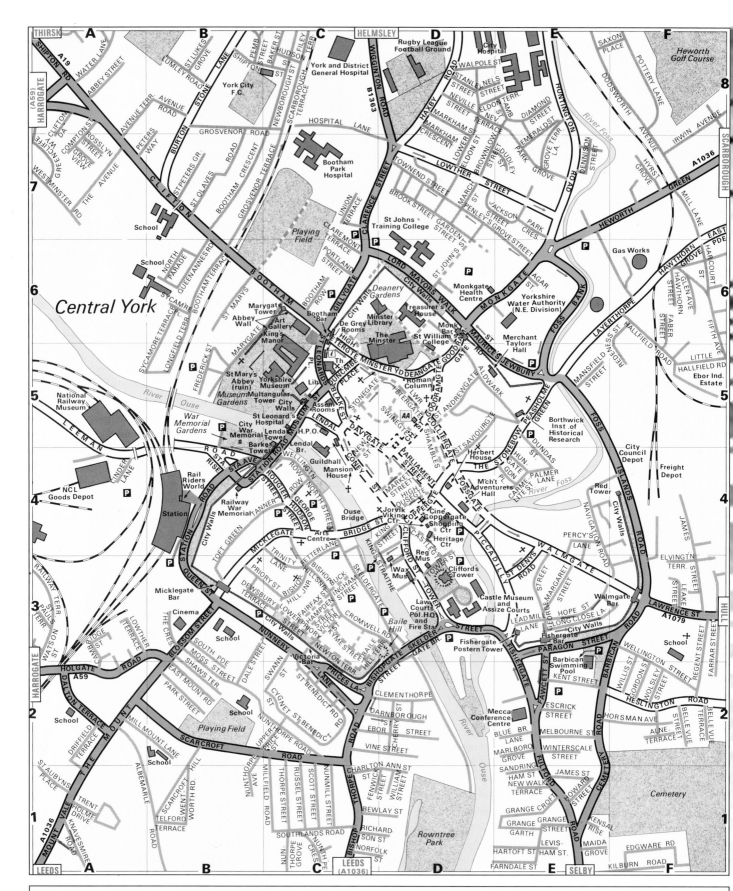

York

York Minster, unquestionably the city's outstanding glory, is considered to be one of the greatest cathedral churches in Europe. It is especially famous for its lovely windows which contain more than half the medieval stained glass in England.

Great medieval walls enclose the historic city centre and their three-mile circuit offers magnificent views of the Minster, York's numerous fine buildings, churches and the River Ouse. The ancient streets consist of a maze of alleys and lanes, some of them so narrow that the overhanging upper storeys of the houses almost touch. The most famous of these picturesque streets is The Shambles, formerly the butchers' quarter of the city, but now colonised by antique and tourist shops. York flourished throughout Tudor, Georgian and Victorian times and handsome buildings from these periods also feature throughout the city.

The Castle Museum gives a fascinating picture of York as it used to be and the Heritage Centre interprets the social and architectural history of the city. Other places of exceptional note in this city of riches include the Merchant Adventurer's Hall; the Treasurer's House, now owned by the National Trust and filled with fine paintings and furniture; the Jorvik Viking Centre, where there is an exciting restoration of the original Viking settlement at York; and the National Railway Museum.

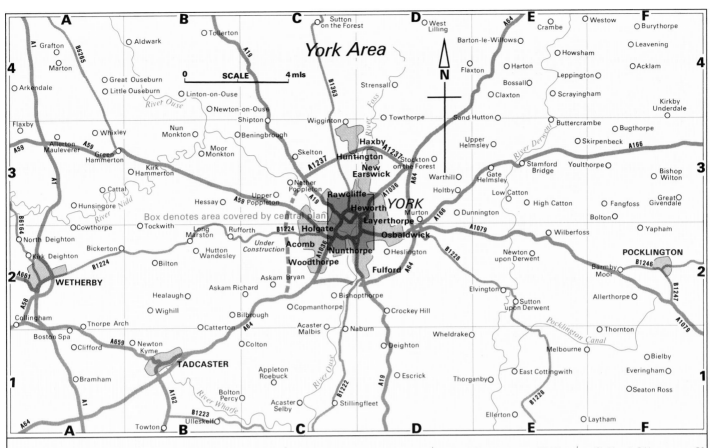

Key to Town Plan and Area Plan

Town Plan

AA Recommended roads
Other roads
Restricted roads
Buildings of interest   Station
Churches
Car Parks
Parks and open spaces
AA Service Centre

Area Plan

A roads
B roads
Locations   Fangfoss
Urban area

Street Index with Grid Reference

York

191

London

Key to Inner London Maps

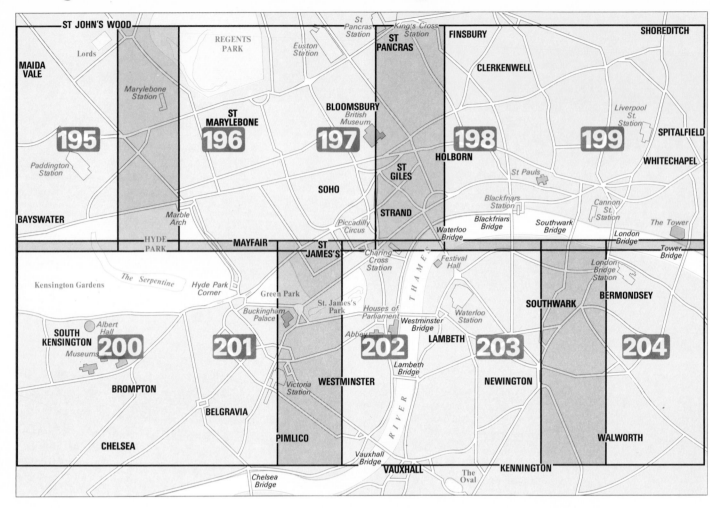

Scale: seven inches to one mile

Map Symbols

Motorway		Hospital	Ⓗ
One-way street		Post office	℗.○
No vehicular access		Church or religious centre	†
Traffic roundabout		Water feature	*Thames*
Banned turn		Park or open space	
Parking	Ⓟ	Place of interest	*Museum*
Garage parking	Ⓖ	AA Service centre	**AA**
British Rail station	*Euston Station*	District name	**STRAND**
London Transport station	*Holborn* ⊖	Overlap extent and number of continuing page	**198**
Police station	℗○ℒ		

OXFORD STREET
Oxford Street, where specially marked, is closed to through traffic (except buses & taxis) 0700 hours-1900 Monday-Saturday

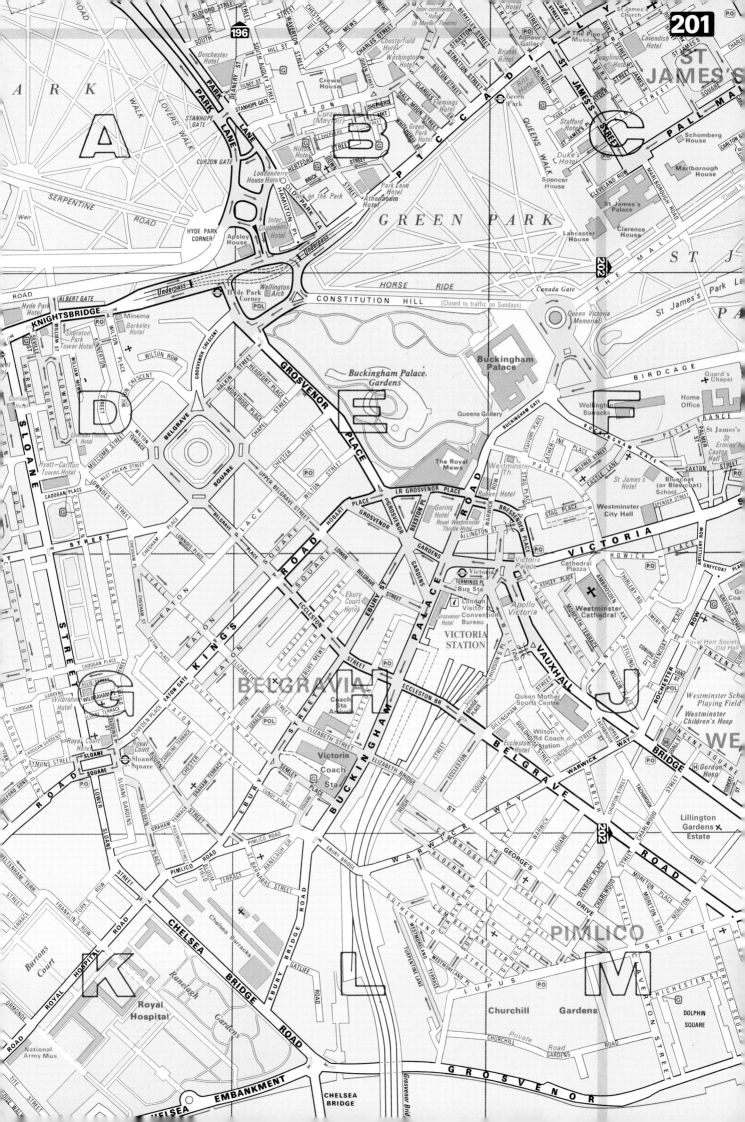

Theatreland

London is the world centre of the performing arts. In addition to the National Theatre and the Royal Shakespeare Company, there are over 40 commercial theatres in the West End. Centring on Shaftesbury Avenue and the Covent Garden area, the map highlights these theatres in red.

Below are the addresses and telephone numbers for the theatres shown. Dial 01 (071 after 6 May 1990) before the telephone number if ringing from outside London.

Theatres

Adelphi, The Strand, WC2 Tel: 836 7611
Albery, St Martin's Lane, WC2 Tel: 867 1115
Aldwych, Aldwych, WC2 Tel: 836 6404
Ambassadors, West Street, WC2 Tel: 836 6111/2
Apollo, Shaftesbury Avenue, W1 Tel: 437 2663

Arts (Theatre Club), Great Newport Street, WC2 Tel: 836 2132
Astoria, Charing Cross Road WC2 Tel: 434 0403
Cambridge, Earlham Street, WC2 Tel: 379 5299
Coliseum, St Martins Lane, WC2 Tel: 836 3161
Comedy, Panton Street, SW1 Tel: 930 2578
Criterion, Piccadilly, W1 Tel: 867 1117
Donmar Warehouse, Earlham Street, WC2 Tel: 240 8230
Duchess, Catherine Street, WC2 Tel: 836 1134
Duke of York's, St Martin's Lane, WC2 Tel: 836 5122
Fortune, Russell Street, WC2 Tel: 836 2238
Garrick, Charing Cross Road, WC2 Tel: 379 6107
Globe, Shaftesbury Avenue, W1 Tel: 437 3667
Her Majesty's, Haymarket, SW1 Tel: 839 2244
Institute of Contemporary Arts, The Mall, SW1 Tel: 930 0493
Lyric, Shaftesbury Avenue, W1 Tel: 437 3686
New London, Parker Street, WC2 Tel: 405 0072
Palace, Shaftesbury Avenue, W1 Tel: 434 0909
Phoenix, Charing Cross Road, WC2 Tel: 836 2294
Players, Villiers Street, WC2 Tel: 839 1134
Playhouse, Northumberland Avenue, WC2 Tel: 839 4401

Prince Edward, Old Compton Street, W1 Tel: 734 8951
Prince of Wales, Coventry Street, W1 Tel: 839 5972
Queen's, Shaftesbury Avenue, W1 Tel: 734 1166
Royal Opera House, Covent Garden, WC2 Tel: 240 1066
Royalty, Portugal Street, WC2 Tel: 831 0660
Savoy, Strand, WC2 Tel: 836 8888
Shaftesbury, Shaftesbury Avenue, WC2 Tel: 379 5399
St Martin's, West Street, WC2 Tel: 836 1443
Strand, Aldwych, WC2 Tel: 836 2660
Theatre Royal (Drury Lane), Catherine Street, WC2 Tel: 836 8108
Theatre Royal, (Haymarket), SW1 Tel: 930 9832
Unicorn, Great Newport Street, WC2 Tel: 836 3334
Vaudeville, Strand, WC2 Tel: 836 9987
Whitehall, Whitehall, SW1 Tel: 867 1119
Wyndham's, Charing Cross Road, WC2 Tel: 867 1116

Scale
0   110   220 yards
0   100   200 metres

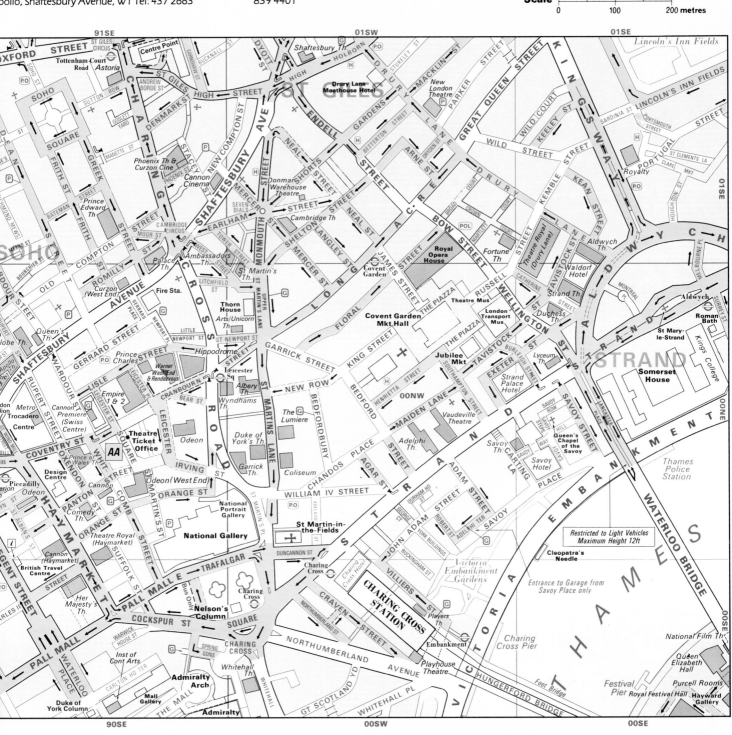

London street index

This map employs an arbitrary system of grid reference. Pages are identified by numbers and divided into twelve squares. Each square contains a blue letter; all references give the page number first, followed by the letter of the square in which a particular street can be found. Reference for Exhibition Road is *200*E, meaning that the relevant map is on page *200* and that the street appears in the square designated E.

Index to atlas

All towns and villages are included in this index.

To locate a place in the atlas, first look up the name of the town or village required in the index. Turn to the page number indicated in **bold** type, and find the location using the last four numbers. Taking Hythe *Kent* .... **15** TR1634 as our example, take the first **bold** figure of the reference, **1**, which refers to the number along the bottom of the page. The second figure, 6, tells you the distance to move in tenths to the right of this numbered line. A vertical line through this point is the first half of the reference. The third, **bold** figure, **3**, refers to the number on the lefthand side of the page. Finally, the fourth figure, 4, indicates the distance to move in tenths above this numbered line. A horizontal line drawn through this point to intersect with the first line gives the precise location of the place in question.

Allbrook Auchmacoy

Allbrook *Hants*	10	SU4521
Allen's Green *Herts*	31	TL4516
Allendale Town *Nthumb*	68	NY8455
Allenheads *Nthumb*	68	NY8645
Allensford *Dur*	68	NZ0749
Allensmore *H & W*	27	SO4635
Allenton *Derbys*	39	SK3732
Aller *Devon*	7	SS7625
Aller *Somset*	8	ST4029
Allerby *Cumb*	58	NY0839
Allercombe *Devon*	7	SY0494
Allerford *Somset*	18	SS9047
Allerston *N York*	63	SE8782
Allerthorpe *Humb*	56	SE7847
Allerton *Mersyd*	46	SJ3987
Allerton *W York*	55	SE1234
Allerton Bywater *W York*	55	SE4127
Allerton Mauleverer *N York*	55	SE4458
Allesley *W Mids*	39	SP2980
Allestree *Derbys*	49	SK3439
Allexton *Leics*	40	SK8100
Allgreave *Ches*	48	SJ9767
Allhallows *Kent*	24	TQ8377
Alligin Shuas *Highld*	91	NG8358
Allington *Dorset*	8	SY4693
Allington *Kent*	14	TQ7557
Allington *Lincs*	50	SK8540
Allington *Wilts*	20	ST8975
Allington *Wilts*	20	SU0663
Allington *Wilts*	10	SU2039
Allithwaite *Cumb*	59	SD3876
Alllen End *Warwks*	38	SP1696
Alloa *Cent*	82	NS8893
Allonby *Cumb*	66	NY0843
Alloway *Strath*	73	NS3318
Allowenshay *Somset*	8	ST3913
Allt Na h'Airbhe (Inn) *Highld*	96	NH1193
Alltchaorunn *Highld*	86	NN1951
Alltmawr *Powys*	26	SO0746
Alltwalis *Dyfed*	17	SN4431
Alltwen *W Glam*	18	SN7303
Alltyblaca *Dyfed*	17	SN5245
Allweston *Dorset*	9	ST6614
Almeley *H & W*	27	SO3351
Almeley Wooton *H & W*	27	SO3352
Almer *Dorset*	9	SY9098
Almholme *S York*	56	SE5808
Almington *Staffs*	37	SJ7034
Alminstone Cross *Devon*	6	SS3420
Almondbank *Tays*	82	NO0625
Almondbury *W York*	55	SE1615
Almondsbury *Avon*	19	ST6083
Alness *Highld*	97	NH6599
Alnham *Nthumb*	68	NT9810
Alnmouth *Nthumb*	69	NU2410
Alnwick *Nthumb*	69	NU1813
Alperton *Gt Lon*	23	TQ1884
Alphamstone *Essex*	24	TL8835
Alpheton *Suffk*	32	TL8850
Alphington *Devon*	5	SX9090
Alport *Derbys*	48	SK2264
Alresford *Essex*	25	TM0721
Alrewas *Staffs*	38	SK1715
Alsager *Ches*	47	SJ7955
Alsagers Bank *Staffs*	47	SJ8048
Alshot *Somset*	19	ST1936
Alsop en le Dale *Derbys*	48	SK1655
Alston *Devon*	8	ST3002
Alston Sutton *Somset*	19	ST4151
Alstone *Gloucs*	28	SO9832
Alstone *Somset*	19	ST3147
Alstone Green *Staffs*	38	SJ8618
Alstonefield *Staffs*	48	SK1355
Alswear *Devon*	7	SS7222
Altandhu *Highld*	98	NB9812
Altarnun *Cnwll*	4	SX2281
Altass *Highld*	96	NC5000
Altcreich *Strath*	79	NM6939
Altgaltraig *Strath*	80	NS0473
Altham *Lancs*	54	SD7733
Althorne *Essex*	24	TQ9199
Althorpe *Humb*	56	SE8309
Altnabreac Station *Highld*	100	ND0045
Altnacealgach Hotel *Highld*	96	NC2810
Altnacraig *Strath*	79	NM8429
Altnaharra *Highld*	99	NC5635
Altofts *W York*	55	SE3723
Alton *Derbys*	49	SK3664
Alton *Hants*	11	SU7139
Alton *Staffs*	48	SK0742
Alton Barnes *Wilts*	20	SU1062
Alton Pancras *Dorset*	9	ST6902
Alton Priors *Wilts*	20	SU1062
Altrincham *Gt Man*	47	SJ7687
Alva *Cent*	82	NS8897
Alvanley *Ches*	46	SJ4974
Alvaston *Derbys*	39	SK3833
Alvechurch *H & W*	38	SP0372
Alvecote *Warwks*	39	SK2404
Alvediston *Wilts*	9	ST9723
Alveley *Shrops*	37	SO7684
Alverdiscott *Devon*	6	SS5225
Alverstoke *Hants*	11	SZ6098
Alverstone *IOW*	11	SZ5785
Alverthorpe *W York*	55	SE3121
Alverton *Notts*	50	SK7942
Alves *Gramp*	93	NJ1362
Alvescot *Oxon*	29	SP2704
Alveston *Avon*	19	ST6387
Alveston *Avon*	19	ST6388
Alveston *Warwks*	29	SP2256
Alvie *Highld*	93	NH8609
Alvingham *Lincs*	51	TF3691
Alvington *Gloucs*	19	SO6000
Alwalton *Cambs*	40	TL1396
Alwinton *Nthumb*	68	NT9106
Alwoodley *W York*	55	SE2840
Alwoodley Gates *W York*	55	SE3141
Alyth *Tays*	88	NO2448
Amberley *Gloucs*	20	SO8401
Amberley *W Susx*	12	TQ0313
Amble *Nthumb*	69	NU2604
Amblecote *W Mids*	38	SO8985
Ambler Thorn *W York*	55	SE0929
Ambleside *Cumb*	59	NY3704
Ambleston *Dyfed*	16	SN0026
Ambrosden *Oxon*	29	SP6019
Amcotts *Humb*	56	SE8514
Amersham *Bucks*	22	SU9597
Amesbury *Wilts*	20	SU1541
Amhuinnsuidhe *W Isls*	102	NB0408
Amisfield Town *D & G*	66	NY0082
Amlwch *Gwynd*	44	SH4492
Ammanford *Dyfed*	17	SN6212
Amotherby *N York*	63	SE7473
Ampleforth *N York*	62	SE5878
Ampney Crucis *Gloucs*	20	SP0602
Ampney St. Mary *Gloucs*	20	SP0802
Ampney St. Peter *Gloucs*	20	SP0801
Amport *Hants*	21	SU2944
Amport *Hants*	21	SU3044
Ampthill *Beds*	30	TL0337
Ampton *Suffk*	32	TL8671
Amroth *Dyfed*	17	SN1608
Amwell *Herts*	31	TL1613
Anaheilt *Highld*	79	NM8162
Ancaster *Lincs*	50	SK9843
Anchor *Shrops*	36	SO1784
Ancroft *Nthumb*	77	NU0045
Ancrum *Border*	76	NT6224
Anderby *Lincs*	51	TF5275
Andersfield *Somset*	8	ST2733
Anderson *Dorset*	9	SY8797
Andover *Hants*	21	SU3645
Andoversford *Gloucs*	28	SP0219
Andreas *IOM*	52	SC4199
Anerley *Gt Lon*	23	TQ3369
Anfield *Mersyd*	46	SJ3692
Angarrack *Cnwll*	2	SW5838
Angelbank *Shrops*	37	SO5776
Angersleigh *Somset*	8	ST1918
Angle *Dyfed*	16	SM8603
Angmering *W Susx*	12	TQ0604
Angram *N York*	55	SE5248
Ankerville *Highld*	97	NH8174
Ankle Hill *Leics*	40	SK7518
Anlaby *Humb*	56	TA0352
Anmer *Norfk*	42	TF7429
Anmore *Hants*	11	SU6711
Anna Valley *Hants*	21	SU3443
Annan *D & G*	67	NY1966
Annat *Highld*	91	NG8954
Annat *Strath*	80	NN0322
Annathill *Strath*	74	NS7270
Annbank *Strath*	73	NS4023
Annelsey Woodhouse *Notts*	49	SK4953
Annesley *Notts*	49	SK5153
Annfield Plain *Dur*	69	NZ1751
Anniesland *Strath*	74	NS5368
Annscroft *Shrops*	36	SJ4508
Ansdell *Lancs*	53	SD3428
Ansford *Somset*	9	ST6432
Ansley *Warwks*	39	SP3091
Anslow *Staffs*	39	SK1924
Anslow Gate *Staffs*	39	SK2125
Anstey *Herts*	31	TL4033
Anstey *Leics*	39	SK5408
Anston *S York*	49	SK5184
Anstruther *Fife*	83	NO5703
Anstruther Easter *Fife*	83	NO5704
Ansty *W Susx*	12	TQ2923
Ansty *Warwks*	39	SP4083
Ansty *Wilts*	9	ST9526
Ansty Cross *Dorset*	9	ST7603
Anthill Common *Hants*	11	SU6412
Anthorn *Cumb*	67	NY1958
Antingham *Norfk*	43	TG2533
Antony *Cnwll*	4	SX3954
Antony *M Glam*	4	SX4054
Antrobus *Ches*	47	SJ6480
Anwick *Lincs*	50	TF1150
Anwoth *D & G*	65	NX5856
Aperfield *Gt Lon*	23	TQ4158
Apes Dale *H & W*	38	SO9973
Apethorpe *Nhants*	40	TL0295
Apley *Lincs*	50	TF1075
Apperknowle *Derbys*	49	SK3878
Apperley *Gloucs*	28	SO8628
Appersett *N York*	60	SD8590
Appin *Strath*	86	NM9346
Appin House *Gramp*	95	NJ9549
Appleby *Humb*	56	SE9414
Appleby Magna *Leics*	39	SK3109
Appleby Parva *Leics*	39	SK3008
Appleby-in-Westmorland *Cumb*	60	NY6820
Applecross *Highld*	91	NG7144
Appledore *Devon*	6	SS4630
Appledore *Devon*	7	ST0614
Appledore *Kent*	14	TQ9529
Appleford *Oxon*	21	SU5293
Applegarth Town *D & G*	67	NY1084
Appleshaw *Hants*	21	SU3048
Appleton *Ches*	46	SJ5186
Appleton *Oxon*	21	SP4401
Appleton Roebuck *N York*	56	SE5542
Appleton Thorn *Ches*	47	SJ6483
Appleton Wiske *N York*	62	NZ3904
Appleton-le-Moors *N York*	63	SE7387
Appleton-le-Street *N York*	63	SE7373
Appletreehall *Border*	76	NT5117
Appletreewick *N York*	55	SE0560
Appley *Somset*	7	ST0721
Appley Bridge *Lancs*	53	SD5209
Apse Heath *IOW*	11	SZ5683
Apsley End *Beds*	30	TL1232
Apuldram *W Susx*	11	SU8403
Arabella *Highld*	97	NH7975
Arbeadie *Gramp*	89	NO6996
Arbirlot *Tays*	83	NO6040
Arboll *Highld*	97	NH8782
Arborfield *Berks*	22	SU7567
Arborfield Cross *Berks*	22	SU7666
Arbory *IOM*	52	SC2470
Arbourthorpe *S York*	49	SK3685
Arbroath *Tays*	89	NO6441
Arbuthnott *Gramp*	89	NO8074
Arcadia *Kent*	14	TQ8736
Archaracle *Highld*	79	NM6767
Archdeacon Newton *Dur*	61	NZ2517
Archiestown *Gramp*	94	NJ2344
Arclid Green *Ches*	47	SJ7962
Ard a'Chapuill *Strath*	80	NS0179
Ardacheranbeg *Strath*	80	NS0085
Ardachu *Highld*	97	NC6603
Ardaily *Strath*	72	NR6450
Ardalanish *Strath*	78	NM3619
Ardanaiseig *Strath*	80	NN0824
Ardaneaskan *Highld*	85	NG8335
Ardarroch *Highld*	85	NG8339
Ardarroch *Strath*	80	NS2394
Ardbeg *Strath*	70	NR4146
Ardbeg *Strath*	72	NS0766
Ardbeg *Strath*	80	NS1583
Ardcharnich *Highld*	96	NH1788
Ardchiavaig *Strath*	78	NM3818
Ardchonnel *Strath*	80	NM9812
Ardchullarie More *Cent*	81	NN5813
Ardchyle *Cent*	81	NN5229
Ardechive *Highld*	86	NN1490
Ardeer *Strath*	73	NS2740
Ardeley *Herts*	31	TL3027
Ardelve *Highld*	85	NG8727
Arden *Strath*	80	NS3684
Ardens Grafton *Warwks*	28	SP1154
Ardentinny *Strath*	80	NS1887
Ardeonaig *Cent*	81	NN6635
Ardersier *Highld*	93	NH7854
Ardessie *Highld*	91	NH0689
Ardfern *Strath*	79	NM8004
Ardgartan *Strath*	80	NN2703
Ardgay *Highld*	97	NH5990
Ardgour *Highld*	86	NN0163
Ardgowan *Strath*	80	NS2073
Ardhallow *Strath*	80	NS1574
Ardhasig *W Isls*	90	NB1303
Ardheslaig *Highld*	91	NG7855
Ardindrean *Highld*	96	NH1588
Ardingly *W Susx*	12	TQ3429
Ardington *Oxon*	21	SU4388
Ardivachar *W Isls*	102	NF7445
Ardlamont House *Strath*	71	NR9865
Ardleigh *Essex*	25	TM0529
Ardleigh Heath *Essex*	25	TM0430
Ardler *Tays*	88	NO2642
Ardley *Oxon*	29	SP5427
Ardley End *Essex*	31	TL5214
Ardlui *Strath*	80	NN3115
Ardlussa *Strath*	71	NR6487
Ardmaddy *Strath*	80	NN0837
Ardmair *Highld*	96	NH1198
Ardmaleish *Strath*	72	NS0768
Ardmay *Strath*	80	NN2802
Ardminish *Strath*	72	NR6448
Ardmolich *Highld*	85	NM7171
Ardmore *Highld*	98	NC2151
Ardmore *Highld*	97	NH7086
Ardmore *Strath*	80	NS3178
Ardnadam *Strath*	80	NS1780
Ardnagrask *Highld*	92	NH5249
Ardnarff *Highld*	85	NG8935
Ardnastang *Highld*	79	NM8061
Ardnave *Strath*	70	NR2873
Ardno *Strath*	80	NN1508
Ardochrig *Strath*	74	NS6346
Ardochy House *Highld*	86	NH3002
Ardpatrick *Strath*	71	NR7660
Ardpeaton *Strath*	80	NS2185
Ardrishaig *Strath*	71	NR8585
Ardroil *W Isls*	102	NB0432
Ardrossan *Strath*	73	NS2342
Ardscalpsie *Strath*	72	NS0558
Ardshealach *Highld*	79	NM6867
Ardsley East *W York*	55	SE3024
Ardslignish *Highld*	79	NM5661
Ardtalnaig *Tays*	81	NN7039
Ardtoe *Highld*	79	NM6270
Ardullie *Highld*	92	NH5862
Ardvaine *Strath*	79	NM7910
Ardvasar *Highld*	84	NG6303
Ardverikie *Highld*	87	NN5087
Ardvorlich *Tays*	81	NN6322
Ardvourlie *W Isls*	90	NB1911
Ardwell *D & G*	64	NX1045
Ardwick *Gt Man*	47	SJ8597
Arford *Hants*	11	SU8236
Argoed *Gwent*	19	SO1700
Argoed *Shrops*	36	SJ3221
Argoed Mill *Powys*	26	SN9962
Argos Hill *E Susx*	13	TQ5628
Aribrauch *W Isls*	102	NB2518
Aridhglas *Strath*	78	NM3123
Arileod *Strath*	78	NM1655
Arinacrinachd *Highld*	91	NG7458
Arinagour *Strath*	78	NM2257
Ariogan *Strath*	79	NM8627
Arisaig *Highld*	85	NM6686
Arisaig House *Highld*	85	NM6984
Arivruach *W Isls*	90	NB2417
Arkendale *N York*	55	SE3861
Arkesden *Essex*	31	TL4834
Arkholme *Lancs*	54	SD5871
Arkleton *D & G*	67	NY3791
Arkley *Gt Lon*	23	TQ2295
Arksey *S York*	56	SE5707
Arksey *S York*	56	SE5807
Arkwright Town *Derbys*	49	SK4270
Arle *Gloucs*	28	SO9223
Arlecdon *Cumb*	58	NY0419
Arleston *Shrops*	37	SJ6610
Arley *Ches*	47	SJ6780
Arley *Warwks*	39	SP2890
Arlingham *Gloucs*	28	SO7010
Arlington *Devon*	6	SS6140
Arlington *E Susx*	13	TQ5407
Arlington Beccott *Devon*	6	SS6240
Armadale *Highld*	99	NC7864
Armadale *Loth*	75	NS9368
Armadale Castle *Highld*	84	NG6304
Armaside *Cumb*	58	NY1527
Armathwaite *Cumb*	67	NY5046
Arminghall *Norfk*	43	TG2504
Armitage *Staffs*	38	SK0816
Armitage Bridge *W York*	55	SE1313
Armley *W York*	55	SE2733
Armston *Nhants*	40	TL0686
Armthorpe *S York*	56	SE6205
Arnabost *Strath*	78	NM2159
Arnburn *Strath*	80	NS3588
Arncliffe *N York*	54	SD9371
Arncroach *Fife*	83	NO5105
Arndilly House *Gramp*	94	NJ2847
Arne *Dorset*	9	SY9788
Arnesby *Leics*	39	SP6192
Arnfield *Derbys*	48	SK0198
Arngask *Tays*	82	NO1411
Arnicle *Strath*	72	NR7138
Arnisdale *Highld*	85	NG8410
Arnish *Highld*	90	NG5948
Arnol *W Isls*	102	NB3148
Arnold *Humb*	57	TA1241
Arnold *Notts*	49	SK5845
Arnprior *Cent*	81	NS6194
Arnside *Cumb*	59	SD4578
Aros Mains *Strath*	79	NM5645
Arotalla *Strath*	70	NR3654
Arrad Foot *Cumb*	58	SD3080
Arram *Humb*	56	TA0344
Arrathorne *N York*	61	SE2093
Arreton *IOW*	11	SZ5386
Arrington *Cambs*	31	TL3250
Arriundle *Highld*	79	NM8264
Arrochar *Strath*	80	NN3004
Arrow *Warwks*	28	SP0856
Arscott *Shrops*	36	SJ4308
Artafallie *Highld*	92	NH6349
Arthington *W York*	55	SE2644
Arthingworth *Nhants*	40	SP7581
Arthrath *Gramp*	95	NJ9636
Artrochie *Gramp*	95	NK0032
Arundel *W Susx*	12	TQ0107
Asby *Cumb*	58	NY0620
Ascog *Strath*	73	NS1062
Ascot *Berks*	22	SU9268
Ascott-under-Whychwood *Oxon*	29	SP3018
Asenby *N York*	62	SE3975
Asfordby *Leics*	40	SK7018
Asfordby Hill *Leics*	40	SK7219
Asgarby *Lincs*	50	TF1145
Asgarby *Lincs*	51	TF3366
Ash *Kent*	14	TQ6064
Ash *Kent*	15	TR2858
Ash *Somset*	8	ST4720
Ash *Surrey*	22	SU8950
Ash Bullayne *Devon*	7	SS7704
Ash Green *Surrey*	22	SU9049
Ash Green *Warwks*	39	SP3385
Ash Magna *Shrops*	37	SJ5739
Ash Mill *Devon*	7	SS7823
Ash Parva *Shrops*	37	SJ5739
Ash Priors *Somset*	8	ST1529
Ash Street *Suffk*	32	TM0146
Ash Thomas *Devon*	7	ST0010
Ash Vale *Surrey*	22	SU8952
Ashampstead *Berks*	21	SU5676
Ashampstead Green *Berks*	21	SU5677
Ashbocking *Suffk*	33	TM1754
Ashbocking Green *Suffk*	33	TM1854
Ashbourne *Derbys*	48	SK1846
Ashbourne Green *Derbys*	48	SK1947
Ashbrittle *Somset*	7	ST0521
Ashburton *Devon*	5	SX7569
Ashbury *Devon*	6	SX5097
Ashby *Humb*	56	SE9008
Ashby Folville *Leics*	40	SK7012
Ashby Magna *Leics*	39	SP5690
Ashby Parva *Leics*	39	SP5288
Ashby Puerorum *Lincs*	51	TF3271
Ashby St. Ledgers *Nhants*	29	SP5768
Ashby St. Mary *Norfk*	43	TG3202
Ashby by Partney *Lincs*	51	TF4266
Ashby cum Fenby *Humb*	51	TA2500
Ashby de la Launde *Lincs*	50	TF0555
Ashby-de-la-Zouch *Leics*	39	SK3516
Ashchurch *Gloucs*	28	SO9233
Ashcombe *Avon*	19	ST3361
Ashcombe *Devon*	5	SX9179
Ashcott *Somset*	19	ST4336
Ashcott Corner *Somset*	19	ST4539
Ashculme *Devon*	8	ST1415
Ashdon *Essex*	31	TL5842
Ashe *Hants*	21	SU5350
Asheldham *Essex*	25	TL9701
Ashen *Essex*	32	TL7442
Ashendon *Bucks*	30	SP7014
Asheridge *Bucks*	22	SP9304
Ashfield *Cent*	81	NN7803
Ashfield *Suffk*	33	TM2162
Ashfield Green *Suffk*	32	TL7656
Ashfield Green *Suffk*	33	TM2673
Ashford *Derbys*	48	SK1969
Ashford *Devon*	5	SX6848
Ashford *Devon*	6	SS5335
Ashford *Kent*	15	TR0142
Ashford *Surrey*	22	TQ0771
Ashford Bowdler *Shrops*	27	SO5170
Ashford Carbonel *Shrops*	27	SO5270
Ashford Hill *Hants*	21	SU5562
Ashgill *Strath*	74	NS7850
Ashill *Devon*	7	ST0811
Ashill *Norfk*	42	TF8804
Ashill *Somset*	8	ST3217
Ashingdon *Essex*	24	TQ8693
Ashington *Nthumb*	69	NZ2787
Ashington *Somset*	8	ST5621
Ashington *W Susx*	12	TQ1315
Ashkirk *Border*	76	NT4722
Ashleworth *Gloucs*	28	SO8125
Ashleworth Quay *Gloucs*	28	SO8125
Ashley *Cambs*	32	TL6961
Ashley *Ches*	47	SJ7784
Ashley *Devon*	7	SS6411
Ashley *Gloucs*	20	ST9394
Ashley *Hants*	10	SU3831
Ashley *Hants*	10	SZ2595
Ashley *Kent*	15	TR3048
Ashley *Nhants*	40	SP7990
Ashley *Staffs*	37	SJ7536
Ashley Green *Bucks*	22	SP9705
Ashmansworth *Hants*	21	SU4157
Ashmansworthy *Devon*	6	SS3317
Ashmore *Dorset*	9	ST9117
Ashmore Green *Berks*	21	SU5069
Ashover *Derbys*	49	SK3463
Ashow *Warwks*	29	SP3170
Ashperton *H & W*	27	SO6441
Ashprington *Devon*	5	SX8157
Ashreigney *Devon*	6	SS6213
Ashtead *Surrey*	23	TQ1858
Ashton *Ches*	46	SJ5069
Ashton *Devon*	5	SX8584
Ashton *H & W*	27	SO5164
Ashton *Hants*	11	SU5519
Ashton *Nhants*	30	SP7649
Ashton *Nhants*	40	TL0588
Ashton *Somset*	19	ST4149
Ashton Common *Wilts*	20	ST8958
Ashton Keynes *Wilts*	20	SU0494
Ashton under Hill *H & W*	28	SO9938
Ashton-under-Lyne *Gt Man*	48	SJ9399
Ashurst *Hants*	10	SU3310
Ashurst *Kent*	13	TQ5138
Ashurst *W Susx*	12	TQ1716
Ashurstwood *W Susx*	13	TQ4136
Ashwater *Devon*	6	SX3895
Ashwell *Herts*	31	TL2639
Ashwell *Leics*	40	SK8613
Ashwell End *Herts*	31	TL2540
Ashwellthorpe *Norfk*	43	TM1497
Ashwick *Somset*	19	ST6447
Ashwicken *Norfk*	42	TF7018
Askam in Furness *Cumb*	58	SD2177
Askern *S York*	56	SE5613
Askerswell *Dorset*	8	SY5292
Askett *Bucks*	22	SP8105
Askham *Cumb*	59	NY5123
Askham *Notts*	50	SK7374
Askham Bryan *N York*	56	SE5548
Askham Richard *N York*	56	SE5347
Asknish *Strath*	71	NR9391
Askrigg *N York*	61	SD9490
Askwith *N York*	55	SE1648
Aslackby *Lincs*	40	TF0830
Aslockton *Notts*	50	SK7440
Asney *Somset*	19	ST4637
Aspatria *Cumb*	58	NY1442
Aspenden *Herts*	31	TL3528
Aspley Guise *Beds*	30	SP9335
Aspley Heath *Beds*	30	SP9334
Aspull *Gt Man*	47	SD6108
Aspull Common *Gt Man*	47	SJ6498
Asselby *Humb*	56	SE7127
Assington *Suffk*	25	TL9338
Assington Green *Suffk*	32	TL7751
Astbury *Ches*	47	SJ8461
Astcote *Nhants*	30	SP6753
Asterby *Lincs*	51	TF2678
Asterley *Shrops*	36	SJ3707
Asterton *Shrops*	36	SO3991
Asterton *Shrops*	36	SO3991
Asthall *Oxon*	29	SP2811
Astle *Highld*	97	NH7391
Astley *H & W*	28	SO7867
Astley *Shrops*	37	SJ5319
Astley *Warwks*	39	SP3189
Astley Abbots *Shrops*	37	SO7196
Astley Bridge *Gt Man*	54	SD7111
Aston *Berks*	22	SU7884
Aston *Ches*	47	SJ6146
Aston *Ches*	47	SJ5578
Aston *Clwyd*	46	SJ3067
Aston *Derbys*	48	SK1883
Aston *H & W*	36	SO4671
Aston *Herts*	31	TL2722
Aston *Oxon*	21	SP3403
Aston *S York*	49	SK4685
Aston *Shrops*	37	SJ5328
Aston *Shrops*	37	SJ6109
Aston *Staffs*	37	SJ7541
Aston *Staffs*	38	SJ9131
Aston Abbotts *Bucks*	30	SP8419
Aston Botterell *Shrops*	37	SO6284
Aston Cantlow *Warwks*	28	SP1360
Aston Clinton *Bucks*	30	SP8812
Aston Crews *H & W*	28	SO6723
Aston End *Herts*	31	TL2724
Aston Eyre *Shrops*	37	SO6594
Aston Fields *H & W*	28	SO9669
Aston Flamville *Leics*	39	SP4692
Aston Heath *Ches*	47	SJ5679
Aston Ingham *H & W*	28	SO6823
Aston Magna *Gloucs*	29	SP1935
Aston Pigott *Shrops*	36	SJ3306
Aston Rogers *Shrops*	36	SJ3406
Aston Rowant *Oxon*	22	SU7299
Aston Somerville *H & W*	28	SP0438
Aston Subedge *Gloucs*	28	SP1341
Aston Tirrold *Oxon*	21	SU5586
Aston Upthorpe *Oxon*	21	SU5586
Aston juxta Mondrum *Ches*	47	SJ6457
Aston le Walls *Nhants*	29	SP4950
Aston on Clun *Shrops*	36	SO3982
Aston-in-Makerfield *Gt Man*	47	SJ5799
Aston-on-Trent *Derbys*	39	SK4129
Astwick *Beds*	31	TL2138
Astwith *Derbys*	49	SK4364
Astwood *Bucks*	30	SP9547
Astwood *H & W*	28	SO9365
Astwood Bank *H & W*	28	SP0462
Aswarby *Lincs*	40	TF0639
Aswardby *Lincs*	51	TF3770
Atch Lench *H & W*	28	SP0350
Atcham *Shrops*	37	SJ5409
Athelhampton *Dorset*	9	SY7694
Athelington *Suffk*	33	TM2171
Athelney *Somset*	8	ST3428
Athelstaneford *Loth*	76	NT5377
Atherington *Devon*	6	SS5923
Atherstone *Somset*	8	ST3816
Atherstone *Warwks*	39	SP3097
Atherstone on Stour *Warwks*	29	SP2050
Atherton *Gt Man*	47	SD6703
Atlow *Derbys*	48	SK2348
Attadale *Highld*	85	NG9238
Attenborough *Notts*	39	SK5134
Atterby *Lincs*	50	SK9893
Attercliffe *S York*	49	SK3788
Atterton *Leics*	39	SP3598
Attleborough *Norfk*	42	TM0495
Attleborough *Warwks*	39	SP3790
Attlebridge *Norfk*	43	TG1317
Attleton Green *Suffk*	32	TL7454
Attonburn *Border*	76	NT8122
Atwick *Humb*	57	TA1850
Atworth *Wilts*	20	ST8565
Aubourn *Lincs*	50	SK9262
Auchachenna *Strath*	80	NN0221
Auchagallon *Strath*	72	NR8934
Auchagoyl *Strath*	71	NR9669
Auchedly *Gramp*	95	NJ8932
Auchenblae *Gramp*	89	NO7278
Auchenbowie *Cent*	81	NS7988
Auchencairn *D & G*	66	NX7951
Auchencairn *D & G*	66	NX9885
Auchencarroch *Strath*	81	NS4182
Auchencastle *D & G*	66	NT0603
Auchencrow *Border*	77	NT8560
Auchendinny *Loth*	75	NT2561
Auchengray *Strath*	75	NS9954
Auchenhalrig *Gramp*	94	NJ3761
Auchenheath *Strath*	74	NS8043
Auchenhessnane *D & G*	66	NX8096
Auchenlochan *Strath*	71	NR9772
Auchenmade *Strath*	73	NS3548
Auchenmalg *D & G*	64	NX2352
Auchentibber *Strath*	74	NS6755
Auchentiber *Strath*	73	NS3647
Auchentroig *Cent*	81	NS5493
Auchindrain *Strath*	80	NN0303
Auchindrean *Highld*	96	NH1980
Auchininna *Gramp*	94	NJ6566
Auchinleck *Strath*	74	NS5521
Auchinloch *Strath*	74	NS6570
Auchinstarry *Strath*	74	NS7176
Auchintore *Highld*	86	NN0972
Auchiries *Gramp*	95	NK0737
Auchlee *Gramp*	89	NO8996
Auchleven *Gramp*	94	NJ6224
Auchlochan *Strath*	74	NS7937
Auchlossan *Gramp*	89	NJ5701
Auchlyne *Cent*	81	NN5029
Auchlyne *Cent*	81	NN5129
Auchmacoy *Gramp*	95	NJ9931

Auchmillan *Strath* 74 NS5129
Auchmithie *Tays* 89 NO6743
Auchmuirbridge *Fife* 82 NO2101
Auchnacraig *Strath* 79 NM7233
Auchnacree *Tays* 89 NO4663
Auchnagarran *Strath* 80 NS0082
Auchnagatt *Gramp* 95 NJ9241
Auchnangoul *Strath* 80 NN0605
Auchronie *Tays* 88 NO4480
Auchtascailt *Highld* 91 NH0987
Auchterarder *Tays* 82 NN9412
Auchteraw *Highld* 92 NH3507
Auchterblair *Highld* 93 NH9222
Auchtercairn *Highld* 91 NG8077
Auchterhouse *Tays* 83 NO3337
Auchterless *Gramp* 95 NJ7141
Auchtermuchty *Fife* 83 NO2311
Auchterneed *Highld* 92 NH4859
Auchtertool *Fife* 82 NT2190
Auchtertyre *Highld* 85 NG8327
Auchton *Cent* 81 NN5520
Auckengill *Highld* 100 ND3664
Auckley *S York* 49 SE6501
Audenshaw *Gt Man* 48 SJ9197
Audlem *Ches* 47 SJ6543
Audley *Staffs* 47 SJ7950
Audley End *Essex* 31 TL5237
Audley End *Essex* 24 TL8037
Audley End *H & W* 32 TL8553
Aughnertree *Cumb* 58 NY2538
Aughton *Humb* 56 SE7038
Aughton *Lancs* 53 SD3950
Aughton *Lancs* 53 SD5467
Aughton *S York* 49 SK4586
Aughton *Wilts* 21 SU2356
Aughton Park *Lancs* 46 SD4006
Auldallan *Tays* 88 NO3158
Auldearn *Highld* 93 NH9155
Aulden *H & W* 27 SO4654
Auldgirth *D & G* 66 NX9186
Auldhame *Loth* 83 NT5984
Auldhouse *Strath* 74 NS6250
Ault Hucknall *Derbys* 49 SK4665
Ault-a-Chruinn *Highld* 85 NG9420
Aultbea *Highld* 91 NG8789
Aultgrishan *Highld* 91 NG7485
Aultguish Inn *Highld* 92 NH3570
Aultiphurst *Highld* 99 NC8065
Aultmore *Gramp* 94 NJ4053
Aultnagoire *Highld* 92 NH5423
Aultnamain Inn *Highld* 97 NH6681
Aunsby *Lincs* 40 TF0438
Aust *Avon* 19 ST5789
Austerfield *Notts* 49 SK6594
Austonley *W York* 48 SE1207
Austrey *Warwks* 39 SK2906
Austwick *N York* 54 SD7668
Authorpe *Lincs* 51 TF3980
Avebury *Wilts* 20 SU1069
Aveley *Essex* 24 TQ5680
Avening *Gloucs* 20 ST8897
Averham *Notts* 50 SK7854
Aveton Gifford *Devon* 5 SX6947
Aviemore *Highld* 93 NH8913
Avinagillan *Strath* 71 NR8367
Avington *Berks* 21 SU3767
Avoch *Highld* 93 NH6955
Avon *Dorset* 10 SZ1498
Avon Dassett *Warwks* 29 SP4150
Avonbridge *Cent* 75 NS9172
Avonmouth *H & W* 19 ST5177
Avonmouth *Avon* 19 ST5278
Avonwick *Devon* 5 SX7158
Awkley *Avon* 19 ST5885
Awliscombe *Devon* 8 ST1301
Awre *Gloucs* 28 SO7008
Awsworth *Notts* 49 SK4844
Axbridge *Somset* 19 ST4354
Axford *Hants* 21 SU6043
Axford *Wilts* 21 SU2370
Axminster *Devon* 8 SY2998
Axmouth *Devon* 8 SY2591
Aycliffe *Dur* 61 NZ2822
Aylburton *Gloucs* 19 SO6101
Aylesbeare *Devon* 5 SY0391
Aylesbury *Bucks* 30 SP8214
Aylesby *Humb* 57 TA2007
Aylesford *Kent* 14 TQ7359
Aylesham *Kent* 15 TR2352
Aylestone *Leics* 39 SK5700
Aylestone Park *Leics* 39 SK5801
Aylmerton *Norfk* 43 TG1839
Aylsham *Norfk* 43 TG1926
Aylton *H & W* 27 SO6537
Aylworth *Gloucs* 28 SP1021
Aymestrey *H & W* 27 SO4265
Aynho *Nhants* 29 SP5133
Ayot Green *Herts* 31 TL2214
Ayot St. Lawrence *Herts* 31 TL1916
Ayot St. Peter *Herts* 31 TL2115
Ayr *Strath* 73 NS3321
Aysgarth *N York* 61 SE0088
Ayshford *Devon* 7 ST0415
Ayside *Cumb* 59 SD3983
Ayston *Leics* 40 SK8601
Aythorpe Roding *Essex* 24 TL5815
Ayton *Border* 77 NT9261
Azrley *N York* 61 SE2574

B

Babbacombe *Devon* 5 SX9265
Babbinswood *Shrops* 36 SJ3330
Babbs Green *Herts* 31 TL3916
Babcary *Somset* 8 ST5628
Babel Green *Suffk* 32 TL7348
Babeny *Devon* 5 SX6774
Babraham *Cambs* 31 TL5150
Babworth *Notts* 49 SK6880
Bache *Shrops* 37 SO4782
Bachelor Bump *E Susx* 14 TQ8312
Back of Keppoch *Highld* 85 NM6587
Backaland *Ork* 103 HY6530
Backfolds *Gramp* 95 NK0252
Backford *Ches* 46 SJ4071
Backhill of Trustach *Gramp* 89 NO6397
Backies *Highld* 97 NC8302
Backlass *Highld* 100 ND2053
Backwell *Avon* 19 ST4968
Bacon End *Essex* 24 TL6018
Bacon's End *W Mids* 38 SP1887
Baconsthorpe *Norfk* 43 TG1237
Bacton *H & W* 27 SO3732
Bacton *Norfk* 43 TG3433
Bacton *Suffk* 32 TM0567
Bachau *Highld* 91 NG7673
Badavanich *Highld* 91 NH1058
Badbury *Wilts* 21 SU1980
Badby *Nhants* 29 SP5559
Badcall *Highld* 98 NC1541
Badcall *Highld* 98 NC2455
Badcaul *Highld* 91 NH0291
Baddesley Clinton *Warwks* 39 SP2071
Baddesley Ensor *Warwks* 39 SP2798
Baddidarach *Highld* 98 NC0822
Badenscallie *Highld* 91 NC0306
Badenscoth *Gramp* 95 NJ7038
Badenyon *Gramp* 94 NJ3319
Badgall *Cnwll* 4 SX2388
Badger *Shrops* 37 SO7699
Badgeworth *Gloucs* 28 SO9019
Badgworth *Somset* 19 ST3952
Badicaul *Highld* 85 NG7528
Badingham *Suffk* 33 TM3068
Badlesmere *Kent* 15 TR0153
Badlieu *Border* 75 NT0518
Badluachrach *Highld* 91 NG9894
Badninish *Highld* 97 NH7594
Badrallach *Highld* 91 NH0691
Badsey *H & W* 28 SP0743

Badshot Lea *Surrey* 22 SU8648
Badsworth *W York* 55 SE4614
Badwell Ash *Suffk* 32 TL9969
Bag Enderby *Lincs* 51 TF3573
Bagber *Dorset* 9 ST7513
Bagby *N York* 62 SE4680
Bagendon *Gloucs* 28 SP0006
Baggrow *Cumb* 58 NY1742
Bagginton *Warwks* 39 SP3474
Baglan *W Glam* 18 SS7492
Bagley *Shrops* 36 SJ4027
Bagley *Somset* 19 ST4545
Bagmore *Hants* 22 SU6642
Bagnall *Staffs* 48 SJ9250
Bagot *Shrops* 37 SO5973
Bagshot *Surrey* 22 SU9063
Bagshot *Wilts* 21 SU3165
Bagstone *Avon* 20 ST6987
Bagthorpe *Notts* 49 SK4751
Bagworth *Leics* 39 SK4408
Bagwy Llydiart *H & W* 27 SO4426
Baildon *W York* 55 SE1539
Baildon Green *W York* 55 SE1439
Baile Boidheach *Strath* 71 NR7473
Baileyhead *Cumb* 67 NY5181
Baillieston *Strath* 74 NS6763
Bainbridge *N York* 61 SD9390
Bainshole *Gramp* 94 NJ6035
Bainton *Cambs* 40 TF0906
Bainton *Humb* 56 SE9652
Baintown *Fife* 83 NO3503
Bairnkine *Border* 76 NT6515
Bakewell *Derbys* 48 SK2168
Bala *Gwynd* 45 SH9236
Balallan *W Isls* 102 NB2720
Balavil *Highld* 87 NH7902
Balbeg *Highld* 92 NH4431
Balbeggie *Tays* 82 NO1629
Balblair *Highld* 92 NH5145
Balblair *Highld* 93 NH7066
Balby *S York* 49 SE5600
Balchladich *Highld* 98 NC0330
Balchraggan *Highld* 92 NH5343
Balchrick *Highld* 98 NC1959
Balcombe *W Susx* 12 TQ3130
Balcombe Links *Fife* 83 NO6209
Balcurvie *Fife* 83 NO3401
Baldersby *N York* 62 SE3578
Baldersby St. James *N York* 62 SE3676
Balderstone *Lancs* 54 SD6332
Balderton *Leics* 50 SK8151
Baldinnie *Fife* 83 NO4211
Baldinnies *Tays* 82 NO0217
Baldock *Herts* 31 TL2434
Baldovie *Tays* 83 NO4533
Baldshaw *E Susx* 14 TQ8013
Baldwin's Gate *Staffs* 37 SJ7940
Bale *Norfk* 42 TG0136
Baledgarno *Tays* 82 NO2730
Balemartine *Strath* 78 NL9841
Balerno *Loth* 75 NT1666
Balfarg *Fife* 83 NO2803
Balfield *Tays* 89 NO5468
Balfour *Ork* 103 HY4716
Balfron *Cent* 81 NS5488
Balgaveny *W Isls* 102 NF7647
Balgavies *Tays* 89 NO5451
Balgedie *Tays* 82 NO1604
Balgonar *Fife* 82 NT0293
Balgowan *Highld* 87 NN6494
Balgowan *D & G* 64 NX1142
Balgown *Highld* 90 NG3868
Balgracie *D & G* 64 NW9761
Balgray *Tays* 83 NO4038
Balhalgardy *Gramp* 95 NJ7623
Balham *Gt Lon* 23 TQ2873
Balhary *Tays* 88 NO2646
Balholmie *Tays* 88 NO1436
Baligill *Highld* 99 NC8565
Balintore *Highld* 97 NH8675
Balintore *Tays* 88 NO2859
Balintraid *Highld* 93 NH7370
Balivanich *W Isls* 102 NF7755
Balk *N York* 62 SE4781
Balkeerie *Tays* 88 NO3344
Balkholme *Humb* 56 SE7828
Balkissock *Strath* 64 NX1482
Ball Haye Green *Staffs* 48 SJ9857
Ball Hill *Hants* 21 SU4263
Ballabeg *IOM* 52 SC2470
Ballacannell *IOM* 52 SC4382
Ballacarnane Beg *IOM* 52 SC3088
Ballachgair *Strath* 72 NR7727
Ballajora *IOM* 52 SC4790
Ballantrae *Strath* 64 NX0882
Ballasalla *IOM* 52 SC2870
Ballasalla *IOM* 52 SC3497
Ballater *Gramp* 88 NO3795
Ballaugh *IOM* 52 SC3493
Ballchraggan *Highld* 97 NH7675
Ballechin *Tays* 87 NN9353
Ballencrieff *Loth* 83 NT4878
Ballevullin *Strath* 78 NL9546
Ballidon *Derbys* 48 SK2054
Balliekine *Strath* 72 NR8739
Balliemore *Strath* 80 NS1099
Balliemore *Strath* 52 NS2882
Ballimore *Cent* 80 NN5317
Ballimore *Strath* 71 NR9283
Ballinaby *Strath* 70 NR2267
Ballindalloch *Gramp* 94 NJ1636
Ballindean *Tays* 83 NO2529
Ballingdon *Essex* 32 TL8640
Ballingham *H & W* 27 SO5731
Ballingry *Fife* 82 NT1797
Ballinluig *Tays* 88 NN9752
Ballinshoe *Tays* 88 NO4153
Ballintuim *Tays* 88 NO1055
Balloch *Highld* 93 NH7246
Balloch *Strath* 64 NX3295
Balloch *Tays* 82 NN8419
Ballochroy *Strath* 71 NR7352
Ballogie *Gramp* 89 NO5795
Balls Cross *W Susx* 12 SU9826
Balls Green *E Susx* 12 TQ4936
Ballygown *Strath* 79 NM4343
Ballygrant *Strath* 70 NR3966
Ballygroggan *Strath* 72 NR6219
Ballyhaugh *Strath* 78 NM1758
Ballymenoch *Strath* 80 NS3086
Ballymichael *Strath* 72 NR9231
Balmacara *Highld* 85 NG8028
Balmaclellan *D & G* 65 NX6579
Balmacneil *Tays* 88 NN9750
Balmae *D & G* 65 NX6845
Balmalcolm *Fife* 83 NO3208
Balmedie *Gramp* 95 NJ9618
Balmerino *Fife* 83 NO3524
Balmore *Strath* 74 NS5973
Balmuchy *Highld* 97 NH8878
Balmuir *Tays* 89 NO5648
Balmule *Fife* 82 NT2088
Balmullo *Fife* 83 NO4320
Balnaboth *Tays* 88 NO3166
Balnacoil Lodge *Highld* 97 NC8011
Balnacra *Highld* 91 NG9746
Balnacroft *Gramp* 88 NO2894
Balnafoich *Highld* 93 NH6835
Balnaguard *Tays* 87 NN9451
Balnahard *Strath* 70 NR4199
Balnain *Highld* 92 NH4430
Balnakeil *Highld* 98 NC3968
Balnapaling *Highld* 93 NH7969
Balnespick *Highld* 93 NH8103
Balquhidder *Cent* 81 NN5320
Balruddery House *Tays* 83 NO3132
Balsall Common *W Mids* 39 SP2376
Balsall Common *W Mids* 39 SP2477
Balsall Heath *W Mids* 38 SP0784
Balscote *Oxon* 29 SP3941
Balsham *Cambs* 31 TL5850
Baltasound *Shet* 103 HP6208

Balterley *Staffs* 47 SJ7550
Baltersan *D & G* 64 NX4261
Balthangie *Gramp* 95 NJ8351
Baltonsborough *Somset* 8 ST5434
Balvarran *Tays* 86 NO0761
Balvicar *Strath* 79 NM7616
Balvraid *Highld* 85 NG8416
Balvraid *Highld* 93 NH8231
Bamber Bridge *Lancs* 53 SD5625
Bamber's Green *Essex* 24 TL5722
Bamburgh *Nthumb* 77 NU1735
Bamff *Tays* 88 NO2251
Bamford *Derbys* 48 SK2083
Bampton *Cumb* 59 NY5118
Bampton *Devon* 7 SS9522
Bampton *Oxon* 21 SP3103
Bampton Grange *Cumb* 59 NY5218
Banavie *Highld* 86 NN1177
Banbury *Oxon* 29 SP4540
Banc-y-ffordd *Dyfed* 17 SN4137
Bancffosfelen *Dyfed* 17 SN4811
Banchory *Gramp* 89 NO6995
Banchory-Devenick *Gramp* 89 NJ9101
Bancycapel *Dyfed* 17 SN4315
Bancyfelin *Dyfed* 17 SN3218
Bandirran *Tays* 82 NO2030
Bandrake Head *Cumb* 67 NY3187
Banff *Gramp* 95 NJ6864
Bangor *Gwynd* 44 SH5872
Bangor *Gwynd* 44 SH5872
Bangor-is-y-coed *Clwyd* 46 SJ3945
Bangors *Cnwll* 6 SX2099
Bangrove *Suffk* 32 TL9463
Banham *Norfk* 32 TM0688
Bank *Hants* 10 SU2807
Bank *Hants* 10 SU2807
Bank Ground *Cumb* 67 NY3196
Bankend *D & G* 66 NY0268
Bankend *Strath* 74 NS8033
Bankfoot *Tays* 82 NO0635
Bankglen *Strath* 66 NS5912
Bankhead *Gramp* 95 NJ8910
Bankhead *Strath* 74 NS3739
Banknock *Cent* 81 NS7779
Banks *Lancs* 53 SD3820
Bankshill *D & G* 67 NY1982
Banningham *Norfk* 43 TG2129
Bannister Green *Essex* 24 TL6921
Bannockburn *Cent* 82 NS8190
Banstead *Surrey* 23 TQ2559
Bantham *Devon* 5 SX6643
Banton *Strath* 81 NS7480
Banwell *Avon* 19 ST3959
Bapchild *Kent* 14 TQ9263
Bapton *Wilts* 20 ST9938
Bar Hill *Cambs* 31 TL3863
Barassie *Strath* 73 NS3232
Barbaraville *Highld* 93 NH7472
Barber Green *Cumb* 67 NY3982
Barbey *D & G* 66 NX8569
Barbieston *Strath* 73 NS4317
Barbon *Cumb* 60 SD6282
Barbreck House *Strath* 79 NM8206
Barby *Warwks* 29 SP5470
Barcaldine *Strath* 86 NM9641
Barcheston *Warwks* 29 SP2639
Barcombe *E Susx* 13 TQ4214
Barcombe Cross *E Susx* 13 TQ4215
Barden *N York* 61 SE1493
Barden Park *Kent* 13 TQ5746
Bardfield End Green *Essex* 24 TL6231
Bardfield Saling *Essex* 24 TL6826
Bardney *Lincs* 50 TF1169
Bardon *Leics* 39 SK4412
Bardowie *Strath* 74 NS5873
Bardsea *Cumb* 59 SD2974
Bardsey *W York* 55 SE3643
Bardwell *Suffk* 32 TL9473
Bare *Lancs* 53 SD4464
Barfad *D & G* 64 NX3266
Barford *Norfk* 43 TG1107
Barford *Warwks* 29 SP2760
Barford St. John *Oxon* 29 SP4332
Barford St. Martin *Wilts* 10 SU0531
Barford St. Michael *Oxon* 29 SP4332
Barfreston *Kent* 15 TR2650
Bargate *Derbys* 49 SK3646
Bargeddie *Strath* 74 NS6865
Bargoed *M Glam* 18 ST1599
Bargrennan *D & G* 64 NX3577
Barham *Cambs* 30 TL1375
Barham *Suffk* 33 TM1451
Barholm *Lincs* 40 TF0810
Barkby *Leics* 39 SK6309
Barkby Thorpe *Leics* 39 SK6309
Barkestone-le-Vale *Leics* 40 SK7734
Barkham *Berks* 22 SU7766
Barking *Gt Lon* 23 TQ4484
Barking *Suffk* 32 TM0753
Barking Tye *Suffk* 32 TM0652
Barkingside *Gt Lon* 23 TQ4489
Barkisland *W York* 55 SE0719
Barkla Shop *Cnwll* 2 SW7350
Barkston *Lincs* 50 SK9341
Barkston *N York* 55 SE4936
Barkway *Herts* 31 TL3835
Barlaston *Staffs* 48 SJ8938
Barlavington *W Susx* 12 SU9716
Barlborough *Derbys* 49 SK4777
Barlby *N York* 56 SE6334
Barlestone *Leics* 39 SK4205
Barley *Herts* 31 TL4038
Barley *Lancs* 54 SD8240
Barley Hole *S York* 49 SK3696
Barleycroft *Herts* 31 TL4327
Barleythorpe *Leics* 40 SK8309
Barlings *Lincs* 50 TF0774
Barlow *Derbys* 49 SK3474
Barlow *N York* 56 SE6428
Barlow *T & W* 69 NZ1561
Barmby Moor *Humb* 56 SE7748
Barmer *Norfk* 42 TF8133
Barmollack *Strath* 72 NR8144
Barmouth *Gwynd* 44 SH6115
Barmpton *Dur* 62 NZ3118
Barmston *Humb* 57 TA1659
Barnabber *Strath* 80 NS1788
Barnacarry *Strath* 80 NS0093
Barnack *Cambs* 40 TF0705
Barnaline *Strath* 80 NM8613
Barnard Castle *Dur* 61 NZ0516
Barnard Gate *Oxon* 29 SP4010
Barnardiston *Suffk* 32 TL7148
Barnburgh *S York* 55 SE4803
Barnby *Suffk* 33 TM4789
Barnby Dun *S York* 55 SE6109
Barnby Moor *Notts* 49 SK6684
Barnby in the Willows *Notts* 50 SK8552
Barnes *Gt Lon* 23 TQ2276
Barnes Street *Kent* 13 TQ6447
Barnet *Gt Lon* 23 TQ2496
Barnetby le Wold *Humb* 56 TA0509
Barney *Norfk* 42 TF9932
Barnham *Suffk* 32 TL8779
Barnham Broom *Norfk* 43 TG0807
Barnhead *Tays* 89 NO6657
Barnhill *Ches* 46 SJ4854
Barnhill *Gramp* 93 NJ1457
Barnhill *Tays* 83 NO4731
Barnhills *D & G* 64 NW9871
Barningham *Dur* 61 NZ0810
Barningham *Suffk* 32 TL9876

Barnwell All Saints *Nhants* 40 TL0584
Barnwell St. Andrew *Nhants* 40 TL0585
Barnwood *Gloucs* 28 SO8518
Barons Wood *Devon* 7 SS6903
Barr *Strath* 64 NX2794
Barrahormid *Strath* 71 NR7183
Barrapoll *Strath* 78 NL9432
Barrasford *Nthumb* 68 NY9173
Barravullin *Strath* 79 NM8207
Barregarrow *IOM* 52 SC3288
Barrets Green *Ches* 47 SJ5859
Barrhead *Strath* 74 NS4958
Barrhill *Strath* 64 NX2382
Barrington *Cambs* 31 TL3848
Barrington *Somset* 8 ST3918
Barripper *Cnwll* 2 SW6338
Barmill *Strath* 73 NS3651
Barrnacarry Bay *Strath* 79 NM8122
Barrock *Highld* 100 ND2571
Barrow *Gloucs* 28 SO8824
Barrow *Lancs* 54 SD7338
Barrow *Leics* 40 SK8815
Barrow *Somset* 9 ST7231
Barrow *Nthumb* 68 NT8610
Barrow Common *Somset* 19 ST5467
Barrow Gurney *Avon* 19 ST5268
Barrow Haven *Humb* 57 TA0622
Barrow Hill *Derbys* 49 SK4375
Barrow upon Soar *Leics* 39 SK5717
Barrow upon Trent *Derbys* 39 SK3528
Barrow-in-Furness *Cumb* 53 SD1971
Barrow-upon-Humber *Humb* 57 TA0720
Barrowby *Lincs* 40 SK8836
Barrowden *Leics* 40 SK9400
Barrowford *Lancs* 54 SD8539
Barry *S Glam* 18 ST1268
Barry *Tays* 83 NO5334
Barsby *Leics* 40 SK6911
Barsham *Suffk* 33 TM3989
Barskimmings *Strath* 73 NS4825
Barston *W Mids* 39 SP2078
Bartestree *H & W* 27 SO5640
Barthol Chapel *Gramp* 95 NJ8134
Bartholomew Green *Essex* 24 TL7221
Barthomley *Ches* 47 SJ7653
Bartley *Hants* 10 SU3012
Bartley Green *W Mids* 38 SP0081
Bartlow *Cambs* 31 TL5646
Barton *Avon* 19 ST3956
Barton *Cambs* 31 TL4055
Barton *Ches* 46 SJ4454
Barton *Devon* 5 SX9067
Barton *Gloucs* 28 SP0925
Barton *Lancs* 53 SD3509
Barton *Lancs* 53 SD5137
Barton *N York* 61 NZ2308
Barton *Oxon* 29 SP5408
Barton Bendish *Norfk* 42 TF7105
Barton End *Gloucs* 20 ST8497
Barton Hartshorn *Bucks* 29 SP6430
Barton Mills *Suffk* 32 TL7273
Barton Seagrave *Nhants* 30 SP8877
Barton St. David *Somset* 8 ST5431
Barton Stacey *Hants* 21 SU4341
Barton Town *Devon* 7 SS6840
Barton Waterside *Humb* 56 TA0222
Barton in Fabis *Notts* 39 SK5232
Barton in the Beans *Leics* 39 SK3906
Barton in the Clay *Beds* 30 TL0831
Barton on Irwell *Gt Man* 47 SJ7698
Barton on Sea *Hants* 10 SZ2493
Barton-Upon-Humber *Humb* 56 TA0322
Barton-le-Street *N York* 63 SE7274
Barton-le-Willows *N York* 56 SE7163
Barton-on-the-Heath *Warwks* 29 SP2532
Barton-under-Needwood *Staffs* 38 SK1818
Barugh Green *S York* 55 SE3106
Barvas *W Isls* 102 NB3649
Barway *Cambs* 31 TL5475
Barwell *Leics* 39 SP4496
Barwick *Devon* 6 SS5907
Barwick *Somset* 8 ST5513
Barwick in Elmet *W York* 55 SE3637
Baschurch *Shrops* 36 SJ4221
Bascote *Warwks* 29 SP4063
Bashall Eaves *Lancs* 54 SD6943
Basildon *Berks* 21 SU6078
Basildon *Essex* 24 TQ7189
Basingstoke *Hants* 21 SU6352
Baslow *Derbys* 48 SK2572
Bason Bridge *Somset* 19 ST3445
Bassaleg *Gwent* 19 ST2787
Bassendean *Border* 76 NT6245
Bassenthwaite *Cumb* 58 NY2332
Bassett *Hants* 10 SU4116
Bassingbourn *Cambs* 31 TL3343
Bassingham *Lincs* 50 SK9059
Bassingham *Lincs* 50 SK9160
Bassingthorpe *Leics* 40 SK9628
Bassus Green *Herts* 31 TL3025
Baston *Lincs* 40 TF1114
Bastwick *Norfk* 43 TG4217
Batchworth *Herts* 22 TQ0694
Batcombe *Dorset* 9 ST6104
Batcombe *Somset* 9 ST6838
Bath *Avon* 20 ST7464
Bath Side *Essex* 25 TM2532
Bathampton *Avon* 20 ST7766
Bathealton *Somset* 7 ST0724
Batheaston *Avon* 20 ST7767
Bathford *Avon* 20 ST7966
Bathgate *Loth* 75 NS9768
Bathley *Notts* 50 SK7759
Bathpool *Cnwll* 4 SX2874
Bathpool *Somset* 8 ST2526
Bathville *Loth* 75 NS9367
Bathway *Somset* 19 ST5952
Batley *W York* 55 SE2424
Batsford *Gloucs* 29 SP1834
Batsworthy *Devon* 7 SS8119
Battersby *N York* 62 NZ5907
Battersea *Gt Lon* 23 TQ2776
Battisborough Cross *Devon* 5 SX6048
Battisford Tye *Suffk* 32 TM0354
Battle *E Susx* 14 TQ7415
Battle *Powys* 26 SO0131
Battledykes *Tays* 88 NO4555
Battlesbridge *Essex* 24 TQ7894
Battleton *Somset* 7 SS9127
Battramsley Cross *Hants* 10 SZ3198
Bauds of Cullen *Gramp* 94 NJ4766
Baughton *H & W* 28 SO8742
Baughurst *Hants* 21 SU5860
Baulds *Gramp* 89 NO6093
Baulking *Oxon* 21 SU3190
Baumber *Lincs* 51 TF2174
Baunton *H & W* 28 SP0204
Baverstock *Wilts* 10 SU0231
Bawburgh *Norfk* 43 TG1508
Bawdeswell *Norfk* 42 TG0420
Bawdrip *Somset* 19 ST3339
Bawdsey *Suffk* 33 TM3440
Bawsey *Norfk* 42 TF6819
Baxenden *Lancs* 54 SD7726
Baxterley *Warwks* 39 SP2896
Bayble *W Isls* 102 NB5231
Baybridge *Hants* 11 SU5223
Baycliff *Cumb* 53 SD2872
Baydon *Wilts* 21 SU2877
Bayford *Herts* 23 TL3108
Bayford *Somset* 9 ST7229
Bayhead *W Isls* 102 NF7668
Bayles *Cumb* 68 NY7044
Baylham *Suffk* 33 TM1051
Baynard's Green *Oxon* 29 SP5529
Baysham *H & W* 27 SO5727
Baythorne End *Essex* 32 TL7242
Bayton *H & W* 37 SO6973
Bayton Common *H & W* 37 SO7172
Bayworth *Oxon* 21 SP4901
Beach *Avon* 20 ST7070
Beachampton *Bucks* 30 SP7736
Beachamwell *Norfk* 42 TF7505
Beachley *Gloucs* 19 ST5591
Beacon *Devon* 8 ST1705
Beacon End *Essex* 25 TL9524
Beacon's Bottom *Bucks* 22 SU7895

Blaen-y-Coed Dyfed	17	SN3427
Blaen-y-cwm Gwent	26	SO1311
Blaen-y-cwm M Glam	18	SS9298
Blaenannerch Dyfed	17	SN2449
Blaenau Ffestiniog Gwynd	45	SH7045
Blaenavon Gwent	27	SO2509
Blaenawey Gwent	27	SO2919
Blaenffos Dyfed	17	SN1937
Blaengarw M Glam	18	SS9092
Blaengeuffardd Dyfed	35	SN6379
Blaengwrach W Glam	26	SN8605
Blaengwynfi W Glam	18	SS8996
Blaenpennal Dyfed	35	SN6264
Blaenplwyf Dyfed	34	SN5775
Blaenporth Dyfed	17	SN2648
Blaenrhondda M Glam	18	SS9299
Blaenwaun Dyfed	17	SN2327
Blagdon Avon	19	ST5059
Blagdon Devon	5	SX8561
Blagdon Somset	8	ST2117
Blagdon Hill Somset	8	ST2117
Blaguegate Lancs	46	SD4506
Blaich Highld	86	NN0476
Blain Highld	79	NM6769
Blair Atholl Tays	87	NN8765
Blair Drummond Cent	81	NS7399
Blairgowrie Tays	88	NO1745
Blairingone Fife	82	NS9896
Blairlogie Cent	82	NS8396
Blairmore Highld	98	NC1960
Blairmore Strath	80	NS1983
Blairnamarrow Gramp	94	NJ2015
Blairs Ferry Strath	71	NR9869
Blaisdon Gloucs	28	SO7017
Blake End Essex	24	TL7023
Blakebrook H & W	37	SO8177
Blakedown H & W	38	SO8878
Blakeley Lane Staffs	48	SJ9747
Blakemere Ches	47	SJ5571
Blakemere H & W	27	SO3640
Blakemore Devon	5	SX7759
Blakeney Gloucs	28	SO6707
Blakeney Norfk	42	TG0243
Blakenhall Ches	47	SJ7247
Blakenhall W Mids	38	SO9197
Blakesley Nhants	29	SP6250
Blanchland Nthumb	68	NY9650
Bland Hill N York	55	SE2053
Blandford Camp Dorset	9	ST9108
Blandford Forum Dorset	9	ST8806
Blandford St. Mary Dorset	9	ST8805
Blankney Lincs	50	TF0660
Blantyre Strath	74	NS6857
Blar a' Chaorainn Highld	86	NN1066
Blargie Highld	87	NN6094
Blarmachfoldach Highld	86	NN0969
Blashford Hants	10	SU1406
Blaston Leics	40	SP8095
Blatherwycke Nhants	40	SP9795
Blawith Cumb	58	SD2888
Blawquhairn D & G	65	NX6282
Blaxhall Suffk	33	TM3657
Blaxton S York	49	SE6600
Blaydon T & W	69	NZ1863
Bleadney Somset	19	ST4845
Bleadon Somset	19	ST3456
Bleak Street Somset	9	ST7531
Blean Kent	15	TR1260
Bleasby Lincs	49	SK7149
Bleasdale Lancs	53	SD5745
Blebocraigs Fife	83	NO4215
Bleddfa Powys	27	SO2168
Bledington Gloucs	29	SP2422
Bledlow Bucks	22	SP7702
Bledlow Ridge Bucks	22	SU7997
Blegbie Loth	76	NT4861
Blencarn Cumb	60	NY6331
Blencogo Cumb	67	NY1947
Blendworth Hants	11	SU7113
Bletchingdon Oxon	29	SP5017
Bletchingley Surrey	12	TQ3250
Bletchley Bucks	30	SP8633
Bletchley Shrops	37	SJ6233
Bletherston Dyfed	16	SN0721
Bletsoe Beds	30	TL0258
Blewbury Oxon	21	SU5385
Blickling Norfk	43	TG1728
Blidworth Notts	49	SK5956
Blidworth Bottoms Notts	49	SK5954
Blindley Heath Surrey	12	TQ3645
Bliss Gate H & W	37	SO7472
Blissford Hants	10	SU1713
Blisworth Nhants	30	SP7253
Blithbury Staffs	38	SK0819
Blo Norton Norfk	32	TM0179
Blockley Gloucs	28	SP1634
Blofield Norfk	43	TG3309
Bloomfield Border	76	NT5824
Blore Staffs	37	SJ7234
Blore Staffs	48	SK1349
Blounts Green Staffs	38	SK0832
Bloxham Oxon	29	SP4235
Bloxwith W Mids	38	SJ9902
Blubberhouses N York	55	SE1655
Blue Anchor Cnwll	3	SW9158
Blue Anchor Somset	7	ST0243
Blue Bell Hill Kent	14	TQ7462
Blughasary Highld	96	NC1301
Blundellsands Mersyd	46	SJ3099
Blundeston Suffk	43	TM5197
Blunham Beds	30	TL1551
Blunsdon St. Andrew Wilts	20	SU1389
Bluntington H & W	38	SO8974
Bluntisham Cambs	31	TL3674
Blunts Cnwll	4	SX3462
Blurton Staffs	48	SJ8942
Blyborough Lincs	50	SK9394
Blyford Suffk	33	TM4276
Blymhill Staffs	37	SJ8112
Blyth Notts	49	SK6287
Blyth Nthumb	69	NZ3181
Blyth Bridge Border	75	NT1345
Blythburgh Suffk	33	TM4575
Blythburgh Suffk	76	NT5849
Blythe Border	76	NT5849
Blythe Bridge Staffs	48	SJ9541
Blythe Bridge Staffs	48	SJ9541
Blyton Lincs	50	SK8594
Bo'Ness Cent	82	NT0081
Boarhills Fife	83	NO5614
Boarhunt Hants	11	SU6008
Boarstall Bucks	29	SP6214
Boat of Garten Highld	93	NH9319
Boath Highld	96	NH5774
Bobbing Kent	14	TQ8865
Bobbington Staffs	37	SO8190
Bochym Cnwll	2	SW6820
Bocking Essex	24	TL7624
Bocking Churchstreet Essex	24	TL7626
Boddam Gramp	95	NK1342
Boddam Shet	103	HU3915
Boddin Tays	89	NO7153
Boddington Gloucs	28	SO8925
Bodedern Gwynd	44	SH3380
Bodelwyddan Clwyd	45	SJ0075
Bodelwyddan Clwyd	45	SJ0075
Bodenham H & W	27	SO5351
Bodenham Wilts	10	SU1626
Bodenham Moor H & W	27	SO5450
Bodewryd Gwynd	44	SH3990
Bodfari Clwyd	45	SJ0970
Bodffordd Gwynd	44	SH4276
Bodfuan Gwynd	44	SH3237
Bodham Street Norfk	43	TG1240
Bodiam E Susx	14	TQ7825
Bodicote Oxon	29	SP4538
Bodinnick Cnwll	3	SX1352
Bodle Street Green E Susx	13	TQ6514
Bodmin Cnwll	3	SX0767
Bodney Norfk	42	TL8398
Bodorgan Gwynd	44	SH3867
Bodsham Green Kent	15	TR1045
Bodwen Cnwll	3	SX0360
Bogallan Highld	93	NH6350
Bogbrae Gramp	95	NK0335
Boghall Loth	75	NS9968
Boghall Loth	75	NT2465
Boghead Strath	74	NS7742

Boghead Farm Gramp	94	NJ3559
Boghole Highld	93	NH9655
Bogmoor Gramp	94	NJ3563
Bogmuir Gramp	89	NO6571
Bogniebrae Gramp	94	NJ5945
Bognor Regis W Susx	11	SZ9399
Bogroy Highld	93	NH9023
Bogue D & G	65	NX6481
Bohortha Cnwll	3	SW8632
Bohuntine Highld	86	NN2883
Bolam Dur	61	NZ1922
Bolberry Devon	5	SX6939
Bold Heath W Mids	38	SP1194
Boldon T & W	69	NZ3461
Boldon Colliery T & W	69	NZ3462
Boldron Dur	61	NZ0314
Bole Notts	50	SK7987
Bolehill Derbys	49	SK2955
Bolfracks Tays	87	NN8248
Bolham Devon	7	SS9514
Bolham Water Devon	8	ST1612
Bolingey Cnwll	2	SW7653
Bollington Ches	47	SJ7286
Bollington Ches	48	SJ9377
Bolney W Susx	12	TQ2622
Bolnhurst Beds	30	TL0859
Bolshan Tays	89	NO6252
Bolsover Derbys	49	SK4770
Bolsterstone S York	49	SK2696
Bolstone H & W	27	SO5532
Bolt Head Devon	5	SX7236
Bolt Tail Devon	5	SX6639
Boltby N York	62	SE4886
Bolton Cumb	60	NY6323
Bolton Gt Man	54	SD7109
Bolton Humb	56	SE7752
Bolton Loth	76	NT5070
Bolton Nthumb	68	NU1013
Bolton Abbey N York	55	SE0754
Bolton Percy N York	56	SE5341
Bolton Town End Lancs	53	SD4767
Bolton Upon Dearne S York	49	SE4602
Bolton-on-Swale N York	61	SE2599
Bolton by Bowland Lancs	54	SD7849
Boltonfellend Cumb	67	NY4768
Boltongate Cumb	58	NY2240
Bolventor Cnwll	4	SX1876
Bomere Heath Shrops	37	SJ4719
Bon-y-Maen W Glam	18	SS6895
Bonar Bridge Highld	97	NH6191
Bonawe Strath	86	NN0141
Bonawe Quarries Strath	80	NN0033
Boncath Dyfed	17	SN2038
Bonchester Bridge Border	67	NT5812
Bondleigh Devon	7	SS6504
Bonds Lancs	53	SD4945
Bonerick D & G	66	NX9076
Boney Hay Staffs	38	SK0510
Bonhill Strath	80	NS3979
Boningale Shrops	38	SJ8202
Bonjedward Border	76	NT6522
Bonnington Kent	15	TR0535
Bonnington Loth	75	NT1269
Bonnington Tays	83	NO5740
Bonnybank Fife	83	NO3802
Bonnykelly Gramp	95	NJ8663
Bonnyrigg Loth	76	NT3065
Bonnyton Tays	83	NO3338
Bont-Dolgadfan Powys	35	SH8800
Bontddu Gwynd	35	SH6719
Bontnewydd Dyfed	35	SN6165
Bontnewydd Gwynd	44	SH4859
Bontuchel Clwyd	46	SJ0857
Bonvilston S Glam	18	ST0673
Boode Devon	6	SS5038
Booham Devon	5	SX8952
Booker Bucks	22	SU8391
Booley Shrops	37	SJ5725
Boon Hill Staffs	47	SJ8050
Boosbeck Cleve	62	NZ6616
Boose's Green Essex	24	TL8531
Boot Cumb	58	NY1701
Booth W York	55	SE0427
Boothby Graffoe Lincs	50	SK9859
Boothby Pagnell Lincs	40	SK9730
Boothe Cumb	58	SD1088
Bootle Mersyd	46	SJ3495
Bootle Station Cumb	58	SD0989
Boquhan Cent	81	NS5387
Boraston Shrops	27	SO6169
Bordeaux Jersey	101	SV0000
Bordon Hants	11	SU7935
Boreham Essex	24	TL7610
Boreham Wilts	20	ST8944
Boreham Street E Susx	13	TQ6611
Borehamwood Herts	23	TQ1996
Boreland D & G	67	NY1790
Boreraig Highld	90	NG1853
Boreston Devon	5	SX7753
Borgie Highld	99	NC6759
Borgue D & G	65	NX6248
Borgue Highld	100	ND1326
Borley Green Essex	32	TL8543
Borneskitaig Highld	90	NG3771
Borness D & G	65	NX6145
Borough Green Kent	14	TQ6057
Boroughbridge N York	55	SE3966
Borrowash Derbys	39	SK4334
Borrowby N York	62	SE4289
Borrowdale Hotel Cumb	58	NY2618
Borrowstoun Cent	82	NS9980
Borstal Kent	14	TQ7366
Borth Dyfed	34	SN6090
Borth-y-Gest Gwynd	44	SH5637
Borthwick Loth	76	NT3659
Borthwickbrae Border	67	NT4113
Borthwickshiels Border	76	NT4315
Borve Highld	90	NG4448
Borve W Isls	102	NB4057
Borve W Isls	102	NF6501
Borve W Isls	102	NF9181
Borwick Lancs	59	SD5273
Borwick Lodge Cumb	67	NY3499
Bosbury H & W	28	SO6943
Boscarne Cnwll	3	SX0367
Boscastle Cnwll	4	SX0990
Boscombe Dorset	10	SZ1191
Boscombe Wilts	10	SU2038
Bosham W Susx	11	SU8004
Bosherton Dyfed	16	SR9694
Boskennal Cnwll	2	SW4323
Bosley Ches	48	SJ9165
Bosoughan Cnwll	3	SW8760
Bossall N York	56	SE7160
Bossiney Cnwll	4	SX0688
Bossingham Kent	15	TR1549
Bossington Somset	7	SS8947
Bostock Green Ches	47	SJ6769
Boston Lincs	51	TF3243
Boston Spa W York	55	SE4245
Boswinger Cnwll	3	SW9941
Botany Bay Gt Lon	23	TQ2999
Botesdale Suffk	32	TM0576
Bothal Nthumb	69	NZ2386
Bothampstead Berks	21	SU5076
Bothamsall Notts	49	SK6773
Bothel Cumb	58	NY1838
Bothenhampton Dorset	8	SY4791
Bothwell Strath	74	NS7058
Botley Bucks	22	SP9802
Botley Hants	11	SU5113
Botley Oxon	29	SP4806
Botolph Claydon Bucks	30	SP7324
Botolphs W Susx	12	TQ1909
Bottesford Humb	56	SE8907
Bottesford Leics	40	SK8038
Bottisham Cambs	31	TL5460
Bottomcraig Fife	83	NO3724
Bottoms W York	54	SD9321
Botusfleming Cnwll	4	SX4060
Botwnnog Gwynd	44	SH2631
Bough Beech Kent	13	TQ4847
Boughrood Powys	26	SO1239
Boughspring Gloucs	19	ST5597
Boughton Cambs	31	TL1965
Boughton Nhants	30	SP7565
Boughton Norfk	42	TF7002
Boughton Notts	49	SK6768

Boughton Aluph Kent	15	TR0348
Boughton Green Kent	14	TQ7651
Boughton Lees Kent	15	TR0246
Boughton Malherbe Kent	14	TQ8849
Boughton Monchelsea Kent	14	TQ7749
Boughton Street Kent	15	TR0559
Boulder Clough W York	55	SE0324
Bouldon Shrops	37	SO5485
Bouley Bay Jersey	101	SV0000
Boulmer Nthumb	69	NU2614
Boultham Lincs	50	SK9568
Boulton Low Houses Cumb	67	NY2344
Bourn Cambs	31	TL3256
Bourne Devon	5	SS6514
Bourne Lincs	40	TF0920
Bourne End Beds	30	SP9644
Bourne End Beds	30	TL0260
Bourne End Bucks	22	SU8987
Bourne End Herts	22	TL0206
Bournebridge Essex	23	TQ5094
Bournebrook W Mids	38	SP0482
Bournemouth Dorset	10	SZ0991
Bournes Green Essex	24	TQ9186
Bournheath H & W	38	SO9474
Bournstream Gloucs	20	ST7594
Bournville W Mids	38	SP0481
Bourton Dorset	9	ST7630
Bourton Oxon	21	SU2386
Bourton Shrops	37	SO5996
Bourton Wilts	20	SU0464
Bourton on Dunsmore Warwks	29	SP4370
Bourton-on-the- Hill Gloucs	29	SP1732
Bourton-on-the-Water Gloucs	28	SP1620
Bousd Highld	78	NM2563
Bouth Cumb	58	SD3385
Bouthwaite N York	55	SE1171
Bovain Cent	81	NN5430
Boveridge Dorset	10	SU0615
Bovey Tracey Devon	5	SX8178
Bovingdon Herts	22	TL0103
Bovinger Essex	31	TL5215
Bow Devon	5	SX8156
Bow Devon	7	SS7201
Bow Ork	103	ND3693
Bow Brickhill Bucks	30	SP9034
Bow End Cumb	67	NY2674
Bow Fife Fife	83	NO3212
Bow Street Dyfed	35	SN6285
Bowbridge Gloucs	28	SO8605
Bowburn Dur	61	NZ3038
Bowcombe IOW	10	SZ4786
Bowd Devon	8	SY1190
Bowden Border	76	NT5530
Bowden Hill Wilts	20	ST9367
Bowdon Gt Man	47	SJ7686
Bower Highld	100	ND2362
Bower House Tye Suffk	32	TL9941
Bower's Row W York	55	SE4027
Bowerchalke Wilts	9	SU0122
Bowermadden Highld	100	ND2464
Bowers Staffs	37	SJ8135
Bowers Gifford Essex	24	TQ7588
Bowershall Fife	82	NT0991
Bowertower Highld	100	ND2361
Bowes Dur	61	NY9913
Bowgreave Lancs	53	SD4943
Bowhill Border	76	NT4227
Bowland Border	76	NT4540
Bowley H & W	27	SO5452
Bowlhead Green Surrey	11	SU9138
Bowling Strath	81	NS4373
Bowling W York	55	SE1731
Bowling Bank Clwyd	46	SJ3949
Bowling Green H & W	28	SO8151
Bowmanstead Cumb	58	SD3096
Bowmore Strath	70	NR3159
Bowness-on-Solway Cumb	67	NY2262
Bowsden Nthumb	77	NT9941
Box Gloucs	20	SO8600
Box Hill Surrey	12	TQ2051
Boxbush Gloucs	28	SO7412
Boxford Berks	21	SU4271
Boxford Suffk	32	TL9640
Boxgrove W Susx	11	SU9007
Boxholme Lincs	50	TF0653
Boxley Kent	14	TQ7758
Boxmoor Herts	22	TL0406
Boxted Essex	25	TL9933
Boxted Suffk	32	TL8251
Boxted Cross Essex	25	TM0032
Boxted Heath Essex	25	TM0031
Boxworth Cambs	31	TL3464
Boyden Gate Kent	15	TR2265
Boylestone Derbys	38	SK1835
Boyndie Gramp	94	NJ6463
Boyndlie Gramp	95	NJ9162
Boynton Humb	57	TA1368
Boys Hill Dorset	9	ST6709
Boysack Tays	89	NO6249
Boyton Cnwll	4	SX3192
Boyton Suffk	33	TM3747
Boyton Wilts	20	ST9539
Boyton Cross Essex	24	TL6409
Boyton End Suffk	32	TL7244
Bozeat Nhants	30	SP9058
Braaid IOM	52	SC3176
Brabourne Kent	15	TR1041
Brabourne Lees Kent	15	TR0840
Brabstermire Highld	100	ND3169
Bracadale Highld	90	NG3538
Braceborough Lincs	40	TF0713
Bracebridge Heath Lincs	50	SK9867
Braceby Lincs	40	TF0135
Bracewell Lancs	54	SD8648
Brackenfield Derbys	49	SK3759
Brackenhurst Strath	74	NS7468
Brackenthwaite Cumb	58	NY1522
Bracketter Highld	86	NN5882
Brackley Nhants	29	SP5837
Brackloch Highld	96	NC1224
Bracknell Berks	22	SU8769
Braco Tays	82	NN8309
Bracobrae Gramp	94	NJ5053
Bracon Ash Norfk	43	TM1899
Bracora Highld	85	NM7192
Bracorina Highld	85	NM7292
Bradbourne Derbys	48	SK2052
Bradbury Dur	62	NZ3128
Bradda IOM	52	SC1970
Bradden Nhants	29	SP6448
Bradenham Bucks	22	SU8297
Bradenstoke Wilts	20	SU0079
Bradfield Devon	7	ST0509
Bradfield Essex	25	TM1430
Bradfield Norfk	43	TG2633
Bradfield Combust Suffk	32	TL8957
Bradfield Green Ches	47	SJ6859
Bradfield Heath Essex	25	TM1430
Bradfield St. Clare Suffk	32	TL9158
Bradfield St. George Suffk	32	TL9060
Bradford Devon	6	SS4207
Bradford W York	55	SE1633
Bradford Abbas Dorset	8	ST5813
Bradford Leigh Wilts	20	ST8362
Bradford Peverell Dorset	9	SY6593
Bradford on Avon Wilts	20	ST8260
Bradford-on-Tone Somset	8	ST1722
Brading IOW	11	SZ6087
Bradley Clwyd	46	SJ3253
Bradley H & W	28	SO9860
Bradley Hants	21	SU6341
Bradley Humb	57	TA2406
Bradley Staffs	38	SJ8717
Bradley W Mids	38	SO9595
Bradley Green Ches	46	SJ5046
Bradley Green Warwks	39	SK2800
Bradley Stoke Avon	19	ST6081
Bradley in the Moors Staffs	48	SK0541
Bradmore Notts	39	SK5831
Bradninch Devon	7	SS9903
Bradnop Staffs	48	SK0155
Bradpole Dorset	8	SY4794
Bradshaw W York	55	SE0729
Bradstone Devon	4	SX3880
Bradwall Green Ches	47	SJ7663
Bradwell Bucks	30	SP8340
Bradwell Norfk	43	TG5003

Bradwell Waterside Essex	25	TL9907
Bradwell-on-Sea Essex	25	TM0007
Bradworthy Devon	6	SS3213
Brae D & G	66	NX8674
Brae Highld	93	NH6662
Brae Shet	103	HU3568
Brae Roy Lodge Highld	86	NN3391
Braeface Cent	81	NS7880
Braefield Highld	92	NH4130
Braegrum Tays	82	NO0025
Braehead D & G	64	NX4252
Braehead Strath	75	NS9550
Braehead Tays	89	NO6952
Braehour Highld	100	ND0953
Braelangwell Lodge Highld	96	NH5192
Braemar Gramp	88	NO1591
Braemore Highld	96	NH2078
Braemore Highld	100	ND0829
Braes The Highld	84	NG5234
Braes of Coul Tays	88	NO2857
Braes of Enzie Gramp	94	NJ3957
Braeside Strath	80	NS2375
Braeswick Ork	103	HY6037
Braevallich Strath	80	NM9507
Brafferton Dur	61	NZ2921
Brafferton N York	55	SE4370
Brafield-on-the-Green Nhants	30	SP8258
Bragar W Isls	102	NB2847
Bragbury End Herts	31	TL2621
Brahen Hill W York	55	SE4317
Braidwood Strath	74	NS8448
Braigo Strath	70	NR2369
Brailsford Green Derbys	48	SK2541
Brain's Green Gloucs	28	SO6608
Braintree Essex	24	TL7523
Braiseworth Suffk	33	TM1372
Braishfield Hants	10	SU3725
Braithwaite Cumb	58	NY2323
Braithwaite Cumb	58	NY2326
Braithwaite W York	55	SE0341
Braithwell S York	55	SK5394
Bramber W Susx	12	TQ1811
Bramcote Warwks	39	SP4088
Bramdean Hants	11	SU6128
Bramerton Norfk	43	TG2904
Bramfield Herts	31	TL2915
Bramfield Suffk	33	TM4074
Bramford Suffk	33	TM1246
Bramhall Gt Man	48	SJ8984
Bramham W York	55	SE4242
Bramhope W York	55	SE2443
Bramley Derbys	49	SK3979
Bramley Hants	21	SU6559
Bramley S York	49	SK4892
Bramley W York	55	TQ0044
Bramley Corner Hants	21	SU6359
Bramleyhead N York	55	SE5218
Bramling Kent	15	TR2256
Brampford Speke Devon	7	SX9398
Brampton Cambs	31	TL2170
Brampton Cumb	60	NY6723
Brampton Cumb	67	NY5361
Brampton Lincs	50	SK8479
Brampton Norfk	43	TG2223
Brampton S York	49	SE4101
Brampton Suffk	33	TM4381
Brampton Abbotts H & W	27	SO6026
Brampton Ash Nhants	40	SP7987
Brampton Bryan H & W	36	SO3672
Brampton-en-le-Morthen S York	49	SK4888
Bramshall Staffs	38	SK0633
Bramshaw Hants	10	SU2615
Bramshaw Hants	10	SU2715
Bramshott Hants	11	SU8432
Bramwell Somset	8	ST4229
Bran End Essex	24	TL6525
Branault Highld	79	NM5269
Brancaster Norfk	42	TF7743
Brancaster Staithe Norfk	42	TF7944
Brancepeth Dur	61	NZ2237
Branch End Nthumb	68	NZ0662
Branchill Gramp	93	NJ0852
Brand End Lincs	51	TF3844
Branderburgh Gramp	94	NJ2371
Brandesburton Humb	57	TA1147
Brandeston Suffk	33	TM2460
Brandis Corner Devon	6	SS4104
Brandiston Norfk	43	TG1421
Brandon Dur	61	NZ2439
Brandon Lincs	50	SK9048
Brandon Suffk	32	TL7886
Brandon Warwks	39	SP4176
Brandon Bank Cambs	41	TL6289
Brandon Parva Norfk	42	TG0708
Brandsby N York	56	SE5872
Brandy Wharf Lincs	50	TF0196
Branksome Dorset	9	SZ0393
Branksome Park Dorset	10	SZ0590
Bransbury Hants	21	SU4242
Bransby Lincs	50	SK8979
Branscombe Devon	8	SY1988
Bransford H & W	28	SO7952
Bransgore Hants	10	SZ1897
Bransley Shrops	37	SO6875
Branston Leics	40	SK8129
Branston Lincs	50	TF0166
Branston Staffs	39	SK2221
Branston Booths Lincs	50	TF0669
Branstone IOW	11	SZ5583
Brant Broughton Lincs	50	SK9154
Brantham Suffk	25	TM1134
Branthwaite Cumb	58	NY0525
Brantingham Humb	56	SE9429
Branton Nthumb	77	NU0416
Branton S York	56	SE6401
Branton Green N York	55	SE4462
Branxton Nthumb	77	NT8937
Brassington Derbys	48	SK2354
Brasted Kent	23	TQ4655
Brasted Chart Gt Lon	13	TQ4653
Brathens Gramp	89	NO6798
Bratoft Lincs	51	TF4764
Brattleby Lincs	50	SK9481
Bratton Shrops	37	SJ6314
Bratton Somset	7	SS9546
Bratton Clovelly Devon	4	SX4691
Bratton Fleming Devon	6	SS6437
Bratton Seymour Somset	9	ST6729
Braughing Herts	31	TL3925
Braunston Leics	40	SK8306
Braunston Nhants	29	SP5466
Braunstone Leics	39	SK5502
Braunton Devon	6	SS4836
Brawby N York	63	SE7378
Brawl Highld	99	NC8166
Brawlbin Highld	100	ND0757
Bray Berks	22	SU9079
Bray Shop Cnwll	4	SX3374
Braybrooke Nhants	40	SP7684
Braydon Wilts	20	SU0588
Braydon Devon	7	SS6934
Braystones Cumb	58	NY0106
Braythorn N York	55	SE2449
Brayton N York	56	SE6030
Braywick Berks	22	SU8979
Braywoodside Berks	22	SU8775
Breacleate W Isls	102	NB1537
Breadsall Derbys	39	SK3639
Breadstone Gloucs	20	SO7000
Breage Cnwll	2	SW6128
Breakachy Highld	92	NH4644
Bream's Meend Gloucs	27	SO5905
Breamore Hants	10	SU1517
Brean Somset	19	ST2955
Brearley W York	55	SE0226
Brearton N York	55	SE3260
Breasclete W Isls	102	NB2135
Breaston Derbys	39	SK4633
Brechfa Dyfed	17	SN5230
Brechin Tays	89	NO5960
Breckles Norfk	42	TL9594
Breckonside D & G	66	NX8489
Breckrey Highld	90	NG5061

Brecon Burnham

Brecon *Powys*	26	SO0428
Bredbury *Gt Man*	48	SJ9291
Bredenbury *H & W*	27	SO6056
Bredfield *Suffk*	33	TM2753
Bredgar *Kent*	14	TQ8860
Bredhurst *Kent*	14	TQ7962
Bredon *H & W*	28	SO9236
Bredon's Hardwick *H & W*	28	SO9135
Bredon's Norton *H & W*	28	SO9339
Bredwardine *H & W*	27	SO3344
Breedon on the Hill *Leics*	39	SK4022
Breich *Loth*	75	NS9560
Breightmet *Gt Man*	54	SD7409
Breighton *Humb*	56	SE7033
Breinton *H & W*	27	SO4739
Bremhill *Wilts*	20	ST9873
Bremley *Devon*	7	SS8128
Brenchley *Kent*	14	TQ6741
Brendon *Devon*	18	SS7648
Brenfield *Strath*	71	NR8482
Brenish *W Isls*	102	NA9926
Brent Eleigh *Suffk*	32	TL9448
Brent Knoll *Somset*	19	ST3350
Brent Knoll *Somset*	19	ST3350
Brent Mill *Devon*	5	SX7059
Brent Pelham *Herts*	31	TL4330
Brentford *Gt Lon*	23	TQ1777
Brentingby *Leics*	40	SK7818
Brentwood *Essex*	24	TQ5993
Brenzett *Kent*	15	TR0027
Brenzett Green *Kent*	15	TR0028
Brereton Green *Ches*	47	SJ7764
Bressingham *Norfk*	32	TM0780
Bressingham Common *Norfk*	33	TM0982
Bretabister *Shet*	103	HU4857
Bretby *Derbys*	39	SK2923
Bretford *Warwks*	39	SP4377
Bretforton *H & W*	28	SP0944
Bretherton *Lancs*	53	SD4720
Brettenham *Norfk*	32	TL9383
Brettenham *Suffk*	32	TL9654
Bretton *Clwyd*	46	SJ3564
Brewhouse *D & G*	66	NY0165
Brewood *Staffs*	38	SJ8808
Brgoed *M Glam*	18	ST1599
Briantspuddle *Dorset*	9	SY8193
Brick Houses *S York*	49	SK3081
Bricket Wood *Herts*	22	TL1302
Bricklehampton *H & W*	28	SO9842
Bride *IOM*	52	NX4501
Bridekirk *Cumb*	58	NY1133
Bridestowe *Devon*	4	SX5189
Brideswell *Gramp*	94	NJ5739
Bridford *Devon*	5	SX8186
Bridge *Cnwll*	2	SW6744
Bridge *Kent*	15	TR1854
Bridge End *Devon*	5	SX7046
Bridge End *Nthumb*	68	NY8965
Bridge End *Surrey*	22	TQ0757
Bridge Fields *Leics*	39	SK4927
Bridge Hewick *N York*	55	SE3370
Bridge Reeve *Devon*	7	SS6613
Bridge Sollers *H & W*	27	SO4142
Bridge Street *Suffk*	32	TL8749
Bridge Trafford *Ches*	46	SJ4571
Bridge of Alford *Gramp*	94	NJ5617
Bridge of Avon *Gramp*	94	NJ1835
Bridge of Balgie *Tays*	87	NN5746
Bridge of Brewlands *Tays*	88	NO1961
Bridge of Brown *Highld*	93	NJ1120
Bridge of Cally *Tays*	88	NO1451
Bridge of Canny *Gramp*	89	NO6597
Bridge of Craigisla *Tays*	88	NO2553
Bridge of Dee *D & G*	65	NX7360
Bridge of Don *Gramp*	95	NJ9409
Bridge of Dulsie *Highld*	93	NH9341
Bridge of Dye *Gramp*	89	NO6586
Bridge of Earn *Tays*	82	NO1318
Bridge of Ericht *Tays*	87	NN5258
Bridge of Feugh *Gramp*	89	NO7095
Bridge of Forss *Highld*	100	ND0368
Bridge of Gairn *Gramp*	88	NO3597
Bridge of Gaur *Tays*	87	NN5056
Bridge of Orchy *Strath*	80	NN2939
Bridge of Tilt *Tays*	87	NN8765
Bridge of Tynet *Gramp*	94	NJ3862
Bridge of Walls *Shet*	103	HU2651
Bridge of Weir *Strath*	73	NS3865
Bridge of Westfield *Highld*	100	ND0664
Bridgehampton *Somset*	8	ST5624
Bridgehouse Gate *N York*	55	SE1565
Bridgemary *Hants*	11	SU5803
Bridgend *Border*	76	NT5235
Bridgend *D & G*	66	NT0708
Bridgend *Devon*	4	SX5547
Bridgend *Fife*	83	NO3911
Bridgend *Gramp*	94	NJ3731
Bridgend *Gramp*	94	NJ5135
Bridgend *Gramp*	95	NJ7249
Bridgend *Loth*	75	NT0475
Bridgend *M Glam*	18	SS9079
Bridgend *Strath*	70	NR3362
Bridgend *Tays*	82	NO1224
Bridgend *Tays*	89	NO5368
Bridgend of Lintrathen *Tays*	88	NO2854
Bridgerule *Devon*	6	SS2703
Bridgeton *Gramp*	94	NJ3251
Bridgetown *Devon*	4	SX3489
Bridgetown *Somset*	7	SS9233
Bridgeyate *Avon*	20	ST6873
Bridgham *Norfk*	32	TL9686
Bridgnorth *Shrops*	37	SO7193
Bridgwater *Somset*	19	ST3037
Bridlington *Humb*	57	TA1766
Bridport *Dorset*	8	SY4692
Bridstow *H & W*	27	SO5824
Brierfield *Lancs*	54	SD8436
Brierley *Gloucs*	27	SO6215
Brierley *W York*	55	SE4011
Brierley Hill *W Mids*	38	SO9187
Brierton *Cleve*	62	NZ4729
Brig o'Turk *Cent*	81	NN5306
Brigg *Humb*	56	TA0007
Brigg of Blair *Gramp*	89	NO8899
Briggate *Norfk*	43	TG3127
Briggswath *N York*	63	NZ8608
Brigham *Cumb*	58	NY0830
Brigham *Humb*	57	TA0753
Brigham *Humb*	57	TA0853
Brighouse *W York*	55	SE1423
Brighstone *IOW*	10	SZ4282
Brighthampton *Oxon*	21	SP3803
Brightholmlee *Derbys*	49	SK2995
Brightley *Devon*	6	SX5997
Brightlingsea *Essex*	25	TM0817
Brighton *E Susx*	12	TQ3105
Brighton le Sands *Mersyd*	46	SJ3199
Brightons *Cent*	75	NS9277
Brightwalton *Berks*	21	SU4279
Brightwell *Oxon*	21	SU5790
Brightwell *Suffk*	33	TM2543
Brightwell Baldwin *Oxon*	21	SU6595
Brightwell Upperton *Oxon*	21	SU6594
Brigland Hall *Cumb*	67	NY3583
Brignall *Dur*	61	NZ0712
Brigsley *Humb*	51	TA2501
Brigsteer *Cumb*	59	SD4889
Brigstock *Nhants*	40	SP9485
Brill *Bucks*	29	SP6513
Brill *Cnwll*	2	SW7229
Brilley *H & W*	27	SO2648
Brimfield Cross *H & W*	27	SO5368
Brimington *Derbys*	49	SK4073
Brimley *Devon*	5	SX7977
Brimpsfield *Gloucs*	28	SO9312
Brimpton *Berks*	21	SU5564
Brimscombe *Gloucs*	20	SO8602
Brimstage *Mersyd*	46	SJ3082
Brincliffe *S York*	49	SK3284
Brind *Humb*	56	SE7430
Brindham *Somset*	19	ST5140
Brindister *Shet*	103	HU2857
Brindle *Lancs*	54	SD6024
Brineton *Staffs*	37	SJ8013
Bringhurst *Leics*	40	SP8492
Brington *Cambs*	30	TL0875
Briningham *Norfk*	42	TG0434
Brinkely *Notts*	49	SK7152
Brinkhill *Lincs*	51	TF3773
Brinkley *Cambs*	32	TL6254
Brinklow *Warwks*	39	SP4379
Brinkworth *Wilts*	20	SU0184
Brinscall *Lancs*	54	SD6221
Brinscombe *Somset*	19	ST4252
Brinsley *Notts*	49	SK4649
Brinton *Norfk*	42	TG0335
Brinyan *Ork*	103	HY4327
Brisley *Norfk*	42	TF9421
Brislington *Avon*	19	ST6170
Brissenden Green *Kent*	14	TQ9339
Bristol *Avon*	19	ST5873
Briston *Norfk*	42	TG0632
Britford *Wilts*	10	SU1628
Brithdir *Gwynd*	35	SH7618
Brithdir *M Glam*	18	SO1401
British Legion Village *Kent*	14	TQ7257
Briton Ferry *W Glam*	18	SS7494
Britwell Salome *Oxon*	22	SU6792
Brixham *Devon*	5	SX9255
Brixton *Devon*	4	SX5452
Brixton *Gt Lon*	23	TQ3175
Brixton Deverill *Wilts*	20	ST8638
Brixworth *Nhants*	30	SP7470
Brize Norton *Oxon*	29	SP2907
Broad Alley *H & W*	28	SO8867
Broad Blunsdon *Wilts*	20	SU1490
Broad Campden *Gloucs*	28	SP1537
Broad Carr *W York*	55	SE0919
Broad Chalke *Wilts*	9	SU0325
Broad Clough *Lancs*	54	SD8624
Broad Green *Cambs*	32	TL6860
Broad Green *Essex*	24	TL8823
Broad Green *H & W*	28	SO7756
Broad Green *Suffk*	32	TL7859
Broad Haven *Dyfed*	16	SM8613
Broad Hinton *Wilts*	20	SU1076
Broad Laying *Hants*	21	SU4362
Broad Marston *H & W*	28	SP1446
Broad Oak *E Susx*	14	TQ8219
Broad Oak *H & W*	27	SO4821
Broad Oak *Mersyd*	46	SJ5395
Broad Street *E Susx*	14	TQ8616
Broad Street *Kent*	14	TQ8356
Broad Street *Kent*	15	TR1139
Broad Street *Wilts*	20	SU1158
Broad Street Green *Essex*	24	TL8610
Broad Town *Wilts*	20	SU0877
Broad's Green *Essex*	24	TL6912
Broadbottom *Derbys*	48	SJ9993
Broadbridge *W Susx*	11	SU8105
Broadbridge Heath *W Susx*	12	TQ1431
Broadclyst *Devon*	7	SX9897
Broadfield *Strath*	80	NS3273
Broadford *Highld*	85	NG6423
Broadford Bridge *W Susx*	12	TQ0921
Broadgairhill *Border*	67	NT2010
Broadgate *Lincs*	41	TF3609
Broadgrass Green *Suffk*	32	TL9763
Broadhaugh *Border*	77	NT8655
Broadheath *Gt Man*	47	SJ7689
Broadhembury *Devon*	8	ST1004
Broadhempston *Devon*	5	SX8066
Broadland Row *E Susx*	14	TQ8319
Broadley *Gramp*	94	NJ3961
Broadmayne *Dorset*	9	SY7286
Broadmoor *Dyfed*	16	SN0906
Broadoak *Dorset*	8	SY4496
Broadoak *E Susx*	13	TQ6022
Broadoak *Kent*	15	TR1761
Broadstairs *Kent*	15	TR3967
Broadstone *Dorset*	9	SZ0095
Broadstone *Gwent*	19	SO5002
Broadstone *Shrops*	37	SO5489
Broadwas *H & W*	28	SO7559
Broadwas *H & W*	28	SO7655
Broadwater *Herts*	31	TL2422
Broadwater *W Susx*	12	TQ1504
Broadwaters *H & W*	38	SO8478
Broadway *Dyfed*	17	SN3808
Broadway *H & W*	28	SP0937
Broadway *Somset*	8	ST3215
Broadwell *Gloucs*	29	SP2027
Broadwell *Oxon*	21	SP2503
Broadwell *Warwks*	29	SP4565
Broadwindsor *Dorset*	8	ST4302
Broadwood Kelly *Devon*	6	SS6105
Broadwoodwidger *Devon*	4	SX4089
Brochel *Highld*	90	NG5846
Brockbridge *Hants*	11	SU6118
Brockdish *Norfk*	33	TM2179
Brockenhurst *Hants*	10	SU2902
Brockenhurst *Hants*	10	SU3002
Brocketsbrae *Strath*	74	NS8240
Brockford Street *Suffk*	33	TM1167
Brockhall *Nhants*	29	SP6362
Brockham *Surrey*	12	TQ1949
Brockhampton *Gloucs*	28	SO9425
Brockhampton *Gloucs*	28	SP0322
Brockhampton *Hants*	11	SU7106
Brockholes *W York*	55	SE1511
Brockhurst *Warwks*	39	SP4683
Brocklebank *Cumb*	67	NY3043
Brocklesby *Lincs*	57	TA1311
Brockley *Avon*	19	ST4667
Brockley *Suffk*	32	TL8371
Brockley Green *Suffk*	32	TL7247
Brockley Green *Suffk*	32	TL8254
Brockleymoor *Cumb*	67	NY4957
Brockmoor *W Mids*	38	SO9187
Brockton *Shrops*	36	SJ3104
Brockton *Shrops*	36	SO3285
Brockton *Shrops*	37	SJ7203
Brockton *Shrops*	37	SO5794
Brockton *Staffs*	37	SJ8131
Brockwell *Gwent*	19	SO5301
Brockworth *Gloucs*	28	SO8916
Brocton *Staffs*	38	SJ9619
Brodick *Strath*	72	NS0135
Brodie *Gramp*	93	NH9757
Brodsworth *S York*	55	SE5007
Brogaig *Highld*	90	NG4768
Brokenborough *Wilts*	20	ST9189
Brokerswood *Wilts*	20	ST8352
Bromborough *Mersyd*	46	SJ3582
Brome *Suffk*	33	TM1376
Brome Street *Suffk*	33	TM1576
Bromeswell *Suffk*	33	TM3050
Bromfield *Cumb*	67	NY1746
Bromfield *Shrops*	37	SO4877
Bromham *Beds*	30	TL0051
Bromham *Wilts*	20	ST9665
Bromley *Gt Lon*	23	TQ4069
Bromley *Shrops*	37	SO7395
Bromlow *Shrops*	36	SJ3201
Brompton *Kent*	14	TQ7668
Brompton *Kent*	14	TQ7668
Brompton *N York*	62	SE3796
Brompton *N York*	63	SE9482
Brompton Ralph *Somset*	7	ST0832
Brompton Regis *Somset*	7	SS9531
Brompton-on-Swale *N York*	61	SE2199
Bromsash *H & W*	27	SO6523
Bromsberrow *Gloucs*	28	SO7434
Bromsberrow Heath *Gloucs*	28	SO7332
Bromsgrove *H & W*	28	SO9570
Bromyard *H & W*	27	SO6554
Bronaber *Gwynd*	45	SH7132
Bronant *Dyfed*	35	SN6467
Brongest *Dyfed*	17	SN3245
Bronington *Clwyd*	37	SJ4839
Bronllys *Powys*	26	SO1434
Bronwydd Arms *Dyfed*	17	SN4124
Bronygarth *Shrops*	36	SJ2637
Brook *Hants*	10	SU2713
Brook *Hants*	10	SU2713
Brook *Hants*	10	SU3428
Brook *IOW*	10	SZ3983
Brook *Kent*	15	TR0644
Brook *Surrey*	11	SU9338
Brook *Surrey*	12	TQ0646
Brook End *Bucks*	30	SP9144
Brook End *Cambs*	38	SP0773
Brook End *Staffs*	38	SK0714
Brook Hill *Hants*	10	SU2714
Brook Hill *Hants*	10	SU2714
Brook Street *Essex*	24	TQ5792
Brook Street *Kent*	14	TQ9334
Brook Street *Suffk*	32	TL8348
Brook Street *W Susx*	12	TQ3026
Brooke *Leics*	40	SK8405
Brooke *Norfk*	43	TM2999
Brookfield *Strath*	73	NS4164
Brookhampton *Oxon*	21	SU6098
Brookhampton *Somset*	9	ST6327
Brookhouse *Lancs*	53	SD5464
Brookhouse *S York*	49	SK5188
Brookhouse Green *Ches*	47	SJ8161
Brookhouses *Derbys*	48	SK0389
Brookland *Kent*	15	TQ9926
Brooklands *Gt Man*	47	SJ7890
Brookmans Park *Herts*	23	TL2404
Brooks End *Kent*	23	TQ2967
Brooks Green *W Susx*	12	TQ1225
Brooksby *Leics*	39	SK6716
Brookthorpe *Gloucs*	28	SO8312
Brookwood *Surrey*	22	SU9557
Broom *Beds*	31	TL1742
Broom *S York*	49	SK4491
Broom *Warwks*	28	SP0953
Broom Green *Norfk*	42	TF9924
Broom Hill *H & W*	38	SO9275
Broom Hill *S York*	49	SE4102
Broom Street *Kent*	15	TR0462
Broom of Dalreoch *Tays*	82	NO0017
Broom's Green *H & W*	28	SO7133
Broome *H & W*	38	SO9078
Broome *Norfk*	33	TM3591
Broome *Shrops*	36	SO3981
Broomedge *Ches*	47	SJ6985
Broomer's Corner *W Susx*	12	TQ1221
Broomfield *Essex*	24	TL7011
Broomfield *Kent*	14	TQ8352
Broomfield *Kent*	15	TR1966
Broomfield *Somset*	8	ST2221
Broomfleet *Humb*	56	SE8727
Broomhaugh *Nthumb*	68	NZ0261
Broomhill *Highld*	93	NH9922
Broomhill *Nthumb*	69	NU2401
Broomhill Green *Ches*	47	SJ6247
Brora *Highld*	97	NC9104
Broseley *Shrops*	37	SJ6701
Brotherlee *Dur*	60	NY9237
Brotherstone *Border*	76	NT6145
Brothertoft *Lincs*	51	TF2746
Brotherton *N York*	55	SE4825
Brotton *Cleve*	62	NZ6819
Broubster *Highld*	100	ND0359
Brough *Cumb*	60	NY7914
Brough *Highld*	100	ND2273
Brough *Humb*	56	SE9326
Brough *Notts*	50	SK8458
Brough *Shet*	103	HU5564
Brough Lodge *Shet*	103	HU5892
Brough Sowerby *Cumb*	60	NY7912
Broughall *Shrops*	37	SJ5741
Broughton *Border*	75	NT1136
Broughton *Bucks*	30	SP8939
Broughton *Cambs*	31	TL2877
Broughton *Clwyd*	46	SJ3363
Broughton *Gt Man*	47	SD8201
Broughton *Hants*	10	SU3132
Broughton *Humb*	56	SE9508
Broughton *Lancs*	53	SD5234
Broughton *N York*	54	SD9451
Broughton *N York*	63	SE7673
Broughton *Nhants*	30	SP8375
Broughton *Oxon*	29	SP4238
Broughton *S Glam*	18	SS9271
Broughton *Staffs*	37	SJ7634
Broughton Astley *Leics*	39	SP5292
Broughton Gifford *Wilts*	20	ST8763
Broughton Green *H & W*	28	SO9561
Broughton Hackett *H & W*	28	SO9254
Broughton Mills *Cumb*	58	SD2290
Broughton Moor *Cumb*	58	NY0533
Broughton Poggs *Oxon*	21	SP2303
Broughton Tower *Cumb*	67	NY2188
Broughty Ferry *Tays*	83	NO4630
Brown Candover *Hants*	11	SU5739
Brown Edge *Staffs*	48	SJ9053
Brown Street *Suffk*	32	TM0664
Brown's Green *W Mids*	38	SP0491
Brownheath *Shrops*	36	SJ4629
Brownhill *Gramp*	95	NJ8640
Brownhills *Fife*	83	NO5215
Brownhills *W Mids*	38	SK0405
Browninghill Green *Hants*	21	SU5859
Brownmuir *Gramp*	89	NO7377
Brownsham *Devon*	6	SS2826
Brownston *Devon*	5	SX6952
Brox *Surrey*	22	TQ0263
Broxa *N York*	63	SE9491
Broxbourne *Herts*	23	TL3607
Broxburn *Loth*	75	NT0872
Broxburn *Loth*	76	NT6977
Broxted *Essex*	24	TL5727
Broxwood *H & W*	27	SO3654
Bruan *Highld*	100	ND3139
Bruar *Tays*	87	NN8266
Brucefield *Highld*	97	NH9386
Bruchag *Strath*	73	NS1157
Brue *W Isls*	102	NB3349
Bruernish *W Isls*	102	NF7102
Bruisyard *Suffk*	33	TM3266
Bruisyard Street *Suffk*	33	TM3365
Brumby *Humb*	56	SE8009
Brund *Staffs*	48	SK1061
Brundall *Norfk*	43	TG3208
Brundish *Suffk*	33	TM2769
Brundish Street *Suffk*	33	TM2671
Brunnian *Cnwll*	2	SW5036
Bruno *Derbys*	48	SK1061
Bruntingthorpe *Leics*	39	SP6090
Brunton *Fife*	83	NO3220
Brunton *Nthumb*	77	NU2024
Brunton *Wilts*	21	SU2456
Brushford *Somset*	7	SS9225
Brushford Barton *Devon*	7	SS6707
Bruton *Somset*	9	ST6834
Bryan's Green *H & W*	28	SO8868
Bryanston *Dorset*	9	ST8706
Bryant's Bottom *Bucks*	22	SU8599
Brydekirk *D & G*	67	NY1870
Brympton *Somset*	8	ST5115
Bryn *W Glam*	18	SS8192
Bryn Du *Gwynd*	44	SH3472
Bryn Gates *Lancs*	47	SD5901
Bryn Saith Marchog *Clwyd*	46	SJ0750
Bryn-Mawr *Gwynd*	44	SH2433
Bryn-henllan *Dyfed*	16	SN0139
Bryn-y-maen *Clwyd*	45	SH8376
Brynamman *Dyfed*	26	SN7114
Brynberian *Dyfed*	16	SN1035
Bryncir *Gwynd*	44	SH4641
Bryncroes *Gwynd*	44	SH2231
Bryncrug *Gwynd*	34	SH6003
Bryneglwys *Clwyd*	46	SJ1447
Brynford *Clwyd*	46	SJ1774
Bryngwran *Gwynd*	44	SH3477
Bryngwyn *Gwent*	27	SO3809
Bryngwyn *Powys*	27	SO1849
Brynhoffnant *Dyfed*	17	SN3351
Bryning *Lancs*	53	SD4030
Brynithel *Gwent*	19	SO2101
Brynmawr *Gwent*	27	SO1911
Brynmenyn *M Glam*	18	SS9085
Brynmill *W Glam*	17	SS6392
Brynna *M Glam*	18	SS9883
Brynrefail *Gwynd*	44	SH4786
Brynrefail *Gwynd*	44	SH5662
Brynsadler *M Glam*	18	ST0280
Brynsiencyn *Gwynd*	44	SH4867
Bualintur *Highld*	84	NG4010
Bubbenhall *Warwks*	39	SP3672
Bubwith *Humb*	56	SE7136
Buccleuch *Border*	67	NT3214
Buchanan Smithy *Cent*	81	NS4689
Buchanhaven *Gramp*	95	NK1247
Buchanty *Tays*	82	NN9328
Buchany *Cent*	81	NN7102
Buchlyvie *Cent*	81	NS5793
Buchtrig *Border*	68	NT7714
Buck's Cross *Devon*	6	SS3523
Buck's Mills *Devon*	6	SS3523
Buckden *Cambs*	31	TL1967
Buckden *N York*	61	SD9477
Buckenham *Norfk*	43	TG3506
Buckerell *Devon*	8	ST1200
Buckfast *Devon*	5	SX7367
Buckfastleigh *Devon*	5	SX7366
Buckfastleigh *Devon*	5	SX7466
Buckhaven *Fife*	83	NT3598
Buckholt *Gwent*	27	SO5016
Buckhorn Weston *Dorset*	9	ST7524
Buckhurst Hill *Essex*	23	TQ4194
Buckie *Gramp*	94	NJ4265
Buckingham *Bucks*	30	SP6933
Buckland *Bucks*	30	SP8812
Buckland *Devon*	5	SX6743
Buckland *Gloucs*	28	SP0836
Buckland *Herts*	31	TL3533
Buckland *Kent*	15	TR3042
Buckland *Oxon*	21	SU3497
Buckland *Surrey*	12	TQ2250
Buckland Brewer *Devon*	6	SS4120
Buckland Common *Bucks*	22	SP9307
Buckland Dinham *Somset*	20	ST7550
Buckland Filleigh *Devon*	6	SS4608
Buckland Monachorum *Devon*	4	SX4868
Buckland Newton *Dorset*	9	ST6905
Buckland Ripers *Dorset*	9	SY6482
Buckland St. Mary *Somset*	8	ST2713
Buckland in the Moor *Devon*	5	SX7273
Buckland-Tout-Saints *Devon*	5	SX7546
Bucklebury *Berks*	21	SU5570
Bucklerheads *Tays*	83	NO4636
Bucklers Hard *Hants*	10	SU4000
Bucklesham *Suffk*	33	TM2442
Buckley *Clwyd*	46	SJ2864
Buckley Green *Warwks*	28	SP1667
Buckley Mountain *Clwyd*	46	SJ2865
Bucklow Hill *Ches*	47	SJ7383
Buckminster *Leics*	40	SK8722
Bucknall *Lincs*	50	TF1668
Bucknall *Staffs*	48	SJ9047
Bucknell *Oxon*	29	SP5626
Bucknell *Shrops*	36	SO3574
Buckpool *Gramp*	94	NJ4265
Bucks Green *W Susx*	12	TQ0732
Bucks Horn Oak *Hants*	11	SU8041
Bucksburn *Gramp*	95	NJ8909
Buckton *Humb*	57	TA1872
Buckton *Nthumb*	77	NU0838
Buckworth *Cambs*	30	TL1476
Budbrooke *Warwks*	29	SP2665
Budby *Notts*	49	SK6169
Budd's Titson *Cnwll*	6	SS2401
Buddon *Tays*	83	NO5232
Bude *Cnwll*	6	SS2006
Budge's Shop *Cnwll*	4	SX3259
Budlake *Devon*	5	SS9700
Budleigh Salterton *Devon*	5	SY0682
Budock Water *Cnwll*	2	SW7832
Buerton *Ches*	47	SJ6843
Bugbrooke *Nhants*	30	SP6757
Bugley *Dorset*	9	ST7824
Bugthorpe *Humb*	56	SE7757
Buildwas *Shrops*	37	SJ6304
Builth Road *Powys*	26	SO0253
Builth Wells *Powys*	26	SO0350
Bulbridge *Wilts*	10	SU0930
Buldoo *Highld*	100	ND0067
Bulford *Wilts*	20	SU1643
Bulkeley *Ches*	46	SJ5254
Bulkington *Warwks*	39	SP3986
Bulkington *Wilts*	20	ST9458
Bulkworthy *Devon*	6	SS3914
Bull's Green *Herts*	31	TL2717
Bullbrook *Berks*	22	SU8869
Bullington *Hants*	21	SU4541
Bullington *Lincs*	50	TF0977
Bullington End *Bucks*	30	SP8144
Bullwood *Strath*	80	NS1675
Bulmer *Essex*	32	TL8440
Bulmer *N York*	56	SE6967
Bulmer Tye *Essex*	32	TL8439
Bulphan *Essex*	24	TQ6386
Bulstrode *Herts*	22	TL0303
Bulval *Cnwll*	2	SW4831
Bulwark *Gramp*	95	NJ9345
Bulwell *Notts*	49	SK5345
Bulwick *Nhants*	40	SP9694
Bumble's Green *Essex*	23	TL4004
Bunacaimb *Highld*	85	NM6588
Bunarkaig *Highld*	86	NN1888
Bunbury *Ches*	47	SJ5658
Bunchrew *Highld*	92	NH6246
Bundalloch *Highld*	85	NG8927
Bunessan *Strath*	78	NM3821
Bungay *Suffk*	33	TM3389
Bunnahabhainn *Strath*	70	NR4173
Bunny *Notts*	39	SK5829
Buntait *Highld*	92	NH4030
Buntingford *Herts*	31	TL3629
Bunwell *Norfk*	33	TM1292
Bunwell Street *Norfk*	43	TM1194
Burbage *Leics*	39	SP4492
Burbage *Wilts*	21	SU2261
Burcher *H & W*	27	SO3360
Burchett's Green *Berks*	22	SU8381
Burcombe *Wilts*	10	SU0630
Burcot *Oxon*	21	SU5595
Burcott *Bucks*	30	SP8723
Bures *Suffk*	24	TL9034
Burford *H & W*	27	SO5868
Burford *Oxon*	29	SP2411
Burg *Strath*	78	NM3845
Burgates *Hants*	11	SU7728
Burgess Hill *W Susx*	12	TQ3118
Burgh *Suffk*	33	TM2351
Burgh Castle *Norfk*	43	TG4805
Burgh Heath *Surrey*	23	TQ2457
Burgh Hill *E Susx*	14	TQ7227
Burgh Le Marsh *Lincs*	51	TF4965
Burgh St. Margaret *Norfk*	43	TG4413
Burgh St. Peter *Norfk*	43	TM4693
Burgh by Sands *Cumb*	67	NY3259
Burgh next Aylsham *Norfk*	43	TG2125
Burgh on Bain *Lincs*	51	TF2186
Burghclere *Hants*	21	SU4761
Burghead *Gramp*	93	NJ1168
Burghfield *Berks*	22	SU6668
Burghfield Common *Berks*	21	SU6566
Burghill *H & W*	27	SO4744
Burghwallis *S York*	56	SE5311
Burghwallis *S York*	56	SE5312
Burham *Kent*	14	TQ7262
Buriton *Hants*	11	SU7320
Burland *Ches*	47	SJ6153
Burlawn *Cnwll*	3	SW9970
Burleigh *Berks*	22	SU9069
Burleigh *Gloucs*	20	SO8601
Burlescombe *Devon*	7	ST0716
Burleston *Dorset*	9	SY7794
Burley *Hants*	10	SU2103
Burley *Leics*	40	SK8810
Burley Gate *H & W*	27	SO5947
Burley Street *Hants*	10	SU2004
Burley Wood Head *W York*	55	SE1544
Burley in Wharfedale *W York*	55	SE1646
Burleydam *Ches*	37	SJ6042
Burlingham Green *Norfk*	43	TG3611
Burlington *Shrops*	37	SJ7611
Burlton *Shrops*	36	SJ4526
Burmington *Warwks*	29	SP2638
Burn *N York*	56	SE5928
Burn Cross *S York*	49	SK3495
Burn of Cambus *Cent*	81	NN7103
Burnage *Gt Man*	47	SJ8692
Burnaston *Derbys*	39	SK2832
Burnbrae *Strath*	74	NS8759
Burnby *Humb*	56	SE8346
Burneside *Cumb*	59	SD5095
Burneston *N York*	61	SE3084
Burnett *Avon*	20	ST6665
Burnfoot *Border*	76	NT5116
Burnfoot *D & G*	66	NX9791
Burnfoot *D & G*	67	NY3388
Burnfoot *D & G*	67	NY3896
Burnfoot *Tays*	82	NN9904
Burnham *Bucks*	22	SU9382
Burnham *Humb*	57	TA0517

Burnham Deepdale *Norfk* 42 TF8044
Burnham Green *Herts* 31 TL2616
Burnham Market *Norfk* 42 TF8342
Burnham Norton *Norfk* 42 TF8243
Burnham Overy *Norfk* 42 TF8442
Burnham Thorpe *Norfk* 42 TF8541
Burnham-on-Crouch *Essex* 25 TQ9496
Burnham-on-Sea *Somset* 19 ST3049
Burnhaven *Gramp* 95 NK1244
Burnhead *D & G* 66 NX8695
Burnhervie *Gramp* 95 NJ7319
Burnhill Green *Staffs* 37 SJ7800
Burnhope *Dur* 69 NZ1948
Burnhouse *Strath* 73 NS3850
Burniston *N York* 63 TA0193
Burnley *Lancs* 54 SD8432
Burnmouth *Border* 77 NT9560
Burnopfield *Dur* 69 NZ1756
Burnsall *N York* 55 SE0361
Burnside *Fife* 83 NO1307
Burnside *Fife* 82 NT0575
Burnside *Gramp* 94 NJ1669
Burnside *Tays* 88 NO4259
Burnside *Tays* 89 NO5050
Burnside of Duntrune *Tays* 83 NO4434
Burnt Heath *Essex* 25 TM0628
Burnt Hill *Berks* 21 SU5774
Burnt Yates *N York* 55 SE2461
Burntisland *Fife* 83 NT2385
Burnworthy *Somset* 8 ST1915
Burpham *Surrey* 12 TQ0151
Burpham *W Susx* 12 TQ0408
Burradon *Nthumb* 68 NT9806
Burrafirth *Shet* 103 HP6113
Burraton *Cnwll* 4 SX4167
Burraton *Devon* 5 SX6152
Burravoe *Shet* 103 HU5279
Burrells *Cumb* 60 NY6718
Burrelton *Tays* 82 NO2037
Burridge *Devon* 8 ST3106
Burridge *Hants* 11 SU5110
Burrill *N York* 61 SE2386
Burringham *Humb* 56 SE8309
Burrington *Avon* 19 ST4759
Burrington *Devon* 7 SS6316
Burrington *H & W* 36 SO4472
Burrough End *Cambs* 32 TL6256
Burrough Green *Cambs* 32 TL6355
Burrough on the Hill *Leics* 40 SK7510
Burrow *Somset* 7 SS9342
Burrow Bridge *Somset* 8 ST3530
Burrowhill *Surrey* 22 SU9763
Burry *W Glam* 17 SS4596
Burry Port *Dyfed* 17 SN4400
Burrygreen *W Glam* 17 SS4591
Burscough *Lancs* 53 SD4310
Burscough Bridge *Lancs* 53 SD4412
Bursea *Humb* 56 SE8033
Bursledon *Hants* 10 SU4809
Burslem *Staffs* 47 SJ8749
Burstall *Suffk* 33 TM1044
Burstock *Dorset* 8 ST4202
Burston *Devon* 7 SS7102
Burston *Norfk* 33 TM1383
Burstwick *Humb* 57 TA2228
Burtersett *N York* 54 SD8959
Burtholme *Cumb* 67 NY5463
Burthorpe Green *Suffk* 32 TL7764
Burtle Hill *Somset* 19 ST3943
Burtoft *Lincs* 41 TF2635
Burton *Ches* 46 SJ3174
Burton *Ches* 46 SJ5063
Burton *Cumb* 59 SD5276
Burton *Dorset* 9 SY6692
Burton *Dorset* 10 SZ1794
Burton *Dyfed* 16 SM9805
Burton *Lincs* 50 SK9574
Burton *Somset* 19 ST1944
Burton *Wilts* 20 ST8179
Burton Agnes *Humb* 57 TA1063
Burton Bradstock *Dorset* 8 SY4889
Burton Coggles *Lincs* 40 SK9725
Burton Dassett *Warwks* 29 SP3951
Burton End *Essex* 31 TL5323
Burton Fleming *Humb* 57 TA0872
Burton Hastings *Warwks* 39 SP4190
Burton Joyce *Notts* 49 SK6443
Burton Latimer *Nhants* 30 SP9074
Burton Lazars *Leics* 40 SK7716
Burton Leonard *N York* 55 SE3263
Burton Overy *Leics* 39 SP6798
Burton Pedwardine *Lincs* 50 TF1142
Burton Pidsea *Humb* 57 TA2431
Burton Salmon *N York* 55 SE4827
Burton in Lonsdale *N York* 54 SD6572
Burton on the Wolds *Leics* 39 SK5921
Burton upon Stather *Humb* 56 SE8617
Burton upon Trent *Staffs* 39 SK2423
Burton's Green *Essex* 24 TL8327
Burton-in-Lonsdale *N York* 54 SD6572
Burtonwood *Ches* 47 SJ5692
Burwarton *Shrops* 37 SO6185
Burwash *E Susx* 14 TQ6724
Burwash Common *E Susx* 13 TQ6423
Burwash Weald *E Susx* 13 TQ6523
Burwell *Cambs* 31 TL5866
Burwell *Lincs* 51 TF3579
Burwen *Gwynd* 44 SH4293
Burwick *Ork* 103 ND4384
Bury *Cambs* 41 TL2883
Bury *Gt Man* 54 SD8111
Bury *Somset* 7 SS9427
Bury *W Susx* 12 TQ0113
Bury End *Bucks* 22 SU9591
Bury St. Edmunds *Suffk* 32 TL8564
Burythorpe *N York* 56 SE7964
Busby *Strath* 74 NS5756
Buscot *Wilts* 21 SU2298
Bush *Gramp* 89 NO7565
Bush Bank *H & W* 27 SO4551
Bush Hill Park *Gt Lon* 23 TQ3395
Bushbury *W Mids* 38 SJ9202
Bushby *Leics* 39 SK6504
Bushey *Herts* 22 TQ1395
Bushey Heath *Herts* 22 TQ1494
Bushley *H & W* 28 SO8734
Bushton *Wilts* 20 SU0677
Buslingthorpe *Lincs* 50 TF0885
Bussex *Somset* 8 ST3435
Butcher's Cross *E Susx* 13 TQ5525
Butcher's Pasture *Essex* 24 TL6024
Butchers Row *W Susx* 12 TQ1720
Butcombe *Avon* 19 ST5162
Butleigh *Somset* 8 ST5233
Butleigh Wootton *Somset* 8 ST5034
Butlers Marston *Warwks* 29 SP3150
Butley *Suffk* 33 TM3751
Butt Green *Ches* 47 SJ6751
Buttercrambe *N York* 56 SE7358
Butterknowle *Dur* 61 NZ1025
Butterleigh *Devon* 7 SS9708
Buttermere *Cumb* 58 NY1726
Buttermere *Wilts* 21 SU3381
Buttershaw *W York* 55 SE1329
Butterstone *Tays* 88 NO0645
Butterton *Staffs* 48 SJ8242
Butterton *Staffs* 48 SK0756
Butterwick *Dur* 62 NZ3829
Butterwick *Lincs* 41 TF3827
Butterwick *N York* 63 SE7371
Butterwick *N York* 56 SE9871
Buttington *Powys* 36 SJ2508
Buttsash *Hants* 10 SU4205
Buxhall *Suffk* 32 TM0057
Buxted *E Susx* 13 TQ4923
Buxton *Derbys* 48 SK0673
Buxton *Norfk* 43 TG2322
Buxton Heath *Norfk* 43 TG1821
Bwlch *Powys* 27 SO1522
Bwlch-y-cibau *Powys* 36 SJ1717
Bwlch-y-ffridd *Powys* 36 SO0796
Bwlch-y-groes *Dyfed* 17 SN2436
Bwlch-y-sarnau *Powys* 36 SO0374
Bwlchgwyn *Clwyd* 46 SJ2653
Bwlchllan *Dyfed* 34 SN5758

Bwlchymyrdd *W Glam* 17 SS5798
Byers Garth *Dur* 62 NZ3141
Byers Green *Dur* 61 NZ2233
Byfield *Nhants* 29 SP5153
Byfield *Nhants* 29 SP5153
Byfleet *Surrey* 22 TQ0661
Byford *H & W* 27 SO3942
Byker *T & W* 69 NZ2764
Bylchau *Clwyd* 45 SH9762
Byre Burnfoot *D & G* 67 NY3877
Byrewalls *Border* 76 NT6643
Byrness *Nthumb* 68 NT7602
Bystock *Devon* 5 SY0283
Bythorn *Cambs* 30 TL0575
Byton *H & W* 27 SO3764
Bywell *Nthumb* 68 NZ0461
Byworth *W Susx* 12 SU9820

C

Cabourne *Lincs* 50 TA1401
Cabrach *Gramp* 94 NJ3826
Cabrach *Strath* 70 NR4964
Cabus *Lancs* 53 SD4948
Cabvie Lodge *Highld* 92 NH1567
Cackle Street *E Susx* 14 TQ8219
Cacrabank *Border* 75 NT3017
Cadbury *Devon* 7 SS9105
Cadder *Strath* 74 NS6172
Caddington *Beds* 30 TL0619
Caddonfoot *Border* 76 NT4535
Cade Street *E Susx* 13 TQ6021
Cadeby *Leics* 39 SK4202
Cadeby *S York* 49 SE5100
Cadeleigh *Devon* 7 SS9107
Cadgwith *Cnwll* 2 SW7214
Cadham *Fife* 83 NO2802
Cadishead *Gt Man* 47 SJ7191
Cadle *W Glam* 17 SS6296
Cadley *Wilts* 21 SU2066
Cadley *Wilts* 21 SU2454
Cadmore End *Bucks* 22 SU7892
Cadnam *Hants* 10 SU2913
Cadney *Humb* 56 TA0103
Cadoxton *S Glam* 18 ST1269
Cadoxton Juxta-Neath *W Glam* 18 SS7598
Caeathro *Gwynd* 44 SH5061
Caenby *Lincs* 50 TF0089
Caeo *Dyfed* 26 SN6739
Caer Farchell *Dyfed* 16 SM7927
Caerau *M Glam* 18 SS8694
Caerau *S Glam* 18 ST1375
Caergeiliog *Gwynd* 44 SH3178
Caergwrle *Clwyd* 46 SJ3057
Caerlanrig *Border* 67 NT3904
Caerleon *Gwent* 19 ST3491
Caernarfon *Gwynd* 44 SH4862
Caerphilly *M Glam* 19 ST1587
Caerphilly *M Glam* 19 ST1598
Caersws *Powys* 35 SO0392
Caerwedros *Dyfed* 34 SN3755
Caerwent *Gwent* 19 ST4790
Caerwys *Clwyd* 46 SJ1272
Cairnbaan *Strath* 71 NR8390
Cairnbrogie *Gramp* 95 NJ8527
Cairnbulg *Gramp* 95 NK0365
Cairncross *Border* 77 NT8963
Cairncurran *Strath* 73 NS3170
Cairndow *Strath* 80 NN1810
Cairneyhill *Fife* 82 NT0486
Cairnfield House *Gramp* 94 NJ4162
Cairngarroch *D & G* 64 NX0649
Cairngrassie *Gramp* 89 NO9095
Cairnie *Gramp* 94 NJ4844
Cairnorrie *Gramp* 95 NJ8641
Cairnryan *D & G* 64 NX0668
Cairnty Auchroisk *Gramp* 94 NJ3351
Cairnwhin *Strath* 64 NX2491
Caister-on-Sea *Norfk* 43 TG5212
Caistor *Lincs* 50 TA1101
Caistor St. Edmund *Norfk* 43 TG2303
Caistron *Nthumb* 68 NT9901
Cake Street *Norfk* 32 TM0790
Calais Street *Suffk* 32 TL9740
Calbost *Highld* 90 NG2148
Calbourne *IOW* 10 SZ4286
Calceby *Lincs* 51 TF3877
Calcot *Clwyd* 46 SJ1775
Calcot *Gloucs* 28 SP0910
Calcot Row *Berks* 22 SU6771
Calcots *Gramp* 94 NJ2563
Calcott *Shrops* 36 SJ4414
Caldback *Shet* 103 HP6104
Caldbeck *Cumb* 59 NY3239
Caldbergh *N York* 61 SE0985
Caldecote *Cambs* 40 TL1488
Caldecote *Cambs* 31 TL3456
Caldecote *Herts* 31 TL2338
Caldecote Highfields *Cambs* 31 TL3559
Caldecott *Leics* 40 SP8693
Caldecott *Nhants* 30 SP9868
Caldecott *Oxon* 21 SU4996
Calder Bridge *Cumb* 58 NY0306
Calder Grove *W York* 55 SE3016
Calder Vale *Lancs* 53 SD5345
Calderbank *Strath* 74 NS7663
Caldercruix *Strath* 74 NS8167
Caldermill *Strath* 74 NS6642
Caldermore *Gt Man* 54 SD9316
Caldicot *Gwent* 19 ST4888
Caldwell *N York* 61 NZ1613
Calfsound *Ork* 103 HY5730
Calgary *Strath* 78 NM3751
Califer *Gramp* 93 NJ0857
California *Cent* 74 NS9076
California *Derbys* 39 SK3335
California *Norfk* 43 TG5114
Calke *Derbys* 39 SK3722
Callander *Cent* 81 NN6208
Callanish *W Isls* 102 NB2133
Callert Cottage *Highld* 86 NN1060
Callestick *Cnwll* 2 SW7750
Calligarry *Highld* 84 NG6203
Callington *Cnwll* 4 SX3669
Callow *H & W* 27 SO4934
Callow End *H & W* 28 SO8349
Callow Hill *H & W* 28 SP0164
Callow Hill *Wilts* 20 SU0385
Callows Grave *H & W* 27 SO5966
Calmore *Hants* 10 SU3314
Calmsden *Gloucs* 28 SP0508
Calne *Wilts* 20 ST9971
Calshot *Hants* 10 SU4701
Calstock *Cnwll* 4 SX4368
Calstone Wellington *Wilts* 20 SU0268
Calthorpe *Norfk* 43 TG1831
Calthorpe Street *Norfk* 43 TG4025
Calthwaite *Cumb* 59 NY4640
Calton *N York* 54 SD9259
Calton *Staffs* 48 SK1050
Calton Green *Staffs* 48 SK1050
Calveley *Ches* 47 SJ5958
Calver *Derbys* 48 SK2474
Calverhall *Shrops* 37 SJ6037
Calverleigh *Devon* 7 SS9214
Calverton *Bucks* 30 SP7938
Calverton *Notts* 49 SK6149
Calvine *Tays* 87 NN8065
Calvo *Cumb* 67 NY1453
Calzeat *Border* 75 NT1135
Cam *Gloucs* 20 ST7599
Camas - Iuinie *Highld* 85 NG9428
Camascross *Highld* 85 NM7660
Camasnacroise *Highld* 79 NM7561
Camasine *Highld* 79 NM6911
Camastianavaig *Highld* 84 NG5039
Camasunary *Highld* 84 NG5118
Camault Muir *Highld* 92 NH5040
Camber *E Susx* 14 TQ9618
Camberley *Surrey* 22 SU8860
Camberwell *Gt Lon* 23 TQ3276
Camblesforth *N York* 56 SE6425
Cambo *Nthumb* 68 NZ0285
Camborne *Cnwll* 2 SW6440

Cambridge *Cambs* 31 TL4558
Cambridge *Gloucs* 20 SO7403
Cambrose *Cnwll* 2 SW6845
Cambus *Cent* 82 NS8593
Cambus O' May *Gramp* 88 NO4198
Cambusavie Platform *Highld* 97 NH6494
Cambusbarron *Cent* 81 NS7792
Cambuskenneth *Cent* 81 NS8094
Cambusmoon *Strath* 81 NS4285
Cambuswallace *Strath* 75 NT0438
Camden Town *Gt Lon* 23 TQ2884
Cameley *Avon* 19 ST6157
Camelford *Cnwll* 3 SX1083
Camelon *Cent* 82 NS8680
Camer's Green *H & W* 28 SO7735
Camerory *Highld* 93 NJ0131
Camerton *Avon* 20 ST6857
Camerton *Cumb* 58 NY0431
Camghouran *Tays* 87 NN5556
Cammachmore *Gramp* 89 NO9195
Cammeringham *Lincs* 50 SK9482
Camore *Highld* 97 NH7889
Campbeltown *Strath* 72 NR7120
Campmuir *Tays* 82 NO2137
Camps *Loth* 75 NT0968
Camps End *Cambs* 31 TL6142
Campsall *S York* 56 SE5313
Campsea Ashe *Suffk* 33 TM3356
Campsie *Strath* 81 NS6179
Campton *Beds* 30 TL1238
Campton *Beds* 30 TL1238
Camptown *Border* 68 NT6813
Camquhart *Strath* 80 NR9985
Camrose *Dyfed* 16 SM9220
Camserney *Tays* 87 NN8149
Camster *Highld* 100 ND2642
Camusnagaul *Highld* 86 NN0874
Camusnagaul *Highld* 91 NH0589
Camusteel *Highld* 91 NG7042
Camusterrach *Highld* 85 NG7141
Canada *Hants* 10 SU2817
Canada *Hants* 10 SU2818
Candacraig *Gramp* 88 NO3499
Candlesby *Lincs* 51 TF4567
Candyburn *Strath* 75 NT0741
Cane End *Oxon* 22 SU6779
Canewdon *Essex* 24 TQ9094
Canfield End *Essex* 24 TL5821
Canford Bottom *Dorset* 9 SU0300
Canford Cliffs *Dorset* 10 SZ0689
Canford Magna *Dorset* 9 SZ0398
Canhams Green *Suffk* 32 TM0565
Canisbay *Highld* 100 ND3472
Canley *W Mids* 39 SP3077
Cann *Dorset* 9 ST8723
Cannich *Highld* 92 NH3331
Cannington *Somset* 19 ST2539
Cannon Bridge *H & W* 27 SO4543
Cannon Frome *H & W* 27 SO6543
Canon Pyon *H & W* 27 SO4548
Canonbie *D & G* 67 NY3976
Canons Ashby *Nhants* 29 SP5750
Canonstown *Cnwll* 2 SW5335
Canterbury *Kent* 15 TR1457
Cantley *Norfk* 43 TG3804
Cantley *S York* 49 SE6202
Canton *S Glam* 19 ST1576
Cantraywood *Highld* 93 NH7847
Cantsfield *Lancs* 54 SD6172
Canvey Island *Essex* 24 TQ7983
Canwick *Lincs* 50 SK9869
Canworthy Water *Cnwll* 4 SX2291
Caol *Highld* 86 NN1075
Caoles *Strath* 78 NM0848
Caonich *Highld* 86 NN0692
Capel *Kent* 13 TQ6344
Capel *Surrey* 12 TQ1740
Capel Bangor *Dyfed* 35 SN6580
Capel Betws Lleucu *Dyfed* 34 SN6058
Capel Coch *Gwynd* 44 SH4582
Capel Curig *Gwynd* 45 SH7258
Capel Dewi *Dyfed* 17 SN4720
Capel Dewi *Dyfed* 34 SN4542
Capel Garmon *Gwynd* 45 SH8155
Capel Green *Suffk* 33 TM3749
Capel Gwyn *Dyfed* 17 SN4521
Capel Gwynfe *Dyfed* 26 SN7222
Capel Hendre *Dyfed* 17 SN5911
Capel Iwan *Dyfed* 17 SN2836
Capel Mawr *Gwynd* 44 SH4171
Capel Seion *Gwynd* 35 SN6379
Capel St. Andrews *Suffk* 33 TM3748
Capel St. Mary *Suffk* 25 TM0838
Capel le Ferne *Kent* 15 TR2439
Capel-Dewi *Dyfed* 35 SN6282
Capelles *Guern* 101 SV0000
Capelulo *Gwynd* 45 SH7476
Capelulo *Gwynd* 45 SH7476
Capenhurst *Ches* 46 SJ3673
Capernwray *Lancs* 53 SD5372
Capheaton *Nthumb* 68 NZ0380
Caplaw *Strath* 73 NS4458
Capon's Green *Suffk* 33 TM2867
Cappeldall *D & G* 67 NT1409
Cappercleuch *Border* 75 NT2423
Capton *Devon* 5 SX8353
Capton *Somset* 7 ST0739
Caputh *Tays* 82 NO0840
Car Colston *Notts* 49 SK7242
Carbeth Inn *Cent* 81 NS5279
Carbis *Cnwll* 3 SW9959
Carbis Bay *Cnwll* 2 SW5238
Carbost *Highld* 84 NG3732
Carbost *Highld* 90 NG4248
Carbrook *S York* 49 SK3888
Carbrooke *Norfk* 42 TF9502
Carburton *Notts* 49 SK6173
Carcary *Tays* 89 NO6455
Cardenden *Fife* 82 NT2195
Cardiff *S Glam* 19 ST1876
Cardigan *Dyfed* 17 SN1846
Cardinal's Green *Cambs* 31 TL6147
Cardington *Beds* 30 TL0847
Cardington *Shrops* 37 SO5095
Cardinham *Cnwll* 3 SX1268
Cardow *Gramp* 94 NJ1943
Cardrona *Border* 75 NT3038
Cardross *Strath* 80 NS3477
Cardurnock *Cumb* 67 NY1758
Careby *Lincs* 40 TF0216
Careston *Tays* 89 NO5260
Carew *Dyfed* 16 SN0404
Carew Cheriton *Dyfed* 16 SN0404
Carew Newton *Dyfed* 16 SN0404
Carey *H & W* 27 SO5730
Carfin *Strath* 74 NS7759
Carfraemill *Border* 76 NT5053
Cargate Green *Norfk* 43 TG3913
Cargen *D & G* 66 NX9672
Cargenbridge *D & G* 66 NX9372
Cargo *Cumb* 67 NY3659
Cargreen *Cnwll* 4 SX4262
Cargurrel *Cnwll* 3 SW8837
Carham *Nthumb* 76 NT7938
Carhampton *Somset* 7 ST0042
Carharrack *Cnwll* 2 SW7341
Carie *Tays* 87 NN6257
Carie *Tays* 81 NN6437
Carinish *W Isls* 102 NF8159
Carisbrooke *IOW* 10 SZ4888
Cark *Cumb* 59 SD3676
Carkeel *Cnwll* 4 SX4060
Carland Cross *Cnwll* 2 SW8454
Carlbury *Dur* 61 NZ2116
Carlby *Lincs* 40 TF0414
Carlcroft *Nthumb* 68 NT8311
Carleen *Cnwll* 2 SW6130
Carlesmoor *N York* 61 SE1973
Carleton *Cumb* 59 NY4253
Carleton *Cumb* 60 NY5330
Carleton Forehoe *Norfk* 43 TG0905
Carleton Rode *Norfk* 33 TM1193
Carleton St. Peter *Norfk* 43 TG3402
Carlin How *Cleve* 62 NZ7018
Carlincraig *Gramp* 95 NJ6743

Carlingcott *Avon* 20 ST6958
Carlisle *Cumb* 67 NY3955
Carloggas *Cnwll* 3 SW8765
Carlops *Border* 75 NT1656
Carloway *W Isls* 102 NB2042
Carlton *Beds* 30 SP9555
Carlton *Cambs* 32 TL6452
Carlton *Cleve* 62 NZ3921
Carlton *Leics* 39 SK3905
Carlton *N York* 56 SE6423
Carlton *N York* 56 SE6423
Carlton *N York* 62 NZ5004
Carlton *N York* 61 SE0684
Carlton *N York* 62 SE6086
Carlton *Notts* 49 SK6041
Carlton *S York* 55 SE3610
Carlton *Suffk* 33 TM3864
Carlton *W York* 55 SE3327
Carlton Colville *Suffk* 33 TM5190
Carlton Curlieu *Leics* 40 SP6997
Carlton Green *Cambs* 32 TL6451
Carlton Husthwaite *N York* 62 SE4976
Carlton Miniott *N York* 62 SE3980
Carlton Scroop *Lincs* 50 SK9445
Carlton in Lindrick *Notts* 49 SK5984
Carlton-on-Trent *Notts* 50 SK7963
Carluke *Strath* 74 NS8450
Carmacoup *Strath* 74 NS7927
Carmarthen *Dyfed* 17 SN4020
Carmel *Dyfed* 17 SN5816
Carmel *Gwynd* 44 SH3882
Carmel *Gwynd* 44 SH4954
Carminowe *Cnwll* 2 SW6624
Carmunnock *Strath* 74 NS5957
Carmyle *Strath* 74 NS6462
Carmyllie *Tays* 89 NO5542
Carn Brea *Cnwll* 2 SW6841
Carn-Gorm *Highld* 85 NG9520
Carnaby *Humb* 57 TA1465
Carnach *W Isls* 90 NG2297
Carnan *W Isls* 102 NF8143
Carnbee *Fife* 83 NO5206
Carnbo *Tays* 82 NO0503
Carndu *Highld* 85 NG8927
Carnduff *Strath* 74 NS6646
Carnell *Strath* 73 NS4731
Carnforth *Lancs* 53 SD4970
Carnhell Green *Cnwll* 2 SW6137
Carnie *Gramp* 89 NJ8005
Carnkie *Cnwll* 2 SW7134
Carno *Powys* 35 SN9696
Carnock *Fife* 82 NT0489
Carnon Downs *Cnwll* 2 SW7940
Carnousie *Gramp* 94 NJ6650
Carnoustie *Tays* 83 NO5534
Carnwath *Strath* 75 NS9746
Carol Green *W Mids* 39 SP2577
Carpalla *Cnwll* 3 SW9654
Carperby *N York* 61 SE0089
Carr *S York* 49 SK5091
Carr Gate *W York* 55 SE3024
Carr Shield *Nthumb* 68 NY8047
Carr Vale *Derbys* 49 SK4670
Carradale *Strath* 72 NR8138
Carragrich *W Isls* 90 NG2098
Carrbridge *Highld* 93 NH9022
Carrefour *Jersey* 101 SV0000
Carreglefn *Gwynd* 44 SH3889
Carrhouse *Humb* 56 SE7706
Carrick *Fife* 83 NO4422
Carrick *Strath* 71 NR9187
Carrick Castle *Strath* 80 NS1994
Carrieden *Cent* 82 NT0281
Carrington *Gt Man* 47 SJ7492
Carrington *Loth* 75 NT3160
Carrington Moss *Gt Man* 47 SJ7592
Carrismerry *Cnwll* 3 SX0158
Carrog *Gwynd* 45 SH7648
Carron *Cent* 82 NS8882
Carron *Gramp* 94 NJ2241
Carron *Highld* 91 NJ1234
Carron Bridge *Cent* 81 NS7483
Carronbridge *D & G* 66 NX8698
Carronshore *Cent* 82 NS8983
Carruth House *Strath* 73 NS3566
Carrutherstown *D & G* 67 NY1071
Carrville *Dur* 69 NZ3243
Carsaig *Strath* 79 NM5421
Carscreugh *D & G* 64 NX2260
Carse Gray *Tays* 88 NO4553
Carseriggen *D & G* 64 NX3167
Carsethorn *D & G* 66 NX9959
Carshalton *Gt Lon* 23 TQ2764
Carsie *Tays* 82 NO1742
Carsington *Derbys* 48 SK2453
Carsphairn *D & G* 65 NX5693
Carstairs *Strath* 75 NS9346
Carstairs Junction *Strath* 75 NS9545
Carswell Marsh *Oxon* 21 SU3298
Carter Bar *Border* 68 NT6907
Carters Green *Essex* 23 TL5111
Carterton *Oxon* 29 SP2706
Carterway Heads *Nthumb* 68 NZ0452
Carthew *Cnwll* 3 SX0056
Carthorpe *N York* 62 SE3083
Cartland *Strath* 74 NS8646
Cartledge *Derbys* 49 SK3477
Cartmel *Cumb* 59 SD3778
Carway *Dyfed* 17 SN4606
Carwinley *Cumb* 67 NY4073
Cashe's Green *Gloucs* 28 SO8305
Cashlie *Tays* 87 NN4942
Cashmoor *Dorset* 9 ST9813
Cassington *Oxon* 29 SP4511
Cassop Colliery *Dur* 62 NZ3438
Castel *Guern* 101 SV0000
Castellau *M Glam* 18 ST0687
Casterton *Cumb* 60 SD6279
Casterton *Lancs* 60 SD6279
Castle *Gwynd* 45 SH7669
Castle Acre *Norfk* 42 TF8115
Castle Ashby *Nhants* 30 SP8659
Castle Bolton *N York* 61 SE0391
Castle Bromwich *W Mids* 38 SP1489
Castle Bytham *Lincs* 40 SK9818
Castle Caereinion *Powys* 36 SJ1605
Castle Camps *Cambs* 32 TL6242
Castle Carrock *Cumb* 67 NY5455
Castle Cary *Somset* 20 ST6332
Castle Combe *Wilts* 20 ST8477
Castle Donington *Leics* 39 SK4427
Castle Douglas *D & G* 65 NX7662
Castle Eaton *Wilts* 20 SU1495
Castle Eden *Dur* 62 NZ4338
Castle End *Cambs* 31 TF1208
Castle Frome *H & W* 28 SO6645
Castle Green *Cumb* 59 SD5391
Castle Gresley *Derbys* 39 SK2717
Castle Hedingham *Essex* 24 TL7835
Castle Hill *Suffk* 33 TM1446
Castle Howard *N York* 62 SE7069
Castle Inn *Cumb* 58 NY2233
Castle Kennedy *D & G* 64 NX0959
Castle Lachlan *Strath* 80 NS0195
Castle O'er *D & G* 67 NY2492
Castle Pulverbatch *Shrops* 36 SJ4202
Castle Rising *Norfk* 42 TF6624
Castle Street *W York* 55 SD9524
Castleford *W York* 55 SE4225
Castlehill *Border* 75 NT2135
Castlehill *Highld* 100 ND1968
Castlehill *Strath* 74 NS8452
Castlemartin *Dyfed* 16 SR9198
Castlemilk *D & G* 67 NY1577
Castlemorton *H & W* 28 SO7937
Castleside *Dur* 68 NZ0848
Castlethorpe *Bucks* 30 SP7944
Castlethorpe *Humb* 56 SE9807
Castleton *Border* 67 NY5189
Castleton *Derbys* 48 SK1582
Castleton *Gt Man* 54 SD8810
Castleton *Gwent* 19 ST2583

Castleton
Clathymore

Castleton *N York*	62	NZ6808
Castleton *Strath*	71	NR8884
Castletown *Highld*	93	NH7442
Castletown *Highld*	100	ND1967
Castletown *IOM*	52	SC2667
Castletown *T & W*	69	NZ3558
Castley *N York*	55	SE2645
Caston *Norfk*	42	TL9597
Castor *Cambs*	40	TL1298
Cat & Fiddle Inn *Derbys*	48	SK0072
Cat's Ash *Gwent*	19	ST3790
Catacol *Strath*	72	NR9149
Catbrain *Avon*	19	ST5780
Catbrook *Gwent*	19	SO5002
Catchall *Cnwll*	2	SW4328
Catcliffe *S York*	49	SK4288
Catcomb *Wilts*	20	SU0076
Catcott *Somset*	19	ST3939
Catcott Burtle *Somset*	19	ST4043
Caterham *Surrey*	23	TQ3455
Catfield *Norfk*	43	TG3821
Catfirth *Shet*	103	HU4354
Catford *Gt Lon*	23	TQ3772
Catforth *Lancs*	53	SD4735
Cath Pair *Border*	76	NT4646
Cathcart *Strath*	74	NS5860
Cathedine *Powys*	26	SO1425
Catherington *Hants*	11	SU6914
Catherston Leweston *Dorset*	8	SY3694
Catisfield *Hants*	11	SU5406
Catlodge *Highld*	87	NN6392
Catlowdy *Cumb*	67	NY4677
Catmere End *Essex*	31	TL4939
Catmore *Berks*	21	SU4580
Caton *Lancs*	53	SD5364
Caton Green *Lancs*	53	SD5564
Catrine *Strath*	74	NS5225
Catsfield *E Susx*	14	TQ7213
Catsham *Somset*	8	ST5534
Catshill *H & W*	38	SO9673
Cattadale *Strath*	72	NR6710
Cattal *N York*	55	SE4454
Cattawade *Suffk*	25	TM1033
Catterall *Lancs*	53	SD5042
Catterick *N York*	61	SE2397
Catterlen *Cumb*	59	NY4833
Catterton *N York*	55	SE5145
Catteshall *Surrey*	12	SU9844
Catthorpe *Leics*	39	SP5578
Cattistock *Dorset*	9	SY5999
Catton *Cumb*	68	NY8257
Catton *N York*	62	SE3678
Catton *Norfk*	43	TG2312
Catwick *Humb*	57	TA1245
Caudle Green *Gloucs*	28	SO9410
Caulcott *Oxon*	29	SP5024
Cauldcots *Tays*	89	NO6547
Cauldhame *Cent*	81	NS6493
Cauldmill *Border*	76	NT5315
Cauldon *Staffs*	48	SK0749
Cauldside *D & G*	67	NY4480
Caulkerbush *D & G*	66	NX9357
Caundle Marsh *Dorset*	9	ST6713
Caunton *Notts*	50	SK7460
Causeway End *D & G*	64	NX4260
Causewayend *Strath*	75	NT0336
Causewayhead *Cent*	81	NS8095
Causey Park *Nthumb*	69	NZ1794
Causeyend *Gramp*	95	NJ9419
Caute *Devon*	6	SS4310
Cautley *Cumb*	60	SD6994
Cavendish *Suffk*	32	TL8046
Cavenham *Suffk*	32	TL7669
Caversfield *Oxon*	29	SP5825
Caversham *Berks*	22	SU7274
Caverswall *Staffs*	48	SJ9542
Caverton Mill *Border*	76	NT7425
Cavil *Humb*	56	SE7630
Cawdor *Highld*	93	NH8450
Cawood *N York*	56	SE5737
Cawsand *Cnwll*	4	SX4350
Cawston *Norfk*	43	TG1323
Cawthorne *S York*	55	SE2807
Caxton *Cambs*	31	TL3058
Caxton End *Cambs*	31	TL2759
Caynham *Shrops*	37	SO5573
Caythorpe *Lincs*	50	SK9348
Caythorpe *Notts*	49	SK6845
Cayton *N York*	63	TA0583
Ceannacroc Lodge *Highld*	92	NH3211
Cefn *Gwent*	19	ST2788
Cefn Cribwr *M Glam*	18	SS8582
Cefn Mably *M Glam*	19	ST2284
Cefn-brith *Clwyd*	45	SH9350
Cefn-mawr *Clwyd*	36	SJ2842
Cefn-y-pant *Dyfed*	17	SN1925
Cefneithin *Dyfed*	17	SN5514
Cefngorwydd *Powys*	26	SN9045
Cellarhead *Staffs*	48	SJ9547
Cemaes *Gwynd*	44	SH3793
Cemmaes *Powys*	35	SH8406
Cemmaes *Powys*	35	SH8406
Cemmaes Road *Powys*	35	SH8104
Cenarth *Dyfed*	17	SN2641
Cennin *Gwynd*	44	SH4645
Ceres *Fife*	83	NO4011
Cerne Abbas *Dorset*	9	ST6601
Cerney Wick *Gloucs*	20	SU0796
Cerrigceinwen *Gwynd*	44	SH4274
Cerrigydrudion *Clwyd*	45	SH9548
Ceunant *Gwynd*	44	SH5361
Chaceley *Gloucs*	28	SO8530
Chacewater *Cnwll*	2	SW7444
Chackmore *Bucks*	30	SP6835
Chacombe *Nhants*	29	SP4943
Chadbury *H & W*	28	SP0146
Chadderton *Gt Man*	54	SD9204
Chadderton Fold *Gt Man*	54	SD9006
Chaddesden *Derbys*	49	SK3737
Chaddesley Corbett *H & W*	38	SO8973
Chaddlehanger *Devon*	4	SX4678
Chaddleworth *Berks*	21	SU4177
Chadlington *Oxon*	29	SP3222
Chadshunt *Warwks*	29	SP3552
Chadwell *Leics*	40	SK7824
Chadwell End *Beds*	30	TL0865
Chadwell Heath *Gt Lon*	23	TQ4888
Chadwell St. Mary *Essex*	24	TQ6478
Chadwick *H & W*	28	SO8369
Chadwick End *W Mids*	39	SP2073
Chaffcombe *Somset*	8	ST3510
Chagford *Devon*	5	SX7087
Chailey *E Susx*	13	TQ3919
Chainbridge *Cambs*	41	TL4299
Chainhurst *Kent*	14	TQ7248
Chaldon *Surrey*	23	TQ3055
Chaldon Herring or East Chaldon *Dorset*	9	SY7983
Chale *IOW*	10	SZ4877
Chale Green *IOW*	10	SZ4879
Chalfont Common *Bucks*	22	TQ0092
Chalfont St. Giles *Bucks*	22	SU9893
Chalfont St. Peter *Bucks*	22	TQ0090
Chalford *Gloucs*	20	SO8902
Chalford *Oxon*	22	SP7101
Chalford *Wilts*	20	ST8750
Chalgrove *Beds*	30	TL0127
Chalgrove *Oxon*	21	SU6396
Chalk *Kent*	14	TQ6773
Chalkwell *Kent*	14	TQ8963
Challaborough *Devon*	5	SX6545
Challacombe *Devon*	7	SS6941
Challoch *D & G*	64	NX3867
Challock Lees *Kent*	15	TR0050
Chalmington *Dorset*	9	ST5901
Chalton *Beds*	30	TL0326
Chalton *Hants*	11	SU7316
Chalvey *Berks*	22	SU9679
Chalvington *E Susx*	13	TQ5109
Chandler's Cross *Herts*	22	TQ0698
Chandler's Ford *Hants*	10	SU4320
Channel's Green *Beds*	30	TL1057
Chantry *Suffk*	33	TM1443
Chapel *Fife*	83	NT2593
Chapel Allerton *Somset*	19	ST4050
Chapel Allerton *W York*	55	SE3037
Chapel Amble *Cnwll*	3	SW9975
Chapel Brampton *Nhants*	30	SP7266
Chapel Chorlton *Staffs*	37	SJ8137
Chapel End *Beds*	30	TL1057
Chapel End *Cambs*	40	TL1282
Chapel Green *Warwks*	29	SP4660
Chapel Haddlesey *N York*	56	SE5826
Chapel Hall *Strath*	73	NS1368
Chapel Hill *Gramp*	95	NK0635
Chapel Hill *Gwent*	19	SO5300
Chapel Hill *Lincs*	51	TF2054
Chapel Hill *N York*	55	SE3346
Chapel Lawn *Shrops*	36	SO3176
Chapel Le Dale *N York*	60	SD7377
Chapel Leigh *Somset*	8	ST1222
Chapel Row *Berks*	21	SU5669
Chapel St. Leonards *Lincs*	51	TF5572
Chapel Stile *Cumb*	58	NY3205
Chapel of Garioch *Gramp*	95	NJ7124
Chapel-en-le-Frith *Derbys*	48	SK0580
Chapelend Way *Essex*	32	TL7139
Chapelhall *Strath*	74	NS7862
Chapelhill *Tays*	82	NO0030
Chapelhope *Border*	67	NT2308
Chapelknowe *D & G*	67	NY3173
Chapelton *Devon*	6	SS5826
Chapelton *Strath*	74	NS6848
Chapelton *Tays*	89	NO6247
Chapeltown *Gramp*	94	NJ2320
Chapeltown *Lancs*	54	SD7315
Chapeltown *S York*	49	SK3596
Chapmans Well *Devon*	4	SX3592
Chapmanslade *Wilts*	20	ST8247
Chapmore End *Herts*	31	TL3216
Chappel *Essex*	24	TL8928
Charaton *M Glam*	4	SX3169
Chard *Somset*	8	ST3208
Chard Junction *Somset*	8	ST3404
Chardleigh Green *Somset*	8	ST3110
Chardstock *Devon*	8	ST3004
Charfield *Avon*	20	ST7292
Charing *Kent*	14	TQ9549
Charing Heath *Kent*	14	TQ9249
Charingworth *Gloucs*	29	SP1939
Charlbury *Oxon*	29	SP3519
Charlcombe *Avon*	20	ST7467
Charlcutt *Wilts*	20	ST9875
Charlecote *Warwks*	29	SP2656
Charles *Devon*	7	SS6832
Charles Tye *Suffk*	32	TM0252
Charleston *Tays*	88	NO3845
Charlestown *Cnwll*	3	SX0351
Charlestown *Fife*	82	NT0683
Charlestown *Gramp*	89	NJ9300
Charlestown *Gt Man*	47	SD8100
Charlestown *Highld*	91	NG8174
Charlestown *Highld*	92	NH6448
Charlestown *W York*	54	SD9726
Charlestown *W York*	55	SE1538
Charlinch *Somset*	19	ST2338
Charlton *Gt Lon*	23	TQ4277
Charlton *Nhants*	29	SP5236
Charlton *Nthumb*	68	NY8184
Charlton *Oxon*	21	SU4088
Charlton *Shrops*	37	SJ5911
Charlton *Somset*	8	ST2827
Charlton *Somset*	19	ST6242
Charlton *W Susx*	11	SU8812
Charlton *Wilts*	20	ST9688
Charlton *Wilts*	9	ST9021
Charlton *Wilts*	20	SU1155
Charlton *Wilts*	10	SU1723
Charlton Abbots *Gloucs*	28	SP0324
Charlton Adam *Somset*	8	ST5328
Charlton Horethorne *Somset*	9	ST6623
Charlton Kings *Gloucs*	28	SO9620
Charlton Mackrell *Somset*	8	ST5228
Charlton Marshall *Dorset*	9	ST8903
Charlton Musgrove *Somset*	9	ST7229
Charlton on the Hill *Dorset*	9	ST8903
Charlton-on-Otmoor *Oxon*	29	SP5616
Charlwood *Hants*	11	SU6731
Charlwood *Surrey*	12	TQ2441
Charminster *Dorset*	9	SY6792
Charmouth *Dorset*	8	SY3693
Charndon *Bucks*	30	SP6724
Charney Bassett *Oxon*	21	SU3894
Charnock Richard *Lancs*	53	SD5515
Charsfield *Suffk*	33	TM2556
Chart Sutton *Kent*	14	TQ8049
Charter Alley *Hants*	21	SU5957
Charterhall *Border*	76	NT7647
Charterhouse *Somset*	19	ST4955
Chartershall *Cent*	81	NS7990
Chartham *Kent*	15	TR1054
Chartham Hatch *Kent*	15	TR1056
Chartridge *Bucks*	22	SP9303
Charwelton *Nhants*	29	SP5355
Chase Terrace *Staffs*	38	SK0409
Chastleton *Oxon*	29	SP2429
Chatburn *Lancs*	54	SD7644
Chatcull *Staffs*	37	SJ7934
Chatham *Gwent*	19	ST2189
Chatham *Kent*	14	TQ7567
Chatham Green *Essex*	24	TL7115
Chathill *Nthumb*	77	NU1827
Chattenden *Kent*	14	TQ7572
Chatteris *Cambs*	41	TL3985
Chattisham *Suffk*	33	TM0942
Chatto *Border*	76	NT7717
Chatton *Nthumb*	77	NU0528
Chawleigh *Devon*	7	SS7112
Chawton *Hants*	11	SU7037
Cheadle *Gt Man*	47	SJ8688
Cheadle *Staffs*	48	SK0043
Cheadle Hulme *Gt Man*	47	SJ8786
Cheam *Gt Lon*	23	TQ2563
Chearsley *Bucks*	22	SP7110
Checkendon *Oxon*	22	SU6683
Checkley *Ches*	47	SJ7346
Checkley *Staffs*	48	SK0237
Chedburgh *Suffk*	32	TL7957
Cheddar *Somset*	19	ST4553
Cheddington *Bucks*	30	SP9217
Cheddleton *Staffs*	48	SJ9752
Cheddon Fitzpaine *Somset*	8	ST2327
Chedglow *Wilts*	20	ST9492
Chedgrave *Norfk*	43	TM3699
Chedington *Dorset*	8	ST4805
Chediston *Suffk*	33	TM3577
Chedworth *Gloucs*	28	SP0511
Chedzoy *Somset*	19	ST3337
Cheeseman's Green *Kent*	15	TR0238
Cheetham Hill *Gt Man*	47	SD8301
Cheetwood *Gt Man*	47	SJ8399
Cheldon *Devon*	7	SS7313
Chelford *Ches*	47	SJ8174
Chellington *Beds*	30	SP9555
Chelmarsh *Shrops*	37	SO7288
Chelmorton *Derbys*	48	SK1169
Chelmsford *Essex*	24	TL7007
Chelmsley Wood *W Mids*	38	SP1886
Chelsea *Gt Lon*	23	TQ2778
Chelsfield *Gt Lon*	23	TQ4864
Chelsworth *Suffk*	32	TL9748
Cheltenham *Gloucs*	28	SO9422
Chelveston *Nhants*	30	SP9969
Chelvey *Avon*	19	ST4668
Chelwood *Avon*	19	ST6361
Chelwood Gate *E Susx*	13	TQ4130
Chelworth Lower Green *Wilts*	20	SU0892
Chelworth Upper Green *Wilts*	20	SU0892
Cheney Longville *Shrops*	36	SO4284
Chenies *Bucks*	22	TQ0198
Chepstow *Gwent*	19	ST5393
Cherhill *Wilts*	20	SU0370
Cherington *Gloucs*	20	ST9098
Cherington *Warwks*	29	SP2936
Cheriton *Devon*	7	SS7346
Cheriton *Devon*	8	ST1001
Cheriton *Kent*	15	TR2037
Cheriton *W Glam*	17	SS4593
Cheriton Bishop *Devon*	5	SX7793
Cheriton Fitzpaine *Devon*	7	SS8606
Cheriton or Stackpole Elidor *Dyfed*	16	SR9997
Cherrington *Shrops*	37	SJ6619
Cherry Burton *Humb*	56	SE9842
Cherry Hinton *Cambs*	31	TL4856
Cherry Orchard *H & W*	28	SO8553
Cherry Willingham *Lincs*	50	TF0272
Cherry Willingham *Lincs*	50	TF0372
Chertsey *Surrey*	22	TQ0466
Cheselbourne *Dorset*	9	SY7699
Chesham *Bucks*	22	SP9601
Chesham Bois *Bucks*	22	SU9699
Cheshunt *Herts*	23	TL3502
Cheslyn Hay *Staffs*	38	SJ9707
Chessetts Wood *Warwks*	38	SP1873
Chessington *Surrey*	23	TQ1863
Chester *Ches*	46	SJ4066
Chester Moor *Dur*	69	NZ2649
Chester-le-Street *T & W*	69	NZ2751
Chesterblade *Somset*	20	ST6641
Chesterfield *Derbys*	49	SK3871
Chesterfield *Staffs*	38	SK1005
Chesterhill *Loth*	76	NT3765
Chesters *Border*	76	NT6022
Chesters *Border*	68	NT6210
Chesterton *Cambs*	31	TL4660
Chesterton *Cambs*	40	TL1295
Chesterton *Gloucs*	20	SP0200
Chesterton *Oxon*	29	SP5621
Chesterton *Shrops*	37	SO7897
Chesterton Green *Warwks*	29	SP3558
Chesterwood *Nthumb*	68	NY8365
Chestfield *Kent*	15	TR1365
Chestnut Street *Kent*	14	TQ8862
Cheston *Devon*	5	SX6758
Cheswardine *Shrops*	37	SJ7130
Cheswick *Nthumb*	77	NU0346
Chetnote *Dorset*	9	ST6008
Chettiscombe *Devon*	7	SS9614
Chettisham *Cambs*	41	TL5483
Chettle *Dorset*	9	ST9513
Chetton *Shrops*	37	SO6690
Chetwode *Bucks*	29	SP6429
Chetwynd *Shrops*	37	SJ7321
Chetwynd Aston *Shrops*	37	SJ7517
Cheveley *Cambs*	32	TL6861
Chevening *Kent*	23	TQ4857
Cheverton *IOW*	10	SZ4584
Chevington *Suffk*	32	TL7860
Chevington Drift *Nthumb*	69	NZ2598
Chevithorne *Devon*	7	SS9715
Chew Magna *Avon*	19	ST5763
Chew Stoke *Avon*	19	ST5561
Chewton Keynsham *Avon*	19	ST6566
Chewton Mendip *Somset*	19	ST5952
Chicheley *Bucks*	30	SP9046
Chichester *W Susx*	11	SU8604
Chicklade *Wilts*	9	ST9134
Chidden *Hants*	11	SU6517
Chiddingfold *Surrey*	12	SU9635
Chiddingly *E Susx*	13	TQ5414
Chiddingstone *Kent*	13	TQ5045
Chiddingstone Causeway *Kent*	13	TQ5146
Chideock *Dorset*	8	SY4292
Chidham *W Susx*	11	SU7903
Chidswell *W York*	55	SE2623
Chieveley *Berks*	21	SU4773
Chignall Smealy *Essex*	24	TL6611
Chignall St. James *Essex*	24	TL6610
Chigwell *Essex*	23	TQ4494
Chigwell Row *Essex*	23	TQ4693
Chilbolton *Hants*	10	SU3939
Chilcomb *Hants*	10	SU5028
Chilcombe *Dorset*	8	SY5291
Chilcompton *Somset*	19	ST6452
Chilcote *Leics*	39	SK2811
Child Okeford *Dorset*	9	ST8312
Child's Ercall *Shrops*	37	SJ6625
Childer Thornton *Ches*	46	SJ3677
Childrey *Oxon*	21	SU3687
Childswickham *H & W*	28	SP0738
Childwall *Mersyd*	46	SJ4189
Childwick Bury *Herts*	22	TL1410
Chilfrome *Dorset*	9	SY5898
Chilgrove *W Susx*	11	SU8314
Chilham *Kent*	15	TR0653
Chilla *Devon*	6	SS4402
Chillaton *Devon*	4	SX4382
Chillenden *Kent*	15	TR2653
Chillerton *IOW*	10	SZ4984
Chillesford *Suffk*	33	TM3852
Chillingham *Nthumb*	77	NU0525
Chillington *Devon*	5	SX7942
Chillington *Somset*	8	ST3811
Chilmark *Wilts*	9	ST9632
Chilmington Green *Kent*	15	TQ9740
Chilson *Oxon*	29	SP3119
Chilsworthy *Cnwll*	4	SX4172
Chilsworthy *Devon*	6	SS3206
Chilthorne Domer *Somset*	8	ST5219
Chiltington *E Susx*	13	TQ3815
Chilton *Bucks*	22	SP6811
Chilton *Oxon*	21	SU4885
Chilton *Suffk*	32	TL8942
Chilton Candover *Hants*	21	SU5940
Chilton Cantelo *Somset*	8	ST5622
Chilton Foliat *Wilts*	21	SU3170
Chilton Polden *Somset*	19	ST3739
Chilton Street *Suffk*	32	TL7547
Chilton Trinity *Somset*	19	ST2939
Chilworth *Hants*	10	SU4118
Chilworth *Surrey*	12	TQ0247
Chimney *Oxon*	21	SP3501
Chineham *Hants*	21	SU6554
Chingford *Gt Lon*	23	TQ3894
Chinley *Derbys*	48	SK0482
Chinnor *Oxon*	22	SP7501
Chipnall *Shrops*	37	SJ7231
Chippenham *Bucks*	22	SU9480
Chippenham *Cambs*	32	TL6669
Chippenham *Wilts*	20	ST9273
Chipperfield *Herts*	22	TL0401
Chipping *Herts*	31	TL3532
Chipping *Lancs*	54	SD6243
Chipping Campden *Gloucs*	28	SP1539
Chipping Norton *Oxon*	29	SP3127
Chipping Ongar *Essex*	24	TL5503
Chipping Sodbury *Avon*	20	ST7281
Chipping Warden *Nhants*	29	SP4948
Chipstable *Somset*	7	ST0427
Chipstead *Kent*	23	TQ5056
Chipstead *Surrey*	23	TQ2757
Chirbury *Shrops*	36	SO2698
Chirk *Clwyd*	36	SJ2938
Chirnside *Border*	77	NT8756
Chirnsidebridge *Border*	77	NT8556
Chirton *Wilts*	20	SU0757
Chisbury *Wilts*	21	SU2766
Chiselborough *Somset*	8	ST4614
Chiseldon *Wilts*	21	SU1879
Chisholme *Border*	67	NT4112
Chislehampton *Oxon*	21	SU5999
Chislehurst *Gt Lon*	23	TQ4470
Chislet *Kent*	15	TR2264
Chisley *W York*	54	SE0028
Chiswellgreen *Herts*	22	TL1304
Chiswick *Gt Lon*	23	TQ2078
Chisworth *Derbys*	48	SJ9991
Chisworth *Derbys*	48	SJ9991
Chithurst *W Susx*	11	SU8423
Chittering *Cambs*	31	TL4969
Chitterne *Wilts*	20	ST9843
Chittlehamholt *Devon*	7	SS6421
Chittlehampton *Devon*	7	SS6325
Chittlehampton *Devon*	7	SS6511
Chittoe *Wilts*	20	ST9566
Chivelstone *Devon*	5	SX7838
Chivelstone *Devon*	5	SX7838
Chlenry *D & G*	64	NX1261
Chobham *Surrey*	22	SU9762
Cholderton *Wilts*	21	SU2242
Cholesbury *Bucks*	22	SP9307
Chollerton *Nthumb*	68	NY9372
Cholstrey *H & W*	27	SO4659
Chop Gate *N York*	62	SE5599
Chop Gate *N York*	62	SE5699
Choppington *T & W*	69	NZ2484
Chopwell *T & W*	69	NZ1158
Chorley *Ches*	47	SJ5751
Chorley *Lancs*	54	SD5817
Chorley *Shrops*	37	SO6983
Chorley *Staffs*	38	SK0711
Chorleywood *Herts*	22	TQ0396
Chorleywood West *Herts*	22	TQ0296
Chorlton *Ches*	47	SJ7250
Chorlton Lane *Ches*	46	SJ4548
Chorlton-cum-Hardy *Gt Man*	47	SJ8193
Choulton *Shrops*	36	SO3788
Chowley *Ches*	46	SJ4756
Chrishall *Essex*	31	TL4439
Chrisswell *Strath*	80	NS2274
Christchurch *Cambs*	41	TL4996
Christchurch *Dorset*	10	SZ1593
Christchurch *Gloucs*	27	SO5713
Christchurch *Gwent*	19	ST3489
Christian Malford *Wilts*	20	ST9678
Christleton *Ches*	46	SJ4465
Christmas Common *Oxon*	22	SU7193
Christon *Avon*	19	ST3956
Christon Bank *Nthumb*	77	NU2123
Christow *Devon*	5	SX8385
Christskirk *Gramp*	94	NJ6027
Chudleigh *Devon*	5	SX8679
Chudleigh Knighton *Devon*	5	SX8477
Chulmleigh *Devon*	7	SS6814
Chunal *Derbys*	48	SK0391
Church *Lancs*	54	SD7429
Church Ashton *Shrops*	37	SJ7317
Church Brampton *Nhants*	30	SP7165
Church Broughton *Derbys*	39	SK2033
Church Crookham *Hants*	22	SU8152
Church End *Beds*	30	TL0334
Church End *Beds*	31	TL1937
Church End *Beds*	30	TL0458
Church End *Beds*	30	TL1059
Church End *Cambs*	41	TF3909
Church End *Cambs*	30	TL0973
Church End *Cambs*	41	TL2083
Church End *Essex*	24	TL6323
Church End *Essex*	24	TL7228
Church End *Essex*	24	TL7416
Church End *Gt Lon*	23	TQ2490
Church End *Hants*	22	SU6756
Church End *Herts*	31	TL4422
Church End *Lincs*	51	TF4195
Church End *Warwks*	39	SP2892
Church Enstone *Oxon*	29	SP3725
Church Fenton *N York*	55	SE5136
Church Green *Devon*	8	SY1796
Church Hanborough *Oxon*	29	SP4212
Church Hill *Ches*	47	SJ6465
Church Hill *Staffs*	38	SK0012
Church Houses *N York*	62	SE6697
Church Knowle *Dorset*	9	SY9481
Church Langton *Leics*	40	SP7293
Church Lawford *Warwks*	39	SP4576
Church Lawton *Staffs*	47	SJ8255
Church Leigh *Staffs*	38	SK0235
Church Lench *H & W*	28	SP0251
Church Mayfield *Staffs*	48	SK1544
Church Minshull *Ches*	47	SJ6660
Church Norton *W Susx*	11	SZ8695
Church Preen *Shrops*	37	SO5498
Church Pulverbatch *Shrops*	36	SJ4303
Church Stoke *Powys*	36	SO2694
Church Stowe *Nhants*	29	SP6357
Church Street *Kent*	14	TQ7174
Church Stretton *Shrops*	36	SO4593
Church Town *Humb*	56	SE7806
Church Village *M Glam*	18	ST0886
Church Warsop *Notts*	49	SK5668
Churcham *Gloucs*	28	SO7618
Churchbridge *Staffs*	38	SJ9808
Churchdown *Gloucs*	28	SO8819
Churchend *Essex*	25	TR0093
Churchill *Avon*	19	ST4359
Churchill *Devon*	8	ST2901
Churchill *H & W*	28	SO9253
Churchill *H & W*	38	SO8879
Churchill *Oxon*	29	SP2824
Churchill Green *Avon*	19	ST4360
Churchingford *Devon*	8	ST2112
Churchover *Warwks*	39	SP5180
Churchstow *Devon*	5	SX7145
Churchthorpe *Lincs*	51	TF3297
Churchtown *Cumb*	59	NY3742
Churchtown *Derbys*	49	SK2663
Churchtown *IOM*	52	SC4294
Churchtown *Lancs*	53	SD4843
Churnsike Lodge *Nthumb*	68	NY6777
Churston Ferrers *Devon*	5	SX9056
Churt *Surrey*	11	SU8538
Churton *Ches*	46	SJ4156
Churwell *W York*	55	SE2729
Chute Lodge *Wilts*	21	SU3151
Chwilog *Gwynd*	44	SH4338
Chyanvounder *Cnwll*	2	SW6522
Cilcain *Clwyd*	46	SJ1765
Cilcennin *Dyfed*	34	SN5160
Cilcewydd *Powys*	36	SJ2304
Cilfrew *W Glam*	18	SN7700
Cilfynydd *M Glam*	18	ST0892
Cilgerran *Dyfed*	17	SN1943
Cilgwyn *Dyfed*	26	SN7429
Ciliau-Aeron *Dyfed*	34	SN5058
Cilmaengwyn *W Glam*	26	SN7406
Cilmery *Powys*	26	SO0051
Cilmery *Powys*	26	SO0051
Cilrhedyn *Dyfed*	17	SN2835
Cilsan *Dyfed*	17	SN5922
Ciltalgarth *Gwynd*	45	SH8840
Cilycwm *Dyfed*	26	SN7540
Cimla *W Glam*	18	SS7696
Cinderford *Gloucs*	27	SO6513
Cirencester *Gloucs*	20	SP0201
Citadilla *N York*	61	NZ2200
Clabhach *Strath*	78	NM1858
Clachaig *Strath*	80	NS1181
Clachan *Highld*	84	NG5436
Clachan *S Glam*	71	NR7656
Clachan *Strath*	79	NM7819
Clachan *Strath*	79	NM8543
Clachan *Strath*	80	NN1812
Clachan *W Isls*	102	NF7746
Clachan *W Isls*	102	NF8163
Clachan Mor *Strath*	78	NL9847
Clachan-Seil *Strath*	79	NM7718
Clachaneasy *D & G*	64	NX3575
Clachbreck *Strath*	71	NR7675
Clachnaharry *Highld*	92	NH6446
Clackavoid *Tays*	88	NO1463
Clackmannan *Cent*	82	NS9191
Clackmarass *Gramp*	94	NJ2458
Clacton-on-Sea *Essex*	25	TM1715
Cladich *Strath*	80	NN0921
Cladswell *H & W*	28	SP0458
Claggan *Highld*	79	NM6949
Claigan *Highld*	90	NG2354
Clandown *Avon*	20	ST6955
Clanfield *Hants*	11	SU6916
Clanfield *Oxon*	21	SP2801
Clanville *Hants*	21	SU3148
Clanville *Somset*	9	ST6232
Clanyard *D & G*	64	NX1037
Claonaig *Strath*	71	NR8656
Clapgate *Herts*	31	TL4424
Clapham *Beds*	30	TL0352
Clapham *Gt Lon*	23	TQ2875
Clapham *N York*	54	SD7469
Clapham *W Susx*	12	TQ0906
Clapton *Somset*	8	ST4106
Clapton *Somset*	19	ST6453
Clapton *Somset*	20	ST6852
Clapton-in-Gordano *Avon*	19	ST4773
Clapton-on-the-Hill *Gloucs*	28	SP1617
Claravale *T & W*	69	NZ1365
Clarbeston *Dyfed*	16	SN0421
Clarbeston Road *Dyfed*	16	SN0121
Clarborough *Notts*	50	SK7383
Clare *Suffk*	32	TL7745
Clarebrand *D & G*	65	NX7666
Claredon Park *Leics*	39	SK6002
Clarencefield *D & G*	67	NY0968
Clarewood *Nthumb*	68	NZ0169
Clarilaw *Border*	76	NT5218
Clarken Green *Hants*	11	SU5631
Clarkston *Strath*	74	NS5757
Clashmore *Highld*	98	NC0331
Clashmore *Highld*	97	NH7489
Clashnessie *Highld*	98	NC0530
Clashnoir *Gramp*	94	NJ2222
Clathy *Tays*	75	NS9920
Clathymore *Tays*	82	NO0121

Clatt
Coton

Place	County	Page	Grid ref
Clatt	Gramp	94	NJ5326
Clatter	Powys	35	SN9994
Clatworthy	Somset	7	ST0530
Claughton	Lancs	53	SD5342
Claughton	Lancs	53	SD5666
Claughton	Mersyd	46	SJ3088
Claverdon	Warwks	29	SP1965
Claverham	Avon	19	ST4566
Clavering	Essex	31	TL4731
Claverley	Shrops	37	SO7993
Claverton	Avon	20	ST7864
Clawdd-coch	S Glam	18	ST0577
Clawdd-newydd	Clwyd	46	SJ0852
Clawton	Devon	6	SX3599
Claxby	Lincs	50	TF1194
Claxton	N York	56	SE6959
Claxton	N York	56	SE6960
Clay Coton	Nhants	39	SP5977
Clay Cross	Derbys	49	SK3963
Clay End	Herts	31	TL3024
Claybrooke Magna	Leics	39	SP4988
Claydon	Oxon	29	SP4549
Claydon	Suffk	33	TM1349
Claygate	D & G	67	NY3979
Claygate	Kent	14	TQ7144
Claygate	Surrey	22	TQ1563
Clayhanger	Devon	7	ST0222
Clayhidon	Devon	8	ST1615
Clayhill	E Susx	14	TQ8323
Clayhill	Hants	10	SU3007
Clayock	Highld	100	ND1659
Claypits	Gloucs	28	SO7606
Claypole	Lincs	50	SK8449
Clayton	S York	55	SE4507
Clayton	W Susx	12	TQ2914
Clayton	W Susx	12	TQ3014
Clayton	W York	55	SE1131
Clayton West	W York	55	SE2511
Clayton-le-Moors	Lancs	54	SD7530
Clayton-le-Woods	Lancs	53	SD5622
Clayworth	Notts	49	SK7288
Cleadale	Highld	84	NM4789
Cleadon	T & W	69	NZ3862
Clearbrook	Devon	4	SX5265
Clearwell	Gloucs	27	SO5608
Cleasby	N York	61	NZ2412
Cleat	Ork	103	ND4584
Cleatlam	Dur	61	NZ1118
Cleator	Cumb	58	NY0123
Cleator Moor	Cumb	58	NY0125
Cleckheaton	W York	55	SE1825
Clee St. Margaret	Shrops	37	SO5684
Cleehill	Shrops	37	SO5975
Cleekhimin	Strath	74	NS7658
Cleethorpes	Humb	57	TA3008
Cleeton St. Mary	Shrops	37	SO6178
Cleeve	Avon	19	ST4666
Cleeve	Oxon	21	SU6081
Cleeve Hill	Gloucs	28	SO9827
Cleeve Prior	H & W	28	SP0849
Clehonger	H & W	27	SO4637
Cleish	Tays	82	NT0998
Cleland	Strath	74	NS7958
Clement Street	Kent	14	TQ5671
Clenamacrie	Strath	80	NM9228
Clenchwarton	Norfk	41	TF5920
Clent	H & W	38	SO9279
Clenterty	Gramp	95	NJ7760
Cleobury Mortimer	Shrops	37	SO6775
Cleobury North	Shrops	37	SO6287
Cleongart	Strath	72	NR6734
Clephanton	Highld	93	NH8150
Cleuch Head	Border	67	NT5910
Cleuch-head	D & G	66	NS8200
Clevancy	Wilts	20	SU0575
Clevedon	Avon	19	ST4071
Cleveleys	Lancs	53	SD3143
Cleverton	Wilts	20	ST9785
Clewer	Somset	19	ST4351
Cley next the Sea	Norfk	42	TG0444
Cliburn	Cumb	59	NY5724
Cliddesden	Hants	21	SU6349
Cliff	Warwks	39	SP2198
Cliff End	E Susx	14	TQ8813
Cliffe	Dur	61	NZ2015
Cliffe	N York	56	SE6631
Clifford	H & W	27	SO2445
Clifford	W York	55	SE4244
Clifford Chambers	Warwks	29	SP1952
Clifford's Mesne	Gloucs	28	SO7023
Clifton	Avon	19	ST5774
Clifton	Beds	31	TL1639
Clifton	Cumb	59	NY5326
Clifton	Derbys	48	SK1644
Clifton	H & W	28	SO8446
Clifton	Lancs	53	SD4630
Clifton	N York	56	SE5953
Clifton	Notts	39	SK5434
Clifton	Oxon	29	SP4931
Clifton	S York	49	SK5196
Clifton	W York	55	SE1622
Clifton	W York	55	SE1948
Clifton Campville	Staffs	39	SK2510
Clifton Hampden	Oxon	21	SU5495
Clifton Reynes	Bucks	30	SP9051
Clifton upon Dunsmore	Warwks	39	SP5376
Clifton upon Teme	H & W	28	SO7161
Cliftonville	Kent	15	TR3771
Climping	W Susx	12	TQ0002
Clink	Somset	20	ST7848
Clint	N York	55	SE2559
Clint Green	Norfk	42	TG0211
Clinterty	Gramp	95	NJ8311
Clintmains	Border	76	NT6132
Clippesby	Norfk	43	TG4214
Clipsham	Leics	40	SK9616
Clipston	Nhants	40	SP7181
Clipston	Notts	39	SK6333
Clipstone	Beds	30	SP9426
Clipstone	Notts	49	SK6064
Clitheroe	Lancs	54	SD7441
Clive	Shrops	37	SJ5124
Cloatley	Wilts	20	ST9890
Clocaenog	Clwyd	46	SJ0854
Cloch Mhor	Highld	92	NH5063
Clochan	Gramp	94	NJ4060
Clochtow	Tays	89	NO4852
Clodock	H & W	27	SO3227
Clola	Gramp	95	NK0043
Clophill	Beds	30	TL0838
Clopton	Nhants	40	TL0680
Clopton	Suffk	33	TM2253
Clopton Corner	Suffk	33	TM2254
Clopton Green	Suffk	32	TL9759
Clos du Valle	Guern	101	SV0000
Closeburn	D & G	66	NX8992
Closeburnmill	D & G	66	NX9094
Closworth	Somset	8	ST5610
Clothall	Herts	31	TL2731
Clotton	Ches	46	SJ5264
Clough Foot	W York	54	SD9123
Clough Head	Staffs	48	SJ9864
Cloughton	N York	63	TA0094
Clousta	Shet	103	HU3157
Clova	Tays	88	NO3273
Clovelly Cross	Devon	6	SS3123
Clovenfords	Border	76	NT4536
Clovulin	Highld	86	NN0063
Clow Bridge	Lancs	54	SD8228
Clowne	Derbys	49	SK4875
Clows Top	H & W	37	SO7171
Cluanie Inn	Highld	85	NH0711
Cluanie Lodge	Highld	85	NH0910
Clun	Shrops	36	SO3081
Clunas	Highld	93	NH8846
Clunbury	Shrops	36	SO3780
Clune	Highld	93	NH7925
Clunes	Highld	86	NN2088
Clungunford	Shrops	36	SO4078
Clunie	Gramp	94	NJ6450
Clunie	Tays	88	NO1043
Clunton	Shrops	36	SO3381
Clutton	Avon	19	ST6159
Clutton	Ches	46	SJ4654
Clutton Hill	Avon	19	ST6359
Clydach	Gwent	27	SO2213
Clydach	W Glam	18	SN6801
Clydach Vale	M Glam	18	SS9792
Clydebank	Strath	74	NS5069
Clydey	Dyfed	17	SN2535
Clyffe Pypard	Wilts	20	SU0776
Clynder	Strath	80	NS2484
Clynderwen	Dyfed	16	SN1219
Clyne	W Glam	18	SN8000
Clynelish	Highld	97	NC8905
Clynnog-fawr	Gwynd	44	SH4149
Clyro	Powys	27	SO2143
Clyst Honiton	Devon	5	SX9893
Clyst Hydon	Devon	7	ST0301
Clyst St. George	Devon	5	SX9888
Clyst St. Lawrence	Devon	7	ST0200
Clyst St. Mary	Devon	5	SX9790
Clyth	Highld	100	ND2836
Cnwch Coch	Dyfed	35	SN6775
Coad's Green	Cnwll	4	SX2976
Coalbrookdale	Shrops	37	SJ6603
Coalburn	Strath	74	NS8134
Coalburns	T & W	69	NZ1261
Coaley	Gloucs	20	SO7701
Coalhill	Essex	24	TQ7598
Coalpit Heath	Avon	20	ST6781
Coalport	Shrops	37	SJ6902
Coalsnaughton	Cent	82	NS9295
Coaltown of Balgonie	Fife	83	NT3099
Coaltown of Wemyss	Fife	83	NT3295
Coalville	Leics	39	SK4214
Coanwood	Nthumb	68	NY6759
Coat	Somset	8	ST4520
Coatbridge	Strath	74	NS7365
Coatdyke	Strath	74	NS7465
Coate	Wilts	20	SU0461
Coate	Wilts	21	SU1783
Coates	Cambs	41	TL3097
Coates	Gloucs	20	SO9700
Coates	W Susx	12	SU9917
Cobbaton	Devon	6	SS6126
Coberley	Gloucs	28	SO9616
Cobham	Kent	14	TQ6768
Cobham	Surrey	22	TQ1060
Cobnash	H & W	27	SO4560
Cobo	Guern	101	SV0000
Cobridge	Staffs	47	SJ8748
Coburby	Gramp	95	NJ9164
Cock Bridge	Gramp	94	NJ2508
Cock Clarks	Essex	24	TL8103
Cock Green	Essex	24	TL6920
Cock Marling	E Susx	14	TQ8719
Cockayne	N York	62	SE6298
Cockayne Hatley	Beds	31	TL2549
Cockburnspath	Border	76	NT7770
Cockenzie and Port Seton	Loth	76	NT4075
Cockerham	Lancs	53	SD4651
Cockermouth	Cumb	58	NY1230
Cockernhoe Green	Herts	30	TL1223
Cockett	W Glam	17	SS6394
Cockfield	Dur	61	NZ1224
Cockfield	Suffk	32	TL9054
Cockfosters	Gt Lon	23	TQ2796
Cocking	W Susx	11	SU8717
Cocking Causeway	W Susx	11	SU8819
Cockington	Devon	5	SX8964
Cocklake	Somset	19	ST4349
Cockley Beck	Cumb	58	NY2501
Cockley Cley	Norfk	42	TF7904
Cockpole Green	Berks	22	SU7981
Cockshutford	Shrops	37	SO5885
Cockshutt	Shrops	36	SJ4328
Cockthorpe	Norfk	42	TF9842
Cockwood	Devon	5	SX9780
Cockwood	Somset	8	ST2223
Coddenham	Suffk	33	TM1354
Coddington	H & W	28	SO7142
Coddington	Notts	50	SK8354
Codford St. Mary	Wilts	20	ST9739
Codford St. Peter	Wilts	20	ST9640
Codicote	Herts	31	TL2118
Codmore Hill	W Susx	12	TQ0520
Codnor	Derbys	49	SK4149
Codrington	Avon	20	ST7278
Codsall	Staffs	38	SJ8603
Codsall Wood	Staffs	38	SJ8405
Coed Talon	Clwyd	46	SJ2658
Coed-y-paen	Gwent	19	ST3398
Coedana	Gwynd	44	SH4381
Coffinswell	Devon	5	SX8868
Coffle End	Beds	30	TL0059
Cofnpennar	Gwent	27	SO3006
Cofton Hackett	H & W	38	SP0075
Cogan	S Glam	19	ST1772
Cogenhoe	Nhants	30	SP8260
Coggeshall	Essex	24	TL8522
Coignafearn	Highld	93	NH7017
Coilacriech	Gramp	88	NO3296
Coilantogle	Cent	81	NN5907
Coillaig	Strath	80	NN0120
Coillore	Highld	84	NG3538
Coiltry	Highld	86	NH3506
Coity	M Glam	18	SS9281
Colaboll	Highld	96	NC5610
Colan	Cnwll	3	SW8661
Colaton Raleigh	Devon	5	SY0787
Colburn	N York	61	SE1999
Colby	Cumb	60	NY6620
Colby	IOM	52	SC2370
Colby	Norfk	43	TG2231
Colchester	Essex	25	TL9925
Cold Ash	Berks	21	SU5169
Cold Ashby	Nhants	39	SP6576
Cold Ashton	Avon	20	ST7472
Cold Aston	Gloucs	28	SP1219
Cold Brayfield	Bucks	30	SP9252
Cold Hanworth	Lincs	50	TF0383
Cold Harbour	Herts	30	TL1415
Cold Harbour	Wilts	20	ST8646
Cold Hatton	Shrops	37	SJ6121
Cold Hesledon	Dur	69	NZ4146
Cold Hiendly	W York	55	SE3714
Cold Higham	Nhants	30	SP6653
Cold Kirby	N York	62	SE5384
Cold Norton	Essex	24	TL8500
Cold Overton	Leics	40	SK8110
Coldbackie	Highld	99	NC6160
Coldbeck	Cumb	60	NY7104
Coldean	E Susx	12	TQ3308
Coldeast	Devon	5	SX8274
Colden	W York	54	SD9628
Colden Common	Hants	10	SU4822
Coldfair Green	Suffk	33	TM4361
Coldham	Cambs	41	TF4302
Coldharbour	Devon	7	ST0612
Coldharbour	Surrey	12	TQ1443
Coldingham	Border	77	NT9065
Coldmeece	Staffs	38	SJ8532
Coldred	Kent	15	TR2747
Coldridge	Devon	7	SS6907
Coldstone	Kent	23	TQ2961
Coldstream	Border	77	NT8439
Coldwaltham	W Susx	12	TQ0216
Coldwell	H & W	27	SO4235
Coldwells	Gramp	95	NJ9538
Coldwells	Gramp	95	NK1039
Cole	Somset	9	ST6633
Cole Green	Herts	23	TL2911
Cole Green	Herts	31	TL4330
Cole Henley	Hants	21	SU4751
Cole's Cross	Devon	5	SX7747
Colebatch	Shrops	36	SO3187
Colebrook	Devon	7	ST0006
Colebrooke	Devon	7	SX7799
Coleby	Humb	56	SE8919
Coleby	Lincs	50	SK9760
Coleford	Devon	7	SS7701
Coleford	Gloucs	27	SO5710
Coleford	Somset	20	ST6848
Coleford Water	Somset	8	ST1234
Colegate End	Norfk	33	TM1988
Coleman's Hatch	E Susx	13	TQ4533
Colemere	Shrops	36	SJ4232
Colemore	Hants	11	SU7030
Colemore Green	Shrops	37	SO7097
Colenden	Tays	82	NO1029
Coleorton	Leics	39	SK3917
Colerne	Wilts	20	ST8171
Colesbourne	Gloucs	28	SP0013
Coleshill	Bucks	22	SU9495
Coleshill	Oxon	21	SU2393
Coley	Avon	19	ST5855
Colgate	W Susx	12	TQ2332
Colgrain	Strath	80	NS3280
Colinsburgh	Fife	83	NO4703
Colinton	Loth	75	NT2268
Colintraive	Strath	80	NS0374
Colkirk	Norfk	42	TF9126
Coll	W Isls	102	NB4539
Collace	Tays	82	NO2032
Collafirth	Shet	103	HU3482
Collaton	Devon	5	SX7338
Collaton St. Mary	Devon	5	SX8660
College Green	Somset	19	ST5736
College Town	Berks	22	SU8560
College of Roseisle	Gramp	93	NJ1466
Collessie	Fife	83	NO2813
Collier Row	Gt Lon	23	TQ4991
Collier Street	Kent	14	TQ7145
Collier's End	Herts	31	TL3720
Collier's Green	Kent	14	TQ7822
Colliers Green	Kent	14	TQ7439
Colliery Row	T & W	69	NZ3349
Collieston	Gramp	95	NK0328
Collin	D & G	66	NY0276
Collingbourne Ducis	Wilts	21	SU2453
Collingbourne Kingston	Wilts	21	SU2355
Collingham	W York	55	SE3845
Collington	H & W	27	SO6460
Collingtree	Nhants	30	SP7555
Collins Green	Ches	47	SJ5694
Colliston	Tays	89	NO6045
Colliton	Devon	7	ST0804
Collyweston	Nhants	40	SK9902
Colmonell	Strath	64	NX1485
Coln Rogers	Gloucs	28	SP0809
Coln St. Aldwyns	Gloucs	28	SP1405
Coln St. Dennis	Gloucs	28	SP0811
Colne	Cambs	31	TL3776
Colne	Lancs	54	SD8940
Colne Engaine	Essex	24	TL8530
Colney	Norfk	43	TG1807
Colney Heath	Herts	23	TL2005
Colney Street	Herts	22	TL1502
Colpy	Gramp	94	NJ6432
Colquhar	Border	75	NT3341
Colsterworth	Lincs	40	SK9324
Colston Bassett	Notts	40	SK7033
Colt Hill	Hants	22	SU7451
Colt's Hill	Kent	13	TQ6443
Coltfield	Gramp	93	NJ1163
Coltishall	Norfk	43	TG2619
Colton	Cumb	58	SD3186
Colton	N York	56	SE5444
Colton	Norfk	43	TG1009
Colton	Staffs	38	SK0520
Colton	W York	55	SE3732
Colva	Powys	27	SO1952
Colvend	D & G	66	NX8654
Colwall Green	H & W	28	SO7441
Colwall Stone	H & W	28	SO7542
Colwell	Nthumb	68	NY9575
Colwich	Staffs	38	SK0121
Colwinston	S Glam	18	SS9375
Colworth	W Susx	11	SU9102
Colwyn Bay	Clwyd	45	SH8479
Colyford	Devon	8	SY2492
Colyton	Devon	8	SY2493
Combe	Berks	21	SU3760
Combe	Devon	5	SX8448
Combe	Devon	5	SX9173
Combe	H & W	27	SO3463
Combe	Oxon	29	SP4116
Combe Almer	Dorset	9	SY9497
Combe Fishacre	Devon	5	SX8465
Combe Florey	Somset	8	ST1531
Combe Hay	Avon	20	ST7359
Combe Martin	Devon	6	SS5846
Combe Moor	H & W	27	SO3663
Combe Raleigh	Devon	8	ST1502
Combe St. Nicholas	Somset	8	ST3011
Combebow	Devon	4	SX4888
Combeinteignhead	Devon	5	SX9071
Comberbach	Ches	47	SJ6477
Comberford	Staffs	39	SK1907
Comberton	Cambs	31	TL3856
Comberton	H & W	27	SO4968
Combrook	Warwks	29	SP3051
Combs	Derbys	48	SK0478
Combs	Suffk	32	TM0456
Combs Ford	Suffk	32	TM0557
Combwich	Somset	8	ST2522
Combwich	Somset	19	ST2542
Comedivock	Cumb	67	NY3449
Comers	Gramp	95	NJ6707
Comhampton	H & W	28	SO8366
Commercial	Dyfed	16	SN1416
Commins Coch	Powys	35	SH8403
Common Moor	Cnwll	4	SX2469
Common The	Wilts	10	SU2432
Commondale	N York	62	NZ6610
Commonside	Ches	47	SJ5573
Compstall	Gt Man	48	SJ9690
Compton	Berks	21	SU5280
Compton	Devon	5	SX8664
Compton	Hants	10	SU3529
Compton	Hants	10	SU4625
Compton	Staffs	38	SO8285
Compton	Surrey	12	SU9547
Compton	W Susx	11	SU7714
Compton Abbas	Dorset	9	ST8718
Compton Bassett	Wilts	20	SU0372
Compton Beauchamp	Oxon	21	SU2886
Compton Bishop	Somset	19	ST3955
Compton Chamberlayne	Wilts	9	SU0229
Compton Dando	Avon	19	ST6464
Compton Dundon	Somset	8	ST4933
Compton Durville	Somset	8	ST4117
Compton Greenfield	Avon	19	ST5682
Compton Martin	Avon	19	ST5456
Compton Pauncefoot	Somset	9	ST6425
Compton Valence	Dorset	9	SY5993
Comrie	Fife	82	NT0289
Comrie	Tays	81	NN7722
Conaglen House	Highld	86	NN0268
Conchra	Highld	85	NG8828
Conchra	Strath	80	NS0288
Concraigie	Tays	88	NO1044
Conderton	H & W	28	SO9637
Condicote	Gloucs	28	SP1528
Condorrat	Strath	74	NS7373
Condover	Shrops	37	SJ4906
Coney Hill	Gloucs	28	SO8516
Coney Weston	Suffk	32	TL9578
Coneyhurst Common	W Susx	12	TQ1024
Coneysthorpe	N York	56	SE7171
Congdon's Shop	Cnwll	4	SX2778
Congerstone	Leics	39	SK3605
Congham	Norfk	42	TF7123
Congleton	Ches	47	SJ8563
Congresbury	Avon	19	ST4363
Congreve	Staffs	38	SJ8914
Conicavel	Gramp	93	NH9853
Conichan	Tays	82	NN8432
Coningsby	Lincs	51	TF2258
Conington	Cambs	40	TL1885
Conington	Cambs	31	TL3266
Conisbrough	S York	49	SK5098
Conisby	Strath	70	NR2661
Conisholme	Lincs	51	TF3995
Coniston	Cumb	58	SD3097
Coniston	Humb	57	TA1535
Coniston Cold	N York	54	SD9054
Conistone	N York	54	SD9867
Connah's Quay	Clwyd	46	SJ2969
Connel	Strath	80	NM9133
Connel Park	Strath	66	NS6012
Connor Downs	Cnwll	2	SW5939
Conon Bridge	Highld	92	NH5455
Cononley	N York	54	SD9847
Consall	Staffs	48	SJ9748
Consett	Dur	69	NZ1150
Constable Burton	N York	61	SE1690
Constable Lee	Lancs	54	SD8123
Constantine	Cnwll	2	SW7329
Contin	Highld	92	NH4556
Convinth	Highld	92	NH5138
Conwy	Gwynd	45	SH7777
Conyer's Green	Suffk	32	TL8867
Cooden	E Susx	14	TQ7107
Coodham	Strath	73	NS3932
Cooil	IOM	52	SC3475
Cook's Green	Essex	25	TM1819
Cookbury	Devon	6	SS4005
Cookbury Wick	Devon	6	SS3805
Cookham	Berks	22	SU8985
Cookham Dean	Berks	22	SU8685
Cookham Rise	Berks	22	SU8885
Cookhill	Warwks	28	SP0558
Cookley	H & W	38	SO8480
Cookley	Suffk	33	TM3475
Cookley Green	Oxon	22	SU6990
Cookney	Gramp	89	NO8693
Cooks Green	Suffk	32	TL9853
Cooksmill Green	Essex	24	TL6306
Cookson Green	Ches	47	SJ5774
Coolham	W Susx	12	TQ1222
Cooling	Kent	14	TQ7575
Coombe	Cnwll	3	SW9551
Coombe	Devon	7	SS9725
Coombe	Devon	5	SX8384
Coombe	Devon	8	SY1092
Coombe	Gloucs	20	ST7693
Coombe	Wilts	20	SU1550
Coombe Bissett	Wilts	10	SU1026
Coombe Cellars	Devon	5	SX9072
Coombe Cross	Hants	11	SU6621
Coombe End	Somset	7	ST0329
Coombe Hill	Gloucs	28	SO8827
Coombe Keynes	Dorset	9	SY8484
Coombe Street	Somset	9	ST7531
Coombes	W Susx	12	TQ1908
Coombeswood	W Mids	38	SO9685
Cooperhill	Gramp	93	NH9953
Coopersale Common	Essex	23	TL4702
Coopersale Street	Essex	23	TL4701
Cop Street	Kent	23	TQ2960
Copford Green	Essex	24	TL9222
Copgrove	N York	55	SE3463
Copister	Shet	103	HU4878
Cople	Beds	30	TL1048
Copley	Dur	61	NZ0825
Copmanthorpe	N York	56	SE5646
Copmere End	Staffs	37	SJ8029
Copp	Lancs	53	SD4239
Coppathorne	Cnwll	6	SS2000
Coppenhall	Staffs	38	SJ9019
Copperhouse	Cnwll	2	SW5738
Coppicegate	Shrops	37	SO7380
Coppingford	Cambs	40	TL1680
Copplestone	Devon	7	SS7702
Coppull	Lancs	53	SD5614
Copsale	W Susx	12	TQ1724
Copston Magna	Warwks	39	SP4588
Copt Heath	W Mids	38	SP1778
Copt Hewick	N York	55	SE3471
Copthall Green	Essex	23	TL4200
Copthorne	W Susx	12	TQ3139
Copy's Green	Norfk	42	TF9439
Copythorne	Hants	10	SU3014
Corbets Tay	Gt Lon	24	TQ5685
Corbiere	Jersey	101	SV0000
Corbridge	Nthumb	68	NY9964
Corby	Nhants	40	SP8988
Corby Glen	Lincs	40	SK9925
Cordon	Strath	72	NS0230
Cordwell Unthank	Derbys	48	SK2076
Coreley	Shrops	37	SO6273
Cores End	Bucks	22	SU9087
Corfe	Somset	8	ST2319
Corfe Castle	Dorset	9	SY9681
Corfe Mullen	Dorset	9	SY9798
Corfton	Shrops	37	SO4985
Corgarff	Gramp	94	NJ2708
Corhampton	Hants	11	SU6120
Corley	Warwks	39	SP3085
Corley Ash	Warwks	39	SP2986
Corley Moor	Warwks	39	SP2885
Cormuir	Tays	88	NO3066
Cornabus	Strath	70	NR3346
Cornard Tye	Suffk	32	TL9041
Corndon	Devon	5	SX6885
Cornelly	M Glam	18	SS8281
Cornforth	Dur	62	NZ3134
Cornheath	D & G	66	NX9969
Cornhill	Gramp	94	NJ5858
Cornhill-on-Tweed	Nthumb	77	NT8639
Cornholme	W York	54	SD9126
Cornoigmore	Strath	78	NL9846
Cornsay	Dur	69	NZ1443
Cornsay Colliery	Dur	69	NZ1643
Corntown	Highld	92	NH5556
Corntown	M Glam	18	SS9177
Cornwell	Oxon	29	SP2727
Cornwood	Devon	5	SX6059
Cornworthy	Devon	5	SX8255
Corpach	Highld	86	NN0976
Corpusty	Norfk	43	TG1130
Corra	Strath	71	NR9765
Corrachree	Gramp	89	NJ4604
Corran	Highld	86	NN0263
Corran	Highld	85	NG8509
Corranbuie	Strath	71	NR8465
Corrie	D & G	67	NY2086
Corrie	Strath	72	NS0242
Corriecravie	Strath	72	NR9223
Corriegour	Highld	86	NN2692
Corriemoille	Highld	92	NH3663
Corrimony	Highld	92	NH3730
Corringham	Essex	24	TQ7083
Corringham	Lincs	50	SK8691
Corris	Gwynd	35	SH7507
Corris Uchaf	Gwynd	35	SH7408
Corrow	Strath	80	NN1800
Corry	Highld	85	NG6424
Corrygills	Strath	72	NS0335
Corsback	Highld	100	ND2372
Corscombe	Devon	6	SX6296
Corscombe	Dorset	8	ST5105
Corse	Gloucs	28	SO7926
Corse	Gramp	94	NJ6040
Corse Lawn	Gloucs	28	SO8330
Corsham	Wilts	20	ST8670
Corsindae	Gramp	95	NJ6808
Corsley	Wilts	20	ST8246
Corsley Heath	Wilts	20	ST8245
Corsock	D & G	65	NX7675
Corston	Avon	20	ST6965
Corston	Wilts	20	ST9283
Corstorphine	Loth	75	NT1972
Cortachy	Tays	88	NO3959
Corton	Suffk	43	TM5497
Corton	Wilts	20	ST9340
Corton Denham	Somset	9	ST6322
Coruanan Lodge	Highld	86	NN0668
Corvallie	IOM	52	SC1968
Corwar	Strath	64	NX2780
Corwen	Clwyd	46	SJ0743
Coryton	Devon	4	SX4583
Coryton	Essex	24	TQ7482
Cosby	Leics	39	SP5495
Coseley	W Mids	38	SO9494
Cosgrove	Nhants	30	SP7942
Cosham	Hants	11	SU6505
Cosheston	Dyfed	16	SN0003
Coshieville	Tays	87	NN7749
Cossall Marsh	Notts	49	SK4842
Cossington	Leics	39	SK6013
Cossington	Somset	19	ST3540
Costessey	Norfk	43	TG1712
Costock	Notts	39	SK5726
Coston	Leics	40	SK8422
Coston	Norfk	42	TG0606
Cote	Oxon	21	SP3502
Cote	Somset	19	ST3544
Cotebrook	Ches	47	SJ5765
Cotehill	Cumb	67	NY4650
Cotes	Cumb	59	SD4886
Cotes	Leics	39	SK5520
Cotesbach	Leics	39	SP5382
Cotgrave	Notts	39	SK6435
Cotham	Notts	50	SK7947
Cotherstone	Dur	61	NZ0119
Cothill	Oxon	21	SU4699
Cotleigh	Devon	8	ST2002
Cotmanhay	Derbys	49	SK4643
Coton	Cambs	31	TL4058

Dagenham
Dudsbury

Dagenham *Gt Lon* 23 TQ5084
Daglingworth *Gloucs* 28 SO9905
Dagnall *Bucks* 30 SP9916
Dailly *Strath* 73 NS2701
Dainton *Devon* 5 SX8466
Dairsie *Fife* 83 NO4117
Dalavich *Strath* 80 NM9612
Dalbeattie *D & G* 66 NX8361
Dalbeg *W Isls* 102 NB2345
Dalblair *Strath* 74 NS6419
Dalbog *Tays* 89 NO5871
Dalby *IOM* 52 SC2178
Dalby *N York* 56 SE6370
Dalcapon *Tays* 88 NN9754
Dalchalm *Highld* 97 NC9105
Dalchenna *Strath* 80 NN0706
Dalchork *Highld* 96 NC5710
Dalchreichart *Highld* 92 NH2912
Dalchriun *Tays* 81 NN7116
Dalcrue *Tays* 82 NO0417
Dalderby *Lincs* 51 TF2465
Dalditch *Devon* 3 SX0483
Dale *Derbys* 49 SK4338
Dale *Dyfed* 16 SM8005
Dale End *N York* 54 SD9646
Dale Head *Cumb* 59 NY4316
Dalelia *Highld* 79 NM7369
Dalgarven *Strath* 73 NS2846
Dalgety Bay *Fife* 82 NT1683
Dalgig *Strath* 73 NS5513
Dalginross *Tays* 81 NN7721
Dalguise *Tays* 88 NN9947
Dalhalvaig *Highld* 99 NC8954
Dalham *Suffk* 32 TL7261
Daliburgh *W Isls* 102 NF7421
Dalkeith *Loth* 75 NT3367
Dall *Tays* 87 NN5956
Dallas *Gramp* 93 NJ1252
Dalleagles *Strath* 73 NS5610
Dallinghoo *Suffk* 33 TM2655
Dallington *E Susx* 13 TQ6519
Dalmally *Strath* 80 NN1527
Dalmarnoch *Tays* 75 NS9945
Dalmary *Cent* 81 NS5195
Dalmellington *Strath* 73 NS4706
Dalmeny *Loth* 75 NT1477
Dalmigavie *Highld* 93 NH7319
Dalmigavie Lodge *Highld* 93 NH7523
Dalmore *Highld* 93 NH6668
Dalnacardoch Lodge *Tays* 87 NN7270
Dalnaspidal *Tays* 87 NN6473
Dalnawillan Lodge *Highld* 100 ND0240
Daloist *Tays* 87 NN7857
Dalqueich *Tays* 82 NO0704
Dalquhairn *Strath* 64 NX3296
Dalreavoch Lodge *Highld* 97 NC7508
Dalry *Strath* 73 NS2949
Dalrymple *Strath* 73 NS3514
Dalserf *Strath* 74 NS7950
Dalsmeran *Strath* 72 NR6413
Dalston *Cumb* 67 NY3650
Dalston *Gt Lon* 23 TQ3384
Dalswinton *D & G* 66 NX9385
Dalton *D & G* 67 NY1173
Dalton *N York* 61 NZ1108
Dalton *N York* 62 SE4376
Dalton *Nthumb* 69 NZ1172
Dalton Magna *S York* 49 SK4693
Dalton Piercy *Cleve* 62 NZ4631
Dalton in Furness *Cumb* 58 SD2273
Dalton-le-Dale *Dur* 69 NZ4047
Dalton-on-Tees *N York* 61 NZ2907
Daltot *Strath* 71 NR7583
Dalveich *Cent* 81 NN6124
Dalwhinnie *Highld* 87 NN6385
Dalwood *Devon* 8 ST2400
Damgate *Norfk* 43 TG4009
Danbury *Essex* 24 TL7805
Danby *N York* 62 NZ7008
Danby Wiske *N York* 62 SE3398
Dandaleith *Gramp* 94 NJ2845
Danderhall *Loth* 75 NT3069
Dane End *Herts* 31 TL3321
Dane Hills *Leics* 39 SK5605
Dane Street *Kent* 15 TR0552
Danebridge *Ches* 48 SJ9665
Danegate *E Susx* 13 TQ5634
Danehill *E Susx* 13 TQ4027
Danesford *Shrops* 37 SO7391
Danesmoor *Derbys* 49 SK4263
Danshillack *Gramp* 95 NJ7157
Danskine *Loth* 76 NT5667
Danthorpe *Humb* 57 TA2732
Darenth *Kent* 23 TQ5571
Daresbury *Ches* 47 SJ5882
Darfield *S York* 55 SE4104
Dargate *Kent* 15 TR0761
Darite *Cnwll* 4 SX2569
Darlaston *W Mids* 38 SO9796
Darlaston Green *W Mids* 38 SO9797
Darley *N York* 55 SE2059
Darley Abbey *Derbys* 49 SK3538
Darley Bridge *Derbys* 49 SK2661
Darley Green *Warwks* 38 SP1874
Darley Head *N York* 55 SE1959
Darleyhall *Herts* 30 TL1422
Darlingscott *Warwks* 29 SP2342
Darlington *Dur* 61 NZ2914
Darlton *Notts* 50 SK7773
Darowen *Powys* 35 SH8301
Darra *Gramp* 95 NJ7447
Darracot *Cnwll* 3 SX2712
Darracott *Devon* 6 SS2317
Darracott *Devon* 6 SS4739
Darrington *W York* 55 SE4919
Darsham *Suffk* 33 TM4170
Dartford *Kent* 23 TQ5474
Dartington *Devon* 5 SX7862
Dartmouth *Devon* 5 SX8751
Darton *S York* 55 SE3110
Darvel *Strath* 74 NS5637
Darwen *Lancs* 54 SD6922
Datchet *Berks* 22 SU9877
Datchworth *Herts* 31 TL2619
Datchworth Green *Herts* 31 TL2618
Daubhill *Gt Man* 47 SD7007
Dauntsey *Wilts* 20 ST9782
Dauntsey Green *Wilts* 20 ST9982
Dava *Highld* 93 NJ0138
Davenham *Ches* 47 SJ6571
Daventry *Nhants* 29 SP5762
David Street *Kent* 14 TQ6466
Davidson's Mains *Loth* 75 NT2175
Davidstow *Cnwll* 4 SX1587
Davington *D & G* 67 NT2302
Davington Hill *Kent* 15 TR0161
Daviot *Gramp* 95 NJ7528
Daviot *Highld* 93 NH7239
Daviot House *Highld* 93 NH7240
Davis Street *Berks* 22 SU7872
Davoch of Grange *Gramp* 94 NJ4851
Dawesgreen *Surrey* 12 TQ2147
Dawley *Shrops* 37 SJ6807
Dawlish *Devon* 5 SX9676
Dawlish Warren *Devon* 5 SX9778
Dawn *Clwyd* 45 SH8672
Daws Green *Somset* 8 ST2021
Daybrook *Notts* 49 SK5745
Daylesford *Gloucs* 29 SP2425
Deal *Kent* 15 TR3752
Dean *Cumb* 58 NY0725
Dean *Devon* 5 SX7364
Dean *Devon* 18 SS7048
Dean *Hants* 10 SU4431
Dean *Hants* 11 SU5619
Dean *Lancs* 54 SD8526
Dean *Oxon* 29 SP3422
Dean *Somset* 20 ST6743
Dean Bottom *Kent* 14 TQ5868
Dean Court *Oxon* 29 SP4705
Dean Cross *Devon* 6 SS5042
Dean End *Dorset* 9 ST9617
Dean Prior *Devon* 5 SX7363
Dean Street *Kent* 14 TQ7451
Deanburnhaugh *Border* 67 NT3912
Deancombe *Devon* 5 SX7264
Deane *Gt Man* 47 SD6907
Deane *Hants* 21 SU5450
Deanhead *W York* 55 SE0415
Deanich Lodge *Highld* 96 NH3683
Deanland *Dorset* 9 ST9918
Deanraw *Nthumb* 68 NY8162
Deanscale *Cumb* 58 NY0926
Deanshanger *Nhants* 30 SP7639
Deanshaugh *Gramp* 94 NJ3550
Deanston *Cent* 81 NN7101
Debach *Suffk* 33 TM2454
Debden Cross *Essex* 24 TL5731
Debden Green *Essex* 23 TQ4398
Debenham *Suffk* 33 TM1763
Deblin's Green *H & W* 28 SO8149
Dechmont *Loth* 75 NT0470
Dechmont Road *Loth* 75 NT0269
Deddington *Oxon* 29 SP4631
Dedham *Essex* 25 TM0533
Dedworth *Berks* 22 SU9476
Deebank *Gramp* 89 NO6994
Deene *Nhants* 40 SP9492
Deenethorpe *Nhants* 40 SP9591
Deepdale *Cumb* 60 SD7284
Deepdale *N York* 60 SD8989
Deeping Gate *Lincs* 40 TF1509
Deeping St. James *Lincs* 40 TF1609
Deeping St. Nicholas *Lincs* 41 TF2115
Deerhurst *Gloucs* 28 SO8729
Defford *H & W* 28 SO9143
Defynnog *Powys* 26 SN9227
Deganwy *Gwynd* 45 SH7779
Degnish *Strath* 79 NM7812
Deighton *N York* 62 NZ3801
Deighton *N York* 56 SE6244
Deiniolen *Gwynd* 44 SH5863
Delabole *Cnwll* 3 SX0683
Delamere *Ches* 47 SJ5668
Delfrigs *Gramp* 95 NJ9620
Dell Quay *W Susx* 11 SU8302
Delliefure *Highld* 93 NJ0731
Delnashaugh Hotel *Gramp* 94 NJ1835
Delnato *Gramp* 93 NJ1517
Delny *Highld* 93 NH7372
Delves *Dur* 69 NZ1149
Delvine *Tays* 82 NO1240
Dembleby *Lincs* 40 TF0437
Denaby *S York* 49 SK4899
Denbigh *Clwyd* 45 SJ0566
Denbrae *Fife* 83 NO3818
Denbury *Devon* 5 SX8268
Denby *Derbys* 49 SK3946
Denby Dale *W York* 55 SE2208
Denchworth *Oxon* 21 SU3891
Dendron *Cumb* 53 SD2470
Denfield *Strath* 75 NS9517
Denford *Nhants* 30 SP9976
Dengie *Essex* 25 TL9802
Denham *Suffk* 33 TM1974
Denham *Bucks* 22 TQ0487
Denham *Suffk* 32 TL7561
Denham End *Suffk* 32 TL7663
Denham Green *Bucks* 22 TQ0388
Denhead *Fife* 83 NO4613
Denhead *Gramp* 95 NJ9952
Denhead of Gray *Tays* 83 NO3431
Denhead of Gray *Tays* 83 NO3531
Denholm *Border* 76 NT5718
Denholme *W York* 55 SE0734
Denmead *Hants* 11 SU6512
Denmore *Gramp* 95 NJ9411
Dennis Park *W Mids* 38 SO9585
Denny *Cent* 81 NS8082
Dennyloanhead *Cent* 82 NS8180
Denside *Gramp* 89 NO8095
Densole *Kent* 15 TR2141
Denston *Suffk* 32 TL7652
Denstone *Staffs* 48 SK0940
Denstroude *Kent* 15 TR1061
Dent *Cumb* 60 SD7087
Dent-de-Lion *Kent* 15 TR3269
Denton *Cambs* 40 TL1487
Denton *Dur* 61 NZ2118
Denton *E Susx* 13 TQ4502
Denton *Gt Man* 48 SJ9295
Denton *Kent* 15 TR2147
Denton *Lincs* 40 SK8632
Denton *N York* 55 SE1448
Denton *Nhants* 30 SP8358
Denton *Norfk* 33 TM2888
Denver *Norfk* 41 TF6101
Denwick *Nthumb* 69 NU2014
Deopham *Norfk* 42 TG0500
Deopham Green *Norfk* 42 TM0499
Deptford *Gt Lon* 23 TQ3777
Deptford *Wilts* 20 SU0038
Derby *Derbys* 39 SK3536
Derbyhaven *IOM* 52 SC2867
Derculich *Tays* 87 NN8852
Deri *M Glam* 18 SO1201
Derringstone *Kent* 15 TR2049
Derrington *Staffs* 38 SJ8922
Derriton *Devon* 6 SS3303
Derry Hill *Wilts* 20 ST9670
Derrythorpe *Humb* 56 SE8208
Dersingham *Norfk* 42 TF6830
Dervaig *Strath* 79 NM4352
Derwen *Clwyd* 46 SJ0750
Derwenlas *Powys* 35 SN7298
Desborough *Nhants* 40 SP8083
Desford *Leics* 39 SK4703
Deskford *Gramp* 94 NJ5061
Detling *Kent* 14 TQ7958
Devauden *Gwent* 19 ST4898
Devil's Bridge *Dyfed* 35 SN7477
Devizes *Wilts* 20 SU0061
Devonport *Devon* 4 SX4554
Devonside *Cent* 82 NS9296
Devoran *Cnwll* 2 SW7939
Dewarton *Loth* 76 NT3763
Dewlish *Dorset* 9 SY7798
Dewsbury *W York* 55 SE2422
Deytheur *Powys* 36 SJ2417
Dhoon *IOM* 52 SC3784
Dhoor *IOM* 52 SC4396
Dhowin *IOM* 52 NX4101
Dial *Avon* 19 ST5367
Dial Green *W Susx* 11 SU9227
Dial Post *W Susx* 12 TQ1519
Dibden *Hants* 10 SU4108
Dibden Purlieu *Hants* 10 SU4106
Dickens Heath *W Mids* 38 SP1076
Dickleburgh *Norfk* 33 TM1682
Didbrook *Gloucs* 28 SP0531
Didcot *Oxon* 21 SU5190
Diddlebury *Shrops* 37 SO5085
Didling *W Susx* 11 SU8318
Didmarton *Gloucs* 20 ST8287
Didsbury *Gt Man* 47 SJ8392
Digby *Lincs* 50 TF0854
Digg *Highld* 90 NG4669
Digmore *Lancs* 46 SD4805
Digswell Water *Herts* 31 TL2414
Dihewyd *Dyfed* 34 SN4855
Dilham *Norfk* 43 TG3325
Dilhorne *Staffs* 48 SJ9743
Dillington *Cambs* 30 TL1365
Dilston *Nthumb* 68 NY9763
Dilton *Wilts* 20 ST8548
Dilton Marsh *Wilts* 20 ST8449
Dilwyn *H & W* 27 SO4154
Dinas *Cnwll* 3 SW9174
Dinas *Dyfed* 16 SN0139
Dinas *Gwynd* 44 SH2732
Dinas Dinlle *Gwynd* 44 SH4356
Dinas Powis *S Glam* 19 ST1571
Dinas-Mawddwy *Gwynd* 35 SH8615
Dinder *Somset* 19 ST5744
Dinedor *H & W* 27 SO5336
Dingle *Mersyd* 46 SJ3687
Dingley *Nhants* 40 SP7787
Dingwall *Highld* 92 NH5458
Dinnet *Gramp* 88 NO4598
Dinnington *S York* 49 SK5386
Dinnington *Somset* 8 ST4012
Dinnington *T & W* 69 NZ2073
Dinorwic *Gwynd* 44 SH5961
Dinton *Bucks* 22 SP7611
Dinton *Wilts* 9 SU0131
Dinwoodie *D & G* 67 NY1090
Dinworthy *Devon* 6 SS3015
Dipford *Somset* 8 ST2022
Dippen *Strath* 72 NR7937
Dippertown *Devon* 4 SX4385
Dippin *Strath* 72 NS0422
Dipple *Gramp* 94 NJ3258
Dipple *Strath* 73 NS2002
Diptford *Devon* 5 SX7256
Dipton *Dur* 69 NZ1554
Dirleton *Loth* 83 NT5184
Dirt Pot *Nthumb* 68 NY8546
Diseworth *Leics* 39 SK4524
Dishforth *N York* 62 SE3873
Diss *Norfk* 33 TM1180
Distillery *Highld* 92 NH5150
Distillery *Highld* 93 NJ0727
Distington *Cumb* 58 NY0023
Ditchampton *Wilts* 10 SU0831
Ditchburn *Nthumb* 77 NU1320
Ditchingham *Norfk* 33 TM3391
Ditchling *E Susx* 12 TQ3215
Ditherington *Shrops* 37 SJ5014
Ditteridge *Wilts* 20 ST8169
Dittisham *Devon* 5 SX8654
Ditton *Ches* 46 SJ4986
Ditton *Kent* 14 TQ7158
Ditton Green *Cambs* 32 TL6558
Ditton Priors *Shrops* 37 SO6089
Dixton *Gloucs* 28 SO9830
Dixton *Gwent* 27 SO5113
Dobcross *Gt Man* 54 SD9906
Dobwalls *Cnwll* 4 SX2165
Doccombe *Devon* 5 SX7786
Dochgarroch *Highld* 92 NH6241
Docker *Lancs* 59 SD5774
Docking *Norfk* 42 TF7636
Docklow *H & W* 27 SO5557
Dockray *Cumb* 59 NY3921
Dodd's Green *Ches* 47 SJ6043
Doddinghurst *Essex* 24 TQ5999
Doddington *Cambs* 41 TL4090
Doddington *Kent* 14 TQ9357
Doddington *Lincs* 50 SK9070
Doddington *Nthumb* 77 NT9932
Doddington *Shrops* 37 SO6176
Doddiscombsleigh *Devon* 5 SX8586
Dodford *H & W* 38 SO9373
Dodford *Nhants* 29 SP6160
Dodington *Avon* 20 ST7580
Dodington *Somset* 19 ST1740
Dodleston *Ches* 46 SJ3661
Dodside *Strath* 74 NS5053
Dodworth *S York* 55 SE3105
Dodworth Bottom *S York* 55 SE3205
Dodworth Green *S York* 55 SE3103
Doe Lea *Derbys* 49 SK4566
Dog Village *Devon* 7 SX9896
Dogdyke *Lincs* 51 TF2055
Dogmersfield *Hants* 22 SU7852
Dogridge *Wilts* 20 SU0787
Dolanog *Powys* 36 SJ0612
Dolau *Powys* 26 SO1367
Dolbenmaen *Gwynd* 44 SH5043
Dolcombe *Devon* 5 SX7786
Dolfor *Powys* 36 SO1087
Dolgarrog *Gwynd* 45 SH7767
Dolgellau *Gwynd* 35 SH7217
Dolgoch *Gwynd* 35 SH6404
Doll *Highld* 97 NC8803
Dollar *Cent* 82 NS9698
Dollarbeg *Cent* 82 NS9796
Dollarfield *Cent* 82 NS9697
Dollwen *Dyfed* 35 SN6981
Dolphin *Clwyd* 46 SJ1973
Dolphinholme *Lancs* 53 SD5253
Dolphinstone *Border* 76 NT6815
Dolphinton *Strath* 75 NT1046
Dolton *Devon* 6 SS5712
Dolwen *Clwyd* 45 SH8874
Dolwyddelan *Gwynd* 45 SH7352
Domgay *Powys* 36 SJ2819
Doncaster *S York* 56 SE5803
Doncaster Carr *S York* 49 SE5901
Donhead St. Mary *Wilts* 9 ST9024
Donibristle *Fife* 82 NT1688
Doniford *Somset* 7 ST0842
Donington *Lincs* 41 TF2035
Donington on Bain *Lincs* 51 TF2382
Donisthorpe *Leics* 39 SK3114
Donkey Street *Kent* 15 TR1233
Donkey Town *Surrey* 22 SU9460
Donnington *Berks* 21 SU4668
Donnington *Gloucs* 29 SP1928
Donnington *Shrops* 37 SJ5808
Donnington *W Susx* 11 SU8502
Donnington Wood *Shrops* 37 SJ7012
Donyatt *Somset* 8 ST3313
Doomsday Green *W Susx* 12 TQ1930
Doon Castle *Strath* 65 NX4895
Doonfoot *Strath* 73 NS3219
Doonholm *Strath* 73 NS3317
Dorback Lodge *Highld* 93 NJ0716
Dorchester *Dorset* 9 SY6990
Dorchester *Oxon* 21 SU5794
Dordon *Warwks* 39 SK2600
Dore *S York* 49 SK3081
Dores *Highld* 92 NH5934
Dorking *Surrey* 12 TQ1649
Dorking Tye *Suffk* 32 TL9257
Dorlin House *Highld* 85 NM6471
Dormans Land *Surrey* 13 TQ4041
Dormans Park *Surrey* 13 TQ3940
Dormington *H & W* 27 SO5840
Dormston *H & W* 28 SO9857
Dornal *Strath* 64 NX3077
Dorney *Berks* 22 SU9378
Dornie *Highld* 85 NG8826
Dornoch *Highld* 97 NH7989
Dornock *D & G* 67 NY2366
Dorrery *Highld* 100 ND0755
Dorridge *W Mids* 38 SP1775
Dorrington *Lincs* 50 TF0852
Dorrington *Shrops* 37 SJ4703
Dorsington *Warwks* 28 SP1349
Dorstone *H & W* 27 SO3141
Dorton *Bucks* 30 SP6714
Douglas *IOM* 52 SC3876
Douglas *Strath* 74 NS8330
Douglas Castle *Strath* 74 NS8431
Douglas Hill *Gwynd* 44 SH6065
Douglas Pier *Strath* 80 NS1999
Douglas Water *Strath* 74 NS8736
Douglas West *Strath* 74 NS8231
Douglas and Angus *Tays* 83 NO4233
Douglastown *Tays* 88 NO4147
Dougrie *Strath* 72 NR8837
Dounby *Ork* 103 HY2920
Doune *Cent* 81 NN7201
Doune *Highld* 96 NC4400
Dounepark *Strath* 64 NX1897
Dounie *Highld* 96 NH5690
Dounreay *Highld* 100 NC9965
Dousland *Devon* 4 SX5368
Dove Holes *Derbys* 48 SK0778
Dovenby *Cumb* 58 NY0933
Dovercourt *Essex* 25 TM2531
Doverdale *H & W* 28 SO8666
Doveridge *Derbys* 38 SK1134
Doversgreen *Surrey* 12 TQ2548
Dowally *Tays* 88 NO0048
Dowdeswell *Gloucs* 28 SP0019
Dowhill *Strath* 73 NS2003
Dowlais *M Glam* 26 SO0607
Dowland *Devon* 6 SS5610
Dowlish Wake *Somset* 8 ST3712
Down Ampney *Gloucs* 20 SU0997
Down Hatherley *Gloucs* 28 SO8622
Down St. Mary *Devon* 7 SS7404
Down Thomas *Devon* 4 SX5050
Downderry *Cnwll* 4 SX3153
Downe *Gt Lon* 23 TQ4361
Downend *Avon* 19 ST6577
Downend *Gloucs* 20 ST8398
Downfield *Tays* 83 NO3932
Downgate *Cnwll* 4 SX2871
Downgate *Cnwll* 4 SX3773
Downham *Cambs* 41 TL5284
Downham *Essex* 24 TQ7296
Downham *Gt Lon* 23 TQ3871
Downham *Lancs* 54 SD7844
Downham Market *Norfk* 41 TF6003
Downhead *Somset* 8 ST5625
Downhead *Somset* 20 ST6945
Downhill *Tays* 82 NO0930
Downholme *N York* 61 SE1197
Downies *Gramp* 89 NO9294
Downley *Bucks* 22 SU8495
Downside *Surrey* 22 TQ1058
Downton *Hants* 10 SZ2693
Downton *Wilts* 10 SU1721
Downton on the Rock *H & W* 36 SO4273
Dowsby *Lincs* 40 TF1129
Doxey *Staffs* 38 SJ9023
Doynton *Avon* 20 ST7173
Draethen *M Glam* 19 ST2287
Draffan *Strath* 74 NS7945
Draice Hole *Notts* 49 SK7090
Drakeland Corner *Devon* 4 SX5758
Drakemyre *Strath* 73 NS2950
Drakes Broughton *H & W* 28 SO9248
Drakewalls *Cnwll* 4 SX4271
Draughton *N York* 55 SE0352
Draughton *Nhants* 30 SP7676
Drax *N York* 56 SE6726
Drax Hales *N York* 56 SE6726
Draycote *Warwks* 29 SP4570
Draycott *Derbys* 39 SK4433
Draycott *Gloucs* 29 SP1835
Draycott *Shrops* 37 SO8192
Draycott *Somset* 19 ST4751
Draycott in the Clay *Staffs* 38 SK1528
Draycott in the Moors *Staffs* 48 SJ9840
Drayford *Devon* 7 SS7913
Drayton *H & W* 38 SO9076
Drayton *Hants* 11 SU6705
Drayton *Leics* 40 SP8392
Drayton *Norfk* 43 TG1813
Drayton *Oxon* 29 SP4241
Drayton *Oxon* 21 SU4794
Drayton *Somset* 8 ST4024
Drayton Bassett *Staffs* 39 SK1900
Drayton Beauchamp *Bucks* 22 SP9011
Drayton Parslow *Bucks* 30 SP8428
Drayton St. Leonard *Oxon* 21 SU5996
Dreenhill *Dyfed* 16 SM9214
Drefach *Dyfed* 17 SN3538
Drefach *Dyfed* 17 SN5213
Drefach *Dyfed* 17 SN5045
Dreghorn *Strath* 73 NS3538
Drellingore *Kent* 15 TR2141
Drem *Loth* 83 NT5079
Drewsteignton *Devon* 5 SX7391
Driby *Lincs* 51 TF3784
Driffield *Gloucs* 20 SU0799
Driffield Cross Roads *Gloucs* 20 SU0699
Drift *Cnwll* 2 SW4328
Drigg *Cumb* 58 SD0699
Drighlington *W York* 55 SE2229
Drimnin *Highld* 79 NM5554
Drimpton *Dorset* 8 ST4104
Drimsallie *Highld* 85 NM9578
Drimsynie *Strath* 80 NN1901
Drimvore *Strath* 71 NR8394
Dringhouses *N York* 56 SE5849
Drinkstone *Suffk* 32 TL9661
Drinkstone Green *Suffk* 32 TL9660
Drinsey Nook *Notts* 50 SK8673
Driver's End *Herts* 31 TL2220
Drointon *Staffs* 38 SK0226
Droitwich Spa *H & W* 28 SO8963
Dron *Tays* 82 NO1416
Dronfield *Derbys* 49 SK3578
Dronfield Woodhouse *Derbys* 49 SK3278
Drongan *Strath* 73 NS4519
Dronley *Tays* 83 NO3435
Droop *Dorset* 9 ST7508
Dropping Well *S York* 49 SK3993
Droxford *Hants* 11 SU6018
Droylsden *Gt Man* 48 SJ9098
Druid *Clwyd* 45 SJ0443
Druidale *IOM* 52 SC3688
Druids Heath *W Mids* 38 SK0601
Druidston *Dyfed* 16 SM8716
Druimachoish *Highld* 86 NN1246
Druimarbin *Highld* 86 NN0870
Druimdrishaig *Strath* 71 NR7370
Druimindarroch *Highld* 85 NM6884
Drum *Strath* 72 NR6625
Drum *Strath* 71 NR9276
Drum *Tays* 82 NO0400
Drum Kildavie *Strath* 72 NR7210
Drumalbin *Strath* 74 NS9038
Drumbeg *Highld* 98 NC1232
Drumblade *Gramp* 94 NJ5840
Drumblair House *Gramp* 94 NJ6343
Drumbuie *Highld* 85 NG7730
Drumburgh *Cumb* 67 NY2659
Drumburn *D & G* 66 NX8855
Drumburn *D & G* 66 NX9762
Drumchapel *Strath* 74 NS5270
Drumchastle *Tays* 87 NN6858
Drumclog *Strath* 74 NS6439
Drumeldrie *Fife* 83 NO4403
Drumelzier *Border* 75 NT1334
Drumfearn *Highld* 85 NG6716
Drumfrennie *Gramp* 89 NO7298
Drumgask *Highld* 87 NN6193
Drumguish *Highld* 81 NN7900
Drumhead *Gramp* 89 NO6092
Drumin *Gramp* 94 NJ1830
Drumjohn *D & G* 65 NX5297
Drumlamford *Strath* 64 NX2876
Drumlasie *Gramp* 89 NJ6405
Drumleaning *Cumb* 67 NY2751
Drumlemble *Strath* 72 NR6619
Drumlithie *Gramp* 89 NO7880
Drummoddie *D & G* 64 NX3945
Drummond *Highld* 92 NH6065
Drummore *D & G* 64 NX1336
Drummore *D & G* 66 NX9075
Drummuir *Gramp* 94 NJ3844
Drumnadrochit *Highld* 92 NH5029
Drumnagorrach *Gramp* 94 NJ5252
Drumore *Strath* 72 NR7022
Drumpark *D & G* 66 NX8780
Drumrash *D & G* 65 NX6871
Drumrunie Lodge *Highld* 96 NC1604
Drumshang *Strath* 73 NS2514
Drumsleet *D & G* 66 NX9474
Drumtroddan *D & G* 64 NX3644
Drumuie *Highld* 90 NG4546
Drumuillie *Highld* 93 NH9420
Drumvaich *Cent* 81 NN6703
Drumwhirn *D & G* 65 NX7480
Drunzie *Tays* 82 NO1308
Dry Doddington *Lincs* 50 SK8546
Dry Drayton *Cambs* 31 TL3862
Dry Sandford *Oxon* 21 SP4900
Drybeck *Cumb* 60 NY6615
Drybridge *Gramp* 94 NJ4362
Drybridge *Strath* 73 NS3536
Drybrook *Gloucs* 27 SO6417
Dryburgh *Border* 76 NT5932
Dryhope *Border* 75 NT2624
Drym *Cnwll* 2 SW6233
Drymen *Cent* 81 NS4788
Drymuir *Gramp* 95 NJ9146
Drynoch *Highld* 84 NG4031
Dryton *Shrops* 37 SJ5905
Dubford *Gramp* 95 NJ7963
Duchally *Highld* 96 NC3817
Duck End *Essex* 24 TL6833
Duck Street *Hants* 21 SU3249
Duckington *Ches* 46 SJ4951
Ducklington *Oxon* 29 SP3507
Duddingston *Loth* 75 NT2872
Duddington *Nhants* 40 SK9800
Duddlestone *Somset* 8 ST2321
Duddlewick *Shrops* 37 SO6583
Duddo *Nthumb* 77 NT9342
Duddon *Ches* 46 SJ5164
Dudleston *Shrops* 36 SJ3438
Dudley *T & W* 69 NZ2573
Dudley *W Mids* 38 SO9490
Dudley Port *W Mids* 38 SO9691
Dudsbury *Dorset* 10 SZ0898

Duffield Derbys 49 SK3443
Duffryn M Glam 18 SS8495
Dufftown Gramp 94 NJ3240
Duffus Gramp 94 NJ1668
Dufton Cumb 60 NY6825
Duggleby N York 56 SE8767
Duirinish Highld 85 NG7831
Duisdalemore Highld 85 NG6913
Duisky Highld 85 NN0076
Duke Street Suffk 32 TM0842
Dukinfield Gt Man 48 SJ9497
Dulcote Somset 19 ST5644
Dulford Devon 7 ST0606
Dull Tays 87 NN8049
Dullatur Strath 74 NS7476
Dullingham Cambs 32 TL6357
Dullingham Ley Cambs 32 TL6456
Dulnain Bridge Highld 93 NH9924
Duloe Beds 30 TL1560
Duloe Cnwll 4 SX2358
Dulverton Somset 4 SS9127
Dulwich Gt Lon 23 TQ3373
Dumbarton Strath 80 NS3975
Dumbleton Gloucs 28 SP0136
Dumcrieff D & G 67 NT1104
Dumfries D & G 66 NX9776
Dumgoyne Cent 81 NS5283
Dummer Hants 21 SU5846
Dumpton Kent 15 TR3866
Dun Tays 89 NO6660
Dunalastair Tays 87 NN7159
Dunan Highld 84 NG5828
Dunan Strath 80 NS1571
Dunan Tays 87 NN4757
Dunans Strath 80 NS0491
Dunaverty Strath 72 NR6807
Dunavourd Tays 75 NS9659
Dunball Somset 19 ST3041
Dunbar Loth 83 NT6778
Dunbar Somset 19 ST3140
Dunbeath Highld 100 ND1630
Dunbeg Strath 79 NM8833
Dunblane Cent 81 NN7801
Dunbog Fife 83 NO2817
Dunbridge Hants 10 SU3126
Duncanston Gramp 94 NJ5726
Duncanston Highld 92 NH5956
Dunchideock Devon 5 SX8787
Dunchurch Warwks 39 SP4871
Duncow D & G 66 NX9683
Duncrievie Tays 82 NO1309
Duncton W Susx 12 SU9617
Dundee Tays 83 NO4030
Dundon Somset 8 ST4732
Dundonald Strath 73 NS3834
Dundonnell Highld 91 NH0886
Dundreggan Highld 92 NH3214
Dundrennan D & G 65 NX7447
Dundry Avon 19 ST5566
Dunecht Gramp 95 NJ7509
Dunfermline Fife 82 NT0987
Dunfield Gloucs 20 SU1497
Dungavel Strath 74 NS6537
Dunglass Loth 76 NT7671
Dungworth S York 49 SK2889
Dunham Notts 50 SK8174
Dunham Town Gt Man 47 SJ7387
Dunham Woodhouses Gt Man 47 SJ7287
Dunham-on-the-Hill Ches 46 SJ4772
Dunhampton H & W 28 SO8466
Dunholme Lincs 50 TF0279
Dunino Fife 83 NO5311
Dunipace Cent 81 NS8083
Dunira Tays 81 NN7323
Dunk's Green Kent 13 TQ6152
Dunkeld Tays 88 NO0242
Dunkerton Avon 20 ST7159
Dunkeswell Devon 8 ST1407
Dunkeswick W York 55 SE3047
Dunkirk Avon 20 ST7886
Dunkirk Kent 15 TR0759
Dunlappie Tays 89 NO5867
Dunley H & W 28 SO7869
Dunlop Strath 73 NS4049
Dunmaglass Highld 92 NH5922
Dunmore Cent 82 NS8989
Dunmore Strath 71 NR7961
Dunnet Highld 100 ND2171
Dunnichen Tays 89 NO5048
Dunning Tays 82 NO0114
Dunnington Humb 57 TA1551
Dunnington N York 56 SE6652
Dunnington Warwks 28 SP0653
Dunnockshaw Lancs 54 SD8227
Dunoon Strath 80 NS1777
Dunphail Gramp 93 NJ0147
Dunragit D & G 64 NX1557
Dunrod Strath 80 NS2273
Duns Border 76 NT7853
Duns Tew Oxon 29 SP4528
Dunsby Lincs 40 TF1026
Dunscore D & G 66 NX8884
Dunscroft Cleve 62 NZ6019
Dunsdale Cleve 62 NZ6019
Dunsden Green Oxon 22 SU7377
Dunsdon Devon 6 SS3008
Dunsfold Surrey 12 TQ0036
Dunsford Devon 5 SX8189
Dunshelt Fife 83 NO2410
Dunshillock Gramp 95 NJ9848
Dunsley N York 63 NZ8511
Dunsley Staffs 38 SO8583
Dunsmore Bucks 22 SP8605
Dunsop Bridge Lancs 54 SD6650
Dunstable Beds 30 TL0122
Dunstall Staffs 39 SK1920
Dunstan Nthumb 77 NU2420
Dunster Somset 7 SS9943
Dunston Lincs 50 TF0663
Dunston Norfk 43 TG2202
Dunston Staffs 38 SJ9217
Dunston T & W 69 NZ2262
Dunston Heath Staffs 38 SJ9117
Dunstone Devon 5 SX5951
Dunstone Devon 5 SX7171
Dunswell Humb 57 TA0736
Dunsyre Strath 75 NT0748
Dunterton Devon 4 SX3779
Duntisbourne Abbots Gloucs 28 SO9607
Duntisbourne Rouse Gloucs 28 SO9806
Duntocher Strath 74 NS4973
Dunton Beds 31 TL2244
Dunton Bucks 30 SP8224
Dunton Norfk 42 TF8830
Dunton Bassett Leics 39 SP5490
Dunton Green Kent 23 TQ5157
Duntulm Highld 90 NG4174
Dunure Strath 73 NS2515
Dunvant W Glam 17 SS5993
Dunvegan Highld 90 NG2548
Durgan Cnwll 2 SW7727
Durham Dur 61 NZ2742
Durisdeer D & G 66 NS8903
Durisdeermill D & G 66 NS8804
Durka W York 55 SE3117
Durleigh Somset 19 ST2736
Durley Hants 11 SU5116
Durley Wilts 21 SU2364
Durley Street Hants 11 SU5217
Durlock Kent 15 TR2758
Durlock Kent 15 TR3164
Durmgley Tays 88 NO4250
Durnamuck Highld 91 NH0192
Durness Highld 98 NC4067
Durno Gramp 95 NJ7128
Duror Highld 86 NM9754
Durran Highld 100 ND1963
Durran Strath 80 NM9607
Durrington W Susx 12 TQ1105
Durrington Wilts 20 SU1544
Dursley Gloucs 20 ST7597
Dursley Cross Gloucs 28 SO6920
Durston Somset 8 ST2828
Durweston Dorset 9 ST8508
Dury Shet 103 SP2261
Duston Nhants 30 SP7261
Duthil Highld 93 NH9324
Dutlas Powys 36 SO2077
Dutson M Glam 4 SX3486
Dutton Ches 47 SJ5779

Duxford Cambs 31 TL4846
Duxford Oxon 21 SU3699
Dwygyfylchi Gwynd 45 SH7376
Dwygyfylchi Gwynd 45 SH7377
Dwyran Gwynd 44 SH4446
Dyce Gramp 95 NJ8812
Dye House Nthumb 68 NY9458
Dyer's End Essex 24 TL7238
Dyfatty Dyfed 17 SN4501
Dyffryn Ardudwy Gwynd 34 SH5822
Dyffryn Ceidrych Dyfed 26 SN7025
Dyffryn Cellwen W Glam 26 SN8510
Dyke Gramp 93 NH9858
Dyke Lincs 40 TF1022
Dykehead Cent 81 NS5997
Dykehead Strath 74 NS8659
Dykehead Tays 88 NO2453
Dykehead Tays 88 NO3860
Dykelands Gramp 89 NO7068
Dykends Tays 88 NO2557
Dykeside Gramp 95 NJ7243
Dymchurch Kent 15 TR1029
Dymock Gloucs 28 SO6931
Dyrham Avon 20 ST7375
Dysart Fife 83 NT3093
Dyserth Clwyd 45 SJ0579

E

Eagland Hill Lancs 53 SD4345
Eagle Lincs 50 SK8767
Eaglescliffe Cleve 62 NZ4215
Eaglesfield Cumb 58 NY0928
Eaglesfield D & G 67 NY2374
Eaglesham Strath 74 NS5751
Eagley Gt Man 54 SD7112
Eakring Notts 49 SK6762
Ealand Humb 56 SE7811
Ealing Gt Lon 23 TQ1780
Eals Nthumb 68 NY6756
Eamont Bridge Cumb 59 NY5228
Earby Lancs 54 SD9046
Eardington Shrops 37 SO7290
Eardisland H & W 27 SO4158
Eardisley H & W 27 SO3149
Eardiston H & W 28 SO6968
Eardiston Shrops 36 SJ3725
Earith Cambs 31 TL3875
Earl Shilton Leics 39 SP4697
Earl Soham Suffk 33 TM2363
Earl Sterndale Derbys 48 SK0967
Earl's Croome H & W 28 SO8642
Earlestown Mersyd 47 SJ5795
Earley Berks 22 SU7472
Earlham Norfk 43 TG2008
Earlish Highld 90 NG3961
Earls Barton Nhants 30 SP8563
Earls Colne Essex 24 TL8528
Earls Common H & W 28 SO9559
Earlsdon W Mids 39 SP3278
Earlsferry Fife 83 NO4800
Earlsfield Gt Lon 23 TQ2673
Earlsford Gramp 95 NJ8334
Earlsheaton W York 55 SE2621
Earlston Border 76 NT5738
Earlston Strath 73 NS4035
Earlswood Surrey 12 TQ2849
Earlswood W Mids 38 SO8995
Earlswood Warwks 38 SP1174
Earlswood Common Gwent 19 ST4595
Earnley W Susx 11 SZ8197
Earsdon Nthumb 69 NZ1993
Earsdon T & W 69 NZ3272
Earsham Norfk 33 TM3289
Eartham W Susx 11 SU9309
Easby N York 62 NZ5708
Easdale Strath 79 NM7417
Easebourne W Susx 11 SU8922
Easenhall Warwks 39 SP4679
Eashing Surrey 12 SU9443
Easington Bucks 22 SP6810
Easington Cleve 63 NZ7417
Easington Dur 62 NZ4143
Easington Humb 57 TA3919
Easington Oxon 21 SU6597
Easington Colliery Dur 62 NZ4344
Easingwold N York 55 SE5269
Eassie and Nevay Tays 88 NO3344
East Aberthaw S Glam 18 ST0366
East Allington Devon 5 SX7648
East Anstey Devon 7 SS8626
East Anton Hants 21 SU3647
East Appleton N York 61 SE2395
East Ashley IOW 11 SZ5888
East Ashling W Susx 11 SU8207
East Aston Hants 21 SU4345
East Ayton N York 63 SE9985
East Bank Gwent 27 SO2206
East Barkwith Lincs 50 TF1681
East Barming Kent 14 TQ7254
East Barnby N York 63 NZ8212
East Barnet Gt Lon 23 TQ2794
East Barns Loth 76 NT7176
East Barsham Norfk 42 TF9134
East Beckham Norfk 43 TG1639
East Bedfont Gt Lon 22 TQ0873
East Bergholt Suffk 25 TM0734
East Bilney Norfk 42 TF9519
East Blatchington E Susx 13 TV4800
East Bloxworth Dorset 9 SY8994
East Boldon T & W 69 NZ3761
East Boldre Hants 10 SU3700
East Bower Somset 8 ST3137
East Bradenham Norfk 42 TF9308
East Brent Somset 19 ST3452
East Bridgford Notts 49 SK6943
East Buckland Devon 7 SS6731
East Budleigh Devon 5 SY0684
East Butterwick Humb 56 SE8306
East Calder Loth 75 NT0867
East Carleton Norfk 43 TG1702
East Carlton Nhants 40 SP8389
East Carlton W York 55 SE2224
East Challow Oxon 21 SU3888
East Charleton Devon 5 SX7642
East Chelborough Dorset 9 ST5405
East Chiltington E Susx 13 TQ3715
East Chinnock Somset 8 ST4913
East Chisenbury Wilts 21 SU2945
East Clandon Surrey 12 TQ0651
East Claydon Bucks 30 SP7325
East Coker Somset 8 ST5412
East Combe Somset 8 ST1631
East Compton Somset 19 ST6141
East Cornworthy Devon 5 SX8455
East Cottingwith Humb 56 SE7042
East Coulston Wilts 20 ST9454
East Cowes IOW 11 SZ5095
East Cowick N York 56 SE6621
East Cowton N York 62 NZ3103
East Cranmore Somset 20 ST6743
East Creech Dorset 9 SY9282
East Dean H & W 27 SO6520
East Dean Hants 10 SU2626
East Dean Hants 10 SU2726
East Dean W Susx 11 SU9013
East Dereham Norfk 42 TF9913
East Down Devon 6 SS6041
East Drayton Notts 50 SK7775
East Dulwich Gt Lon 23 TQ3375
East Dundry Avon 19 ST5766
East Ella Humb 57 TA0529
East End Hants 10 SU4160
East End Hants 10 SZ3697
East End Humb 57 TA1930
East End Kent 14 TQ2727
East End Kent 14 TQ8335
East End Oxon 29 SP3914
East End Somset 20 ST6746
East Everleigh Wilts 21 SU2053

East Farleigh Kent 14 TQ7353
East Farndon Nhants 40 SP7184
East Ferry Lincs 50 SK8199
East Flexford Surrey 12 SU9448
East Fortune Loth 83 NT5579
East Garforth W York 55 SE4133
East Garston Berks 21 SU3576
East Goscote Leics 39 SK6413
East Grafton Wilts 21 SU2560
East Grange Gramp 93 NJ0981
East Grimstead Wilts 10 SU2227
East Grinstead W Susx 13 TQ3938
East Guldeford E Susx 14 TQ9321
East Haddon Nhants 30 SP6668
East Hagbourne Oxon 21 SU5388
East Halton Humb 57 TA1319
East Ham Gt Lon 23 TQ4283
East Hanney Oxon 21 SU4193
East Hanningfield Essex 24 TL7701
East Hardwick W York 55 SE4618
East Harling Norfk 32 TL9986
East Harlsey N York 62 SE4299
East Harnham Wilts 10 SU1428
East Harptree Avon 19 ST5655
East Hartburn Cleve 62 NZ4111
East Hartford Nthumb 69 NZ2679
East Harting W Susx 11 SU8019
East Hatch Wilts 9 ST9228
East Hatley Cambs 31 TL2850
East Hauxwell N York 61 SE1693
East Haven Tays 83 NO5836
East Heath Berks 22 SU6867
East Heckington Lincs 50 TF1944
East Hedleyhope Dur 61 NZ1540
East Helmsdale Highld 97 ND0315
East Hendred Oxon 21 SU4588
East Herrington T & W 69 NZ3453
East Hesleton N York 63 SE9276
East Hewish Avon 19 ST3964
East Hoathly E Susx 13 TQ5216
East Holme Dorset 9 SY8986
East Horndon Essex 24 TQ6389
East Horrington Somset 19 ST5846
East Horsley Surrey 12 TQ0953
East Horton Nthumb 77 NU0331
East Howe Dorset 10 SZ0795
East Huntington N York 56 SE6155
East Hyde Beds 30 TL1217
East Ilkerton Devon 7 SS7146
East Ilsley Berks 21 SU4980
East Keal Lincs 51 TF3764
East Kennett Wilts 20 SU1167
East Keswick W York 55 SE3644
East Kilbride Strath 74 NS6354
East Kimber Devon 4 SX4989
East Kirkby Lincs 51 TF3362
East Knighton Dorset 9 SY8185
East Knoyle Wilts 9 ST8830
East Kyloe Nthumb 77 NU0639
East Lambrook Somset 8 ST4319
East Langdon Kent 15 TR3346
East Langton Leics 40 SP7292
East Langwell Highld 97 NC7206
East Laroch Highld 86 NN0858
East Lavant W Susx 11 SU8606
East Lavington W Susx 11 SU9416
East Layton N York 61 NZ1609
East Leake Notts 39 SK5526
East Leigh Devon 5 SX7657
East Leigh Devon 7 SS6905
East Lexham Norfk 42 TF8617
East Linton Loth 76 NT5877
East Lockinge Oxon 21 SU4287
East Lound Humb 50 SK7899
East Lulworth Dorset 9 SY8581
East Lutton N York 56 SE9469
East Lydford Somset 8 ST5731
East Mains Gramp 89 NO6797
East Malling Kent 14 TQ7057
East Marden W Susx 11 SU8014
East Markham Notts 50 SK7472
East Martin Hants 10 SU0719
East Marton N York 54 SD9051
East Meon Hants 11 SU6822
East Mersea Essex 25 TM0514
East Molesey Surrey 22 TQ1467
East Morden Dorset 9 SY9194
East Morton D & G 66 NS8801
East Norton Leics 40 SK7800
East Ogwell Devon 5 SX8370
East Orchard Dorset 9 ST8317
East Ord Nthumb 77 NT9175
East Parley Dorset 10 SZ1098
East Pennar Dyfed 16 SM9602
East Pennard Somset 19 ST5937
East Perry Cambs 30 TL1467
East Plean Cent 82 NS8387
East Poringland Norfk 43 TG2701
East Portlemouth Devon 5 SX7438
East Prawle Devon 5 SX7736
East Preston W Susx 11 TQ0702
East Pulham Dorset 9 ST7109
East Putford Devon 6 SS3616
East Quantoxhead Somset 18 ST1343
East Rainton T & W 69 NZ3347
East Ravendale Lincs 51 TF2399
East Raynham Norfk 42 TF8825
East Rigton W York 55 SE3743
East Rounton N York 62 NZ4203
East Rudham Norfk 42 TF8328
East Runton Norfk 43 TG1942
East Ruston Norfk 43 TG3427
East Saltoun Loth 76 NT4767
East Sheen Gt Lon 23 TQ2075
East Shefford Berks 21 SU3874
East Stoke Dorset 9 SY8787
East Stoke Notts 50 SK7549
East Stour Dorset 9 ST8022
East Stourmouth Kent 15 TR2662
East Stowford Devon 7 SS6326
East Stratton Hants 21 SU5440
East Sutton Kent 14 TQ8249
East Taphouse Cnwll 3 SX1863
East Thirston Nthumb 69 NZ1900
East Tilbury Essex 24 TQ6877
East Tisted Hants 11 SU7032
East Torrington Lincs 50 TF1483
East Tuddenham Norfk 42 TG0811
East Tytherley Hants 10 SU2929
East Tytherton Wilts 20 ST9674
East Village Devon 7 SS8405
East Wall Shrops 37 SO5293
East Walton Norfk 42 TF7416
East Week Devon 5 SX6692
East Wellow Hants 10 SU3020
East Wemyss Fife 83 NT3497
East Whitburn Loth 75 NS9665
East Wickham Gt Lon 23 TQ4576
East Williamston Dyfed 16 SN0005
East Winch Norfk 42 TF6916
East Winterslow Wilts 10 SU2434
East Wittering W Susx 11 SZ7996
East Witton N York 61 SE1486
East Woodburn Nthumb 68 NY9086
East Woodhay Hants 21 NU4061
East Woodlands Somset 20 ST7943
East Worldham Hants 11 SU7438
East Wretham Norfk 32 TL9190
East Youlstone Devon 6 SS2715
Eastbourne Dur 61 NZ3013
Eastbridge Suffk 33 TM4566
Eastburn W York 54 SE0144
Eastbury Berks 21 SU3477
Eastbury Gt Lon 22 TQ1092
Eastbury Herts 22 TQ1092
Eastby N York 54 SE0154
Eastchurch Kent 15 TR0171
Eastcombe Gloucs 28 SO8804
Eastcote Gt Lon 22 TQ1088
Eastcote Nhants 30 SP6853
Eastcote W Mids 39 SP1979
Eastcott Wilts 20 SU0255
Eastcourt Wilts 20 ST9792
Eastcourt Wilts 21 SU2361
Eastend Essex 25 TQ9492
Eastend Essex 25 TQ9492

Eastend Strath 75 NS9437
Easter Balmoral Gramp 88 NO2693
Easter Compton Avon 19 ST6782
Easter Dalziel Highld 93 NH7550
Easter Elchies Gramp 94 NJ2744
Easter Fearn Highld 97 NH6486
Easter Howgate Tays 75 NT2463
Easter Kinkell Highld 92 NH5755
Easter Lednathie Tays 88 NO3463
Easter Moniack Highld 92 NH5543
Easter Ord Gramp 89 NJ8304
Easter Pitkierie Fife 83 NO5606
Easter Skeld Shet 103 HU3144
Eastergate W Susx 12 SU9405
Easterhouse Strath 74 NS6765
Eastern Green W Mids 39 SP2879
Easterton Wilts 20 SU0154
Eastertown Somset 19 ST3454
Eastertown Strath 74 NS8260
Eastfield Cent 74 NS8964
Eastfield Strath 74 NS7575
Eastgate Dur 61 NY9538
Eastgate Norfk 43 TG1423
Easthampstead Berks 22 SU8667
Easthampton H & W 27 SO4063
Easthope Shrops 37 SO5695
Easthorpe Essex 24 TL9121
Easthorpe Notts 49 SK7053
Eastington Devon 7 SS7409
Eastington Gloucs 28 SP1213
Eastlands D & G 66 NX8172
Eastleach Martin Gloucs 29 SP2005
Eastleach Turville Gloucs 29 SP1905
Eastleigh Devon 6 SS4827
Eastleigh Hants 10 SU4519
Eastling Kent 15 TQ9656
Eastney Hants 11 SZ6698
Eastnor H & W 28 SO7337
Eastoft Humb 56 SE8016
Easton Berks 21 SU4271
Easton Cambs 31 TL1371
Easton Cumb 67 NY2759
Easton Devon 5 SX7288
Easton Hants 11 SU5132
Easton IOW 10 SZ3486
Easton Lincs 40 SK9326
Easton Norfk 43 TG1510
Easton Somset 19 ST5147
Easton Suffk 33 TM2858
Easton Wilts 20 ST8970
Easton Grey Wilts 20 ST8787
Easton Maudit Nhants 30 SP8858
Easton Royal Wilts 21 SU2060
Easton-in-Gordano Avon 19 ST5175
Easton-on-the-Hill Nhants 40 TF0104
Eastpeak Devon 6 SX3494
Eastrea Cambs 41 TL2997
Eastriggs D & G 67 NY2465
Eastrington Humb 56 SE7929
Eastrop Wilts 21 SU2092
Eastry Kent 15 TR3055
Eastville Lincs 51 TF4056
Eastwell Leics 40 SK7728
Eastwick Herts 24 TL4311
Eastwood Essex 24 TQ8688
Eastwood Notts 49 SK4646
Eastwood W York 54 SD9727
Eathorpe Warwks 29 SP3969
Eaton Ches 47 SJ5763
Eaton Ches 47 SJ8765
Eaton Leics 40 SK7928
Eaton Norfk 43 TG2006
Eaton Notts 49 SK7077
Eaton Oxon 21 SP4403
Eaton Shrops 37 SO5090
Eaton Shrops 37 SJ5906
Eaton Bray Beds 30 SP9620
Eaton Constantine Shrops 37 SJ5906
Eaton Green Beds 30 SP9621
Eaton Hastings Oxon 21 SU2698
Eaton Mascott Shrops 37 SJ5305
Eaton Socon Beds 31 TL1659
Eaton upon Tern Shrops 37 SJ6523
Eaves Brow Ches 47 SJ6493
Ebberston N York 63 SE8982
Ebbesborne Wake Wilts 9 ST9924
Ebbw Vale Gwent 27 SO1609
Ebbw Vale Gwent 19 ST2094
Ebchester Dur 68 NZ1055
Ebford Devon 5 SX9887
Ebley Gloucs 28 SO8205
Ebnal Ches 46 SJ4948
Ebnall Shrops 29 SP3840
Ebrington Gloucs 29 SP1840
Ebsworthy Town Devon 4 SX5090
Ebsworthy Turbary Humb 56 SE7604
Ecchinswell Hants 21 SU5059
Ecclaw Loth 76 NT7568
Ecclefechan D & G 67 NY1974
Eccles Border 76 NT7641
Eccles Gt Man 47 SJ7798
Eccles Kent 14 TQ7360
Eccles Road Norfk 32 TM0190
Ecclesfield S York 49 SK3393
Ecclesgreig Gramp 89 NO7365
Eccleshall Staffs 37 SJ8329
Eccleshall S York 49 SK3184
Eccleshill W York 55 SE1736
Ecclesmachan Loth 75 NT0673
Eccleston Ches 46 SJ4162
Eccleston Lancs 53 SD5217
Eccleston Mersyd 46 SJ4895
Echt Gramp 95 NJ7405
Eckford Border 76 NT7026
Eckington Derbys 49 SK4279
Eckington H & W 28 SO9241
Ecton Nhants 30 SP8263
Edale Derbys 48 SK1285
Edburton W Susx 12 TQ2311
Edderton Highld 97 NH7084
Edderton Highld 97 NH7183
Eddleston Border 75 NT2447
Eddlewood Strath 74 NS7153
Eden Mount Cumb 59 SD4078
Edenbridge Kent 13 TQ4446
Edenfield Lancs 54 SD8019
Edenhall Cumb 59 NY5632
Edenham Lincs 40 TF0621
Edensor Derbys 48 SK2469
Edentaggart Strath 80 NS3293
Edenthorpe S York 56 SE6206
Ederline Strath 79 NM8702
Edern Gwynd 44 SH2739
Edgarley Somset 19 ST5138
Edgbaston W Mids 38 SP0684
Edgcombe Cnwll 2 SW7233
Edgcott Bucks 30 SP6722
Edgcott Devon 7 SS8438
Edge Shrops 28 SO8409
Edge Gloucs 36 SJ3909
Edge Shrops 36 SJ3909
Edge End Gloucs 27 SO5913
Edgebolton Shrops 37 SJ5721
Edgefield Norfk 43 TG0934
Edgefield Green Norfk 43 TG0934
Edgeside Lancs 54 SD8322
Edgeworth W York 55 SE1217
Edgeworth Gloucs 28 SO9406
Edgmond Shrops 37 SJ7119
Edgton Shrops 36 SO3888
Edgware Gt Lon 23 TQ1991
Edgworth Lancs 54 SD7416
Edial Staffs 38 SK0708
Edinample Cent 81 NN6022
Edinbane Highld 90 NG3451
Edinburgh Loth 75 NT2573
Edingale Staffs 39 SK2112
Edingight D & G 66 NX8363
Edingley Notts 49 SK6655
Edingthorpe Norfk 43 TG3132
Edingthorpe Green Norfk 43 TG3131
Edington Border 77 NT8956
Edington Nthumb 69 NZ1582
Edington Somset 19 ST3940
Edington Wilts 20 ST9252
Edington Burtle Somset 19 ST3943
Edingworth Somset 19 ST3553
Edith Weston Leics 40 SK9205
Edithmead Somset 19 ST3249
Edlesborough Bucks 30 SP9719
Edlingham Nthumb 69 NU1109
Edlington Lincs 51 TF2371

F

Fifehead St. Quinton

Gatelawbridge

Fifehead St. Quinton *Dorset*	9	ST7710
Fifield *Berks*	22	SU9076
Fifield *Oxon*	29	SP2318
Figheldean *Wilts*	20	SU1547
Filby *Norfk*	43	TG4613
Filey *N York*	63	TA1180
Filgrave *Bucks*	30	SP8648
Filkins *Oxon*	29	SP2304
Filleigh *Devon*	7	SS6628
Filleigh *Devon*	7	SS7410
Fillingham *Lincs*	50	SK9485
Fillongley *Warwks*	39	SP2887
Filton *Avon*	19	ST6079
Fimber *Humb*	56	SE8960
Finavon *Tays*	89	NO4956
Fincham *Norfk*	42	TF6806
Finchampstead *Berks*	22	SU7963
Fincharr *Strath*	79	NM9003
Finchdean *Hants*	11	SU7312
Finchingfield *Essex*	24	TL6832
Finchley *Gt Lon*	23	TQ2690
Find O' Gask *Tays*	82	NO0019
Findern *Derbys*	39	SK3030
Findhorn *Gramp*	93	NJ0463
Findhorn Bridge *Highld*	93	NH8027
Findochty *Gramp*	94	NJ4667
Findon *Gramp*	89	NO9397
Findon *W Susx*	12	TQ1208
Findon Mains *Highld*	92	NH6060
Findrack House *Gramp*	89	NJ6004
Finedon *Nhants*	30	SP9172
Fingal Street *Suffk*	33	TM2270
Fingask *Gramp*	95	NJ7827
Fingask *Tays*	82	NO1619
Fingest *Bucks*	22	SU7791
Finghall *N York*	61	SE1789
Fingland *D & G*	74	NS7517
Fingringhoe *Essex*	25	TM0320
Finkle Street *S York*	49	SK3099
Finlarig *Cent*	81	NN5733
Finmere *Oxon*	29	SP6333
Finnart *Tays*	87	NN5157
Finningham *Suffk*	32	TM0669
Finningley *Notts*	49	SK6699
Finsbay *W Isls*	102	NG0786
Finstall *H & W*	28	SO9870
Finstock *Oxon*	29	SP3616
Finstown *Ork*	103	HY3514
Fintry *Cent*	81	NS6186
Fintry *Gramp*	95	NJ7554
Finzean *Gramp*	89	NO5993
Fionnphort *Strath*	78	NM3023
Fir Tree *Dur*	61	NZ1434
Firbank *Cumb*	60	SD6293
Firbeck *S York*	49	SK5688
Firby *N York*	61	SE2686
Firby *N York*	56	SE7466
Firsby *Lincs*	51	TF4562
Fishbourne *IOW*	11	SZ5592
Fishbourne *W Susx*	11	SU8304
Fishburn *Dur*	62	NZ3632
Fishcross *Cent*	82	NS8995
Fisher *W Susx*	11	SU8700
Fisher's Pond *Hants*	10	SU4820
Fisherford *Gramp*	95	NJ6735
Fisherrow *Loth*	75	NT3472
Fisherstreet *W Susx*	12	SU9531
Fisherton *Highld*	93	NH7451
Fisherton *Strath*	73	NS2717
Fisherton de la Mere *Wilts*	20	ST9938
Fishery Estate *Berks*	22	SU8980
Fishguard *Dyfed*	16	SM9637
Fishlake *S York*	56	SE6513
Fishnish Pier *Strath*	79	NM6542
Fishponds *Avon*	19	ST6375
Fishtoft *Lincs*	51	TF3642
Fishtoft Drove *Lincs*	51	TF3148
Fishtown of Usan *Tays*	89	NO7254
Fishwick *Border*	77	NT9151
Fishwick *Lancs*	53	SD5529
Fiskavaig *Highld*	84	NG3334
Fiskerton *Lincs*	50	TF0472
Fiskerton *Notts*	50	SK7351
Fittleworth *W Susx*	12	TQ0119
Fitz *Shrops*	36	SJ4418
Fitzhead *Somset*	8	ST1228
Fitzwilliam *W York*	55	SE4115
Fiunary *Highld*	79	NM6246
Five Ash Down *E Susx*	13	TQ4724
Five Bells *Somset*	7	ST0642
Five Oak Green *Kent*	13	TQ6445
Five Oaks *Jersey*	101	SV0000
Five Oaks *W Susx*	12	TQ0928
Fivecrosses *Ches*	46	SJ5376
Fivehead *Somset*	8	ST3522
Fivelanes *Cnwll*	4	SX2280
Flackwell Heath *Bucks*	22	SU8990
Fladbury *H & W*	28	SO9946
Fladdabister *Shet*	103	HU4332
Flagg *Derbys*	48	SK1368
Flamborough *Humb*	57	TA2270
Flamstead *Herts*	30	TL0714
Flansham *W Susx*	12	SU9601
Flanshow *W York*	55	SE3020
Flasby *N York*	54	SD9456
Flash *Staffs*	48	SK0267
Flashader *Highld*	90	NG3453
Flatt *Strath*	74	NS6551
Flaunden *Herts*	22	TL0100
Flawborough *Notts*	50	SK7842
Flawith *N York*	55	SE4865
Flax Bourton *Avon*	19	ST5069
Flaxby *N York*	55	SE3957
Flaxley *Gloucs*	28	SO6815
Flaxmere *Ches*	47	SJ5672
Flaxpool *Somset*	8	ST1435
Flaxton *N York*	56	SE6762
Fleckney *Leics*	39	SP6493
Flecknoe *Warwks*	29	SP5163
Fledborough *Notts*	50	SK8072
Fleet *Dorset*	9	SY6380
Fleet *Hants*	22	SU8053
Fleet *Lincs*	41	TF3923
Fleet Hargate *Lincs*	41	TF3924
Fleetwood *Lancs*	53	SD3348
Flemingston *S Glam*	18	ST0170
Flemington *Strath*	74	NS6559
Flempton *Suffk*	32	TL8169
Fletching *E Susx*	13	TQ4223
Fleur-de-lis *M Glam*	36	SO1596
Flexbury *Cnwll*	6	SS2107
Flexford *Surrey*	22	SU9350
Flimby *Cumb*	58	NY0233
Flimwell *E Susx*	14	TQ7131
Flint *Clwyd*	46	SJ2472
Flintham *Notts*	50	SK7445
Flinton *Humb*	57	TA2136
Flitcham *Norfk*	42	TF7326
Flitton *Beds*	30	TL0535
Flixborough *Humb*	56	SE8715
Flixborough Stather *Humb*	56	SE8614
Flixton *N York*	63	TA0479
Flixton *Suffk*	33	TM3186
Flockton Green *W York*	55	SE2514
Flodda *W Isls*	102	NF8455
Flodigarry *Highld*	90	NG4671
Flookburgh *Cumb*	59	SD3675
Flordon *Norfk*	43	TM1897
Flore *Nhants*	29	SP6460
Flowton *Suffk*	32	TM0847
Flushdyke *W York*	55	SE2821
Fluxton *Devon*	8	SY0892
Flyford Flavell *H & W*	28	SO9854
Fobbing *Essex*	24	TQ7184
Fochabers *Gramp*	94	NJ3458
Fockerby *Humb*	56	SE8519
Fodderty *Highld*	92	NH5159
Foddington *Somset*	9	ST5829
Foel *Powys*	35	SH9911
Foel y Dyffryn *M Glam*	18	SS8594
Foelgastell *Dyfed*	17	SN5415
Foffarty *Tays*	88	NO4145
Foggathorpe *Humb*	56	SE7537
Fogo *Border*	76	NT7749
Fogwatt *Gramp*	94	NJ2356
Foindle *Highld*	98	NC1948
Folda *Tays*	88	NO1963
Fole *Staffs*	48	SK0437
Foleshill *W Mids*	39	SP3582
Folke *Dorset*	9	ST6513
Folkestone *Kent*	15	TR2336
Folkingham *Lincs*	40	TF0733
Folkington *E Susx*	13	TQ5603
Folksworth *Cambs*	40	TL1489
Folkton *N York*	63	TA0579
Folla Rule *Gramp*	95	NJ7332
Follifoot *N York*	55	SE3452
Folly Gate *Devon*	6	SX5797
Font-y-gary *S Glam*	18	ST0566
Fonthill Bishop *Wilts*	9	ST9332
Fonthill Gifford *Wilts*	9	ST9231
Fontmell Magna *Dorset*	9	ST8616
Fontmell Parva *Dorset*	9	ST8214
Fontwell *W Susx*	12	SU9507
Foolow *Derbys*	48	SK1976
Foord *Kent*	15	TR2236
Footbridge *Cumb*	67	NY4148
Forbestown *Gramp*	94	NJ3613
Forcett *N York*	61	NZ1712
Ford *Bucks*	22	SP7709
Ford *Derbys*	49	SK4080
Ford *Devon*	5	SX6150
Ford *Devon*	5	SX7945
Ford *Devon*	6	SS4024
Ford *Gloucs*	28	SP0829
Ford *Nthumb*	77	NT9437
Ford *Somset*	7	ST0928
Ford *Somset*	19	ST5853
Ford *Staffs*	48	SK0653
Ford *Strath*	79	NM8603
Ford *W Susx*	12	TQ0003
Ford *Wilts*	20	ST8475
Ford Barton *Devon*	7	SS9118
Ford End *Essex*	24	TL6716
Ford Street *Somset*	8	ST1518
Forda *Devon*	4	SX5391
Fordcombe *Kent*	13	TQ5240
Fordell *Fife*	82	NT1588
Forden *Powys*	36	SJ2201
Forder *Devon*	5	SX6789
Forder Green *Devon*	5	SX7867
Fordham *Cambs*	32	TL6370
Fordham *Essex*	25	TL9328
Fordham *Norfk*	41	TL6199
Fordingbridge *Hants*	10	SU1413
Fordon *Humb*	63	TA0475
Fordoun *Gramp*	89	NO7475
Fordton *Devon*	7	SX8298
Fordwells *Oxon*	29	SP3014
Fordwich *Kent*	15	TR1859
Fordyce *Gramp*	94	NJ5563
Forebridge *Staffs*	38	SJ9222
Foremark *Derbys*	39	SK3326
Forest *Dur*	60	NY8629
Forest *Guern*	101	SV0000
Forest Becks *Lancs*	54	SD7851
Forest Gate *Gt Lon*	23	TQ4085
Forest Green *Surrey*	12	TQ1241
Forest Hill *Gt Lon*	23	TQ3671
Forest Hill *Oxon*	29	SP5807
Forest Lane Head *N York*	55	SE3356
Forest Lodge *Strath*	86	NN2642
Forest Mill *Cent*	82	NS9694
Forest Moor *N York*	55	SE2256
Forestfield *Strath*	74	NS8566
Forestside *W Susx*	11	SU7512
Forfar *Tays*	88	NO4550
Forgandenny *Tays*	82	NO0818
Forge-Hammer *Gwent*	19	ST2895
Forgie *Gramp*	94	NJ3854
Forgieside *Gramp*	94	NJ4053
Forgorig *Border*	76	NT7748
Formby *Mersyd*	46	SD3007
Forncett End *Norfk*	43	TM1494
Forncett St. Mary *Norfk*	43	TM1694
Forncett St. Peter *Norfk*	43	TM1693
Forneth *Tays*	88	NO1044
Fornham All Saints *Suffk*	32	TL8367
Fornham St. Martin *Suffk*	32	TL8567
Fornside *Cumb*	58	NY3230
Forres *Gramp*	93	NJ0358
Forsbrook *Staffs*	48	SJ9641
Forse *Highld*	100	ND2234
Forse House *Highld*	100	ND2135
Forsinard *Highld*	99	NC8943
Fort Augustus *Highld*	92	NH3709
Fort George *Highld*	93	NH7656
Fort Hommet *Guern*	101	SV0000
Fort William *Highld*	86	NN1074
Fort le Marchant *Guern*	101	SV0000
Forter *Tays*	88	NO1864
Fortescue *Devon*	8	SY1388
Forteviot *Tays*	82	NO0517
Forth *Strath*	75	NS9453
Forthampton *Gloucs*	28	SO8532
Fortingall *Tays*	87	NN7447
Fortnighty *Highld*	93	NH9350
Forton *Hants*	21	SU4243
Forton *Lancs*	53	SD4851
Forton *Shrops*	36	SJ4216
Forton *Somset*	8	ST3306
Forton *Staffs*	37	SJ7521
Fortrose *Highld*	93	NH7256
Fortuneswell *Dorset*	9	SY6873
Forty Hill *Gt Lon*	23	TQ3398
Forward Green *Suffk*	33	TM1060
Fosbury *Wilts*	21	SU3157
Foscot *Oxon*	29	SP2421
Fosdyke *Lincs*	41	TF3133
Fosdyke Bridge *Lincs*	41	TF3132
Foss *Tays*	87	NN7958
Foss-y-ffin *Dyfed*	34	SN4460
Fossebridge *Gloucs*	28	SP0811
Foster Street *Essex*	23	TL4709
Foston *Derbys*	38	SK1831
Foston *Leics*	39	SP6094
Foston *Lincs*	50	SK8542
Foston *N York*	56	SE6965
Foston on the Wolds *Humb*	57	TA1055
Fotherby *Lincs*	51	TF3191
Fotheringhay *Nhants*	40	TL0593
Fotrie *Gramp*	94	NJ6645
Foul End *Warwks*	39	SP2494
Foul Mile *E Susx*	13	TQ6115
Foulden *Border*	77	NT9256
Foulridge *Lancs*	54	SD8942
Foulsham *Norfk*	42	TG0325
Fountainhall *Border*	76	NT4349
Four Ashes *Suffk*	32	TM0070
Four Crosses *Powys*	36	SJ2618
Four Elms *Kent*	13	TQ4648
Four Foot *Somset*	8	ST5733
Four Forks *Somset*	19	ST2336
Four Gates *Gt Man*	47	SD6507
Four Gotes *Cambs*	41	TF4516
Four Lane Ends *Ches*	47	SJ5661
Four Lanes *Cnwll*	2	SW6838
Four Marks *Hants*	11	SU6634
Four Mile Bridge *Gwynd*	44	SH2778
Four Oaks *W Mids*	39	SP2480
Four Points *Berks*	21	SU5579
Four Roads *Dyfed*	17	SN4409
Four Shire Stone *Warwks*	29	SP2332
Four Throws *Kent*	14	TQ7729
Four cabots *Guern*	101	SV0000
Fourpenny *Highld*	97	NH8094
Fourstones *Nthumb*	68	NY8867
Fovant *Wilts*	9	SU0028
Foveran *Gramp*	95	NJ9824
Fowey *Cnwll*	3	SX1251
Fowley Common *Ches*	47	SJ6796
Fowlhall *Kent*	14	TQ6946
Fowlis *Tays*	83	NO3233
Fowlis Wester *Tays*	82	NN9324
Fowlmere *Cambs*	31	TL4245
Fownhope *H & W*	27	SO5834
Fox Corner *Surrey*	22	SU9655
Fox House Inn *S York*	49	SK2680
Foxbar *Strath*	73	NS4561
Foxcote *Somset*	20	ST7155
Foxdale *IOM*	52	SC2778
Foxearth *Essex*	32	TL8344
Foxendown *Kent*	14	TQ6666
Foxfield *Cumb*	58	SD2085
Foxhole *Highld*	92	NH5239
Foxholes *N York*	63	TA0173
Foxley *Norfk*	42	TG0321
Foxley *Wilts*	20	ST8985
Foxt *Staffs*	48	SK0348
Foxton *Cambs*	31	TL4148
Foxton *Leics*	40	SP7089
Foxton *N York*	62	SE4295
Foxwood *Shrops*	37	SO6276
Foy *H & W*	27	SO5928
Foyers *Highld*	92	NH4921
Foynesfield *Highld*	93	NH8855
Fraddon *Cnwll*	3	SW9158
Fradley *Staffs*	38	SK1513
Fradswell *Staffs*	38	SJ9931
Fraisthorpe *Humb*	57	TA1561
Framfield *E Susx*	13	TQ4920
Framingham Earl *Norfk*	43	TG2702
Framingham Pigot *Norfk*	43	TG2703
Framlingham *Suffk*	33	TM2863
Frampton *Dorset*	9	SY6294
Frampton *Lincs*	41	TF3239
Frampton Cotterell *Avon*	20	ST6682
Frampton Mansell *Gloucs*	20	SO9202
Frampton West End *Lincs*	51	TF2941
Frampton on Severn *Gloucs*	28	SO7407
Framsden *Suffk*	33	TM1959
Framwellgate Moor *Dur*	69	NZ2644
Frances Green *Lancs*	54	SD6236
Franche *H & W*	37	SO8178
Frankaborough *Devon*	4	SX3992
Frankby *Mersyd*	46	SJ2486
Frankley *H & W*	38	SO9980
Frankton *Warwks*	29	SP4270
Frant *E Susx*	13	TQ5835
Fraserburgh *Gramp*	95	NJ9966
Frating *Essex*	25	TM0822
Frating Green *Essex*	25	TM0923
Fratton *Hants*	11	SU6500
Freathy *Cnwll*	4	SX3952
Freckenham *Suffk*	32	TL6672
Freckleton *Lancs*	53	SD4329
Freebirch *Derbys*	49	SK3173
Freeby *Leics*	40	SK8020
Freefolk *Hants*	21	SU4848
Freeland *Oxon*	29	SP4112
Freethorpe *Norfk*	43	TG4005
Freethorpe Common *Norfk*	43	TG4004
Freiston *Lincs*	51	TF3743
Fremington *Devon*	6	SS5132
French Street *Kent*	13	TQ4652
Frenich *Tays*	87	NN8258
Frensham *Surrey*	11	SU8441
Freshfield *Mersyd*	46	SD2908
Freshiebridge *Highld*	87	NH8504
Freshwater *IOW*	10	SZ3487
Fressingfield *Suffk*	33	TM2677
Freston *Suffk*	33	TM1739
Freswick *Highld*	100	ND3667
Fretherne *Gloucs*	28	SO7210
Frettenham *Norfk*	43	TG2417
Freuchie *Fife*	83	NO2806
Freystrop *Dyfed*	16	SM9511
Friar Waddon *Dorset*	9	SY6485
Friars' Hill *N York*	63	SE7385
Friday Bridge *Cambs*	41	TF4605
Friday Street *Suffk*	33	TM3352
Friday Street *Suffk*	33	TM3760
Fridaythorpe *Humb*	56	SE8759
Fridaythorpe *Humb*	56	SE8759
Friden *Derbys*	48	SK1660
Friern Barnet *Gt Lon*	23	TQ2892
Friesland Bay *Strath*	78	NM1954
Friesthorpe *Lincs*	50	TF0683
Frieston *Lincs*	50	SK9347
Frieth *Bucks*	22	SU7990
Friezeland *Notts*	49	SK4750
Frilford *Oxon*	21	SU4497
Frilsham *Berks*	21	SU5473
Frimley *Surrey*	22	SU8758
Frindsbury *Kent*	14	TQ7369
Fring *Norfk*	42	TF7334
Fringford *Oxon*	29	SP6029
Frinsted *Kent*	14	TQ8957
Frinton-on-Sea *Essex*	25	TM2320
Friockheim *Tays*	89	NO5949
Friog *Gwynd*	35	SH6111
Frisby on the Wreake *Leics*	40	SK6917
Friskney *Lincs*	51	TF4655
Friston *Suffk*	33	TM4160
Fritham *Hants*	10	SU2413
Frithelstock *Devon*	6	SS4619
Frithelstock Stone *Devon*	6	SS4518
Frithville *Lincs*	51	TF3150
Frittenden *Kent*	14	TQ8140
Frittiscombe *Devon*	5	SX8043
Fritton *Norfk*	43	TG4700
Fritton *Norfk*	43	TM2293
Fritwell *Oxon*	29	SP5229
Frizinghall *W York*	55	SE1436
Frizington *Cumb*	58	NY0316
Frocester *Gloucs*	20	SO7803
Frodesley *Shrops*	37	SJ5101
Frodsham *Ches*	46	SJ5177
Frog End *Cambs*	31	TL3946
Frog Pool *H & W*	28	SO8065
Frogbury *Devon*	7	SS6806
Frogden *Border*	76	NT7628
Froggatt *Derbys*	48	SK2476
Froghall *Staffs*	48	SK0247
Frogmore *Devon*	5	SX7742
Frognall *Lincs*	40	TF1610
Frogwell *Cnwll*	4	SX3468
Frolesworth *Leics*	39	SP5090
Frome *Somset*	20	ST7747
Frome St. Quintin *Dorset*	9	ST5902
Fromes Hill *H & W*	28	SO6846
Fron *Gwynd*	44	SH5055
Fron *Powys*	36	SJ2303
Fron Cysyllte *Clwyd*	36	SJ2740
Fron Isaf *Clwyd*	36	SJ2740
Fron-goch *Gwynd*	45	SH9039
Frostenden *Suffk*	33	TM4881
Frosterley *Dur*	61	NZ0237
Froxfield *Wilts*	21	SU2968
Froxfield Green *Hants*	11	SU7025
Fryern Hill *Hants*	10	SU4321
Fryerning *Essex*	24	TL6300
Fulbeck *Lincs*	50	SK9449
Fulbourn *Cambs*	31	TL5256
Fulbrook *Oxon*	29	SP2513
Fulflood *Hants*	10	SU4730
Fulford *N York*	56	SE6149
Fulford *Somset*	8	ST2129
Fulford *Staffs*	48	SJ9537
Fulham *Gt Lon*	23	TQ2576
Fulking *W Susx*	12	TQ2411
Full Sutton *Humb*	56	SE7455
Fullabrook *Devon*	6	SS5240
Fullarton *Strath*	73	NS3238
Fuller Street *Essex*	24	TL7416
Fullerton *Hants*	10	SU3739
Fulletby *Lincs*	51	TF2973
Fullready *Warwks*	29	SP2846
Fullwood *Strath*	73	NS4450
Fulmer *Bucks*	22	SU9985
Fulmodeston *Norfk*	42	TF9931
Fulnetby *Lincs*	50	TF0979
Fulwell *Oxon*	29	SP3723
Fulwell *T & W*	69	NZ3959
Fulwood *Lancs*	53	SD5431
Fulwood *S York*	49	SK3085
Fundenhall *Norfk*	43	TM1596
Funtington *W Susx*	11	SU8008
Funtullich *Guern*	81	NN7526
Furley *Devon*	8	ST2704
Furnace *Dyfed*	17	SN5001
Furnace *Strath*	80	NN0200
Furnace End *Warwks*	39	SP2491
Furnace Vale *Derbys*	48	SK0083
Furzehill *Dorset*	9	SU0002
Furzehills *Lincs*	51	TF2572
Furzley *Hants*	10	SU2816
Furzley *Hants*	10	SU2816
Fyfield *Essex*	24	TL5707
Fyfield *Hants*	21	SU2946
Fyfield *Hants*	21	SU2946
Fyfield *Oxon*	21	SU4298
Fyfield *Wilts*	20	SU1468
Fyfield *Wilts*	21	SU1760
Fyfield Wick *Oxon*	21	SU4196
Fylingthorpe *N York*	63	NZ9404
Fyning *W Susx*	11	SU8124
Fyvie *Gramp*	95	NJ7637

G

Gabroc Hill *Strath*	73	NS4551
Gaddesby *Leics*	39	SK6813
Gaddesden Row *Herts*	30	TL0512
Gadfa *Gwynd*	44	SH4589
Gadoirth *Strath*	73	NS4022
Gaer *Powys*	27	SO1721
Gaer-llwyd *Gwent*	19	ST4496
Gaerwen *Gwynd*	44	SH4871
Gailes *Strath*	73	NS3235
Gailey *Staffs*	38	SJ9110
Gainford *Dur*	61	NZ1716
Gainsborough *Lincs*	50	SK8189
Gainsford End *Essex*	24	TL7335
Gairloch *Highld*	91	NG8076
Gairlochy *Highld*	86	NN1784
Gairney Bank *Tays*	82	NT1299
Gairneybridge *Tays*	82	NT1397
Gaisby *W York*	55	SE1536
Gaisland *Cent*	81	NS5390
Gaitsgill *Cumb*	67	NY3847
Galashiels *Border*	76	NT4936
Galby *Leics*	40	SK6900
Galcantray *Highld*	93	NH8147
Galgate *Lancs*	53	SD4855
Galhampton *Somset*	9	ST6329
Gallaberry *D & G*	66	NX9682
Gallanach *Strath*	78	NM2160
Gallanach *Strath*	79	NM8326
Gallatown *Fife*	83	NT2994
Galley Common *Warwks*	39	SP3192
Galleywood *Essex*	24	TL7003
Gallovie *Highld*	87	NN5589
Gallowfauld *Tays*	88	NO4342
Gallowhill *Tays*	82	NO1635
Gallows Green *Essex*	32	TL9246
Gallows Green *H & W*	28	SO9363
Gallows Green *Staffs*	48	SK0741
Galltair *Highld*	85	NG8120
Gallypot Street *E Susx*	13	TQ4635
Galmisdale *Highld*	84	NM4784
Galmpton *Devon*	5	SX6940
Galmpton *Devon*	5	SX8856
Galphay *N York*	55	SE2572
Galston *Strath*	74	NS5036
Galton *Dorset*	9	SY7785
Galtrigill *Highld*	90	NG1854
Gambles Green *Essex*	24	TL7615
Gamblesby *Cumb*	59	NY6039
Gambling *Humb*	57	TA1057
Gamlingay *Cambs*	31	TL2452
Gamlingay Great Heath *Beds*	31	TL2151
Gamrie *Gramp*	95	NJ7962
Gamston *Notts*	49	SK7076
Ganavan Bay *Strath*	79	NM8632
Ganllwyd *Gwynd*	35	SH7224
Gannachy *Tays*	89	NO5970
Ganstead *Humb*	57	TA1434
Ganthorpe *N York*	56	SE6870
Ganton *N York*	63	SE9877
Ganwick Corner *Herts*	23	TQ2599
Garbat *Highld*	92	NH4168
Garbity *Gramp*	94	NJ3052
Garboldisham *Norfk*	32	TM0081
Garchory *Gramp*	94	NJ2909
Garden Village *Derbys*	49	SK2698
Gardeners Green *Berks*	22	SU8266
Gardenstown *Gramp*	95	NJ7964
Garderhouse *Shet*	103	HU3347
Gare Hill *Somset*	20	ST7840
Garelochhead *Strath*	80	NS2491
Garenin *W Isls*	102	NB1944
Garford *Oxon*	21	SU4296
Garforth *W York*	55	SE4033
Gargrave *N York*	54	SD9354
Gargunnock *Cent*	81	NS7094
Garlandhayes *Devon*	8	ST1716
Garlic Street *Norfk*	33	TM2183
Garlieston *D & G*	65	NX4746
Garlinge *Kent*	15	TR3369
Garlinge Green *Kent*	15	TR1152
Garlogie *Gramp*	89	NJ7805
Garmond *Gramp*	95	NJ8052
Garmony House *Strath*	79	NM6640
Garmouth *Gramp*	94	NJ3364
Garmston *Shrops*	37	SJ6006
Garn *Gwynd*	44	SH2734
Garn-Dolbenmaen *Gwynd*	44	SH4944
Garnant *Dyfed*	26	SN6813
Garnett Bridge *Cumb*	59	SD5298
Garnkirk *Strath*	74	NS6768
Garnlydan *Gwent*	27	SO1612
Garnoch *Highld*	85	NM8696
Garrabost *W Isls*	102	NB5133
Garrallan *Strath*	74	NS5418
Garraron *Strath*	79	NM8008
Garras *Cnwll*	2	SW7023
Garreg *Gwynd*	45	SH6141
Garrigill *Cumb*	60	NY7441
Garroch *D & G*	65	NX5981
Garrochtrie *D & G*	64	NX1038
Garrochty *Strath*	73	NS0953
Garros *Highld*	90	NG4963
Garsdale Head *Cumb*	60	SD7892
Garsdon *Wilts*	20	ST9687
Garshall Green *Staffs*	38	SJ9634
Garsington *Oxon*	21	SP5802
Garstang *Lancs*	53	SD4945
Garston *Herts*	22	TL1100
Garston *Mersyd*	46	SJ4084
Gartachossan *Strath*	70	NR3461
Gartcosh *Strath*	74	NS6968
Garth *Clwyd*	36	SJ2542
Garth *Powys*	26	SN9549
Garth Penrhyncoch *Dyfed*	35	SN6484
Garth Row *Cumb*	59	SD5297
Garthbrengy *Powys*	26	SO0433
Garthorpe *Humb*	56	SE8419
Garthorpe *Leics*	40	SK8320
Gartly *Gramp*	94	NJ5232
Gartmore *Cent*	81	NS5297
Gartnatra *Strath*	70	NR3260
Gartness *Cent*	81	NS5086
Gartness *Strath*	74	NS7864
Gartocharn *Strath*	81	NS4286
Garton *Humb*	57	TA2635
Garton End *Cambs*	40	TF1909
Garton-on-the-Wolds *Humb*	56	SE9759
Gartsherrie *Strath*	74	NS7265
Gartymore *Highld*	97	ND0114
Garvald *Loth*	76	NT5870
Garvalt *Strath*	80	NS0296
Garvan *Highld*	85	NM9777
Garvard *Strath*	70	NR3691
Garve *Highld*	92	NH3961
Garvestone *Norfk*	42	TG0207
Garvock *Strath*	73	NS2570
Garway *H & W*	27	SO4522
Garway Common *H & W*	27	SO4622
Garynahine *W Isls*	102	NB2331
Gasper *Wilts*	9	ST7533
Gass *Strath*	73	NS4105
Gastard *Wilts*	20	ST8868
Gasthorpe *Norfk*	32	TL9781
Gaston Green *Essex*	31	TL4917
Gatcombe *IOW*	10	SZ4885
Gate Burton *Lincs*	50	SK8382
Gate Helmsley *N York*	56	SE6855
Gateforth *N York*	56	SE5628
Gatehead *Strath*	73	NS3936
Gatehouse *Nthumb*	68	NY7989
Gatehouse *Strath*	71	NR8160
Gatehouse of Fleet *D & G*	65	NX5956
Gatelawbridge *D & G*	66	NX8996

Gatelawbridge Great Warley

Gatelawbridge *D & G* 66 NX9096
Gateley *Norfk* 42 TF9624
Gatenby *N York* 62 SE3287
Gatesgarth *Cumb* 58 NY1925
Gateshaw *Border* 76 NT7722
Gateshead *T & W* 69 NZ2562
Gateside *Fife* 82 NO1809
Gateside *Strath* 73 NS3653
Gateside *Strath* 73 NS4858
Gateside *Tays* 88 NO4344
Gateslack *D & G* 66 NS8902
Gatley *Gt Man* 47 SJ8488
Gatton *Surrey* 12 TQ2752
Gattonside *Border* 76 NT5435
Gauldry *Fife* 83 NO3723
Gauldswell *Tays* 88 NO2151
Gaunt's End *Essex* 24 TL5525
Gautby *Lincs* 50 TF1772
Gavinton *Border* 76 NT7652
Gawcott *Bucks* 30 SP6831
Gawsworth *Ches* 48 SJ8969
Gawthrop *Cumb* 60 SD6987
Gawthwaite *Cumb* 58 SD2784
Gaydon *Warwks* 29 SP3654
Gayhurst *Bucks* 30 SP8446
Gayle *N York* 60 SD8688
Gayles *N York* 61 NZ1207
Gayton *Nhants* 30 SP7054
Gayton *Norfk* 42 TF7219
Gayton *Staffs* 38 SJ9828
Gayton Thorpe *Norfk* 42 TF7418
Gayton le Marsh *Lincs* 51 TF4284
Gaywood *Norfk* 41 TF6320
Gazeley *Suffk* 32 TL7264
Geary *Highld* 90 NG2661
Gedding *Suffk* 32 TL9458
Geddinge *Kent* 15 TR2346
Geddington *Nhants* 40 SP8983
Gedintailor *Highld* 84 NG5235
Gedling *Notts* 49 SK6142
Gedney *Lincs* 41 TF4024
Gedney Broadgate *Lincs* 41 TF4022
Gedney Drove End *Lincs* 41 TF4629
Gedney Dyke *Lincs* 41 TF4126
Gedney Hill *Lincs* 41 TF3311
Geldeston *Norfk* 33 TM3991
Gelli *Gwent* 19 ST2793
Gelli Gynan *Clwyd* 46 SJ1854
Gellideg *M Glam* 26 SO0207
Gellifor *Clwyd* 46 SJ1262
Gelligaer *M Glam* 18 ST1397
Gelligroes *Gwent* 19 ST1794
Gellilydan *Gwynd* 45 SH6839
Gellinudd *W Glam* 18 SN7303
Gellinudd *W Glam* 26 SN7304
Gellyburn *Tays* 82 NO0939
Gellywen *Dyfed* 17 SN2723
Gelston *D & G* 66 NX7758
Gelston *Lincs* 50 SK9145
Gentleshaw *Staffs* 38 SK0511
George Green *Bucks* 22 TQ0081
George Nympton *Devon* 7 SS7023
Georgefield *D & G* 67 NY3091
Georgeham *Devon* 6 SS4639
Georgetown *Gwent* 27 SO1508
Georth *Ork* 103 HY3626
Germansweek *Devon* 6 SX4394
Gerrans *Cnwll* 3 SW8735
Gerrards Cross *Bucks* 22 TQ0088
Gerrick *Cleve* 62 NZ7012
Geshader *W Isls* 102 NB1131
Gestingthorpe *Essex* 24 TL8138
Geuffordd *Powys* 36 SJ2114
Gibraltar *Lincs* 51 TF5558
Gibsmere *Notts* 49 SK7248
Giddy Green *Dorset* 9 SY8286
Gidea Park *Gt Lon* 23 TQ5290
Gidleigh *Devon* 5 SX6788
Giffnock *Strath* 74 NS5658
Gifford *Loth* 76 NT5368
Giffordtown *Fife* 83 NO2811
Giggleswick *N York* 54 SD8163
Gilberdyke *Humb* 56 SE8329
Gilbert Street *Hants* 11 SU6532
Gilbert's Cross *Staffs* 37 SO8186
Gilbert's End *H & W* 28 SO8242
Gilchriston *Loth* 76 NT4865
Gilcrux *Cumb* 58 NY1138
Gildersome *W York* 55 SE2429
Gildingwells *S York* 49 SK5585
Gilesgate Moor *Dur* 69 NZ2943
Gileston *S Glam* 18 ST0167
Gilfach *M Glam* 19 ST1598
Gilfach Goch *M Glam* 18 SS9890
Gilfachrheda *Dyfed* 34 SN4159
Gilgarran *Cumb* 58 NY0323
Gillamore *N York* 62 SE6890
Gillesbie *D & G* 67 NY1691
Gilling *N York* 61 NZ1805
Gilling East *N York* 62 SE6176
Gillingham *Dorset* 9 ST8026
Gillingham *Kent* 14 TQ7768
Gillingham *Norfk* 33 TM4191
Gillock *Highld* 100 ND2159
Gills *Highld* 100 ND3272
Gilmanscleuch *Border* 75 NT3321
Gilmerton *Loth* 75 NT2968
Gilmerton *Tays* 82 NN8823
Gilmonby *Dur* 61 NY9912
Gilmorton *Leics* 39 SP5787
Gilsland *Nthumb* 68 NY6366
Gilson *Warwks* 38 SP1890
Gilstead *W York* 55 SE1131
Gilwern *Gwent* 27 SO2414
Gimingham *Norfk* 43 TG2836
Gipping *Suffk* 32 TM0763
Gipsey Bridge *Lincs* 51 TF2849
Girdle Toll *Strath* 73 NS3440
Girlsta *Shet* 103 HU4250
Girsby *Cleve* 62 NZ3508
Girton *Cambs* 31 TL4262
Girvan *Strath* 64 NX1897
Gisburn *Lancs* 54 SD8248
Gisleham *Suffk* 33 TM5188
Gislingham *Suffk* 32 TM0771
Gissing *Norfk* 33 TM1485
Gittisham *Devon* 8 SY1398
Gladestry *Powys* 27 SO2355
Gladsmuir *Loth* 76 NT4573
Glais *W Glam* 18 SN7000
Glaisdale *N York* 63 NZ7705
Glamis *Tays* 88 NO3846
Glan-y-don *Clwyd* 46 SJ1679
Glan-y-llyn *M Glam* 18 ST1184
Glanafon *Dyfed* 16 SM9517
Glanaman *Dyfed* 26 SN6713
Glandford *Norfk* 42 TG0441
Glandwr *Dyfed* 17 SN1928
Glangrwyne *Powys* 27 SO2316
Glanllynfi *M Glam* 18 SS8690
Glanton *Nthumb* 68 NU0714
Glanvilles Wootton *Dorset* 9 ST6708
Glapthorn *Nhants* 40 TL0290
Glapwell *Derbys* 49 SK4766
Glasbury *Powys* 27 SO1739
Glascoed *Gwent* 19 SO3201
Glascwm *Powys* 27 SO1552
Glasfryn *Clwyd* 45 SH9250
Glasgow *Strath* 74 NS5865
Glasinfryn *Gwynd* 44 SH5868
Glaslaw *Gramp* 89 NO8585
Glasnacardoch Bay *Highld* 85 NM6795
Glasnakille *Highld* 84 NG5313
Glassburn *Highld* 92 NH3634
Glassel *Gramp* 89 NO6599
Glassford *Strath* 74 NS7247
Glasshouse *Gloucs* 28 SO7021
Glasshouses *N York* 55 SE1764
Glasson *Cumb* 67 NY2560
Glasson *Lancs* 53 SD4456
Glassonby *Cumb* 59 NY5738
Glasterlaw *Tays* 89 NO5951
Glaston *Leics* 40 SK8900
Glastonbury *Somset* 19 ST4938
Glatton *Cambs* 40 TL1586
Glazebury *Ches* 47 SJ6797
Glazeley *Shrops* 37 SO7088
Gleaston *Cumb* 53 SD2570
Gledhow *W York* 55 SE3137
Gleding *Notts* 39 SK5132
Gledrid *Shrops* 36 SJ2936
Glehearn *Tays* 82 NO1016
Glemanault *Strath* 72 NR6407
Glemsford *Suffk* 32 TL8348
Glen Auldyn *IOM* 52 SC4393
Glen Clunie Lodgĕ *Gramp* 88 NO1383
Glen Nevis House *Highld* 86 NN1272
Glen Parva *Leics* 39 SP5798
Glen Trool Lodge *D & G* 64 NX4080
Glen Village *Cent* 82 NS8878
Glen Vine *IOM* 52 SC3378
Glen of Foudland *Gramp* 94 NJ6035
Glenancross *Highld* 85 NM6691
Glenaros House *Strath* 79 NM5544
Glenbarr *Strath* 72 NR6736
Glenbeg *Highld* 79 NM5862
Glenbervie *Gramp* 89 NO7680
Glenboig *Strath* 74 NS7269
Glenborrodale *Highld* 79 NM6061
Glenbranter *Strath* 80 NS1197
Glenbreck *Border* 75 NT0521
Glenbrittle House *Highld* 84 NG4121
Glenbuck *Strath* 74 NS7429
Glencally *Tays* 88 NO3562
Glencalvie Lodge *Highld* 96 NH4689
Glencaple *D & G* 66 NX9968
Glencarron Lodge *Highld* 91 NH0650
Glencarse *Tays* 82 NO1922
Glenceitlein *Highld* 86 NN1548
Glencoe *Highld* 86 NN1058
Glencothe *Border* 75 NT0829
Glencraig *Fife* 82 NT1894
Glencrosh *D & G* 65 NX7689
Glendaruel *Strath* 80 NR9983
Glendevon *Tays* 82 NN9904
Glendoe Lodge *Highld* 92 NH4009
Glendoik *Tays* 82 NO2022
Glenduckie *Fife* 83 NO2818
Gleneagles *Tays* 82 NN9209
Glenegedale *Strath* 70 NR3351
Glenelg *Highld* 85 NG8119
Glenerney *Gramp* 93 NJ0146
Glenfarg *Tays* 82 NO1310
Glenfeshie Lodge *Highld* 87 NN8493
Glenfield *Leics* 39 SK5306
Glenfinnan *Highld* 85 NM8980
Glenfinntaig Lodge *Highld* 86 NN2286
Glenfoot *Tays* 82 NO1815
Glenfyne Lodge *Strath* 80 NN2215
Glengarnock *Strath* 73 NS3252
Glengolly *Highld* 100 ND1065
Glengorm Castle *Strath* 79 NM4357
Glengrasco *Highld* 90 NG4444
Glenholm *Border* 75 NT1033
Glenhoul *D & G* 65 NX6187
Glenkerry *Border* 67 NT2711
Glenkiln *D & G* 66 NX8477
Glenkin *Strath* 80 NS1280
Glenkindie *Gramp* 94 NJ4314
Glenlee *D & G* 65 NX6080
Glenlochar *D & G* 65 NX7364
Glenloig *Strath* 72 NR9435
Glenluce *D & G* 64 NX1957
Glenmallan *Strath* 80 NS2595
Glenmark *Tays* 88 NO4283
Glenmassan *Strath* 80 NS1087
Glenmavis *Strath* 74 NS7467
Glenmaye *IOM* 52 SC2380
Glenmore *Highld* 84 NG4340
Glenmore *Strath* 79 NM8412
Glenmore Lodge *Highld* 93 NH9709
Glenmuirshaw *Strath* 74 NS6920
Glenquiech *Tays* 88 NO4266
Glenralloch *Strath* 71 NR8569
Glenrisdell *Strath* 71 NR8658
Glenrothes *Fife* 83 NO2700
Glenshero Lodge *Highld* 87 NN5593
Glenstriven *Strath* 80 NS0878
Glentham *Lincs* 50 TF0090
Glentromie Lodge *Highld* 87 NN7897
Glentrool Village *D & G* 64 NX3578
Glentruim House *Highld* 87 NN6894
Glentworth *Lincs* 50 SK9488
Glenuig *Highld* 85 NM6676
Glenure *Strath* 86 NN0448
Glenurquhart *Highld* 93 NH7462
Glenvarragill *Highld* 84 NG4739
Glenwhilly *D & G* 64 NX1771
Glespin *Strath* 74 NS8128
Glewstone *H & W* 27 SO5521
Glinton *Cambs* 40 TF1505
Glooston *Leics* 40 SP7595
Glossop *Derbys* 48 SK0493
Gloster Hill *Nthumb* 69 NU2504
Gloucester *Gloucs* 28 SO8318
Glover's Hill *Staffs* 38 SK0416
Glusburn *N York* 55 SE0344
Glutt Lodge *Highld* 100 ND0036
Gluvian *Cnwll* 3 SW9164
Glympton *Oxon* 29 SP4221
Glyn Ceiriog *Clwyd* 36 SJ2038
Glyn-Neath *W Glam* 26 SN8806
Glynarthen *Dyfed* 17 SN3148
Glyncoch *M Glam* 18 ST0792
Glyncorrwg *W Glam* 18 SS8799
Glynde *E Susx* 13 TQ4509
Glyndyfrdwy *Clwyd* 36 SJ1442
Glynogwr *M Glam* 18 SS9585
Glyntawe *Powys* 26 SN8416
Glynteg *Dyfed* 17 SN3638
Gnosall *Staffs* 38 SJ8220
Gnosall Heath *Staffs* 38 SJ8220
Goadby *Leics* 40 SP7598
Goadby Marwood *Leics* 40 SK7826
Goatacre *Wilts* 20 SU0176
Goatfield *Strath* 80 NN0100
Goathill *Dorset* 9 ST6717
Goathland *N York* 63 NZ8301
Goathurst *Somset* 8 ST2534
Goathurst Common *Kent* 13 TQ4952
Gobowen *Shrops* 36 SJ3033
Godalming *Surrey* 12 SU9743
Goddard's Green *Kent* 14 TQ8134
Godmanchester *Cambs* 31 TL2470
Godmanstone *Dorset* 9 SY6697
Godmersham *Kent* 15 TR0550
Godney *Somset* 19 ST4842
Godolphin Cross *Cnwll* 2 SW6031
Godre'r-graig *W Glam* 26 SN7506
Godshill *Hants* 10 SU1714
Godshill *IOW* 11 SZ5281
Godstone *Staffs* 38 SK0134
Godstone *Surrey* 12 TQ3551
Goetre *Gwent* 27 SO3206
Goff's Oak *Herts* 23 TL3203
Gogar *Loth* 75 NT1672
Goginan *Dyfed* 35 SN6981
Golan *Gwynd* 44 SH5242
Golant *Cnwll* 3 SX1254
Golborne *Gt Man* 47 SJ6097
Golcar *W York* 55 SE0915
Goldcliff *Gwent* 19 ST3683
Golden Green *Kent* 13 TQ6348
Golders Green *Gt Lon* 23 TQ2487
Goldhanger *Essex* 24 TL9009
Goldington *Beds* 30 TL0750
Goldsborough *N York* 55 SE3856
Goldsborough *N York* 63 NZ8314
Goldsithney *Cnwll* 2 SW5430
Goldsworth *Surrey* 22 SU9958
Goldthorpe *S York* 55 SE4604
Goldworthy *Devon* 6 SS3923
Gollanfield *Highld* 93 NH8053
Gollinglith Foot *N York* 61 SE1480
Golsoncott *Somset* 7 ST0338
Golspie *Highld* 87 NH8300
Gomeldon *Wilts* 10 SU1936
Gomshall *Surrey* 12 TQ0847
Gonachan *Cent* 81 NS6386
Gonalston *Notts* 49 SK6747
Gonfirth *Shet* 103 HU3761
Good Easter *Essex* 24 TL6212
Gooderstone *Norfk* 42 TF7602
Goodleigh *Devon* 6 SS6034
Goodmanham *Humb* 56 SE8842
Goodnestone *Kent* 15 TR0461
Goodnestone *Kent* 15 TR2554
Goodrich *H & W* 27 SO5719
Goodrich Cross *H & W* 27 SO5619
Goodrington *Devon* 5 SX8958
Goodshaw Fold *Lancs* 54 SD8026
Goodstone *Devon* 5 SX7871
Goodwick *Dyfed* 16 SM9438
Goodworth Clatford *Hants* 21 SU3642
Goole *Humb* 56 SE7423
Goonbell *Cnwll* 2 SW7249
Goonhavern *Cnwll* 2 SW7853
Goonvrea *Cnwll* 2 SW7149
Goose Green *Avon* 20 ST6774
Goose Green *Essex* 25 TM1425
Goose Green *Essex* 25 TM1425
Goosecruives *Gramp* 89 NO7583
Gooseford *Devon* 5 SX6892
Goosetrey *Ches* 47 SJ7770
Goosey *Oxon* 21 SU3591
Goosnargh *Lancs* 53 SD5536
Gordon *Border* 76 NT6443
Gordon Arms Hotel *Border* 75 NT3125
Gordonbush *Highld* 97 NC8409
Gordonstown *Gramp* 94 NJ5656
Gordonstown *Gramp* 95 NJ7138
Gore *Powys* 27 SO2658
Gore Street *Kent* 23 TQ2765
Gorebridge *Loth* 75 NT3461
Gores *Wilts* 20 SU1158
Gorey *Jersey* 101 SV0000
Goring *Oxon* 21 SU6080
Goring-by-Sea *W Susx* 12 TQ1102
Gorleston on Sea *Norfk* 43 TG5204
Gorrachie *Gramp* 95 NJ7358
Gorran Churchtown *Cnwll* 3 SW9942
Gorran Haven *Cnwll* 3 SX0141
Gorran High Lanes *Cnwll* 3 SW9843
Gorrenberry *Border* 67 NY4699
Gorse Hill *Wilts* 20 SU1586
Gorsedd *Clwyd* 46 SJ1576
Gorseinon *W Glam* 17 SS5998
Gorsgoch *Dyfed* 17 SN4850
Gorslas *Dyfed* 17 SN5713
Gorsley *Gloucs* 28 SO6925
Gorst Hill *H & W* 37 SO7473
Gorstan *Highld* 92 NH3863
Gorstello *Ches* 46 SJ3562
Gorsty Common *H & W* 27 SO4437
Gorsty Common *H & W* 27 SO4537
Gorsty Hill *Staffs* 38 SK1029
Gorten *Strath* 79 NM7432
Gorton *Gt Man* 47 SJ8896
Gosbeck *Suffk* 33 TM1555
Gosberton *Lincs* 41 TF2331
Gosfield *Essex* 24 TL7829
Gosford *Devon* 6 SX1197
Gosforth *Cumb* 58 NY0603
Gosforth *T & W* 69 NZ2467
Gosling Street *Somset* 8 ST5633
Gospel End *Staffs* 38 SO8993
Gospel Green *W Susx* 11 SU9331
Gosport *Hants* 11 SZ6199
Goswick *Nthumb* 77 NU0645
Gotham *Notts* 39 SK5330
Gotherington *Gloucs* 28 SO9629
Gotton *Somset* 8 ST2428
Goudhurst *Kent* 14 TQ7237
Goulceby *Lincs* 51 TF2579
Gourdas *Gramp* 95 NJ7741
Gourdie *Tays* 83 NO3532
Gourdon *Gramp* 89 NO8271
Gourock *Strath* 80 NS2477
Govan *Strath* 74 NS5465
Goveton *Devon* 5 SX7546
Govilon *Gwent* 27 SO2614
Gowdall *Humb* 56 SE6122
Gower *Highld* 92 NH5058
Gowerton *W Glam* 17 SS5896
Gowkhall *Fife* 82 NT0589
Goxhill *Humb* 57 TA1021
Goxhill *Humb* 57 TA1844
Graffham *W Susx* 11 SU9217
Grafham *Cambs* 31 TL1669
Grafham *Surrey* 12 TQ0241
Grafton *H & W* 28 SO9837
Grafton *H & W* 27 SO5761
Grafton *N York* 55 SE4163
Grafton *Oxon* 21 SP2600
Grafton *Shrops* 36 SJ4319
Grafton Flyford *H & W* 28 SO9656
Grafton Regis *Nhants* 30 SP7546
Grafton Underwood *Nhants* 40 SP9280
Grafty Green *Kent* 14 TQ8748
Graig *Clwyd* 46 SJ0872
Graig *Gwynd* 45 SH8071
Graig-fechan *Clwyd* 46 SJ1454
Grains *Kent* 14 TQ8876
Grains o'the Beck Bridge *Dur* 60 NY8621
Grainsby *Lincs* 51 TF2799
Grainthorpe *Lincs* 51 TF3896
Gramisdale *W Isls* 102 NF8155
Grampound *Cnwll* 3 SW9348
Grampound Road *Cnwll* 3 SW9150
Gramsdale *W Isls* 102 NF8255
Granborough *Bucks* 30 SP7625
Granby *Notts* 40 SK7536
Grand Chemins *Jersey* 101 SV0000
Grandborough *Warwks* 29 SP4967
Grandes Rocques *Guern* 101 SV0000
Grandtully *Tays* 87 NN9153
Grange *Cumb* 58 NY2517
Grange *Kent* 14 TQ7968
Grange *Tays* 83 NO2625
Grange Crossroads *Gramp* 94 NJ4754
Grange Hall *Gramp* 93 NJ0660
Grange Hill *Gt Lon* 23 TQ4492
Grange Lindores *Fife* 83 NO2516
Grange Moor *W York* 55 SE2216
Grange Villa *Dur* 69 NZ2352
Grangehall *Strath* 75 NS9642
Grangemill *Derbys* 48 SK2457
Grangemouth *Cent* 82 NS9282
Grangepans *Cent* 82 NT0181
Gransmoor *Humb* 57 TA1259
Granston *Dyfed* 16 SM8934
Grantchester *Cambs* 31 TL4355
Grantham *Lincs* 40 SK9135
Granton *Fife* 75 NT2277
Grantown-on-Spey *Highld* 93 NJ0328
Grantsfield *H & W* 27 SO5360
Grantshouse *Border* 76 NT8165
Grasby *Lincs* 57 TA0804
Grasmere *Cumb* 59 NY3307
Grassendale *Mersyd* 46 SJ3985
Grassington *N York* 54 SE0063
Grassmoor *Derbys* 49 SK4067
Grassthorpe *Notts* 50 SK7967
Grateley *Hants* 21 SU2741
Grateley *Hants* 21 SU2742
Graveley *Cambs* 31 TL2564
Graveley *Herts* 31 TL2327
Gravelsbank *Shrops* 36 SJ3600
Graveney *Kent* 15 TR0562
Gravesend *Kent* 14 TQ6474
Gravir *W Isls* 90 NB3715
Grayingham *Lincs* 50 SK9396
Grayrigg *Cumb* 59 SD5796
Grays *Essex* 24 TQ6177
Grayshott *Hants* 11 SU8735
Grayswood *Surrey* 11 SU9134
Grazeley *Berks* 22 SU6966
Grazies Hill *Oxon* 22 SU7980
Greasbrough *S York* 49 SK4195
Greasby *Mersyd* 46 SJ2587
Greasley *Notts* 49 SK4947
Great Abington *Cambs* 31 TL5348
Great Addington *Nhants* 30 SP9675
Great Alne *Warwks* 28 SP1259
Great Altcar *Lancs* 46 SD3306
Great Amwell *Herts* 31 TL3712
Great Asby *Cumb* 60 NY6713
Great Ayton *N York* 62 NZ5510
Great Baddow *Essex* 24 TL7305
Great Badminton *Avon* 20 ST8082
Great Bardfield *Essex* 24 TL6730
Great Barford *Beds* 30 TL1352
Great Barrington *Gloucs* 29 SP2013
Great Barrow *Ches* 46 SJ4768
Great Barton *Suffk* 32 TL8967
Great Barugh *N York* 63 SE7478
Great Bavington *Nthumb* 68 NY9880
Great Bealings *Suffk* 33 TM2349
Great Bedwyn *Wilts* 21 SU2764
Great Bentley *Essex* 25 TM1021
Great Billing *Nhants* 30 SP8162
Great Bircham *Norfk* 42 TF7732
Great Blakenham *Suffk* 33 TM1150
Great Bookham *Surrey* 22 TQ1354
Great Bosullow *Cnwll* 2 SW4133
Great Bourton *Oxon* 29 SP4545
Great Bowden *Leics* 40 SP7488
Great Bradley *Suffk* 32 TL6753
Great Braxted *Essex* 24 TL8614
Great Bricett *Suffk* 32 TM0350
Great Brickhill *Bucks* 30 SP9030
Great Bridge *W Mids* 38 SO9792
Great Bridgeford *Staffs* 38 SJ8827
Great Brington *Nhants* 30 SP6665
Great Bromley *Essex* 25 TM0826
Great Broughton *Cumb* 58 NY0731
Great Broughton *N York* 62 NZ5405
Great Budworth *Ches* 47 SJ6677
Great Burdon *Dur* 62 NZ3116
Great Burstead *Essex* 24 TQ6892
Great Busby *N York* 62 NZ5205
Great Canfield *Essex* 24 TL5918
Great Carlton *Lincs* 51 TF4085
Great Casterton *Leics* 40 TF0009
Great Chart *Kent* 15 TQ9741
Great Chatfield *Wilts* 20 ST8663
Great Chatwell *Staffs* 37 SJ7914
Great Chell *Staffs* 47 SJ8752
Great Chesterford *Essex* 31 TL5042
Great Cheverell *Wilts* 20 ST9858
Great Chishill *Cambs* 31 TL4238
Great Clacton *Essex* 25 TM1716
Great Cliffe *W York* 55 SE3015
Great Clifton *Cumb* 58 NY0429
Great Coates *Humb* 57 TA2309
Great Comberton *H & W* 28 SO9542
Great Corby *Cumb* 67 NY4754
Great Cornard *Suffk* 32 TL8840
Great Cowden *Humb* 57 TA2342
Great Coxwell *Oxon* 21 SU2693
Great Cressingham *Norfk* 42 TF8501
Great Crosthwaite *Cumb* 58 NY2624
Great Cubley *Derbys* 48 SK1638
Great Dalby *Leics* 40 SK7414
Great Doddington *Nhants* 30 SP8864
Great Driffield *Humb* 56 TA0257
Great Dunham *Norfk* 42 TF8714
Great Dunmow *Essex* 24 TL6222
Great Durnford *Wilts* 10 SU1338
Great Easton *Essex* 24 TL6025
Great Easton *Leics* 40 SP8493
Great Eccleston *Lancs* 53 SD4240
Great Ellingham *Norfk* 42 TM0196
Great Elm *Somset* 20 ST7449
Great Englebourne *Devon* 5 SX7756
Great Everdon *Nhants* 29 SP5957
Great Eversden *Cambs* 31 TL3653
Great Finborough *Suffk* 32 TM0158
Great Fransham *Norfk* 42 TF8913
Great Gaddesden *Herts* 22 TL0211
Great Gidding *Cambs* 40 TL1183
Great Givendale *Humb* 56 SE8153
Great Glemham *Suffk* 33 TM3361
Great Glen *Leics* 39 SP6597
Great Gonerby *Lincs* 40 SK8938
Great Gransden *Cambs* 31 TL2655
Great Green *Cambs* 31 TL2844
Great Green *Suffk* 32 TL9156
Great Green *Suffk* 32 TL9365
Great Habton *N York* 63 SE7576
Great Hale *Lincs* 50 TF1442
Great Hallingbury *Essex* 31 TL5119
Great Hanwood *Shrops* 36 SJ4409
Great Harrowden *Nhants* 30 SP8770
Great Harwood *Lancs* 54 SD7332
Great Haseley *Oxon* 21 SP6401
Great Hatfield *Humb* 57 TA1842
Great Haywood *Staffs* 38 SJ9922
Great Heck *N York* 56 SE5921
Great Henny *Essex* 24 TL8637
Great Hinton *Wilts* 20 ST9058
Great Hockham *Norfk* 32 TL9592
Great Holland *Essex* 25 TM2019
Great Horkesley *Essex* 25 TL9731
Great Hormead *Herts* 31 TL4030
Great Horton *W York* 55 SE1411
Great Horwood *Bucks* 30 SP7731
Great Houghton *Nhants* 30 SP7958
Great Houghton *S York* 55 SE4206
Great Hucklow *Derbys* 48 SK1777
Great Kelk *Humb* 57 TA1058
Great Kimble *Bucks* 22 SP8206
Great Kingshill *Bucks* 22 SU8797
Great Langdale *Cumb* 58 NY2906
Great Langton *N York* 61 SE2996
Great Leighs *Essex* 24 TL7217
Great Limber *Lincs* 57 TA1308
Great Linford *Bucks* 30 SP8542
Great Livermere *Suffk* 32 TL8871
Great Longstone *Derbys* 48 SK1971
Great Lumley *T & W* 69 NZ2949
Great Malvern *H & W* 28 SO7845
Great Maplestead *Essex* 24 TL8134
Great Marton *Lancs* 53 SD3235
Great Massingham *Norfk* 42 TF7923
Great Milton *Oxon* 21 SP6202
Great Missenden *Bucks* 22 SP8901
Great Mitton *Lancs* 54 SD7138
Great Mongeham *Kent* 15 TR3551
Great Moulton *Norfk* 33 TM1690
Great Munden *Herts* 31 TL3524
Great Ness *Shrops* 36 SJ3919
Great Oak *Gwent* 27 SO3809
Great Oakley *Essex* 25 TM1927
Great Oakley *Nhants* 40 SP8686
Great Offley *Herts* 30 TL1427
Great Ormside *Cumb* 60 NY7017
Great Orton *Cumb* 67 NY3254
Great Ouseburn *N York* 55 SE4461
Great Oxendon *Nhants* 40 SP7383
Great Oxney Green *Essex* 24 TL6606
Great Pattenden *Kent* 14 TQ7345
Great Paxton *Cambs* 31 TL2063
Great Plumpton *Lancs* 53 SD3833
Great Plumstead *Norfk* 43 TG3010
Great Ponton *Lincs* 40 SK9230
Great Preston *W York* 55 SE4029
Great Raveley *Cambs* 41 TL2581
Great Rissington *Gloucs* 29 SP1917
Great Rollright *Oxon* 29 SP3231
Great Ryburgh *Norfk* 42 TF9527
Great Ryle *Nthumb* 68 NU0212
Great Saling *Essex* 24 TL7026
Great Salkeld *Cumb* 59 NY5436
Great Sampford *Essex* 24 TL6435
Great Saughall *Ches* 46 SJ3669
Great Shefford *Berks* 21 SU3875
Great Shelford *Cambs* 31 TL4652
Great Smeaton *N York* 62 NZ3404
Great Snoring *Norfk* 42 TF9434
Great Somerford *Wilts* 20 ST9682
Great Soudley *Shrops* 37 SJ7229
Great Stainton *Dur* 62 NZ3322
Great Stambridge *Essex* 24 TQ8992
Great Staughton *Cambs* 30 TL1264
Great Steeping *Lincs* 51 TF4364
Great Stoke *Avon* 19 ST6280
Great Strickland *Cumb* 59 NY5522
Great Stukeley *Cambs* 31 TL2274
Great Sturton *Lincs* 51 TF2176
Great Swinburne *Nthumb* 68 NY9375
Great Tew *Oxon* 29 SP3929
Great Tey *Essex* 24 TL8925
Great Torrington *Devon* 6 SS4919
Great Tosson *Nthumb* 68 NU0200
Great Totham *Essex* 24 TL8611
Great Totham *Essex* 24 TL8713
Great Wakering *Essex* 25 TQ9487
Great Waldingfield *Suffk* 32 TL9144
Great Walsingham *Norfk* 42 TF9437
Great Waltham *Essex* 24 TL6913
Great Warley *Essex* 24 TQ5890

Great Washbourne Hartland

Great Washbourne *Gloucs*	28	SO9834
Great Weeke *Devon*	5	SX7187
Great Weldon *Nhants*	40	SP9289
Great Wenham *Suffk*	25	TM0738
Great Whittington *Nthumb*	68	NZ0070
Great Wigborough *Essex*	25	TL9615
Great Wilbraham *Cambs*	31	TL5557
Great Wishford *Wilts*	10	SU0835
Great Witcombe *Gloucs*	28	SO9114
Great Witley *H & W*	28	SO7566
Great Wolford *Warwks*	29	SP2534
Great Wratting *Essex*	32	TL6848
Great Wymondley *Herts*	31	TL2128
Great Wyrley *Staffs*	38	SJ9907
Great Yarmouth *Norfk*	43	TG5207
Great Yeldham *Essex*	24	TL7638
Greatford *Lincs*	40	TF0811
Greatgate *Staffs*	48	SK0540
Greatham *Cleve*	62	NZ4927
Greatham *Hants*	11	SU7730
Greatham *W Susx*	12	TQ0415
Greatstone-on-Sea *Kent*	15	TR0822
Greatworth *Nhants*	29	SP5542
Green Bank *Cumb*	67	NY3780
Green Cross *Surrey*	11	SU8634
Green End *Herts*	31	TL3333
Green End *Warwks*	39	SP2686
Green Hammerton *N York*	55	SE4656
Green Heath *Staffs*	38	SJ9913
Green Hill *Nthumb*	68	NY8647
Green Moor *S York*	49	SK2899
Green Ore *Somset*	19	ST5749
Green Quarter *Cumb*	59	NY4603
Green Street *H & W*	28	SO8749
Green Street *Herts*	23	TQ1998
Green Street *Herts*	31	TL4521
Green Street Green *Kent*	14	TQ5870
Green The *Cumb*	58	SD1784
Green Tye *Herts*	31	TL4418
Green end *Herts*	31	TL3122
Greenburn *Loth*	75	NS9360
Greenfield *Beds*	30	TL0534
Greenfield *Clwyd*	46	SJ1977
Greenfield *Highld*	86	NH2000
Greenfield *Strath*	80	NS2490
Greenford *Gt Lon*	22	TQ1482
Greengairs *Strath*	74	NS7870
Greenhalgh *Lancs*	53	SD4035
Greenham *Somset*	7	ST0719
Greenhaugh *Nthumb*	68	NY7987
Greenhill *Cent*	82	NS8279
Greenhill *D & G*	67	NY1079
Greenhill *Kent*	15	TR1666
Greenhill *S York*	49	SK3481
Greenhill *Strath*	75	NS9333
Greenhithe *Kent*	14	TQ5875
Greenholm *Strath*	74	NS5437
Greenhouse *Border*	76	NT5624
Greenhow Hill *N York*	55	SE1164
Greenland *Highld*	100	ND2367
Greenland *S York*	49	SK3988
Greenlaw *Border*	76	NT7146
Greenlea *D & G*	66	NY0375
Greenloaning *Tays*	82	NN8307
Greenmount *Gt Man*	54	SD7714
Greenock *Strath*	80	NS2776
Greenodd *Cumb*	58	SD3182
Greens Norton *Nhants*	30	SP6649
Greenside *T & W*	69	NZ1362
Greenside *W York*	55	SE1616
Greenstead *Essex*	25	TM0125
Greenstead Green *Essex*	24	TL8227
Greensted *Essex*	23	TL5303
Greenstreet Green *Suffk*	32	TM0450
Greenway *Gloucs*	28	SO7032
Greenway *S Glam*	18	ST0574
Greenway *Somset*	8	ST3124
Greenwich *Gt Lon*	23	TQ3877
Greet *Gloucs*	28	SP0230
Greete *Shrops*	37	SO5771
Greetham *Leics*	40	SK9214
Greetham *Lincs*	51	TF3070
Greetland *W York*	55	SE0821
Greinton *Somset*	19	ST4136
Grenaby *IOM*	52	SC2672
Grendon *Nhants*	30	SP8760
Grendon *Warwks*	39	SP2799
Grendon Underwood *Bucks*	30	SP6820
Grenofen *Devon*	4	SX5671
Grenoside *S York*	49	SK3394
Gresford *Clwyd*	46	SJ3454
Gresham *Norfk*	43	TG1638
Greshornish *Highld*	90	NG3454
Gressenhall *Norfk*	42	TF9615
Gressenhall Green *Norfk*	42	TF9616
Gressingham *Lancs*	53	SD5769
Grestey Green *Ches*	47	SJ7054
Greta Bridge *Dur*	61	NZ0813
Gretna *D & G*	67	NY3167
Gretna Green *D & G*	67	NY3268
Gretton *Gloucs*	28	SP0030
Gretton *Nhants*	40	SP8994
Gretton *Shrops*	37	SO5195
Grewelthorpe *N York*	61	SE2376
Grey Friars *Suffk*	33	TM4770
Grey's Green *Oxon*	22	SU7183
Greyrigg *D & G*	66	NY0889
Greysouthen *Cumb*	58	NY0729
Greysouthern *Cumb*	58	NY0629
Greystoke *Cumb*	59	NY4330
Greystone *Tays*	89	NO5343
Greywell *Hants*	22	SU7151
Gribb *Dorset*	8	ST3703
Griff *Warwks*	39	SP3689
Griffithstown *Gwent*	19	ST2999
Grigghall *Cumb*	59	SD4691
Grimeford Village *Lancs*	54	SD6112
Grimley *H & W*	28	SO8360
Grimmet *Strath*	73	NS3210
Grimoldby *Lincs*	51	TF3988
Grimpo *Shrops*	36	SJ3526
Grimsargh *Lancs*	54	SD5834
Grimsby *Humb*	57	TA2710
Grimscote *Nhants*	29	SP6553
Grimscott *Cnwll*	6	SS2607
Grimshader *W Isls*	102	NB4026
Grimsthorpe *Lincs*	40	TF0422
Grimston *Leics*	39	SK6821
Grimston *Norfk*	42	TF7222
Grimston Hill *Notts*	49	SK6865
Grimstone End *Suffk*	32	TL9368
Grindale *Humb*	57	TA1271
Grindleford *Derbys*	48	SK2477
Grindleton *Lancs*	54	SD7545
Grindley Brook *Shrops*	37	SJ5242
Grindlow *Derbys*	48	SK1878
Grindon *Staffs*	48	SK0854
Gringley on the Hill *Notts*	50	SK7390
Grinsdale *Cumb*	67	NY3758
Grinshill *Shrops*	37	SJ5223
Grinton *N York*	61	SE0498
Grishipoll *Strath*	78	NM1959
Grisling Common *E Susx*	13	TQ4422
Gristhorpe *N York*	63	TA0881
Griston *Norfk*	42	TL9499
Gritley *Ork*	103	HY5604
Grittenham *Wilts*	20	SU0382
Grittleton *Wilts*	20	ST8580
Grizebeck *Cumb*	58	SD2384
Grizedale *Cumb*	59	SD3394
Groby *Leics*	39	SK5207
Groes *Clwyd*	45	SJ0064
Groes *W Glam*	18	SS7986
Groes-Wen *M Glam*	18	ST1286
Groes-faen *M Glam*	18	ST0680
Groesffordd *Gwynd*	44	SH2739
Groesffordd Marli *Clwyd*	45	SJ0073
Grogport *Strath*	72	NR8044
Gronant *Clwyd*	46	SJ0883
Groom's Hill *H & W*	28	SP0154
Groombridge *E Susx*	13	TQ5337
Grosebay *W Isls*	90	NG1592
Grosmont *Gwent*	27	SO4024
Grosmont *N York*	63	NZ8305
Grossington *Gloucs*	20	SO7302
Grouville *Jersey*	101	SV0000
Grove *Notts*	50	SK7379
Grove *Oxon*	21	SU4090
Grove Green *Kent*	14	TQ7856
Grove Park *Gt Lon*	23	TQ4072
Grovesend *Avon*	19	ST6489
Grovesend *W Glam*	17	SN5900
Gruids *Highld*	96	NC5603
Gruinard *Highld*	91	NG9489
Gruinart Flats *Strath*	70	NR2866
Grula *Highld*	84	NG3826
Gruline *Strath*	79	NM5440
Grundisburgh *Suffk*	33	TM2251
Gruting *Shet*	103	HU2849
Gualachulain *Highld*	86	NN1145
Gualin House *Highld*	98	NC3056
Guardbridge *Fife*	83	NO4518
Guarlford *H & W*	28	SO8145
Guay *Tays*	89	NO9949
Guestling Green *E Susx*	14	TQ8513
Guestling Thorn *E Susx*	14	TQ8516
Guestwick *Norfk*	42	TG0627
Guide *Lancs*	54	SD7025
Guide Bridge *Gt Man*	45	SH9297
Guilden Down *Shrops*	36	SO3083
Guilden Morden *Cambs*	31	TL2744
Guilden Sutton *Ches*	46	SJ4468
Guildford *Surrey*	12	SU9949
Guildstead *Kent*	14	TQ8262
Guildtown *Tays*	82	NO1331
Guilreehill *Strath*	73	NS3610
Guilsborough *Nhants*	30	SP6772
Guilsfield *Powys*	36	SJ2211
Guisborough *Cleve*	62	NZ6115
Guiseley *W York*	55	SE1942
Guist *Norfk*	42	TF9925
Guiting Power *Gloucs*	28	SP0924
Gullane *Loth*	83	NT4882
Gulling Green *Suffk*	32	TL8356
Gulworthy *Devon*	4	SX4572
Gumfreston *Dyfed*	16	SN1101
Gumley *Leics*	39	SP6890
Gun Hill *E Susx*	13	TQ5614
Gunby *Humb*	56	SE7135
Gunby *Lincs*	40	SK9121
Gunby *Lincs*	51	TF4667
Gundleton *Hants*	11	SU6133
Gunn *Devon*	7	SS6333
Gunnerside *N York*	61	SD9598
Gunnerton *Nthumb*	68	NY9074
Gunness *Humb*	56	SE8411
Gunnislake *Devon*	4	SX4371
Gunnista *Shet*	103	HU5043
Gunthorpe *Cambs*	40	TF1803
Gunthorpe *Norfk*	42	TG0134
Gunthorpe *Notts*	49	SK6844
Gunville *IOW*	10	SZ4889
Gupworthy *Somset*	7	SS9735
Gurnard *IOW*	10	SZ4795
Gurnett *Ches*	48	SJ9271
Gurney Slade *Somset*	19	ST6249
Gurnos *W Glam*	26	SN7709
Gussage All Saints *Dorset*	9	SU0010
Gussage St. Michael *Dorset*	9	ST9811
Guston *Kent*	15	TR3244
Gutcher *Shet*	103	HU5499
Guthrie *Tays*	89	NO5650
Guyhirn *Cambs*	41	TF4003
Guyhirn Gull *Cambs*	41	TF3903
Guyzance *Nthumb*	69	NU2104
Gwaenysgor *Clwyd*	46	SJ0780
Gwalchmai *Gwynd*	44	SH3876
Gwaun-Cae-Gurwen *W Glam*	26	SN7011
Gwbert-on-Sea *Dyfed*	17	SN1649
Gwealavellan *Cnwll*	2	SW5942
Gweek *Cnwll*	2	SW7026
Gwenddwr *Powys*	26	SO0643
Gwendreath *Cnwll*	2	SW7216
Gwennap *Cnwll*	2	SW7340
Gwern-y-Steeple *S Glam*	18	ST0775
Gwernesney *Gwent*	19	SO4101
Gwernogle *Dyfed*	17	SN5334
Gwernymynydd *Clwyd*	46	SJ2162
Gwinear *Cnwll*	2	SW5937
Gwithian *Cnwll*	2	SW5841
Gwredog *Gwynd*	44	SH4086
Gwyddelwern *Clwyd*	46	SJ0746
Gwyddgrug *Dyfed*	17	SN4635
Gwytherin *Clwyd*	45	SH8761

H

Habberley *H & W*	37	SO8176
Habberley *Shrops*	36	SJ3903
Habergham *Lancs*	54	SD8033
Habertoft *Lincs*	51	TF5069
Habrough *Humb*	57	TA1413
Haccombe *Devon*	5	SX8970
Hacconby *Lincs*	40	TF1025
Haceby *Lincs*	40	TF0236
Hacheston *Suffk*	33	TM3059
Hackenthorpe *S York*	49	SK4183
Hackford *Norfk*	42	TG0502
Hackforth *N York*	61	SE2493
Hackland *Ork*	103	HY3920
Hackleton *Nhants*	30	SP8055
Hacklinge *Kent*	15	TR3454
Hackness *N York*	63	SE9790
Hackney *Gt Lon*	23	TQ3484
Hackthorn *Lincs*	50	SK9982
Hackthorpe *Cumb*	59	NY5323
Hadden *Border*	76	NT7836
Haddenham *Bucks*	22	SP7308
Haddenham *Cambs*	31	TL4675
Haddington *Lincs*	50	SK9163
Haddington *Loth*	76	NT5173
Haddiscoe *Norfk*	43	TM4497
Haddo *Gramp*	95	NJ8337
Haddon *Cambs*	40	TL1392
Hadham Ford *Herts*	31	TL4321
Hadleigh *Essex*	24	TQ8187
Hadleigh *Suffk*	32	TM0242
Hadley *H & W*	28	SO8664
Hadley *Shrops*	37	SJ6712
Hadley Wood *Gt Lon*	23	TQ2698
Hadlow *Kent*	13	TQ6350
Hadlow Down *E Susx*	13	TQ5324
Hadnall *Shrops*	37	SJ5220
Hadstock *Essex*	31	TL5644
Hadzor *H & W*	28	SO9162
Hafodunos *Clwyd*	45	SH8667
Hafodyrynys *Gwent*	19	ST2299
Hafodyrynys *Gwent*	19	ST2499
Haggbeck *Cumb*	67	NY4774
Haggerston *Nthumb*	77	NU0443
Haggington Hill *Devon*	6	SS5647
Haggs *Cent*	81	NS7979
Hagley *H & W*	27	SO5641
Hagley *H & W*	38	SO9181
Hagworthingham *Lincs*	51	TF3469
Hail Weston *Cambs*	31	TL1662
Haile *Cumb*	58	NY0308
Hailsham *E Susx*	13	TQ5909
Hainault *Gt Lon*	23	TQ4591
Hainford *Norfk*	43	TG2318
Hainton *Lincs*	50	TF1784
Hainworth *W York*	55	SE0639
Haisthorpe *Humb*	57	TA1264
Hakin *Dyfed*	16	SM8905
Halam *Notts*	49	SK6754
Halbeath *Fife*	82	NT1289
Halberton *Devon*	7	ST0012
Halcro *Highld*	100	ND2360
Hale *Ches*	46	SJ4782
Hale *Cumb*	59	SD5078
Hale *Gt Man*	47	SJ7786
Hale *Hants*	10	SU1919
Hale *Somset*	9	ST7527
Hale *Surrey*	22	SU8448
Hale Bank *Ches*	46	SJ4884
Hale Green *E Susx*	13	TQ5514
Hale Street *Kent*	14	TQ6749
Hales *Norfk*	43	TM3897
Hales *Staffs*	37	SJ7134
Hales Place *Kent*	15	TR1459
Halesowen *W Mids*	38	SO9683
Halesworth *Suffk*	33	TM3877
Halford *Shrops*	36	SO4383
Halford *Warwks*	29	SP2545
Halford Blackpool *Devon*	5	SX8175
Halfpenny Green *Staffs*	38	SO8291
Halfway *Powys*	26	SN8332
Halfway Bridge *W Susx*	11	SU9322
Halfway House *Shrops*	36	SJ3411
Halfway Houses *Kent*	14	TQ9372
Halifax *W York*	55	SE0925
Halistra *Highld*	90	NG2459
Halket *Strath*	73	NS4252
Halkirk *Highld*	100	ND1359
Halkyn *Clwyd*	46	SJ2171
Hall *Strath*	73	NS4154
Hall Cliffe *W York*	55	SE2918
Hall Dunnerdale *Cumb*	58	SD2195
Hall End *Beds*	30	TL0045
Hall Green *W Mids*	38	SP1181
Hall's Green *Herts*	31	TL2728
Halland *E Susx*	13	TQ4916
Hallaton *Leics*	40	SP7896
Hallatrow *Avon*	19	ST6356
Hallbankgate *Cumb*	67	NY5859
Hallen *Avon*	19	ST5480
Hallfield Gate *Derbys*	49	SK3958
Hallgarth *Dur*	69	NZ3343
Hallin *Highld*	90	NG2558
Halling *Kent*	14	TQ7063
Hallington *Lincs*	51	TF3085
Hallington *Nthumb*	68	NY9875
Hallins *Derbys*	49	SK3371
Halliwell *Gt Man*	54	SD6910
Halloughton *Notts*	49	SK6951
Hallow *H & W*	28	SO8258
Hallrule *Border*	67	NT5914
Hallsands *Devon*	5	SX8138
Hallthwaites *Cumb*	58	SD1785
Hallworthy *Cnwll*	4	SX1887
Hallyne *Border*	75	NT1940
Halmer End *Staffs*	47	SJ7949
Halmond's Frome *H & W*	28	SO6647
Halmore *Gloucs*	20	SO6902
Halnaker *W Susx*	11	SU9008
Halsall *Lancs*	53	SD3710
Halse *Nhants*	29	SP5640
Halse *Somset*	8	ST1327
Halse *Somset*	8	ST1428
Halsetown *Cnwll*	2	SW5038
Halstead *Essex*	24	TL8130
Halstead *Kent*	23	TQ4961
Halstead *Leics*	40	SK7505
Halstock *Dorset*	8	ST5308
Halsway *Somset*	18	ST1338
Haltham *Lincs*	51	TF2463
Halton *Bucks*	22	SP8710
Halton *Clwyd*	36	SJ3039
Halton *Lancs*	53	SD5064
Halton *Nthumb*	68	NY9967
Halton *W York*	55	SE3533
Halton East *N York*	55	SE0454
Halton Gill *N York*	60	SD8876
Halton Lea Gate *Nthumb*	68	NY6458
Halton Shields *Nthumb*	68	NZ0168
Halton West *N York*	54	SD8454
Haltwhistle *Nthumb*	68	NY7064
Halvergate *Norfk*	43	TG4207
Halwell *Devon*	5	SX7753
Halwill *Devon*	6	SX4299
Halwill *Devon*	4	SX4392
Halwill Junction *Devon*	6	SS4400
Halwill Junction *Devon*	6	SX4599
Ham *Devon*	8	ST2301
Ham *Gloucs*	20	ST6898
Ham *Gt Lon*	23	TQ1772
Ham *Kent*	15	TR3354
Ham *Somset*	8	ST2825
Ham *Wilts*	21	SU3262
Ham Street *Somset*	8	ST5534
Hamble *Hants*	10	SU4806
Hambleden *Bucks*	22	SU7886
Hambledon *Hants*	11	SU6415
Hambledon *Surrey*	12	SU9638
Hambleton *Lancs*	53	SD3742
Hambleton *N York*	56	SE5430
Hambridge *Somset*	8	ST3921
Hambrook *Avon*	19	ST6378
Hambrook *W Susx*	11	SU7806
Hamels *Herts*	31	TL3724
Hameringham *Lincs*	51	TF3067
Hamerton *Cambs*	40	TL1379
Hamilton *Strath*	74	NS7255
Hamlet *Dorset*	9	ST5908
Hamlins *E Susx*	13	TQ5909
Hammerpot *W Susx*	12	TQ0705
Hammersmith *Gt Lon*	23	TQ2378
Hammerwich *Staffs*	38	SK0607
Hammond Street *Herts*	23	TL3304
Hammoon *Dorset*	9	ST8114
Hamnavoe *Shet*	103	HU3735
Hamnavoe *Shet*	103	HU4971
Hampden Park *E Susx*	13	TQ6002
Hampden Row *Bucks*	22	SP8501
Hamperden End *Essex*	24	TL5730
Hampnett *Gloucs*	28	SP0915
Hampole *S York*	55	SE5010
Hampreston *Dorset*	10	SZ0598
Hampsfield *Cumb*	59	SD4080
Hampstead *Gt Lon*	23	TQ2685
Hampstead Norrey's *Berks*	21	SU5276
Hampsthwaite *N York*	55	SE2558
Hampt *M Glam*	4	SX3974
Hampton *Devon*	6	SX2696
Hampton *Gt Lon*	22	TQ1369
Hampton *H & W*	28	SP0243
Hampton *Kent*	15	TR1568
Hampton *Wilts*	21	SU1892
Hampton Bishop *H & W*	27	SO5537
Hampton Heath *Ches*	46	SJ4949
Hampton Loade *Shrops*	37	SO7486
Hampton Lovett *H & W*	28	SO8865
Hampton Lucy *Warwks*	29	SP2557
Hampton Poyle *Oxon*	29	SP5015
Hampton Wick *Gt Lon*	23	TQ1769
Hampton in Arden *W Mids*	39	SP2081
Hampton on the Hill *Warwks*	29	SP2564
Hamptworth *Wilts*	10	SU2419
Hamsey *E Susx*	13	TQ4012
Hamsey Green *Gt Lon*	23	TQ3760
Hamstall Ridware *Staffs*	38	SK1019
Hamstead Marshall *Berks*	21	SU4165
Hamsterley *Dur*	61	NZ1131
Hamsterley *Dur*	69	NZ1156
Hamstreet *Kent*	15	TR0034
Hamworthy *Dorset*	9	SY9990
Hanbury *H & W*	28	SO9664
Hanbury *Staffs*	38	SK1727
Hanchurch *Staffs*	38	SJ8441
Hand and Pen *Devon*	7	SY0495
Handbridge *Ches*	46	SJ4065
Handcross *W Susx*	12	TQ2629
Handley *Ches*	46	SJ4657
Handley *Derbys*	49	SK3761
Handley Green *Essex*	24	TL6601
Handsacre *Staffs*	38	SK0916
Handsworth *S York*	49	SK4186
Handsworth *W Mids*	38	SP0589
Handy Cross *Bucks*	22	SU8490
Hanford *Dorset*	9	ST8410
Hanford *Staffs*	38	SJ8642
Hanging Langford *Wilts*	20	SU0237
Hangleton *E Susx*	12	TQ2607
Hanham *Avon*	19	ST6372
Hankelow *Ches*	47	SJ6745
Hankerton *Wilts*	20	ST9690
Hanley *Staffs*	47	SJ8847
Hanley Child *H & W*	27	SO6565
Hanley Swan *H & W*	28	SO8143
Hanley William *H & W*	28	SO6766
Hanlith *N York*	54	SD8960
Hanmer *Clwyd*	36	SJ4540
Hannaford *Devon*	6	SS6029
Hannington *Hants*	21	SU5455
Hannington *Nhants*	30	SP8170
Hannington *Wilts*	21	SU1793
Hannington Wick *Wilts*	21	SU1795
Hanslope *Bucks*	30	SP8046
Hanthorpe *Lincs*	40	TF0823
Hanwell *Gt Lon*	22	TQ1579
Hanwell *Oxon*	29	SP4343
Hanworth *Gt Lon*	22	TQ1271
Hanworth *Norfk*	43	TG1935
Happendon *Strath*	74	NS8533
Happisburgh *Norfk*	43	TG3831
Happisburgh Common *Norfk*	43	TG3729
Hapsford *Ches*	46	SJ4774
Hapton *Lancs*	54	SD7931
Hapton *Norfk*	43	TM1796
Harberton *Devon*	5	SX7758
Harbertonford *Devon*	5	SX7856
Harbledown *Kent*	15	TR1357
Harborne *W Mids*	38	SP0284
Harborough Magna *Warwks*	39	SP4778
Harborough Parva *Warwks*	39	SP4778
Harbottle *Nthumb*	68	NT9304
Harbours Hill *H & W*	28	SO9566
Harbridge *Hants*	10	SU1409
Harbridge Green *Hants*	10	SU1411
Harburn *Loth*	75	NT0462
Harbury *Warwks*	29	SP3760
Harby *Leics*	40	SK7431
Harby *Notts*	50	SK8770
Harcombe *Devon*	5	SX8881
Harcombe *Devon*	8	SY1590
Harcombe Bottom *Devon*	8	SY3395
Harden *W Mids*	38	SK0101
Harden *W York*	55	SE0838
Hardenhuish *Wilts*	20	ST9074
Hardgate *Gramp*	89	NJ7901
Hardgate *Strath*	74	NS5073
Hardham *W Susx*	12	TQ0317
Hardingham *Norfk*	42	TG0403
Hardingstone *Nhants*	30	SP7657
Hardington *Somset*	20	ST7452
Hardington Mandeville *Somset*	8	ST5111
Hardington Marsh *Somset*	8	ST5009
Hardington Moor *Somset*	8	ST5212
Hardisworthy *Devon*	3	SX2320
Hardley *Hants*	10	SU4205
Hardley Street *Norfk*	43	TG3801
Hardraw *N York*	60	SD8691
Hardstoft *Derbys*	49	SK4463
Hardway *Hants*	11	SU6101
Hardway *Somset*	9	ST7134
Hardwick *Bucks*	30	SP8019
Hardwick *Cambs*	31	TL3758
Hardwick *Nhants*	30	SP8469
Hardwick *Norfk*	33	TM2290
Hardwick *Oxon*	29	SP3706
Hardwick *Oxon*	29	SP5729
Hardwicke *Gloucs*	28	SO7912
Hardwicke *Gloucs*	28	SO9027
Hardy's Green *Essex*	25	TL9320
Hare Croft *W York*	55	SE0835
Hare Green *Essex*	25	TM1025
Hare Hatch *Berks*	22	SU8077
Hare Street *Essex*	23	TL4209
Hare Street *Essex*	23	TL5300
Hare Street *Herts*	31	TL3929
Hareby *Lincs*	51	TF3365
Harefield *Gt Lon*	22	TQ0590
Harehill *Derbys*	38	SK1735
Harehills *W York*	55	SE3135
Harelaw *Border*	76	NT5323
Harelaw *Dur*	69	NZ1552
Hareplain *Kent*	14	TQ8140
Haresceugh *Cumb*	68	NY6043
Harescombe *Gloucs*	28	SO8310
Haresfield *Gloucs*	28	SO8110
Harestock *Hants*	10	SU4631
Harewood *W York*	55	SE3245
Harewood End *H & W*	27	SO5227
Harford *Devon*	5	SX6359
Hargate *Norfk*	33	TM1291
Hargatewell *Derbys*	48	SK1274
Hargrave *Ches*	46	SJ4862
Hargrave *Nhants*	30	TL0370
Hargrave Green *Suffk*	32	TL7759
Harkstead *Suffk*	25	TM1834
Harlaston *Staffs*	39	SK2110
Harlaxton *Lincs*	40	SK8832
Harlech *Gwynd*	44	SH5831
Harlescott *Shrops*	37	SJ5115
Harlesden *Gt Lon*	23	TQ2383
Harlesthorpe *Derbys*	49	SK4976
Harleston *Devon*	5	SX7945
Harleston *Norfk*	33	TM2483
Harleston *Suffk*	32	TM0160
Harlestone *Nhants*	30	SP7064
Harley *S York*	49	SK3698
Harleyholm *Strath*	75	NS9238
Harlington *Beds*	30	TL0330
Harlington *Gt Lon*	22	TQ0877
Harlington *S York*	49	SE4802
Harlosh *Highld*	84	NG2841
Harlow *Herts*	23	TL4711
Harlow Hill *Nthumb*	68	NZ0768
Harlthorpe *Humb*	56	SE7337
Harlton *Cambs*	31	TL3852
Harlyn Bay *Cnwll*	3	SW8775
Harman's Cross *Dorset*	9	SY9880
Harmby *N York*	61	SE1289
Harmer Green *Herts*	31	TL2515
Harmer Hill *Shrops*	37	SJ4822
Harmston *Lincs*	50	SK9762
Harnage *Shrops*	37	SJ5604
Harnhill *Gloucs*	20	SP0600
Harold Hill *Gt Lon*	23	TQ5392
Harold Wood *Gt Lon*	24	TQ5590
Haroldston West *Dyfed*	16	SM8615
Haroldswick *Shet*	103	HP6312
Harome *N York*	62	SE6481
Harpenden *Herts*	30	TL1314
Harpford *Devon*	8	SY0890
Harpham *Humb*	57	TA0961
Harpley *H & W*	28	SO6861
Harpley *Norfk*	42	TF7825
Harpole *Nhants*	30	SP6961
Harpsdale *Highld*	100	ND1355
Harpsden *Oxon*	22	SU7680
Harpswell *Lincs*	50	SK9389
Harpurhey *Gt Man*	47	SD8501
Harraby *Cumb*	67	NY4154
Harracott *Devon*	6	SS5627
Harrapool *Highld*	85	NG6522
Harrietfield *Tays*	82	NN9829
Harrietsham *Kent*	14	TQ8652
Harringay *Gt Lon*	23	TQ3188
Harrington *Cumb*	58	NX9926
Harrington *H & W*	38	SO8774
Harrington *Lincs*	51	TF3671
Harrington *Nhants*	40	SP7780
Harringworth *Nhants*	40	SP9197
Harris *Highld*	88	NO3396
Harriseahead *Staffs*	47	SJ8656
Harriston *Cumb*	58	NY1641
Harrogate *N York*	55	SE3055
Harrold *Beds*	30	SP9456
Harrop Dale *Gt Man*	54	SE0008
Harrow *Gt Lon*	22	TQ1588
Harrow Green *Suffk*	32	TL8654
Harrow Weald *Gt Lon*	22	TQ1591
Harrow on the Hill *Gt Lon*	22	TQ1587
Harrowbarrow *Cnwll*	4	SX3969
Harrowden *Beds*	30	TL0646
Harsgeir *W Isls*	102	NB1040
Harston *Cambs*	31	TL4250
Harston *Leics*	40	SK8331
Harswell *Humb*	56	SE8240
Hart *Cleve*	62	NZ4734
Hartburn *Nthumb*	68	NZ0886
Hartest *Suffk*	32	TL8352
Hartford *Cambs*	31	TL2572
Hartford *Ches*	47	SJ6372
Hartford *Somset*	7	SS9629
Hartford End *Essex*	24	TL6817
Hartfordbridge *Hants*	22	SU7757
Hartforth *N York*	61	NZ1606
Harthill *Ches*	46	SJ4955
Harthill *Loth*	74	NS9064
Harthill *S York*	49	SK4980
Hartington *Derbys*	48	SK1260
Hartland *Devon*	6	SS2624

Place	Pg	Grid
Hartland Quay Devon	6	SS2224
Hartlebury H & W	38	SO8471
Hartlepool Cleve	62	NZ5032
Hartley Cumb	60	NY7808
Hartley Kent	14	TQ6166
Hartley Kent	14	TQ7634
Hartley Green Kent	14	TQ6066
Hartley Wintney Hants	22	SU7656
Hartlip Kent	14	TQ8364
Hartoft End N York	63	SE7592
Harton N York	56	SE7061
Harton T & W	69	NZ3765
Hartpury Gloucs	28	SO7924
Hartshead W York	55	SE1822
Hartshill Staffs	47	SJ8645
Hartshill Warwks	39	SP3294
Hartshorne Derbys	39	SK3221
Hartside Nthumb	77	NT9716
Hartswell Somset	7	ST0826
Hartwell Nhants	30	SP7850
Hartwith N York	55	SE2161
Hartwood Strath	74	NS8459
Hartwood Myres Border	76	NT4424
Harvel Kent	14	TQ6563
Harvington H & W	28	SP0548
Harwell Notts	49	SK6891
Harwell Oxon	21	SU4989
Harwich Essex	25	TM2531
Harwood Nthumb	60	NY9133
Harwood Dale N York	63	SE9695
Harwood Lee Gt Man	54	SD7412
Harworth Notts	49	SK6291
Hasbury W Mids	38	SO9583
Hascombe Surrey	12	TQ0039
Haselbeach Nhants	30	SP7177
Haselbury Plucknett Somset	8	ST4711
Haselor Warwks	28	SP1257
Hasfield Gloucs	28	SO8227
Haskayne Lancs	46	SD3508
Hasketon Suffk	33	TM2450
Haslemere Surrey	11	SU9032
Haslingden Lancs	54	SD7823
Haslingfield Cambs	31	TL4052
Haslington Ches	47	SJ7355
Haslington Grane Lancs	54	SD7523
Hassendean Border	76	NT5420
Hassingham Norfk	43	TG3705
Hassness Cumb	58	NY1826
Hassocks W Susx	12	TQ3015
Hassop Derbys	48	SK2272
Haste Hill Surrey	11	SU9032
Haster Highld	100	ND3251
Hastigrow Highld	100	ND2660
Hastingleigh Kent	15	TR0945
Hastings E Susx	14	TQ8209
Hastings Somset	8	ST3316
Hastings Somset	8	ST3316
Hastingwood Essex	23	TL4807
Hastoe Herts	22	SP9209
Haswell Dur	69	NZ3743
Haswell Plough Dur	62	NZ3741
Hatch Beauchamp Somset	8	ST3020
Hatch End Herts	22	TQ1391
Hatching Green Herts	30	TL1313
Hatchmere Ches	47	SJ5571
Hatcliffe Humb	51	TA2100
Hatfield H & W	28	SO7760
Hatfield H & W	27	SO5959
Hatfield Herts	23	TL2308
Hatfield S York	56	SE6609
Hatfield Broad Oak Essex	24	TL5416
Hatfield Heath Essex	31	TL5215
Hatfield Peverel Essex	24	TL7911
Hatfield Woodhouse S York	56	SE6708
Hatford Oxon	21	SU3294
Hatford Oxon	21	SU3294
Hatherden Hants	21	SU3450
Hatherleigh Devon	6	SS5404
Hathern Leics	39	SK5022
Hatherop Gloucs	28	SP1505
Hathersage Derbys	48	SK2383
Hathersage Booths Derbys	48	SK2480
Hatherton Ches	47	SJ6847
Hatherton Staffs	38	SJ9510
Hatley St. George Cambs	31	TL2751
Hatt Cnwll	4	SX3961
Hatton Ches	47	SJ5982
Hatton Derbys	39	SK2130
Hatton Gramp	95	NK0537
Hatton Gt Lon	22	TQ0975
Hatton Lincs	50	TF1776
Hatton Shrops	36	SO4690
Hatton Tays	89	NO4642
Hatton of Fintray Gramp	95	NJ8316
Haugh Strath	74	NS4925
Haugh of Glass Gramp	94	NJ4239
Haugh of Urr D & G	66	NX8066
Haugham Lincs	51	TF3381
Haughhead Inn Strath	81	NS6178
Haughley Suffk	32	TM0262
Haughley Green Suffk	32	TM0364
Haughton Notts	49	SK6772
Haughton Shrops	37	SJ7408
Haughton Shrops	36	SJ3726
Haughton Staffs	38	SJ8620
Haughton Moss Ches	47	SJ5756
Haughton le Skerne Dur	62	NZ3116
Haultwick Herts	31	TL3323
Haunton Staffs	39	SK2310
Hautes Croix Jersey	101	SV0000
Hauxley Nthumb	69	NU2703
Hauxton Cambs	31	TL4352
Havannah Ches	47	SJ8764
Havant Hants	11	SU7106
Havenhouse Station Lincs	51	TF5259
Havenstreet IOW	11	SZ5690
Havercroft W York	55	SE3813
Haverfordwest Dyfed	16	SM9515
Haverhill Suffk	32	TL6745
Haverigg Cumb	58	SD1578
Havering-atte-Bower Essex	23	TQ5193
Haversham Bucks	30	SP8242
Havyat Avon	19	ST4761
Hawarden Clwyd	46	SJ3165
Hawbridge H & W	28	SO9049
Hawbush Green Essex	24	TL7820
Hawcoat Cumb	67	NY2271
Hawe's Green Norfk	43	TM2499
Hawen Dyfed	17	SN3447
Hawes N York	60	SD8789
Haweford H & W	28	SO8460
Hawick Border	67	NT5014
Hawkchurch Devon	8	ST3400
Hawkedon Suffk	32	TL7953
Hawkeridge Wilts	20	ST8653
Hawkerland Devon	5	SY0589
Hawkes End W Mids	39	SP2983
Hawkesbury Avon	20	ST7686
Hawkesbury Upton Avon	20	ST7786
Hawkhurst Kent	14	TQ7530
Hawkhurst Common E Susx	13	TQ5317
Hawkinge Kent	15	TR2139
Hawkley Hants	11	SU7429
Hawkridge Devon	7	SS8630
Hawkshead Cumb	59	SD3598
Hawkshead Hill Cumb	67	NY3398
Hawksland Strath	74	NS8439
Hawkspur Green Essex	24	TL6532
Hawkstone Shrops	37	SJ5830
Hawkswick N York	54	SD9570
Hawksworth Notts	50	SK7543
Hawksworth W York	55	SE1641
Hawkwell Essex	24	TQ8591
Hawley Hants	22	SU8586
Hawley Kent	23	TQ5571
Hawling Gloucs	28	SP0623
Hawnby N York	62	SE5489
Haworth W York	55	SE0337
Hawstead Suffk	32	TL8559
Hawthorn Dur	69	NZ4145
Hawthorn Hill Lincs	51	TF2155
Hawton Notts	50	SK7851
Haxby N York	56	SE6058
Haxey Humb	50	SK7699
Haxted Surrey	13	TQ4245
Haxton Wilts	20	SU1549
Hay Green Norfk	41	TF5418
Hay Street Herts	31	TL3926

Place	Pg	Grid
Hay-on-Wye Powys	27	SO2342
Haydock Mersyd	47	SJ5697
Haydon Dorset	9	ST6615
Haydon Bridge Nthumb	68	NY8464
Haydon Wick Wilts	20	SU1387
Hayes Gt Lon	23	TQ4066
Hayes Gt Lon	22	TQ0980
Hayes End Gt Lon	22	TQ0882
Hayfield Derbys	48	SK0186
Hayfield Strath	80	NN0723
Hayhillock Tays	89	NO5242
Hayle Cnwll	2	SW5537
Hayley Green W Mids	38	SO9482
Hayne Devon	7	SS9515
Hayne Devon	5	SX7685
Haynes Beds	30	TL0740
Haynes West End Beds	30	TL0640
Haynscastle Dyfed	16	SM8925
Hayscastle Cross Dyfed	16	SM9125
Haysden Kent	13	TQ5645
Hayton Cumb	67	NY5057
Hayton Cumb	66	SE8145
Hayton Humb	56	SE8145
Hayton Notts	49	SK7284
Haytor Vale Devon	5	SX7677
Haytown Devon	6	SS3814
Haywards Heath W Susx	12	TQ3324
Haywood S York	56	SE5812
Hazel Grove Gt Man	48	SJ9287
Hazelbank Strath	74	NS8345
Hazelbury Bryan Dorset	9	ST7408
Hazeleigh Essex	24	TL8203
Hazeley Hants	22	SU7459
Hazelton Walls Fife	83	NO3322
Hazelwood Derbys	49	SK3245
Hazlemere Bucks	22	SU8895
Hazleton Gloucs	28	SP0718
Head of Muir Cent	42	TF6737
Head of Muir Cent	81	NS8080
Headbourne Worthy Hants	10	SU4831
Headcorn Kent	14	TQ8344
Headingley W York	55	SE2836
Headington Oxon	29	SP5307
Headlam Dur	61	NZ1818
Headless Cross Strath	75	NS9158
Headley Hants	21	SU5162
Headley Hants	11	SU8236
Headley Surrey	23	TQ2054
Headley Down Hants	11	SU8436
Headon Notts	50	SK7476
Heads Strath	74	NS7147
Heads Nook Cumb	67	NY4955
Heads Nook Cumb	67	NY5054
Heage Derbys	49	SK3650
Healaugh N York	61	SE0198
Healaugh N York	55	SE4947
Heald Green Gt Man	47	SJ8486
Heale Somset	8	ST2420
Heale Somset	8	ST3825
Healey Lancs	54	SD8817
Healey N York	61	SE1780
Healeyfield Dur	68	NZ0648
Healing Humb	57	TA2110
Heamoor Cnwll	2	SW4631
Heanor Derbys	49	SK4346
Heanton Punchardon Devon	6	SS5035
Heapham Lincs	50	SK8788
Hearthstone Border	75	NT1126
Heasley Mill Devon	7	SS7332
Heasley Highld	85	NG6417
Heath Derbys	49	SK4467
Heath W York	55	SE3520
Heath Common W Susx	12	TQ1014
Heath End Bucks	22	SU8798
Heath End Hants	21	SU4162
Heath End Hants	21	SU5762
Heath End Surrey	22	SU8449
Heath Green H & W	38	SP0771
Heath Hill Shrops	37	SJ7614
Heath Town W Mids	38	SO9399
Heath and Reach Beds	30	SP9228
Heathcote Derbys	48	SK1460
Heathcote Nhants	30	SP7047
Heather Leics	39	SK3910
Heathfield E Susx	13	TQ5821
Heathfield Somset	8	ST1626
Heathton Shrops	37	SO8192
Heatley Staffs	38	SK0626
Heaton Staffs	48	SJ9562
Heaton T & W	69	NZ2666
Heaton W York	55	SE1335
Heaton's Bridge Lancs	53	SD3905
Heaverham Kent	14	TQ5758
Heavitree Devon	5	SX9392
Hebburn T & W	69	NZ3263
Hebden N York	55	SE0263
Hebden Bridge W York	55	SD9927
Hebing End Herts	31	TL3122
Hebron Dyfed	17	SN1827
Hebron Nthumb	69	NZ1989
Heckfield Hants	22	SU7260
Heckfield Green Suffk	33	TM1875
Heckfordbridge Essex	25	TL9421
Heckington Lincs	50	TF1444
Heckmondwike W York	55	SE2123
Heddington Wilts	20	ST9966
Heddon-on-the-Wall Nthumb	69	NZ1366
Hedenham Norfk	43	TM3193
Hedge End Hants	10	SU4912
Hedgerley Bucks	22	SU9687
Hedging Somset	8	ST3029
Hedley on the Hill Nthumb	68	NZ0759
Hednesford Staffs	38	SK0012
Hedon Humb	57	TA1928
Hedsor Bucks	22	SU9086
Heglibister Shet	103	HU3851
Heighington Dur	61	NZ2422
Heighington Lincs	50	TF0269
Heightington H & W	37	SO7671
Heiton Border	76	NT7130
Hele Cnwll	6	SX2197
Hele Devon	6	SS5347
Hele Devon	7	SS9902
Hele Somset	8	ST1824
Helensburgh Strath	80	NS2982
Helenton Strath	73	NS3820
Helford Cnwll	2	SW7526
Helford Passage Cnwll	2	SW7627
Helhoughton Norfk	42	TF8626
Helions Bumpstead Essex	32	TL6541
Helland Cnwll	3	SX0771
Hellescott Cnwll	4	SX2888
Hellesdon Norfk	43	TG2010
Hellidon Nhants	29	SP5157
Hellidon Nhants	29	SP5158
Hellifield N York	54	SD8556
Hellingly E Susx	13	TQ5812
Hellmdon Nhants	29	SP5943
Helme W York	55	SE0912
Helmingham Suffk	33	TM1957
Helmsdale Highld	97	ND0315
Helmshore Lancs	54	SD7821
Helmsley N York	62	SE6183
Helperby N York	55	SE4369
Helperthorpe N York	56	SE9570
Helpringham Lincs	50	TF1340
Helpston Cambs	40	TF1205
Helsby Ches	46	SJ4975
Helston Cnwll	2	SW6527
Helstone Cnwll	3	SX0881
Helton Cumb	59	NY5021
Hemblington Norfk	43	TG3411
Hemel Hempstead Herts	22	TL0507
Hemerdon Devon	4	SX5657
Hemerdon Devon	4	SX5657
Hemingbrough N York	56	SE6730
Hemingby Lincs	51	TF2375
Hemingford Abbots Cambs	31	TL2871
Hemingford Grey Cambs	31	TL2970
Hemingstone Suffk	33	TM1454
Hemington Leics	40	TL0985
Hemington Somset	20	ST7253
Hemley Suffk	33	TM2842
Hempnall Norfk	43	TM2494
Hempnall Green Norfk	43	TM2493
Hempriggs Gramp	93	NJ0963
Hempstead Essex	24	TL6338
Hempstead Kent	14	TQ7964
Hempstead Norfk	43	TG1037
Hempstead Norfk	43	TG4028

Place	Pg	Grid
Hempton Norfk	42	TF9129
Hempton Oxon	29	SP4431
Hemsby Norfk	43	TG4917
Hemswell Lincs	50	SK9290
Hemsworth W York	55	SE4213
Hemyock Devon	8	ST1313
Henbury Ches	47	SJ8873
Hendersyde Park Border	76	NT7435
Hendomen Powys	36	SO2198
Hendon Gt Lon	23	TQ2389
Hendon T & W	69	NZ4055
Hendy Dyfed	17	SN5803
Henfield W Susx	12	TQ2116
Hengoed M Glam	19	ST1595
Hengoed Powys	27	SO2253
Hengrave Suffk	32	TL8269
Henham Essex	24	TL5428
Henhurst Kent	14	TQ6669
Heniarth Powys	36	SJ1208
Henlade Somset	8	ST2624
Henley Dorset	9	ST6904
Henley Somset	8	ST4232
Henley Suffk	33	TM1551
Henley W Susx	11	SU8925
Henley on Thames Oxon	22	SU7682
Henley's Down E Susx	14	TQ7312
Henley-in-Arden Warwks	28	SP1566
Henllan Clwyd	45	SJ0268
Henllan Dyfed	17	SN3540
Henllan Amgoed Dyfed	17	SN1820
Henllys Gwent	19	ST2691
Henlow Beds	31	TL1738
Hennock Devon	5	SX8381
Henny Street Essex	24	TL8738
Henry's Moat (Castell Hen Dyfed	16	SN0428
Henryd Gwynd	45	SH7674
Henryd Gwynd	45	SH7774
Hensall N York	56	SE5923
Henshaw Nthumb	68	NY7664
Hensingham Cumb	58	NX9816
Henstead Suffk	33	TM4986
Hensting Hants	10	SU4922
Henstride Ash Somset	9	ST7220
Henstridge Somset	9	ST7219
Henstridge Marsh Somset	9	ST7420
Henton Oxon	22	SP7602
Henton Somset	19	ST4845
Henwick H & W	28	SO8354
Henwood Cnwll	4	SX2673
Heol-y-Cyw M Glam	18	SS9484
Hepscott Nthumb	69	NZ2284
Heptonstall W York	54	SD9828
Hepworth Suffk	32	TL9874
Hepworth W York	55	SE1606
Herbrandston Dyfed	16	SM8707
Hereford H & W	27	SO5039
Hereson Kent	15	TR3865
Hergest H & W	27	SO2555
Heribusta Highld	90	NG3970
Heriot Loth	76	NT3952
Hermiston Loth	75	NT1870
Hermitage Berks	21	SU5072
Hermitage Dorset	67	NY5095
Hermitage Dorset	9	ST6306
Hermon Dyfed	17	SN2032
Hermon Gwynd	44	SH3868
Herne Kent	15	TR1865
Herne Bay Kent	15	TR1768
Herne Common Kent	15	TR1764
Herne Pound Kent	14	TQ6554
Herner Devon	6	SS5926
Hernhill Kent	15	TR0660
Herodsfoot Cnwll	4	SX2160
Heronden Kent	15	TR2954
Herongate Essex	24	TQ6391
Heronsford Strath	64	NX1283
Herringfleet Suffk	43	TM4797
Herringswell Suffk	32	TL7270
Herrington T & W	69	NZ3443
Hersden Kent	15	TR2062
Hersham Surrey	22	TQ1164
Herstmonceux E Susx	13	TQ6410
Herston Dorset	9	SZ0278
Herston Ork	103	ND4291
Hertford Herts	31	TL3212
Hertford Heath Herts	23	TL3510
Hertingfordbury Herts	23	TL3011
Hesket Newmarket Cumb	59	NK0438
Hesketh Lane Lancs	54	SD6141
Hesleden Dur	62	NZ4438
Heslington N York	56	SE6250
Heslington N York	56	SE6250
Hessay N York	55	SE5253
Hessenford Cnwll	4	SX3057
Hessett Suffk	32	TL9361
Hessle Humb	56	TA0226
Hessle W York	54	SE4217
Heston Gt Lon	22	TQ1277
Hestwall Ork	103	HY2616
Heswall Mersyd	46	SJ2781
Hethe Oxon	29	SP5929
Hethersett Norfk	43	TG1505
Hethersgill Cumb	67	NY4767
Hetherson Green Ches	46	SJ5249
Hethpool Nthumb	77	NT8928
Hett Dur	61	NZ2836
Hetton N York	54	SD9658
Hetton-le-Hole T & W	69	NZ3548
Heugh Nthumb	68	NZ0873
Heugh Head Border	77	NT8762
Heugh-Head Gramp	94	NJ3811
Heveningham Suffk	33	TM3372
Hever Kent	13	TQ4745
Heversham Cumb	59	SD4983
Hevingham Norfk	43	TG2021
Hewas Water Cnwll	3	SW9649
Hewelsfield Gloucs	19	SO5602
Hewish Avon	19	ST4064
Hewish Somset	8	ST4108
Hewood Dorset	8	ST3502
Hextable Kent	23	TQ5170
Hexthorpe S York	49	SE5602
Hexton Herts	30	TL1030
Hexworthy Devon	5	SX6572
Hexworthy M Glam	18	SX3681
Heybridge Essex	24	TL8508
Heybridge Essex	24	TQ6398
Heybrook Bay Devon	4	SX4948
Heydon Cambs	31	TL4340
Heydon Norfk	43	TG1127
Heydour Lincs	40	TF0039
Heylipoll Strath	78	NL9743
Heylor Shet	103	HU2980
Heysham Lancs	53	SD4160
Heyshott W Susx	11	SU8918
Heytesbury Wilts	20	ST9242
Heythrop Oxon	29	SP3527
Heywood Gt Man	54	SD8510
Heywood Wilts	20	ST8753
Hibaldstow Humb	50	SE9702
Hickleton S York	55	SE4805
Hickling Norfk	43	TG4124
Hickling Notts	40	SK6928
Hickling Green Norfk	43	TG4123
Hickstead W Susx	12	TQ2620
Hidcote Bartrim Gloucs	29	SP1742
Hidcote Boyce Gloucs	29	SP1741
High Auldgirth D & G	66	NX9187
High Bankhill Cumb	59	NY5542
High Barrans Cumb	59	NY4200
High Beach Essex	23	TQ4198
High Bentham N York	54	SD6669
High Bickington Devon	6	SS5920
High Biggin Cumb	54	SD5978
High Blantyre Strath	74	NS6756
High Bonnybridge Cent	82	NS9879
High Bray Devon	6	SS6934
High Brooms Kent	13	TQ5841
High Catton Humb	56	SE7153
High Close N York	61	NZ1714
High Coniscliffe Dur	61	NZ2215
High Crosby Cumb	67	NY4559
High Cross Hants	11	SU7126
High Cross Herts	31	TL3618
High Cross Strath	73	NS4046
High Cross W Susx	12	TQ2517

Place	Pg	Grid
High Cross Warwks	29	SP1868
High Disley Ches	48	SJ9784
High Easter Essex	24	TL6214
High Ellington N York	61	SE2083
High Ercall Shrops	37	SJ5917
High Etherley Dur	61	NZ1628
High Ferry Lincs	51	TF3449
High Fremington N York	61	SE0499
High Garrett Essex	24	TL7727
High Grantley N York	55	SE2369
High Green Cumb	59	NY4003
High Green H & W	28	SO8745
High Green Norfk	43	TG1305
High Halden Kent	14	TQ8937
High Halstow Kent	14	TQ7875
High Ham Somset	8	ST4231
High Harrogate N York	55	SE3155
High Hartington Nthumb	68	NZ0288
High Hatton Shrops	37	SJ6124
High Hesket Cumb	67	NY4745
High Hoyland S York	55	SE2710
High Hurstwood E Susx	13	TQ4926
High Hutton N York	56	SE7268
High Ireby Cumb	58	NY2332
High Kilburn N York	62	SE5279
High Lands Dur	61	NZ1225
High Lane Gt Man	48	SJ9585
High Lane H & W	28	SO6760
High Lanes Cnwll	2	SW5637
High Laver Essex	23	TL5208
High Legh Ches	47	SJ7084
High Leven Cleve	62	NZ4512
High Lorton Cumb	58	NY1625
High Marnham Notts	50	SK8070
High Melton S York	49	SE5001
High Mickley Nthumb	68	NZ0761
High Moorsley T & W	62	NZ3445
High Newport T & W	69	NZ3864
High Newton Cumb	59	SD4082
High Newtown By-The-Sea Nthumb	77	NU2325
High Nibthwaite Cumb	58	SD2989
High Offley Staffs	37	SJ7826
High Ongar Essex	24	TL5603
High Onn Staffs	38	SJ8216
High Park Corner Essex	25	TM0320
High Pennyvenie Strath	73	NS4907
High Roding Essex	24	TL6017
High Row Cumb	59	NY3832
High Salvington W Susx	12	TQ1206
High Spen T & W	69	NZ1359
High Street Cnwll	3	SW9653
High Street Kent	15	TR0862
High Street Suffk	33	TM4355
High Town Staffs	38	SJ9912
High Toynton Lincs	51	TF2869
High Trewhitt Nthumb	68	NU0105
High Urpeth Dur	69	NZ2353
High Westwood Dur	69	NZ1356
High Wray Cumb	59	SD3799
High Wych Herts	31	TL4614
High Wycombe Bucks	22	SU8693
Higham Derbys	49	SK4059
Higham Kent	13	TQ6068
Higham Kent	14	TQ7171
Higham Lancs	54	SD8136
Higham S York	55	SE3207
Higham Suffk	25	TM0335
Higham Dykes Nthumb	69	NZ1375
Higham Ferrers Nhants	30	SP9568
Higham Gobion Beds	30	TL1032
Higham Hill Gt Lon	23	TQ3590
Higham on the Hill Leics	39	SP3895
Highampton Devon	6	SS4804
Highams Park Gt Lon	23	TQ3891
Highbridge Somset	19	ST3147
Highbrook W Susx	12	TQ3630
Highbury Gt Lon	23	TQ3186
Highbury Somset	20	ST6849
Highclere Hants	21	SU4360
Highcliffe Dorset	10	SZ2193
Highclifflane Derbys	49	SK2947
Higher Alham Somset	8	ST6841
Higher Bartle Lancs	53	SD5033
Higher Bockhampton Dorset	9	SY7292
Higher Brixham Devon	5	SX9255
Higher Burrowton Devon	7	SY0097
Higher Burwardsley Ches	46	SJ5156
Higher Chillington Somset	8	ST3910
Higher Combe Somset	7	SS9030
Higher Coombe Dorset	8	SY5491
Higher Gabwell Devon	5	SX9169
Higher Green Gt Man	37	SJ7000
Higher Harpers Lancs	54	SD8238
Higher Irlam Gt Man	47	SJ7295
Higher Kingscombe Dorset	8	SY5499
Higher Melcombe Dorset	9	ST7402
Higher Muddiford Devon	6	SS5638
Higher Penwortham Lancs	53	SD5128
Higher Prestacott Devon	6	SX3896
Higher Tale Devon	7	ST0601
Higher Town Cnwll	2	SW8044
Higher Town Cnwll	3	SX0061
Higher Town IOS	2	SV9215
Higher Tregantle M Glam	4	SX3952
Higher Walreddon Devon	4	SX4771
Higher Walton Ches	47	SJ5985
Higher Walton Lancs	53	SD5727
Higher Wambrook Somset	8	ST2908
Higher Waterston Dorset	9	SY7295
Higher Whatcombe Dorset	9	ST8302
Higher Wheelton Lancs	54	SD6022
Higher Wraxhall Dorset	8	ST5601
Higher Wych Ches	46	SJ4943
Highfield T & W	73	NS3150
Highfield T & W	72	NZ1459
Highgate E Susx	13	TQ4233
Highgate Gt Lon	23	TQ2887
Highlane S York	49	SK4082
Highlaws Cumb	67	NY1450
Highleadon Gloucs	28	SO7623
Highleigh W Susx	11	SZ8498
Highmoor Oxon	22	SU7084
Highmoor Oxon	22	SU7085
Highmoor Cross Oxon	22	SU7084
Highnam Gloucs	28	SO7918
Highnam Green Gloucs	28	SO7920
Highstead Kent	15	TQ2166
Highsted Kent	14	TQ9061
Highstreet Green Essex	24	TL7634
Highstreet Green Surrey	12	SU9835
Hightae D & G	67	NY0979
Hightown Mersyd	53	SD3005
Hightown Mersyd	46	SD3005
Hightown Green Suffk	32	TL9756
Highweek Devon	5	SX8472
Highwood Hill Gt Lon	23	TQ2193
Highworth Wilts	20	SU2092
Hilden Park Kent	13	TQ5746
Hildenborough Kent	13	TQ5648
Hildersham Cambs	31	TL5448
Hilderstone Staffs	38	SJ9434
Hilderthorpe Humb	57	TA1765
Hilfield Dorset	8	ST6305
Hilgay Norfk	41	TL6298
Hill Avon	19	ST6495
Hill Devon	7	SS6926
Hill Warwks	29	SP4567
Hill Brow Hants	11	SU7826
Hill Chorlton Staffs	37	SJ7937
Hill Common Somset	8	ST1526
Hill Dyke Lincs	51	TF3547
Hill End Fife	82	NT0396
Hill End Gloucs	28	SO9037
Hill Head Hants	11	SU5402
Hill Ridware Staffs	38	SK0718
Hill Side W York	55	SE1717
Hill The Cumb	58	SD1783
Hill Top Dur	60	NY9984
Hill Top W York	55	SE3315
Hill View Dorset	9	SY9896
Hill of Beath Fife	82	NT1590
Hill of Fearn Highld	97	NH8377
Hillam N York	55	SE5029
Hillberry IOM	52	SC3879
Hillborough Kent	15	TR2167
Hillbrae Gramp	95	NJ6926
Hillbutts Dorset	9	ST9901
Hillcott Wilts	20	SU1158

225

Hillend Hythe End

Hillend *Fife* 82 NT1483
Hillend *Loth* 75 NT2566
Hillend *Strath* 74 NS8267
Hillend *W Glam* 17 SS4291
Hillesden *Bucks* 30 SP6828
Hillesley *Avon* 20 ST7689
Hillfarrance *Somset* 8 ST1624
Hillfoot *Strath* 74 NS5472
Hillhead *Devon* 5 SX9053
Hillhead *Strath* 75 NS9840
Hillhead of Cocklaw *Gramp* 95 NK0844
Hilliclay *Highld* 100 ND1764
Hillingdon *Gt Lon* 22 TQ0783
Hillington *Norfk* 42 TF7225
Hillington *Strath* 74 NS5164
Hillmorton *Warwks* 39 SP5373
Hillowtan *D & G* 66 NX7763
Hillpound *Hants* 11 SU5815
Hills Town *Derbys* 49 SK4869
Hillside *Gramp* 89 NO9197
Hillside *T & W* 89 NO7060
Hillstreet *Hants* 10 SU3416
Hillswick *Shet* 103 HU2877
Hilltown *Devon* 4 SX5380
Hillwell *Shet* 103 HU3714
Hilmarton *Wilts* 20 SU0175
Hilperton *Wilts* 20 ST8759
Hilsea *Hants* 11 SU6503
Hilston *Humb* 57 TA2833
Hiltingbury *Hants* 10 SU4222
Hilton *Border* 77 NT8750
Hilton *Cambs* 31 TL2966
Hilton *Cleve* 62 NZ4611
Hilton *Cumb* 60 NY7320
Hilton *Derbys* 39 SK2430
Hilton *Dorset* 9 ST7802
Hilton *Dur* 61 NZ1621
Hilton *Shrops* 37 SO7795
Hilton of Cadboll *Highld* 97 NH8776
Himbleton *H & W* 28 SO9458
Himley *Staffs* 38 SO8891
Hinckley *Leics* 39 SP4294
Hinderclay *Suffk* 32 TM0276
Hinderwell *N York* 63 NZ7916
Hindhead *Surrey* 11 SU8835
Hindle Fold *Lancs* 54 SD7332
Hindley *Gt Man* 47 SD6204
Hindlip *H & W* 28 SO8758
Hindolveston *Norfk* 42 TG0329
Hindon *Wilts* 9 ST9032
Hindringham *Norfk* 42 TF9836
Hingham *Norfk* 42 TG0202
Hinnington *Shrops* 37 SJ7404
Hinstock *Shrops* 37 SJ6926
Hintlesham *Suffk* 32 TM0843
Hinton *Avon* 20 ST7376
Hinton *H & W* 27 SO3338
Hinton *Hants* 10 SZ2095
Hinton *Shrops* 36 SJ4008
Hinton Admiral *Hants* 10 SZ2196
Hinton Ampner *Hants* 11 SU5927
Hinton Blewett *Somset* 19 ST5956
Hinton Charterhouse *Avon* 20 ST7758
Hinton Marsh *Hants* 11 SU5927
Hinton Martell *Dorset* 9 SU0106
Hinton Parva *Wilts* 21 SU2283
Hinton St. George *Somset* 8 ST4212
Hinton St. Mary *Dorset* 9 ST7816
Hinton Waldrist *Oxon* 21 SU3799
Hinton on the Green *H & W* 28 SP0244
Hinton-in-the-Hedges *Nhants* 29 SP5636
Hints *Staffs* 38 SK1503
Hinwick *Beds* 30 SP9361
Hinxhill *Kent* 15 TR0442
Hinxton *Cambs* 31 TL4945
Hinxton *Cambs* 31 TL4945
Hinxworth *Herts* 31 TL2340
Hipperholme *W York* 55 SE1225
Hipswell *N York* 61 SE1798
Hirn *Gramp* 89 NJ7200
Hirnant *Powys* 35 SN8869
Hirnant *Powys* 36 SJ0423
Hirst *Nthumb* 69 NZ2787
Hirst Courtney *N York* 56 SE6124
Hirwaun *M Glam* 26 SN9605
Hiscott *Devon* 6 SS5426
Histon *Cambs* 31 TL4363
Hitcham *Suffk* 32 TL9851
Hitcham Causeway *Suffk* 32 TL9852
Hitcham Street *Suffk* 32 TL9851
Hitchin *Herts* 31 TL1829
Hither Green *Gt Lon* 23 TQ3874
Hittisleigh Cross *Devon* 7 SX7394
Hive *Humb* 56 SE8230
Hixon *Staffs* 38 SK0025
Hoaden *Kent* 15 TR2659
Hoaldalbert *Gwent* 27 SO3923
Hoar Cross *Staffs* 38 SK1323
Hoarwithy *H & W* 27 SO5429
Hoath *Kent* 15 TR2064
Hobarris *Shrops* 36 SO3178
Hobkirk *Border* 67 NT5811
Hobson *Dur* 69 NZ1755
Hoby *Leics* 39 SK6617
Hoccum *Shrops* 37 SO7393
Hockering *Norfk* 42 TG0713
Hockerton *Notts* 49 SK7156
Hockley *Essex* 24 TQ8392
Hockley Heath *W Mids* 38 SP1572
Hockliffe *Beds* 30 SP9726
Hockwold cum Wilton *Norfk* 32 TL7288
Hockworthy *Devon* 7 ST0319
Hoddesdon *Herts* 23 TL3708
Hoddleston *Lancs* 54 SD7122
Hoddom Cross *D & G* 67 NY1873
Hoddom Mains *D & G* 67 NY1572
Hodgeston *Dyfed* 16 SS0399
Hodnet *Shrops* 37 SJ6128
Hodsall Street *Kent* 14 TQ6263
Hodsock *Notts* 49 SK6185
Hodson *Wilts* 21 SU1787
Hodthorpe *Derbys* 49 SK5376
Hoe *Norfk* 42 TF9916
Hog Hill *E Susx* 14 TQ8816
Hogben's Hill *Kent* 15 TR0356
Hoggeston *Bucks* 30 SP8024
Hoghton *Lancs* 54 SD6125
Hognaston *Derbys* 48 SK2350
Hogrill's End *Warwks* 39 SP2292
Hogsthorpe *Lincs* 51 TF5372
Holbeach *Lincs* 41 TF3624
Holbeach Clough *Lincs* 41 TF3427
Holbeach Drove *Lincs* 41 TF3212
Holbeach Hurn *Lincs* 41 TF3926
Holbeach St. Johns *Lincs* 41 TF3518
Holbeach St. Mark's *Lincs* 41 TF3731
Holbeach St. Matthew *Lincs* 41 TF4132
Holbeck *Notts* 49 SK5473
Holbeck Woodhouse *Notts* 49 SK5373
Holberrow Green *H & W* 28 SP0259
Holborn *Gt Lon* 23 TQ3181
Holbrook *Derbys* 49 SK3644
Holbrook *S York* 49 SK4581
Holbrook *Suffk* 25 TM1736
Holbrook Moor *Derbys* 49 SK3645
Holbury *Hants* 10 SU4303
Holcombe *Devon* 5 SX9574
Holcombe *Somset* 20 ST6649
Holcombe Burnell Barton *Devon* 5 SX8591
Holcombe Rogus *Devon* 7 ST0519
Holcot *Nhants* 30 SP7969
Holden *Lancs* 54 SD8833
Holden *Lancs* 54 SD7749
Holdenby *Nhants* 30 SP6967
Holder's Green *Essex* 24 TL6329
Holdgate *Shrops* 37 SO5689
Holdingham *Lincs* 50 TF0547
Holditch *Dorset* 8 ST3402
Hole Street *W Susx* 12 TQ1414
Holehouse *Derbys* 48 SK0092
Holford *Somset* 19 ST1541
Holgate *N York* 56 SE5851
Holker *Cumb* 59 SD3677
Holkham *Norfk* 42 TF8944
Hollacombe *Devon* 6 SS3703
Hollacombe *Devon* 7 SS8000
Holland Fen *Lincs* 51 TF2349
Holland-on-Sea *Essex* 25 TM1916
Hollandstoun *Ork* 103 HY7553
Hollesley *Suffk* 33 TM3544
Hollicombe *Devon* 5 SX8763
Hollingbourne *Kent* 14 TQ8455
Hollingbury *E Susx* 12 TQ0107
Hollingthorpe *W York* 55 SE3832
Hollington *Bucks* 30 SP8727
Hollington *Derbys* 48 SK2239
Hollington *Staffs* 48 SK0539
Hollingworth *Gt Man* 48 SK0096
Hollins End *S York* 49 SK3883
Hollins Green *Ches* 47 SJ6990
Hollinsclough *Staffs* 48 SK0666
Hollinswood *Shrops* 37 SJ7009
Hollinwood *Shrops* 37 SJ5236
Holllingrove *E Susx* 14 TQ6821
Hollocombe *Devon* 7 SS6311
Holloway *Derbys* 49 SK3256
Holloway *Gt Lon* 23 TQ3086
Hollowell *Nhants* 30 SP6972
Hollowmoor Heath *Ches* 46 SJ4868
Hollybush *Gwent* 19 SO1603
Hollybush *H & W* 28 SO7636
Hollybush *Strath* 73 NS3915
Hollym *Humb* 57 TA3425
Holmacott *Devon* 6 SS5028
Holmbridge *W York* 55 SE1106
Holmbury St. Mary *Surrey* 12 TQ1144
Holmbush *Cnwll* 3 SX0352
Holmcroft *Staffs* 38 SJ9125
Holme *Cambs* 40 TL1987
Holme *Cumb* 59 SD5278
Holme *Humb* 56 SE9106
Holme *N York* 62 SE3582
Holme *Notts* 50 SK8059
Holme *W York* 55 SE1005
Holme Chapel *Lancs* 54 SD8728
Holme Green *N York* 56 SE5541
Holme Hale *Norfk* 42 TF8807
Holme Lacy *H & W* 27 SO5535
Holme Marsh *H & W* 27 SO3454
Holme Pierrepont *Notts* 49 SK6238
Holme Street *Cumb* 67 NY1047
Holme next the Sea *Norfk* 42 TF7043
Holme on the Wolds *Humb* 56 SE9646
Holme upon Spalding Moor *Humb* 56 SE8138
Holmer *H & W* 27 SO5042
Holmer Green *Bucks* 22 SU9097
Holmes Chapel *Ches* 47 SJ7667
Holmes Hill *E Susx* 13 TQ5313
Holmesfield *Derbys* 49 SK3277
Holmeswood *Lancs* 53 SD4316
Holmethorpe *Surrey* 12 TQ2851
Holmewood *Derbys* 49 SK4365
Holmfirth *W York* 55 SE1408
Holmhead *Strath* 74 NS5620
Holmpton *Humb* 57 TA3623
Holmrook *Cumb* 58 SD0799
Holmsey Green *Suffk* 32 TL6977
Holmwood *Surrey* 12 TQ1647
Holne *Devon* 5 SX7069
Holnest *Dorset* 9 ST6509
Holnicote *Somset* 7 SS9146
Holsworthy *Devon* 6 SS3403
Holsworthy Beacon *Devon* 6 SS3508
Holt *Clwyd* 46 SJ4053
Holt *Dorset* 9 SU0203
Holt *H & W* 28 SO8262
Holt *Norfk* 42 TG0838
Holt *Wilts* 20 ST8661
Holt End *H & W* 28 SP0769
Holt Green *Lancs* 46 SD3905
Holt Heath *H & W* 28 SO8163
Holtby *N York* 56 SE6754
Holton *Oxon* 29 SP6006
Holton *Oxon* 29 SP6006
Holton *Somset* 9 ST6826
Holton *Suffk* 33 TM4077
Holton Heath *Dorset* 9 SY9491
Holton St. Mary *Suffk* 25 TM0537
Holton cum Beckering *Lincs* 50 TF1181
Holton le Clay *Lincs* 51 TA2802
Holton le Moor *Lincs* 50 TF0797
Holwell *Dorset* 9 ST7011
Holwell *Herts* 31 TL1633
Holwell *Leics* 40 SK7323
Holwell *Oxon* 29 SP2309
Holwick *Dur* 60 NY9126
Holy Cross *H & W* 28 SO9256
Holy Island *Nthumb* 77 NU1241
Holybourne *Hants* 11 SU7340
Holyhead *Gwynd* 44 SH2482
Holylee *Border* 83 NT3978
Holymoorside *Derbys* 49 SK3368
Holystone *Nthumb* 68 NT9502
Holytown *Strath* 74 NS7660
Holywell *Cambs* 31 TL3370
Holywell *Clwyd* 46 SJ1875
Holywell *Cnwll* 2 SW7658
Holywell *Dorset* 9 ST5904
Holywell Green *W York* 55 SE0819
Holywell Lake *Somset* 8 ST1020
Holywell Row *Suffk* 32 TL7077
Holywood *D & G* 66 NX9480
Homer *Shrops* 37 SJ6101
Homer Green *Mersyd* 46 SD3402
Homersfield *Suffk* 33 TM2885
Homeston *Strath* 72 NR6716
Homington *Wilts* 10 SU1226
Honey Tye *Suffk* 25 TL9535
Honeybourne *H & W* 28 SP1144
Honeychurch *Devon* 6 SS6203
Honeystreet *Wilts* 20 SU1061
Honiley *Warwks* 39 SP2472
Honing *Norfk* 43 TG3227
Honingham *Norfk* 43 TG1011
Honington *Lincs* 50 SK9443
Honington *Suffk* 32 TL9174
Honington *Warwks* 29 SP2642
Honiton *Devon* 8 ST1600
Honley *W York* 55 SE1311
Hoo *Kent* 23 TQ2964
Hoo *Kent* 14 TQ7872
Hoo End *Herts* 31 TL1820
Hoo Green *Ches* 47 SJ7182
Hooe *Devon* 4 SX4952
Hooe *E Susx* 14 TQ6809
Hooe Common *E Susx* 14 TQ6910
Hoohill *Lancs* 53 SD3237
Hook *Cambs* 41 TL4393
Hook *Dyfed* 16 SM9811
Hook *Hants* 22 SU7254
Hook *Humb* 56 SE7525
Hook *Kent* 14 TQ6171
Hook *Surrey* 23 TQ1864
Hook *Wilts* 20 SU0784
Hook Green *Kent* 13 TQ6535
Hook Norton *Oxon* 29 SP3533
Hookagate *Shrops* 36 SJ4508
Hooke *Dorset* 8 ST5300
Hookway *Devon* 7 SX8598
Hooton Levitt *S York* 49 SK5291
Hooton Pagnell *S York* 55 SE4808
Hooton Roberts *S York* 49 SK4897
Hope *Clwyd* 46 SJ3158
Hope *Derbys* 48 SK1783
Hope *Devon* 5 SX6740
Hope *Shrops* 37 SO5974
Hope *Staffs* 48 SK1254
Hope Bowdler *Shrops* 37 SO4792
Hope End Green *Essex* 24 TL5720
Hope Mansell *H & W* 27 SO6219
Hope under Dinmore *H & W* 27 SO5052
Hopefield *Highld* 93 NH7359
Hopehouse *Border* 75 NT2916
Hopeman *Gramp* 93 NJ1469
Hopes Nose *Devon* 5 SX9563
Hopesay *Shrops* 36 SO3983
Hopperton *N York* 55 SE4258
Hopstone *Shrops* 37 SO7894
Hopton *Derbys* 49 SK2653
Hopton *Staffs* 38 SJ9426
Hopton *Suffk* 32 TL9979
Hopton Cangeford *Shrops* 37 SO5480
Hopton Castle *Shrops* 36 SO3678
Hopton Wafers *Shrops* 37 SO6376
Hopton on Sea *Norfk* 43 TG5300
Hoptonheath *Shrops* 36 SO3877
Hopwas *Staffs* 38 SK1705
Hopwood *H & W* 38 SP0375
Horam *E Susx* 13 TQ5717
Horbling *Lincs* 40 TF1135
Horbury *W York* 55 SE2918
Horderley *Shrops* 36 SO4087
Hordle *Hants* 10 SZ2795
Hordley *Shrops* 36 SJ3731
Horeb *Dyfed* 17 SN4905
Horfield *Avon* 19 ST5877
Horham *Suffk* 33 TM2072
Horkesley Green *Essex* 25 TL9832
Horkesley Heath *Essex* 25 TL9829
Horkstow *Humb* 56 SE9817
Horkstow *Humb* 56 SE9818
Horley *Oxon* 29 SP4144
Horley *Surrey* 12 TQ2843
Hornby *Lancs* 54 SD5868
Hornby *N York* 62 NZ3605
Hornby *N York* 61 SE2293
Horncastle *Lincs* 51 TF2669
Hornchurch *Gt Lon* 23 TQ5387
Horncliffe *Nthumb* 77 NT9249
Horndean *Border* 77 NT9049
Horndean *Hants* 11 SU7013
Horndon *Devon* 4 SX5080
Horndon on the Hill *Essex* 24 TQ6783
Horne *Surrey* 12 TQ3344
Horner *Somset* 7 SS9045
Horners Green *Suffk* 32 TL9641
Horning *Norfk* 43 TG3417
Horninghold *Leics* 40 SP8097
Horninglow *Staffs* 39 SK2425
Horningsea *Cambs* 31 TL4962
Horningtoft *Norfk* 42 TF9323
Horns Cross *Devon* 6 SS3823
Hornsby *Cumb* 67 NY5050
Hornsea *Humb* 57 TA1947
Hornsey *Gt Lon* 23 TQ3089
Hornton *Oxon* 29 SP3945
Horra *Shet* 103 HU4693
Horrabridge *Devon* 4 SX5170
Horridge *Devon* 5 SX7674
Horringer *Suffk* 32 TL8261
Horrocksford *Lancs* 54 SD7543
Horsebridge *Devon* 4 SX4074
Horsebridge *E Susx* 13 TQ5810
Horsebridge *E Susx* 13 TQ5811
Horsebridge *Hants* 10 SU3430
Horseheath *Cambs* 31 TL6147
Horsehouse *N York* 61 SE0480
Horsell *Surrey* 22 TQ0059
Horseman's Green *Clwyd* 36 SJ4441
Horsenden *Bucks* 22 SP7902
Horsepath *Oxon* 29 SP5704
Horseshoes *Wilts* 20 ST9159
Horsey *Norfk* 43 TG4622
Horsey *Somset* 19 ST3239
Horsford *Norfk* 43 TG1916
Horsforth *W York* 55 SE2337
Horsham *H & W* 28 SO7358
Horsham *W Susx* 12 TQ1730
Horsham St. Faith *Norfk* 43 TG2114
Horsington *Lincs* 50 TF1868
Horsington *Somset* 9 ST7023
Horsley *Gloucs* 20 ST8397
Horsley *Nthumb* 68 NY8496
Horsley *Nthumb* 68 NZ0965
Horsley Woodhouse *Derbys* 49 SK3945
Horsleycross Street *Essex* 25 TM1228
Horsleyhill *Border* 76 NT5319
Horsmonden *Kent* 14 TQ7040
Horstead *Norfk* 43 TG2619
Horsted Keynes *W Susx* 13 TQ3828
Horton *Avon* 20 ST7584
Horton *Berks* 22 TQ0175
Horton *Bucks* 30 SP9219
Horton *Dorset* 9 SU0307
Horton *Gt Lon* 31 TL1962
Horton *Lancs* 54 SD8550
Horton *Nhants* 30 SP8154
Horton *Shrops* 37 SJ6814
Horton *Somset* 8 ST3214
Horton *Staffs* 48 SJ9457
Horton *W Glam* 17 SS4785
Horton *Wilts* 20 SU0463
Horton Green *Ches* 46 SJ4549
Horton Heath *Hants* 10 SU4917
Horton Kirby *Kent* 14 TQ5668
Horton in Ribblesdale *N York* 54 SD8172
Horton-cum-Studley *Oxon* 29 SP5912
Horwich *Gt Man* 54 SD6311
Horwood *Devon* 6 SS5027
Hoscar *Lancs* 53 SD4711
Hoscote *Border* 67 NT3911
Hose *Leics* 40 SK7329
Hoses *Cumb* 58 SD2393
Hosh *Tays* 82 NN8523
Hoswick *Shet* 103 HU4123
Hotham *Humb* 56 SE8934
Hothfield *Kent* 15 TQ9644
Hoton *Leics* 39 SK5722
Hott *Nthumb* 68 NY7785
Houdston *Strath* 64 NX2097
Hough *Ches* 47 SJ7151
Hough Green *Ches* 46 SJ4886
Hough-on-the-Hill *Lincs* 50 SK9246
Hougham *Lincs* 50 SK8844
Hougharry *W Isls* 102 NF7071
Houghton *Cambs* 31 TL2872
Houghton *Dyfed* 16 SM9807
Houghton *Hants* 10 SU3432
Houghton *W Susx* 12 TQ0111
Houghton Conquest *Beds* 30 TL0441
Houghton Green *E Susx* 14 TQ9222
Houghton Regis *Beds* 30 TL0123
Houghton St. Giles *Norfk* 42 TF9235
Houghton le Spring *T & W* 69 NZ3350
Houghton on the Hill *Leics* 39 SK6703
Hound Green *Hants* 22 SU7259
Houndslow *Border* 76 NT6347
Houndwood *Border* 77 NT8463
Hounslow *Gt Lon* 22 TQ1375
Hounslow Green *Essex* 24 TL6518
Househill *Highld* 93 NH8855
Houses Hill *W York* 55 SE1916
Housieside *Gramp* 95 NJ8926
Houston *Strath* 73 NS4067
Houstry *Highld* 100 ND1535
Houton *Ork* 103 HY3104
Hove *E Susx* 12 TQ2804
Hoveringham *Notts* 49 SK6946
Hoveton *Norfk* 43 TG3018
Hovingham *N York* 62 SE6675
How *Cumb* 67 NY5056
How Caple *H & W* 27 SO6030
Howden *Humb* 56 SE7428
Howden-le-Wear *Dur* 61 NZ1633
Howe *Cumb* 59 SD4588
Howe *Highld* 100 ND3061
Howe *N York* 62 SE3580
Howe *Norfk* 43 TM2799
Howe Green *Essex* 24 TL7503
Howe Street *Essex* 24 TL6914
Howe Street *Essex* 24 TL6934
Howe of Teuchar *Gramp* 95 NJ7946
Howegreen *Essex* 24 TL8301
Howell *Lincs* 50 TF1346
Howes *D & G* 67 NY1867
Howgate *Loth* 75 NT2457
Howick *Nthumb* 77 NU2417
Howle *Dur* 61 NZ0925
Howle *Shrops* 37 SJ6924
Howle Hill *H & W* 27 SO6020
Howlett End *Essex* 24 TL5834
Howley *Somset* 8 ST2609
Howmore *W Isls* 102 NF7636
Hownam *Border* 76 NT7719
Howrigg *Cumb* 67 NY3247
Howsham *Humb* 57 TA0404
Howsham *N York* 56 SE7362
Howt Green *Kent* 14 TQ8964
Howtel *Nthumb* 77 NT8934
Howwood *Strath* 73 NS3960
Hoxne *Suffk* 33 TM1877
Hoylake *Mersyd* 46 SJ2189
Hoyland Common *S York* 49 SE3600
Hoyland Nether *S York* 49 SE3600
Hoyland Swaine *S York* 55 SE2604
Hubberston *Dyfed* 16 SM8806
Huby *N York* 55 SE2747
Huby *N York* 56 SE5665
Hucclecote *Gloucs* 28 SO8717
Hucking *Kent* 14 TQ8458
Hucknall *Notts* 49 SK5349
Huddersfield *W York* 55 SE1416
Huddington *H & W* 28 SO9457
Hudscott *Devon* 7 SS6525
Hudswell *N York* 61 NZ1400
Huggate *Humb* 56 SE8855
Hugh Town *IOS* 2 SV9010
Hughenden Valley *Bucks* 22 SU8597
Hughley *Shrops* 37 SO5698
Huish *Devon* 6 SS5311
Huish *Wilts* 20 SU1463
Huish Champflower *Somset* 7 ST0429
Huish Episcopi *Somset* 8 ST4226
Hulcott *Bucks* 30 SP8516
Hulham *Devon* 3 SX0182
Hulland *Derbys* 48 SK2446
Hulland Ward *Derbys* 48 SK2547
Hullavington *Wilts* 20 ST8982
Hullbridge *Essex* 24 TQ8095
Hulme *Gt Man* 47 SJ8396
Hulme *Staffs* 48 SJ9345
Hulme End *Staffs* 48 SK1059
Hulme Walfield *Ches* 47 SJ8465
Hulver Street *Suffk* 33 TM4686
Hulverstone *IOW* 10 SZ3984
Humber Court *H & W* 27 SO5356
Humberston *Humb* 57 TA3105
Humberstone *Leics* 39 SK6305
Humbie *Loth* 76 NT4662
Humbleton *Humb* 57 TA2234
Humby *Lincs* 40 TF0032
Hume *Border* 76 NT7041
Humshaugh *Nthumb* 68 NY9171
Huna *Highld* 100 ND3573
Huncote *Leics* 39 SP5197
Hundalee *Border* 76 NT6418
Hundall *Derbys* 49 SK3877
Hunderthwaite *Dur* 61 NY9821
Hundleby *Lincs* 51 TF3866
Hundleton *Dyfed* 16 SM9600
Hundred End *Lancs* 53 SD4122
Hungarton *Leics* 40 SK6907
Hungerford *Berks* 21 SU3368
Hungerford *Somset* 7 ST0440
Hungerford Newtown *Berks* 21 SU3571
Hungerstone *H & W* 27 SO4435
Hungryhatton *Shrops* 37 SJ6726
Hunmanby *N York* 63 TA0977
Hunningham *Warwks* 29 SP3768
Hunny Hill *IOW* 10 SZ4989
Hunsdon *Herts* 31 TL4114
Hunsingore *N York* 55 SE4253
Hunslet *W York* 55 SE3130
Hunsonby *Cumb* 59 NY5835
Hunstanton *Norfk* 42 TF6740
Hunstanworth *Dur* 68 NY9448
Hunston *Suffk* 32 TL9768
Hunston *W Susx* 11 SU8601
Hunstrete *Avon* 19 ST6462
Hunsworth *W York* 55 SE1827
Hunters Quay *Strath* 80 NS1879
Hunterston *Ches* 47 SJ6946
Hunthill Lodge *Tays* 89 NO4771
Huntingdon *Cambs* 31 TL2471
Huntingdon *H & W* 27 SO2553
Huntingfield *Suffk* 33 TM3374
Huntingford *Dorset* 9 ST8129
Huntington *Loth* 76 NT4874
Huntington *N York* 56 SE6156
Huntington *N York* 56 SE6156
Huntington *Staffs* 38 SJ9713
Huntingtower *Tays* 82 NO0725
Huntley *Gloucs* 28 SO7219
Huntly *Gramp* 94 NJ5339
Hunton *Hants* 21 SU4840
Hunton *Kent* 14 TQ7149
Hunton *N York* 61 SE1892
Hunton Bridge *Herts* 22 TL0900
Huntscott *Somset* 7 SS9244
Huntsham *Devon* 7 ST0020
Huntshaw *Devon* 6 SS5023
Huntspill *Somset* 19 ST3045
Huntstile *Somset* 8 ST2633
Huntworth *Somset* 8 ST3134
Huntworth *Somset* 8 ST3134
Hunwick *Dur* 61 NZ1832
Hunworth *Norfk* 42 TG0635
Hurdcott *Wilts* 10 SU1633
Hurdsfield *Ches* 48 SJ9274
Hurley *Warwks* 39 SP2495
Hurley Bottom *Berks* 22 SU8283
Hurley Common *Warwks* 39 SP2496
Hurlford *Strath* 73 NS4536
Hurlston Green *Lancs* 53 SD4011
Hurn *Dorset* 10 SZ1296
Hurn's Head *Lincs* 51 TF4248
Hursebridge *Shrops* 36 SJ3606
Hursley *Hants* 10 SU4225
Hurst *Berks* 22 SU7973
Hurst Green *E Susx* 14 TQ7327
Hurst Green *Essex* 30 TL0916
Hurst Green *Lancs* 54 SD6838
Hurst Green *Surrey* 13 TQ3951
Hurst Hill *W Mids* 38 SO9394
Hurst Wickham *W Susx* 12 TQ2916
Hurstbourne Priors *Hants* 21 SU4346
Hurstbourne Tarrant *Hants* 21 SU3853
Hurstley *H & W* 27 SO3548
Hurstwood *Lancs* 54 SD8831
Hurtiso *Ork* 103 HY5001
Hurtmore *Surrey* 12 SU9545
Hurworth-on-Tees *Dur* 61 NZ3010
Husbands Bosworth *Leics* 39 SP6484
Husborne Crawley *Beds* 30 SP9535
Husinish *W Isls* 102 NA9812
Husthwaite *N York* 62 SE5175
Hut Green *N York* 56 SE5623
Huthwaite *Notts* 49 SK4659
Huttoft *Lincs* 51 TF5176
Hutton *Avon* 19 ST3458
Hutton *Border* 77 NT9053
Hutton *Essex* 24 TQ6395
Hutton *Humb* 56 TA0253
Hutton *Lancs* 53 SD4926
Hutton Bonville *N York* 62 NZ3300
Hutton Buscel *N York* 63 SE9784
Hutton Conyers *N York* 62 SE3273
Hutton End *Cumb* 59 NY4538
Hutton Henry *Dur* 62 NZ4236
Hutton Lowcross *Cleve* 62 NZ5913
Hutton Magna *Dur* 61 NZ1212
Hutton Mulgrave *N York* 63 NZ8310
Hutton Roof *Cumb* 59 SD5777
Hutton Roof *Cumb* 59 NY3734
Hutton Rudby *N York* 62 NZ4606
Hutton Sessay *N York* 62 SE4776
Hutton Wandesley *N York* 55 SE5050
Hutton-le-Hole *N York* 62 SE7090
Huxham *Devon* 7 SX9497
Huxley *Ches* 46 SJ5161
Huyton *Mersyd* 46 SJ4490
Hycemoor *Cumb* 58 SD0989
Hyde *Gt Man* 48 SJ9494
Hyde End *Berks* 21 SU6266
Hyde Heath *Bucks* 22 SP9300
Hyde Lea *Staffs* 38 SJ9020
Hydestile *Surrey* 12 SU9740
Hynish *Strath* 78 NL9839
Hyssington *Powys* 36 SO3194
Hythe *Hants* 10 SU4207
Hythe *Kent* 15 TR1634
Hythe End *Berks* 22 TQ0172

Ibberton Kimberworth

I

Ibberton *Dorset* 9 ST7807
Ible *Derbys* 48 SK2457
Ibsley *Hants* 10 SU1509
Ibstock *Leics* 39 SK4010
Ibstone *Bucks* 22 SU7593
Ibthorpe *Hants* 21 SU3753
Iburndale *N York* 63 NZ8707
Ibworth *Hants* 21 SU5654
Ickburgh *Norfk* 42 TL8195
Ickenham *Gt Lon* 22 TQ0886
Ickford *Bucks* 29 SP6407
Ickham *Kent* 15 TR2158
Ickleford *Herts* 31 TL1831
Icklesham *E Susx* 14 TQ8716
Ickleton *Cambs* 31 TL4943
Icklingham *Suffk* 32 TL7772
Ickornshaw *N York* 54 SD9643
Ickwell Green *Beds* 30 TL1545
Icomb *Gloucs* 29 SP2122
Idbury *Oxon* 29 SP2320
Iddesleigh *Devon* 5 SS5708
Ide *Devon* 5 SX8990
Ide Hill *Kent* 13 TQ4851
Ideford *Devon* 5 SX8977
Iden *E Susx* 14 TQ9123
Iden Green *Kent* 14 TQ7437
Iden Green *Kent* 14 TQ8031
Idle *W York* 55 SE1737
Idless *Cnwll* 2 SW8247
Idlicote *Warwks* 29 SP2844
Idmiston *Wilts* 10 SU1937
Idridgehay *Derbys* 49 SK2849
Idrigill *Highld* 90 NG3863
Idstone *Oxon* 21 SU2584
Idvies *Tays* 89 NO5347
Iffley *Oxon* 21 SP5303
Ifield *W Susx* 12 TQ2537
Iford *Dorset* 10 SZ1493
Iford *E Susx* 13 TQ4007
Ifton *Gwent* 19 ST4688
Ifton Heath *Shrops* 36 SJ3337
Ightfield *Shrops* 37 SJ5938
Iken *Suffk* 33 TM4156
Ilam *Staffs* 48 SK1350
Ilchester *Somset* 8 ST5222
Ilderton *Nthumb* 77 NU0121
Ilford *Gt Lon* 23 TQ4486
Ilfracombe *Devon* 6 SS5147
Ilkeston *Derbys* 49 SK4642
Ilketshall St. Andrew *Suffk* 33 TM3887
Ilketshall St. Margaret *Suffk* 33 TM3485
Ilkley *W York* 55 SE1147
Illey *W Mids* 38 SO9881
Illston on the Hill *Leics* 40 SP7099
Ilmer *Bucks* 22 SP7605
Ilmington *Warwks* 29 SP2143
Ilsington *Devon* 5 SX7876
Ilston *W Glam* 17 SS5590
Ilton *N York* 61 SE1878
Ilton *Somset* 8 ST3517
Imachar *Strath* 72 NR8640
Immingham *Humb* 57 TA1714
Immingham Dock *Humb* 57 TA1916
Ince *Ches* 46 SJ4576
Ince Blundell *Mersyd* 46 SD3203
Ince-in-Makerfield *Gt Man* 47 SD5904
Inchbae Lodge *Highld* 92 NH4069
Inchbare *Tays* 89 NO6065
Inchberry *Gramp* 94 NJ3055
Inchinnan *Strath* 73 NS4868
Inchlaggan *Highld* 86 NH1801
Inchmagranachan *Tays* 88 NO0044
Inchmichael *Tays* 83 NO2425
Inchnacardoch *Highld* 92 NH3810
Inchnadamph *Highld* 96 NC2522
Inchture *Tays* 83 NO2728
Inchvuilt *Highld* 92 NH2438
Inchyra *Tays* 82 NO1820
Indian Queens *Cnwll* 3 SW9159
Ingatestone *Essex* 24 TQ6499
Ingbirchworth *S York* 55 SE2205
Ingestre *Staffs* 38 SJ9724
Ingham *Lincs* 50 SK9483
Ingham *Norfk* 43 TG3926
Ingham *Suffk* 32 TL8570
Ingham Corner *Norfk* 43 TG3927
Ingleby *Derbys* 39 SK3426
Ingleby Arncliffe *N York* 62 NZ4400
Ingleby Greenhow *N York* 62 NZ5806
Ingleigh Green *Devon* 6 SS6007
Inglesbatch *Avon* 20 ST7061
Inglesham *Wilts* 21 SU2098
Ingleston *D & G* 66 NX9765
Ingleton *Dur* 61 NZ1720
Ingleton *N York* 54 SD6972
Inglewhite *Lancs* 53 SD5440
Ingliston *Tays* 88 NO4248
Ingoe *Nthumb* 68 NZ0374
Ingoldisthorpe *Norfk* 42 TF6832
Ingoldmells *Lincs* 51 TF5668
Ingoldsby *Lincs* 40 TF0130
Ingon *Warwks* 29 SP2158
Ingram *Nthumb* 77 NU0116
Ingrow *W York* 55 SE0539
Ingst *Avon* 19 ST5887
Ingst *Avon* 19 ST5887
Ingthorpe *Leics* 40 SK9908
Ingworth *Norfk* 43 TG1929
Inkberrow *H & W* 28 SP0157
Inkerman *Dur* 61 NZ1140
Inkhorn *Gramp* 95 NJ9239
Inkpen *Berks* 21 SU3664
Inkstack *Highld* 100 ND2570
Innellan *Strath* 73 NS1470
Innerleithen *Border* 75 NT3336
Innerleven *Fife* 83 NO3700
Innermessan *D & G* 64 NX0863
Innerwick *Loth* 76 NT7273
Innesmill *Gramp* 94 NJ2863
Insch *Gramp* 94 NJ6328
Insh *Highld* 87 NH8101
Inskip *Lancs* 53 SD4637
Instow *Devon* 6 SS4730
Insworke *Cnwll* 4 SX4252
Intake *S York* 49 SK3884
Intake *S York* 49 SK3884
Inver *Gramp* 88 NO2393
Inver *Highld* 97 NH8682
Inver *Tays* 88 NO0142
Inver-Boyndie *Gramp* 94 NJ6664
Inverailort *Highld* 85 NM7681
Inverallign *Highld* 86 NG8427
Inverallochy *Gramp* 95 NK0464
Inveran *Highld* 96 NH5797
Inveraray *Strath* 80 NN0908
Inverarish *Highld* 84 NG5535
Inverarity *Tays* 88 NO4544
Inverarnan *Cent* 80 NN3218
Inveravon *Cent* 82 NS9579
Inverawe *Strath* 80 NN0231
Inverbervie *Gramp* 89 NO8372
Inverbroom *Highld* 96 NH1883
Invercharolain *Strath* 80 NS0975
Invercreran House Hotel *Strath* 86 NN0147
Inverdruie *Highld* 93 NH8910
Inveresk *Loth* 75 NT3571
Inveresragan *Strath* 80 NM9935
Inverey *Gramp* 88 NO0889
Inverfarigaig *Highld* 92 NH5223
Inverfolla *Strath* 86 NM9544
Invergarry *Highld* 86 NH3101
Invergeldie *Tays* 81 NN7327
Invergloy *Highld* 86 NN2288
Invergordon *Highld* 93 NH7068
Invergowrie *Tays* 83 NO3430
Inverguseran *Highld* 85 NG7407
Inverhadden *Tays* 87 NN6757
Inverherive *Cent* 80 NN3626
Inverie *Highld* 85 NG7600
Inverinan *Strath* 80 NM9917
Inverinate *Highld* 85 NG9221
Inverkeilor *Tays* 89 NO6649
Inverkeithing *Fife* 82 NT1383
Inverkeithny *Gramp* 94 NJ6246
Inverkip *Strath* 80 NS2071
Inverkirkaig *Highld* 98 NC0819
Inverlael *Highld* 96 NH1886
Inverlair *Highld* 86 NN3379
Inverliever Lodge *Strath* 79 NM8905
Inverlochlarig *Cent* 81 NN4318
Inverlochy *Strath* 80 NN1927
Invermarkie *Gramp* 94 NJ4239
Invermoriston *Highld* 92 NH4217
Invernaver *Highld* 99 NC7060
Inverneg *Strath* 80 NS3497
Inverneil *Strath* 71 NR8481
Inverness *Highld* 93 NH6645
Invernoaden *Strath* 80 NS1297
Inveroran Hotel *Strath* 86 NN2741
Inverquharity *Tays* 88 NO4057
Inverquhomery *Gramp* 95 NK0246
Inverroy *Highld* 86 NN2581
Inversanda *Highld* 86 NM9459
Invershiel *Highld* 85 NG9319
Invershin *Highld* 96 NH5796
Invershore *Highld* 100 ND2435
Inversnaid *Cent* 80 NN3408
Inverugie *Gramp* 95 NK0947
Inveruglas *Strath* 80 NN3109
Inveruglass *Highld* 87 NH8000
Inverurie *Gramp* 95 NJ7721
Inwardleigh *Devon* 6 SX5699
Inworth *Essex* 24 TL8718
Iping *W Susx* 11 SU8522
Ipplepen *Devon* 5 SX8366
Ipsden *Oxon* 21 SU6285
Ipstones *Staffs* 48 SK0249
Ipswich *Suffk* 33 TM1644
Irby *Mersyd* 46 SJ2584
Irby in the Marsh *Lincs* 51 TF4763
Irby upon Humber *Humb* 57 TA1904
Irchester *Nhants* 30 SP9265
Ireby *Cumb* 58 NY2338
Ireby *Lancs* 60 SD6575
Ireland *Beds* 30 TL1341
Irelands's Cross *Shrops* 37 SJ7341
Ireleth *Cumb* 58 SD2277
Ireshopeburn *Dur* 60 NY8638
Ireton Wood *Derbys* 49 SK2847
Irlam *Gt Man* 47 SJ7294
Irnham *Lincs* 40 TF0226
Iron Acton *Avon* 20 ST6783
Iron Bridge *Cambs* 41 TL4897
Ironmacannie *D & G* 65 NX6675
Irons Bottom *Surrey* 12 TQ2546
Ironville *Derbys* 49 SK4351
Irstead *Norfk* 43 TG3620
Irthington *Cumb* 67 NY4961
Irthlingborough *Nhants* 30 SP9470
Irton *N York* 63 TA0184
Irvine *Strath* 73 NS3239
Isauld *Highld* 99 NC9865
Isbister *Shet* 103 HU3790
Isfield *E Susx* 13 TQ4417
Isham *Nhants* 30 SP8873
Isington *Hants* 11 SU7742
Islandpool *H & W* 38 SO8680
Isle Abbotts *Somset* 8 ST3520
Isle Brewers *Somset* 8 ST3621
Isle of Whithorn *D & G* 65 NX4736
Isleham *Cambs* 32 TL6474
Isleornsay *Highld* 85 NG6912
Islet Village *Guern* 101 SV0000
Isley Walton *Leics* 39 SK4225
Islington *Gt Lon* 23 TQ3184
Islip *Nhants* 40 SP9879
Islip *Oxon* 29 SP5214
Islivig *W Isls* 102 NA9927
Isombridge *Shrops* 37 SJ6113
Istead Rise *Kent* 14 TQ6369
Itchen Abbas *Hants* 11 SU5332
Itchen Stoke *Hants* 11 SU5532
Itchingfield *W Susx* 12 TQ1328
Itteringham *Norfk* 43 TG1430
Itton *Devon* 7 SX6898
Itton *Gwent* 19 ST4995
Itton Common *Gwent* 19 ST4895
Ivegill *Cumb* 67 NY4143
Iver *Bucks* 22 TQ0381
Iver Heath *Bucks* 22 TQ0283
Iveston *Dur* 69 NZ1350
Ivinghoe *Bucks* 30 SP9416
Ivinghoe Aston *Bucks* 30 SP9517
Ivington *H & W* 27 SO4756
Ivington Green *H & W* 27 SO4655
Ivington Green *H & W* 27 SO4656
Ivy Hatch *Kent* 14 TQ5854
Ivybridge *Devon* 5 SX6356
Ivychurch *Kent* 15 TR0227
Iwade *Kent* 14 TQ8967
Iwerne Courney *Dorset* 9 ST8512
Iwerne Minster *Dorset* 9 ST8614
Ixworth *Suffk* 32 TL9370
Ixworth Thorpe *Suffk* 32 TL9173

J

Jack-in-the-Green *Devon* 7 SY0195
Jackson Bridge *W York* 55 SE1606
Jackton *Strath* 74 NS5952
Jacobstow *Cnwll* 6 SX1995
Jacobstowe *Devon* 6 SS5801
Jameston *Dyfed* 16 SS0599
Jamestown *Highld* 92 NH4756
Jamestown *Strath* 80 NS3981
Janets-town *Highld* 100 ND3551
Janetstown *Highld* 100 ND1932
Jardine Hall *D & G* 67 NY1088
Jarrow *T & W* 69 NZ3065
Jasper's Green *Essex* 24 TL7226
Jawcraig *Cent* 74 NS8475
Jaywick *Essex* 25 TM1513
Jedburgh *Border* 76 NT6420
Jeffreyston *Dyfed* 16 SN0806
Jemimaville *Highld* 93 NH7165
Jerbourg *Guern* 101 SV0000
Jesmond *T & W* 69 NZ2566
Jevington *E Susx* 13 TQ5601
Jockey End *Herts* 30 TL0413
John O'Groats *Highld* 100 ND3872
Johnby *Cumb* 59 NY4333
Johnshaven *Gramp* 89 NO7967
Johnston *Dyfed* 16 SM9310
Johnstone *D & G* 67 NT1400
Johnstone *Strath* 73 NS4263
Johnstonebridge *D & G* 67 NY1092
Joppa *Dyfed* 34 SN5666
Joppa *Strath* 73 NS4119
Jordanston *Dyfed* 16 SM9232
Jordanthorpe *S York* 49 SK3581
Jump *S York* 49 SE3701
Juniper Green *Loth* 75 NT1968
Jurby *IOM* 52 SC3598

K

Kaber *Cumb* 60 NY7911
Kaimes *Loth* 75 NT2768
Kalnakill *Highld* 91 NG6955
Kames *Strath* 71 NR9771
Kames *Strath* 74 NS6926
Kames *Strath* 79 NM8211
Kea *Cnwll* 2 SW8142
Keal Cotes *Lincs* 51 TF3661
Kearby Town End *N York* 55 SE3446
Kearnsey *Kent* 15 TR2844
Kearsley *Gt Man* 47 SD7504
Kearstwick *Cumb* 59 SD6079
Kedington *Suffk* 32 TL7046
Kedleston *Derbys* 49 SK3041
Keelby *Lincs* 57 TA1610
Keele *Staffs* 47 SJ8045
Keele University *Staffs* 47 SJ8145
Keelham *W York* 55 SE0732
Keeston *Dyfed* 16 SM9019
Keevil *Wilts* 20 ST9157
Kegworth *Leics* 39 SK4826
Keig *Gramp* 94 NJ6119
Keighley *W York* 55 SE0641
Keilarsbrae *Cent* 82 NS8993
Keillmore *Strath* 71 NR6880
Keillour *Tays* 82 NN9725
Keiloch *Gramp* 88 NO1891
Keils *Strath* 70 NR5268
Keinton Mandeville *Somset* 8 ST5430
Keir Mill *D & G* 66 NX8593
Keisley *Cumb* 60 NY7124
Keiss *Highld* 100 ND3461
Keith *Gramp* 94 NJ4250
Keithick *Tays* 82 NO2038
Keithock *Tays* 89 NO6063
Keithtown *Gramp* 92 NH5256
Kelbrook *Lancs* 54 SD9044
Kelburn *Strath* 73 NS2156
Kelby *Lincs* 50 TF0041
Keld *N York* 60 NY8901
Kelfield *N York* 56 SE5938
Kelham *Notts* 50 SK7755
Kelhead *D & G* 67 NY1469
Kellacott *Devon* 4 SX4089
Kellas *Gramp* 94 NJ1654
Kellas *Tays* 83 NO4535
Kellaton *Devon* 5 SX8039
Kelling *Norfk* 43 TG0942
Kellington *N York* 56 SE5524
Kelloe *Dur* 62 NZ3436
Kelly *Devon* 4 SX3981
Kelly Bray *Cnwll* 4 SX3571
Kelmarsh *Nhants* 40 SP7379
Kelmscot *Oxon* 21 SU2499
Kelsale *Suffk* 33 TM3865
Kelsall *Ches* 46 SJ5268
Kelshall *Herts* 31 TL3236
Kelsick *Cumb* 67 NY1950
Kelso *Border* 76 NT7234
Kelstedge *Derbys* 49 SK3363
Kelstern *Lincs* 51 TF2489
Kelston *Avon* 20 ST7067
Keltneyburn *Tays* 87 NN7749
Kelton *D & G* 66 NX9970
Kelty *Fife* 82 NT1494
Kelvedon *Essex* 24 TL8619
Kelvedon Hatch *Essex* 24 TQ5698
Kelynack *Cnwll* 2 SW3729
Kemback *Fife* 83 NO4115
Kemberton *Shrops* 37 SJ7204
Kemble *Wilts* 20 ST9897
Kemerton *H & W* 28 SO9437
Kemnay *Gramp* 95 NJ7316
Kemneys Commander *Gwent* 27 SO3404
Kemp Town *E Susx* 12 TQ3303
Kempley *Gloucs* 28 SO6729
Kempley Green *Gloucs* 28 SO6728
Kempsey *H & W* 28 SO8549
Kempsford *Gloucs* 20 SU1597
Kempshott *Hants* 21 SU6050
Kempston *Beds* 30 TL0347
Kempton *Shrops* 36 SO3682
Kemsing *Kent* 23 TQ5558
Kenardington *Kent* 15 TQ9732
Kenchester *H & W* 27 SO4342
Kencot *Oxon* 29 SP2504
Kendal *Cumb* 59 SD5192
Kenfig *M Glam* 18 SS8081
Kenilworth *Warwks* 39 SP2971
Kenley *Gt Lon* 23 TQ3260
Kenley *Shrops* 37 SJ5600
Kenmore *Highld* 91 NG7557
Kenmore *Tays* 87 NN7745
Kenn *Avon* 19 ST4269
Kenn *Devon* 5 SX9285
Kennacley *W Isls* 90 NG1794
Kennacraig *Strath* 71 NR8262
Kenneggy *Cnwll* 2 SW5629
Kennerleigh *Devon* 7 SS8107
Kennessee Green *Mersyd* 46 SD3801
Kennet *Cent* 82 NS9291
Kennethmont *Gramp* 94 NJ5428
Kennett *Cambs* 32 TL7068
Kennford *Devon* 5 SX9186
Kenninghall *Norfk* 32 TM0386
Kennington *Kent* 15 TR0245
Kennington *Oxon* 21 SP5101
Kennoway *Fife* 83 NO3502
Kenny *Somset* 8 ST3118
Kennyhill *Suffk* 32 TL6680
Kennythorpe *N York* 56 SE7865
Kenovay *Strath* 78 NL9946
Kensaleyre *Highld* 90 NG4251
Kensington *Gt Lon* 23 TQ2579
Kensworth *Beds* 30 TL0319
Kensworth Common *Beds* 30 TL0318
Kent's Green *Gloucs* 28 SO7423
Kentallen *Highld* 86 NN0057
Kentchurch *H & W* 27 SO4125
Kentford *Suffk* 32 TL7066
Kentisbeare *Devon* 7 ST0608
Kentisbury *Devon* 6 SS6244
Kentish Town *Gt Lon* 23 TQ2984
Kentmere *Cumb* 59 NY4504
Kenton *Devon* 5 SX9583
Kenton *Gt Lon* 23 TQ1788
Kenton *Suffk* 33 TM1965
Kenton *T & W* 69 NZ2267
Kentra *Highld* 79 NM6569
Kents Bank *Cumb* 59 SD3976
Kenwyn *Cnwll* 2 SW8145
Keoldale *Highld* 98 NC3866
Keppoch *Highld* 85 NG8924
Keprigan *Strath* 72 NR6810
Kepwick *N York* 62 SE4690
Keresley *W Mids* 39 SP3282
Keresley Green *Warwks* 39 SP3184
Kernborough *Devon* 5 SX7940
Kerridge *Ches* 48 SJ9377
Kerridge-end *Ches* 48 SJ9475
Kerris *Cnwll* 2 SW4427
Kerry Powys 36 SO1490
Kerry's Gate *H & W* 27 SO3933
Kerrycroy *Strath* 73 NS1061
Kersall *Notts* 49 SK7162
Kersbrook *Devon* 5 SY0683
Kersey *Suffk* 32 TM0044
Kershader *W Isls* 102 NB3419
Kersoe *H & W* 28 SO9939
Kerswell *Devon* 7 ST0806
Kerswell Green *H & W* 28 SO8646
Kesgrave *Suffk* 33 TM2245
Kessingland *Suffk* 33 TM5286
Kestle *Cnwll* 3 SW9845
Kestle Mill *Cnwll* 3 SW8459
Keston *Gt Lon* 23 TQ4164
Keswick *Cumb* 58 NY2623
Keswick *Norfk* 43 TG2004
Ketsby *Lincs* 51 TF3676
Kettering *Nhants* 30 SP8678
Ketteringham *Norfk* 43 TG1603
Kettins *Tays* 83 NO2339
Kettlebaston *Suffk* 32 TL9650
Kettlebridge *Fife* 83 NO3007
Kettleburgh *Suffk* 33 TM2660
Kettleshulme *Ches* 48 SJ9879
Kettlesing *N York* 55 SE2155
Kettlesing Bottom *N York* 55 SE2257
Kettlestoft *Ork* 103 HY6538
Kettlestone *Norfk* 42 TF9631
Kettlethorpe *Lincs* 50 SK8475
Kettlewell *N York* 54 SD9772
Ketton *Leics* 40 SK9804
Kew *Gt Lon* 23 TQ1877
Kexbrough *S York* 55 SE2909
Kexby *Lincs* 50 SK8785
Kexby *N York* 56 SE7050
Key Green *Ches* 48 SJ8963
Key Street *Kent* 14 TQ8864
Keyham *Leics* 39 SK6706
Keyhaven *Hants* 10 SZ3091
Keyingham *Humb* 57 TA2425
Keymer *W Susx* 12 TQ3115
Keynsham *Avon* 19 ST6568
Keysoe Row *Beds* 30 TL0861
Keyston *Cambs* 30 TL0475
Keyworth *Notts* 39 SK6130
Kibbear *Somset* 8 ST2122
Kibblesworth *T & W* 69 NZ2456
Kibworth Beauchamp *Leics* 39 SP6893
Kibworth Harcourt *Leics* 39 SP6894
Kidbrooke *Gt Lon* 23 TQ4076
Kidderminster *H & W* 38 SO8376
Kidlington *Oxon* 29 SP4913
Kidmore End *Oxon* 22 SU6979
Kidwelly *Dyfed* 17 SN4006
Kiel Crofts *Strath* 79 NM9039
Kielder *Nthumb* 68 NY6293
Kiells *Strath* 70 NR4168
Kilbagie *Cent* 82 NS9290
Kilbeg *Highld* 85 NG6506
Kilberry *Strath* 71 NR7164
Kilbirnie *Strath* 73 NS3154
Kilbride *Highld* 84 NG5820
Kilbride *Strath* 71 NR7279
Kilbride *Strath* 72 NS0367
Kilbride *Strath* 79 NM8525
Kilbride *W Isls* 102 NF7514
Kilburn *Derbys* 49 SK3845
Kilburn *Gt Lon* 23 TQ2483
Kilburn *N York* 62 SE5179
Kilby *Leics* 39 SP6295
Kilcadzow *Strath* 74 NS8848
Kilchamaig *Strath* 71 NR8060
Kilchattan *Strath* 70 NR3795
Kilchattan *Strath* 73 NS1054
Kilchenzie *Strath* 72 NR6724
Kilcheran *Strath* 79 NM8238
Kilchiaran *Strath* 70 NR2060
Kilchoan *Highld* 79 NM4964
Kilchrenan *Strath* 80 NN0322
Kilconquhar *Fife* 83 NO4802
Kilcot *Gloucs* 28 SO6925
Kilcoy *Highld* 92 NH5751
Kilcreggan *Strath* 80 NS2380
Kildale *N York* 62 NZ6009
Kildalloig *Strath* 72 NR7518
Kildary *Highld* 97 NH7674
Kildavanan *Strath* 72 NS0266
Kildermorie Lodge *Highld* 96 NH5277
Kildonan *Highld* 97 NC9120
Kildonan *Strath* 72 NS0321
Kildonan Lodge *Highld* 97 NC9022
Kildonnan *Highld* 84 NM4985
Kildrummy *Gramp* 94 NJ4617
Kildwick *N York* 54 SE0046
Kilehoman *Strath* 70 NR2163
Kilfinan *Strath* 71 NR9378
Kilfinnan *Highld* 86 NN2795
Kilgetty *Dyfed* 16 SN1207
Kilgrammie *Strath* 73 NS2502
Kilgwrrwg Common *Gwent* 19 ST4798
Kilham *Humb* 57 TA0664
Kilkenneth *Strath* 78 NL9444
Kilkerran *Strath* 73 NS3003
Kilkhampton *Cnwll* 6 SS2511
Killay *W Glam* 17 SS6092
Killean *Strath* 72 NR6944
Killearn *Cent* 81 NS5286
Killen *Highld* 93 NH6758
Killerby *Dur* 61 NZ1919
Killerton *Devon* 7 SS9700
Killichonan *Tays* 87 NN5458
Killiechronan *Strath* 79 NM5441
Killiecrankie *Tays* 87 NN9162
Killilan *Highld* 85 NG9430
Killimster *Highld* 100 ND3156
Killin *Cent* 81 NN5733
Killinghall *N York* 55 SE2858
Killington *Cumb* 59 SD6188
Killingworth *T & W* 69 NZ2870
Killinochonoch *Strath* 71 NR8395
Killochyett *Border* 76 NT4545
Killocraw *Strath* 72 NR6630
Killundine *Highld* 79 NM5849
Kilmacolm *Strath* 73 NS3569
Kilmahog *Cent* 81 NN6108
Kilmahumaig *Strath* 71 NR7893
Kilmaluag *Highld* 90 NG4373
Kilmansharachan *Strath* 72 NR7107
Kilmany *Fife* 83 NO3821
Kilmarie *Highld* 84 NG5517
Kilmarnock *Strath* 73 NS4238
Kilmartin *Strath* 71 NR8398
Kilmaurs *Strath* 73 NS4141
Kilmelford *Strath* 79 NM8512
Kilmeny *Strath* 70 NR3865
Kilmersdon *Somset* 20 ST6952
Kilmeston *Hants* 11 SU5926
Kilmichael Glassary *Strath* 71 NR8593
Kilmichael of Inverlussa *Strath* 71 NR7786
Kilmington *Devon* 8 SY2798
Kilmington *Wilts* 20 ST7736
Kilmington Common *Wilts* 20 ST7736
Kilmington Street *Wilts* 9 ST7835
Kilmor *Strath* 79 NM8825
Kilmorack *Highld* 92 NH4944
Kilmore *Highld* 85 NG6507
Kilmory *Highld* 79 NM5369
Kilmory *Highld* 84 NG3603
Kilmory *Strath* 71 NR7075
Kilmuir *Highld* 90 NG2547
Kilmuir *Highld* 90 NG3770
Kilmuir *Highld* 93 NH6749
Kilmuir *Highld* 97 NH7573
Kilmun *Strath* 80 NS1781
Kiln Green *Berks* 22 SU8178
Kiln Pit Hill *Nthumb* 68 NZ0354
Kilnave *Strath* 70 NR2871
Kilndown *Kent* 14 TQ7035
Kilninian *Strath* 79 NM3946
Kilninver *Strath* 79 NM8221
Kilnsea *Humb* 57 TA4015
Kilnsey *N York* 54 SD9767
Kilnwick *Humb* 56 SE9949
Kiloran *Strath* 70 NR3996
Kilpeck *H & W* 27 SO4430
Kilpheder *W Isls* 102 NF7419
Kilphedir *Highld* 97 NC9818
Kilpin *Humb* 56 SE7726
Kilsby *Nhants* 39 SP5671
Kilspindie *Tays* 82 NO2125
Kilstay *D & G* 64 NX1238
Kilsyth *Strath* 81 NS7178
Kiltarlity *Highld* 92 NH5041
Kilton *Cleve* 62 NZ7018
Kilton *Somset* 19 ST1644
Kilton Thorpe *Cleve* 62 NZ6917
Kilvaxter *Highld* 90 NG3869
Kilve *Somset* 18 ST1443
Kilvington *Notts* 50 SK8042
Kilwinning *Strath* 73 NS2943
Kimberley *Norfk* 42 TG0704
Kimberley *Notts* 49 SK4944
Kimberworth *S York* 49 SK4092

Langley Moor

Little Singleton

Langley Moor Dur 61 NZ2440
Langley Park Dur 69 NZ2144
Langley Street Norfk 43 TG3601
Langleybury Herts 22 TL0700
Langney E Susx 13 TQ6302
Langold Notts 49 SK5886
Langore Cnwll 4 SX2986
Langore Cnwll 4 SX3086
Langport Somset 8 ST4226
Langrick Lincs 51 TF2648
Langridge Avon 20 ST7469
Langrigg Cumb 67 NY1645
Langrish Hants 11 SU7023
Langsett S York 48 SE2100
Langshaw Border 76 NT5139
Langside Tays 81 NN7913
Langstone Gwent 19 ST3789
Langstone Hants 11 SU7105
Langthorne N York 61 SE2491
Langthorpe N York 55 SE3867
Langthwaite N York 61 NZ0001
Langtoft Humb 56 TA0166
Langtoft Lincs 40 TF1212
Langton Dur 61 NZ1719
Langton Lincs 51 TF2368
Langton Lincs 51 TF3970
Langton N York 56 SE7967
Langton Green Kent 13 TQ5439
Langton Green Kent 13 TQ5439
Langton Herring Dorset 9 SY6182
Langton by Wragby Lincs 50 TF1476
Langtree Devon 6 SS4515
Langtree Week Devon 6 SS4705
Langwathby Cumb 59 NY5733
Langwell Highld 96 NC1703
Langwell House Highld 100 ND1122
Langworth Lincs 50 TF0676
Langworthy Devon 4 SX4895
Lank Cnwll 3 SX0975
Lanlivery Cnwll 3 SX0759
Lanner Cnwll 2 SW7139
Lanreath Cnwll 3 SX1857
Lansallos Cnwll 3 SX1751
Lanteglos Cnwll 3 SX0882
Lanteglos Highway Cnwll 3 SX1453
Lantilio-Crossenny Gwent 27 SO3914
Lanton Border 76 NT6122
Lanton Nthumb 77 NT9231
Lapford Devon 7 SS7308
Laphroaig Strath 70 NR3845
Lapley Staffs 38 SJ8713
Lapworth Warwks 38 SP1671
Larachbeg Highld 79 NM6948
Larbert Cent 82 NS8582
Largie Gramp 94 NJ6131
Largiemore Strath 71 NR9486
Largoward Fife 83 NO4607
Largs Strath 73 NS2059
Largybeg Strath 72 NS0423
Largymore Strath 72 NS0424
Larkfield Kent 14 TQ7058
Larkfield Strath 80 NS2376
Larkhall Strath 74 NS7651
Larkhill Wilts 20 SU1243
Larling Norfk 32 TL9889
Larrick Cnwll 4 SX3078
Larriston Border 67 NY5494
Lartington Dur 61 NZ0117
Lasham Hants 11 SU6742
Lask Edge Staffs 48 SJ9156
Lassodie Fife 82 NT1292
Lastingham N York 63 SE7290
Latchingdon and Snoreham Essex 24 TL8800
Latchley Cnwll 4 SX4173
Latebrook Staffs 47 SJ8453
Lathbury Bucks 30 SP8744
Latheron Highld 100 ND2033
Latheronwheel House Highld 100 ND1832
Lathones Fife 83 NO4708
Latimer Bucks 22 TQ0199
Latteridge Avon 20 ST6684
Lattiford Somset 9 ST6926
Latton Wilts 20 SU0995
Lauder Border 76 NT5347
Laugharne Dyfed 17 SN3011
Laughterton Lincs 50 SK8375
Laughton E Susx 13 TQ4913
Laughton Leics 39 SP6688
Laughton Lincs 40 TF0731
Laughton Lincs 50 SK8497
Laughton-en-le-Morthen S York 49 SK5188
Launcells Cnwll 6 SS2405
Launceston Cnwll 4 SX3384
Launton Oxon 29 SP6022
Laurencekirk Gramp 89 NO7171
Laurieston Cent 82 NS9179
Laurieston D & G 65 NX6864
Lavendon Bucks 30 SP9153
Lavenham Suffk 32 TL9149
Lavernock S Glam 19 ST1868
Laversdale Cumb 67 NY4762
Laverstock Wilts 10 SU1530
Laverstoke Hants 21 SU4948
Laverton Gloucs 28 SP0735
Laverton N York 61 SE2273
Laverton Somset 20 ST7753
Lavister Clwyd 46 SJ3758
Law Strath 74 NS8152
Law Hill Strath 74 NS8251
Lawers Tays 81 NN6739
Lawers Tays 81 NN7923
Lawford Essex 25 TM0831
Lawford Somset 18 ST1437
Lawgrove Tays 82 NO0926
Lawhitton Cnwll 4 SX3582
Lawkland N York 54 SD7766
Lawkland Green N York 54 SD7865
Lawnhead Staffs 38 SJ8224
Lawrence End Herts 30 TL1419
Lawrenny Dyfed 16 SN0107
Lawshall Suffk 32 TL8654
Laxay W Isls 102 NB3321
Laxdale W Isls 102 NB4234
Laxey IOM 52 SC4384
Laxfield Suffk 33 TM2972
Laxford Bridge Highld 98 NC2346
Laxo Shet 103 HU4463
Laxton Humb 56 SE7825
Laxton Nhants 40 SP9596
Laxton Notts 49 SK7266
Layer Breton Essex 25 TL9418
Layer Marney Essex 24 TL9217
Layer-de-la-Haye Essex 25 TL9620
Layham Suffk 32 TM0340
Laymore Dorset 8 ST3804
Laysters Pole H & W 27 SO5563
Laytham Humb 56 SE7439
Laythes Cumb 67 NY2455
Lazonby Cumb 67 NY5449
Le Bigard Guern 101 SV0000
Le Bourg Guern 101 SV0000
Le Bron Guern 101 SV0000
Le Haquais Jersey 101 SV0000
Le Hocq Jersey 101 SV0000
Le Villocq Guern 101 SV0000
Lea Derbys 49 SK3257
Lea H & W 27 SO6521
Lea Lincs 50 SK8286
Lea Shrops 36 SO3589
Lea Wilts 20 ST9586
Lea Marston Warwks 39 SP2093
Leachkin Highld 92 NH6445
Leadburn Loth 75 NT2355
Leaden Roding Essex 24 TL5913
Leadenham Lincs 50 SK9452
Leadgate Cumb 68 NY7043
Leadgate Dur 69 NZ1251
Leadhills Strath 74 NS8815
Leafield Oxon 29 SP3115
Leagrave Beds 30 TL0523
Leahead Ches 47 SJ6964
Leaholm Side N York 63 NZ7607
Leake Common Side Lincs 51 TF3952
Lealt Highld 90 NG5060
Leamington Hastings Warwks 29 SP4467
Leargybreck Strath 70 NR5371
Leasgill Cumb 59 SD4984
Leasingham Lincs 50 TF0548
Leasingthorne Dur 61 NZ2530
Leatherhead Surrey 23 TQ1656
Leathley N York 55 SE2346
Leaths D & G 66 NX7863
Leaton Shrops 36 SJ4618
Leaveland Kent 15 TR0053
Leavenheath Suffk 25 TL9537
Leavening N York 56 SE7863
Leaves Green Gt Lon 23 TQ4161
Lebberston N York 63 TA0782
Lechampstead Thicket Berks 21 SU4276
Lechlade Wilts 21 SU2199
Leck Lancs 60 SD6476
Leckbuie Tays 81 NN7040
Leckford Hants 10 SU3737
Leckfurin Highld 99 NC7059
Leckgruinart Strath 70 NR2768
Leckhampstead Berks 21 SU4375
Leckhampstead Bucks 30 SP7237
Leckhampton Gloucs 28 SO9419
Leckhamstead Bucks 30 SP7237
Leckmelm Highld 96 NH1790
Leconfield Humb 56 TA0143
Ledaig Strath 79 NM9037
Ledburn Bucks 30 SP9021
Ledbury H & W 28 SO7037
Ledgemoor H & W 27 SO4150
Ledmore Junction Highld 96 NC2412
Ledsham W York 55 SE4529
Ledston W York 55 SE4328
Ledwell Oxon 29 SP4128
Lee Devon 6 SS4846
Lee Gt Lon 23 TQ3875
Lee Strath 78 NM4022
Lee Brockhurst Shrops 37 SJ5427
Lee Chapel Essex 24 TQ6987
Lee Clump Bucks 22 SP9004
Lee Common Bucks 22 SP9303
Lee Green Ches 47 SJ6562
Lee Mill Devon 5 SX5855
Lee-on-the-Solent Hants 11 SU5600
Leebotwood Shrops 37 SO4798
Leece Cumb 53 SD2469
Leeds Kent 14 TQ8253
Leeds W York 55 SE3034
Leedstown Cnwll 2 SW6034
Leek Wootton Warwks 29 SP2968
Leeming N York 61 SE2989
Leeming Bar N York 61 SE2889
Lees Derbys 49 SK2637
Lees Gt Man 54 SD9504
Lees Gt Man 54 SD9504
Lees Green Derbys 49 SK2637
Leesthorpe Leics 40 SK7813
Leetown Tays 82 NO2121
Leftwich Ches 47 SJ6672
Legbourne Lincs 51 TF3684
Legerwood Border 76 NT5843
Legsby Lincs 50 TF1385
Leicester Leics 39 SK5804
Leicester Forest East Leics 39 SK5303
Leigh Devon 7 SS9115
Leigh Dorset 9 ST6108
Leigh Gloucs 28 SO8626
Leigh H & W 28 SO7853
Leigh Kent 13 TQ5446
Leigh Mersyd 47 SJ6599
Leigh Surrey 12 TQ2246
Leigh Wilts 20 SU0692
Leigh Beck Essex 24 TQ8183
Leigh Delamere Wilts 20 ST8879
Leigh Green Kent 14 TQ9033
Leigh Knoweglass Strath 74 NS6350
Leigh Sinton H & W 28 SO7750
Leigh Woods Avon 19 ST5572
Leigh upon Mendip Somset 20 ST6847
Leigh-on-Sea Essex 24 TQ8286
Leighterton Gloucs 20 ST8290
Leighton Powys 36 SJ2406
Leighton Shrops 37 SJ6105
Leighton Bromswold Cambs 30 TL1175
Leighton Buzzard Beds 30 SP9225
Leinthall Earls H & W 27 SO4467
Leinthall Starkes H & W 27 SO4369
Leintwardine H & W 36 SO4074
Leire Leics 39 SP5290
Leiston Suffk 33 TM4462
Leitfie Tays 88 NO2545
Leith Loth 75 NT2676
Leitholm Border 76 NT7944
Lelant Cnwll 2 SW5437
Lelley Humb 57 TA2032
Lempitlaw Border 76 NT7832
Lemreway W Isls 90 NB3711
Lemsford Herts 31 TL2212
Lenchwick H & W 28 SP0347
Lendalfoot Strath 64 NX1390
Lendrick Cent 81 NN5506
Lendrum Terrace Gramp 95 NK1141
Lenham Kent 14 TQ8952
Lenie Highld 92 NH5126
Lennel Border 77 NT8540
Lennoxlove Loth 76 NT5172
Lennoxtown Strath 74 NS6277
Lenton Lincs 40 TF0230
Lenzie Strath 74 NS6572
Leochel-Cushnie Gramp 94 NJ5210
Leominster H & W 27 SO4958
Leonard Stanley Gloucs 20 SO8003
Leorin Strath 70 NR3548
Leoville Jersey 101 SV0000
Lepe Hants 10 SZ4598
Lephin Highld 90 NG1749
Lephinchapel Strath 71 NR9690
Lephinmore Strath 71 NR9892
Leppington N York 56 SE7661
Lepton W York 55 SE2015
Lerags Strath 79 NM8324
Lerryn Cnwll 3 SX1457
Lerwick Shet 103 HU4741
Les Arquets Guern 101 SV0000
Les Hubits Guern 101 SV0000
Les Lohiers Guern 101 SV0000
Les Murchez Guern 101 SV0000
Les Nicolles Guern 101 SV0000
Les Quartiers Guern 101 SV0000
Les Quennevais Jersey 101 SV0000
Les Sages Guern 101 SV0000
Les Villets Guern 101 SV0000
Lesbury Nthumb 69 NU2312
Leslie Fife 83 NO2501
Leslie Gramp 94 NJ5924
Lesmahagow Strath 74 NS8139
Lesnewth Cnwll 4 SX1390
Lessingham Norfk 43 TG3928
Lessonhall Cumb 67 NY2249
Leswalt D & G 64 NX0164
Letchmore Heath Herts 22 TQ1597
Letchworth Herts 31 TL2232
Letcombe Bassett Oxon 21 SU3785
Letcombe Regis Oxon 21 SU3786
Letham Border 68 NT6708
Letham Fife 83 NO3014
Letham Tays 89 NO5348
Letham Grange Tays 89 NO6345
Lethenty Gramp 94 NJ5820
Lethenty Gramp 95 NJ8140
Letheringham Suffk 33 TM2757
Letheringsett Norfk 42 TG0639
Lett's Green Kent 23 TQ4558
Letterfearn Highld 85 NG8823
Letterfinlay Lodge Hotel Highld 86 NN2591
Lettermorar Highld 85 NM7389
Letters Highld 96 NH1687
Lettershaw Strath 74 NS8920
Letterston Dyfed 16 SM9429
Lettoch Highld 93 NJ0219
Lettoch Highld 93 NJ0932
Letton H & W 27 SO3346
Letty Green Herts 23 TL2810
Letwell S York 49 SK5587
Leuchars Fife 83 NO4521
Leurbost W Isls 102 NB3725
Levedale Staffs 38 SJ9016
Level's Green Essex 31 TL4724
Leven Fife 83 NO3800
Leven Humb 57 TA1045
Levencorroch Strath 72 NS0021
Levens Green Herts 31 TL3522
Levenshulme Gt Man 47 SJ8794
Levenwick Shet 103 HU4021
Leverburgh W Isls 102 NG0186
Leverington Cambs 41 TF4411
Leverstock Green Herts 22 TL0806
Leverton Lincs 51 TF3947
Levington Suffk 33 TM2339
Levisham N York 63 SE8390
Lew Oxon 29 SP3206
Lew Middleton Nthumb 77 NU1036
Lewannick Cnwll 4 SX2780
Lewdown Devon 4 SX4486
Lewes E Susx 13 TQ4110
Leweston Dyfed 16 SM9422
Lewisham Gt Lon 23 TQ3774
Lewiston Highld 92 NH5129
Lewknor Oxon 22 SU7197
Lewson Street Kent 15 TQ9661
Lewtrenchard Devon 4 SX4686
Lexworthy Somset 8 ST2535
Leybourne Kent 14 TQ6858
Leyburn N York 61 SE1190
Leygreen Herts 31 TL1624
Leyland Lancs 53 SD5422
Leylodge Gramp 95 NJ7613
Leys Gramp 95 NK0052
Leys Tays 83 NO2537
Leys of Cossans Tays 88 NO3849
Leysdown-on-Sea Kent 15 TR0370
Leysmill Tays 89 NO6047
Leyton Gt Lon 23 TQ3886
Leytonstone Gt Lon 23 TQ3987
Lezant Cnwll 4 SX3379
Lezayre IOM 52 SC4294
Lhanbryde Gramp 94 NJ2761
Lhen The IOM 52 NX3801
Libberton Strath 75 NS9943
Liberton Loth 75 NT2769
Lichfield Staffs 38 SK1109
Lickey H & W 38 SO9975
Lickey End H & W 38 SO9772
Lickfold W Susx 11 SU9226
Liddesdale Highld 79 NM7759
Liddington Wilts 21 SU2081
Lidgate Suffk 32 TL7258
Lidlington Beds 30 SP9839
Lienassie Highld 85 NG9621
Liff Tays 83 NO3332
Lifford W Mids 38 SP0580
Lifton Devon 4 SX3885
Liftondown Devon 4 SX3685
Lighthorne Warwks 29 SP3355
Lightwater Surrey 22 SU9362
Lightwood Green Ches 49 SK6342
Lilbourne Nhants 39 SP5677
Lileshall Shrops 37 SJ7315
Lilley Herts 31 TL1226
Lilliesleaf Border 76 NT5325
Lillingstone Dayrell Bucks 30 SP7039
Lillingstone Lovell Bucks 30 SP7140
Lillington Dorset 9 ST6212
Lilstock Somset 19 ST1644
Limbury Beds 30 TL0724
Lime Street H & W 28 SO8130
Limefield Gt Man 54 SD8013
Limekilnburn Strath 74 NS7050
Limekilns Fife 82 NT0883
Limerigg Cent 74 NS8570
Limerstone IOW 10 SZ4482
Limington Somset 8 ST5422
Limmerhaugh Strath 74 NS6127
Limpenhoe Norfk 43 TG3903
Limpley Stoke Wilts 20 ST7760
Limpsfield Surrey 13 TQ4053
Linby Notts 49 SK5351
Linchmere W Susx 11 SU8731
Lincoln Lincs 50 SK9771
Lincomb H & W 28 SO8269
Lincombe Devon 5 SX7340
Lincombe Devon 5 SX7458
Lindal in Furness Cumb 58 SD2475
Lindale Cumb 59 SD4180
Lindean Border 76 NT4931
Lindfield W Susx 12 TQ3425
Lindford Hants 11 SU8036
Lindford Magna Lincs 50 TF1988
Lindley Green N York 55 SE2248
Lindores Fife 83 NO2617
Lindridge H & W 28 SO6769
Lindsell Essex 24 TL6427
Lindsey Suffk 32 TL9745
Lindsey Tye Suffk 32 TL9845
Linford Hants 10 SU1707
Lingague IOM 52 SC2172
Lingdale Cleve 62 NZ6716
Lingen H & W 27 SO3667
Lingfield Surrey 13 TQ3843
Lingfield Common Surrey 13 TQ3844
Lingley Green Ches 47 SJ5589
Lingwood Norfk 43 TG3608
Liniclett W Isls 102 NF7949
Linicro Highld 90 NG3967
Linkend H & W 28 SO8231
Linkenholt Hants 21 SU3658
Linkhill Kent 14 TQ8128
Linkinhorne Cnwll 4 SX3173
Linktown Fife 83 NT2890
Linkwood Gramp 94 NJ2361
Linley Shrops 36 SO3592
Linley Green H & W 28 SO6953
Linleygreen Shrops 37 SO6898
Linlithgow Loth 75 NS9977
Linnels Bridge Nthumb 68 NY9562
Linsidemore Highld 96 NH5499
Linslade Beds 30 SP9125
Linstead Parva Suffk 33 TM3377
Linstock Cumb 67 NY4258
Linthurst H & W 38 SO9972
Linthwaite W York 55 SE0913
Linthwaite W York 55 SE1014
Lintlaw Border 77 NT8258
Lintmill Gramp 94 NJ5165
Linton Border 76 NT7726
Linton Cambs 31 TL5646
Linton Derbys 39 SK2716
Linton Gloucs 28 SO7918
Linton H & W 28 SO6625
Linton Kent 14 TQ7550
Linton N York 54 SD9962
Linton W York 55 SE3846
Linton Hill Gloucs 28 SO6624
Linton-on-Ouse N York 55 SE4860
Linwood Lincs 50 TF1186
Linwood Strath 73 NS4464
Lionel W Isls 102 NB5263
Liphook Hants 11 SU8431
Liscard Mersyd 46 SJ2991
Liscombe Devon 7 SS8732
Liskeard Cnwll 4 SX2564
Liss Hants 11 SU7727
Liss Forest Hants 11 SU7829
Lissett Humb 57 TA1458
Lissington Lincs 50 TF1083
Lisvane S Glam 19 ST1983
Liswerry Gwent 19 ST3487
Litcham Norfk 42 TF8817
Litchard M Glam 18 SS9182
Litchborough Nhants 29 SP6354
Litchfield Hants 21 SU4653
Litherland Mersyd 46 SJ3397
Litlington Cambs 31 TL3142
Litlington E Susx 13 TQ5201
Little Abington Cambs 31 TL5349
Little Addington Nhants 30 SP9673
Little Almshoe Herts 31 TL2025
Little Alne Warwks 28 SP1461
Little Amwell Herts 23 TL3511
Little Asby Cumb 60 NY6909
Little Aston Staffs 38 SK0900
Little Atherfield IOW 10 SZ4680
Little Ayton N York 62 NZ5610
Little Baddow Essex 24 TL7708
Little Badminton Avon 20 ST8084
Little Bampton Cumb 67 NY2755
Little Bardfield Essex 24 TL6531
Little Barford Beds 31 TL1756
Little Barningham Norfk 43 TG1333
Little Barrington Gloucs 29 SP2012
Little Barrow Ches 46 SJ4770
Little Barugh N York 63 SE7579
Little Bavington Nthumb 68 NY9878
Little Bedwyn Wilts 21 SU2966
Little Bentley Essex 25 TM1125
Little Berkhamsted Herts 23 TL2907
Little Billing Nhants 30 SP8061
Little Billington Beds 30 SP9322
Little Birch H & W 27 SO5130
Little Blakenham Suffk 33 TM1049
Little Blencow Cumb 59 NY4532
Little Bognor W Susx 12 TQ0020
Little Bolehill Derbys 49 SK2954
Little Bookham Surrey 22 TQ1254
Little Bourton Oxon 29 SP4543
Little Bradley Suffk 32 TL6852
Little Brampton Shrops 36 SO3681
Little Braxted Essex 24 TL8314
Little Brechin Tays 89 NO5862
Little Brickhill Bucks 30 SP9032
Little Brington Nhants 30 SP6663
Little Bromley Essex 25 TM0928
Little Budworth Ches 47 SJ6065
Little Burstead Essex 24 TQ6692
Little Bytham Lincs 40 TF0118
Little Carlton Lincs 51 TF3985
Little Casterton Leics 40 TF0109
Little Catwick Humb 57 TA1444
Little Cawthorpe Lincs 51 TF3583
Little Chalfont Bucks 22 SU9997
Little Chart Kent 14 TQ9446
Little Chesterford Essex 31 TL5141
Little Chishill Cambs 31 TL4237
Little Clacton Essex 25 TM1618
Little Clanfield Oxon 21 SP2701
Little Clifton Cumb 58 NY0528
Little Comberton H & W 28 SO9643
Little Common E Susx 14 TQ7108
Little Comp Kent 14 TQ6357
Little Compton Warwks 29 SP2530
Little Cornard Suffk 32 TL9039
Little Cowarne H & W 27 SO6051
Little Coxwell Oxon 21 SU2893
Little Crakehall N York 61 SE2490
Little Cransley Nhants 30 SP8376
Little Creaton Nhants 30 SP7171
Little Cressingham Norfk 42 TF8700
Little Crosby Mersyd 46 SD3201
Little Cubley Derbys 38 SK1537
Little Dalby Leics 40 SK7714
Little Dens Gramp 95 NK0643
Little Dewchurch H & W 27 SO5231
Little Ditton Cambs 32 TL6658
Little Driffield Humb 56 TA0058
Little Dunham Norfk 42 TF8612
Little Dunkeld Tays 88 NO0342
Little Dunmow Essex 24 TL6521
Little Durnford Wilts 10 SU1234
Little Easton Essex 24 TL6023
Little Eaton Derbys 49 SK3641
Little Ellingham Norfk 42 TM0099
Little Elm Somset 20 ST7246
Little Everdon Nhants 29 SP5957
Little Eversden Cambs 31 TL3753
Little Faringdon S York 21 SP2201
Little Fencote N York 61 SE2793
Little Fenton N York 55 SE5135
Little Fransham Norfk 42 TF9011
Little Gaddesden Herts 30 SP9913
Little Glemham Suffk 33 TM3458
Little Gorsley H & W 28 SO6824
Little Gransden Cambs 31 TL2755
Little Green Somset 20 ST7248
Little Grimsby Lincs 51 TF3291
Little Hadham Herts 31 TL4322
Little Hale Lincs 50 TF1441
Little Hallam Derbys 49 SK4640
Little Hanford Dorset 9 ST8311
Little Harrowden Nhants 30 SP8771
Little Haseley Oxon 21 SP6400
Little Hatfield Humb 57 TA1743
Little Haven Dyfed 16 SM8513
Little Hay Staffs 38 SK1202
Little Haywood Staffs 38 SK0021
Little Heath Berks 21 SU6537
Little Heath W Mids 39 SP3482
Little Hereford H & W 27 SO5568
Little Horkesley Essex 25 TL9632
Little Hormead Herts 31 TL4028
Little Horsted E Susx 13 TQ4718
Little Horton W York 55 SE1531
Little Horwood Bucks 30 SP7930
Little Houghton Nhants 30 SP8059
Little Houghton S York 55 SE4205
Little Hucklow Derbys 48 SK1678
Little Hutton N York 62 SE4576
Little Irchester Nhants 30 SP9066
Little Keyford Somset 20 ST7746
Little Kimble Bucks 22 SP8207
Little Kineton Warwks 29 SP3350
Little Kingshill Bucks 22 SU8899
Little Knox D & G 66 NX8060
Little Langdale Cumb 58 NY3103
Little Langford Wilts 10 SU0436
Little Lashbrook Devon 6 SS4007
Little Laver Essex 24 TL5409
Little Leigh Ches 47 SJ6175
Little Leighs Essex 24 TL7117
Little Lever Gt Man 47 SD7507
Little Linford Bucks 30 SP8434
Little Load Somset 8 ST4624
Little London E Susx 13 TQ5720
Little London Essex 31 TL4729
Little London Essex 24 TL6835
Little London Hants 21 SU3749
Little London Hants 21 SU6259
Little London Lincs 41 TF3375
Little London Norfk 41 TF5620
Little London Powys 36 SO0489
Little Longstone Derbys 48 SK1871
Little Malvern H & W 28 SO7640
Little Maplestead Essex 24 TL8234
Little Marcle H & W 28 SO6736
Little Marlow Bucks 22 SU8787
Little Massingham Norfk 42 TF7924
Little Melton Norfk 43 TG1607
Little Mill Gwent 19 SO3203
Little Milton Oxon 21 SP6100
Little Missenden Bucks 22 SU9298
Little Mongham Kent 15 TR3351
Little Musgrave Cumb 60 NY7613
Little Ness Shrops 36 SJ4019
Little Neston Ches 46 SJ3076
Little Newcastle Dyfed 16 SM9829
Little Newsham Dur 61 NZ1217
Little Norton Somset 8 ST4815
Little Norton Staffs 38 SK0208
Little Oakley Essex 25 TM2129
Little Oakley Nhants 40 SP8985
Little Offley Herts 30 TL1228
Little Onn Staffs 38 SJ8315
Little Orton Cumb 67 NY3555
Little Oxendon Nhants 40 SP7184
Little Packington Warwks 39 SP2184
Little Paxton Cambs 31 TL1862
Little Petherick Cnwll 3 SW9172
Little Plumstead Norfk 43 TG3112
Little Ponton Lincs 40 SK9232
Little Preston Nhants 29 SP5854
Little Preston W York 55 SE3830
Little Raveley Cambs 41 TL2579
Little Reedness Humb 56 SE8022
Little Ribston N York 55 SE3853
Little Rissington Gloucs 29 SP1819
Little Rollright Oxon 29 SP2930
Little Rowsley Derbys 48 SK2566
Little Ryburgh Norfk 42 TF9628
Little Ryton Shrops 37 SJ4803
Little Salkeld Cumb 59 NY5636
Little Sampford Essex 24 TL6533
Little Saughall Ches 46 SJ3769
Little Saxham Suffk 32 TL8063
Little Scatwell Highld 92 NH3856
Little Sessay N York 62 SE4674
Little Shelford Cambs 31 TL4551
Little Silver Devon 7 SS8601
Little Singleton Lancs 53 SD3739

Little Skipwith

Lostwithiel

Little Skipwith *N York*	56	SE6538
Little Smeaton *N York*	55	SE5217
Little Snoring *Norfk*	42	TF9532
Little Sodbury *Avon*	20	ST7583
Little Somborne *Hants*	10	SU3832
Little Somerford *Wilts*	20	ST9684
Little Soudley *Shrops*	37	SJ7128
Little Stainton *Dur*	62	NZ3420
Little Staughton *Beds*	30	TL1062
Little Steeping *Lincs*	51	TF4362
Little Stonham *Suffk*	33	TM1160
Little Stretton *Leics*	39	SK6600
Little Stretton *Shrops*	36	SO4492
Little Strickland *Cumb*	59	NY5619
Little Stukeley *Cambs*	31	TL2175
Little Sugnall *Staffs*	37	SJ8031
Little Tew *Oxon*	29	SP3828
Little Tey *Essex*	24	TL8923
Little Thetford *Cambs*	31	TL5376
Little Thirkleby *N York*	62	SE4778
Little Thorpe *Dur*	62	NZ4242
Little Thurlow Green *Suffk*	32	TL6851
Little Thurrock *Essex*	24	TQ6277
Little Torrington *Devon*	6	SS4916
Little Totham *Essex*	24	TL8912
Little Town *Lancs*	54	SD6635
Little Urswick *Cumb*	67	NY2673
Little Wakering *Essex*	25	TQ9388
Little Walden *Essex*	31	TL5541
Little Waldingfield *Suffk*	32	TL9245
Little Walsingham *Norfk*	42	TF9336
Little Waltham *Essex*	24	TL7013
Little Washbourne *Gloucs*	28	SO9833
Little Weighton *Humb*	56	SE9833
Little Weldon *Nhants*	40	SP9289
Little Welnetham *Suffk*	32	TL8960
Little Wenham *Suffk*	32	TM0839
Little Wenlock *Shrops*	37	SJ6407
Little Weston *Somset*	9	ST6125
Little Whitefield *IOW*	11	SZ5989
Little Wilbraham *Cambs*	31	TL5458
Little Witcombe *Gloucs*	28	SO9115
Little Witley *H & W*	28	SO7864
Little Wittenham *Oxon*	21	SU5693
Little Wolford *Warwks*	29	SP2635
Little Woodcote *Surrey*	23	TQ2861
Little Wratting *Suffk*	32	TL6847
Little Wymington *Beds*	30	SP9565
Little Wymondley *Herts*	31	TL2127
Little Wyrley *Staffs*	38	SK0105
Little Yeldham *Essex*	32	TL7839
Littlebeck *N York*	63	NZ8704
Littleborough *Notts*	50	SK8282
Littlebourne *Kent*	15	TR2057
Littlebredy *Dorset*	9	SY5888
Littlebury *Essex*	31	TL5139
Littlebury Green *Essex*	31	TL4938
Littlecott *Wilts*	20	SU1451
Littledean *Gloucs*	28	SO6713
Littledown *Hants*	21	SU3558
Littleferry *Highld*	97	NH8095
Littleham *Devon*	6	SS4323
Littleham *Devon*	5	SY0281
Littlehampton *W Susx*	12	TQ0202
Littlehempston *Devon*	5	SX8162
Littlemill *Gramp*	88	NO3295
Littlemill *Highld*	93	NH9150
Littlemill *Strath*	73	NS4515
Littlemore *Oxon*	21	SP5302
Littleover *Derbys*	39	SK3234
Littleport *Cambs*	41	TL5686
Littlestone-on-Sea *Kent*	15	TR0824
Littlethorpe *Leics*	39	SP5496
Littlethorpe *N York*	55	SE3268
Littleton *Avon*	19	ST5564
Littleton *Ches*	46	SJ4466
Littleton *Hants*	10	SU4532
Littleton *Somset*	8	ST4830
Littleton *Surrey*	22	TQ0668
Littleton Drew *Wilts*	20	ST8380
Littleton Pannell *Wilts*	20	ST9954
Littleton-on-Severn *Avon*	19	ST5990
Littletown *Dur*	69	NZ3343
Littlewick Green *Berks*	22	SU8379
Littlewindsor *Dorset*	8	ST4303
Littleworth *H & W*	28	SO8850
Littleworth *Oxon*	21	SU3197
Littleworth *Staffs*	38	SJ9323
Littleworth *Staffs*	38	SK0112
Littley Green *Essex*	24	TL6917
Litton *Derbys*	48	SK1675
Litton *N York*	60	SD9074
Litton *Somset*	19	ST5954
Litton Cheney *Dorset*	8	SY5490
Liverpool *Mersyd*	46	SJ3490
Liverton *Cleve*	63	NZ7115
Liverton *Devon*	5	SX8075
Liverton Street *Kent*	14	TQ8749
Livingston *Loth*	75	NT0668
Livingston Village *Loth*	75	NT0366
Lixton *Devon*	5	SX6950
Lizard *Cnwll*	2	SW7012
Llaingoch *Gwynd*	44	SH2282
Llanaelhaearn *Gwynd*	44	SH3844
Llanafan *Dyfed*	35	SN6872
Llanafan-fechan *Powys*	26	SN9650
Llanallgo *Gwynd*	44	SH5085
Llanarmon Dyffryn Ceiriog *Clwyd*	36	SJ1532
Llanarmon-yn-Ial *Clwyd*	46	SJ1956
Llanarth *Dyfed*	34	SN4257
Llanarth *Gwent*	27	SO3710
Llanarthney *Dyfed*	17	SN5320
Llanasa *Clwyd*	46	SJ1081
Llanbabo *Gwynd*	44	SH3786
Llanbadarn Fawr *Dyfed*	34	SN6080
Llanbadarn Fynydd *Powys*	36	SO0977
Llanbadoc *Gwent*	19	ST3799
Llanbeder *Gwent*	19	ST3890
Llanbedr *Gwynd*	44	SH5826
Llanbedr *Powys*	27	SO2320
Llanbedr *Powys*	26	SO1346
Llanbedr-Dyffryn-Clwyd *Clwyd*	46	SJ1459
Llanbedrgoch *Gwynd*	44	SH5180
Llanbedrog *Gwynd*	44	SH3231
Llanberis *Gwynd*	44	SH5760
Llanbethery *S Glam*	18	ST0369
Llanbister *Powys*	36	SO1073
Llanblethian *S Glam*	18	SS9873
Llanboidy *Dyfed*	17	SN2123
Llanbradach *M Glam*	18	ST1490
Llancadle *S Glam*	19	ST2368
Llancarfan *S Glam*	18	ST0570
Llancloudy *H & W*	27	SO4920
Llandaff *S Glam*	19	ST1578
Llandanwg *Gwynd*	44	SH5728
Llanddaniel Fab *Gwynd*	44	SH4970
Llanddarog *Dyfed*	17	SN5016
Llanddeiniol *Dyfed*	34	SN5572
Llanddeiniolen *Gwynd*	44	SH5465
Llandderfel *Gwynd*	45	SH9837
Llanddeusant *Gwynd*	44	SH3485
Llanddewi *W Glam*	17	SS4685
Llanddewi Brefi *Dyfed*	26	SN6655
Llanddewi Rhydderch *Gwent*	27	SO3513
Llanddewi Velfrey *Dyfed*	16	SN1416
Llanddewi Ystradenni *Powys*	26	SO1068
Llanddoget *Gwynd*	45	SH8063
Llanddona *Gwynd*	44	SH5779
Llanddowror *Dyfed*	17	SN2514
Llanddrew *Powys*	26	SO0530
Llanddulas *Clwyd*	45	SH9078
Llanddyfnan *Gwynd*	44	SH5078
Llandefaelogtrer-graig *Powys*	26	SO1229
Llandefalle *Powys*	26	SO1035
Llandegai *Gwynd*	44	SH5971
Llandegfan *Gwynd*	44	SH5674
Llandegfan *Gwynd*	44	SH5674
Llandegla *Clwyd*	46	SJ1952
Llandegley *Powys*	26	SO1463
Llandegveth *Gwent*	19	ST3395
Llandegwning *Gwynd*	44	SH2630
Llandeilo *Dyfed*	17	SN6322
Llandeilo Graban *Powys*	26	SO0944
Llandeloy *Dyfed*	16	SM8526
Llandenny *Gwent*	27	SO4104
Llandenny Walks *Gwent*	19	SO4003
Llandevaud *Gwent*	19	ST4090
Llandevenny *Gwent*	19	ST4186
Llandinam *Powys*	35	SO0288
Llandissilio *Dyfed*	16	SN1221
Llandogo *Gwent*	19	SO5203
Llandough *S Glam*	18	SS9972
Llandough *S Glam*	19	ST1673
Llandovery *Dyfed*	26	SN7634
Llandow *S Glam*	18	SS9473
Llandre *Dyfed*	35	SN6286
Llandre *Dyfed*	26	SN6741
Llandre Isaf *Dyfed*	16	SN1328
Llandrillo *Clwyd*	36	SJ0337
Llandrillo-yn-Rhos *Clwyd*	45	SH8380
Llandrindod Wells *Powys*	26	SO0561
Llandrinio *Powys*	36	SJ2817
Llandudno *Gwynd*	45	SH7882
Llandudno Junction *Gwynd*	45	SH7977
Llandudwen *Gwynd*	44	SH2736
Llandulas *Powys*	26	SN8841
Llandwrog *Gwynd*	44	SH4556
Llandybie *Dyfed*	17	SN6215
Llandyfaelog *Dyfed*	17	SN4111
Llandyfriog *Dyfed*	17	SN3341
Llandygwydd *Dyfed*	17	SN2443
Llandyssil *Powys*	36	SO1995
Llandysul *Dyfed*	17	SN4140
Llanedeyrn *S Glam*	19	ST2282
Llanegryn *Gwynd*	34	SH5905
Llanegryn *Gwynd*	34	SH6005
Llanegwad *Dyfed*	17	SN5121
Llaneilian *Gwynd*	44	SH4692
Llanelian-yn-Rhos *Clwyd*	45	SH8676
Llanelidan *Clwyd*	46	SJ1150
Llanelieu *Powys*	27	SO1834
Llanelli *Dyfed*	17	SN5000
Llanelltyd *Gwynd*	35	SH7119
Llanelwedd *Powys*	26	SO0451
Llanenddwyn *Gwynd*	34	SH5823
Llanengan *Gwynd*	44	SH2926
Llanerch *Powys*	36	SO3094
Llanerchymedd *Gwynd*	44	SH4184
Llanerfyl *Powys*	36	SJ0309
Llanfachraeth *Gwynd*	44	SH3182
Llanfachreth *Gwynd*	35	SH7522
Llanfaelog *Gwynd*	44	SH3373
Llanfaelrhys *Gwynd*	44	SH2227
Llanfaenor *Gwent*	27	SO4217
Llanfaethlu *Gwynd*	44	SH3186
Llanfair *Gwynd*	44	SH5729
Llanfair *H & W*	27	SO2444
Llanfair Caereinion *Powys*	36	SJ1006
Llanfair Clydogau *Dyfed*	17	SN6251
Llanfair Dyffryn Clwyd *Clwyd*	46	SJ1355
Llanfair Kilgeddin *Gwent*	27	SO3407
Llanfair P G *Gwynd*	44	SH5371
Llanfair Talhaiarn *Clwyd*	45	SH9269
Llanfair Waterdine *Shrops*	36	SO2376
Llanfair-is-gaer *Gwynd*	44	SH5267
Llanfair-y-Cwmmwd *Gwynd*	44	SH4466
Llanfair-yn-Neubwll *Gwynd*	44	SH3077
Llanfairfechan *Gwynd*	45	SH6874
Llanfairynghornwy *Gwynd*	44	SH3290
Llanfallteg *Dyfed*	17	SN1520
Llanfallteg West *Dyfed*	16	SN1419
Llanfaredd *M Glam*	26	SO0651
Llanfarian *Dyfed*	34	SN5977
Llanfechain *Powys*	36	SJ1820
Llanfechelli *Gwynd*	44	SH3691
Llanfendigaid *Gwynd*	34	SH5605
Llanferres *Clwyd*	46	SJ1960
Llanfflewyn *Gwynd*	44	SH3689
Llanfihangel Glyn Myfyr *Clwyd*	45	SH9849
Llanfihangel Nant Bran *Powys*	26	SN9434
Llanfihangel Rhydithon *Powys*	27	SO1566
Llanfihangel Rogiet *Gwent*	19	ST4487
Llanfihangel ar-Arth *Dyfed*	17	SN4539
Llanfihangel yn Nhowyn *Gwynd*	44	SH3277
Llanfihangel-nant-Melan *Powys*	27	SO1858
Llanfihangel-uwch-Gwili *Dyfed*	17	SN4923
Llanfihangel-y-Creuddyn *Dyfed*	35	SN6675
Llanfihangel-y-pennant *Gwynd*	44	SH5245
Llanfihangel-y-traethau *Gwynd*	44	SH5935
Llanfihangel-yng-Ngwynfa *Powys*	36	SJ0816
Llanfilo *Powys*	26	SO1132
Llanfoist *Gwent*	27	SO2813
Llanfor *Gwynd*	45	SH9336
Llanfrechfa *Gwent*	19	ST3293
Llanfrynach *Powys*	26	SO0725
Llanfwrog *Clwyd*	46	SJ1157
Llanfwrog *Gwynd*	44	SH3083
Llanfyllin *Powys*	36	SJ1419
Llanfynydd *Clwyd*	46	SJ2756
Llanfynydd *Dyfed*	17	SN5527
Llanfyrnach *Dyfed*	17	SN2231
Llangadfan *Powys*	35	SJ0111
Llangadog *Dyfed*	26	SN7028
Llangadwaladr *Gwynd*	44	SH3869
Llangaffo *Gwynd*	44	SH4468
Llangammarch Wells *Powys*	26	SN9347
Llangan *S Glam*	18	SS9577
Llangarron *H & W*	27	SO5220
Llangathen *Dyfed*	17	SN5822
Llangattock *Powys*	27	SO2117
Llangattock Lingoed *Gwent*	27	SO3620
Llangedwyn *Clwyd*	36	SJ1824
Llangefni *Gwynd*	44	SH4675
Llangeinor *M Glam*	18	SS9187
Llangeinwen *Gwynd*	44	SH4465
Llangeitho *Dyfed*	35	SN6259
Llangeler *Dyfed*	17	SN3739
Llangelynin *Gwynd*	34	SH5707
Llangendeirne *Dyfed*	17	SN4514
Llangennech *Dyfed*	17	SN5601
Llangenny *Powys*	27	SO2418
Llangernyw *Clwyd*	45	SH8767
Llangian *Gwynd*	44	SH2928
Llangloffan *Dyfed*	16	SM9032
Llanglydwen *Dyfed*	17	SN1827
Llangoed *Gwynd*	44	SH6079
Llangoedmor *Dyfed*	17	SN1945
Llangollen *Clwyd*	36	SJ2141
Llangolman *Dyfed*	16	SN1127
Llangorse *Powys*	26	SO1327
Llangower *Gwynd*	45	SH9032
Llangranog *Dyfed*	34	SN3154
Llangristiolus *Gwynd*	44	SH4373
Llangrove *H & W*	27	SO5219
Llangunllo *Powys*	36	SO2171
Llangunnor *Dyfed*	17	SN4320
Llangurig *Powys*	35	SN9080
Llangwm *Clwyd*	45	SH9644
Llangwm *Gwent*	19	ST4299
Llangwm-isaf *Gwent*	19	SO4300
Llangwyfan *Clwyd*	46	SJ1266
Llangwyryfon *Dyfed*	34	SN5970
Llangybi *Dyfed*	17	SN6053
Llangybi *Gwent*	19	ST3797
Llangybi *Gwynd*	44	SH4240
Llangynhafal *Clwyd*	46	SJ1263
Llangynidr *Powys*	27	SO1519
Llangynin *Dyfed*	17	SN2519
Llangynog *Dyfed*	17	SN3314
Llangynog *Powys*	26	SO0145
Llangynog *Powys*	36	SJ0526
Llangynwyd *M Glam*	18	SS8588
Llangynwyd *M Glam*	18	SS8988
Llanhamlach *Powys*	26	SO0926
Llanharan *M Glam*	18	ST0083
Llanharry *M Glam*	18	ST0080
Llanhennock *Gwent*	19	ST3592
Llanhilleth *Gwent*	19	SO2100
Llanidloes *Powys*	35	SN9584
Llaniestyn *Gwynd*	44	SH2633
Llanigon *Powys*	27	SO2139
Llanilar *Dyfed*	35	SN6275
Llanilid *M Glam*	18	SS9781
Llanina *Dyfed*	34	SN4059
Llanishen *Gwent*	19	SO4703
Llanishen *S Glam*	19	ST1781
Llanllechid *Gwynd*	45	SH6268
Llanllowell *Gwent*	19	ST3998
Llanllugan *Powys*	36	SJ0502
Llanllwch *Dyfed*	17	SN3818
Llanllwchaiarn *Powys*	36	SO1292
Llanllwni *Dyfed*	17	SN4741
Llanllyfni *Gwynd*	44	SH4651
Llanmadoc *W Glam*	17	SS4493
Llanmaes *S Glam*	18	SS9869
Llanmartin *Gwent*	19	ST3989
Llanmerewig *Powys*	36	SO1593
Llanmihangel *S Glam*	18	SS9872
Llanmiloe *Dyfed*	17	SN2508
Llanmorlais *W Glam*	17	SS5294
Llannefydd *Clwyd*	45	SH9870
Llannon *Dyfed*	17	SN5308
Llannor *Gwynd*	44	SH3537
Llanon *Dyfed*	34	SN5166
Llanover *Gwent*	27	SO3109
Llanpumsaint *Dyfed*	17	SN4229
Llanrhaeadr *Clwyd*	46	SJ0763
Llanrhaeadr-ym-Mochnant *Clwyd*	36	SJ1226
Llanrhidian *W Glam*	17	SS4992
Llanrhos *Gwynd*	45	SH7880
Llanrhychwyn *Gwynd*	45	SH7761
Llanrhyddlad *Gwynd*	44	SH3389
Llanrhystud *Dyfed*	34	SN5369
Llanrian *Dyfed*	16	SM8131
Llanrothal *H & W*	27	SO4618
Llanrothal *H & W*	27	SO4718
Llanrug *Gwynd*	44	SH5363
Llanrumney *S Glam*	19	ST2280
Llanrwst *Gwynd*	45	SH7961
Llansadurnen *Dyfed*	17	SN2810
Llansadwrn *Dyfed*	26	SN6931
Llansadwrn *Gwynd*	44	SH5575
Llansamlet *W Glam*	18	SS6897
Llansannan *Clwyd*	45	SH9365
Llansantffraed *Powys*	26	SO1223
Llansantffraed-Cwmdeuddwr *Powys*	35	SN9667
Llansantffraed-in-Elvel *Powys*	26	SO0954
Llansantffraid *Dyfed*	34	SN5167
Llansantffraid Glan Conwy *Gwynd*	45	SH8075
Llansantffraid-ym-Mechain *Powys*	36	SJ2220
Llansawel *Dyfed*	17	SN6136
Llansilin *Clwyd*	36	SJ2128
Llansoy *Gwent*	19	SO4402
Llanspyddid *Powys*	26	SO0128
Llanstadwell *Dyfed*	16	SM9505
Llanstephan *Dyfed*	17	SN3511
Llantarnam *Gwent*	19	ST3093
Llanteg *Dyfed*	17	SN1810
Llanthewy Skirrid *Gwent*	27	SO3416
Llanthony *Gwent*	27	SO2827
Llantilio Pertholey *Gwent*	27	SO3116
Llantrisant *Gwent*	19	ST3997
Llantrisant *Gwynd*	44	SH3683
Llantrisant *M Glam*	18	ST0483
Llantrithyd *S Glam*	18	ST0472
Llantwit Fardre *M Glam*	18	ST0886
Llantwit Major *S Glam*	18	SS9668
Llanuwchllyn *Gwynd*	45	SH8730
Llanvaches *Gwent*	19	ST4391
Llanvair Discoed *Gwent*	19	ST4492
Llanvapley *Gwent*	27	SO3614
Llanvetherine *Gwent*	27	SO3617
Llanvihangel Crucorney *Gwent*	27	SO3220
Llanwddyn *Powys*	35	SJ0219
Llanwenog *Dyfed*	17	SN4945
Llanwinio *Dyfed*	17	SN2626
Llanwnda *Dyfed*	16	SM9339
Llanwnda *Gwynd*	44	SH4758
Llanwnen *Dyfed*	17	SN5347
Llanwnog *Powys*	35	SO0293
Llanwrda *Dyfed*	26	SN7131
Llanwrin *Powys*	35	SH7803
Llanwrthwl *Powys*	35	SN9763
Llanwrtyd Wells *Powys*	26	SN8846
Llanwyddelan *Powys*	36	SJ0801
Llanyblodwel *Shrops*	36	SJ2423
Llanybri *Dyfed*	17	SN3312
Llanybydder *Dyfed*	17	SN5244
Llanycefn *Dyfed*	16	SN0923
Llanychaer Bridge *Dyfed*	16	SM9835
Llanymawddwy *Gwynd*	35	SH9019
Llanymynech *Shrops*	36	SJ2620
Llanynghenedl *Gwynd*	44	SH3181
Llanynis *Powys*	26	SN9950
Llanynys *Clwyd*	46	SJ1062
Llanyre *Powys*	26	SO0462
Llanystumdwy *Gwynd*	44	SH4738
Llanywern *Powys*	26	SO1028
Llawhaden *Dyfed*	16	SN0717
Llawryglyn *Powys*	35	SN9291
Llay *Clwyd*	46	SJ3355
Llechcynfarwy *Gwynd*	44	SH3881
Llechryd *Dyfed*	17	SN2243
Llechryd *M Glam*	26	SO1009
Lledrod *Dyfed*	35	SN6470
Llidiart-y-parc *Clwyd*	46	SJ1243
Llithfaen *Gwynd*	44	SH3542
Llowes *Powys*	27	SO1941
Llwydcoed *M Glam*	26	SN9904
Llwydiarth *Powys*	36	SJ0315
Llwyncelyn *Dyfed*	34	SN4459
Llwyndafydd *Dyfed*	34	SN3755
Llwynderw *Powys*	36	SJ2004
Llwyngwril *Gwynd*	34	SH5909
Llwynmawr *Clwyd*	36	SJ2237
Llwynypia *M Glam*	18	SS9993
Llyn-y-pandy *Clwyd*	46	SJ2065
Llynclys *Shrops*	36	SJ2823
Llynfaes *Gwynd*	44	SH4178
Llys-y-fran *Dyfed*	16	SN0424
Llysfaen *Clwyd*	45	SH8977
Llysfaen *Clwyd*	45	SH8977
Llyswen *Dyfed*	34	SN4561
Llyswen *Powys*	26	SO1337
Llysworney *S Glam*	18	SS9674
Llywel *Powys*	26	SN8730
Loan *Cent*	75	NS9675
Loanhead *Loth*	75	NT2865
Loaningfoot *D & G*	66	NX9656
Loans *Strath*	73	NS3431
Lobb *Devon*	6	SS4637
Lobhillcross *Devon*	4	SX4686
Loceport *W Isls*	102	NF8563
Loch Katrine Pier *Cent*	81	NN4907
Loch Loyal Lodge *Highld*	99	NC6146
Loch Maree Hotel *Highld*	91	NG9668
Loch Skipport *W Isls*	102	NF8238
Lochailort *Highld*	85	NM7682
Lochans *D & G*	64	NX0656
Lochassynt Lodge *Highld*	98	NC1727
Lochavich *Strath*	80	NM9415
Lochawe *Strath*	80	NN1227
Lochboisdale *W Isls*	102	NF7820
Lochbuie *Strath*	79	NM6125
Lochcarron *Highld*	85	NG8939
Lochdochart House *Cent*	81	NN4327
Lochdrum *Highld*	96	NH2585
Lochead *Strath*	71	NR7778
Lochearnhead *Cent*	81	NN5823
Lochee *Tays*	83	NO3731
Locheilside Station *Highld*	85	NM9978
Lochend *Highld*	92	NH5937
Locherben *D & G*	66	NX9797
Lochfoot *D & G*	66	NX8973
Lochgair *Strath*	71	NR9290
Lochgarthside *Highld*	92	NH5219
Lochgelly *Fife*	82	NT1893
Lochgilphead *Strath*	71	NR8688
Lochgoilhead *Strath*	80	NN2001
Lochieheads *Fife*	83	NO2513
Lochill *Gramp*	94	NJ2964
Lochindorb Lodge *Highld*	93	NH9635
Lochinver *Highld*	98	NC0922
Lochlane *Tays*	82	NN8320
Lochluichart *Highld*	92	NH3363
Lochmaben *D & G*	66	NY0882
Lochmaddy *W Isls*	102	NF9169
Lochmore Lodge *Highld*	98	NC2938
Lochore *Fife*	82	NT1896
Lochranza *Strath*	72	NR9350
Lochside *Gramp*	89	NO7364
Lochside *Highld*	93	NH8152
Lochslin *Highld*	97	NH8481
Lochton *Strath*	64	NX2579
Lochty *Fife*	83	NO5208
Lochty *Tays*	89	NO5362
Lochuisge *Highld*	79	NM7956
Lochwinnoch *Strath*	73	NS3558
Lochwood *D & G*	66	NY0896
Lochwood *Strath*	74	NS6966
Lockengate *Cnwll*	3	SX0361
Lockerbie *D & G*	67	NY1381
Lockeridge *Wilts*	20	SU1467
Lockerley *Hants*	10	SU2925
Lockerley *Hants*	10	SU3026
Locking *Avon*	19	ST3659
Lockington *Humb*	56	SE9947
Lockleywood *Shrops*	37	SJ6928
Lockmaddy *W Isls*	102	NF9168
Locksbottom *Gt Lon*	23	TQ4265
Lockton *N York*	63	SE8490
Loddington *Leics*	40	SK7902
Loddington *Nhants*	30	SP8178
Loddiswell *Devon*	5	SX7148
Loddon *Norfk*	43	TM3698
Lode *Cambs*	31	TL5362
Lode Heath *W Mids*	38	SP1580
Loders *Dorset*	8	SY4994
Lodsworth *W Susx*	11	SU9223
Lofthouse *N York*	61	SE1073
Lofthouse *W York*	55	SE3325
Loftus *Cleve*	63	NZ7118
Logan *Strath*	74	NS5820
Loganlea *Loth*	75	NS9762
Loggerheads *Staffs*	37	SJ7336
Logie *Fife*	83	NO4020
Logie *Gramp*	93	NJ0150
Logie *Tays*	89	NO6963
Logie Coldstone *Gramp*	88	NJ4304
Logie Pert *Tays*	89	NO6664
Logierait *Tays*	88	NN9752
Login *Dyfed*	17	SN1623
Lolworth *Cambs*	31	TL3664
Lonbain *Highld*	91	NG6852
Londesborough *Humb*	56	SE8645
London *Gt Lon*	23	TQ2980
London Apprentice *Cnwll*	3	SX0050
London Colney *Herts*	23	TL1803
London End *Nhants*	30	SP9265
Londonderry *N York*	61	SE3087
Londonthorpe *Lincs*	40	SK9537
Londubh *Highld*	91	NG8680
Long Ashton *Avon*	19	ST5470
Long Bank *H & W*	37	SO7674
Long Bennington *Lincs*	50	SK8344
Long Bredy *Dorset*	8	SY5690
Long Buckby *Nhants*	29	SP6367
Long Cause *Devon*	5	SX7461
Long Clawson *Leics*	40	SK7227
Long Compton *Staffs*	38	SJ8522
Long Compton *Warwks*	29	SP2832
Long Crendon *Bucks*	22	SP6908
Long Crichel *Dorset*	9	ST9710
Long Ditton *Surrey*	23	TQ1766
Long Drax *N York*	56	SE6828
Long Duckmanton *Derbys*	49	SK4471
Long Eaton *Derbys*	39	SK4933
Long Green *Ches*	46	SJ4770
Long Green *H & W*	28	SO8433
Long Hedges *Lincs*	51	TF3546
Long Itchington *Warwks*	29	SP4165
Long Lane *Shrops*	37	SJ6315
Long Lawford *Warwks*	39	SP4776
Long Load *Somset*	8	ST4623
Long Marston *Herts*	30	SP8915
Long Marston *N York*	55	SE5051
Long Marston *Warwks*	28	SP1548
Long Marton *Cumb*	60	NY6624
Long Meadowend *Shrops*	36	SO4081
Long Melford *Suffk*	32	TL8645
Long Newnton *Gloucs*	20	ST9092
Long Newton *Loth*	76	NT5164
Long Preston *N York*	54	SD8358
Long Riston *Humb*	57	TA1242
Long Sight *Gt Man*	54	SD9207
Long Stratton *Norfk*	33	TM1992
Long Street *Bucks*	30	SP7947
Long Sutton *Hants*	22	SU7347
Long Sutton *Lincs*	41	TF4322
Long Sutton *Somset*	8	ST4625
Long Thurlow *Suffk*	32	TM0168
Long Waste *Shrops*	37	SJ6115
Long Whatton *Leics*	39	SK4723
Long Wittenham *Oxon*	21	SU5493
Longbenton *T & W*	69	NZ2768
Longborough *Gloucs*	29	SP1729
Longbridge *W Mids*	38	SP0177
Longbridgemuir *D & G*	66	NY0669
Longburgh *Cumb*	67	NY3159
Longburton *Dorset*	9	ST6412
Longcliffe *Derbys*	48	SK2255
Longcombe *Devon*	5	SX8359
Longcot *Oxon*	21	SU2790
Longden *Shrops*	36	SJ4406
Longden Common *Shrops*	36	SJ4404
Longdon *H & W*	28	SO8336
Longdon Green *Staffs*	38	SK0813
Longdon upon Tern *Shrops*	37	SJ6116
Longdown *Devon*	5	SX8691
Longdowns *Cnwll*	2	SW7434
Longfield *Kent*	14	TQ6069
Longford *Derbys*	48	SK2137
Longford *Gloucs*	28	SO8320
Longford *Kent*	23	TQ5156
Longford *Shrops*	37	SJ6434
Longford *Shrops*	37	SJ7218
Longforgan *Tays*	83	NO2929
Longformacus *Border*	76	NT6957
Longframlington *Nthumb*	69	NU1201
Longham *Dorset*	10	SZ0697
Longham *Norfk*	42	TF9415
Longhill *Gramp*	95	NJ9953
Longhirst *Nthumb*	69	NZ2289
Longhope *Gloucs*	28	SO6819
Longhorsley *Nthumb*	69	NZ1494
Longhoughton *Nthumb*	77	NU2415
Longlane *Derbys*	48	SK2538
Longlevens *Gloucs*	28	SO8519
Longleys *Tays*	88	NO2643
Longmanhill *Gramp*	95	NJ7462
Longmoor Camp *Hants*	11	SU7931
Longmorn *Gramp*	94	NJ2358
Longnewton *Border*	76	NT5827
Longney *Gloucs*	28	SO7612
Longniddry *Loth*	76	NT4476
Longnor *Shrops*	37	SJ4800
Longnor *Staffs*	48	SK0865
Longparish *Hants*	21	SU4344
Longpark *Cumb*	67	NY4261
Longridge *Lancs*	54	SD6037
Longridge *Loth*	75	NS9562
Longriggend *Strath*	74	NS8270
Longrock *Cnwll*	2	SW4931
Longshaw Common *Gt Man*	46	SD5302
Longside *Gramp*	95	NK0347
Longsleddale *Cumb*	59	NY4902
Longstanton *Cambs*	31	TL3966
Longstock *Hants*	10	SU3536
Longstone Wells *Devon*	7	SS7634
Longstowe *Cambs*	31	TL3054
Longstreet *Wilts*	20	SU1451
Longthorpe *Cambs*	40	TL1698
Longthwaite *Cumb*	59	NY4323
Longton *Lancs*	53	SD4825
Longton *Staffs*	48	SJ9143
Longtown *Cumb*	67	NY3768
Longtown *H & W*	27	SO3129
Longueville *Jersey*	101	SV0000
Longville in the Dale *Shrops*	37	SO5494
Longwick *Bucks*	22	SP7805
Longwitton *Nthumb*	68	NZ0788
Longwood *D & G*	65	NX7061
Longwood House *Hants*	11	SU5424
Longworth *Oxon*	21	SU3899
Longyester *Loth*	76	NT5465
Lonmay *Gramp*	95	NK0159
Lonmore *Highld*	90	NG2646
Looe *Cnwll*	4	SX2553
Loose *Kent*	14	TQ7552
Loosley Row *Bucks*	22	SP8100
Lootcherbrae *Gramp*	94	NJ6053
Lopcombe Corner *Wilts*	10	SU2435
Lopen *Somset*	8	ST4214
Lornty *Tays*	88	NO1746
Loscoe *Derbys*	49	SK4247
Loscombe *Dorset*	8	SY4998
Losonford *Warwks*	29	SP1867
Lossiemouth *Gramp*	94	NJ2370
Lostock Gralam *Ches*	47	SJ6975
Lostock Green *Ches*	47	SJ6973
Lostwithiel *Cnwll*	3	SX1059

Lothbeg Marston St. Lawrence

Lothbeg Highld 97 NC9410
Lothersdale N York 54 SD9646
Lothmore Highld 97 NC9611
Loudwater Bucks 22 SU8990
Loughborough Leics 39 SK5319
Loughton Bucks 30 SP8337
Loughton Essex 23 TQ4296
Loughton Shrops 37 SO6183
Lound Lincs 40 TF0618
Lound Suffk 43 TM5099
Lounston Devon 5 SX7874
Lount Leics 39 SK3819
Louth Lincs 51 TF3287
Lovaton Devon 4 SX5466
Love Clough Lancs 54 SD8127
Lovedean Hants 11 SU6812
Loversall S York 49 SK5798
Loves Green Essex 24 TL6404
Loveston Dyfed 16 SN0808
Lovington Somset 9 ST5931
Low Ackworth W York 55 SE4517
Low Barbeth D & G 64 NX0166
Low Bell End N York 63 SE7196
Low Borrowbridge Cumb 59 NY6101
Low Bradfield S York 49 SK2691
Low Bradley N York 54 SE0048
Low Brunton Nthumb 68 NY9269
Low Burnham Humb 50 SE7702
Low Catton Humb 56 SE7053
Low Crosby Cumb 67 NY4459
Low Dinsdale Dur 62 NZ3411
Low Eggborough N York 56 SE5523
Low Ellington N York 61 SE1983
Low Fremington N York 61 SE0398
Low Gartachorrans Cent 81 NS4685
Low Gate Nthumb 68 NY9064
Low Grantley N York 55 SE2370
Low Ham Somset 8 ST4329
Low Harrogate N York 55 SE2855
Low Hawsker N York 63 NZ9207
Low Hesket Cumb 67 NY4646
Low Hutton N York 56 SE7567
Low Leighton Derbys 48 SK0085
Low Lorton Cumb 58 NY1525
Low Marnham Notts 50 SK8069
Low Mill N York 62 SE6795
Low Moor Lancs 54 SD7341
Low Moor W York 55 SE1629
Low Moorsley T & W 69 NZ3346
Low Mowthorpe N York 56 SE9066
Low Row Cumb 67 NY5863
Low Row Cumb 67 NY5863
Low Row N York 61 SD9897
Low Salchrie D & G 64 NX0365
Low Salter Lancs 54 SD6063
Low Santon Humb 56 SE9312
Low Street Essex 24 TQ6677
Low Street Norfk 43 TG3424
Low Tharston Norfk 43 TM1895
Low Valleyfield Fife 82 NT0086
Low Wood Cumb 59 NY3483
Low Worsall N York 62 NZ3909
Low Wray Cumb 59 NY3731
Lowbands H & W 28 SO7831
Lowdham Notts 49 SK6646
Lower Aisholt Somset 8 ST2035
Lower Apperley Gloucs 28 SO8527
Lower Assendon Oxon 22 SU7484
Lower Bartle Lancs 53 SD4933
Lower Beeding W Susx 12 TQ2227
Lower Benefield Nhants 40 SP9888
Lower Bentham N York 54 SD6469
Lower Bentley H & W 28 SO9865
Lower Boddington Nhants 29 SP4851
Lower Boscaswell Cnwll 2 SW3834
Lower Bourne Surrey 22 SU8444
Lower Brailes Warwks 29 SP3139
Lower Broadheath H & W 28 SO8057
Lower Breakish Highld 85 NG6723
Lower Bullingham H & W 27 SO5038
Lower Bullingham H & W 27 SO5137
Lower Burgate Hants 10 SU1515
Lower Burrowton Devon 7 SY0096
Lower Caldecote Beds 31 TL1746
Lower Cam Gloucs 20 SO7400
Lower Catesby Nhants 29 SP5159
Lower Chapel Powys 26 SO0235
Lower Chicksgrove Wilts 9 ST9730
Lower Chute Wilts 21 SU3153
Lower Clapton Gt Lon 23 TQ3486
Lower Clent H & W 38 SO9279
Lower Crossings Derbys 48 SK0480
Lower Cumberworth W York 55 SE2209
Lower Dalveen D & G 66 NS8807
Lower Dean Beds 30 TL0569
Lower Denby W York 55 SE2307
Lower Diabaig Highld 91 NG7960
Lower Dicker E Susx 13 TQ5511
Lower Down Shrops 36 SO3384
Lower Dunsforth N York 55 SE4464
Lower Egleton H & W 27 SO6245
Lower End Bucks 30 SP9237
Lower Exbury Hants 10 SZ4298
Lower Eythorne Kent 15 TR2749
Lower Failand Avon 19 ST5173
Lower Farringdon Hants 11 SU7035
Lower Feltham Gt Lon 22 TQ0972
Lower Fittleworth W Susx 12 TQ0118
Lower Froyle Hants 22 SU7644
Lower Gabwell Devon 5 SX9169
Lower Gledfield Highld 96 NH5890
Lower Godney Somset 19 ST4742
Lower Gravenhurst Beds 30 TL1034
Lower Green Gt Man 47 SJ7099
Lower Green Herts 31 TL4232
Lower Green Kent 13 TQ5640
Lower Green Kent 13 TQ6341
Lower Green Norfk 42 TF9837
Lower Green Suffk 32 TL7465
Lower Grove Common H & W 27 SO5525
Lower Hacheston Suffk 33 TM3157
Lower Halliford Surrey 22 TQ0867
Lower Halstow Kent 14 TQ8567
Lower Hamworthy Dorset 9 SY9990
Lower Hardres Kent 15 TR1453
Lower Hartwell Bucks 30 SP7912
Lower Hawthwaite Cumb 58 SD2189
Lower Hergest H & W 27 SO2755
Lower Heyford Oxon 29 SP4824
Lower Holbrook Suffk 25 TM1835
Lower Irlam Gt Man 47 SJ7193
Lower Kilburn Derbys 49 SK3745
Lower Killeyan Strath 70 NR2743
Lower Kinnerton Ches 46 SJ3462
Lower Largo Fife 83 NO4102
Lower Leigh Staffs 38 SK0136
Lower Lovacott Devon 6 SS5326
Lower Loxhore Devon 6 SS6137
Lower Lydbrook Gloucs 27 SO5916
Lower Lye H & W 27 SO4067
Lower Machen Gwent 19 ST2288
Lower Mannington Dorset 10 SU0705
Lower Marston Somset 20 ST7643
Lower Meend Gloucs 27 SO5504
Lower Middleton Cheney Nhants 29 SP5041
Lower Milton Somset 19 ST5446
Lower Moor W Mids 28 SO9747
Lower Morton Avon 19 ST6492
Lower Nazeing Essex 23 TL3906
Lower Norton Warwks 29 SP2364
Lower Nyland Dorset 9 ST7421
Lower Penarth S Glam 19 ST1869
Lower Penn Staffs 38 SO8796
Lower Pond Street Essex 31 TL4537
Lower Quinton Warwks 29 SP1847
Lower Raydon Suffk 25 TM0338
Lower Roadwater Somset 7 ST0139
Lower Shelton Beds 30 SP9942
Lower Shiplake Oxon 22 SU7679
Lower Shuckburgh Warwks 29 SP4862
Lower Shurlach Ches 47 SJ6772
Lower Slaughter Gloucs 28 SP1622
Lower Smerlay Strath 72 NR7522
Lower Standen Kent 15 TR2340
Lower Stanton St. Quintin Wilts 20 ST9180
Lower Stoke Kent 14 TQ8375
Lower Stone Gloucs 20 ST6794
Lower Stow Bedon Norfk 42 TL9694
Lower Street Dorset 9 SY8399
Lower Street E Susx 14 TQ7012
Lower Street Norfk 43 TG2635
Lower Street Suffk 32 TL7852
Lower Street Suffk 33 TM1052
Lower Sundon Beds 30 TL0526
Lower Swanwick Hants 10 SU4909
Lower Swell Gloucs 29 SP1725
Lower Tean Staffs 48 SK0138
Lower Town Devon 5 SX7172
Lower Town Dyfed 16 SM9637
Lower Tysoe Warwks 29 SP3445
Lower Ufford Suffk 33 TM2952
Lower Upcott Devon 5 SX8880
Lower Upham Hants 11 SU5219
Lower Vexford Somset 8 ST1135
Lower Westmancote H & W 28 SO9337
Lower Whatley Somset 20 ST7347
Lower Whitley Ches 47 SJ6179
Lower Wick Gloucs 20 ST7196
Lower Wield Hants 21 SU6340
Lower Willingdon E Susx 13 TQ5803
Lower Winchendon Bucks 30 SP7312
Lower Woodford Wilts 10 SU1235
Lower Wraxhall Dorset 8 ST5700
Lowertown Devon 4 SX4584
Lowesby Leics 40 SK7207
Lowestoft Suffk 43 TM5493
Loweswater Cumb 58 NY1420
Lowfield Heath W Susx 12 TQ2740
Lowgill Cumb 60 SD6297
Lowick Cumb 58 SD2985
Lowick Nhants 40 SP9881
Lowick Nthumb 77 NU0139
Lowick Bridge Cumb 67 NY2886
Lowick Green Cumb 67 NY3085
Lowtherton D & G 67 NY2566
Lowthorpe Humb 57 TA0860
Loxbeare Devon 7 SS9116
Loxhill Surrey 12 TQ0038
Loxhore Devon 6 SS6138
Loxhore Cott Devon 6 SS6138
Loxley Warwks 29 SP2552
Loxton Avon 19 ST3755
Loxwood W Susx 12 TQ0331
Lubcroy Highld 96 NC3502
Lubenham Nhants 40 SP7087
Lucas Green Surrey 22 SU9460
Luccombe Somset 7 SS9144
Luccombe Village IOW 11 SZ5880
Lucker Nthumb 77 NU1530
Luckett Cnwll 4 SX3873
Lucking Street Essex 24 TL8134
Luckington Wilts 20 ST8383
Lucklawhill Fife 83 NO4221
Luckwell Bridge Somset 7 SS9038
Lucton H & W 27 SO4364
Ludag W Isls 102 NF7714
Ludborough Lincs 51 TF2995
Ludbrook Devon 5 SX6654
Ludchurch Dyfed 16 SN1411
Luddenden W York 55 SE0426
Luddenden Foot W York 55 SE0325
Luddenham Court Kent 15 TQ9962
Luddesdown Kent 14 TQ6766
Luddington Humb 56 SE8216
Luddington Warwks 28 SP1652
Luddington in the Brook Nhants 40 TL1083
Ludford Lincs 50 TF1989
Ludford Shrops 37 SO5174
Ludgershall Bucks 29 SP6517
Ludgershall Wilts 21 SU2650
Ludgershall Wilts 21 SU2650
Ludgvan Cnwll 2 SW5033
Ludham Norfk 43 TG3818
Ludlow Shrops 37 SO5175
Ludney Somset 8 ST3812
Ludwell Wilts 9 ST9122
Ludworth Dur 62 NZ3641
Luffenhall Herts 31 TL2928
Luffincott Devon 6 SX3394
Lufflands Devon 6 SS3209
Luffness Loth 83 NT4780
Lugar Strath 74 NS5821
Luggate Burn Loth 76 NT6074
Luggiebank Strath 74 NS7672
Lugton Strath 73 NS4152
Lugwardine H & W 27 SO5540
Luib Highld 84 NG5627
Lulham H & W 27 SO4141
Lullington Derbys 39 SK2513
Lullington Somset 20 ST7851
Lulsgate Bottom Avon 19 ST5165
Lulsley H & W 28 SO7455
Lumb Lancs 54 SD8324
Lumb W York 55 SE0321
Lumbutts W York 54 SD9528
Lumby N York 55 SE4830
Lumloch Strath 74 NS6370
Lumphanan Gramp 89 NJ5804
Lumphinnans Fife 82 NT1692
Lumsden Gramp 94 NJ4722
Lunan Tays 89 NO6851
Lunanhead Tays 89 NO4752
Luncarty Tays 82 NO0929
Lund Humb 56 SE9647
Lund N York 56 SE6532
Lundie Cent 81 NN7304
Lundie Tays 83 NO2836
Lundin Links Fife 83 NO4002
Lunna Shet 103 HU4869
Lunsford Kent 14 TQ6959
Lunsford's Cross E Susx 14 TQ7210
Lunt Mersyd 46 SD3402
Luppitt Devon 8 ST1606
Lupridge Devon 5 SX7153
Lupset W York 55 SE3119
Lupton Cumb 59 SD5581
Lurgashall W Susx 11 SU9327
Lurley Devon 7 SS9214
Lusby Lincs 51 TF3367
Luscombe Devon 5 SX7957
Luskentyre W Isls 102 NG0699
Luss Strath 80 NS3692
Lusta Highld 90 NG2756
Lustleigh Devon 5 SX7881
Luston H & W 27 SO4863
Luthermuir Gramp 89 NO6568
Luthrie Fife 83 NO3319
Lutley W Mids 38 SO9483
Luton Beds 30 TL0921
Luton Devon 5 SX9076
Luton Devon 7 ST0802
Luton Kent 14 TQ7766
Lutterworth Leics 39 SP5484
Lutton Devon 5 SX5959
Lutton Lincs 41 TF4325
Lutton Nhants 40 TL1187
Lutworthy Devon 7 SS7615
Luxborough Somset 7 SS9738
Luxulyan Cnwll 3 SX0458
Luzley Gt Man 48 SD9601
Lybster Highld 100 ND2435
Lydbury North Shrops 36 SO3486
Lydd Kent 15 TR0420
Lydden Kent 15 TR2645
Lydden Kent 15 TR3567
Lyddington Leics 40 SP8797
Lyde Green Hants 22 SU7057
Lydeard St. Lawrence Somset 8 ST1232
Lydford Devon 4 SX5084
Lydford on Fosse Somset 8 ST5630
Lydgate Derbys 49 SK3177
Lydgate Gt Man 54 SD9526
Lydgate W York 54 SD9225
Lydham Shrops 36 SO3391
Lydiard Millicent Wilts 20 SU0986
Lydiard Tregoze Wilts 20 SU1085
Lydiate Mersyd 46 SD3604
Lydiate Ash H & W 38 SO9775
Lydlinch Dorset 9 ST7413
Lydney Gloucs 19 SO6303
Lydstep Dyfed 16 SS0898
Lye W Mids 38 SO9284
Lye Green E Susx 13 TQ5034
Lye Green Warwks 29 SP1965
Lye's Green Wilts 20 ST8246
Lyford Oxon 21 SU3994
Lymbridge Green Kent 15 TR1244
Lyme Border 75 NT2041
Lyme Regis Dorset 8 SY3492
Lyminge Kent 15 TR1641
Lymington Hants 10 SZ3295
Lyminster W Susx 12 TQ0204
Lymm Ches 47 SJ6887
Lympne Kent 15 TR1135
Lympstone Devon 5 SX9984
Lynch Green Norfk 43 TG1505
Lynchat Highld 87 NH7801
Lyndhurst Hants 10 SU2907
Lyndon Leics 40 SK9004
Lyne Surrey 22 TQ0166
Lyne Down H & W 27 SO6530
Lyne Hill Staffs 38 SJ9212
Lyne of Gorthleck Highld 92 NH5420
Lyne of Skene Gramp 95 NJ7610
Lyneal Shrops 36 SJ4433
Lynegar Highld 100 ND2256
Lyneham Oxon 29 SP2720
Lyneham Wilts 20 SU0278
Lyness Ork 103 ND3094
Lyng Norfk 42 TG0717
Lyng Somset 8 ST3328
Lynmouth Devon 18 SS7249
Lynn Staffs 46 SD0804
Lynn of Shenval Gramp 94 NJ2129
Lynsted Kent 14 TQ9460
Lynton Devon 18 SS7149
Lyon's Gate Dorset 9 ST6605
Lyonshall H & W 27 SO3355
Lytchett Matravers Dorset 9 SY9495
Lytham Lancs 53 SD3627
Lytham St. Anne's Lancs 53 SD3427
Lythe Highld 100 ND2762
Lythe N York 63 NZ8413
Lythmore Highld 100 ND0566

M

Maaruig W Isls 90 NB1906
Mabe Burnthouse Cnwll 2 SW7634
Mabie D & G 66 NX9570
Mablethorpe Lincs 51 TF5085
Macclesfield Ches 48 SJ9173
Macclesfield Forest Ches 48 SJ9772
Macduff Gramp 95 NJ7064
Macharioch Strath 72 NR7309
Machen M Glam 19 ST2189
Machire Strath 70 NR2064
Machrie Farm Strath 72 NR9033
Machrihanish Strath 72 NR6320
Machrins Strath 70 NR3693
Machynlleth Powys 35 SH7400
Machynys Dyfed 17 SS5198
Mackworth Derbys 49 SK3137
Macmerry Loth 76 NT4372
Maddaford Devon 6 SX5495
Madderty Tays 82 NN9522
Maddington Wilts 20 SU0643
Maddiston Cent 75 NS9476
Madeley Staffs 47 SJ7744
Madingley Cambs 31 TL3960
Madley H & W 27 SO4238
Madresfield H & W 28 SO8047
Madron Cnwll 2 SW4532
Maen-y-groes Dyfed 34 SN3858
Maenclochog Dyfed 16 SN0827
Maendy S Glam 18 ST0076
Maentwrog Gwynd 45 SH6640
Maer Staffs 37 SJ7938
Maerdy Clwyd 45 SJ0144
Maerdy M Glam 18 SS9798
Maes-glas Gwent 19 ST2986
Maes-y-cwmmer M Glam 19 ST1794
Maesbrook Shrops 36 SJ3021
Maesbury Marsh Shrops 36 SJ3125
Maesllyn Dyfed 17 SN3644
Maesmynis Powys 26 SO0147
Maesmynis Powys 26 SO0350
Maesteg M Glam 18 SS8590
Maesybont Dyfed 17 SN5616
Maesycwmmer M Glam 19 ST1594
Magdalen Laver Essex 23 TL5108
Maggieknockater Gramp 94 NJ3145
Maggots End Essex 31 TL4727
Magham Down E Susx 13 TQ6011
Maghull Mersyd 46 SD3703
Magor Gwent 19 ST4287
Maidenhead D & G 64 NX1058
Maiden Bradley Wilts 20 ST7938
Maiden Head Avon 19 ST5666
Maiden Newton Dorset 9 SY5997
Maiden Wells Dyfed 16 SR9799
Maidencombe Devon 5 SX9268
Maidenhayne Devon 8 SY2795
Maidenhead Berks 22 SU8980
Maidens Strath 73 NS2107
Maidenwell Lincs 51 TF3179
Maidford Nhants 29 SP6052
Maids Moreton Bucks 30 SP7035
Maidstone Kent 14 TQ7555
Maidwell Nhants 30 SP7476
Maindee Gwent 19 ST3288
Mains of Allardice Gramp 89 NO8375
Mains of Bainakettle Gramp 89 NO6274
Mains of Balhall Tays 89 NO5163
Mains of Cairnbarrow Gramp 94 NJ4640
Mains of Dalvey Highld 93 NJ1031
Mains of Dillavaird Gramp 89 NO7482
Mains of Haulkerton Gramp 89 NO7172
Mains of Throsk Cent 82 NS8690
Mainsforth Dur 62 NZ3131
Mainsriddle D & G 66 NX9557
Mainstone Shrops 36 SO2787
Maisemore Gloucs 28 SO8121
Makeney Derbys 49 SK3544
Malborough Devon 5 SX7039
Malden Surrey 23 TQ2175
Maldon Essex 24 TL8507
Malham N York 54 SD9062
Mallaig Highld 85 NM6796
Mallaigvaig Highld 85 NM6897
Malleny Mills Loth 75 NT1665
Malltraeth Gwynd 44 SH4069
Mallwyd Gwynd 35 SH8612
Malmesbury Wilts 20 ST9387
Malmsmead Somset 18 SS7947
Malpas Ches 46 SJ4847
Malpas Cnwll 3 SW8442
Malpas Gwent 19 ST3090
Malshanger House Hants 21 SU5652
Maltby Cleve 62 NZ4613
Maltby Lincs 51 TF3083
Maltby S York 49 SK5392
Maltby le Marsh Lincs 51 TF4681
Malting Green Essex 25 TL9720
Maltman's Hill Kent 15 TQ9043
Malton N York 56 SE7871
Malvern Link H & W 28 SO7847
Malvern Wells H & W 28 SO7741
Mamble H & W 37 SO6971
Mamhilad Gwent 19 SO3003
Manaccan Cnwll 2 SW7625
Manafon Powys 36 SJ1102
Manaton Devon 5 SX7581
Manby Lincs 51 TF3986
Mancetter Warwks 39 SP3296
Manchester Gt Man 47 SJ8497
Mandally Highld 86 NH2900
Manea Cambs 41 TL4789
Maneight Strath 73 NS5409
Maney W Mids 38 SP1295
Manfield N York 61 NZ2213
Mangersta W Isls 102 NB0131
Mangotsfield Avon 20 ST6676
Mangrove End Herts 30 TL1223
Manish W Isls 102 NA9513
Manish W Isls 90 NG1089
Mankinholes W York 54 SD9623
Manley Ches 46 SJ5071
Manmoel Gwent 19 SO1803
Manning's Heath W Susx 12 TQ2028
Manningford Bohune Wilts 20 SU1357
Manningford Bruce Wilts 20 SU1359
Manningham W York 55 SE1435
Mannington Dorset 10 SU0605
Manningtree Essex 25 TM1032
Mannofield Gramp 89 NJ9204
Manor Park Gt Lon 23 TQ4286
Manorbier Dyfed 16 SS0697
Manorbier Newton Dyfed 16 SN0400
Manorhill Border 76 NT6632
Manorowen Dyfed 16 SM9336
Mansell Gamage H & W 27 SO3944
Mansell Lacy H & W 27 SO4245
Mansfield Notts 49 SK5361
Mansfield Strath 66 NS6214
Mansfield Woodhouse Notts 49 SK5363
Mansriggs Cumb 58 SD2880
Manston Dorset 9 ST8115
Manston W York 55 SE3634
Manswood Dorset 9 ST9708
Manthorpe Lincs 40 SK9237
Manthorpe Lincs 40 TF0715
Manton Humb 50 SE9302
Manton Lincs 40 SK8704
Manuden Essex 31 TL4926
Maolachy Strath 79 NM8912
Maperton Somset 9 ST6726
Maple Cross Herts 22 TQ0392
Maplebeck Notts 49 SK7160
Mapledurham Oxon 22 SU6776
Mapledurwell Hants 22 SU6851
Maplehurst W Susx 12 TQ1824
Maplescombe Kent 14 TQ5664
Mapleton Derbys 48 SK1648
Mapperley Derbys 49 SK4343
Mapperley Park Notts 49 SK5742
Mapperton Dorset 8 SY5099
Mappleborough Green Warwks 28 SP0866
Mappleton Humb 57 TA2243
Marazanvose Cnwll 2 SW8050
Marazion Cnwll 2 SW5130
March Cambs 41 TL4297
March Strath 66 NS9914
Marcham Oxon 21 SU4596
Marchamley Shrops 37 SJ5929
Marchington Staffs 38 SK1330
Marchros Gwynd 44 SH3126
Marchwiel Clwyd 46 SJ3547
Marchwood Hants 10 SU3810
Marcross S Glam 18 SS9269
Marden H & W 27 SO5146
Marden Kent 14 TQ7444
Marden Wilts 20 SU0857
Marden Beech Kent 14 TQ7343
Marden Thorn Kent 14 TQ7643
Mardleybury Herts 31 TL2618
Mardy Gwent 27 SO3015
Mare Green Somset 8 ST3326
Mareham le Fen Lincs 51 TF2761
Mareham on the Hill Lincs 51 TF2867
Marehay Derbys 49 SK3948
Marehill W Susx 12 TQ0618
Maresfield E Susx 13 TQ4624
Marfleet Humb 57 TA1329
Marford Clwyd 36 SJ3635
Margam W Glam 18 SS7887
Margaret Marsh Dorset 9 ST8218
Margaretting Essex 24 TL6701
Margaretting Tye Essex 24 TL6801
Margate Kent 15 TR3571
Margnaheglish Strath 72 NS0332
Margrove Park Cleve 62 NZ6515
Marham Norfk 42 TF7110
Marhamchurch Cnwll 6 SS2203
Marholm Cambs 40 TF1402
Mariansleigh Devon 7 SS7422
Marine Town Kent 14 TQ9274
Marionburgh Gramp 89 NJ7006
Marishader Highld 90 NG4963
Maristow Devon 4 SX4764
Marjoriebanks D & G 66 NY0883
Mark D & G 64 NX1158
Mark Somset 19 ST3747
Mark Cross E Susx 13 TQ5010
Mark Cross E Susx 13 TQ5831
Mark's Corner IOW 10 SZ4792
Markbeech Kent 13 TQ4742
Markby Lincs 51 TF4878
Markeaton Derbys 49 SK3337
Market Bosworth Leics 39 SK4003
Market Drayton Shrops 37 SJ6734
Market Harborough Leics 40 SP7387
Market Lavington Wilts 20 SU0154
Market Overton Leics 40 SK8816
Market Rasen Lincs 50 TF1089
Market Stainton Lincs 51 TF2279
Market Street Norfk 43 TG2921
Market Weighton Humb 56 SE8741
Market Weston Suffk 32 TL9877
Markfield Leics 39 SK4810
Markham Gwent 19 SO1601
Markham Moor Notts 49 SK7274
Markinch Fife 83 NO2901
Markington N York 55 SE2864
Marks Tey Essex 24 TL9023
Marksbury Avon 20 ST6623
Markshall Essex 24 TL8425
Markwell Cnwll 4 SX3658
Markyate Herts 30 TL0616
Marlborough Wilts 21 SU1869
Marlbrook H & W 27 SO5054
Marlcliff Warwks 28 SP0950
Marldon Devon 5 SX8663
Marlesford Suffk 33 TM3258
Marley Kent 15 TR1750
Marley Kent 15 TR3352
Marley Green Ches 47 SJ5745
Marlingford Norfk 43 TG1309
Marloes Dyfed 16 SM7908
Marlow Bucks 22 SU8486
Marlpit Hill Kent 13 TQ4447
Marnhull Dorset 9 ST7718
Marnoch Gramp 94 NJ5950
Marple Gt Man 48 SJ9588
Marple Bridge Gt Man 48 SJ9789
Marr S York 55 SE5105
Marrel Highld 97 ND0117
Marrick N York 61 SE0798
Marros Dyfed 17 SN2009
Marsden T & W 69 NZ4064
Marsden W York 55 SE0411
Marsh W York 55 SE0236
Marsh Baldon Oxon 21 SU5699
Marsh Gibbon Bucks 29 SP6422
Marsh Green Devon 5 SY0493
Marsh Green Kent 13 TQ4344
Marsh Green Staffs 47 SJ8859
Marsh Lane Derbys 49 SK4079
Marsh Street Somset 7 SS9944
Marshalswick Herts 23 TL1608
Marsham Norfk 43 TG1924
Marshborough Kent 15 TR2958
Marshbrook Shrops 36 SO4489
Marshchapel Lincs 51 TF3599
Marshfield Avon 20 ST7773
Marshfield Gwent 19 ST2582
Marshgate Cnwll 4 SX1592
Marshland St. James Norfk 41 TF5209
Marshwood Dorset 8 SY3899
Marske N York 61 NZ1000
Marske-by-the-Sea Cleve 62 NZ6322
Marston H & W 27 SO3557
Marston Lincs 50 SK8943
Marston Oxon 29 SP5208
Marston Staffs 38 SJ8314
Marston Staffs 38 SJ9227
Marston Warwks 39 SP2195
Marston Wilts 20 ST9656
Marston Green W Mids 38 SP1785
Marston Magna Somset 9 ST5922
Marston Meysey Wilts 20 SU1297
Marston Montgomery Derbys 48 SK1338
Marston Moretaine Beds 30 SP9941
Marston St. Lawrence Nhants 29 SP5342

Marston Stannet

Montford Bridge

Marston Stannet *H & W* 27 SO5655
Marston Trussell *Nhants* 40 SP6985
Marston on Dove *Derbys* 39 SK2329
Marstow *H & W* 27 SO5518
Marsworth *Bucks* 30 SP9214
Marten *Wilts* 21 SU2860
Marthall *Ches* 47 SJ8075
Martham *Norfk* 43 TG4518
Martin *Hants* 10 SU0719
Martin *Kent* 15 TR3347
Martin *Lincs* 50 TF1259
Martin *Lincs* 51 TF2366
Martin Dales *Lincs* 50 TF1762
Martin Drove End *Hants* 10 SU0420
Martin Hussingtree *H & W* 28 SO8860
Martinhoe *Devon* 18 SS6648
Martinscroft *Ches* 47 SJ6589
Martinstown *Dorset* 9 SY6488
Martlesham *Suffk* 33 TM2547
Martletwy *Dyfed* 16 SN0310
Martock *Somset* 8 ST4619
Marton *Ches* 47 SJ8568
Marton *Cleve* 62 NZ5115
Marton *Humb* 57 TA1839
Marton *N York* 55 SE4162
Marton *N York* 63 SE7383
Marton *Shrops* 36 SJ2802
Marton *Warwks* 29 SP4069
Marton-le-Moor *N York* 55 SE3670
Martyr Worthy *Hants* 11 SU5132
Martyr's Green *Surrey* 22 TQ0857
Marwick *Ork* 103 HY2324
Marybank *Highld* 92 NH4853
Maryburgh *Highld* 92 NH5456
Maryculter *Gramp* 89 NO8599
Maryfield *Cnwll* 4 SX4256
Maryhill *Gramp* 95 NJ8245
Maryhill *Strath* 74 NS5669
Marykirk *Gramp* 89 NO6865
Marylebone *Gt Man* 47 SD5807
Marypark *Gramp* 94 NJ1938
Maryport *Cumb* 58 NY0336
Maryport *D & G* 64 NX1434
Marystow *Devon* 4 SX4383
Maryton *Tays* 89 NO6856
Marywell *Gramp* 89 NO9399
Marywell *Tays* 89 NO6544
Marywell *Tays* 89 NO5896
Masham *N York* 61 SE2280
Masongill *N York* 60 SD6675
Mastin Moor *Derbys* 49 SK4575
Matching *Essex* 31 TL5212
Matching Green *Essex* 23 TL5311
Matching Tye *Essex* 23 TL5111
Matfen *Nthumb* 68 NZ0371
Matfield *Kent* 13 TQ6541
Mathern *Gwent* 19 ST5291
Mathon *H & W* 28 SO7345
Mathry *Dyfed* 16 SM8832
Matlaske *Norfk* 43 TG1534
Matlock *Derbys* 49 SK3060
Matlock Bank *Derbys* 49 SK3060
Matson *Gloucs* 28 SO8515
Matterdale End *Cumb* 59 NY3933
Mattersey Thorpe *Notts* 49 SK6889
Mattingley *Hants* 22 SU7357
Mattishall *Norfk* 42 TG0511
Mattishall Burgh *Norfk* 42 TG0512
Mauchline *Strath* 74 NS4927
Maud *Gramp* 95 NJ9247
Maufant *Jersey* 101 SV0000
Maufant *Jersey* 101 SV0000
Maugersbury *Gloucs* 29 SP1925
Maughold *IOM* 52 SC4991
Mauld *Highld* 92 NH4038
Maulden *Beds* 30 TL0538
Maulds Meaburn *Cumb* 60 NY6216
Maunby *N York* 62 SE3486
Maund Bryan *H & W* 27 SO5650
Maundown *Somset* 7 ST0528
Mautby *Norfk* 43 TG4812
Mavesyn Ridware *Staffs* 38 SK0816
Mavis Enderby *Lincs* 51 TF3666
Maw Green *Ches* 47 SJ7157
Mawbray *Cumb* 66 NY0846
Mawdesley *Lancs* 53 SD4914
Mawdlam *M Glam* 18 SS8081
Mawgan Porth *Cnwll* 3 SW8467
Mawla *Cnwll* 2 SW7045
Mawnan *Cnwll* 2 SW7827
Mawnan Smith *Cnwll* 2 SW7728
Maxstoke *Warwks* 39 SP2386
Maxted Street *Kent* 15 TR1244
Maxton *Border* 76 NT6130
Maxton *Kent* 15 TR3041
Maxwellheugh *Border* 76 NT7333
Maxwelltown *D & G* 66 NX9676
Maxworthy *Cnwll* 4 SX2593
May Bank *Staffs* 47 SJ8547
May's Green *Oxon* 22 SU7580
Mayals *W Glam* 17 SS6090
Maybole *Strath* 73 NS2909
Maybury *Surrey* 22 TQ0158
Mayfield *E Susx* 13 TQ5827
Mayfield *Loth* 75 NT3565
Mayfield *Staffs* 48 SK1545
Mayford *Surrey* 22 SU9956
Maymore *Strath* 80 NR9986
Maynard's Green *E Susx* 13 TQ5818
Maypole *W Mids* 38 SP0878
Maypole Green *Norfk* 43 TM4195
Maypole Green *Suffk* 32 TL9159
Meadgate *Avon* 20 ST6758
Meadle *Bucks* 22 SP8006
Meadowtown *Shrops* 36 SJ3101
Meadwell *Devon* 4 SX4081
Mealrigg *Cumb* 67 NY1345
Mealsgate *Cumb* 58 NY2141
Meamskirk *Strath* 74 NS5455
Meanwood *W York* 55 SE2837
Meare *Somset* 19 ST4541
Meare Green *Somset* 8 ST2922
Mears Ashby *Nhants* 30 SP8366
Measham *Leics* 39 SK3312
Meathop *Cumb* 59 SD4380
Meavy *Devon* 4 SX5467
Med *Avon* 20 ST7358
Medbourne *Leics* 40 SP8093
Meden Vale *Notts* 56 SE5870
Medmenham *Berks* 22 SU8084
Medomsley *Dur* 69 NZ1254
Medstead *Hants* 11 SU6537
Meer End *W Mids* 39 SP2474
Meerbrook *Staffs* 48 SJ9860
Meesden *Herts* 31 TL4322
Meeson *Shrops* 37 SJ6420
Meeth *Devon* 6 SS5408
Meeting Green *Suffk* 32 TL7455
Meeting House Hill *Norfk* 43 TG3028
Meidrim *Dyfed* 17 SN2820
Meifod *Powys* 36 SJ1513
Meigle *Tays* 88 NO2944
Meikle Carco *D & G* 66 NS7813
Meikle Earnock *Strath* 74 NS7053
Meikle Grenach *Strath* 72 NS0760
Meikle Kilmory *Strath* 72 NS0561
Meikle Obney *Tays* 82 NO0337
Meikle Wartle *Gramp* 95 NJ7231
Meikleour *Tays* 82 NO1539
Meinciau *Dyfed* 17 SN4610
Meir *Staffs* 48 SJ9342
Melbourn *Cambs* 31 TL3844
Melbourne *Humb* 56 SE7543
Melbury Abbas *Dorset* 9 ST8820
Melbury Bubb *Dorset* 9 ST5906
Melbury Osmond *Dorset* 8 ST5707
Melchbourne *Beds* 30 TL0365
Melcombe Bingham *Dorset* 9 ST7602
Meldon *Devon* 4 SX5592
Meldon *Devon* 4 SX5692
Meldon *Nthumb* 69 NZ1183
Meldreth *Cambs* 31 TL3746
Meldrum *Cent* 81 NS7199
Melfort *Strath* 79 NM8313
Melgund Castle *Tays* 89 NO5455
Meliden *Clwyd* 45 SJ0580
Melin-y-ddol *Powys* 36 SJ0907
Melin-y-wig *Clwyd* 45 SJ0448
Melkinthorpe *Cumb* 59 NY5525
Melkridge *Nthumb* 68 NY7363
Melksham *Wilts* 20 ST9063
Melldalloch *Strath* 71 NR9375
Mellguards *Cumb* 67 NY4446
Melling *Lancs* 54 SD5970
Melling *Mersyd* 46 SD3800
Mellis *Suffk* 33 TM0974
Mellon Charles *Highld* 91 NG8491
Mellon Udrigle *Highld* 91 NG8895
Mellor *Gt Man* 48 SJ9988
Mellor *Lancs* 54 SD6530
Mellor Brook *Lancs* 54 SD6431
Mells *Somset* 20 ST7249
Melmerby *Cumb* 59 NY6137
Melmerby *N York* 61 SE0785
Melmerby *N York* 62 SE3376
Melness *Highld* 99 NC5861
Melplash *Dorset* 8 SY4797
Melrose *Border* 76 NT5434
Melsetter *Ork* 103 ND2689
Melsonby *N York* 61 NZ1908
Meltham *W York* 55 SE0910
Meltham Mills *W York* 55 SE1010
Melton *Humb* 56 SE9726
Melton *Suffk* 33 TM2850
Melton Constable *Norfk* 42 TG0433
Melton Mowbray *Leics* 40 SK7518
Melton Ross *Humb* 57 TA0610
Melvaig *Highld* 91 NG7486
Melverley *Shrops* 36 SJ3316
Melvich *Highld* 99 NC8764
Membury *Devon* 8 ST2703
Memsie *Gramp* 95 NJ9762
Menai Bridge *Gwynd* 44 SH5571
Mendham *Suffk* 33 TM2783
Mendlesham *Suffk* 33 TM1065
Mendlesham Green *Suffk* 33 TM0963
Menethorpe *N York* 56 SE7667
Menheniot *Cnwll* 4 SX2862
Mennock *D & G* 66 NS8008
Menston *W York* 55 SE1743
Menstrie *Cent* 82 NS8596
Menthorpe *N York* 56 SE6934
Mentmore *Bucks* 30 SP9019
Meoble *Highld* 85 NM7987
Meole Brace *Shrops* 37 SJ4810
Meonstoke *Hants* 11 SU6119
Mepal *Cambs* 41 TL4481
Meppershall *Beds* 30 TL1336
Mere *Ches* 47 SJ7281
Mere *Wilts* 9 ST8132
Mere Brow *Lancs* 53 SD4218
Mere Green *W Mids* 38 SP1298
Mereclough *Lancs* 54 SD8730
Mereworth *Kent* 13 TQ6553
Meriden *W Mids* 39 SP2482
Merkadale *Highld* 84 NG3931
Merriott *Somset* 8 ST4412
Merrow *Surrey* 12 TQ0250
Merry Hill *Herts* 22 TQ1394
Merry Hill *W Mids* 38 SO9386
Merryhill *W Mids* 38 SO8897
Merrymeet *Cnwll* 4 SX2766
Mersham *Kent* 15 TR0540
Merstham *Surrey* 12 TQ2953
Merston *W Susx* 11 SU8903
Merstone *IOW* 11 SZ5285
Merther *Cnwll* 3 SW8644
Merthyr Cynog *Powys* 26 SN9837
Merthyr Dyfan *S Glam* 18 ST1169
Merthyr Mawr *M Glam* 18 SS8877
Merthyr Tydfil *M Glam* 26 SO0506
Merthyr Vale *M Glam* 18 ST0799
Merthyr Vale *M Glam* 18 ST0899
Merton *Devon* 6 SS5212
Merton *Gt Lon* 23 TQ2570
Merton *Norfk* 42 TL9098
Merton *Oxon* 29 SP5717
Mervinslaw *Border* 68 NT6713
Meshaw *Devon* 7 SS7519
Messing *Essex* 24 TL8919
Messingham *Humb* 56 SE8904
Metcombe *Devon* 5 SY0791
Metfield *Suffk* 33 TM2980
Metherell *Cnwll* 4 SX4069
Metheringham *Lincs* 50 TF0661
Methil *Fife* 83 NT3799
Methley *W York* 55 SE3826
Methlick *Gramp* 95 NJ8537
Methven *Tays* 82 NO0226
Methwold *Norfk* 42 TL7394
Methwold Hythe *Norfk* 42 TL7195
Mettingham *Suffk* 33 TM3690
Metton *Norfk* 43 TG1937
Mevagissey *Cnwll* 3 SX0144
Mexborough *S York* 49 SE4700
Mey *Highld* 100 ND2872
Meyllteyrn *Gwynd* 44 SH2332
Meyllteyrn *Gwynd* 44 SH2333
Meysey Hampton *Gloucs* 20 SU1199
Miavaig *W Isls* 102 NB0834
Michaelchurch *H & W* 27 SO5125
Michaelchurch Escley *H & W* 27 SO3134
Michaelston-le-Pit *S Glam* 19 ST1573
Michaelstone-y-Fedw *Gwent* 19 ST2484
Michaelstow *Cnwll* 3 SX0878
Michelcombe *Devon* 5 SX6968
Micheldever *Hants* 11 SU5139
Micheldever Station *Hants* 21 SU5143
Michelmersh *Hants* 10 SU3426
Mickfield *Suffk* 33 TM1361
Mickle Trafford *Ches* 46 SJ4469
Micklebring *S York* 49 SK5194
Mickleby *N York* 63 NZ8012
Micklefield *W York* 55 SE4432
Mickleham *Surrey* 12 TQ1753
Mickleover *Derbys* 39 SK3034
Mickleton *Dur* 61 NY9623
Mickleton *Gloucs* 28 SP1643
Mickleton *W York* 55 SE4027
Mickley *Derbys* 49 SK3379
Mickley *N York* 61 SE2576
Mickley Green *Suffk* 32 TL8457
Mickley Square *Nthumb* 68 NZ0762
Mid Ardlaw *Gramp* 95 NJ9464
Mid Beltie *Gramp* 89 NJ6200
Mid Calder *Loth* 75 NT0767
Mid Clyth *Highld* 100 ND2937
Mid Lavant *W Susx* 11 SU8508
Mid Mains *Highld* 92 NH4239
Mid Sannox *Strath* 72 NS0145
Mid Yell *Shet* 103 HU5191
Midbea *Ork* 103 HY4444
Middle Aston *Oxon* 29 SP4726
Middle Chinnock *Somset* 8 ST4713
Middle Claydon *Bucks* 30 SP7225
Middle Duntisbourne *Gloucs* 28 SO9806
Middle Handley *Derbys* 49 SK4077
Middle Kames *Strath* 71 NR9189
Middle Mayfield *Staffs* 48 SK1444
Middle Quarter *Kent* 14 TQ8937
Middle Rasen *Lincs* 50 TF0889
Middle Rocombe *Devon* 5 SX9069
Middle Stoke *Kent* 14 TQ8275
Middle Stoughton *Somset* 19 ST4248
Middle Street *Essex* 23 TL4005
Middle Street *Gloucs* 20 SO7803
Middle Town *IOS* 2 SV8808
Middle Tysoe *Warwks* 29 SP3344
Middle Wallop *Hants* 10 SU2937
Middle Wallop *Hants* 10 SU2938
Middle Winterslow *Wilts* 10 SU2432
Middle Woodford *Wilts* 10 SU1136
Middle Yard *Gloucs* 20 SO8103
Middlebie *D & G* 67 NY2176
Middlegill *D & G* 66 NT0407
Middleham *N York* 61 SE1287
Middlehope *Shrops* 37 SO4988
Middlemarsh *Dorset* 9 ST6707
Middlemore *Devon* 4 SX5073
Middlesbrough *Cleve* 62 NZ4920
Middlesceugh *Cumb* 59 NY3942
Middleshaw *Cumb* 59 SD5589
Middleshaw *D & G* 67 NY1475
Middlesmoor *N York* 61 SE0973
Middlestone *Dur* 61 NZ2531
Middlethird *Border* 76 NT6743
Middleton *Derbys* 48 SK1963
Middleton *Derbys* 49 SK2756
Middleton *Essex* 32 TL8739
Middleton *Gt Man* 47 SD8705
Middleton *H & W* 27 SO5469
Middleton *Hants* 21 SU4244
Middleton *Loth* 76 NT3758
Middleton *N York* 63 SE7885
Middleton *Nhants* 40 SP8489
Middleton *Norfk* 42 TF6616
Middleton *Nthumb* 68 NZ0584
Middleton *Nthumb* 77 NU0024
Middleton *Shrops* 37 SO5477
Middleton *Strath* 78 NL9443
Middleton *Strath* 73 NS3952
Middleton *Suffk* 33 TM4267
Middleton *Tays* 82 NO1206
Middleton *W Glam* 17 SS4287
Middleton *W York* 55 SE3027
Middleton *W York* 55 SE1249
Middleton *Warwks* 38 SP1798
Middleton Cheney *Nhants* 29 SP4941
Middleton Moor *Suffk* 33 TM4167
Middleton Quernhow *N York* 62 SE3378
Middleton Scriven *Shrops* 37 SO6887
Middleton St. George *Dur* 62 NZ3412
Middleton Stoney *Oxon* 29 SP5323
Middleton Tyas *N York* 61 NZ2205
Middleton one Tow *Dur* 62 NZ3512
Middleton-in-Teesdale *Dur* 61 NY9425
Middleton-on-the-Hill *H & W* 27 SO5364
Middleton-on-the-Wolds *Humb* 56 SE9449
Middletown *Avon* 19 ST4571
Middletown *Powys* 36 SJ3012
Middlewich *Ches* 47 SJ7066
Middlewood *Cnwll* 4 SX2775
Middlewood *H & W* 27 SO2844
Middlewood Green *Suffk* 33 TM0961
Middleyard *Strath* 74 NS5132
Middlezoy *Somset* 8 ST3733
Middridge *Dur* 61 NZ2526
Midford *Avon* 20 ST7660
Midge Hall *Lancs* 53 SD5123
Midgham *Berks* 21 SU5567
Midgley *W York* 55 SE0226
Midgley *W York* 55 SE2714
Midhopestones *S York* 48 SK2399
Midhurst *W Susx* 11 SU8821
Midlem *Border* 76 NT5227
Midpark *Strath* 72 NS0259
Midsomer Norton *Avon* 20 ST6654
Midtown *Highld* 91 NG8285
Midtown *Highld* 99 NC5861
Midway *Ches* 48 SJ9282
Migvie *Gramp* 88 NJ4306
Milarrochy *Cent* 80 NS4092
Milborne Port *Somset* 9 ST6718
Milborne St. Andrew *Dorset* 9 SY8097
Milborne Wick *Somset* 9 ST6620
Milbourne *Nthumb* 69 NZ1175
Milbourne *Wilts* 20 ST9587
Milburn *Cumb* 60 NY6529
Milbury Heath *Avon* 20 ST6790
Milby *N York* 55 SE4067
Milcombe *Oxon* 29 SP4134
Milden *Suffk* 32 TL9546
Mildenhall *Suffk* 32 TL7174
Mildenhall *Wilts* 21 SU2069
Mile End *Gloucs* 27 SO5811
Mile End *Gloucs* 27 SO5911
Mile Head *Lancs* 53 SD4970
Mile Oak *E Susx* 12 TQ2407
Mile Town *Kent* 14 TQ9274
Mileham *Norfk* 42 TF9119
Milehead *Highld* 87 NH8406
Miles Hope *H & W* 27 SO5764
Miles Platting *Gt Man* 47 SJ8599
Milesmark *Fife* 82 NT0688
Milfield *Nthumb* 77 NT9333
Milford *Derbys* 49 SK3545
Milford *Staffs* 38 SJ9721
Milford *Surrey* 12 SU9442
Milford Haven *Dyfed* 16 SM9006
Milford on Sea *Hants* 10 SZ2891
Milkwall *Gloucs* 27 SO5809
Mill Bank *W York* 55 SE0321
Mill Brow *Gt Man* 48 SJ9889
Mill Common *Norfk* 43 TG3301
Mill Common *Suffk* 33 TM4082
Mill Cross *Devon* 5 SX7361
Mill End *Bucks* 22 SU7885
Mill End *Cambs* 41 TL3180
Mill End *Herts* 31 TL3332
Mill Green *Cambs* 32 TL6245
Mill Green *Essex* 24 TL6301
Mill Green *Lincs* 41 TF2223
Mill Green *Suffk* 32 TL9542
Mill Green *Suffk* 32 TL9957
Mill Green *Suffk* 33 TM1360
Mill Hill *E Susx* 13 TQ6104
Mill Hill *Gt Lon* 23 TQ2292
Mill Meece *Staffs* 38 SJ8333
Mill Street *Suffk* 32 TM0672
Mill of Cammie *Gramp* 89 NO6993
Mill of Drummond *Tays* 82 NN8315
Mill of Grange *Gramp* 93 NJ0460
Mill of Haldane *Strath* 80 NS4083
Mill of Uras *Gramp* 89 NO8680
Millais *Jersey* 101 SV0000
Milland *W Susx* 11 SU8328
Millbreck *Gramp* 95 NK0044
Millbrex *Gramp* 95 NJ8144
Millbrook *Beds* 30 TL0138
Millbrook *Hants* 10 SU3813
Millbrook *Jersey* 101 SV0000
Millbrook *Jersey* 101 SV0000
Millbuie *Gramp* 95 NJ7909
Millburn *Strath* 73 NS4429
Millcombe *Devon* 5 SX8050
Millcorner *E Susx* 14 TQ8223
Millcraig *Highld* 93 NH6571
Milldale *Staffs* 48 SK1354
Millend *Gloucs* 27 SO5608
Miller's Dale *Derbys* 48 SK1373
Millerhill *Loth* 75 NT3269
Millers Green *Derbys* 49 SK2752
Millerston *Strath* 74 NS6467
Millhalf *H & W* 27 SO2847
Millheugh *Strath* 74 NS7450
Millholme *Cumb* 59 SD5690
Millhouse *Strath* 71 NR9570
Millhouse Green *S York* 55 SE2203
Millhousebridge *D & G* 67 NY1085
Millhouses *S York* 49 SK3484
Millikenpark *Strath* 73 NS4162
Millington *Humb* 56 SE8351
Millness *Cumb* 59 SD5383
Millom *Cumb* 58 SD1780
Millport *Strath* 73 NS1655
Millthrop *Cumb* 60 SD6691
Milltimber *Gramp* 89 NJ8501
Milltown *D & G* 67 NY3375
Milltown *Devon* 6 SS5539
Milltown *Gramp* 94 NJ2609
Milltown *Gramp* 94 NJ4716
Milltown of Campfield *Gramp* 89 NJ6500
Milltown of Edinvillie *Gramp* 94 NJ2639
Milltown of Learney *Gramp* 89 NJ6303
Milnathort *Tays* 82 NO1204
Milngavie *Strath* 74 NS5574
Milnmark *D & G* 65 NX6582
Milnrow *Gt Man* 54 SD9212
Milnthorpe *Cumb* 59 SD4981
Milovaig *Highld* 90 NG1550
Milson *Shrops* 37 SO6472
Milsted *Kent* 14 TQ9058
Milthorpe *Lincs* 40 TF1030
Milthorpe *Nhants* 29 SP5946
Milton *Avon* 19 ST3462
Milton *Cambs* 31 TL4762
Milton *Cent* 81 NS4490
Milton *Cent* 81 NN5001
Milton *Cumb* 67 NY5560
Milton *D & G* 64 NX2154
Milton *D & G* 66 NX8470
Milton *Derbys* 39 SK3126
Milton *Dyfed* 16 SN0303
Milton *Gramp* 94 NJ5163
Milton *Gwent* 19 ST3688
Milton *Highld* 85 NG7134
Milton *Highld* 92 NH4930
Milton *Highld* 92 NH5030
Milton *Highld* 92 NH5749
Milton *Highld* 97 NH7674
Milton *Highld* 100 ND3451
Milton *Kent* 14 TQ6573
Milton *Notts* 49 SK7173
Milton *Oxon* 21 SU4892
Milton *Somset* 8 ST4621
Milton *Staffs* 48 SJ9050
Milton *Strath* 73 NS3468
Milton *Strath* 81 NS4274
Milton *Tays* 88 NO1357
Milton Abbas *Dorset* 9 ST8001
Milton Abbot *Devon* 4 SX4079
Milton Bridge *Fife* 75 NT2562
Milton Bryan *Beds* 30 SP9730
Milton Clevedon *Somset* 20 ST6637
Milton Combe *Devon* 4 SX4866
Milton Damerel *Devon* 6 SS3810
Milton End *Gloucs* 20 SP1401
Milton Ernest *Beds* 30 TL0156
Milton Green *Ches* 46 SJ4658
Milton Hill *Devon* 5 SX9278
Milton Hill *Oxon* 21 SU4790
Milton Keynes *Bucks* 30 SP8537
Milton Lilbourne *Wilts* 21 SU1860
Milton Malsor *Nhants* 30 SP7355
Milton Morenish *Tays* 81 NN6136
Milton Regis *Kent* 14 TQ9064
Milton of Auchinhove *Gramp* 89 NJ5503
Milton of Balgonie *Fife* 83 NO3200
Milton of Campsie *Strath* 74 NS6576
Milton of Cushnie *Gramp* 94 NJ5111
Milton of Tullich *Gramp* 88 NO3897
Milton on Stour *Dorset* 9 ST7828
Milton-under-Wychwood *Oxon* 29 SP2618
Milverton *Somset* 8 ST1226
Milverton *Warwks* 29 SP3066
Milwich *Staffs* 38 SJ9632
Minard *Strath* 71 NR9796
Minchinhampton *Gloucs* 20 SO8700
Mindrum *Nthumb* 77 NT8332
Minehead *Somset* 7 SS9746
Minera *Clwyd* 46 SJ2651
Minffordd *Gwynd* 44 SH5938
Mingarry Park *Highld* 79 NM6869
Mingary *W Isls* 102 NF7426
Miningsby *Lincs* 51 TF3264
Minions *Cnwll* 4 SX2671
Minishant *Strath* 73 NS3314
Minllyn *Gwynd* 35 SH8514
Minmore Hotel *Gramp* 94 NJ1929
Minnigaff *D & G* 64 NX4166
Minnonie *Gramp* 95 NJ7760
Minskip *N York* 55 SE3864
Minstead *Hants* 10 SU2711
Minstead *Hants* 10 SU2811
Minsted *W Susx* 11 SU8520
Minster *Kent* 14 TQ9572
Minster *Kent* 15 TR3064
Minster Lovell *Oxon* 29 SP3111
Minsterley *Shrops* 36 SJ3705
Minsterworth *Gloucs* 28 SO7816
Minterne Magna *Dorset* 9 ST6504
Minting *Lincs* 50 TF1873
Mintlaw *Gramp* 95 NJ9948
Minto *Border* 76 NT5620
Minton *Shrops* 36 SO4390
Minworth *W Mids* 38 SP1692
Mirehouse *Cumb* 58 NX9715
Mireland *Highld* 100 ND3160
Mirfield *W York* 55 SE2019
Miskin *M Glam* 18 ST0481
Misson *Notts* 49 SK6895
Misterton *Leics* 39 SP5584
Misterton *Notts* 50 SK7694
Misterton *Somset* 8 ST4508
Mistley *Essex* 25 TM1231
Mitcham *Gt Lon* 23 TQ2768
Mitchel Troy *Gwent* 27 SO4910
Mitcheldean *Gloucs* 28 SO6618
Mitchell *Cnwll* 3 SW8654
Mitchellslacks *D & G* 66 NX9696
Mitcheltroy Common *Gwent* 27 SO4909
Mitford *Nthumb* 69 NZ1786
Mithian *Cnwll* 2 SW7450
Mixbury *Oxon* 29 SP6033
Mobberley *Ches* 47 SJ7879
Mobberley *Staffs* 48 SK0041
Moccas *H & W* 27 SO3543
Mochdre *Powys* 36 SO0788
Mochrum *D & G* 64 NX3446
Mockbeggar *Kent* 14 TQ7246
Mockerkin *Cumb* 58 NY0923
Modbury *Devon* 5 SX6652
Moddershall *Staffs* 38 SJ9236
Modsary *Gramp* 99 NC6562
Moelfre *Clwyd* 36 SJ1828
Moelfre *Gwynd* 44 SH5186
Moffat *D & G* 66 NT0805
Mogerhanger *Beds* 30 TL1439
Mogworthy *Devon* 7 SS8517
Moira *Leics* 39 SK3215
Mol-Chlach *Highld* 84 NG4513
Molash *Kent* 15 TR0251
Mold *Clwyd* 46 SJ2363
Moldgreen *W York* 55 SE1516
Molehill Green *Essex* 24 TL5624
Molescroft *Humb* 56 TA0140
Molesworth *Cambs* 30 TL0775
Molland *Devon* 7 SS8028
Mollington *Ches* 46 SJ3870
Mollington *Oxon* 29 SP4347
Mollinsburn *Strath* 74 NS7171
Monachty *Dyfed* 34 SN5062
Monachylemore *Cent* 81 NN4719
Monboddo *Gramp* 89 NO7478
Mondynes *Gramp* 89 NO7779
Monewden *Suffk* 33 TM2458
Moneydie *Tays* 82 NO0629
Moneygrow Green *Berks* 22 SU8977
Moniaive *D & G* 66 NX7791
Monifieth *Tays* 83 NO4932
Monikie *Tays* 83 NO4938
Monimail *Fife* 83 NO2914
Monk Fryston *N York* 55 SE5029
Monk Hesleden *Dur* 62 NZ4536
Monk Sherborne *Hants* 21 SU6056
Monk Soham *Suffk* 33 TM2165
Monk Street *Essex* 24 TL6128
Monk's Gate *W Susx* 12 TQ2027
Monken Hadley *Gt Lon* 23 TQ2497
Monkhide *H & W* 27 SO6144
Monkhill *Cumb* 67 NY3458
Monkhopton *Shrops* 37 SO6293
Monkland *H & W* 27 SO4557
Monkleigh *Devon* 6 SS4520
Monknash *S Glam* 18 SS9170
Monkokehampton *Devon* 6 SS5805
Monks Eleigh *Suffk* 32 TL9647
Monks Heath *Ches* 47 SJ8474
Monkseaton *T & W* 69 NZ3472
Monksilver *Somset* 7 ST0737
Monksthorpe *Lincs* 51 TF4465
Monkswood *Gwent* 19 SO3402
Monkton *E Susx* 8 ST1803
Monkton *Kent* 15 TR2864
Monkton *S Glam* 18 SS9271
Monkton *Strath* 73 NS3527
Monkton *T & W* 69 NZ3463
Monkton Combe *Avon* 20 ST7762
Monkton Deverill *Wilts* 20 ST8537
Monkton Farleigh *Wilts* 20 ST8065
Monkton Heathfield *Somset* 8 ST2526
Monkton Wyld *Dorset* 8 SY3396
Monkwear-Mouth *T & W* 69 NZ4058
Monkwood *Hants* 11 SU6730
Monmore Green *W Mids* 38 SO9297
Monnington on Wye *H & W* 27 SO3743
Monreith *D & G* 64 NX3641
Mont Saint *Guern* 101 SV0000
Montacute *Somset* 8 ST4916
Montcliffe *Gt Man* 54 SD6511
Montford *Shrops* 36 SJ4114
Montford Bridge *Shrops* 36 SJ4215

Montgarrie Newby Wiske

Montgarrie *Gramp* 94 NJ5717
Montgarswood *Strath* 74 NS5227
Montgomery *Powys* 36 SO2296
Montgreenan *Strath* 73 NS3343
Montrave *Fife* 83 NO3806
Montrose *Tays* 89 NO7157
Monxton *Hants* 21 SU3144
Monyash *Derbys* 48 SK1566
Monybachach *Strath* 71 NR9058
Monymusk *Gramp* 95 NJ6815
Monzie *Tays* 82 NN8725
Moodiesburn *Strath* 74 NS6970
Moonzie *Fife* 83 NO3317
Moor Allerton *W York* 55 SE3038
Moor Crichel *Dorset* 9 ST9908
Moor End *Devon* 7 SS6608
Moor End *N York* 56 SE5938
Moor End *W York* 55 SE0528
Moor Green *Herts* 31 TL3226
Moor Head *W York* 55 SE1337
Moor Monkton *N York* 55 SE5156
Moor Row *Cumb* 58 NY0114
Moor Street *W Mids* 38 SP0083
Moor The *Kent* 14 TQ7529
Moorby *Lincs* 51 TF2964
Moorcock Inn *N York* 60 SD8092
Moordown *Dorset* 10 SZ0994
Moore *Ches* 47 SJ5884
Moorend *Glouc*s 28 SO7303
Moorhall *Derbys* 49 SK3174
Moorhouse *Notts* 50 SK7566
Moorhouse *W York* 56 SE4311
Moorhouse Bank *Surrey* 13 TQ4253
Moorlinch *Somset* 19 ST3936
Moorsgreen *Notts* 49 SK4847
Moorsholm *Cleve* 62 NZ6814
Moorside *Dorset* 9 ST7919
Moorside *Gt Man* 54 SD9507
Moorside *Gt Man* 54 SD9507
Moorswater *Cnwll* 4 SX2364
Moorthorpe *W York* 55 SE4511
Moortown *Hants* 10 SU1504
Moortown *Lincs* 50 TF0699
Morangie *Highld* 97 NH7683
Morar *Highld* 85 NM6793
Morborne *Cambs* 40 TL1391
Morchard Bishop *Devon* 7 SS7707
Morcombelake *Dorset* 8 SY4093
Morcott *Leics* 40 SK9200
Morda *Shrops* 36 SJ2827
Morden *Dorset* 9 SY9195
Morden *Gt Lon* 23 TQ2567
Mordiford *H & W* 27 SO5737
Mordon *Dur* 62 NZ3226
More *Shrops* 36 SO3491
Morebath *Devon* 7 SS9525
Morebattle *Border* 76 NT7724
Morecambe *Lancs* 53 SD4364
Moredon *Wilts* 20 SU1387
Morefield *Highld* 96 NH1195
Morehall *Kent* 15 TR2137
Moreleigh *Devon* 5 SX7652
Morenish *Tays* 81 NN6035
Moresby Parks *Cumb* 58 NY0019
Morestead *Hants* 10 SU5025
Moreton *Dorset* 9 SY8089
Moreton *Essex* 23 TL5307
Moreton *H & W* 27 SO5164
Moreton *Mersyd* 46 SJ2690
Moreton *Oxon* 22 SP6904
Moreton Corbet *Shrops* 37 SJ5523
Moreton Jeffries *H & W* 27 SO6048
Moreton Mill *Shrops* 37 SJ5823
Moreton Morrell *Warwks* 29 SP3155
Moreton Paddox *Warwks* 29 SP3054
Moreton Pinkney *Nhants* 29 SP5749
Moreton Say *Shrops* 37 SJ6234
Moreton Valence *Glouc*s 28 SO7809
Moreton on Lugg *H & W* 27 SO5045
Moreton-in-Marsh *Glouc*s 29 SP2032
Moretonhampstead *Devon* 5 SX7586
Morfa Glas *W Glam* 26 SN8706
Morfa Nefyn *Gwynd* 44 SH2840
Morgan's Vale *Wilts* 10 SU1921
Morham *Loth* 76 NT5571
Morland *Cumb* 59 NY6022
Morley *Ches* 47 SJ8282
Morley *Derbys* 49 SK3941
Morley *W York* 55 SE2627
Morley Green *Ches* 47 SJ8281
Morley St. Botolph *Norfk* 42 TM0799
Mornick *Cnwll* 4 SX3172
Morningside *Loth* 75 NT2470
Morningside *Strath* 74 NS8355
Morningthorpe *Norfk* 33 TM2192
Morpeth *Nthumb* 69 NZ2085
Morphie *Gramp* 89 NO7164
Morrey *Staffs* 38 SK1218
Morriston *W Glam* 18 SS6697
Morston *Norfk* 42 TG0043
Mortehoe *Devon* 6 SS4545
Morthen *S York* 49 SK4789
Mortimer *Berks* 21 SU6564
Mortimer West End *Hants* 21 SU6363
Mortimer's Cross *H & W* 27 SO4263
Mortlake *Gt Lon* 23 TQ2075
Morton *Cumb* 67 NY3855
Morton *Derbys* 49 SK4060
Morton *IOW* 11 SZ6086
Morton *Lincs* 40 TF0923
Morton *Lincs* 50 SK8091
Morton *Norfk* 43 TG1217
Morton *Notts* 49 SK7252
Morton *Shrops* 36 SJ2924
Morton Bagot *Warwks* 28 SP1164
Morton-on-Swale *N York* 62 SE3292
Morvah *Cnwll* 2 SW4035
Morval *Cnwll* 4 SX2656
Morvich *Highld* 85 NG9621
Morville *Shrops* 37 SO6794
Morwenstow *Cnwll* 6 SS2015
Mosborough *S York* 49 SK4281
Moscow *Strath* 73 NS4840
Moseley *H & W* 28 SO8159
Moseley *W Mids* 38 SO9398
Moseley *W Mids* 38 SP0783
Moss *S York* 56 SE5914
Moss *Strath* 78 NL9644
Moss Bank *Mersyd* 46 SJ5198
Moss Nook *Gt Man* 47 SJ8385
Moss-Side *Highld* 93 NH8554
Mossat *Gramp* 94 NJ4719
Mossbank *Shet* 103 HU4575
Mossbay *Cumb* 58 NX9927
Mossblown *Strath* 73 NS3925
Mossbrow *Gt Man* 47 SJ7189
Mossburnford *Border* 76 NT6616
Mossdale *D & G* 65 NX6570
Mossdale *Strath* 73 NS4904
Mossend *Strath* 74 NS7360
Mossgiel *Strath* 73 NS4828
Mossknowe *D & G* 67 NY2769
Mossley *Gt Man* 48 SD9702
Mosspaul Hotel *Border* 67 NY4099
Mosstodloch *Gramp* 94 NJ3259
Mossy Lea *Lancs* 53 SD5312
Mossyard *D & G* 65 NX5551
Mosterton *Dorset* 8 ST4505
Moston *Gt Man* 47 SD8701
Motcombe *Dorset* 9 ST8425
Motherby *Cumb* 59 NY4228
Mothercombe *Devon* 5 SX6147
Motherwell *Strath* 74 NS7457
Motspur Park *Gt Lon* 23 TQ2267
Mottingham *Gt Lon* 23 TQ4272
Mottistone *IOW* 10 SZ4083
Mottram in Longdendale *Gt Man* 48 SJ9995
Mottram in Longdendale *Gt Man* 48 SJ9995
Mouilpied *Guern* 101 SV0000
Mouldsworth *Ches* 46 SJ5071
Moulin *Tays* 87 NN9459
Moulsecoomb *E Susx* 12 TQ3307
Moulsford *Oxon* 21 SU5984
Moulsoe *Bucks* 30 SP9041
Moultavie *Highld* 92 NH6371
Moulton *Ches* 47 SJ6569
Moulton *Lincs* 41 TF3023
Moulton *N York* 61 NZ2303
Moulton *Nhants* 30 SP7866
Moulton *S Glam* 18 ST0770
Moulton *Suffk* 32 TL6964
Moulton Chapel *Lincs* 41 TF2918
Moulton Seas End *Lincs* 41 TF3227
Moulton St. Mary *Norfk* 43 TG3907
Mount *Cnwll* 3 SX1468
Mount *W York* 55 SE0918
Mount Ambrose *Cnwll* 2 SW7143
Mount Bures *Essex* 24 TL9032
Mount Hawke *Cnwll* 2 SW7147
Mount Lothian *Loth* 75 NT2757
Mount Pleasant *Derbys* 49 SK3448
Mount Pleasant *E Susx* 13 TQ4216
Mount Pleasant *Suffk* 32 TL7347
Mount Tabor *W York* 55 SE0527
Mountain Ash *M Glam* 18 ST0499
Mountain Cross *Border* 75 NT1547
Mountblairy *Gramp* 95 NJ6954
Mountfield *E Susx* 14 TQ7320
Mountgerald House *Highld* 92 NH5661
Mountjoy *Cnwll* 3 SW8760
Mountnessing *Essex* 24 TQ6297
Mounton *Gwent* 19 ST5193
Mountsorrel *Leics* 39 SK5814
Mountstuart *Strath* 73 NS1159
Mousehill *Surrey* 12 SU9441
Mouswald *D & G* 66 NY0672
Mowacre Hill *Leics* 39 SK5707
Mowhaugh *Border* 76 NT8120
Mowsley *Leics* 39 SP6489
Mowtie *Gramp* 89 NO8388
Moy *Highld* 86 NN4282
Moy *Highld* 93 NH7634
Moye *Highld* 85 NG8818
Moylgrove *Dyfed* 16 SN1144
Muasdale *Strath* 72 NR6840
Much Birch *H & W* 27 SO5030
Much Cowarne *H & W* 27 SO6147
Much Dewchurch *H & W* 27 SO4831
Much Hadham *Herts* 31 TL4219
Much Hoole *Lancs* 53 SD4723
Much Marcle *H & W* 27 SO6533
Much Wenlock *Shrops* 37 SO6299
Muchalls *Gramp* 89 NO9092
Muchelney *Somset* 8 ST4224
Muchelney Ham *Somset* 8 ST4323
Muchlarnick *Cnwll* 4 SX2156
Muckingford *Essex* 24 TQ6779
Muckleford *Dorset* 9 SY6393
Mucklestone *Staffs* 37 SJ7237
Muckton *Lincs* 51 TF3781
Mucomir *Highld* 86 NN1884
Mudale *Highld* 99 NC5335
Muddiford *Devon* 6 SS5638
Muddlebridge *Devon* 6 SS5132
Muddles Green *E Susx* 13 TQ5413
Mudeford *Dorset* 10 SZ1892
Mudford *Somset* 8 ST5719
Mudford Sock *Somset* 8 ST5519
Mudgley *Somset* 19 ST4445
Mugdock *Cent* 74 NS5577
Mugeary *Highld* 84 NG4438
Mugginton *Derbys* 49 SK2843
Muggleswick *Dur* 68 NZ0449
Muie *Highld* 97 NC6704
Muir of Fowlis *Gramp* 94 NJ5612
Muir of Miltonduff *Gramp* 94 NJ1859
Muir of Ord *Highld* 92 NH5250
Muir of Thorn *Tays* 82 NO0637
Muirden *Gramp* 95 NJ7054
Muirdrum *Tays* 83 NO5637
Muiresk *Gramp* 95 NJ6948
Muirhead *Fife* 83 NO2805
Muirhead *Strath* 74 NS6869
Muirhead *Tays* 83 NO3434
Muirhouselaw *Border* 76 NT6328
Muirhouses *Cent* 82 NT0180
Muirkirk *Strath* 74 NS6927
Muirmill *Cent* 81 NS7283
Muirshearlich *Highld* 86 NN1380
Muirtack *Gramp* 95 NJ9937
Muirton Mains *Highld* 92 NH3553
Muirton of Ardblair *Tays* 88 NO1643
Muirtown *Tays* 82 NN9211
Muker *N York* 60 SD9098
Mulbarton *Norfk* 43 TG1901
Mulben *Gramp* 94 NJ3550
Mullfra *Cnwll* 2 SW4534
Mulindry *Strath* 70 NR3659
Mullion *Cnwll* 2 SW6719
Mumby *Lincs* 51 TF5174
Muncher's Green *Herts* 31 TL3126
Munderfield Row *H & W* 27 SO6451
Munderfield Stocks *H & W* 27 SO6550
Mundesley *Norfk* 43 TG3136
Mundford *Norfk* 42 TL8093
Mundham *Norfk* 43 TM3397
Mundon Hill *Essex* 24 TL8602
Munerigie *Highld* 86 NH2602
Mungrisdale *Cumb* 59 NY3630
Munlochy *Highld* 92 NH6453
Munnoch *Strath* 73 NS2548
Munsley *H & W* 28 SO6641
Munslow *Shrops* 37 SO5287
Munslow Aston *Shrops* 37 SO5186
Munslow Aston *Shrops* 37 SO5187
Murchington *Devon* 5 SX6888
Murcott *Oxon* 29 SP5815
Murkle *Highld* 100 ND1668
Murlaggan *Highld* 85 NN0192
Murroes *Tays* 83 NO4635
Murrow *Cambs* 41 TF3707
Mursley *Bucks* 30 SP8128
Murthill *Tays* 89 NO4657
Murthly *Tays* 82 NO1038
Murton *Cumb* 60 NY7221
Murton *Dur* 69 NZ3947
Murton *N York* 56 SE6452
Murton *N York* 56 SE6452
Murton *Nthumb* 77 NT9748
Musbury *Devon* 8 SY2794
Muston *Leics* 40 SK8237
Muston *N York* 63 TA0979
Mustow Green *H & W* 38 SO8774
Muswell Hill *Gt Lon* 23 TQ2889
Mutehill *D & G* 65 NX6848
Mutford *Suffk* 33 TM4888
Muthill *Tays* 82 NN8616
Mutterton *Devon* 7 ST0305
Muxton *Shrops* 37 SJ7114
Mybster *Highld* 100 ND1652
Myddfai *Dyfed* 26 SN7730
Myddle *Shrops* 36 SJ4623
Mydroilyn *Dyfed* 34 SN4555
Mylor Bridge *Cnwll* 2 SW8036
Mynachlog-ddu *Dyfed* 16 SN1430
Myndtown *Shrops* 36 SO3999
Mynydd Isa *Clwyd* 46 SJ2363
Mynydd-bach *Gwent* 19 ST4894
Mynydd-bach *W Glam* 18 SS6597
Myrebird *Gramp* 89 NO7398
Myredykes *Border* 67 NY5998
Mytchett *Surrey* 22 SU8855
Mytholm *W York* 54 SD9827
Mytholmroyd *W York* 54 SE0126
Myton-on-Swale *N York* 55 SE4466

N

Naast *Highld* 91 NG8283
Nab's Head *Lancs* 54 SD6229
Naburn *N York* 56 SE5945
Nackington *Kent* 15 TR1554
Nacton *Suffk* 33 TM2240
Nafferton *Humb* 57 TA0559
Nag's Head *Gloucs* 20 ST8898
Nailbridge *Gloucs* 27 SO6416
Nailsbourne *Somset* 8 ST2128
Nailsea *Avon* 19 ST4770
Nailstone *Leics* 39 SK4107
Nailsworth *Gloucs* 20 ST8499
Nairn *Highld* 93 NH8756
Nalderswood *Surrey* 12 TQ2345
Nannerch *Clwyd* 46 SJ1669
Nanpantan *Leics* 39 SK5017
Nanpean *Cnwll* 3 SW9656
Nant Peris *Gwynd* 44 SH6058
Nant-ddu *Powys* 26 SO0015
Nant-y-gollen *Shrops* 36 SJ2429
Nant-y-pandy *Gwynd* 45 SH6974
Nanternis *Dyfed* 34 SN3756
Nantgaredig *Dyfed* 17 SN4921
Nantglyn *Clwyd* 45 SJ0061
Nantlle *Gwynd* 44 SH5053
Nantmel *Powys* 26 SO0366
Nantmor *Gwynd* 44 SH6046
Nantwich *Ches* 47 SJ6552
Nantyffyllon *M Glam* 18 SS8592
Nantyglo *Gwent* 27 SO1910
Naphill *Bucks* 22 SU8496
Napleton *H & W* 28 SO8648
Napton on the Hill *Warwks* 29 SP4661
Narberth *Dyfed* 16 SN1114
Narborough *Leics* 39 SP5497
Narborough *Norfk* 42 TF7412
Nasareth *Gwynd* 44 SH4749
Naseby *Nhants* 30 SP6978
Nash *Bucks* 30 SP7833
Nash *Gwent* 19 ST3483
Nash *Shrops* 37 SO6071
Nash's Green *Hants* 22 SU6745
Nassington *Nhants* 40 TL0696
Nateby *Cumb* 60 NY7706
Nateby *Lancs* 53 SD4644
Natland *Cumb* 59 SD5289
Naughton *Suffk* 32 TM0249
Naunton *Gloucs* 28 SP1123
Naunton *H & W* 28 SO8645
Naunton *H & W* 28 SO8739
Naunton Beauchamp *H & W* 28 SO9652
Navenby *Lincs* 50 SK9857
Navestock *Essex* 23 TQ5397
Navestock Side *Essex* 24 TQ5697
Navidale *Highld* 97 ND0316
Navity *Highld* 93 NH7864
Nawton *N York* 62 SE6584
Nayland *Suffk* 25 TL9734
Nazeing *Essex* 23 TL4106
Neacroft *Hants* 10 SZ1897
Neap *Shet* 103 HU5058
Near Cotton *Staffs* 48 SK0646
Near Sawry *Cumb* 59 SD3795
Nearsden *Gt Lon* 23 TQ2185
Neasham *Dur* 62 NZ3210
Neath *W Glam* 18 SS7597
Neatham *Hants* 11 SU7440
Neatishead *Norfk* 43 TG3421
Nebo *Gwynd* 44 SH4750
Nebo *Gwynd* 45 SH8356
Necton *Norfk* 42 TF8709
Nedd *Highld* 98 NC1331
Nedging *Suffk* 32 TM0048
Nedging Tye *Suffk* 32 TM0250
Needham *Norfk* 33 TM2281
Needham Market *Suffk* 32 TM0855
Needingworth *Cambs* 31 TL3472
Neen Savage *Shrops* 37 SO6777
Neen Sollars *Shrops* 37 SO6572
Neenton *Shrops* 37 SO6388
Nefyn *Gwynd* 44 SH3040
Neilston *Strath* 73 NS4857
Nelson *Lancs* 54 SD8638
Nelson *M Glam* 18 ST1195
Nemphlar *Strath* 74 NS8544
Nempnett Thrubwell *Avon* 19 ST5260
Nenthead *Cumb* 68 NY7743
Nenthorn *Border* 76 NT6837
Neopardy *Devon* 7 SX7998
Nercwys *Clwyd* 46 SJ2360
Nereabolls *Strath* 70 NR2255
Nerston *Strath* 74 NS6457
Nesbit *Nthumb* 77 NT9833
Nesfield *N York* 55 SE0949
Nesscliffe *Shrops* 36 SJ3819
Neston *Ches* 46 SJ2977
Neston *Wilts* 20 ST8667
Netchwood *Shrops* 37 SO6291
Nether Alderley *Ches* 47 SJ8476
Nether Blainslie *Border* 76 NT5443
Nether Broughton *Notts* 40 SK6925
Nether Burrow *Lancs* 59 SD6174
Nether Cassock *D & G* 67 NT2303
Nether Cerne *Dorset* 9 SY6698
Nether Compton *Dorset* 9 ST5917
Nether Crimond *Gramp* 95 NJ8222
Nether Dallachy *Gramp* 94 NJ3664
Nether Exe *Devon* 7 SS9300
Nether Fingland *Strath* 66 NS9310
Nether Handwick *Tays* 88 NO3641
Nether Haugh *S York* 49 SK4196
Nether Headon *Notts* 50 SK7477
Nether Heage *Derbys* 49 SK3650
Nether Heyford *Nhants* 30 SP6658
Nether Howeclevch *Strath* 66 NT0312
Nether Kellet *Lancs* 53 SD5067
Nether Kinmundy *Gramp* 95 NK0543
Nether Moor *Derbys* 49 SK3866
Nether Newton *Cumb* 59 SD4082
Nether Poppleton *N York* 56 SE5654
Nether Row *Cumb* 58 NY3238
Nether Silton *N York* 62 SE4592
Nether Skyborry *Shrops* 36 SO2773
Nether Stowey *Somset* 19 ST1939
Nether Wallop *Hants* 10 SU3036
Nether Wasdale *Cumb* 58 NY1204
Nether Wellwood *Strath* 74 NS6526
Nether Westcote *Oxon* 29 SP2220
Nether Whitacre *Warwks* 39 SP2392
Nether Whitecleuch *Strath* 74 NS8319
Netheravon *Wilts* 20 SU1448
Netherbrae *Gramp* 95 NJ7959
Netherburn *Strath* 74 NS7947
Netherbury *Dorset* 8 SY4799
Nethercleuch *D & G* 67 NY1186
Netherend *Gloucs* 19 SO5900
Netherfield *E Susx* 14 TQ7019
Netherfield Road *E Susx* 14 TQ7417
Netherhampton *Wilts* 10 SU1029
Netherhay *Dorset* 8 ST4105
Netherlaw *D & G* 65 NX7445
Netherley *Gramp* 89 NO8493
Nethermill *D & G* 66 NY0487
Nethermuir *Gramp* 95 NJ9144
Netherplace *Strath* 74 NS5255
Netherseal *Derbys* 39 SK2813
Netherstreet *Wilts* 20 ST9764
Netherthong *W York* 55 SE1309
Netherthorpe *Derbys* 49 SK4574
Netherton *Cent* 81 NS5579
Netherton *Devon* 5 SX8971
Netherton *H & W* 27 SO5126
Netherton *Nthumb* 69 NZ2382
Netherton *Nthumb* 68 NT9807
Netherton *Oxon* 19 ST4199
Netherton *Shrops* 37 SO7382
Netherton *Strath* 74 NS7854
Netherton *Tays* 88 NO1452
Netherton *Tays* 89 NO5457
Netherton *W Mids* 38 SO9488
Netherton *W York* 55 SE2716
Nethertown *Cumb* 58 NX9807
Nethertown *Highld* 100 ND3578
Nethertown *Staffs* 38 SK1017
Netherwitton *Nthumb* 69 NZ0990
Nethy Bridge *Highld* 93 NJ0020
Netley *Hants* 10 SU4508
Netley Marsh *Hants* 10 SU3313
Nettacott *Devon* 7 SX9099
Nettlebed *Oxon* 22 SU6986
Nettlebridge *Somset* 19 ST6448
Nettlecombe *Dorset* 8 SY5195
Nettleden *Herts* 22 TL0110
Nettleham *Lincs* 50 TF0075
Nettlestead *Kent* 14 TQ6852
Nettlestead Green *Kent* 14 TQ6850
Nettlestone *IOW* 11 SZ6290
Nettlesworth *Dur* 69 NZ2547
Nettleton *Lincs* 50 TA1100
Nettleton *Wilts* 20 ST8178
Netton *Wilts* 10 SU1236
Neuadd Fawr *Dyfed* 26 SN7541
Neuadd-ddu *Powys* 35 SN9275
Nevern *Dyfed* 16 SN0840
Nevill Holt *Leics* 40 SP8193
New Abbey *D & G* 66 NX9666
New Aberdour *Gramp* 95 NJ8863
New Addington *Gt Lon* 23 TQ3763
New Alresford *Hants* 11 SU5832
New Alyth *Tays* 88 NO2447
New Ash Green *Kent* 14 TQ6064
New Balderton *Notts* 50 SK8152
New Barn *Kent* 14 TQ6168
New Barnet *Gt Lon* 23 TQ2695
New Bewick *Nthumb* 77 NU0620
New Bilton *Warwks* 39 SP4975
New Bolingbroke *Lincs* 51 TF3057
New Bradwell *Bucks* 30 SP8341
New Brampton *Derbys* 49 SK3671
New Brancepeth *Dur* 61 NZ2241
New Brighton *Mersyd* 46 SJ3193
New Brinsley *Notts* 49 SK4650
New Brotton *Cleve* 62 NZ6820
New Buckenham *Norfk* 32 TM0890
New Bury *Gt Man* 47 SD7305
New Byth *Gramp* 95 NJ8254
New Clipstone *Notts* 49 SK5863
New Costessey *Norfk* 43 TG1810
New Crofton *W York* 55 SE3817
New Cross *Gt Lon* 23 TQ3676
New Cross *Somset* 8 ST4219
New Cumnock *Strath* 66 NS6113
New Cut *E Susx* 14 TQ8115
New Deer *Gramp* 95 NJ8847
New Denham *Bucks* 22 TQ0485
New Duston *Nhants* 30 SP7162
New Eastwood *Notts* 49 SK4646
New Edlington *S York* 49 SK5399
New Elgin *Gramp* 94 NJ2261
New Ellerby *Humb* 57 TA1639
New Eltham *Gt Lon* 23 TQ4472
New End *H & W* 28 SP0560
New England *Notts* 55 SE5163
New Farnley *W York* 55 SE2431
New Fletton *Cambs* 40 TL1997
New Galloway *D & G* 65 NX6377
New Gilston *Fife* 83 NO4208
New Grimsby *IOS* 2 SV8915
New Hedges *Dyfed* 16 SN1302
New Holkham *Norfk* 42 TF8839
New Holland *Humb* 57 TA0823
New Houghton *Derbys* 49 SK5065
New Houghton *Norfk* 42 TF7927
New Hutton *Cumb* 59 SD5691
New Inn *Devon* 6 SS4408
New Inn *Dyfed* 17 SN4736
New Inn *Gwent* 19 SO4800
New Inn *Gwent* 19 ST3099
New Inn *N York* 54 SD8072
New Invention *Shrops* 36 SO2976
New Kelso *Highld* 91 NG9442
New Lakenham *Norfk* 43 TG2306
New Lanark *Strath* 74 NS8842
New Langholm *D & G* 67 NY3584
New Leake *Lincs* 51 TF4057
New Leeds *Gramp* 95 NJ9954
New Luce *D & G* 64 NX1764
New Machar *Gramp* 95 NJ8919
New Malden *Gt Lon* 23 TQ2168
New Marske *Cleve* 62 NZ6110
New Marston *Oxon* 29 SP5307
New Mill *Gramp* 89 NO7883
New Mill *W York* 55 SE1608
New Mills *Powys* 36 SJ0901
New Milton *Hants* 10 SZ2495
New Mistley *Essex* 25 TM1131
New Moat *Dyfed* 16 SN0625
New Ollerton *Notts* 49 SK6668
New Pitsligo *Gramp* 95 NJ8855
New Prestwick *Strath* 73 NS3424
New Quay *Dyfed* 34 SN3859
New Rackheath *Norfk* 43 TG2812
New Radnor *Powys* 27 SO2161
New Ridley *Nthumb* 68 NZ0559
New Romney *Kent* 15 TR0624
New Rossington *Notts* 49 SK6198
New Sauchie *Cent* 82 NS8994
New Scone *Tays* 82 NO1326
New Sharlston *W York* 55 SE3820
New Silksworth *T & W* 69 NZ3853
New Somerby *Lincs* 40 SK9235
New Spilsby *Lincs* 51 TF4165
New Stevenston *Strath* 74 NS7659
New Town *Dorset* 9 ST8318
New Town *Dorset* 9 ST9515
New Town *Dorset* 9 ST9918
New Town *E Susx* 13 TQ4720
New Town *Loth* 76 NT4470
New Tredegar *M Glam* 18 SO1403
New Trows *Strath* 74 NS8038
New Ulva *Strath* 71 NR7080
New Village *Humb* 56 SE8530
New Walsoken *Cambs* 41 TF4609
New Waltham *Humb* 57 TA2804
New Whittington *Derbys* 49 SK4075
New Wimpole *Cambs* 31 TL3449
New Wimpole *Cambs* 31 TL3450
New Winton *Loth* 76 NT4271
New York *Lincs* 51 TF2455
New York *N York* 55 SE1962
New Zealand *Derbys* 39 SK3336
Newall *W York* 55 SE1946
Newark *D & G* 66 NS7809
Newark-on-Trent *Notts* 50 SK7953
Newarthill *Strath* 74 NS7859
Newbattle *Loth* 75 NT3365
Newbie *D & G* 67 NY1764
Newbiggin *Cumb* 58 SD0993
Newbiggin *Cumb* 59 NY4729
Newbiggin *Cumb* 67 NY5549
Newbiggin *Cumb* 60 NY6228
Newbiggin *Dur* 60 NY9127
Newbiggin *N York* 61 SE0085
Newbiggin *Nthumb* 68 NY9461
Newbiggin-by-the-Sea *Nthumb* 69 NZ3087
Newbigging *Strath* 75 NT0145
Newbigging *Tays* 88 NO2842
Newbigging *Tays* 83 NO4237
Newbold Pacey *Warwks* 29 SP2957
Newbold Verdon *Leics* 39 SK4403
Newbold on Avon *Warwks* 39 SP4877
Newbold on Stour *Warwks* 29 SP2446
Newborough *Cambs* 41 TF2006
Newborough *Gwynd* 44 SH4265
Newborough *Staffs* 38 SK1325
Newbourn *Suffk* 33 TM2743
Newbridge *Cnwll* 2 SW4231
Newbridge *D & G* 66 NX9579
Newbridge *Gwent* 19 ST2097
Newbridge *Hants* 10 SU2915
Newbridge *Hants* 10 SU2915
Newbridge *IOW* 10 SZ4187
Newbridge *Loth* 75 NT1272
Newbridge Green *H & W* 28 SO8439
Newbridge on Wye *Powys* 26 SO0158
Newbrough *Nthumb* 68 NY8767
Newbuildings *Devon* 7 SS7903
Newbuildings *Devon* 7 SS7903
Newburgh *Fife* 83 NO2318
Newburgh *Gramp* 95 NJ9659
Newburgh *Gramp* 95 NJ9925
Newburgh *Lancs* 53 SD4810
Newburgh Priory *N York* 62 SE5476
Newburn *T & W* 69 NZ1665
Newbury *Berks* 21 SU4666
Newbury *Somset* 20 ST6950
Newbury *Wilts* 20 ST8241
Newby *Cumb* 59 NY5921
Newby *Lancs* 54 SD8146
Newby *N York* 54 SD7269
Newby *N York* 62 NZ5012
Newby *N York* 63 TA0190
Newby Bridge *Cumb* 59 SD3686
Newby East *Cumb* 67 NY4758
Newby West *Cumb* 67 NY3654
Newby Wiske *N York* 62 SE3687

Newcastle Odsal

Newcastle *Gwent*	27	SO4417
Newcastle *Shrops*	36	SO2482
Newcastle Emlyn *Dyfed*	17	SN3040
Newcastle upon Tyne *T & W*	69	NZ2464
Newcastle-under-Lyme *Staffs*	47	SJ8445
Newcastleton *D & G*	67	NY4887
Newchapel *Dyfed*	17	SN2239
Newchapel *Surrey*	12	TQ3642
Newchurch *Gwent*	27	SO1710
Newchurch *Gwent*	19	ST4597
Newchurch *IOW*	11	SZ5685
Newchurch *Kent*	15	TR0531
Newchurch *Powys*	27	SO2150
Newchurch *Staffs*	38	SK1423
Newcott *Devon*	8	ST2309
Newcraighall *Loth*	75	NT2973
Newdigate *Surrey*	12	TQ1942
Newell Green *Berks*	22	SU8771
Newenden *Kent*	14	TQ8327
Newent *Gloucs*	28	SO7226
Newfield *Dur*	61	NZ2033
Newfield *Highld*	97	NH7877
Newgale *Dyfed*	16	SM8422
Newgate Street *Herts*	23	TL3005
Newhall *Ches*	47	SJ6145
Newhall *Derbys*	39	SK2821
Newham *Gt Lon*	23	TQ4081
Newhaven *E Susx*	13	TQ4401
Newholm *N York*	63	NZ8610
Newhouse *Strath*	74	NS7961
Newick *E Susx*	13	TQ4121
Newington *Kent*	14	TQ8564
Newington *Kent*	15	TR1837
Newington *Oxon*	21	SU6096
Newington *Shrops*	36	SO4283
Newland *Cumb*	67	NY2979
Newland *Gloucs*	27	SO5409
Newland *H & W*	28	SO7948
Newland *Humb*	57	TA0631
Newland *N York*	56	SE6824
Newland *Somset*	7	SS8338
Newlandrig *Loth*	76	NT3762
Newlands *Border*	67	NY5194
Newlands *Nthumb*	68	NZ0855
Newlands of Dundurlas *Gramp*	94	NJ2950
Newlyn *Cnwll*	2	SW4628
Newlyn East *Cnwll*	2	SW8256
Newmains *Strath*	74	NS8256
Newman's Green *Suffk*	32	TL8843
Newmarket *Cumb*	59	NY3338
Newmarket *Suffk*	32	TL6463
Newmill *Border*	67	NT4510
Newmill *Gramp*	94	NJ4352
Newmill of Inshewan *Tays*	88	NO4260
Newmillerdam *W York*	55	SE3215
Newmills *Fife*	82	NT0186
Newmills *Gwent*	27	SO5107
Newmills *Loth*	75	NT1667
Newmiln *Tays*	82	NO1230
Newmilns *Strath*	74	NS5337
Newney Green *Essex*	24	TL6507
Newnham *Gloucs*	28	SO6911
Newnham *H & W*	27	SO6469
Newnham *Hants*	22	SU7054
Newnham *Herts*	31	TL2437
Newnham *Kent*	14	TQ9557
Newnham Paddox *Warwks*	39	SP4783
Newport *Devon*	6	SS5631
Newport *Essex*	31	TL5234
Newport *Gloucs*	20	ST7097
Newport *Gwent*	19	ST3188
Newport *Highld*	100	ND1324
Newport *IOW*	10	SZ4989
Newport *Norfk*	43	TG5016
Newport *Shrops*	37	SJ7419
Newport Bagnell *Bucks*	30	SP8743
Newport-on-Tay *Fife*	83	NO4228
Newquay *Cnwll*	2	SW8161
Newseat *Gramp*	95	NJ7033
Newsham *Lancs*	53	SD5136
Newsham *N York*	61	NZ1010
Newsham *N York*	62	SE3884
Newsham *Nthumb*	69	NZ3080
Newsholme *Humb*	56	SE7129
Newstead *Border*	76	NT5634
Newstead *Notts*	49	SK5152
Newstead *Nthumb*	77	NU1527
Newtack *Gramp*	94	NJ4446
Newthorpe *N York*	55	SE4632
Newton *Beds*	31	TL2344
Newton *Border*	76	NT6020
Newton *Cambs*	31	TL4349
Newton *Cambs*	41	TF4314
Newton *Ches*	46	SJ4167
Newton *Ches*	46	SJ5059
Newton *Cumb*	53	SD2271
Newton *D & G*	67	NY1194
Newton *Derbys*	49	SK4459
Newton *Gramp*	94	NJ1663
Newton *Gramp*	94	NJ3362
Newton *H & W*	27	SO3432
Newton *H & W*	27	SO5153
Newton *Highld*	92	NH5850
Newton *Highld*	93	NH7448
Newton *Highld*	93	NH7866
Newton *Highld*	100	ND3449
Newton *Lancs*	53	SD3436
Newton *Lancs*	53	SD4430
Newton *Lancs*	59	SD5974
Newton *Lancs*	54	SD6950
Newton *Lincs*	40	TF0436
Newton *Loth*	75	NT0977
Newton *M Glam*	18	SS8377
Newton *Nhants*	40	SP8883
Newton *Norfk*	42	TF8315
Newton *Notts*	49	SK6841
Newton *Nthumb*	68	NZ0364
Newton *Nthumb*	68	NT9407
Newton *S Glam*	19	ST2378
Newton *Staffs*	38	SK0325
Newton *Strath*	74	NS6560
Newton *Strath*	75	NS9331
Newton *Strath*	80	NS0498
Newton *Suffk*	32	TL9240
Newton *W Glam*	17	SS6088
Newton *W Isls*	102	NF8877
Newton *W York*	55	SE4427
Newton *Warwks*	39	SP5378
Newton Abbot *Devon*	5	SX8671
Newton Arlosh *Cumb*	67	NY2055
Newton Aycliffe *Dur*	61	NZ2724
Newton Bewley *Cleve*	62	NZ4626
Newton Blossomville *Bucks*	30	SP9251
Newton Bromswold *Beds*	30	SP9966
Newton Burgoland *Leics*	39	SK3709
Newton Ferrers *Devon*	4	SX5447
Newton Ferrers *M Glam*	4	SX3466
Newton Flotman *Norfk*	43	TM2198
Newton Harcourt *Leics*	39	SP6497
Newton Heath *Gt Man*	47	SD8700
Newton Hill *Gramp*	89	NO9193
Newton Kyme *N York*	55	SE4644
Newton Longville *Bucks*	30	SP8431
Newton Mearns *Strath*	74	NS5355
Newton Morrel *N York*	61	NZ2309
Newton Mountain *Dyfed*	16	SM9807
Newton Poppleford *Devon*	8	SY0889
Newton Purcell *Oxon*	29	SP6230
Newton Regis *Warwks*	39	SK2707
Newton Reigny *Cumb*	59	NY4731
Newton Solney *Derbys*	39	SK2825
Newton St. Cyres *Devon*	7	SX8797
Newton St. Faith *Norfk*	43	TG2217
Newton St. Loe *Avon*	20	ST7064
Newton St. Petrock *Devon*	6	SS4112
Newton Stacey *Hants*	21	SU4140
Newton Stewart *D & G*	64	NX4165
Newton Toney *Wilts*	21	SU2140
Newton Tracey *Devon*	6	SS5226
Newton Valence *Hants*	11	SU7232
Newton by Toft *Lincs*	50	TF0487
Newton of Balcanquhal *Tays*	82	NO1610
Newton on Ouse *N York*	55	SE5159
Newton on Trent *Lincs*	50	SK8374
Newton under Roseberry *Cleve*	62	NZ5613
Newton upon Derwent *Humb*	56	SE7149
Newton-le-Willows *Mersyd*	47	SJ5995
Newton-le-Willows *N York*	61	SE2189
Newton-on-the-Moor *Nthumb*	69	NU1705
Newtonairds *D & G*	66	NX8880
Newtongarry Croft *Gramp*	94	NJ5735
Newtongrange *Loth*	75	NT3364
Newtonloan *Loth*	75	NT3362
Newtonmill *Tays*	89	NO6064
Newtonmore *Highld*	87	NN7198
Newtown *Beds*	31	TL1945
Newtown *Ches*	46	SJ5374
Newtown *Ches*	48	SJ9060
Newtown *Cnwll*	4	SX2978
Newtown *Cumb*	67	NY0948
Newtown *Cumb*	67	NY5262
Newtown *D & G*	66	NS7710
Newtown *Devon*	4	SX0699
Newtown *Devon*	7	SS7625
Newtown *Dorset*	8	ST4701
Newtown *Dorset*	9	SZ0393
Newtown *Gloucs*	20	SO6702
Newtown *Gt Man*	47	SD5605
Newtown *H & W*	27	SO5333
Newtown *H & W*	27	SO6145
Newtown *H & W*	28	SO7037
Newtown *H & W*	28	SO8655
Newtown *Hants*	10	SU2710
Newtown *Hants*	11	SU6113
Newtown *Highld*	86	NH3504
Newtown *IOM*	52	SC3273
Newtown *IOW*	10	SZ4290
Newtown *Nthumb*	68	NU0300
Newtown *Powys*	36	SO1091
Newtown *Shrops*	36	SJ4222
Newtown *Shrops*	37	SJ4831
Newtown *Somset*	8	ST2712
Newtown *Wilts*	9	ST9128
Newtown Linford *Leics*	39	SK5110
Newtown St. Boswells *Border*	76	NT5732
Newtown of Beltrees *Strath*	73	NS3758
Newtyle *Tays*	88	NO2941
Newyork *Strath*	80	NM9611
Neyland *Dyfed*	16	SM9605
Nibley Green *Gloucs*	20	ST7296
Nicholashayne *Devon*	8	ST1016
Nicholaston *W Glam*	17	SS5288
Nickies Hill *Cumb*	67	NY5467
Nidd *N York*	55	SE3060
Nigg *Gramp*	89	NJ9402
Nigg *Highld*	93	NH8071
Nightcott *Devon*	7	SS8925
Nine Ashes *Essex*	24	TL5902
Nine Elms *Wilts*	20	SU1085
Nine Elms *Wilts*	10	SU1236
Nine Wells *Dyfed*	16	SM7824
Ninebanks *Nthumb*	68	NY7853
Ninemile Bar or Crocketford *D & G*	66	NX8373
Nineveh *H & W*	27	SO6265
Ningwood *IOW*	10	SZ3989
Nisbet *Border*	76	NT6725
Nisbet Hill *Border*	76	NT7850
Niton *IOW*	10	SZ5076
Nitshill *Strath*	74	NS5260
No Man's Heath *Ches*	46	SJ5148
No Man's Heath *Warwks*	39	SK2909
Nocton *Lincs*	50	TF0564
Noke *Oxon*	29	SP5413
Nolton *Dyfed*	16	SM8718
Nolton Haven *Dyfed*	16	SM8618
Nomansland *Devon*	7	SS8313
Nomansland *Wilts*	10	SU2517
Noneley *Shrops*	37	SJ4728
Nonington *Kent*	15	TR2552
Nook *Cumb*	59	SD5482
Norbiton Common *Gt Lon*	23	TQ2167
Norbury *Ches*	47	SJ5547
Norbury *Derbys*	48	SK1241
Norbury *Gt Lon*	23	TQ3069
Norbury *Shrops*	36	SO3693
Norbury *Staffs*	37	SJ7823
Norby *N York*	62	SE4381
Norchard *H & W*	28	SO8568
Norcott Brook *Ches*	47	SJ6180
Nordelph *Norfk*	41	TF5501
Nordley *Shrops*	37	SO6997
Norham *Nthumb*	77	NT9047
Norland Town *W York*	55	SE0622
Norley *Ches*	47	SJ5772
Norley *Devon*	6	SS4900
Norleywood *Hants*	10	SZ3597
Norman Cross *Cambs*	40	TL1691
Norman's Green *Devon*	7	ST0503
Normanby *Cleve*	62	NZ5518
Normanby *Humb*	56	SE8716
Normanby *Lincs*	50	TF0088
Normanby *N York*	63	SE7381
Normanby le Wold *Lincs*	50	TF1295
Normansland *Wilts*	10	SU2517
Normanton *Derbys*	39	SK3433
Normanton *Leics*	50	SK8140
Normanton *Lincs*	50	SK9446
Normanton *Notts*	49	SK7054
Normanton *W York*	55	SE3822
Normanton le Heath *Leics*	39	SK3712
Normanton on Soar *Notts*	39	SK5123
Normanton on Trent *Notts*	50	SK7868
Normanton on the Wolds *Notts*	39	SK6232
Normoss *Lancs*	53	SD3437
Norney *Surrey*	12	SU9444
Norristhorpe *W York*	55	SE2123
North Anston *S York*	49	SK5184
North Aston *Oxon*	29	SP4728
North Baddesley *Hants*	10	SU3920
North Ballchulish *Highld*	86	NN0560
North Barrow *Somset*	9	ST6029
North Barsham *Norfk*	42	TF9135
North Benfleet *Essex*	24	TQ7690
North Bersted *W Susx*	11	SU9200
North Berwick *Loth*	83	NT5485
North Biddick *T & W*	69	NZ5153
North Bitchburn *Dur*	61	NZ1733
North Boarhunt *Hants*	11	SU6010
North Bovey *Devon*	5	SX7483
North Bradley *Wilts*	20	ST8554
North Brentor *Devon*	4	SX4881
North Brewham *Somset*	20	ST7236
North Brook End *Cambs*	31	TL2844
North Buckland *Devon*	6	SS4840
North Burlingham *Norfk*	43	TG3610
North Cadbury *Somset*	9	ST6327
North Cairn *D & G*	64	NW9770
North Carlton *Lincs*	50	SK9477
North Carlton *Notts*	49	SK5885
North Cave *Humb*	56	SE8832
North Cerney *Gloucs*	28	SP0208
North Charford *Hants*	10	SU1919
North Charlton *Nthumb*	77	NU1622
North Cheam *Gt Lon*	23	TQ2365
North Cheriton *Somset*	9	ST6825
North Chideock *Dorset*	8	SY4294
North Cliffe *Humb*	56	SE8737
North Clifton *Notts*	50	SK8272
North Cockerington *Lincs*	51	TF3790
North Collingham *Notts*	50	SK8362
North Common *E Susx*	13	TQ3921
North Connel *Strath*	80	NM9135
North Cornelly *M Glam*	18	SS8281
North Corner *Cnwll*	2	SW7818
North Corry *Highld*	79	NM8353
North Cotes *Lincs*	51	TA3400
North Cottingham *Notts*	50	SK8061
North Cove *Suffk*	33	TM4689
North Cowton *N York*	61	NZ2803
North Creake *Norfk*	42	TF8538
North Curry *Somset*	8	ST3125
North Dalton *Humb*	56	SE9352
North Deighton *N York*	55	SE3851
North Duffield *N York*	56	SE6837
North Elham *Kent*	15	TR1844
North Elmham *Norfk*	42	TF9820
North Elmsall *W York*	55	SE4712
North End *Avon*	19	ST4267
North End *Essex*	24	TL6619
North End *Hants*	10	SU1016
North End *Hants*	11	SU5829
North End *Hants*	11	SU6502
North End *Humb*	57	TA2931
North End *Humb*	57	TA3007
North End *Nhants*	30	SP9668
North End *Nthumb*	67	NT1301
North End *W Susx*	12	SU9804
North End *W Susx*	12	TQ1209
North Erradale *Highld*	91	NG7481
North Evington *Leics*	39	SK6204
North Fambridge *Essex*	24	TQ8597
North Feorline *Strath*	72	NR9129
North Ferriby *Humb*	56	SE9826
North Frodingham *Humb*	57	TA1053
North Gorley *Hants*	10	SU1611
North Green *Suffk*	33	TM3162
North Grimston *N York*	56	SE8467
North Hayling *Hants*	11	SU7303
North Hill *Cnwll*	4	SX2776
North Hillingdon *Gt Lon*	22	TQ0784
North Hinksey *Oxon*	29	SP4805
North Huish *Devon*	5	SX7156
North Hykeham *Lincs*	50	SK9466
North Kelsey *Humb*	50	TA0401
North Kessock *Highld*	93	NH6548
North Killingholme *Humb*	57	TA1417
North Kilvington *N York*	62	SE4284
North Kilworth *Leics*	39	SP6183
North Kingston *Hants*	10	SU1603
North Kyme *Lincs*	50	TF1552
North Lee *Bucks*	22	SP8308
North Lees *N York*	61	SE3073
North Leigh *Kent*	15	TR1447
North Leigh *Oxon*	29	SP3813
North Leverton with Habblesthorpe *Notts*	50	SK7882
North Lopham *Norfk*	32	TM0383
North Luffenham *Leics*	40	SK9303
North Marden *W Susx*	11	SU8016
North Marston *Bucks*	30	SP7722
North Middleton *Loth*	75	NT3559
North Milmain *D & G*	64	NX0952
North Molton *Devon*	7	SS7329
North Moreton *Oxon*	21	SU5689
North Mundham *W Susx*	11	SU8702
North Muskham *Notts*	50	SK7958
North Newbald *Humb*	56	SE9136
North Newington *Oxon*	29	SP4139
North Newnton *Wilts*	20	SU1257
North Newton *Gwent*	8	ST2931
North Newton *Somset*	8	ST3031
North Nibley *Gloucs*	20	ST7395
North Ormsby *Lincs*	51	TF2893
North Otterington *N York*	62	SE3689
North Owersby *Lincs*	50	TF0594
North Perrott *Somset*	8	ST4709
North Petherton *Somset*	8	ST2832
North Petherwin *Cnwll*	4	SX2889
North Pickenham *Norfk*	42	TF8607
North Piddle *H & W*	28	SO9654
North Pool *Devon*	5	SX7741
North Poorton *Dorset*	8	SY5197
North Queensferry *Fife*	82	NT1380
North Radworthy *Devon*	7	SS7534
North Rauceby *Lincs*	50	TF0246
North Reston *Lincs*	51	TF3883
North Rigton *N York*	55	SE2749
North Runcton *Norfk*	42	TF6416
North Scarle *Lincs*	50	SK8466
North Shian *Strath*	79	NM9143
North Shields *T & W*	69	NZ3568
North Shoebury *Essex*	24	TQ9286
North Shore *Lancs*	53	SD3037
North Side *Cambs*	41	TL2799
North Side *Cumb*	58	NY0029
North Skirlaugh *Humb*	57	TA1439
North Somercotes *Lincs*	51	TF4296
North Stainley *N York*	61	SE2876
North Stainmore *Cumb*	60	NY8215
North Stifford *Essex*	24	TQ6080
North Stoke *Avon*	20	ST7068
North Stoke *Oxon*	21	SU6186
North Stoke *W Susx*	12	TQ0210
North Street *Berks*	21	SU6371
North Street *Kent*	15	TR0157
North Sunderland *Nthumb*	77	NU2131
North Tamerton *Cnwll*	6	SX3197
North Tawton *Devon*	7	SS6601
North Third *Cent*	81	NS7589
North Tidworth *Wilts*	21	SU2248
North Town *Berks*	22	SU8882
North Town *Devon*	6	SS5109
North Town *Somset*	19	ST5642
North Tuddenham *Norfk*	42	TG0414
North Walsham *Norfk*	43	TG2830
North Waltham *Hants*	21	SU5646
North Warnborough *Hants*	22	SU7351
North Weald Basset *Essex*	23	TL4904
North Weston *Avon*	19	ST4674
North Wheatley *Notts*	50	SK7685
North Widcombe *Somset*	19	ST5758
North Willingham *Lincs*	50	TF1688
North Wingfield *Derbys*	49	SK4064
North Witham *Lincs*	40	SK9221
North Wootton *Dorset*	9	ST6614
North Wootton *Norfk*	42	TF6424
North Wootton *Somset*	19	ST5641
North Wraxall *Wilts*	20	ST8175
Northall *Bucks*	30	SP9520
Northall Green *Norfk*	42	TF9915
Northallerton *N York*	62	SE3793
Northam *Devon*	6	SS4429
Northam *Hants*	10	SU4312
Northampton *H & W*	28	SO8365
Northampton *Nhants*	30	SP7560
Northaw *Herts*	23	TL2702
Northay *Somset*	8	ST2811
Northborough *Cambs*	40	TF1507
Northbourne *Kent*	15	TR3352
Northbridge Street *E Susx*	14	TQ7423
Northbrook *Hants*	11	SU5139
Northchapel *W Susx*	12	SU9529
Northchurch *Herts*	22	SP9708
Northcott *Devon*	4	SX3392
Northcott *Devon*	8	ST1109
Northcourt *Oxon*	21	SU5098
Northdown *Kent*	15	TR3770
Northedge *Derbys*	49	SK3565
Northend *Warwks*	29	SP3852
Northenden *Gt Man*	47	SJ8290
Northfield *Gramp*	95	NJ9008
Northfield *Humb*	56	TA0328
Northfield *W Mids*	38	SP0279
Northfields *Lincs*	40	TF0208
Northfleet *Essex*	14	TQ6274
Northiam *E Susx*	14	TQ8324
Northill *Beds*	30	TL1446
Northington *Hants*	11	SU5637
Northlands *Lincs*	51	TF3453
Northleach *Gloucs*	28	SP1114
Northleigh *Devon*	6	SS6034
Northleigh *Devon*	8	SY1995
Northlew *Devon*	6	SX5099
Northmoor *Oxon*	21	SP4202
Northmoor Green or Moorland *Somset*	8	ST3332
Northmuir *Tays*	88	NO3854
Northney *Hants*	11	SU7303
Northolt *Gt Lon*	22	TQ1384
Northop *Clwyd*	46	SJ2468
Northop Hall *Clwyd*	46	SJ2667
Northorpe *Lincs*	41	TF2036
Northorpe *Lincs*	50	SK8996
Northorpe *W York*	55	SE2121
Northowram *W York*	55	SE1127
Northport *Dorset*	9	SY9288
Northrepps *Norfk*	43	TG2439
Northton *W Isls*	102	NF9889
Northway *Somset*	8	ST1329
Northway *W Glam*	17	SS5889
Northwich *Ches*	47	SJ6673
Northwick *H & W*	28	SO8458
Northwold *Norfk*	42	TL7597
Northwood *Gt Lon*	22	TQ0990
Northwood *IOW*	10	SZ4893
Northwood *Shrops*	36	SJ4633
Northwood *Staffs*	48	SJ8948
Northwood End *Beds*	30	TL0941
Northwood Green *Gloucs*	28	SO7216
Norton *Ches*	47	SJ5582
Norton *Cleve*	62	NZ4421
Norton *E Susx*	13	TQ4601
Norton *Gloucs*	28	SO8524
Norton *H & W*	28	SO8751
Norton *H & W*	28	SP0448
Norton *IOW*	10	SZ3489
Norton *N York*	56	SE7971
Norton *Nhants*	29	SP5963
Norton *Notts*	49	SK5772
Norton *Powys*	27	SO3067
Norton *S York*	56	SE5415
Norton *S York*	49	SK3561
Norton *Shrops*	37	SJ7200
Norton *Shrops*	37	SO6482
Norton *Suffk*	32	TL9565
Norton *W Glam*	17	SS6188
Norton *W Susx*	11	SU9306
Norton *Wilts*	20	ST8884
Norton Bavant *Wilts*	20	ST9043
Norton Bridge *Staffs*	38	SJ8730
Norton Brook *Staffs*	48	SJ9052
Norton Canon *H & W*	27	SO3847
Norton Disney *Lincs*	50	SK8859
Norton Fitzwarren *Somset*	8	ST1925
Norton Green *IOW*	10	SZ3388
Norton Green *Staffs*	38	SK0107
Norton Hawkfield *Avon*	19	ST5964
Norton Heath *Essex*	24	TL6004
Norton Lindsey *Warwks*	29	SP2263
Norton Little Green *Suffk*	32	TL9766
Norton Malreward *Avon*	19	ST6065
Norton St. Philip *Somset*	20	ST7755
Norton Subcourse *Norfk*	43	TM4198
Norton Wood *H & W*	27	SO3648
Norton in Hales *Shrops*	37	SJ7038
Norton sub Hamdon *Somset*	8	ST4615
Norton-Juxta-Twycross *Leics*	39	SK3207
Norton-le-Clay *N York*	55	SE4071
Norwell *Notts*	50	SK7661
Norwell Woodhouse *Notts*	50	SK7362
Norwich *Norfk*	43	TG2308
Norwick *Shet*	103	HP6514
Norwood *Cent*	82	NS8793
Norwood *Kent*	15	TR0430
Norwood Green *Gt Lon*	22	TQ1378
Norwood Green *W York*	55	SE1427
Norwood Hill *Surrey*	12	TQ2443
Noseley *Leics*	40	SP7398
Noss Mayo *Devon*	4	SX5447
Nosterfield *N York*	61	SE2780
Nostie *Highld*	85	NG8527
Notgrove *Gloucs*	28	SP1020
Nottage *M Glam*	18	SS8278
Notter *M Glam*	4	SX3961
Nottingham *Notts*	49	SK5739
Nottington *Dorset*	9	SY6582
Notton *W York*	55	SE3413
Notton *Wilts*	20	ST9169
Noutard's Green *H & W*	28	SO8066
Nox *Shrops*	36	SJ4110
Nuffield *Oxon*	22	SU6687
Nun Monkton *N York*	55	SE5057
Nuneaton *Warwks*	39	SP3692
Nuneham Courtenay *Oxon*	21	SU5599
Nunhead *Gt Lon*	23	TQ3475
Nunkeeling *Humb*	57	TA1449
Nunnerie *Strath*	66	NS9612
Nunney *Somset*	20	ST7345
Nunnington *N York*	62	SE6679
Nunsthorpe *Humb*	57	TA2508
Nunthorpe *N York*	56	SE6050
Nunthorpe Village *Cleve*	62	NZ5313
Nunton *W Isls*	102	NF7653
Nunton *Wilts*	10	SU1525
Nunwick *N York*	62	SE3274
Nupend *Gloucs*	28	SO7806
Nuptow *Berks*	22	SU8873
Nursling *Hants*	10	SU3616
Nursted *Hants*	11	SU7621
Nutbourne *W Susx*	11	SU7705
Nutbourne *W Susx*	12	TQ0718
Nutfield *Surrey*	12	TQ3050
Nuthall *Notts*	49	SK5144
Nuthampstead *Herts*	31	TL4034
Nuthurst *W Susx*	12	TQ1926
Nutley *E Susx*	13	TQ4427
Nutley *Hants*	21	SU6144
Nybster *Highld*	100	ND3663
Nyetimber *W Susx*	11	SZ8998
Nyewood *W Susx*	11	SU8021
Nymet Rowland *Devon*	7	SS7108
Nymet Tracey *Devon*	7	SS7200
Nympsfield *Gloucs*	20	SO8000
Nynehead *Somset*	8	ST1423
Nyton *W Susx*	11	SU9322

O

Oad Street *Kent*	14	TQ8662
Oadby *Leics*	39	SK6200
Oak Cross *Devon*	6	SX5399
Oakamoor *Staffs*	48	SK0544
Oakbank *Loth*	75	NT0766
Oakdale *Gwent*	19	ST1898
Oake *Somset*	8	ST1525
Oaken *Staffs*	38	SJ8502
Oakenclough *Lancs*	53	SD5447
Oakengates *Shrops*	37	SJ7010
Oakenshaw *Dur*	61	NZ1937
Oakenshaw *W York*	55	SE1728
Oaker Side *Derbys*	49	SK2761
Oakford *Devon*	7	SS9021
Oakford *Dyfed*	34	SN4558
Oakfordbridge *Devon*	7	SS9122
Oakham *Leics*	40	SK8608
Oakhanger *Ches*	47	SJ7654
Oakhanger *Hants*	11	SU7635
Oakhill *Somset*	19	ST6347
Oakhurst *Kent*	13	TQ5450
Oakington *Cambs*	31	TL4164
Oakle Street *Gloucs*	28	SO7517
Oakley *Suffk*	33	TM1678
Oakley *Beds*	30	TL0053
Oakley *Bucks*	29	SP6412
Oakley *Hants*	21	SU5650
Oakley *Oxon*	22	SP7400
Oakridge *Gloucs*	20	SO9103
Oaks *Dur*	61	NZ1526
Oaks *Lancs*	54	SD6733
Oaksey *Wilts*	20	ST9893
Oakshaw *Cumb*	67	NY5076
Oakthorpe *Leics*	39	SK3213
Oakwood *Border*	76	NT4225
Oakwoodhill *Surrey*	12	TQ1337
Oakworth *W York*	55	SE0339
Oape *Highld*	96	NC4101
Oare *Kent*	15	TR0063
Oare *Somset*	18	SS8047
Oare *Wilts*	20	SU1563
Oasby *Lincs*	40	TF0039
Oath *Somset*	8	ST3827
Oathlaw *Tays*	89	NO4756
Oatlands Park *Surrey*	22	TQ0865
Oban *Strath*	79	NM8630
Obinan *Highld*	91	NG8796
Obney *Tays*	82	NO0237
Oborne *Dorset*	9	ST6518
Obthorpe *Lincs*	40	TF0915
Occlestone Green *Ches*	47	SJ6962
Occold *Suffk*	33	TM1570
Ochertyre *Tays*	82	NN8323
Ochiltree *Strath*	74	NS5121
Ockbrook *Derbys*	39	SK4235
Ockle *Highld*	79	NM5570
Ockley *Surrey*	12	TQ1440
Ocle Pychard *H & W*	27	SO5946
Odcombe *Somset*	8	ST5015
Odd Down *Avon*	20	ST7462
Oddingley *H & W*	28	SO9159
Oddington *Gloucs*	29	SP2225
Oddington *Oxon*	29	SP5514
Odell *Beds*	30	SP9657
Odiham *Hants*	22	SU7451
Odsal *W York*	55	SE1529

Odsey
Pennygown

Odsey *Herts* 31 TL2938
Odstock *Wilts* 10 SU1426
Odstone *Leics* 39 SK3907
Offchurch *Warwks* 29 SP3566
Offenham *H & W* 28 SP0546
Offham *E Susx* 13 TQ4012
Offham *Kent* 14 TQ6557
Offham *W Susx* 12 TQ0208
Offleymarsh *Shrops* 37 SJ7829
Offord Cluny *Cambs* 31 TL2267
Offord Darcy *Cambs* 31 TL2266
Offton *Suffk* 32 TM0649
Offwell *Devon* 8 SY1999
Ogbourne Maizey *Wilts* 21 SU1871
Ogbourne St. Andrew *Wilts* 21 SU1872
Ogbourne St. George *Wilts* 21 SU2074
Ogle *Nthumb* 69 NZ1378
Oglet *Mersyd* 46 SJ4481
Ogmore *M Glam* 18 SS8876
Ogmore Vale *M Glam* 18 SS9390
Ogmore-by-Sea *M Glam* 18 SS8675
Okeford Fitzpaine *Dorset* 9 ST8010
Okehampton *Devon* 6 SX5895
Okehampton Camp *Devon* 5 SX5893
Olchard *Devon* 5 SX8776
Old *Nhants* 30 SP7873
Old Aberdeen *Gramp* 95 NJ9407
Old Alresford *Hants* 11 SU5834
Old Auchenbrack *D & G* 65 NX7597
Old Basford *Notts* 49 SK5543
Old Basing *Hants* 22 SU6652
Old Bewick *Nthumb* 77 NU0621
Old Bolingbroke *Lincs* 51 TF3564
Old Bramhope *W York* 55 SE2343
Old Brampton *Derbys* 49 SK3371
Old Bridge of Tilt *Tays* 87 NN8866
Old Bridge of Urr *D & G* 66 NX7767
Old Buckenham *Norfk* 32 TM0691
Old Burghclere *Hants* 21 SU4657
Old Byland *N York* 62 SE5485
Old Castle *M Glam* 18 SS9079
Old Church Stoke *Powys* 36 SO2894
Old Clee *Humb* 57 TA2808
Old Cleeve *Somset* 7 ST0342
Old Dailly *Strath* 64 NX2299
Old Dalby *Leics* 39 SK6723
Old Dam *Derbys* 48 SK1179
Old Deer *Gramp* 95 NJ9747
Old Edington *S York* 49 SK5397
Old Ellerby *Humb* 57 TA1637
Old Felixstowe *Suffk* 25 TM3136
Old Fletton *Cambs* 40 TL1997
Old Forge *H & W* 27 SO5518
Old Grimsby *IOS* 2 SV8915
Old Hall Green *Herts* 31 TL3622
Old Harlow *Essex* 23 TL4711
Old Huntstanton *Norfk* 42 TF6842
Old Hutton *Cumb* 59 SD5088
Old Hutton *Cumb* 59 SD5688
Old Kea *Cnwll* 3 SW8441
Old Kilpatrick *Strath* 81 NS4673
Old Knebworth *Herts* 31 TL2320
Old Lakenham *Norfk* 43 TG2206
Old Langho *Lancs* 54 SD7035
Old Leake *Lincs* 51 TF4050
Old Malton *N York* 56 SE7972
Old Micklefield *W York* 55 SE4432
Old Milton *Hants* 10 SZ2494
Old Milverton *Warwks* 29 SP2967
Old Newton *Suffk* 32 TM0662
Old Radnor *Powys* 27 SO2559
Old Ratray *Gramp* 95 NK0857
Old Rayne *Gramp* 95 NJ6728
Old Romney *Kent* 15 TR0325
Old Scone *Tays* 82 NO1226
Old Shoreham *W Susx* 12 TQ2006
Old Shoremore *Highld* 98 NC2059
Old Soar *Kent* 14 TQ6154
Old Sodbury *Avon* 20 ST7581
Old Somerby *Lincs* 40 SK9633
Old Stratford *Nhants* 30 SP7741
Old Sunnford *W Mids* 38 SO9083
Old Thirsk *N York* 62 SE4382
Old Town *Cumb* 59 SD5983
Old Town *IOS* 2 SV9110
Old Trafford *Gt Man* 47 SJ8196
Old Warden *Beds* 30 TL1343
Old Weston *Cambs* 30 TL0977
Old Wick *Highld* 100 ND3649
Old Windsor *Berks* 22 SU9874
Old Wives Lees *Kent* 15 TR0754
Old Woking *Surrey* 22 TQ0156
Oldany *Highld* 98 NC0932
Oldberrow *Warwks* 28 SP1266
Oldborough *Devon* 7 SS7706
Oldburry *Kent* 14 TQ5956
Oldbury *Shrops* 37 SO7192
Oldbury *Warwks* 39 SP3194
Oldbury on the Hill *Gloucs* 20 ST8287
Oldbury-on-Severn *Avon* 19 ST6092
Oldcastle *Gwent* 27 SO3224
Oldcotes *Notts* 49 SK5888
Oldfield *H & W* 28 SO8465
Oldford *Somset* 20 ST7849
Oldhall Green *Suffk* 32 TL8956
Oldham *Gt Man* 54 SD9215
Oldhamstocks *Loth* 76 NT7470
Oldhurst *Cambs* 31 TL3077
Oldland *Avon* 20 ST6771
Oldley *Shrops* 36 SO3378
Oldmeldrum *Gramp* 95 NJ8027
Oldmill *Cnwll* 4 SX3774
Oldmixon *Avon* 19 ST3358
Oldridge *Devon* 7 SX8295
Oldstead *N York* 62 SE5279
Oldwall *Cumb* 67 NY4761
Oldwalls *W Glam* 17 SS4891
Oldways End *Devon* 7 SS8624
Oldwhat *Gramp* 95 NJ8661
Olive Green *Staffs* 38 SK1118
Oliver *Border* 75 NT0924
Oliver's Battery *Hants* 10 SU4527
Ollaberry *Shet* 103 HU3680
Ollach *Highld* 84 NG5137
Ollerton *Ches* 47 SJ7776
Ollerton *Notts* 49 SK6567
Ollerton *Shrops* 37 SJ6425
Olney *Bucks* 30 SP8851
Olney *Nhants* 30 SP6643
Olrig House *Highld* 100 ND1866
Olveston *Avon* 19 ST6087
Ombersley *H & W* 28 SO8463
Onchan *IOM* 52 SC4078
Onecote *Staffs* 48 SK0455
Onibury *Shrops* 36 SO4579
Onich *Highld* 86 NN0261
Onllwyn *W Glam* 26 SN8410
Onneley *Staffs* 47 SJ7543
Onslow Village *Surrey* 12 SU9849
Onston *Ches* 47 SJ5973
Opinan *Highld* 91 NG7472
Orbliston *Gramp* 94 NJ3057
Orbost *Highld* 90 NG2543
Orby *Lincs* 51 TF4967
Orchard Portman *Somset* 8 ST2421
Orcheston *Wilts* 20 SU0545
Orcop *H & W* 27 SO4726
Orcop Hill *H & W* 27 SO4828
Ord *Gramp* 94 NJ6259
Ord *Highld* 84 NG6113
Ordhead *Gramp* 94 NJ6610
Ordie *Gramp* 88 NJ4501
Ordiequish *Gramp* 94 NJ3356
Ordley *Nthumb* 68 NY9559
Ordsall *Notts* 49 SK7079
Ore *E Susx* 14 TQ8311
Oreton *Shrops* 37 SO6581
Orford *Ches* 47 SJ6190
Orford *Suffk* 33 TM4250
Organford *Dorset* 9 SY9392
Orlestone *Kent* 15 TR0034
Orleton *H & W* 27 SO4967
Orleton *H & W* 28 SO7067
Orlingbury *Nhants* 30 SP8572
Ormesby *Cleve* 62 NZ5317
Ormesby St. Margaret *Norfk* 43 TG4914
Ormesby St. Michael *Norfk* 43 TG4814
Ormidale *Strath* 80 NS0081
Ormiscaig *Highld* 91 NG8590
Ormiston *Loth* 76 NT4269
Ormsaigmore *Highld* 79 NM4763
Ormsary *Strath* 71 NR7472
Ormskirk *Lancs* 46 SD4108
Oronsay *Strath* 70 NR3588
Orosay *W Isls* 90 NB3612
Orphir *Ork* 103 HY3405
Orpington *Gt Lon* 23 TQ4666
Orrell *Gt Man* 46 SD5303
Orrell *Mersyd* 46 SJ3496
Orrisdale *IOM* 52 SC3293
Orrisdale Head *IOM* 52 SC3192
Orsett *Essex* 24 TQ6482
Orslow *Staffs* 37 SJ8015
Orston *Notts* 50 SK7740
Orton *Cumb* 60 NY6208
Orton *Nhants* 40 SP8079
Orton *Staffs* 38 SO8795
Orton Longueville *Cambs* 40 TL1696
Orton Waterville *Cambs* 40 TL1596
Orton-on-the-Hill *Leics* 39 SK3003
Orwell *Cambs* 31 TL3650
Osbaldeston *Lancs* 54 SD6431
Osbaldwick *N York* 56 SE6251
Osbaston *Leics* 39 SK4204
Osbaston *Shrops* 36 SJ3222
Osbournby *Lincs* 40 TF0638
Oscroft *Ches* 46 SJ5067
Osgathorpe *Leics* 39 SK4219
Osgodby *Lincs* 50 TF0792
Osgodby *N York* 56 SE6433
Osgodby *N York* 63 TA0584
Oskaig *Highld* 84 NG5438
Oskamull *Strath* 79 NM4540
Osmaston *Derbys* 48 SK1943
Osmington *Dorset* 9 SY7282
Osmington Mills *Dorset* 9 SY7381
Osmonthorpe *W York* 55 SE3333
Osmotherley *N York* 62 SE4596
Osney *Oxon* 29 SP5006
Ospringe *Kent* 15 TR0060
Ossett *W York* 55 SE2720
Ossington *Notts* 50 SK7564
Oswaldkirk *N York* 62 SE6278
Oswaldtwistle *Lancs* 54 SD7327
Oswestry *Shrops* 36 SJ2829
Otford *Kent* 23 TQ5359
Otham *Kent* 14 TQ7954
Otham Hole *Kent* 14 TQ7952
Othery *Somset* 8 ST3831
Otley *Suffk* 33 TM2055
Otley *W York* 55 SE2045
Otter Ferry *Strath* 71 NR9384
Otterbourne *Hants* 10 SU4523
Otterburn *N York* 54 SD8857
Otterburn *Nthumb* 68 NY8893
Otterham *Cnwll* 4 SX1690
Otterhampton *Somset* 8 ST2423
Ottershaw *Surrey* 22 TQ0264
Otterswick *Shet* 103 HU5185
Otterton *Devon* 5 SY0785
Ottery *Devon* 4 SX4475
Ottery St. Mary *Devon* 7 SY0995
Ottinge *Kent* 15 TR1642
Ottringham *Humb* 57 TA2624
Oughtershaw *N York* 60 SD8781
Oughterside *Cumb* 58 NY1140
Oughtibridge *S York* 49 SK3093
Oulston *N York* 62 SE5474
Oulton *Cumb* 67 NY2451
Oulton *Norfk* 43 TG1328
Oulton *Staffs* 38 SJ9135
Oulton *Suffk* 43 TM5294
Oulton *W York* 55 SE3627
Oulton Broad *Suffk* 33 TM5292
Oulton Street *Norfk* 43 TG1527
Oundle *Nhants* 40 TL0488
Ousby *Cumb* 59 NY6134
Ousden *Suffk* 32 TL7459
Ousefleet *Humb* 56 SE8323
Ouston *Dur* 69 NZ2554
Out Elmstead *Kent* 12 TQ2050
Out Newton *Humb* 51 TA3801
Outgate *Cumb* 59 SD3599
Outhgill *Cumb* 60 NY7801
Outhill *Warwks* 28 SP1066
Outlands *Staffs* 37 SJ7730
Outlane *W York* 55 SE0817
Outwell *Norfk* 41 TF5104
Outwood *Surrey* 12 TQ3245
Outwood *W York* 55 SE3223
Outwoods *Staffs* 37 SJ7818
Ouzlewell Green *W York* 55 SE3426
Over *Avon* 19 ST5882
Over *Cambs* 31 TL3770
Over *Ches* 47 SJ6466
Over Compton *Dorset* 9 ST5917
Over End *Cambs* 40 TL0893
Over Green *Warwks* 38 SP1694
Over Haddon *Derbys* 48 SK2066
Over Kellet *Lancs* 53 SD5169
Over Kiddington *Oxon* 29 SP4122
Over Monnow *Gwent* 27 SO4912
Over Norton *Oxon* 29 SP3128
Over Silton *N York* 62 SE4593
Over Stenton *Fife* 83 NT2799
Over Stowey *Somset* 19 ST1838
Over Stratton *Somset* 8 ST4315
Over Tabley *Ches* 47 SJ7280
Over Wallop *Hants* 10 SU2838
Over Wallop *Hants* 10 SU2838
Over Whitacre *Warwks* 39 SP2590
Over Worton *Oxon* 29 SP4329
Overbury *H & W* 28 SO9537
Overleigh *Somset* 8 ST5035
Overpool *Ches* 46 SJ3877
Overscaig Hotel *Highld* 96 NC4223
Overseal *Derbys* 39 SK2915
Oversland *Kent* 15 TR0557
Overstone *Nhants* 30 SP8066
Overstrand *Norfk* 43 TG2440
Overstreet *Wilts* 10 SU0637
Overthorpe *Nhants* 29 SP4840
Overton *Clwyd* 36 SJ3741
Overton *Gramp* 95 NJ8714
Overton *Hants* 21 SU5149
Overton *Lancs* 53 SD4358
Overton *N York* 56 SE5555
Overton *Shrops* 37 SO5072
Overton *W Glam* 17 SS4685
Overton *W York* 55 SE2516
Overtown *Lancs* 60 SD6275
Overtown *Strath* 74 NS8053
Overtown *W York* 55 SE3516
Overy *Oxon* 21 SU5894
Overy Staithe *Norfk* 42 TF8444
Oving *Bucks* 30 SP7821
Oving *W Susx* 11 SU9005
Ovingdean *E Susx* 12 TQ3503
Ovingham *Nthumb* 68 NZ0863
Ovington *Dur* 61 NZ1314
Ovington *Essex* 32 TL7742
Ovington *Hants* 11 SU5631
Ovington *Norfk* 42 TF9202
Ovington *Nthumb* 68 NZ0663
Ower *Hants* 10 SU3216
Owermoigne *Dorset* 9 SY7685
Owler Bar *Derbys* 49 SK2978
Owlerton *S York* 49 SK3389
Owlsmoor *Berks* 22 SU8462
Owlswick *Bucks* 22 SP7806
Owmby *Lincs* 48 SK0087
Owmby *Lincs* 57 TA0724
Owmby *Lincs* 50 TF0087
Owslebury *Hants* 11 SU5123
Owston *Leics* 40 SK7707
Owston *S York* 56 SE5511
Owston Ferry *Humb* 50 SE8000
Owstwick *Humb* 57 TA2732
Owthorne *Humb* 57 TA3327
Owthorpe *Notts* 39 SK6733
Oxborough *Norfk* 42 TF7401
Oxbridge *Dorset* 8 SY4797
Oxcombe *Lincs* 51 TF3177
Oxen End *Essex* 24 TL6629
Oxenhope *W York* 55 SE0335
Oxenpill *Somset* 19 ST4441
Oxenton *Gloucs* 28 SO9531
Oxenwood *Wilts* 21 SU3059
Oxford *Oxon* 29 SP5305
Oxhey *Herts* 22 TQ1295
Oxhill *Warwks* 29 SP3145
Oxley *W Mids* 38 SJ9001
Oxley Green *Essex* 24 TL9114
Oxley's Green *E Susx* 14 TQ6921
Oxlode *Cambs* 41 TL4886
Oxnam *Border* 76 NT7018
Oxnead *Norfk* 43 TG2224
Oxshott *Surrey* 22 TQ1460
Oxspring *S York* 49 SE2601
Oxted *Surrey* 13 TQ3852
Oxton *Border* 76 NT4953
Oxton *N York* 55 SE5043
Oxton *Notts* 49 SK6351
Oxwich *W Glam* 17 SS4986
Oxwich Green *W Glam* 17 SS4986
Oykel Bridge *Highld* 96 NC3801
Oyne *Gramp* 95 NJ6725

P

Packers hill *Dorset* 9 ST7011
Packington *Leics* 39 SK3614
Packmores *Warwks* 29 SP2865
Padanaram *Tays* 88 NO4251
Padbury *Bucks* 30 SP7230
Paddington *Gt Lon* 23 TQ2681
Paddlesworth *Kent* 14 TQ6862
Paddlesworth *Kent* 15 TR1939
Paddock Wood *Kent* 14 TQ6644
Paddon *Devon* 6 SS3509
Padfield *Derbys* 48 SK0396
Padiham *Lancs* 54 SD7933
Padside *N York* 56 SE5719
Padstow *Cnwll* 3 SW9175
Padworth *Berks* 21 SU6166
Pagham *W Susx* 11 SZ8897
Paglesham *Essex* 24 TQ9293
Paible *W Isls* 102 NF7367
Paible *W Isls* 102 NG0299
Paignton *Devon* 5 SX8960
Pailton *Warwks* 39 SP4781
Paincastle *Powys* 27 SO1646
Painshawfield *Nthumb* 68 NZ0560
Painsthorpe *Humb* 56 SE8158
Painswick *Gloucs* 28 SO8609
Painter's Forstal *Kent* 15 TQ9958
Paisley *Strath* 73 NS4864
Pakefield *Suffk* 33 TM5390
Pakenham *Suffk* 32 TL9267
Palestine *Hants* 21 SU2640
Palfrey *W Mids* 38 SP0197
Palgrave *Suffk* 33 TM1178
Pallington *Dorset* 9 SY7891
Palmers Green *Gt Lon* 23 TQ3193
Palmerston *Strath* 74 NS5019
Palnackie *D & G* 66 NX8257
Palnure *D & G* 65 NX4563
Palterton *Derbys* 49 SK4768
Pamber End *Hants* 21 SU6158
Pamber Green *Hants* 21 SU6059
Pamber Heath *Hants* 21 SU6162
Pamington *Gloucs* 28 SO9333
Pamphill *Dorset* 9 ST9900
Pampisford *Cambs* 31 TL4948
Panbride *Tays* 83 NO5635
Pancrasweek *Devon* 6 SS2905
Pandy *Gwent* 27 SO3322
Pandy *Gwent* 27 SO3322
Pandy *Gwynd* 35 SH6203
Pandy *M Glam* 19 ST1587
Pandy Tudur *Clwyd* 45 SH8564
Panfield *Essex* 24 TL7425
Pangbourne *Berks* 21 SU6376
Pangdean *W Susx* 12 TQ2911
Pannal *N York* 55 SE3051
Pannal Ash *N York* 55 SE2853
Pannanich Wells Hotel *Gramp* 88 NO4097
Pant *Shrops* 36 SJ2722
Pant-glas *Gwynd* 44 SH4747
Pant-y-dwr *Powys* 35 SN9874
Pant-y-mwyn *Clwyd* 46 SJ1964
Pant-yr-awel *M Glam* 18 SS9287
Pantglas *Powys* 35 SN7797
Panton *Lincs* 50 TF1778
Pantside *Gwent* 19 ST2297
Pantygasseg *Gwent* 19 SO2501
Panxworth *Norfk* 43 TG3513
Papigoe *Highld* 100 ND3851
Papple *Loth* 76 NT5972
Papplewick *Notts* 49 SK5451
Papworth Everard *Cambs* 31 TL2862
Papworth St. Agnes *Cambs* 31 TL2664
Par *Cnwll* 3 SX0753
Paramour Street *Kent* 23 TQ2861
Parbold *Lancs* 53 SD4911
Parbrook *W Susx* 12 TQ0824
Parc *Gwynd* 45 SH8834
Parc Seymour *Gwent* 19 ST4091
Pardshaw *Cumb* 58 NY0925
Parham *Suffk* 33 TM3060
Park *D & G* 66 NX9091
Park *Gramp* 89 NO7898
Park *Nthumb* 68 NY6861
Park Corner *Berks* 22 SU8583
Park Corner *Oxon* 22 SU6988
Park End *Beds* 30 SP9853
Park Gate *Hants* 11 SU5108
Park Gate *W York* 55 SE1841
Park Head *W York* 55 SE1907
Park Hill *Gloucs* 19 ST5699
Park Royal *Gt Lon* 23 TQ2082
Park Street *W Susx* 12 TQ1131
Parkend *Gloucs* 27 SO6108
Parkers Green *Kent* 13 TQ6138
Parkfield *M Glam* 4 SX5267
Parkgate *D & G* 66 NY0288
Parkgate *Surrey* 12 TQ2043
Parkhall *Strath* 81 NS4871
Parkham *Devon* 6 SS3821
Parkhill House *Gramp* 95 NJ8914
Parkhouse *Gwent* 19 SO5002
Parkmill *W Glam* 17 SS5489
Parkside *Dur* 69 NZ4148
Parkstone *Dorset* 10 SZ0491
Parlington *W York* 55 SE4235
Parndon *Essex* 23 TL4308
Parr Bridge *Gt Man* 47 SD7001
Parracombe *Devon* 7 SS6645
Parrog *Dyfed* 16 SN0439
Parson Drove *Cambs* 41 TF3708
Parson's Cross *S York* 49 SK3491
Parson's Heath *Essex* 25 TM0226
Partick *Strath* 74 NS5567
Partington *Gt Man* 47 SJ7191
Partney *Lincs* 51 TF4168
Parton *Cumb* 58 NX9720
Parton *Cumb* 58 NY2715
Parton *D & G* 65 NX6970
Partridge Green *W Susx* 12 TQ1919
Parwich *Derbys* 48 SK1854
Passenham *Nhants* 30 SP7839
Passfield *Hants* 11 SU8234
Passingford Bridge *Essex* 23 TQ5098
Paston *Norfk* 43 TG3234
Pasturefields *Staffs* 38 SJ9925
Patcham *E Susx* 12 TQ3009
Patching *W Susx* 12 TQ0806
Patchway *Avon* 19 ST6081
Pateley Bridge *N York* 55 SE1565
Path of Condie *Tays* 82 NO0711
Pathhead *Gramp* 89 NO7263
Pathhead *Loth* 76 NT3964
Pathhead *Strath* 66 NS6114
Patna *Strath* 73 NS4110
Patney *Wilts* 20 SU0758
Patrick *IOM* 52 SC2482
Patrick Brompton *N York* 61 SE2290
Patricroft *Gt Man* 47 SJ7597
Patrington *Humb* 57 TA3122
Patrixbourne *Kent* 15 TR1855
Patterdale *Cumb* 59 NY3915
Pattingham *Staffs* 38 SO8299
Pattishall *Nhants* 30 SP6754
Pattiswick Green *Essex* 24 TL8224
Paul *Cnwll* 2 SW4627
Paul's Dene *Wilts* 10 SU1432
Paulerspury *Bucks* 30 SP7144
Paull *Humb* 57 TA1626
Paulton *Avon* 19 ST6456
Pauperhaugh *Nthumb* 68 NZ1099
Pave Lane *Shrops* 37 SJ7516
Pavenham *Beds* 30 SP9955
Pawlett *Somset* 19 ST2942
Paxford *Gloucs* 29 SP1837
Paxton *Border* 77 NT9353
Payden Street *Kent* 14 TQ9253
Payhembury *Devon* 7 ST0801
Paythorne *Lancs* 54 SD8251
Peacehaven *E Susx* 13 TQ4101
Peak Hill *Lincs* 41 TF2614
Peakirk *Cambs* 40 TF1606
Pean *Kent* 15 TR1837
Peanmeanach *Highld* 85 NM7180
Pearsie *Tays* 88 NO3659
Pease Pottage *W Susx* 12 TQ2633
Peasedown St. John *Avon* 20 ST7057
Peaseland *Norfk* 42 TG0516
Peasemore *Berks* 21 SU4576
Peasenhall *Suffk* 33 TM3569
Peaslake *Surrey* 12 TQ0844
Peasley Cross *Mersyd* 46 SJ5294
Peasmarsh *E Susx* 14 TQ8822
Peasmarsh *Somset* 8 ST3313
Peat Inn *Fife* 83 NO4509
Peathill *Gramp* 95 NJ9365
Peatling Magna *Leics* 39 SP5992
Peatling Parva *Leics* 39 SP5989
Pebmarsh *Essex* 24 TL8533
Pebworth *H & W* 28 SP1347
Pecket Well *W York* 54 SD9929
Peckforton *Ches* 46 SJ5356
Peckham *Gt Lon* 23 TQ3476
Peckleton *Leics* 39 SK4701
Pedlinge *Kent* 15 TR1335
Pedmore *W Mids* 38 SO9182
Pedwell *Somset* 19 ST4236
Peebles *Border* 75 NT2540
Peel *IOM* 52 SC2484
Peel Common *Hants* 11 SU5804
Pegsdon *Beds* 30 TL1130
Pegswood *Nthumb* 69 NZ2287
Pegwell *Kent* 15 TR3664
Peinchorran *Highld* 84 NG5233
Peinlich *Highld* 90 NG4158
Pelaw *T & W* 69 NZ2962
Peldon *Essex* 25 TL9817
Pell Green *E Susx* 14 TQ6736
Pelsall *W Mids* 38 SK0103
Pelsall Wood *W Mids* 38 SK0103
Pelton Fell *Dur* 69 NZ2552
Pelynt *Cnwll* 4 SX2055
Pemberton *Devon* 6 SS5300
Pemberton *Dyfed* 17 SN5300
Pemberton *Gt Man* 47 SD5503
Pembles Cross *Kent* 14 TQ8847
Pembrey *Dyfed* 17 SN4201
Pembridge *H & W* 27 SO3958
Pembroke *Dyfed* 16 SM9901
Pembroke Dock *Dyfed* 16 SM9603
Pembury *Kent* 13 TQ6240
Pen Rhiwfawr *W Glam* 26 SN7410
Pen-Sarn *Gwynd* 44 SH4344
Pen-Sarn *Gwynd* 44 SH5728
Pen-bont Rhydybeddau *Dyfed* 35 SN6783
Pen-ffordd *Dyfed* 16 SN0722
Pen-groes-oped *Gwent* 27 SO3107
Pen-llyn *Gwynd* 44 SH3482
Pen-lon *Gwynd* 44 SH4364
Pen-twyn *Gwent* 27 SO5209
Pen-y-Gwryd Hotel *Gwynd* 45 SH6555
Pen-y-bont *Clwyd* 36 SJ2123
Pen-y-bryn *Dyfed* 17 SN1743
Pen-y-cae-mawr *Gwent* 19 ST4095
Pen-y-clawdd *Gwent* 27 SO4507
Pen-y-coedcae *M Glam* 18 ST0687
Pen-y-cwn *Dyfed* 16 SM8423
Pen-y-darren *M Glam* 26 SO0506
Pen-y-felin *Clwyd* 46 SJ1569
Pen-y-genffordd *Powys* 27 SO1730
Pen-y-graig *Gwynd* 44 SH1933
Pen-y-stryt *Clwyd* 46 SJ1952
Pen-y-stryt *Clwyd* 46 SJ2052
Penallt *Gwent* 27 SO5210
Penally *Dyfed* 16 SS1199
Penalt *H & W* 27 SO5629
Penarth *S Glam* 19 ST1872
Penbryn *Dyfed* 17 SN2952
Pencader *Dyfed* 17 SN4436
Pencaitland *Loth* 76 NT4468
Pencarnisiog *Gwynd* 44 SH3573
Pencarreg *Dyfed* 17 SN5345
Pencarrow *Cnwll* 3 SX1082
Pencelli *Powys* 26 SO0925
Penclawdd *W Glam* 17 SS5495
Pencoed *M Glam* 18 SS9681
Pencombe *H & W* 27 SO5952
Pencraig *H & W* 27 SO5620
Pencraig *Powys* 36 SJ0426
Pendeen *Cnwll* 2 SW3834
Penderyn *M Glam* 26 SN9408
Pendine *Dyfed* 17 SN2308
Pendlebury *Gt Man* 47 SD7802
Pendleton *Lancs* 54 SD7539
Pendock *H & W* 28 SO7832
Pendoggett *Cnwll* 3 SX0279
Pendomer *Somset* 8 ST5210
Pendoylan *S Glam* 18 ST0576
Penegoes *Powys* 35 SH7701
Pengam *Gwent* 19 ST1597
Pengam *S Glam* 19 ST2178
Penge *Gt Lon* 23 TQ3570
Pengelly *Cnwll* 3 SX0783
Pengover Green *Cnwll* 4 SX2865
Pengrugla *Cnwll* 3 SW9947
Pengwern *Clwyd* 45 SJ0176
Penhallow *Cnwll* 2 SW7651
Penhalvean *Cnwll* 2 SW7037
Penhill *Wilts* 20 SU1588
Penhow *Gwent* 19 ST4290
Penifiler *Highld* 84 NG4841
Peninver *Strath* 72 NR7524
Penisar Waun *Gwynd* 44 SH5564
Penistone *S York* 48 SE2402
Penkill *Strath* 64 NX2398
Penkridge *Staffs* 38 SJ9214
Penlean *Cnwll* 6 SX2098
Penllyn *S Glam* 18 SS9776
Penmachno *Gwynd* 45 SH7950
Penmaen *Gwent* 19 ST1897
Penmaen *W Glam* 17 SS5388
Penmaenmawr *Gwynd* 45 SH7176
Penmaenmawr *Gwynd* 45 SH7176
Penmaenpool *Gwynd* 35 SH6918
Penmark *S Glam* 18 ST0568
Penmon *Gwynd* 45 SH6381
Penmorfa *Gwynd* 44 SH5440
Penmynydd *Gwynd* 44 SH5174
Penn *Bucks* 22 SU9193
Penn Green *Notts* 49 SK5375
Penn Street *Bucks* 22 SU9295
Pennal *Gwynd* 35 SH6900
Pennan *Gramp* 95 NJ8465
Pennant *Powys* 35 SN8897
Pennard *W Glam* 17 SS5688
Pennerley *Shrops* 36 SO3599
Pennington *Cumb* 58 SD2677
Pennington *Hants* 10 SZ3194
Pennorth *Powys* 26 SO1125
Penny Bridge *Cumb* 58 SD3183
Penny Hill *Lincs* 41 TF3626
Pennycross *Strath* 79 NM5025
Pennyghael *Strath* 79 NM5125
Pennyglen *Strath* 73 NS2710
Pennygown *Strath* 79 NM6042

Pennymoor

Priestcliffe Ditch

Pennymoor *Devon*	7	SS8611
Penparc *Dyfed*	17	SN2148
Penperlleni *Gwent*	27	SO3204
Penpillick *Cnwll*	3	SX0756
Penpoll *Cnwll*	3	SX1454
Penponds *Cnwll*	2	SW6339
Penpont *D & G*	66	NX8494
Penrest *M Glam*	4	SX3378
Penrherber *Dyfed*	17	SN2839
Penrhiw *Dyfed*	17	SN2440
Penrhiwceiber *M Glam*	18	ST0597
Penrhiwllan *Dyfed*	17	SN3742
Penrhiwpal *Dyfed*	17	SN3445
Penrhos *Gwent*	27	SO4111
Penrhos *Gwynd*	44	SH3433
Penrhyn Bay *Gwynd*	45	SH8281
Penrhyncoch *Dyfed*	35	SN6384
Penrhyndeudraeth *Gwynd*	45	SH6138
Penrice *W Glam*	17	SS4987
Penrioch *Strath*	72	NR8744
Penrith *Cumb*	59	NY5130
Penrose *Cnwll*	3	SW8770
Penruddock *Cumb*	59	NY4227
Penryn *Cnwll*	2	SW7834
Pensarn *Clwyd*	45	SH9478
Pensax *H & W*	28	SO7269
Penselwood *Somset*	9	ST7531
Pensford *Avon*	19	ST6263
Pensham *H & W*	28	SO9444
Penshurst *Kent*	13	TQ5243
Pensilva *Cnwll*	4	SX2969
Pentewan *Cnwll*	3	SX0147
Pentir *Gwynd*	44	SH5767
Pentire *Cnwll*	2	SW7961
Pentlow *Essex*	32	TL8146
Pentney *Norfk*	42	TF7214
Penton Grafton *Hants*	21	SU3247
Penton Mewsey *Hants*	21	SU3347
Pentraeth *Gwynd*	44	SH5278
Pentre *Clwyd*	46	SJ3267
Pentre *M Glam*	18	SS9796
Pentre *Powys*	36	SO0686
Pentre *Shrops*	36	SJ3617
Pentre Bach *Clwyd*	46	SJ2176
Pentre Berw *Gwynd*	44	SH4772
Pentre Hodrey *Shrops*	36	SO3277
Pentre Meyrick *S Glam*	18	SS9675
Pentre-Cagal *Dyfed*	17	SN3440
Pentre-Dolau-Honddu *Powys*	26	SN9943
Pentre-Gwenlais *Dyfed*	17	SN6116
Pentre-Maw *Powys*	35	SH8903
Pentre-bach *Powys*	26	SN9133
Pentre-celyn *Clwyd*	46	SJ1453
Pentre-celyn *Powys*	35	SH8905
Pentre-cwrt *Dyfed*	17	SN3838
Pentre-llyn *Dyfed*	35	SN6174
Pentre-piod *Gwent*	19	SO2602
Pentre-poeth *Gwent*	19	ST2687
Pentre-tafarn-y-fedw *Gwynd*	45	SH8162
Pentrebach *M Glam*	26	SO0604
Pentrebeirdd *Powys*	36	SJ1913
Pentredwr *Clwyd*	46	SJ1946
Pentrefelin *Gwynd*	44	SH5239
Pentrefoelas *Clwyd*	45	SH8751
Pentregalar *Dyfed*	17	SN1831
Pentregat *Dyfed*	17	SN3551
Pentrich *Derbys*	49	SK3852
Pentridge Hill *Dorset*	9	SU0317
Pentyrch *M Glam*	18	ST1081
Penwithick *Cnwll*	3	SX0256
Penybanc *Dyfed*	17	SN6124
Penybont *Powys*	26	SO1164
Penybontfawr *Powys*	36	SJ0824
Penybryn *M Glam*	18	ST1395
Penycae *Clwyd*	46	SJ2745
Penyffordd *Clwyd*	46	SJ3061
Penygarnedd *Powys*	36	SJ1023
Penygraig *M Glam*	18	SS9990
Penygroes *Dyfed*	17	SN5813
Penygroes *Gwynd*	44	SH4753
Penysarn *Gwynd*	44	SH4690
Penywaun *M Glam*	26	SN9804
Penzance *Cnwll*	2	SW4730
Peopleton *H & W*	28	SO9350
Peover Heath *Ches*	47	SJ7973
Peper Harow *Surrey*	22	SU9344
Peplow *Shrops*	37	SJ6324
Pepper's Green *Essex*	24	TL6210
Pepperstock *Beds*	30	TL0817
Percie *Gramp*	89	NO5991
Percyhorner *Gramp*	95	NJ9665
Perelle *Guern*	101	SV0000
Periton *Somset*	7	SS9645
Perivale *Gt Lon*	23	TQ1682
Perkin's Beach *Shrops*	36	SJ3600
Perkins Village *Devon*	5	SY0291
Perkinsville *Dur*	69	NZ2553
Perlethorpe *Notts*	49	SK6471
Permathorn *Loth*	75	NT2459
Perran Wharf *Cnwll*	2	SW7738
Perranporth *Cnwll*	2	SW7554
Perranuthnoe *Cnwll*	2	SW5329
Perranwell *Cnwll*	2	SW7739
Perranwell *Cnwll*	2	SW7752
Perry *W Mids*	38	SP0792
Perry Barr *W Mids*	38	SP0791
Perry Green *Essex*	24	TL8122
Perry Green *Somset*	19	ST2738
Perry Green *Wilts*	20	ST9689
Perry Street *Somset*	8	ST3405
Pershall *Staffs*	37	SJ8129
Pershore *H & W*	28	SO9445
Perth *Tays*	82	NO1123
Perthcelyn *M Glam*	18	ST0595
Perthy *Shrops*	36	SJ3633
Perton *Staffs*	38	SO8699
Pertwood *Wilts*	20	ST8936
Peter Tavy *Devon*	4	SX5177
Peterborough *Cambs*	40	TL1989
Peterchurch *H & W*	27	SO3438
Peterculter *Gramp*	89	NJ8400
Peterhead *Gramp*	95	NK1246
Peterlee *Dur*	62	NZ4341
Peters Marland *Devon*	6	SS4713
Petersfield *Hants*	11	SU7423
Petersham *Gt Lon*	23	TQ1873
Peterstone Wentlooge *Gwent*	19	ST2679
Peterstonsuper-Ely *S Glam*	18	ST0876
Peterstow *H & W*	27	SO5624
Petham *Kent*	15	TR1251
Petherwin Gate *Cnwll*	4	SX2889
Petrockstow *Devon*	17	SS5190
Pett *E Susx*	14	TQ8714
Pettaugh *Suffk*	33	TM1659
Petterden *Tays*	83	NO4240
Pettinain *Strath*	75	NS9542
Pettistree *Suffk*	33	TM3055
Petton *Devon*	7	ST0024
Petts Wood *Gt Lon*	23	TQ4567
Pettycur *Fife*	83	NT2686
Pettymuk *Gramp*	95	NJ9024
Petworth *W Susx*	12	SU9721
Pevensey *E Susx*	13	TQ6405
Pewsey *Wilts*	20	SU1660
Pheasant's Hill *Bucks*	22	SU7887
Phepson *H & W*	28	SO9459
Philham *Devon*	6	SS2522
Philiphaugh *Border*	76	NT4327
Phillack *Cnwll*	2	SW5638
Philleigh *Cnwll*	3	SW8739
Philpot End *Essex*	24	TL6118
Philpstoun *Loth*	75	NT0677
Phocle Green *H & W*	27	SO6226
Phoenix Green *Hants*	22	SU7555
Phoines *Highld*	87	NN7093
Pibsbury *Somset*	8	ST4326
Pica *Cumb*	58	NY0222
Pickering *N York*	63	SE7983
Picket Piece *Hants*	21	SU3947
Picket Post *Hants*	10	SU1905
Pickford *W Mids*	39	SP2781
Pickhill *N York*	62	SE3483
Picklescott *Shrops*	36	SO4399
Pickmere *Ches*	47	SJ6977
Pickney *Somset*	8	ST2128
Pickup Bank *Lancs*	54	SD7122
Pickwell *Devon*	6	SS4540
Pickwell *Leics*	40	SK7811
Pickworth *Leics*	40	SK9913
Pickworth *Lincs*	40	TF0433
Pictillum *Gramp*	95	NJ7317
Picton *Ches*	46	SJ4371
Picton *Clwyd*	46	SJ1282
Picton *N York*	62	NZ4107
Piddinghoe *E Susx*	13	TQ4303
Piddington *Nhants*	30	SP8054
Piddington *Oxon*	29	SP6317
Piddlehinton *Dorset*	9	SY7197
Piddletrenthide *Dorset*	9	SY7099
Pidley *Cambs*	31	TL3377
Piercebridge *Dur*	61	NZ2015
Pierowall *Ork*	103	HY4348
Piff's Elm *Gloucs*	28	SO8926
Pilgrims Hatch *Essex*	24	TQ5895
Pilham *Lincs*	50	SK8693
Pillaton *Cnwll*	4	SX3664
Pillatonmill *M Glam*	4	SX3063
Pillerton Hersey *Warwks*	29	SP2948
Pillerton Priors *Warwks*	29	SP2947
Pilley *Hants*	10	SZ3398
Pilley *S York*	49	SE3300
Pillgwenlly *Gwent*	19	ST3186
Pilling *Lancs*	53	SD4048
Pilning *Avon*	19	ST5684
Pilsbury *Derbys*	48	SK1163
Pilsdon *Dorset*	8	SY4199
Pilsley *Derbys*	48	SK2471
Pilsley *Derbys*	49	SK4262
Pilson Green *Norfk*	43	TG3713
Piltdown *E Susx*	13	TQ4422
Pilton *Leics*	40	SK9102
Pilton *Nhants*	40	TL0284
Pilton *Somset*	19	ST5940
Pimlico *Lancs*	54	SD7543
Pimperne *Dorset*	9	ST9009
Pin Green *Herts*	31	TL2525
Pinchbeck *Lincs*	41	TF2425
Pinchbeck Bars *Lincs*	40	TF1905
Pincock *Lancs*	53	SD5517
Pinford End *Suffk*	32	TL8559
Pinhoe *Devon*	7	SX9694
Pinmill *Suffk*	25	TM2037
Pinminnoch *Strath*	64	NX1993
Pinmore *Strath*	64	NX2091
Pinn *Devon*	4	SX0986
Pinner *Gt Lon*	22	TQ1289
Pinner Green *Gt Lon*	22	TQ1290
Pinvin *H & W*	28	SO9549
Pinwherry *Strath*	64	NX2086
Pinxton *Derbys*	49	SK4555
Pipe Gate *Shrops*	37	SJ7340
Pipe and Lyde *H & W*	27	SO5043
Pipehill *Staffs*	38	SK0908
Piperhill *Highld*	93	NH8650
Pipewell *Nhants*	40	SP8385
Pippin Street *Lancs*	54	SD5824
Pirbright *Surrey*	22	SU9455
Pirbright Camp *Surrey*	22	SU9257
Pirnie *Border*	76	NT6528
Pirton *H & W*	28	SO8847
Pirton *Herts*	30	TL1431
Pishill *Oxon*	22	SU7389
Pistyll *Gwynd*	44	SH3242
Pitagowan *Tays*	87	NN8165
Pitblae *Gramp*	95	NJ9864
Pitcairngreen *Tays*	82	NO0627
Pitcalnie *Highld*	93	NH8172
Pitcaple *Gramp*	95	NJ7225
Pitcarity *Tays*	88	NO3365
Pitch Green *Bucks*	22	SP7703
Pitch Place *Surrey*	11	SU8939
Pitchcombe *Gloucs*	28	SO8508
Pitchcott *Bucks*	30	SP7720
Pitchford *Shrops*	37	SJ5303
Pitchroy *Gramp*	94	NJ1738
Pitcombe *Somset*	9	ST6732
Pitcot *M Glam*	18	SS8974
Pitcox *Loth*	76	NT6475
Pitcur *Tays*	83	NO2437
Pitfichie *Gramp*	95	NJ6716
Pitfour Castle *Tays*	82	NO1921
Pitglassie *Gramp*	95	NJ6943
Pitgrudy *Highld*	97	NH7991
Pitkennedy *Tays*	89	NO5454
Pitlessie *Fife*	83	NO3309
Pitlochry *Tays*	87	NN9458
Pitmachie *Gramp*	95	NJ6728
Pitmain *Highld*	87	NH7400
Pitmedden *Gramp*	95	NJ8827
Pitminster *Somset*	8	ST2119
Pitmuies *Tays*	89	NO5649
Pitmunie *Gramp*	94	NJ6615
Pitney *Somset*	8	ST4428
Pitroddie *Tays*	82	NO2125
Pitscottie *Fife*	83	NO4112
Pitsea *Essex*	24	TQ7488
Pitsford *Nhants*	30	SP7568
Pitsford Hill *Somset*	7	ST0930
Pitt *Devon*	7	ST0316
Pittarrow *Gramp*	89	NO7274
Pittenweem *Fife*	83	NO5502
Pitteuchar *Fife*	83	NT2899
Pittington *Dur*	69	NZ3244
Pittodrie *Gramp*	95	NJ6925
Pitton *Wilts*	10	SU2131
Pittulie *Gramp*	95	NJ9567
Pity Me *Dur*	69	NZ2645
Pityme *Cnwll*	3	SW9575
Pixham *Surrey*	12	TQ1750
Plains *Strath*	74	NS7966
Plaish *Shrops*	37	SO5296
Plaistow *Derbys*	49	SK3556
Plaistow *Gt Lon*	23	TQ4082
Plaistow *W Susx*	12	TQ0030
Plaitford *Hants*	10	SU2719
Plaitford *Hants*	10	SU2719
Plas Llanfair *Gwynd*	44	SH5371
Plas Llysyn *Powys*	35	SN9596
Plastow Green *Hants*	21	SU5361
Platt *Kent*	14	TQ6257
Plawsworth *Dur*	69	NZ2647
Plaxtol *Kent*	13	TQ6053
Play Hatch *Oxon*	22	SU7376
Playden *E Susx*	14	TQ9121
Playford *Suffk*	33	TM2147
Playing Place *Cnwll*	2	SW8141
Playley Green *Gloucs*	28	SO7631
Plealey *Shrops*	36	SJ4206
Plean *Cent*	82	NS8386
Pleasance *Fife*	83	NO2312
Pleasey Hill *Notts*	55	SE5064
Pleasington *Lancs*	54	SD6426
Pleck *Dorset*	9	ST7011
Pleinheaume *Guern*	101	SV0000
Plemont *Jersey*	101	SV0000
Plemstall *Ches*	46	SJ4570
Plenmeller *Nthumb*	68	NY7162
Pleshey *Essex*	24	TL6614
Plockton *Highld*	85	NG8033
Ploughfield *H & W*	27	SO3841
Plowden *Shrops*	36	SO3888
Ploxgreen *Shrops*	36	SJ3604
Pluckley *Kent*	14	TQ9245
Pluckley Thorne *Kent*	15	TQ9644
Plumley *Ches*	47	SJ7275
Plumpton *E Susx*	12	TQ3613
Plumpton End *Nhants*	30	SP7245
Plumpton Green *E Susx*	12	TQ3616
Plumstead *Gt Lon*	23	TQ4478
Plumstead *Norfk*	43	TG1335
Plumstead Green *Norfk*	43	TG1334
Plumtree *Notts*	39	SK6133
Plungar *Leics*	40	SK7633
Plurenden *Kent*	14	TQ9237
Plush *Dorset*	9	ST7102
Plwmp *Dyfed*	17	SN3652
Plymouth *Devon*	4	SX4755
Plympton *Devon*	4	SX5356
Plymtree *Devon*	7	ST0502
Pockley *N York*	62	SE6385
Pocklington *Humb*	56	SE8048
Podimore *Somset*	8	ST5424
Podington *Beds*	30	SP9462
Podmore *Staffs*	37	SJ7835
Pointon *Lincs*	40	TF1131
Pokesdown *Dorset*	10	SZ1292
Polbae *D & G*	64	NX2873
Polbain *Highld*	91	NB9910
Polbathic *Cnwll*	4	SX3456
Polbeth *Loth*	75	NT0364
Polchar *Highld*	93	NH8909
Pole Elm *H & W*	28	SO8450
Polebrook *Nhants*	40	TL0687
Polegate *E Susx*	13	TQ5804
Polesworth *Warwks*	39	SK2602
Polglass *Highld*	91	NC0307
Polgooth *Cnwll*	3	SW9950
Polgown *D & G*	66	NS7104
Poling *W Susx*	12	TQ0404
Poling Corner *W Susx*	12	TQ0405
Polkerris *Cnwll*	3	SX0952
Polla *Highld*	98	NC3854
Pollington *Humb*	56	SE6119
Polloch *Highld*	79	NM7868
Pollokshaws *Strath*	74	NS5661
Pollokshields *Strath*	74	NS5773
Polmassick *Cnwll*	3	SW9745
Polmear *Cnwll*	3	SX0833
Polmont *Cent*	82	NS9378
Polnish *Highld*	85	NM7582
Polperro *Cnwll*	4	SX2051
Polruan *Cnwll*	3	SX1250
Polsham *Somset*	19	ST5142
Polstead *Suffk*	25	TL9938
Poltalluch *Strath*	71	NR8196
Poltescoe *Cnwll*	2	SW7215
Poltimore *Devon*	7	SX9696
Polton *Loth*	75	NT2864
Polwarth *Border*	76	NT7450
Polyphant *Cnwll*	4	SX2682
Polzeath *Cnwll*	3	SW9378
Ponders End *Gt Lon*	23	TQ3596
Pondersbridge *Cambs*	41	TL2692
Ponsanooth *Cnwll*	2	SW7537
Ponsworthy *Devon*	5	SX7073
Pont Pen-y-benglog *Gwynd*	45	SH6460
Pont Robert *Powys*	36	SJ1112
Pont-Ebbw *Gwent*	19	ST2986
Pont-Nedd-Fechan *Powys*	26	SN9007
Pont-ar-gothi *Dyfed*	17	SN5021
Pont-faen *Powys*	26	SN9934
Pont-rhyd-y-fen *W Glam*	18	SS7994
Pont-y-pant *Gwynd*	45	SH7554
Pontac *Jersey*	101	SV0000
Pontantwn *Dyfed*	17	SN4412
Pontarddulais *W Glam*	17	SN5903
Pontarsais *Dyfed*	17	SN4428
Pontblyddyn *Clwyd*	46	SJ2760
Pontefract *W York*	55	SE4521
Ponteland *Nthumb*	69	NZ1673
Ponterwyd *Dyfed*	35	SN7481
Pontesbury *Shrops*	36	SJ3906
Pontesbury Hill *Shrops*	36	SJ3905
Pontesford *Shrops*	36	SJ4106
Pontfadog *Clwyd*	36	SJ2338
Pontfaen *Dyfed*	16	SN0234
Pontgarreg *Dyfed*	34	SN3354
Ponthenry *Dyfed*	17	SN4709
Ponthir *Gwent*	19	ST3293
Ponthirwaun *Dyfed*	17	SN2645
Pontllanfraith *Gwent*	19	ST1895
Pontlliw *W Glam*	17	SN6101
Pontlyfni *Gwynd*	•4	SH4352
Pontnewydd *Gwent*	19	ST2896
Pontop *Dur*	69	NZ1453
Pontrhydfendigaid *Dyfed*	35	SN7366
Pontrhydygroes *Dyfed*	35	SN7472
Pontrilas *H & W*	27	SO3927
Ponts Green *E Susx*	14	TQ6716
Pontshaen *Dyfed*	17	SN4446
Pontshill *H & W*	27	SO6321
Pontsticill *M Glam*	26	SO0511
Pontwelly *Dyfed*	17	SN4140
Pontyates *Dyfed*	17	SN4708
Pontyberem *Dyfed*	17	SN5011
Pontybodkin *Clwyd*	46	SJ2659
Pontyclun *M Glam*	18	ST0381
Pontycymer *M Glam*	18	SS9091
Pontypool *Gwent*	19	SO2800
Pontypridd *M Glam*	18	ST0790
Pontywaun *Gwent*	19	ST2292
Pool *Cnwll*	2	SW6741
Pool *IOS*	2	SV8714
Pool *W York*	55	SE2445
Pool O' Muckhart *Cent*	82	NO0000
Pool Street *Essex*	24	TL7637
Poole *Dorset*	9	SZ0190
Poole Keynes *Wilts*	20	ST9995
Poolewe *Highld*	91	NG8580
Pooley Bridge *Cumb*	59	NY4724
Poolfold *Staffs*	48	SJ8959
Poolhill *Gloucs*	28	SO7329
Poolmill *H & W*	27	SO5724
Pooting's *Kent*	13	TQ4449
Popham *Hants*	21	SU5543
Poplar *Gt Lon*	23	TQ3780
Porchfield *IOW*	10	SZ4491
Porin *Highld*	92	NH3155
Porkellis *Cnwll*	2	SW6933
Porlock *Somset*	7	SS8846
Porlock Weir *Somset*	18	SS8647
Port Akaig *Strath*	70	NR4369
Port Appin *Strath*	79	NM9045
Port Bannatyne *Strath*	73	NS0867
Port Carlisle *Cumb*	67	NY2461
Port Charlotte *Strath*	70	NR2558
Port Clarence *Cleve*	62	NZ5022
Port Cornaa *IOM*	52	SC4787
Port Dinorwic *Gwynd*	44	SH5267
Port Driseach *Strath*	80	NR9973
Port Ellen *Strath*	70	NR3645
Port Elphinstone *Gramp*	95	NJ7720
Port Erin *IOM*	52	SC1969
Port Erroll *Gramp*	95	NK0935
Port Glasgow *Strath*	80	NS3274
Port Henderson *Highld*	91	NG7573
Port Isaac *Cnwll*	3	SW9980
Port Logan *D & G*	64	NX0940
Port Mor *Highld*	84	NM4279
Port Na-Craig *Tays*	75	NS9357
Port Quin *Cnwll*	3	SW9780
Port Ramsay *Strath*	79	NM8845
Port Soderick *IOM*	52	SC3472
Port St. Mary *IOM*	52	SC2067
Port Talbot *W Glam*	18	SS7589
Port Wemyss *Strath*	70	NR1751
Port William *D & G*	64	NX3343
Port e Vullen *IOM*	52	SC4793
Port of Menteith *Cent*	81	NN5801
Port of Ness *W Isls*	102	NB5363
Portachoillan *Strath*	71	NR7557
Portavadie *Strath*	71	NR9369
Portbury *Avon*	19	ST5075
Portchester *Hants*	11	SU6105
Portencalzie *D & G*	64	NX0171
Portencross *Strath*	73	NS1748
Portesham *Dorset*	9	SY6085
Portessie *Gramp*	94	NJ4366
Portgate *Devon*	4	SX4285
Portgordon *Gramp*	94	NJ3964
Portgower *Highld*	97	ND0013
Porth *Cnwll*	2	SW8262
Porth *M Glam*	18	ST0291
Porth Mellin *Cnwll*	2	SW6618
Porth Navas *Cnwll*	2	SW7527
Porth-y-Waen *Shrops*	36	SJ2642
Porthallow *Cnwll*	4	SX2251
Porthcawl *M Glam*	18	SS8177
Porthcothan *Cnwll*	3	SW8572
Porthcurno *Cnwll*	2	SW3822
Porthgain *Dyfed*	16	SM8132
Porthill *Staffs*	47	SJ8548
Porthkerry *S Glam*	18	ST0866
Porthleven *Cnwll*	2	SW6225
Porthmadog *Gwynd*	44	SH5638
Porthpean *Cnwll*	3	SX0350
Porthtowan *Cnwll*	2	SW6947
Porthyrhyd *Dyfed*	17	SN5215
Porthyrhyd *Dyfed*	26	SN7137
Portincaple *Strath*	80	NS2393
Portinfer *Jersey*	101	SV0000
Portington *Humb*	56	SE7830
Portinnisherrich *Strath*	80	NM9711
Portinscale *Cumb*	58	NY2524
Portishead *Avon*	19	ST4675
Portknockie *Gramp*	94	NJ4868
Portlethen *Gramp*	89	NO9296
Portloe *Cnwll*	3	SW9339
Portmahomack *Highld*	97	NH9184
Portmeirion *Gwynd*	44	SH5937
Portmellon *Cnwll*	3	SX0143
Portnacroish *Strath*	79	NM9247
Portnaguiran *W Isls*	102	NB5537
Portnahaven *Strath*	70	NR1652
Portnalong *Highld*	84	NG3435
Portnancon *Highld*	98	NC4260
Portneora *Highld*	85	NG7731
Portobello *Loth*	75	NT3073
Portobello *T & W*	69	NZ2755
Portobello *W Mids*	38	SO9598
Porton *Wilts*	10	SU1836
Portpatrick *D & G*	64	NX0054
Portreath *Cnwll*	2	SW6545
Portreath *Cnwll*	3	SW9679
Portree *Highld*	90	NG4843
Portrye *Strath*	73	NS1757
Portscatho *Cnwll*	3	SW8735
Portsea *Hants*	11	SU6300
Portskerra *Highld*	99	NC8765
Portskewett *Gwent*	19	ST4988
Portslade *E Susx*	12	TQ2506
Portslade-by-Sea *E Susx*	12	TQ2604
Portsmouth *Hants*	11	SU6400
Portsmouth *W York*	54	SD9026
Portsoy *Gramp*	94	NJ5866
Portswood *Hants*	10	SU4314
Portuairk *Highld*	79	NM4468
Portvasgo *Highld*	99	NC5865
Portway *Cnwll*	4	SX3553
Portway *H & W*	27	SO4844
Portway *H & W*	36	SO0872
Portway *W Mids*	38	SO9788
Portwrinkle *Cnwll*	4	SX3553
Poslingford *Suffk*	32	TL7748
Posso *Border*	75	NT2033
Post Green *Dorset*	9	SY9583
Postbridge *Devon*	5	SX6579
Postcombe *Oxon*	22	SU7099
Postling *Kent*	15	TR1439
Postwick *Norfk*	43	TG2907
Pothole *Cnwll*	3	SW9750
Potsgrove *Beds*	30	SP9529
Pott Shrigley *Ches*	48	SJ9479
Potten Street *Kent*	23	TQ2567
Potter Brompton *N York*	63	SE9776
Potter Heigham *Norfk*	43	TG4119
Potter Somersal *Derbys*	38	SK1436
Potter's Forstal *Kent*	14	TQ8946
Potter's Green *Herts*	31	TL3520
Pottergate Street *Norfk*	33	TM1591
Potterhanworth *Lincs*	50	TF0566
Potterhanworth Booths *Lincs*	50	TF0767
Potterne *Wilts*	20	ST9958
Potterne Wick *Wilts*	20	ST9957
Potters Bar *Herts*	23	TL2501
Potters Crouch *Herts*	22	TL1105
Potters Green *W Mids*	39	SP3781
Potters Marston *Leics*	39	SP4996
Pottersheath *Herts*	31	TL2318
Potterspury *Nhants*	30	SP7543
Potterton *W York*	55	SE4038
Pottle Street *Wilts*	20	ST8141
Potto *N York*	62	NZ4703
Potton *Beds*	31	TL2249
Poughill *Cnwll*	6	SS2207
Poughill *Devon*	7	SS8508
Poulshot *Wilts*	20	ST9659
Poulton *Gloucs*	20	SP0900
Poulton-le-Fylde *Lancs*	53	SD3439
Pound Green *E Susx*	13	TQ5123
Pound Green *Hants*	21	SU5759
Pound Hill *W Susx*	12	TQ2937
Poundffald *W Glam*	17	SS5694
Poundgates *E Susx*	13	TQ4918
Poundon *Bucks*	29	SP6425
Poundsgate *Devon*	5	SX7072
Poundstock *Cnwll*	6	SX2099
Povey Cross *Surrey*	12	TQ2642
Pow Green *H & W*	28	SO7044
Powburn *Nthumb*	77	NU0616
Powderham *Devon*	5	SX9684
Powerstock *Dorset*	8	SY5196
Powfoot *D & G*	67	NY1465
Powhill *Cumb*	67	NY2355
Powick *H & W*	28	SO8351
Powler's Piece *Devon*	6	SS3618
Powmill *Tays*	82	NT0297
Poxwell *Dorset*	9	SY7484
Poynings *W Susx*	12	TQ2612
Poynter's Lane End *Cnwll*	2	SW6743
Poyntington *Dorset*	9	ST6419
Poynton *Ches*	48	SJ9283
Poynton *Shrops*	37	SJ5717
Poynton Green *Shrops*	37	SJ5618
Poys Street *Suffk*	33	TM3570
Poystreet Green *Suffk*	32	TL9858
Praa Sands *Cnwll*	2	SW5828
Pratt's Bottom *Gt Lon*	23	TQ4762
Prawle Point *Devon*	5	SX7734
Praze-an-Beeble *Cnwll*	2	SW6336
Prees *Shrops*	37	SJ5533
Prees Green *Shrops*	37	SJ5531
Prees Higher Heath *Shrops*	37	SJ5636
Preesall *Lancs*	53	SD3647
Pren-gwyn *Dyfed*	17	SN4244
Prendwick *Nthumb*	68	NU0012
Prenteg *Gwynd*	44	SH5841
Prescot *Mersyd*	46	SJ4692
Prescott *Devon*	7	ST0814
Presnerb *Tays*	88	NO1866
Prestatyn *Clwyd*	45	SJ0682
Prestbury *Ches*	48	SJ9077
Prestbury *Gloucs*	28	SO9723
Presteigne *Powys*	27	SO3164
Prestleigh *Somset*	19	ST6340
Preston *Border*	76	NT7957
Preston *Devon*	5	SX7351
Preston *Devon*	5	SX8574
Preston *Devon*	5	SX8862
Preston *Dorset*	9	SY7083
Preston *E Susx*	12	TQ3106
Preston *Gloucs*	28	SO6734
Preston *Gloucs*	20	SP0400
Preston *Herts*	31	TL1824
Preston *Kent*	15	TR0260
Preston *Lancs*	53	SD5329
Preston *Leics*	40	SK8602
Preston *Loth*	76	NT5977
Preston *Nthumb*	77	NU1825
Preston *Shrops*	37	SJ5215
Preston *Somset*	18	ST1036
Preston *Suffk*	32	TL9450
Preston *Wilts*	21	SU2774
Preston Bagot *Warwks*	29	SP1766
Preston Bissett *Bucks*	29	SP6529
Preston Bowyer *Somset*	8	ST1326
Preston Brook *Ches*	47	SJ5680
Preston Candover *Hants*	21	SU6041
Preston Capes *Nhants*	29	SP5754
Preston Green *Warwks*	28	SP1665
Preston Gubbals *Shrops*	37	SJ4919
Preston Patrick *Cumb*	59	SD5483
Preston Plucknett *Somset*	8	ST5515
Preston Streeet *Kent*	23	TQ2561
Preston Wynne *H & W*	27	SO5546
Preston on Stour *Warwks*	29	SP2049
Preston on Wye *H & W*	27	SO3842
Preston on the Hill *Ches*	47	SJ5780
Preston upon the Weald Moors *Shrops*	37	SJ6815
Preston-under-Scar *N York*	61	SE0791
Prestonpans *Loth*	76	NT3874
Prestwich *Gt Man*	47	SD8104
Prestwick *Strath*	73	NS3525
Prestwood *Bucks*	22	SP8700
Prestwood *Staffs*	38	SO8686
Prickwillow *Cambs*	41	TL5982
Priddy *Somset*	19	ST5250
Priest Hutton *Lancs*	59	SD5273
Priestacott *Devon*	6	SS4206
Priestcliffe *Derbys*	48	SK1471
Priestcliffe Ditch *Derbys*	48	SK1271

Rockland All Saints Seafield

Rockland All Saints *Norfk* 42 TL9996
Rockland St. Mary *Norfk* 43 TG3104
Rockland St. Peter *Norfk* 42 TL9897
Rockley *Notts* 49 SK7174
Rockley *Wilts* 20 SU1571
Rockwell End *Bucks* 22 SU7988
Rockwell Green *Somset* 8 ST1320
Rodborough *Gloucs* 28 SO8304
Rodborough *Wilts* 20 SU1485
Rodbourne *Wilts* 20 ST9383
Rodden *Dorset* 9 SY6184
Rode *Somset* 20 ST8053
Rode Heath *Ches* 47 SJ8767
Rodel *W Isls* 102 NG0483
Roden *Shrops* 37 SJ5716
Rodhuish *Somset* 7 ST0139
Rodington *Shrops* 37 SJ5814
Rodington Heath *Shrops* 37 SJ5814
Rodley *Gloucs* 28 SO7411
Rodmarton *Gloucs* 20 ST9497
Rodmell *E Susx* 13 TQ4106
Rodmersham *Kent* 14 TQ9261
Rodmersham Green *Kent* 14 TQ9161
Rodney Stoke *Somset* 19 ST4849
Rodono *Border* 75 NT2321
Rodsley *Derbys* 48 SK2040
Roe Green *Herts* 23 TL2107
Roe Green *Herts* 31 TL3133
Roecliffe *N York* 55 SE3765
Roehampton *Gt Lon* 23 TQ2273
Roewen *Gwynd* 45 SH7571
Roewen *Gwynd* 45 SH7672
Roffey *W Susx* 12 TQ1932
Rogart *Highld* 97 NC7304
Rogate *W Susx* 11 SU8023
Roger Ground *Cumb* 67 NY3597
Rogerstone *Gwent* 19 ST2788
Rogiet *Gwent* 19 ST4587
Roke *Oxon* 21 SU6293
Roker *T & W* 69 NZ4059
Rollesby *Norfk* 43 TG4415
Rolleston *Leics* 40 SK7300
Rolleston *Staffs* 39 SK2327
Rolston *Humb* 57 TA2145
Rolstone *Avon* 19 ST3862
Rolvenden *Kent* 14 TQ8431
Rolvenden Layne *Kent* 14 TQ8530
Romaldkirk *Dur* 61 NY9921
Romanby *N York* 62 SE3693
Romanno Bridge *Border* 75 NT1647
Romansleigh *Devon* 7 SS7220
Romesdal *Highld* 84 NG4033
Romford *Dorset* 10 SU0709
Romford *Gt Lon* 23 TQ5188
Romiley *Gt Man* 48 SJ9490
Romney Street *Kent* 23 TQ5461
Romsey *Hants* 10 SU3521
Romsley *H & W* 38 SO9679
Romsley *Shrops* 37 SO7883
Ronachan *Strath* 71 NR7454
Ronague *IOM* 52 SC2472
Rookhope *Dur* 61 NY9342
Rookley *IOW* 10 SZ5084
Rooks Bridge *Somset* 19 ST3752
Rooks Nest *Somset* 7 ST0339
Rookwith *N York* 61 SE2086
Roos *Humb* 57 TA2830
Roosebeck *Cumb* 67 NY2567
Roothams Green *Beds* 30 TL1057
Ropley *Hants* 11 SU6431
Ropley Dean *Hants* 11 SU6332
Ropsley *Lincs* 40 SK9934
Rora *Gramp* 95 NK0650
Rorrington *Shrops* 36 SJ3000
Rosarie *Gramp* 94 NJ3850
Rose *Cnwll* 2 SW7754
Rose Ash *Devon* 7 SS7821
Rose Green *Essex* 24 TL9028
Rose Green *Suffk* 25 TL9337
Rose Green *Suffk* 32 TL9744
Rose Green *W Susx* 11 SZ9099
Rose Hill *Lancs* 54 SD8231
Rose Lands *E Susx* 13 TQ6200
Rosebank *Strath* 74 NS8049
Rosebush *Dyfed* 16 SN0729
Rosedale Abbey *N York* 63 SE7296
Rosehall *Highld* 96 NC4701
Rosehearty *Gramp* 95 NJ9367
Rosehill *Shrops* 37 SJ4717
Roseisle *Gramp* 93 NJ1466
Rosemarket *Dyfed* 16 SM9508
Rosemarkie *Highld* 93 NH7357
Rosemary Lane *Devon* 8 ST1514
Rosemount *Tays* 88 NO1843
Rosenannon *Cnwll* 3 SW9566
Rosenithon *Cnwll* 2 SW8021
Rosewarne *Cnwll* 2 SW6137
Rosewell *Loth* 75 NT2862
Roseworth *Cleve* 62 NZ4121
Rosgill *Cumb* 59 NY5316
Roshven *Highld* 85 NM7078
Roskhill *Highld* 90 NG2745
Roskorwell *Cnwll* 2 SW7923
Rosley *Cumb* 67 NY3245
Roslin *Loth* 75 NT2763
Rosliston *Derbys* 39 SK2416
Rosneath *Strath* 80 NS2583
Ross *D & G* 65 NX6444
Ross *Tays* 81 NN7621
Ross-on-Wye *H & W* 27 SO6024
Rossett *Clwyd* 46 SJ3657
Rossett Green *N York* 55 SE2952
Rossie Orchill *Tays* 82 NO0912
Rossington *Notts* 49 SK6298
Rosskeen *Highld* 93 NH6869
Rossland *Strath* 73 NS4370
Roster *Highld* 100 ND2639
Rostherne *Ches* 47 SJ7483
Roston *Derbys* 48 SK1241
Rosyth *Loth* 82 NT1182
Rothbury *Nthumb* 68 NU0501
Rotherby *Leics* 39 SK6716
Rotherfield *E Susx* 13 TQ5529
Rotherfield Greys *Oxon* 22 SU7282
Rotherfield Peppard *Oxon* 22 SU7082
Rotherham *S York* 49 SK4392
Rothersthorpe *Nhants* 30 SP7156
Rotherwick *Hants* 22 SU7156
Rothes *Gramp* 94 NJ2749
Rothesay *Strath* 73 NS0864
Rothiebrisbane *Gramp* 95 NJ7437
Rothiemay *Gramp* 94 NJ5448
Rothienorman *Gramp* 95 NJ7235
Rothley *Leics* 39 SK5812
Rothmaise *Gramp* 95 NJ6832
Rothwell *Lincs* 50 TF1499
Rothwell *Nhants* 40 SP8181
Rothwell *W York* 55 SE3428
Rottal *Tays* 88 NO3769
Rottingdean *E Susx* 12 TQ3602
Rottington *Cumb* 58 NX9613
Roucan *D & G* 66 NY0277
Rough Common *Kent* 15 TR1359
Rougham *Norfk* 42 TF8320
Rougham Green *Suffk* 32 TL9061
Roughton *Lincs* 51 TF2364
Roughton *Norfk* 43 TG2237
Roughton *Shrops* 37 SO7594
Round Bush *Herts* 22 TQ1498
Round Green *Suffk* 32 TL7154
Roundbush *Essex* 24 TL8601
Roundbush Green *Essex* 24 TL5815
Roundham *Somset* 8 ST4209
Roundhay *W York* 55 SE3235
Rounds Green *W Mids* 38 SO9889
Roundstone Foot *D & G* 67 NT1308
Roundway *Wilts* 20 SU0163
Roundyhill *Tays* 88 NO3750
Rous Lench *H & W* 28 SP0153
Rousdon *Devon* 8 SY2990
Rousham *Oxon* 29 SP4724
Rout's Green *Bucks* 22 SU7899
Routenburn *Strath* 73 NS1961
Routh *Humb* 57 TA0942
Row *Cnwll* 3 SX0976
Row *Cumb* 59 SD4589
Row *Cumb* 60 NY6235
Row Green *Essex* 24 TL7420
Rowanburn *D & G* 67 NY4177
Rowardennan *Cent* 80 NS3698
Rowarth *Derbys* 48 SK0189
Rowberrow *Somset* 19 ST4558
Rowborough *IOW* 10 SZ4685
Rowde *Wilts* 20 ST9762
Rowfield *Derbys* 48 SK1949
Rowfoot *Nthumb* 68 NY6860
Rowhedge *Essex* 25 TM0321
Rowington *Warwks* 29 SP2069
Rowland *Derbys* 48 SK2172
Rowland's Castle *Hants* 11 SU7310
Rowland's Gill *T & W* 69 NZ1658
Rowledge *Surrey* 11 SU8243
Rowley *Dur* 68 NZ0848
Rowley *Humb* 56 SE9732
Rowley Green *W Mids* 39 SP3483
Rowley Hill *W York* 55 SE1915
Rowlstone *H & W* 27 SO3727
Rowly *Surrey* 12 TQ0441
Rowner *Hants* 11 SU5801
Rowney Green *H & W* 38 SP0471
Rownhams *Hants* 10 SU3817
Rowsham *Bucks* 30 SP8418
Rowstock *Oxon* 21 SU4788
Rowston *Lincs* 50 TF0856
Rowthorne *Derbys* 49 SK4864
Rowton *Ches* 46 SJ4564
Rowton *Shrops* 37 SJ6120
Roxburgh *Border* 76 NT6930
Roxby *Humb* 56 SE9217
Roxton *Beds* 30 TL1554
Roxwell *Essex* 24 TL6408
Roy Bridge *Highld* 86 NN2681
Royal Leamington Spa *Warwks* 29 SP3265
Royal Tunbridge Wells *Kent* 13 TQ5839
Roydon *Essex* 23 TL4009
Roydon *Norfk* 42 TF7023
Roydon *Norfk* 33 TM0980
Roydon Hamlet *Essex* 23 TL4107
Royston *Herts* 31 TL3540
Royston *S York* 55 SE3611
Royton *Gt Man* 54 SD9107
Rozel *Jersey* 101 SV0001
Ruabon *Clwyd* 46 SJ3043
Ruaig *Strath* 78 NM0747
Ruan Lanihorne *Cnwll* 3 SW8942
Ruan Major *Cnwll* 2 SW7016
Ruardean *Gloucs* 27 SO6117
Ruardean Hill *Gloucs* 27 SO6317
Ruardean Woodside *Gloucs* 27 SO6215
Rubery *H & W* 38 SO9877
Ruckinge *Kent* 15 TR0233
Ruckley *Shrops* 37 SJ5300
Rudchester *Nthumb* 69 NZ1167
Ruddington *Notts* 39 SK5733
Rudge *Somset* 20 ST8252
Rudgeway *Avon* 19 ST6386
Rudgwick *W Susx* 12 TQ0833
Rudhall *H & W* 27 SO6225
Rudley Green *Essex* 24 TL8303
Rudry *M Glam* 19 ST2086
Rudston *Humb* 57 TA0967
Rudway Barton *Devon* 7 SS9301
Rudyard *Staffs* 48 SJ9558
Ruecastle *Border* 76 NT6120
Rufford *Lancs* 53 SD4615
Rufforth *N York* 55 SE5251
Rugby *Warwks* 39 SP5075
Rugeley *Staffs* 38 SK0418
Ruggaton *Devon* 6 SS5645
Ruishton *Somset* 8 ST2624
Ruislip *Gt Lon* 22 TQ0987
Ruletown Head *Border* 68 NT6113
Rumbach *Gramp* 94 NJ3852
Rumbling Bridge *Tays* 82 NT0199
Rumburgh *Suffk* 33 TM3481
Rumford *Cent* 75 NS9377
Rumford *Cnwll* 3 SW8970
Rumney *S Glam* 19 ST2179
Runcorn *Ches* 46 SJ5182
Runcton *W Susx* 11 SU8802
Runcton Holme *Norfk* 41 TF6109
Runfold *Surrey* 22 SU8747
Runhall *Norfk* 42 TG0507
Runham *Norfk* 43 TG4610
Running Waters *Dur* 62 NZ3340
Runnington *Somset* 8 ST1121
Runswick *N York* 63 NZ8016
Runtaleave *Tays* 88 NO2867
Runwell *Essex* 24 TQ7594
Ruscombe *Berks* 22 SU8076
Rush Green *Essex* 25 TM1615
Rush Green *Gt Lon* 23 TQ5187
Rushall *H & W* 27 SO6435
Rushall *Norfk* 33 TM1982
Rushall *W Mids* 38 SK0201
Rushall *Wilts* 20 SU1255
Rushbury *Shrops* 37 SO5092
Rushden *Herts* 31 TL3031
Rushden *Nhants* 30 SP9566
Rushford *Devon* 4 SX4476
Rushford *Norfk* 32 TL9281
Rushlake Green *E Susx* 13 TQ6218
Rushmere *Suffk* 33 TM4987
Rushmoor *Surrey* 11 SU8740
Rushock *H & W* 38 SO8871
Rushock *H & W* 27 SO3058
Rusholme *Gt Man* 47 SJ8595
Rushton *Ches* 47 SJ5864
Rushton *Nhants* 40 SP8483
Rushton Spencer *Staffs* 48 SJ9362
Rushwick *H & W* 28 SO8254
Rushyford *Dur* 61 NZ2828
Ruskie *Cent* 81 NN6200
Ruskington *Lincs* 50 TF0850
Rusland *Cumb* 59 SD3488
Rusper *W Susx* 12 TQ2037
Ruspidge *Gloucs* 28 SO6611
Russ Hill *Surrey* 12 TQ2340
Russell's Water *Oxon* 22 SU7089
Rusthall *Kent* 13 TQ5639
Rusthall *Kent* 13 TQ5639
Rustington *W Susx* 12 TQ0502
Ruston *N York* 63 SE9583
Ruston Parva *Humb* 57 TA0661
Ruswarp *N York* 63 NZ8809
Rutherford *Border* 76 NT6430
Rutherglen *Strath* 74 NS6162
Ruthernbridge *Cnwll* 3 SX0166
Ruthin *Clwyd* 46 SJ1258
Ruthrieston *Gramp* 89 NJ9204
Ruthven *Gramp* 94 NJ5046
Ruthven *Highld* 93 NH8132
Ruthven *Highld* 87 NN7699
Ruthven *Tays* 88 NO2848
Ruthven House *Tays* 88 NO3047
Ruthvoes *Cnwll* 3 SW9260
Ruthwell *D & G* 67 NY1067
Ruxley Corner *Gt Lon* 23 TQ4770
Ruyton-XI-Towns *Shrops* 36 SJ3922
Ryal *Nthumb* 68 NZ0174
Ryall *Dorset* 8 SY4094
Ryarsh *Kent* 14 TQ6660
Rydal *Cumb* 59 NY3606
Ryde *IOW* 11 SZ5992
Rye *E Susx* 14 TQ9220
Rye Foreign *E Susx* 14 TQ8922
Rye Street *H & W* 28 SO7835
Ryebank *Shrops* 37 SJ5131
Ryeish Green *Nhants* 21 SU6267
Ryhall *Leics* 40 TF0310
Ryhope *T & W* 69 NZ4152
Ryland *Lincs* 50 TF0179
Rylands *Notts* 39 SK5336
Rylstone *N York* 54 SD9658
Ryme Intrinseca *Dorset* 9 ST5810
Ryther *N York* 56 SE5539
Ryton *Shrops* 37 SJ7602
Ryton *T & W* 69 NZ1564
Ryton *Warwks* 39 SP3986
Ryton-on-Dunsmore *Warwks* 39 SP3874

S

Sabden *Lancs* 54 SD7837
Sacombe *Herts* 31 TL3319
Sacombe Green *Herts* 31 TL3419
Sacriston *T & W* 69 NZ2447
Sadberge *Dur* 62 NZ3416
Saddell *Strath* 72 NR7832
Saddington *Leics* 39 SP6591
Saddle Bow *Norfk* 41 TF6015
Saddlescombe *W Susx* 12 TQ2711
Saffron Walden *Essex* 24 TL5438
Sageston *Dyfed* 16 SN0503
Saham Hills *Norfk* 42 TF9003
Saham Toney *Norfk* 42 TF9001
Saighton *Ches* 46 SJ4462
Saintbury *Gloucs* 28 SP1139
Salachail *Strath* 86 NN0551
Salcombe *Devon* 5 SX7338
Salcombe Regis *Devon* 8 SY1588
Salcott *Essex* 25 TL9413
Sale *Gt Man* 47 SJ7991
Sale Green *H & W* 28 SO9358
Saleby *Lincs* 51 TF4578
Salehurst *E Susx* 14 TQ7424
Salem *Dyfed* 17 SN6236
Salem *Dyfed* 35 SN6684
Salem *Gwynd* 44 SH5456
Salen *Highld* 79 NM6864
Salen *Strath* 79 NM5743
Salesbury *Lancs* 54 SD6832
Salford *Beds* 30 SP9339
Salford *Gt Man* 47 SJ8198
Salford *Oxon* 29 SP2828
Salford Priors *Warwks* 28 SP0751
Salfords *Surrey* 12 TQ2846
Salhouse *Norfk* 43 TG3014
Saline *Fife* 82 NT0292
Salisbury *Wilts* 10 SU1429
Salkeld Dykes *Cumb* 59 NY5437
Sall *Norfk* 43 TG1025
Sallachy *Highld* 85 NG9130
Sallachy *Highld* 96 NC5408
Salmonby *Lincs* 51 TF3273
Salmond's Muir *Tays* 83 NO5838
Salperton *Gloucs* 28 SP0720
Salsburgh *Strath* 74 NS8262
Salt *Staffs* 38 SJ9527
Saltaire *W York* 55 SE1337
Saltash *Cnwll* 4 SX4258
Saltburn *Highld* 93 NH7270
Saltburn-by-the-Sea *Cleve* 62 NZ6621
Saltby *Leics* 40 SK8526
Saltcoats *Strath* 73 NS2441
Saltdean *E Susx* 13 TQ3802
Salterbeck *Cumb* 58 NX9926
Salterforth *IOM* 54 SD8845
Salterton *Wilts* 10 SU1236
Saltfleet *Lincs* 51 TF4593
Saltfleetby All Saints *Lincs* 51 TF4590
Saltfleetby St. Clements *Lincs* 51 TF4591
Saltfleetby St. Peter *Lincs* 51 TF4489
Saltford *Avon* 20 ST6867
Salthouse *Norfk* 42 TG0743
Saltley *W Mids* 38 SP0987
Saltmarsh *Gwent* 19 ST3483
Saltmarshe *Humb* 56 SE7824
Saltney *Ches* 46 SJ3865
Salton *N York* 63 SE7179
Saltrens *Devon* 6 SS4521
Saltwood *Kent* 15 TR1535
Salvington *W Susx* 12 TQ1305
Salwarpe *H & W* 28 SO8762
Salwayash *Dorset* 8 SY4596
Sambourne *Warwks* 28 SP0662
Sambrook *Shrops* 37 SJ7124
Samlesbury *Lancs* 54 SD5930
Sampford Arundel *Somset* 8 ST1018
Sampford Brett *Somset* 7 ST0941
Sampford Courtnay *Devon* 7 SS6301
Sampford Moor *Somset* 8 ST1118
Sampford Peverell *Devon* 7 ST0214
Sampford Spiney *Devon* 4 SX5372
Samsonlane *Ork* 103 HY6525
Samuelston *Loth* 76 NT4870
Sanaigmore *Strath* 70 NR2370
Sancreed *Cnwll* 2 SW4129
Sancton *Humb* 56 SE8939
Sand Hills *W York* 55 SE3739
Sand Hole *Humb* 56 SE8037
Sand Hutton *N York* 56 SE6958
Sandaig *Highld* 85 NG7102
Sandal Magna *W York* 55 SE3417
Sandavore *Highld* 84 NM4785
Sandbach *Ches* 47 SJ7560
Sandbank *Strath* 80 NS1580
Sandbanks *Dorset* 10 SZ0487
Sandend *Gramp* 94 NJ5566
Sanderstead *Gt Lon* 23 TQ3461
Sandford *Avon* 19 ST4159
Sandford *Cumb* 60 NY7216
Sandford *Devon* 7 SS8202
Sandford *Hants* 10 SU1601
Sandford *IOW* 11 SZ5481
Sandford *Shrops* 37 SJ5834
Sandford *Strath* 74 NS7143
Sandford Batch *Avon* 19 ST4158
Sandford Orcas *Dorset* 9 ST6220
Sandford St. Martin *Oxon* 29 SP4226
Sandford-on-Thames *Oxon* 21 SP5301
Sandgate *Kent* 15 TR2035
Sandhaven *Gramp* 95 NJ9667
Sandhead *D & G* 64 NX0949
Sandhills *Surrey* 12 SU9438
Sandhoe *Nthumb* 68 NY9666
Sandhole *Strath* 80 NS0098
Sandholme *Humb* 56 SE8230
Sandholme *Lincs* 41 TF3337
Sandhurst *Berks* 22 SU8361
Sandhurst *Gloucs* 28 SO8223
Sandhurst *Kent* 14 TQ8028
Sandhutton *N York* 62 SE3881
Sandilands *Lincs* 51 TF5280
Sandleheath *Hants* 10 SU1214
Sandley *Dorset* 9 ST7724
Sandness *Shet* 103 HU1957
Sandon *Essex* 24 TL7404
Sandon *Herts* 31 TL3234
Sandon *Staffs* 38 SJ9429
Sandon Bank *Staffs* 38 SJ9428
Sandown *IOW* 11 SZ5984
Sandplace *Cnwll* 4 SX2556
Sandridge *Herts* 23 TL1710
Sandringham *Norfk* 42 TF6928
Sands *Bucks* 22 SU8393
Sandsend *N York* 63 NZ8612
Sandside House *Highld* 99 NC9565
Sandtoft *Humb* 56 SE7408
Sandwich *Kent* 15 TR3358
Sandwick *Shet* 103 HU4323
Sandwith *Cumb* 58 NX9615
Sandy *Beds* 31 TL1649
Sandy Bank *Lincs* 51 TF2654
Sandy Lane *Clwyd* 36 SJ4040
Sandy Lane *W York* 55 SE1136
Sandy Lane *Wilts* 20 ST9668
Sandy Park *Devon* 5 SX7189
Sandyford *D & G* 67 NY2093
Sandygate *Devon* 5 SX8674
Sandygate *IOM* 52 SC3797
Sandylands *Lancs* 53 SD4163
Sandystones *Border* 76 NT5926
Sangobeg *Highld* 98 NC4266
Sangomore *Highld* 98 NC4067
Sankyn's Green *H & W* 28 SO7964
Sanna Bay *Highld* 79 NM4469
Santon Bridge *Cumb* 58 NY1101
Santon Downham *Suffk* 32 TL8187
Sapcote *Leics* 39 SP4993
Sapey Common *H & W* 28 SO7064
Sapiston *Suffk* 32 TL9175
Sapperton *Gloucs* 20 SO9403
Sapperton *Lincs* 40 TF0133
Saracen's Head *Lincs* 41 TF3427
Sarclet *Highld* 100 ND3443
Sarisbury *Hants* 10 SU5008
Sarn *Gwynd* 44 SH2432
Sarn *Gwynd* 44 SH2432
Sarn *Powys* 36 SO2091
Sarnau *Dyfed* 17 SN3151
Sarnau *Gwynd* 45 SH9739
Sarnau *Powys* 36 SJ2315
Sarnesfield *H & W* 27 SO3750
Saron *Dyfed* 17 SN6012
Saron *Gwynd* 44 SH5365
Sarratt *Herts* 22 TQ0499
Sarre *Kent* 15 TR2565
Sarsden *Oxon* 29 SP2822
Satley *Dur* 69 NZ1143
Satterleigh *Devon* 7 SS6622
Satterthwaite *Cumb* 59 SD3392
Sauchen *Gramp* 95 NJ7011
Saucher *Tays* 82 NO1933
Sauchieburn *Gramp* 89 NO6669
Saughtree *Border* 67 NY5696
Saul *Gloucs* 28 SO7409
Saundby *Notts* 50 SK7888
Saundersfoot *Dyfed* 16 SN1304
Saunderton *Bucks* 22 SP7901
Saunton *Devon* 6 SS4637
Sausthorpe *Lincs* 51 TF3868
Savile Town *W York* 55 SE2420
Sawbridge *Warwks* 29 SP5065
Sawbridgeworth *Herts* 31 TL4814
Sawdon *N York* 63 SE9485
Sawley *Derbys* 39 SK4731
Sawley *Lancs* 54 SD7746
Sawley *N York* 55 SE2467
Sawry *Cumb* 59 SD3795
Sawston *Cambs* 31 TL4849
Saxby *Leics* 40 SK8219
Saxby *Lincs* 50 TF0086
Saxby *W Susx* 12 SU9604
Saxby All Saints *Humb* 56 SE9816
Saxelbye *Leics* 40 SK7021
Saxham Street *Suffk* 32 TM0861
Saxilby *Lincs* 50 SK8875
Saxlingham *Norfk* 42 TG0239
Saxlingham Green *Norfk* 43 TM2496
Saxlingham Nethergate *Norfk* 43 TM2397
Saxlingham Thorpe *Norfk* 43 TM2198
Saxmundham *Suffk* 33 TM3863
Saxon Street *Cambs* 32 TL6579
Saxondale *Notts* 49 SK6839
Saxtead *Suffk* 33 TM2665
Saxtead Green *Suffk* 33 TM2564
Saxtead Little Green *Suffk* 33 TM2566
Saxthorpe *Norfk* 43 TG1130
Saxton *N York* 55 SE4736
Sayers Common *W Susx* 12 TQ2618
Scackleton *N York* 56 SE6472
Scadabay *W Isls* 90 NG1792
Scaftworth *Notts* 49 SK6691
Scagglethorpe *N York* 56 SE8372
Scalasaig *Strath* 70 NR3994
Scaldwell *Nhants* 30 SP7672
Scaleby *Cumb* 67 NY4463
Scalebyhill *Cumb* 67 NY4363
Scales *Cumb* 53 SD2772
Scales *Cumb* 59 NY3426
Scales *Cumb* 59 NY3427
Scalesceough *Cumb* 67 NY4450
Scalford *Leics* 40 SK7624
Scaling *N York* 63 NZ7413
Scalloway *Shet* 103 HU4039
Scalpay *W Isls* 90 NG2395
Scamblesby *Lincs* 51 TF2778
Scamodale *Highld* 85 NM8373
Scampston *N York* 63 SE8575
Scampton *Lincs* 50 SK9479
Scancroft Hill *W York* 55 SE3741
Scaniport *Highld* 92 NH6239
Scapegoat Hill *W York* 55 SE0916
Scarborough *N York* 63 TA0388
Scarcewater *Cnwll* 3 SW9154
Scarcliffe *Derbys* 49 SK4968
Scarcroft *W York* 55 SE3540
Scarfskerry *Highld* 100 ND2674
Scargill *Dur* 61 NZ0510
Scarinish *Strath* 78 NM0444
Scarness *Cumb* 58 NY2130
Scarning *Norfk* 42 TF9512
Scarrington *Notts* 50 SK7341
Scarthingwell *N York* 55 SE4837
Scartho *Humb* 57 TA2606
Scawby *Humb* 56 SE9605
Scawthorpe *S York* 56 SE5506
Scawton *N York* 62 SE5483
Scayne's Hill *W Susx* 12 TQ3623
Scethrog *Powys* 26 SO1025
Scholes *Gt Man* 47 SD5905
Scholes *S York* 49 SK3896
Scholes *W York* 55 SE1507
Scholes *W York* 55 SE1726
Schoolgreen *Berks* 21 SU6367
Scissett *W York* 55 SE2510
Scleddau *Dyfed* 16 SM9434
Sco Ruston *Norfk* 43 TG2822
Scofton *Notts* 49 SK6280
Scole *Norfk* 33 TM1579
Sconser *Highld* 84 NG5131
Scoonie *Fife* 83 NO3801
Scopwick *Lincs* 50 TF0757
Scoraig *Highld* 91 NH0096
Scorborough *Humb* 56 TA0145
Scorrier *Cnwll* 2 SW7244
Scorton *Lancs* 53 SD5048
Scorton *N York* 61 NZ2500
Scot Hay *Staffs* 47 SJ8047
Scot's Gap *Nthumb* 68 NZ0386
Scotby *Cumb* 67 NY4455
Scotforth *Lancs* 53 SD4859
Scothern *Lincs* 50 TF0377
Scotlandwell *Tays* 82 NO1801
Scotsburn *Highld* 97 NH7275
Scotscalder *Highld* 100 ND0956
Scotscraig *Fife* 83 NO4428
Scotsmill *Gramp* 94 NJ5618
Scotstoun *Strath* 74 NS5367
Scotswood *T & W* 69 NZ2064
Scotter *Lincs* 50 SE8800
Scotterthorpe *Lincs* 50 SE8701
Scotton *Lincs* 50 SK8899
Scotton *N York* 61 SE1895
Scotton *N York* 55 SE3259
Scoughall *Loth* 83 NT6183
Scoulton *Norfk* 42 TF9800
Scourie *Highld* 98 NC1544
Scouriemore *Highld* 98 NC1443
Scousburgh *Shet* 103 HU3717
Scrabster *Highld* 100 ND1070
Scraesburgh *Border* 76 NT6718
Scrafield *Lincs* 51 TF3069
Scrane End *Lincs* 51 TF3841
Scraptoft *Leics* 39 SK6405
Scratby *Norfk* 43 TG5115
Scrayingham *N York* 56 SE7359
Scrayingham *N York* 56 SE7360
Scredington *Lincs* 50 TF0940
Screel *D & G* 66 NX7953
Scremby *Lincs* 51 TF4467
Scremerston *Nthumb* 77 NU0148
Screveton *Notts* 50 SK7343
Scriven *N York* 55 SE3458
Scrooby *Notts* 49 SK6590
Scropton *Derbys* 39 SK1930
Scrub Hill *Lincs* 51 TF2355
Scruschloch *Tays* 88 NO2357
Scruton *N York* 61 SE2992
Sculthorpe *Norfk* 42 TF8931
Scunthorpe *Humb* 56 SE8910
Sea Palling *Norfk* 43 TG4226
Seaborough *Dorset* 8 ST4205
Seabrook *Kent* 15 TR1835
Seaburn *T & W* 69 NZ4160
Seacroft *W York* 55 SE3536
Seafield *Highld* 90 NG4743

Seafield Soberton

Seafield Loth	75	NT0066
Seaford E Susx	13	TV4899
Seaforth Mersyd	46	SJ3297
Seagrave Leics	39	SK6217
Seaham Dur	69	NZ4149
Seahouses Nthumb	77	NU2232
Seal Kent	23	TQ5556
Seale Surrey	22	SU8947
Seamer N York	70	NZ4910
Seamer N York	63	TA0183
Seamill Strath	73	NS2047
Searby Lincs	57	TA0605
Seasalter Kent	15	TR0864
Seascale Cumb	58	NY0301
Seathwaite Cumb	58	SD2296
Seatoller Cumb	58	NY2414
Seaton Cnwll	4	SX3054
Seaton Cumb	58	NY0130
Seaton Devon	8	SY2490
Seaton Humb	57	TA1646
Seaton Kent	15	TR2258
Seaton Leics	40	SP9098
Seaton Nthumb	69	NZ3276
Seaton Delaval Nthumb	69	NZ3075
Seaton Ross Humb	56	SE7740
Seaton Sluice Nthumb	69	NZ3376
Seatown Dorset	8	SY4191
Seave Green N York	62	NZ5600
Seaview IOW	11	SZ6291
Seaville Cumb	67	NY1553
Seavington St. Mary Somset	8	ST4014
Seavington St. Michael Somset	8	ST4015
Sebergham Cumb	59	NY3542
Seckington Warwks	39	SK2607
Sedbergh Cumb	60	SD6592
Sedbury Gloucs	19	ST5493
Sedbusk N York	60	SD8891
Sedgeberrow H & W	28	SP0238
Sedgebrook Lincs	40	SK8537
Sedgefield Dur	62	NZ3528
Sedgeford Norfk	42	TF7136
Sedgehill Wilts	9	ST8627
Sedgley W Mids	38	SO9193
Sedgwick Cumb	59	SD5186
Sedlescombe E Susx	14	TQ7818
Sedrup Bucks	22	SP7911
Seend Wilts	20	ST9461
Seend Cleeve Wilts	20	ST9360
Seer Green Bucks	22	SU9691
Seething Norfk	43	TM3197
Sefton Mersyd	46	SD3501
Seighford Staffs	38	SJ8725
Seilebost W Isls	102	NG0696
Seion Gwynd	44	SH5467
Seisdon Staffs	38	SO8495
Selattyn Shrops	36	SJ2633
Selborne Hants	11	SU7433
Selby N York	56	SE6132
Selham W Susx	11	SU9320
Selkirk Border	76	NT4728
Sellack H & W	27	SO5627
Sellafirth Shet	103	HU5297
Sellick's Green Somset	8	ST2119
Sellindge Kent	15	TR0938
Selling Kent	15	TR0456
Sells Green Wilts	20	ST9462
Selly Oak W Mids	38	SP0482
Selmeston E Susx	13	TQ5007
Selsden Gt Lon	23	TQ3562
Selsey W Susx	11	SZ8593
Selside Cumb	59	SD5298
Selside Gt Lon	23	TQ3267
Selside N York	60	SD7875
Selstead Kent	15	TR2144
Selston Notts	49	SK4653
Selworthy Somset	7	SS9146
Semer Suffk	32	TL9947
Semington Wilts	20	ST8960
Semley Wilts	9	ST8926
Send Surrey	22	TQ0255
Send Marsh Surrey	22	TQ0455
Senghenydd M Glam	18	ST1190
Sennen Cnwll	2	SW3525
Sennen Cove Cnwll	2	SW3526
Sennybridge Powys	26	SN9228
Sessay N York	62	SE4575
Setchey Norfk	41	TF6313
Seton Mains Loth	76	NT4275
Settle N York	54	SD8322
Settrington N York	56	SE8370
Seven Ash Somset	8	ST1533
Seven Ash Somset	8	ST1533
Seven Kings Gt Lon	23	TQ4587
Seven Sisters W Glam	26	SN8208
Seven Wells Gloucs	28	SP1134
Sevenhampton Gloucs	28	SP0321
Sevenhampton Wilts	21	SU2090
Sevenoaks Kent	23	TQ5255
Sevenoaks Weald Kent	13	TQ5250
Sever Star Green Essex	25	TL9326
Severn Beach Avon	19	ST5484
Severn Stoke H & W	28	SO8544
Sevicks End Beds	30	TL0954
Sevington Kent	15	TR0340
Sewards End Essex	24	TL5738
Sewell Beds	30	SP9922
Sewerby Humb	57	TA2068
Seworgan Cnwll	2	SW7030
Sewstern Leics	40	SK8821
Shabbington Bucks	22	SP6606
Shackleford Surrey	22	SU9345
Shader W Isls	102	NB3854
Shadforth Dur	62	NZ3441
Shadingfield Suffk	33	TM4384
Shadoxhurst Kent	15	TQ9737
Shadwell Norfk	32	TL9383
Shafton S York	55	SE3812
Shafton Two Gates S York	55	SE3910
Shalbourne Wilts	21	SU3163
Shalden Hants	11	SU6941
Shalden Green Hants	11	SU6943
Shaldon Devon	5	SX9372
Shalfleet IOW	10	SZ4189
Shalford Essex	24	TL7229
Shalford Surrey	12	TQ0047
Shalford Green Essex	24	TL7127
Shallowford Devon	7	SS7144
Shalmsford Street Kent	15	TR0954
Shalstone Bucks	29	SP6436
Shamley Green Surrey	12	TQ0343
Shandford Tays	89	NO4962
Shandon Strath	80	NS2586
Shandwick Highld	97	NH8575
Shangton Leics	40	SP7196
Shank End Border	67	NT5205
Shanklin IOW	11	SZ5881
Shap Cumb	59	NY5615
Shapwick Dorset	9	ST9301
Shapwick Somset	19	ST4137
Shardlow Derbys	39	SK4330
Shareshill Staffs	38	SJ9406
Sharkham Point Devon	5	SX9354
Sharlston W York	55	SE3818
Sharman's Cross W Mids	38	SP1379
Sharnbrook Beds	30	SP9959
Sharnford Leics	39	SP4891
Sharnhill Green Dorset	9	ST7105
Sharoe Green Lancs	53	SD5333
Sharow N York	55	SE3371
Sharpenhoe Beds	30	TL0630
Sharperton Nthumb	68	NT9503
Sharpness Gloucs	20	SO6702
Sharrington Norfk	42	TG0337
Shatterford H & W	37	SO7981
Shaugh Prior Devon	4	SX5463
Shaughlaige-e-Caine IOM	52	SC3187
Shavington Ches	47	SJ6951
Shaw Berks	21	SU4768
Shaw Gt Man	54	SD9309
Shaw Wilts	20	ST8865
Shaw Common Gloucs	28	SO6927
Shaw Green Herts	31	TL2932
Shaw Green Lancs	53	SD5218
Shaw Hill Lancs	53	SD5721
Shaw Mills N York	55	SE2562
Shawbost W Isls	102	NB2646
Shawbury Shrops	37	SJ5521
Shawell Leics	39	SP5480
Shawford Hants	10	SU4624
Shawhead D & G	66	NX8676
Shawton Strath	74	NS6749
Shearington D & G	66	NY0266
Shearsby Leics	39	SP6291
Shebbear Devon	6	SS4309
Shebdon Staffs	37	SJ7625
Shebster Highld	100	ND0164
Shedfield Hants	11	SU5513
Sheen Derbys	48	SK1161
Sheepscar W York	55	SE3134
Sheepscombe Gloucs	28	SO8910
Sheepstor Devon	4	SX5667
Sheepwash Devon	6	SS4806
Sheepy Magna Leics	39	SK3201
Sheepy Parva Leics	39	SK3301
Sheering Essex	31	TL5014
Sheerness Kent	14	TQ9174
Sheerwater Surrey	22	TQ0461
Sheet Hants	11	SU7524
Sheffield S York	49	SK3587
Shefford Beds	30	TL1439
Shegra Highld	98	NC1860
Sheinton Shrops	37	SJ6104
Shelderton Shrops	36	SO4077
Sheldon Derbys	48	SK1768
Sheldon Devon	8	ST1208
Sheldon W Mids	38	SP1584
Sheldwich Lees Kent	15	TR0156
Shelfanger Norfk	33	TM1083
Shelfield Green Warwks	28	SP1262
Shelford Notts	49	SK6642
Shelford Warwks	39	SP4289
Shelley Suffk	25	TM0338
Shelley W York	55	SE2011
Shellingford Oxon	21	SU3193
Shellow Bowells Essex	24	TL6108
Shelsley Beauchamp H & W	28	SO7363
Shelsley Walsh H & W	28	SO7263
Shelston D & G	66	NX8285
Shelton Beds	30	TL0368
Shelton Norfk	33	TM2291
Shelton Notts	50	SK7844
Shelton Lock Derbys	39	SK3630
Shelton Under Harley Staffs	38	SJ8139
Shelve Shrops	36	SO3399
Shelwick H & W	27	SO5242
Shenfield Essex	24	TQ6095
Shenington Oxon	29	SP3742
Shenley Herts	23	TL1800
Shenley Brook End Bucks	30	SP8335
Shenley Church End Bucks	30	SP8336
Shenleybury Herts	23	TL1803
Shenmore H & W	27	SO3937
Shennanton D & G	64	NX3463
Shenstone H & W	38	SO8673
Shenstone Staffs	38	SK1004
Shenton Leics	39	SK3800
Sheperdswell Kent	15	TR2647
Shephall Herts	31	TL2623
Shepherd's Bush Gt Lon	23	TQ2379
Shepherds Green Oxon	22	SU7183
Shepley W York	55	SE1909
Shepperdine Avon	19	ST6295
Shepperton Surrey	22	TQ0776
Shepperton Green Surrey	22	TQ0768
Shepreth Cambs	31	TL3947
Shepshed Leics	39	SK4719
Shepton Beauchamp Somset	8	ST4016
Shepton Mallet Somset	19	ST6143
Shepton Montague Somset	9	ST6731
Shepway Kent	14	TQ7753
Sheraton Dur	62	NZ4435
Sherborne Dorset	9	ST6316
Sherborne Gloucs	29	SP1714
Sherborne Somset	19	ST5855
Sherborne St. John Hants	21	SU6255
Sherbourne Warwks	29	SP2661
Sherburn Dur	62	NZ3142
Sherburn N York	63	SE9577
Sherburn Hill Dur	62	NZ3342
Sherburn in Elmet N York	55	SE4933
Shere Surrey	12	TQ0747
Shereford Norfk	42	TF8829
Sherfield English Hants	10	SU2922
Sherfield English Hants	10	SU2922
Sherfield on Loddon Hants	22	SU6757
Sherford Devon	5	SX7844
Sherford Dorset	9	SY9193
Sheriff Hutton N York	56	SE6566
Sheriffhales Shrops	37	SJ7512
Sheringham Norfk	43	TG1543
Sherington Bucks	30	SP8846
Shernborne Norfk	42	TF7132
Sherril Devon	5	SX6774
Sherrington Wilts	20	ST9638
Sherston Wilts	20	ST8585
Sherwood Notts	49	SK5743
Sherwood Green Devon	6	SS5520
Shettleston Strath	74	NS6464
Shevington Gt Man	47	SD5408
Sheviock Cnwll	4	SX3655
Shewglie Highld	92	NH4129
Shide IOW	10	SZ4988
Shidlaw Nthumb	76	NT8038
Shiel Bridge Highld	85	NG9318
Shieldaig Highld	91	NG8153
Shieldhill Cent	74	NS8976
Shieldhill D & G	66	NY0385
Shieldhill Strath	75	NT0040
Shields Strath	74	NS7755
Shielhill Strath	80	NS2471
Shielhill Tays	88	NO4257
Shifnal Shrops	37	SJ7407
Shilbottle Nthumb	69	NU1908
Shildon Dur	61	NZ2326
Shillingford Devon	7	SS9723
Shillingford Oxon	21	SU5992
Shillingford Abbot Devon	5	SX9187
Shillingford St. George Devon	5	SX9087
Shillingstone Dorset	9	ST8211
Shillington Beds	30	TL1234
Shiltenish W Isls	102	NB2819
Shilton Oxon	29	SP2608
Shilton Warwks	39	SP4084
Shimpling Norfk	33	TM1583
Shimpling Suffk	32	TL8651
Shimpling Street Suffk	32	TL8753
Shincliffe Dur	61	NZ2940
Shinfield Berks	22	SU7368
Shinnersbridge Devon	5	SX7863
Shinness Highld	96	NC5215
Shipbourne Kent	13	TQ5952
Shipdham Norfk	42	TF9607
Shipham Somset	19	ST4457
Shiphay Devon	5	SX8965
Shiplake Oxon	22	SU7678
Shiplake Row Oxon	22	SU7478
Shipley Shrops	37	SO8096
Shipley W Susx	12	TQ1422
Shipley W York	55	SE1437
Shipley Bridge Surrey	12	TQ3040
Shipmeadow Suffk	33	TM3890
Shippon Oxon	21	SU4898
Shipston on Stour Warwks	29	SP2540
Shipton N York	56	SE5558
Shipton Shrops	37	SO5692
Shipton Bellinger Hants	21	SU2345
Shipton Gorge Dorset	8	SY4991
Shipton Green W Susx	11	SU8000
Shipton Moyne Gloucs	20	ST8989
Shipton-on-Cherwell Oxon	29	SP4617
Shipton-under-Wychwood Oxon	29	SP2717
Shiptonthorpe Humb	56	SE8543
Shirburn Oxon	22	SU6995
Shirdley Hill Lancs	53	SD3612
Shirebrook Notts	49	SK5267
Shiregreen S York	49	SK3691
Shirehampton Avon	19	ST5377
Shiremoor T & W	69	NZ3171
Shirenewton Gwent	19	ST4793
Shireoaks Notts	49	SK5580
Shirlett Shrops	37	SO6597
Shirley Derbys	48	SK2141
Shirley Gt Lon	23	TQ3565
Shirley Hants	10	SU4013
Shirley W Mids	38	SP1278
Shirrell Heath Hants	11	SU5714
Shirven Strath	71	NR8784
Shirwell Devon	6	SS6037
Shirwell Cross Devon	6	SS5937
Shittlehope Dur	61	NZ0038
Shobdon H & W	27	SO4062
Shobrooke Devon	7	SS8600
Shoby Leics	39	SK6820
Shoeburyness Essex	25	TQ9484
Sholden Kent	15	TR3552
Sholing Hants	10	SU4511
Shop Cnwll	6	SS2214
Shop Street Suffk	33	TM2268
Shore Gt Man	54	SD9217
Shoreditch Gt Lon	23	TQ3382
Shoreditch Somset	8	ST2422
Shoreham Kent	23	TQ5261
Shoreham-by-Sea W Susx	12	TQ2105
Shorley Hants	11	SU5726
Shorne Kent	14	TQ6971
Short Heath W Mids	38	SJ9701
Shorta Cross Cnwll	4	SX2857
Shortfield Common Surrey	11	SU8442
Shortgate E Susx	13	TQ4915
Shortlanesend Cnwll	2	SW8047
Shorwell IOW	10	SZ4582
Shoscombe Avon	20	ST7156
Shotesham Norfk	43	TM2599
Shotgate Essex	24	TQ7593
Shotley Suffk	25	TM2335
Shotley Bridge Nthumb	68	NZ0853
Shotley Gate Suffk	25	TM2433
Shotley Street Suffk	25	TM2335
Shotleyfield Nthumb	68	NZ0653
Shottenden Kent	15	TR0454
Shottery Warwks	29	SP1954
Shotteswell Warwks	29	SP4245
Shottisham Suffk	33	TM3244
Shottle Derbys	49	SK3149
Shottlegate Derbys	49	SK3147
Shotton Clwyd	46	SJ3168
Shotwick Ches	46	SJ3472
Shougle Gramp	94	NJ2155
Shouldham Norfk	42	TF6709
Shouldham Thorpe Norfk	42	TF6607
Shoulton H & W	28	SO8158
Shrawardine Shrops	36	SJ3915
Shrawley H & W	28	SO8065
Shreding Green Bucks	22	TQ0281
Shrewley Warwks	29	SP2167
Shrewsbury Shrops	37	SJ4912
Shrewton Wilts	20	SU0643
Shripney W Susx	11	SU9302
Shrivenham Oxon	21	SU2388
Shropham Norfk	42	TL9893
Shroton Dorset	9	ST8512
Shucknall H & W	27	SO5842
Shudy Camps Cambs	32	TL6244
Shurdington Gloucs	28	SO9118
Shurlock Row Berks	22	SU8374
Shurnock H & W	28	SP0260
Shurrery Highld	100	ND0458
Shurrery Lodge Highld	100	ND0456
Shurton Somset	19	ST2044
Shustoke Warwks	39	SP2290
Shut Heath Staffs	38	SJ8621
Shute Devon	8	SY2597
Shutford Oxon	29	SP3840
Shuthonger Gloucs	28	SO8935
Shutlanger Nhants	30	SP7249
Shutterton Devon	5	SX9678
Shuttington Warwks	39	SK2505
Shuttlewood Derbys	49	SK4672
Shuttleworth Lancs	54	SD8017
Sibbertoft Nhants	39	SP6882
Sibdon Carwood Shrops	36	SO4081
Sibford Ferris Oxon	29	SP3537
Sibford Gower Oxon	29	SP3537
Sible Hedingham Essex	24	TL7734
Sibley's Green Essex	24	TL6128
Sibsey Lincs	51	TF3550
Sibson Cambs	40	TL0997
Sibson Leics	39	SK3500
Sibster Highld	100	ND3253
Sibthorpe Notts	50	SK7645
Sibthorpe Notts	49	SK7272
Sicklesmere Suffk	32	TL8760
Sicklinghall N York	55	SE3548
Sid Devon	8	SY1388
Sidborough Devon	7	SS9014
Sidbury Devon	8	SY1491
Sidbury Shrops	37	SO6885
Sidcot Somset	19	ST4257
Sidcup Gt Lon	23	TQ4672
Siddick Cumb	58	NY0131
Siddington Ches	47	SJ8470
Siddington Gloucs	20	SU0399
Sidestrand Norfk	43	TG2539
Sidford Devon	8	SY1390
Sidinish W Isls	102	NF8763
Sidlesham W Susx	11	SZ8598
Sidlesham Common W Susx	11	SU8500
Sidley E Susx	14	TQ7409
Sidmouth Devon	8	SY1287
Siggelsthorne Humb	57	TA1545
Sigingstone S Glam	18	SS9771
Silchester Hants	21	SU6262
Sileby Leics	39	SK6015
Silecroft Cumb	58	SD1281
Silfield Norfk	43	TM1299
Silk Willoughby Lincs	50	TF0542
Silkstone S York	55	SE2905
Silkstone Common S York	55	SE2904
Silksworth T & W	69	NZ3752
Silloth Cumb	67	NY1153
Silpho N York	63	SE9692
Silsden W York	54	SE0446
Silsoe Beds	30	TL0835
Silver End Beds	30	TL1042
Silver End Essex	24	TL8119
Silver Street H & W	38	SP0776
Silver Street Kent	14	TQ8761
Silverburn Loth	75	NT2060
Silverdale Lancs	53	SD4574
Silverdale Staffs	47	SJ8146
Silverford Gramp	95	NJ7763
Silverstone Nhants	30	SP6643
Silverton Devon	7	SS9503
Silvington Shrops	37	SO6279
Simonburn Nthumb	68	NY8773
Simons Burrow Devon	8	ST1416
Simonsbath Somset	7	SS7739
Simonstone Lancs	54	SD7734
Simpson Bucks	30	SP8835
Simpson Cross Dyfed	16	SM8919
Sinclair's Hill Border	76	NT8150
Sinclairston Strath	73	NS4716
Sincliffe N York	55	SE2458
Sinderby N York	62	SE3481
Sinderland Green Gt Man	47	SJ7390
Sindlesham Berks	22	SU7769
Singleton Lancs	53	SD3838
Singleton W Susx	11	SU8713
Singlewell Kent	14	TQ6571
Sinnahard Gramp	94	NJ4713
Sinton H & W	28	SO8160
Sinton Green H & W	28	SO8160
Sirhowy Gwent	27	SO1510
Sissinghurst Kent	14	TQ7937
Siston Avon	20	ST6875
Sithney Cnwll	2	SW6329
Sittingbourne Kent	14	TQ9063
Six Ashes Staffs	37	SO7988
Six Mile Bottom Cambs	31	TL5756
Six Rues Jersey	101	SV0000
Sixhills Lincs	50	TF1787
Sixpenny Handley Dorset	9	ST9917
Skail Highld	99	NC7146
Skaill Ork	103	HY5806
Skaith D & G	64	NX3766
Skares Strath	74	NS5217
Skateraw Loth	76	NT7375
Skeabost Highld	90	NG4148
Skeeby N York	61	NZ1902
Skeffington Leics	40	SK7402
Skeffling Humb	57	TA3719
Skegby Notts	49	SK4961
Skegby Notts	50	SK7869
Skegness Lincs	51	TF5663
Skelbo Highld	97	NH7895
Skelbo Street Highld	97	NH7994
Skelbrook S York	55	SE5112
Skellingthorpe Lincs	50	SK9272
Skelmanthorpe W York	55	SE2210
Skelmersdale Lancs	46	SD4606
Skelmorlie Strath	73	NS1967
Skelpick Highld	99	NC7255
Skelton Cleve	62	NZ6619
Skelton Cumb	59	NY4335
Skelton Humb	56	SE7725
Skelton N York	55	SE3668
Skelton N York	56	SE5656
Skelwith Bridge Cumb	59	NY3403
Skendleby Lincs	51	TF4369
Skene House Gramp	95	NJ7610
Skenfrith Gwent	27	SO4520
Skerne Humb	57	TA0455
Skerray Highld	99	NC6563
Skerton Lancs	53	SD4763
Sketchley Leics	39	SP4292
Sketty W Glam	17	SS6292
Skewsby N York	56	SE6270
Skidby Humb	56	TA0133
Skigersta W Isls	102	NB5461
Skilgate Somset	7	SS9827
Skillington Lincs	40	SK8925
Skinburness Cumb	67	NY1356
Skinflats Cent	82	NS9082
Skinidin Highld	90	NG2247
Skipness Strath	71	NR9057
Skipper's Bridge Cumb	67	NY3783
Skipsea Brough Humb	57	TA1554
Skipton N York	54	SD9851
Skipton-on-Swale N York	62	SE3679
Skipwith N York	56	SE6638
Skirling Border	75	NT0739
Skirmett Bucks	22	SU7790
Skirpenbeck Humb	56	SE7457
Skirwith Cumb	59	NY6132
Skirza Highld	100	ND3868
Skulamus Highld	85	NG6722
Skullomie Highld	99	NC6161
Skye Green Essex	24	TL8722
Skye of Curr Highld	93	NH9824
Slack W York	54	SD9728
Slackadale Gramp	95	NJ7454
Slackhall Derbys	48	SK0781
Slacks of Cairnbanno Gramp	95	NJ8445
Slad Gloucs	28	SO8707
Slade Devon	6	SS5046
Slade Somset	7	SS8427
Slade End Oxon	21	SU5890
Slade Green Kent	23	TQ5276
Slade Heath Staffs	38	SJ9206
Slade Hooton S York	49	SK5288
Sladen Derbys	48	SK0772
Slades Green H & W	28	SO8134
Slaggan Highld	91	NG8494
Slaggyford Nthumb	68	NY6752
Slaid Hill W York	55	SE3340
Slaidburn Lancs	54	SD7152
Slaithwaite W York	55	SE0813
Slaley Nthumb	68	NY9757
Slamannan Cent	74	NS8573
Slapton Bucks	30	SP9320
Slapton Devon	5	SX8244
Slapton Nhants	29	SP6446
Slaugham W Susx	12	TQ2528
Slaughterford Wilts	20	ST8473
Slawston Leics	40	SP7794
Sleaford Hants	11	SU8038
Sleaford Lincs	50	TF0645
Sleagill Cumb	59	NY5919
Sleasdairidh Highld	97	NH6496
Sledmere Humb	56	SE9364
Sleightholme Dur	61	NY9510
Sleights N York	63	NZ8607
Slickly Highld	100	ND2966
Sliddery Strath	72	NR9322
Sligachan Highld	84	NG4829
Sligrachan Strath	80	NS1791
Slimbridge Gloucs	20	SO7303
Slindon Staffs	38	SJ8232
Slindon W Susx	12	SU9608
Slingsby N York	62	SE6974
Slip End Beds	30	TL0818
Slip End Herts	31	TL2837
Slipton Nhants	40	SP9579
Slitting Mill Staffs	38	SK0217
Slockavullin Strath	71	NR8297
Slogarie D & G	65	NX6568
Sloncombe Devon	5	SX7386
Sloothby Lincs	51	TF4970
Slough Berks	22	SU9879
Slough Green Somset	8	ST2720
Slumbay Highld	85	NG8838
Slyfield Green Surrey	12	TQ0052
Slyne Lancs	53	SD4765
Smailholm Border	76	NT6436
Small Dole W Susx	12	TQ2112
Small Heath W Mids	38	SP1085
Small Hythe Kent	14	TQ8930
Smallburgh Norfk	43	TG3324
Smalldale Derbys	48	SK1781
Smalley Derbys	49	SK4044
Smallfield Surrey	12	TQ3143
Smallholm D & G	67	NY0977
Smallridge Devon	8	ST3001
Smallworth Norfk	32	TM0181
Smannell Hants	21	SU3849
Smarden Kent	14	TQ8742
Smarden Bell Kent	14	TQ8742
Smart's Hill Kent	13	TQ5242
Smearisary Highld	85	NM6477
Smeatharpe Devon	8	ST1910
Smeeth Kent	15	TR0739
Smeeton Westerby Leics	39	SP6792
Smerclate W Isls	102	NF7415
Smerral Highld	100	ND1733
Smestow Staffs	38	SO8591
Smethwick W Mids	38	SP0288
Smisby Derbys	39	SK3419
Smith's End Herts	31	TL4037
Smith's Green Essex	24	TL5821
Smith's Green Essex	32	TL6640
Smitheclose IOW	11	SZ5391
Smithstown Highld	91	NG7977
Smithton Highld	93	NH7145
Smithy Green Ches	47	SJ7474
Smithy Houses Derbys	49	SK3847
Smoo Highld	98	NC4167
Smythe's Green Essex	24	TL9218
Snade D & G	66	NX8486
Snaigow House Tays	88	NO0843
Snailwell Cambs	32	TL6467
Snainton N York	63	SE9181
Snaith Humb	56	SE6422
Snape N York	61	SE2684
Snape Suffk	33	TM3959
Snape Green Mersyd	53	SD3814
Snape Street Suffk	33	TM3958
Snarestone Leics	39	SK3409
Snarford Lincs	50	TF0482
Snargate Kent	15	TQ9928
Snave Kent	15	TR0130
Sneath Common Norfk	33	TM1589
Sneaton N York	63	NZ8907
Snelland Lincs	50	TF0780
Snelston Derbys	48	SK1543
Snetterton Norfk	32	TL9991
Snettisham Norfk	42	TF6834
Snibston Leics	39	SK4113
Snig's End Gloucs	28	SO7828
Sniperhill Kent	14	TQ9163
Snitter Nthumb	68	NU0203
Snitterby Lincs	50	SK9894
Snitterfield Warwks	29	SP2159
Snitton Shrops	37	SO5575
Snoadhill Kent	14	TQ9342
Snodland Kent	14	TQ7061
Snoll Hatch Kent	14	TQ6637
Snow End Herts	31	TL4032
Snowshill Gloucs	28	SP0933
Soake Hants	11	SU6611
Soar Gwynd	44	SH3872
Soar Powys	26	SN9732
Soberton Hants	11	SU6116

Stanshope Sutton Wick

Stanshope *Staffs* 48 SK1254
Stanstead *Suffk* 32 TL8449
Stanstead Abbots *Herts* 23 TL3811
Stanstead Street *Suffk* 32 TL8448
Stansted *Kent* 14 TQ6062
Stansted Mountfitchet *Essex* 31 TL5125
Stanton *Derbys* 39 SK2719
Stanton *Gloucs* 28 SP0634
Stanton *Nthumb* 69 NZ1390
Stanton *Staffs* 48 SK1246
Stanton *Suffk* 32 TL9673
Stanton Drew *Avon* 19 ST5963
Stanton Fitzwarren *Wilts* 21 SU1790
Stanton Harcourt *Oxon* 29 SP4105
Stanton Lacy *Shrops* 37 SO4979
Stanton Long *Shrops* 37 SO5691
Stanton Prior *Avon* 20 ST6762
Stanton St. Bernard *Wilts* 20 SU0962
Stanton St. John *Oxon* 29 SP5709
Stanton St. Quintin *Wilts* 20 ST9079
Stanton Street *Suffk* 32 TL9566
Stanton Wick *Avon* 19 ST6162
Stanton by Bridge *Derbys* 39 SK3627
Stanton by Dale *Derbys* 49 SK4637
Stanton in Peak *Derbys* 48 SK2464
Stanton on the Wolds *Notts* 39 SK6330
Stanton under Bardon *Leics* 39 SK4610
Stanton upon Hine Heath *Shrops* 37 SJ5624
Stanway *Essex* 25 TL9424
Stanway *Gloucs* 28 SP0632
Stanway Green *Essex* 25 TL9623
Stanwell *Surrey* 22 TQ0574
Stanwick *Nhants* 30 SP9871
Stanwix *Cumb* 67 NY3957
Stape *N York* 63 SE7994
Stapeley *Ches* 47 SJ6749
Stapenhill *Staffs* 39 SK2521
Staple *Kent* 15 TR2756
Staple *Somset* 18 ST1141
Staple Cross *Devon* 7 ST0320
Staple Fitzpaine *Somset* 8 ST2618
Staplefield *W Susx* 12 TQ2728
Stapleford *Cambs* 31 TL4751
Stapleford *Herts* 31 TL3117
Stapleford *Leics* 40 SK8018
Stapleford *Lincs* 50 SK8857
Stapleford *Notts* 49 SK4837
Stapleford Abbotts *Essex* 23 TQ5194
Staplegrove *Somset* 8 ST2126
Staplehay *Somset* 8 ST2121
Staplehurst *Kent* 14 TQ7843
Staplestreet *Kent* 15 TR0660
Stapleton *H & W* 27 SO3265
Stapleton *Leics* 39 SP4398
Stapleton *N York* 61 NZ2612
Stapleton *Shrops* 36 SJ4604
Stapleton *Somset* 8 ST4621
Stapley *Somset* 8 ST1813
Staploe *Beds* 30 TL1560
Staplow *H & W* 28 SO6941
Star *Dyfed* 17 SN2435
Star *Fife* 83 NO3103
Star *Somset* 19 ST4358
Star Hill *Gwent* 19 SO4702
Starbotton *N York* 61 SD9574
Starcross *Devon* 5 SX9781
Stareton *Warwks* 39 SP3371
Starlings Green *Essex* 31 TL4531
Starston *Norfk* 33 TM2384
Start *Devon* 5 SX8144
Start Point *Devon* 5 SX8337
Startforth *Dur* 61 NZ0415
Startley *Wilts* 20 ST9482
Statenborough *Kent* 15 TR3155
Stathe *Somset* 8 ST3728
Stathern *Leics* 40 SK7731
Staughton Green *Cambs* 30 TL1365
Staughton Highway *Cambs* 30 TL1364
Staunton *Gloucs* 27 SO5512
Staunton *Gloucs* 28 SO7929
Staunton Green *H & W* 27 SO3661
Staunton on Arrow *H & W* 27 SO3760
Staunton on Wye *H & W* 27 SO3644
Staveley *Cumb* 59 SD3786
Staveley *Cumb* 59 SD4698
Staveley *Derbys* 49 SK4374
Staveley *N York* 55 SE3662
Staverton *Devon* 5 SX7964
Staverton *Gloucs* 28 SO8923
Staverton *Nhants* 29 SP5461
Staverton *Wilts* 20 ST8560
Stawell *Somset* 19 ST3638
Stawley *Somset* 7 ST0622
Staxigoe *Highld* 100 ND3852
Staxton *N York* 63 TA0179
Staylittle *Powys* 35 SN8892
Staynall *Lancs* 53 SD3643
Stean *N York* 61 SE0973
Steane *Nhants* 29 SP5538
Stearsby *N York* 56 SE6071
Steart *Somset* 19 ST2745
Stebbing *Essex* 24 TL6624
Stebbing Green *Essex* 24 TL6823
Stebbing Park *Essex* 24 TL6524
Stechford *W Mids* 38 SP1387
Stede Quarter *Kent* 14 TQ8737
Stedham *W Susx* 11 SU8622
Steele Road *Border* 67 NY5292
Steen's Bridge *H & W* 27 SO5357
Steep *Hants* 11 SU7425
Steep Lane *W York* 55 SE0223
Steephill *IOW* 11 SZ5477
Steeple *Dorset* 9 SY9080
Steeple *Essex* 25 TL9303
Steeple Ashton *Wilts* 20 ST9056
Steeple Aston *Oxon* 29 SP4725
Steeple Barton *Oxon* 29 SP4424
Steeple Bumpstead *Essex* 32 TL6841
Steeple Claydon *Bucks* 30 SP7026
Steeple Gidding *Cambs* 40 TL1381
Steeple Langford *Wilts* 20 SU0337
Steeple Morden *Cambs* 31 TL2842
Steeton *W York* 55 SE0344
Stein *Highld* 90 NG2656
Stelling Minnis *Kent* 15 TR1447
Stenhouse *D & G* 66 NX7993
Stenhousemuir *Cent* 82 NS8682
Stenigot *Lincs* 51 TF2481
Stenscholl *Highld* 90 NG4767
Stenton *Loth* 76 NT6274
Stepaside *Dyfed* 16 SN1307
Stepney *Gt Lon* 23 TQ3581
Steppingley *Beds* 30 TL0135
Stepps *Strath* 74 NS6568
Sternfield *Suffk* 33 TM3861
Sterridge *Devon* 6 SS5546
Stert *Wilts* 20 SU0259
Stetchworth *Cambs* 32 TL6459
Stevenage *Herts* 31 TL2325
Stevenston *Strath* 73 NS2742
Steventon *Hants* 21 SU5447
Steventon *Oxon* 21 SU4691
Steventon End *Essex* 31 TL5942
Stevington *Beds* 30 SP9853
Stewartby *Beds* 30 TL0142
Stewarton *Strath* 72 NR6919
Stewarton *Strath* 73 NS4246
Stewkley *Bucks* 30 SP8525
Stewley *Somset* 8 ST3118
Stewton *Lincs* 51 TF3687
Steyning *W Susx* 12 TQ1711
Steynton *Dyfed* 16 SM9108
Stibb *Cnwll* 6 SS2210
Stibb Cross *Devon* 6 SS4314
Stibb Green *Wilts* 21 SU2262
Stibbard *Norfk* 42 TF9828
Stibbington *Cambs* 40 TL0998
Stichill *Border* 76 NT7138
Stickford *Lincs* 51 TF3560
Sticklepath *Devon* 7 SX6494
Sticklepath *Somset* 7 ST0435
Stickling Green *Essex* 31 TL4732
Stickney *Lincs* 51 TF3456
Stiffkey *Norfk* 42 TF9743
Stifford's Bridge *H & W* 28 SO7448
Stile Bridge *Kent* 14 TQ7547
Stileway *Somset* 19 ST4640
Stilligarry *W Isls* 102 NF7638
Stillingfleet *N York* 56 SE5940
Stillington *Cleve* 62 NZ3723
Stillington *N York* 56 SE5867
Stilton *Cambs* 40 TL1689
Stinchcombe *Gloucs* 20 ST7398
Stinsford *Dorset* 9 SY7191
Stirchley *Shrops* 37 SJ6906
Stirling *Cent* 81 NS7993
Stirling *Gramp* 95 NK1242
Stirtloe *Cambs* 31 TL1966
Stirton *N York* 54 SD9753
Stisted *Essex* 24 TL8024
Stithians *Cnwll* 2 SW7336
Stittenham *N York* 56 SE6767
Stivichall *W Mids* 39 SP3376
Stixwould *Lincs* 50 TF1765
Stoak *Ches* 46 SJ4273
Stobo *Border* 75 NT1838
Stoborough *Dorset* 9 SY9286
Stoborough Green *Dorset* 9 SY9285
Stobs Castle *Border* 67 NT5008
Stobswood *Nthumb* 69 NZ2195
Stock *Avon* 19 ST4561
Stock *Essex* 24 TQ6999
Stock Gifford *Avon* 19 ST6279
Stock Green *H & W* 28 SO9859
Stock Wood *H & W* 28 SP0058
Stockbridge *Hants* 10 SU3535
Stockbriggs *Strath* 74 NS7936
Stockbury *Kent* 14 TQ8461
Stockcross *Berks* 21 SU4368
Stockerston *Leics* 40 SP8397
Stocking *H & W* 27 SO6230
Stocking Pelham *Herts* 31 TL4529
Stockingford *Warwks* 39 SP3391
Stockinish *W Isls* 90 NG1391
Stockland *Devon* 8 ST2404
Stockland Bristol *Somset* 19 ST2443
Stockleigh English *Devon* 7 SS8406
Stockleigh Pomeroy *Devon* 7 SS8703
Stockley *Wilts* 20 ST9967
Stocklinch *Somset* 8 ST3817
Stockmoor *H & W* 27 SO3954
Stockport *Gt Man* 48 SJ8990
Stocksbridge *S York* 49 SK2698
Stocksfield *Nthumb* 68 NZ0561
Stockstreet *Essex* 24 TL8322
Stockton *H & W* 27 SO5261
Stockton *Norfk* 43 TM3894
Stockton *Shrops* 37 SJ7716
Stockton *Shrops* 37 SO7299
Stockton *Shrops* 37 SO7399
Stockton *Warwks* 29 SP4364
Stockton *Wilts* 20 ST9738
Stockton Brook *Staffs* 48 SJ9152
Stockton Heath *Ches* 47 SJ6186
Stockton on Teme *H & W* 28 SO7167
Stockton on the Forest *N York* 56 SE6556
Stockton-on-Tees *Cleve* 62 NZ4419
Stockwell End *W Mids* 38 SJ8800
Stockwood *Avon* 19 ST6268
Stockwood *Dorset* 9 ST5806
Stodmarsh *Kent* 15 TR2160
Stody *Norfk* 42 TG0535
Stoer *Highld* 98 NC0428
Stoford *Somset* 8 ST5613
Stoford *Wilts* 10 SU0835
Stogumber *Somset* 7 ST0936
Stogumber *Somset* 7 ST0937
Stogursey *Somset* 19 ST1942
Stogursey *Somset* 19 ST2042
Stoke *Devon* 6 SS2324
Stoke *Hants* 21 SU4051
Stoke *Hants* 11 SU7202
Stoke *Kent* 14 TQ8274
Stoke *W Mids* 39 SP3678
Stoke Abbott *Dorset* 8 ST4500
Stoke Albany *Nhants* 40 SP8088
Stoke Ash *Suffk* 33 TM1170
Stoke Bardolph *Notts* 49 SK6441
Stoke Bliss *H & W* 27 SO6563
Stoke Bruerne *Nhants* 30 SP7449
Stoke Canon *Devon* 7 SX9397
Stoke Charity *Hants* 10 SU4839
Stoke Cross *H & W* 27 SO6250
Stoke D'Abernon *Surrey* 22 TQ1259
Stoke Doyle *Nhants* 40 TL0286
Stoke Dry *Leics* 40 SP8596
Stoke End *Warwks* 38 SP1696
Stoke Farthing *Wilts* 10 SU0525
Stoke Ferry *Norfk* 42 TF7000
Stoke Fleming *Devon* 5 SX8648
Stoke Gabriel *Devon* 5 SX8457
Stoke Gabriel *Devon* 5 SX8557
Stoke Golding *Leics* 39 SP3997
Stoke Goldington *Bucks* 30 SP8348
Stoke Green *Bucks* 22 SU9882
Stoke Hammond *Bucks* 30 SP8829
Stoke Heath *W Mids* 39 SP3580
Stoke Holy Cross *Norfk* 43 TG2301
Stoke Lacy *H & W* 27 SO6149
Stoke Lyne *Oxon* 29 SP5628
Stoke Mandeville *Bucks* 22 SP8310
Stoke Newington *Gt Lon* 23 TQ3386
Stoke Orchard *Gloucs* 28 SO9128
Stoke Poges *Bucks* 22 SU9783
Stoke Prior *H & W* 27 SO5256
Stoke Prior *H & W* 28 SO9467
Stoke Rivers *Devon* 7 SS6335
Stoke Rochford *Lincs* 40 SK9127
Stoke Row *Oxon* 22 SU6884
Stoke St. Gregory *Somset* 8 ST3426
Stoke St. Mary *Somset* 8 ST2622
Stoke St. Michael *Somset* 20 ST6646
Stoke St. Milborough *Shrops* 37 SO5682
Stoke Talmage *Oxon* 22 SU6799
Stoke Trister *Somset* 9 ST7328
Stoke Wake *Dorset* 9 ST7606
Stoke by Clare *Suffk* 32 TL7443
Stoke sub Hamdon *Somset* 8 ST4717
Stoke upon Tern *Shrops* 37 SJ6328
Stoke-by-Nayland *Suffk* 25 TL9836
Stoke-on-Trent *Staffs* 47 SJ8745
Stoke-upon-Trent *Staffs* 47 SJ8745
Stokeford *Dorset* 9 SY8787
Stokeham *Notts* 50 SK7876
Stokeinteignhead *Devon* 5 SX9170
Stokenchurch *Bucks* 22 SU7696
Stokenham *Devon* 5 SX8042
Stokesay *Shrops* 36 SO4381
Stokesby *Norfk* 43 TG4310
Stokesley *N York* 62 NZ5208
Stolford *Somset* 7 ST0332
Stolford *Somset* 19 ST2245
Ston Easton *Somset* 19 ST6253
Stondon Massey *Essex* 24 TL5800
Stone *Bucks* 30 SP7812
Stone *Gloucs* 20 ST6895
Stone *H & W* 38 SO8675
Stone *Kent* 14 TQ9427
Stone *S York* 49 SK5589
Stone *Staffs* 38 SJ9034
Stone Allerton *Somset* 19 ST3950
Stone Cross *E Susx* 13 TQ6431
Stone Cross *Kent* 15 TR3257
Stone House *Cumb* 60 SD7785
Stone Street *Kent* 14 TQ5754
Stone Street *Suffk* 32 TL9639
Stone Street *Suffk* 33 TM3882
Stonea *Cambs* 41 TL4693
Stonebridge *Avon* 19 ST3959
Stonebroom *Derbys* 49 SK4159
Stonebury *Herts* 31 TL3828
Stonechrubie *Highld* 96 NC2419
Stonecrouch *Kent* 14 TQ7033
Stoneferry *Humb* 57 TA1231
Stonefield *Strath* 71 NR8671
Stonegate *E Susx* 14 TQ6628
Stonegate *N York* 63 NZ7709
Stonegrave *N York* 62 SE6577
Stonehall *H & W* 28 SO8848
Stonehaven *Gramp* 89 NO8786
Stonehill Green *Gt Lon* 23 TQ4870
Stonehouse *Ches* 46 SJ5070
Stonehouse *D & G* 66 NX8268
Stonehouse *Devon* 4 SX4653
Stonehouse *Gloucs* 28 SO8005
Stonehouse *Nthumb* 68 NY6958
Stonehouse *Strath* 74 NS7546
Stoneleigh *Warwks* 39 SP3372
Stones Green *Essex* 25 TM1626
Stonesby *Leics* 40 SK8224
Stonesfield *Oxon* 29 SP3917
Stonewells *Gramp* 94 NJ2865
Stoney Cross *Hants* 10 SU2511
Stoney Middleton *Derbys* 48 SK2275
Stoney Stanton *Leics* 39 SP4994
Stoney Stoke *Somset* 9 ST7032
Stoney Stratton *Somset* 19 ST6539
Stoney Stretton *Shrops* 36 SJ3809
Stoneybridge *W Isls* 102 NF7433
Stoneyburn *Loth* 75 NS9862
Stoneykirk *D & G* 64 NX0853
Stoneywood *Cent* 81 NS7982
Stoneywood *Gramp* 95 NJ8811
Stonham Aspal *Suffk* 33 TM1359
Stonnall *Staffs* 38 SK0603
Stonor *Oxon* 22 SU7388
Stonton Wyville *Leics* 40 SP7395
Stony Cross *Devon* 6 SS5125
Stony Cross *H & W* 27 SO5467
Stony Houghton *Derbys* 49 SK4966
Stony Stratford *Bucks* 30 SP7840
Stonywell *Staffs* 38 SK0812
Stoodleigh *Devon* 7 SS6532
Stopham *W Susx* 12 TQ0218
Stopsley *Beds* 30 TL1023
Stormy Corner *Lancs* 46 SD4707
Stornoway *W Isls* 102 NB4333
Storrington *W Susx* 12 TQ0814
Storth *Cumb* 59 SD4780
Storwood *Humb* 56 SE7144
Stotfold *Beds* 31 TL2136
Stottesdon *Shrops* 37 SO6782
Stoughton *Leics* 39 SK6402
Stoughton *Surrey* 12 SU9851
Stoughton *W Susx* 11 SU8011
Stoul *Highld* 85 NM7594
Stour Provost *Dorset* 9 ST7921
Stour Row *Dorset* 9 ST8220
Stourbridge *W Mids* 38 SO9084
Stourpaine *Dorset* 9 ST8509
Stourport-on-Severn *H & W* 37 SO8171
Stourton *Staffs* 38 SO8684
Stourton *Warwks* 29 SP3036
Stourton *Wilts* 9 ST7733
Stourton Caundle *Dorset* 9 ST7114
Stove *Shet* 103 HU4224
Stoven *Suffk* 33 TM4481
Stow *Border* 76 NT4644
Stow *Lincs* 50 SK8781
Stow Bardolph *Norfk* 41 TF6206
Stow Bedon *Norfk* 42 TL9596
Stow Longa *Cambs* 30 TL1171
Stow Maries *Essex* 24 TQ8399
Stow cum Quy *Cambs* 31 TL5260
Stow-on-the-Wold *Gloucs* 29 SP1926
Stowbridge *Norfk* 41 TF6007
Stowe *Shrops* 36 SO3173
Stowe by Chartley *Staffs* 38 SK0027
Stowell *Somset* 9 ST6822
Stowey *Somset* 19 ST5959
Stowford *Devon* 4 SX4387
Stowford *Devon* 7 SS6541
Stowlangtoft *Suffk* 32 TL9568
Stowmarket *Suffk* 32 TM0458
Stowting *Kent* 15 TR1242
Stowting Common *Kent* 15 TR1242
Stowupland *Suffk* 32 TM0760
Straad *Strath* 72 NS0462
Straanruie *Highld* 93 NH9916
Strachan *Gramp* 89 NO6692
Strachur *Strath* 80 NN0901
Stradbroke *Suffk* 33 TM2374
Stradbrook *Wilts* 20 ST9152
Stradishall *Suffk* 32 TL7552
Stradsett *Norfk* 42 TF6605
Stragglethorpe *Lincs* 50 SK9152
Straight Soley *Wilts* 21 SU3272
Straiton *Loth* 75 NT2766
Straiton *Strath* 73 NS3805
Straloch *Gramp* 95 NJ8621
Straloch *Tays* 88 NO0463
Stramshall *Staffs* 38 SK0735
Strang *IOM* 52 SC3678
Strangford *H & W* 27 SO5727
Stranraer *D & G* 64 NX0660
Stratfield Mortimer *Berks* 22 SU6664
Stratfield Saye *Hants* 22 SU6861
Stratfield Turgis *Hants* 22 SU6959
Stratford *Gt Lon* 23 TQ3984
Stratford St. Andrew *Suffk* 33 TM3560
Stratford St. Mary *Suffk* 25 TM0434
Stratford Tony *Wilts* 10 SU0926
Stratford sub Castle *Wilts* 10 SU1331
Stratford-upon-Avon *Warwks* 29 SP2055
Strath *Highld* 91 NG7978
Strath *Highld* 100 ND2652
Strathan *Highld* 85 NM9791
Strathan *Highld* 98 NC0821
Strathan *Highld* 99 NC5764
Strathaven *Strath* 74 NS6944
Strathblane *Cent* 81 NS5679
Strathcarron *Highld* 91 NG9442
Strathcoil *Strath* 79 NM6830
Strathdon *Gramp* 94 NJ3512
Strathkanaird *Highld* 96 NC1501
Strathkinness *Fife* 83 NO4616
Strathlene *Gramp* 94 NJ4567
Strathmashie House *Tays* 87 NN5891
Strathmiglo *Fife* 82 NO2109
Strathpeffer *Highld* 92 NH4858
Strathwhillan *Strath* 72 NS0235
Strathy *Highld* 99 NC8464
Strathy Inn *Highld* 99 NC8365
Strathyre *Cent* 81 NN5617
Stratton *Cnwll* 6 SS2206
Stratton *Dorset* 9 SY6593
Stratton *Gloucs* 20 SP0103
Stratton Audley *Oxon* 29 SP6026
Stratton St. Margaret *Wilts* 21 SU1786
Stratton St. Michael *Norfk* 43 TM2093
Stratton Strawless *Norfk* 43 TG2220
Stratton-on-the-Fosse *Somset* 19 ST6550
Stravithie *Fife* 83 NO5313
Stream *Somset* 7 ST0639
Streat *E Susx* 12 TQ3515
Streatham *Gt Lon* 23 TQ3171
Streatley *Beds* 30 TL0728
Streatley *Berks* 21 SU5980
Street *Devon* 6 SX1895
Street *Devon* 8 SY1888
Street *Somset* 19 ST4836
Street Ashton *Warwks* 39 SP4682
Street Dinas *Shrops* 36 SJ3338
Street End *Kent* 15 TR1453
Street Gate *T & W* 69 NZ2159
Street Houses *N York* 56 SE5346
Street of Kincardine *Highld* 93 NH9417
Street on the Fosse *Somset* 19 ST6139
Streethay *Staffs* 38 SK1410
Streetlam *N York* 61 SE3098
Streetly End *Cambs* 31 TL6418
Strelitz *Tays* 82 NO1836
Strelley *Notts* 49 SK5141
Strensall *N York* 56 SE6360
Strete *Devon* 5 SX8447
Stretford *Gt Man* 47 SJ7994
Strethall *Essex* 31 TL4839
Stretham *Cambs* 31 TL5174
Strettington *W Susx* 11 SU8907
Stretton *Ches* 47 SJ6282
Stretton *Derbys* 49 SK3961
Stretton *Leics* 40 SK9415
Stretton *Staffs* 38 SJ8811
Stretton *Staffs* 39 SK2526
Stretton Grandison *H & W* 27 SO6344
Stretton Sugwas *H & W* 27 SO4642
Stretton Westwood *Shrops* 37 SO5998
Stretton en le Field *Leics* 39 SK3012
Stretton on Fosse *Warwks* 29 SP2238
Stretton under Fosse *Warwks* 39 SP4581
Stretton-on-Dunsmore *Warwks* 39 SP4172
Strichen *Gramp* 95 NJ9455
Stringston *Somset* 19 ST1742
Strixton *Nhants* 30 SP9061
Stroat *Gloucs* 19 ST5797
Stromeferry *Highld* 85 NG8634
Stromness *Ork* 103 HY2509
Stronachlachar *Cent* 80 NN4010
Stronachullin *Strath* 71 NR8479
Stronafian *Strath* 80 NS0281
Strond *W Isls* 102 NG0384
Strone *Highld* 86 NN1481
Strone *Highld* 92 NH5228
Strone *Strath* 80 NS1980
Stronenaba *Highld* 86 NN2084
Stronmilchan *Strath* 80 NN1528
Strontian *Highld* 79 NM8161
Strood *Kent* 14 TQ7269
Stroud *Gloucs* 28 SO8505
Stroud *Hants* 11 SU7223
Stroud Green *Essex* 24 TQ8690
Stroud Green *Gloucs* 28 SO8007
Stroxton *Lincs* 40 SK9030
Struan *Highld* 84 NG3438
Struan *Tays* 87 NN8065
Strumpshaw *Norfk* 43 TG3507
Strutherhill *Strath* 74 NS7649
Struthers *Fife* 83 NO3709
Struy *Highld* 92 NH4039
Stuartfield *Gramp* 95 NJ9745
Stub Place *Cumb* 58 SD0892
Stubbington *Hants* 11 SU5503
Stubley *Derbys* 49 SK3372
Stubshaw Cross *Gt Man* 47 SD5800
Stubton *Lincs* 50 SK8748
Stuckgowan *Strath* 80 NN3203
Stuckton *Hants* 10 SU1613
Studfold *N York* 54 SD8169
Studham *Beds* 30 TL0215
Studholme *Cumb* 67 NY2656
Studland *Dorset* 9 SZ0382
Studley *Oxon* 29 SP6012
Studley *Warwks* 28 SP0764
Studley *Wilts* 20 ST9671
Studley Common *H & W* 28 SP0665
Studley Roger *N York* 55 SE2969
Studley Royal *N York* 55 SE2770
Stuntney *Cambs* 31 TL5578
Sturgate *Lincs* 50 SK8788
Sturmer *Essex* 32 TL6943
Sturminster Common *Dorset* 9 ST7812
Sturminster Marshall *Dorset* 9 ST9400
Sturminster Newton *Dorset* 9 ST7813
Sturry *Kent* 15 TR1760
Sturton *Humb* 56 SE9704
Sturton by Stow *Lincs* 50 SK8980
Sturton le Steeple *Notts* 50 SK7884
Stuston *Suffk* 33 TM1378
Stutton *N York* 55 SE4741
Styal *Ches* 47 SJ8383
Stynie *Gramp* 94 NJ3360
Styrrup *Notts* 49 SK6090
Succoth *Strath* 80 NN2905
Suckley *H & W* 28 SO7251
Sudborough *Nhants* 40 SP9682
Sudbourne *Suffk* 33 TM4153
Sudbrook *Gwent* 19 ST5087
Sudbrook *Lincs* 50 SK9744
Sudbrooke *Lincs* 50 TF0276
Sudbury *Derbys* 38 SK1632
Sudbury *Gt Lon* 23 TQ1685
Sudbury *Suffk* 32 TL8741
Suddie *Highld* 93 NH6554
Suddington *H & W* 28 SO8463
Sudgrove *Gloucs* 28 SO9307
Suffield *N York* 63 SE9890
Suffield *Norfk* 43 TG2332
Sugdon *Shrops* 37 SJ6014
Sugnall *Staffs* 37 SJ7931
Sugwas Pool *H & W* 27 SO4541
Suishnish *Highld* 84 NG5816
Sulby *IOM* 52 SC3894
Sulgrave *Nhants* 29 SP5545
Sulham *Berks* 21 SU6474
Sulhamstead Abbots *Berks* 21 SU6467
Sulhamstead Bannister *Berks* 21 SU6368
Sullom *Shet* 103 HU3573
Sullom Voe *Shet* 103 HU4075
Sully *S Glam* 19 ST1568
Summerbridge *N York* 55 SE2062
Summercourt *Cnwll* 3 SW8856
Summerfield *Norfk* 42 TF7538
Summerhouse *Dur* 61 NZ2019
Summerleaze *Gwent* 19 ST4284
Summersdale *W Susx* 11 SU8606
Summerseat *Gt Man* 54 SD7914
Summertown *Oxon* 29 SP5009
Sunadale *Strath* 72 NR8145
Sunbiggin *Cumb* 60 NY6508
Sunbury *Surrey* 22 TQ1169
Sundaywell *D & G* 66 NX8284
Sunderland *Cumb* 58 NY1735
Sunderland *Lancs* 53 SD4255
Sunderland *Strath* 70 NR2464
Sunderland *T & W* 69 NZ3957
Sunderland Bridge *Dur* 61 NZ2637
Sundhope *Border* 75 NT3325
Sundridge *Kent* 23 TQ4858
Sunk Island *Humb* 57 TA2618
Sunningdale *Surrey* 22 SU9567
Sunninghill *Surrey* 22 SU9367
Sunningwell *Oxon* 21 SP4900
Sunniside *Dur* 61 NZ1438
Sunny Bank *Cumb* 58 SD2992
Sunnyhill *Derbys* 39 SK3332
Sunnyhurst *Lancs* 54 SD6722
Sunnylaw *Cent* 81 NS7998
Sunnymead *Oxon* 29 SP5010
Sunwick *Border* 77 NT9052
Surbiton *Gt Lon* 23 TQ1867
Surfleet *Lincs* 41 TF2528
Surlingham *Norfk* 43 TG3106
Surrex *Essex* 24 TL8722
Sustead *Norfk* 43 TG1837
Susworth *Lincs* 50 SE8302
Sutcombe *Devon* 6 SS3412
Sutcombemill *Devon* 6 SS3411
Sutterby *Lincs* 51 TF3872
Sutterton *Lincs* 41 TF2835
Sutton *Beds* 31 TL2247
Sutton *Cambs* 40 TL0998
Sutton *Cambs* 41 TL4479
Sutton *Devon* 5 SX7042
Sutton *Dyfed* 16 SM9116
Sutton *E Susx* 13 TV4999
Sutton *Gt Lon* 23 TQ2564
Sutton *Kent* 15 TR3349
Sutton *N York* 55 SE4925
Sutton *Norfk* 43 TG3823
Sutton *Notts* 40 SK7637
Sutton *Notts* 49 SK6784
Sutton *Oxon* 29 SP4106
Sutton *Shrops* 37 SJ6632
Sutton *Shrops* 37 SO7286
Sutton *Staffs* 37 SJ7622
Sutton *Suffk* 33 TM3046
Sutton *W Susx* 12 SU9715
Sutton Bassett *Nhants* 40 SP7790
Sutton Benger *Wilts* 20 ST9478
Sutton Bingham *Somset* 8 ST5411
Sutton Bonington *Notts* 39 SK5025
Sutton Bridge *Lincs* 41 TF4821
Sutton Cheney *Leics* 39 SK4100
Sutton Coldfield *W Mids* 38 SP1296
Sutton Courtenay *Oxon* 21 SU5093
Sutton Grange *N York* 61 SE2873
Sutton Green *Surrey* 22 TQ0054
Sutton Howgrave *N York* 62 SE3179
Sutton Maddock *Shrops* 37 SJ7201
Sutton Mallet *Somset* 19 ST3736
Sutton Mandeville *Wilts* 9 ST9828
Sutton Montis *Somset* 9 ST6224
Sutton Scotney *Hants* 10 SU4639
Sutton St. Edmund *Lincs* 41 TF3613
Sutton St. James *Lincs* 41 TF3918
Sutton St. Nicholas *H & W* 27 SO5245
Sutton Street *Kent* 14 TQ8055
Sutton Valence *Kent* 14 TQ8149
Sutton Veny *Wilts* 20 ST9041
Sutton Waldron *Dorset* 9 ST8615
Sutton Weaver *Ches* 47 SJ5479
Sutton Wick *Avon* 19 ST5758

Place	Pg	Grid
Sutton Wick Oxon	21	SU4894
Sutton at Hone Kent	23	TQ5569
Sutton in Ashfield Notts	49	SK4959
Sutton le Marsh Lincs	51	TF5280
Sutton on Sea Lincs	51	TF5181
Sutton on Trent Notts	50	SK7965
Sutton on the Hill Derbys	39	SK2333
Sutton upon Derwent Humb	56	SE7046
Sutton-in-Craven N York	55	SE0044
Sutton-on-Hull Humb	57	TA1113
Sutton-on-Hull Humb	57	TA1132
Sutton-on-the-Forest N York	56	SE5864
Sutton-under-Brailes Warwks	29	SP3037
Sutton-under-Whitestonecliffe N York	62	SE4882
Swaby Lincs	51	TF3877
Swadlincote Derbys	39	SK3019
Swaffham Norfk	42	TF8209
Swaffham Bulbeck Cambs	31	TL5562
Swaffham Prior Cambs	31	TL5764
Swafield Norfk	43	TG2832
Swainby N York	62	NZ4701
Swainsthorpe Norfk	43	TG2201
Swainswick Avon	20	ST7668
Swalcliffe Oxon	29	SP3737
Swalecliffe Kent	15	TR1367
Swallow Lincs	57	TA1703
Swallow Beck Lincs	50	SK9567
Swallow Nest S York	49	SK4584
Swallowcliffe Wilts	9	ST9626
Swallowfield Berks	22	SU7264
Swallows Cross Essex	24	TQ6199
Swan Green Ches	47	SJ7373
Swan Village W Mids	38	SO9992
Swanage Dorset	9	SZ0278
Swanbourne Bucks	30	SP8026
Swanland Humb	56	SE9927
Swanley Kent	23	TQ5168
Swanley Village Kent	23	TQ5269
Swanmore Hants	11	SU5716
Swannington Leics	39	SK4116
Swannington Norfk	43	TG1319
Swanpool Garden Suberb Lincs	50	SK9569
Swanscombe Kent	14	TQ6074
Swansea W Glam	18	SS6592
Swanton Abbot Norfk	43	TG2625
Swanton Morley Norfk	43	TG0117
Swanton Novers Norfk	42	TG0231
Swanwick Derbys	49	SK4053
Swanwick Hants	11	SU5109
Swarby Lincs	50	TF0440
Swardeston Norfk	43	TG2002
Swarkestone Derbys	39	SK3728
Swarland Nthumb	69	NU1602
Swarraton Hants	11	SU5637
Swarthmoor Cumb	58	SD2277
Swaton Lincs	40	TF1337
Swavesey Cambs	31	TL3668
Sway Hants	10	SZ2798
Swayfield Lincs	40	SK9922
Swaythling Hants	10	SU4315
Sweetham Devon	7	SX8899
Sweethaws E Susx	13	TQ5028
Sweets Cnwll	6	SX1595
Sweetshouse Cnwll	3	SX0861
Swefling Suffk	33	TM3463
Swepstone Leics	39	SK3610
Swerford Oxon	29	SP3731
Swettenham Ches	47	SJ8067
Swffryd Gwent	19	ST2199
Swiftsden E Susx	14	TQ7228
Swilland Suffk	33	TM1853
Swillington W York	55	SE3830
Swimbridge Devon	6	SS6229
Swimbridge Newland Devon	6	SS6230
Swinbrook Oxon	29	SP2812
Swinderby Lincs	50	SK8663
Swindon Gloucs	28	SO9325
Swindon Staffs	38	SO8690
Swindon Wilts	20	SU1484
Swine Humb	57	TA1335
Swinefleet Humb	56	SE7621
Swineford Avon	20	ST6968
Swineshead Beds	30	TL0565
Swineshead Lincs	51	TF2340
Swineshead Bridge Lincs	51	TF2142
Swiney Highld	100	ND2335
Swinford Leics	39	SP6779
Swingfield Minnis Kent	15	TR2142
Swingfield Street Kent	15	TR2143
Swingleton Green Suffk	32	TL9647
Swinhill Strath	74	NS7748
Swinhoe Nthumb	77	NU2128
Swinithwaite N York	61	SE0489
Swinscoe Staffs	48	SK1348
Swinside Cumb	58	NY2421
Swinstead Lincs	40	TF0122
Swinton Border	77	NT8447
Swinton Gt Man	47	SD7701
Swinton N York	61	SE2179
Swinton N York	63	SE7573
Swinton S York	49	SK4599
Swithland Leics	39	SK5413
Swordale Highld	92	NH5765
Swordland Highld	85	NM7891
Swordly Highld	99	NC7463
Sworton Heath Ches	47	SJ6984
Swynnerton Staffs	38	SJ8535
Sychtyn Powys	35	SH9907
Syde Gloucs	28	SO9511
Sydenham Gt Lon	23	TQ3571
Sydenham Oxon	22	SP7301
Sydenham Damerel Devon	4	SX4075
Syderstone Norfk	42	TF8332
Sydling St. Nicholas Dorset	8	SY6399
Sydmonton Hants	21	SU4857
Syerston Notts	50	SK7447
Sykehouse S York	56	SE6216
Symbister Shet	103	HU5462
Symington Strath	73	NS3831
Symington Strath	75	NS9935
Symonds Yat H & W	27	SO5515
Symondsbury Dorset	8	SY4493
Synton Border	76	NT4822
Syre Highld	99	NC6943
Syreford Gloucs	28	SP0320
Syresham Nhants	29	SP6241
Syston Leics	39	SK6211
Syston Lincs	50	SK9240
Sytchampton H & W	28	SO8466
Sywell Nhants	30	SP8267

T

Place	Pg	Grid
Tackley Oxon	29	SP4720
Tacolneston Norfk	43	TM1495
Tadcaster N York	55	SE4843
Tadley Hants	21	SU6061
Tadlow Cambs	31	TL2847
Tadmarton Oxon	29	SP3937
Tadworth Surrey	23	TQ2356
Tafarnaubach M Glam	26	SO1110
Taff Merthyr Garden Villa M Glam	18	ST1198
Taff's Well M Glam	18	ST1283
Tafolwern Powys	35	SH8902
Tai'n-lon Gwynd	44	SH4450
Tai'r Bull Powys	26	SN9926
Taibach W Glam	18	SS7788
Tain Highld	97	NH7781
Tain Highld	100	ND2266
Takeley Essex	24	TL5621
Takeley Street Essex	24	TL5421
Tal-y-Bont Gwynd	45	SH7668
Tal-y-Bont Gwynd	45	SH7668
Tal-y-Waun Gwent	54	SO2604
Tal-y-bont Gwynd	44	SH5921
Tal-y-bont Gwynd	45	SH6070
Tal-y-cafn Gwynd	45	SH7971
Tal-y-coed Gwent	27	SO4115
Tal-y-garn M Glam	18	ST0379

Place	Pg	Grid
Talachddu Powys	26	SO0833
Talacre Clwyd	46	SJ1283
Talaton Devon	7	SY0699
Talbenny Dyfed	16	SM8412
Taleford Devon	6	SX0996
Talerddig Powys	35	SH9300
Talgarreg Dyfed	17	SN4251
Talgarth Powys	27	SO1533
Taliesin Dyfed	35	SN6591
Talisker Highld	84	NG3230
Talke Staffs	47	SJ8352
Talke Pits Staffs	47	SJ8352
Talkin Cumb	67	NY5457
Talla Linnfoots Border	75	NT1320
Talladale Highld	91	NG9270
Tallaminnoc Strath	64	NX4098
Tallarn Green Clwyd	46	SJ4444
Talley Dyfed	17	SN6332
Tallington Lincs	40	TF0908
Talmine Highld	99	NC5863
Talog Dyfed	17	SN3325
Talsarn Dyfed	34	SN5456
Talsarnau Gwynd	45	SH6135
Talskiddy Cnwll	3	SW9165
Talwrn Gwynd	44	SH4877
Talybont Dyfed	35	SN6589
Talybont-on-Usk Powys	26	SO1122
Talysarn Gwynd	44	SH4852
Tamerton Foliot Devon	4	SX4761
Tamworth Staffs	39	SK2004
Tan Hill N York	60	NY8907
Tan Office Green Suffk	32	TL7858
Tan-y-fron Clwyd	45	SH9664
Tan-y-groes Dyfed	17	SN2849
Tandlemuir Strath	73	NS3361
Tandridge Surrey	13	TQ3750
Tanfield Dur	69	NZ1855
Tanfield Lea Dur	69	NZ1854
Tangley Hants	21	SU3252
Tangmere W Susx	11	SU9006
Tangusdale W Isls	102	NF6500
Tankersley S York	103	HY5108
Tankerton Kent	15	TR1167
Tannach Highld	100	ND3247
Tannachie Gramp	89	NO7884
Tannadice Tays	89	NO4758
Tanner Green H & W	38	SP0874
Tannington Suffk	33	TM2467
Tannochside Strath	74	NS6962
Tansley Derbys	49	SK3259
Tansor Nhants	40	TL0590
Tantobie Dur	69	NZ1754
Tanton N York	62	NZ5210
Tanworth in Arden Warwks	28	SP1170
Tanygrisiau Gwynd	45	SH4945
Taplow Bucks	22	SU9182
Tarbert Strath	71	NR6182
Tarbert Strath	72	NR6551
Tarbert Strath	71	NR8668
Tarbert W Isls	90	NB1500
Tarbet Highld	85	NM7992
Tarbet Highld	91	NC1649
Tarbet Highld	86	NN3104
Tarbolton Strath	73	NS4327
Tarbrax Strath	75	NT0255
Tardebigge H & W	28	SO9969
Tardy Gate Lancs	53	SD5426
Tarfside Tays	89	NO4979
Tarland Gramp	89	NJ4804
Tarleton Lancs	53	SD4520
Tarlton Gloucs	20	ST9599
Tarnock Somset	19	ST3852
Tarns Cumb	67	NY1247
Tarporley Ches	47	SJ5562
Tarr Somset	7	SS8632
Tarr Somset	8	ST1030
Tarrant Crawford Dorset	9	ST9203
Tarrant Gunville Dorset	9	ST9212
Tarrant Hinton Dorset	9	ST9310
Tarrant Keynston Dorset	9	ST9204
Tarrant Launceston Dorset	9	ST9409
Tarrant Monkton Dorset	9	ST9408
Tarrant Rawston Dorset	9	ST9306
Tarrant Rushton Dorset	9	ST9305
Tarring Neville E Susx	13	TQ4404
Tarrington H & W	27	SO6240
Tarrylin Strath	72	NR9621
Tarskavaig Highld	84	NG5810
Tarves Gramp	95	NJ8631
Tarvie Tays	88	NO0164
Tarvin Ches	46	SJ4966
Tasburgh Norfk	43	TM2096
Taston Oxon	29	SP3621
Tatenhill Staffs	39	SK2022
Tathall End Bucks	30	SP8047
Tathwell Lincs	51	TF3281
Tatsfield Surrey	23	TQ4156
Tattenhall Ches	46	SJ4858
Tatterford Norfk	42	TF8628
Tattersett Norfk	42	TF8429
Tattershall Lincs	51	TF2157
Tattershall Thorpe Lincs	51	TF2159
Tattingstone Suffk	25	TM1337
Tattingstone White Horse Suffk	25	TM1338
Tatworth Somset	8	ST3205
Tauchers Gramp	94	NJ3649
Taunton Somset	8	ST2324
Taverham Norfk	43	TG1614
Tavernspite Dyfed	17	SN1812
Tavistock Devon	4	SX4774
Taw green Devon	7	SX6597
Tawstock Devon	6	SS5629
Taxal Derbys	48	SK0079
Taychreggan Hotel Strath	80	NN0421
Tayinloan Strath	72	NR7044
Taynish Strath	71	NR7282
Taynton Gloucs	28	SO7222
Taynton Oxon	29	SP2313
Taynuilt Strath	80	NN0031
Tayport Fife	83	NO4628
Tayvallich Strath	71	NR7487
Tealby Lincs	51	TF1590
Teangue Highld	85	NG6609
Teanord Highld	92	NH5964
Tebay Cumb	59	NY6104
Tebworth Beds	30	SP9926
Tedburn St. Mary Devon	7	SX8194
Teddington Gloucs	28	SO9632
Teddington Gt Lon	23	TQ1671
Tedstone Delamere H & W	28	SO6958
Tedstone Wafer H & W	28	SO6759
Teeton Nhants	30	SP6970
Teffont Evias Wilts	9	ST9831
Teffont Magna Wilts	9	ST9832
Tegryn Dyfed	17	SN2233
Teigh Leics	40	SK8615
Teigncombe Devon	5	SX6787
Teigngrace Devon	5	SX8474
Teignmouth Devon	5	SX9473
Telford Shrops	37	SJ6908
Tellisford Somset	20	ST8055
Telscombe E Susx	13	TQ4003
Tempar Tays	87	NN6857
Templand D & G	66	NY0886
Temple Cnwll	3	SX1473
Temple Loth	75	NT3158
Temple Bar Dyfed	34	SN5354
Temple Cloud Avon	19	ST6157
Temple Ewell Kent	15	TR2844
Temple Grafton Warwks	28	SP1255
Temple Guiting Gloucs	28	SP0928
Temple Hirst N York	56	SE6024
Temple Normanton Derbys	49	SK4167
Temple Pier Highld	92	NH5330
Temple Sowerby Cumb	59	NY6127
Templecombe Somset	9	ST7022
Templehall Tays	73	NO4936
Templeton Devon	7	SS8813
Templeton Dyfed	16	SN1111
Templeton Bridge Devon	7	SS8714
Templetown Dur	69	NZ1049
Tempsford Beds	31	TL1653
Ten Mile Bank Norfk	41	TL5996
Tenbury Wells H & W	27	SO5968
Tenby Dyfed	16	SN1300
Tendring Essex	25	TM1424
Tendring Green Essex	25	TM1326
Tendring Heath Essex	25	TM1326
Tenterden Kent	14	TQ8833

Place	Pg	Grid
Terling Essex	24	TL7715
Ternhill Shrops	37	SJ6332
Terregles D & G	66	NX9377
Terrington N York	56	SE6670
Terrington St. Clement Norfk	41	TF5520
Terrington St. John Norfk	41	TF5514
Terry's Cross W Susx	12	TQ2314
Teston Kent	14	TQ7053
Testwood Hants	10	SU3514
Tetbury Gloucs	20	ST8993
Tetbury Upton Gloucs	20	ST8795
Tetchill Shrops	36	SJ3932
Tetcott Devon	6	SX3396
Tetney Lincs	51	TA3100
Tetsworth Oxon	22	SP6801
Tettenhall W Mids	38	SJ8800
Tettenhall Wood W Mids	38	SO8799
Teversal Notts	49	SK4861
Teversham Cambs	31	TL4958
Teviothead Border	67	NT4005
Tewel Gramp	89	NO8085
Tewin Herts	31	TL2714
Tewkesbury Gloucs	28	SO8933
Teynham Kent	14	TQ9562
Thackthwaite Cumb	58	NY1524
Thakeham W Susx	12	TQ1017
Thame Oxon	22	SP7005
Thames Ditton Surrey	23	TQ1567
Thamesmead Gt Lon	23	TQ4780
Thanington Kent	15	TR1356
Thankerton Strath	75	NS9737
Tharston Norfk	43	TM1894
Thatcham Berks	21	SU5167
Thaxted Essex	24	TL6131
The Abbey Gwynd	45	SH7865
The Beeches Gloucs	20	SP0201
The Brunt Loth	76	NT6873
The Bryn Gwent	27	SO3309
The Bungalow IOM	52	SC3987
The Butts Gloucs	28	SO8916
The Chart Surrey	13	TQ4251
The City Bucks	22	SU7896
The Corner Shrops	36	SO4387
The Crossways H & W	27	SO3538
The Den Strath	73	NS3251
The Fence Gloucs	27	SO5405
The Forstal E Susx	23	TQ5455
The Forstal Kent	15	TR0439
The Green Essex	24	TL7719
The Grove H & W	28	SO8740
The Hirsel Border	77	NT8240
The Holt Berks	22	SU8078
The Howe IOM	52	SC1967
The Lees Bucks	22	SP9004
The Lochs Gramp	94	NJ3020
The Marsh Ches	48	SJ8463
The Mound Highld	97	NH7798
The Mumbles W Glam	17	SS6187
The Mythe Gloucs	28	SO8934
The Nant Clwyd	46	SJ2850
The Neuk Gramp	89	NO7397
The Pill Gwent	19	ST4887
The Quarry Gloucs	20	ST7399
The Reddings Gloucs	28	SO9021
The Shoe Wilts	20	ST8074
The Stair Kent	13	TQ6037
The Stocks Kent	14	TQ9127
The Wrythe Gt Lon	23	TQ2765
Theakston N York	61	SE3085
Theale Berks	21	SU6471
Theale Somset	19	ST4646
Thearne Humb	57	TA0736
Theberton Suffk	33	TM4365
Theddingworth Leics	39	SP6685
Theddlethorpe All Saints Lincs	51	TF4688
Theddlethorpe St. Helen Lincs	51	TF4788
Thelbridge Barton Devon	7	SS7812
Thelbridge Cross Devon	7	SS7812
Thelnetham Suffk	32	TM0178
Thelveton Norfk	33	TM1681
Thelwall Ches	47	SJ6587
Themelthorpe Norfk	43	TG0524
Thenford Nhants	29	SP5241
Theobald's Green Wilts	20	SU0268
Therfield Herts	31	TL3337
Thetford Norfk	32	TL8783
Theydon Bois Essex	23	TQ4499
Thickwood Wilts	20	ST8272
Thimbleby Lincs	51	TF2369
Thimbleby N York	62	SE4495
Thingwall Mersyd	46	SJ2884
Thirlby N York	62	SE4883
Thirlestane Border	76	NT5647
Thirlspot Cumb	58	NY3118
Thirn N York	61	SE2185
Thistleton Lancs	53	SD4037
Thistleton Leics	40	SK9117
Thistley Green Suffk	32	TL6776
Thixendale N York	56	SE8461
Thockrington Nthumb	68	NY9578
Tholomas Drove Cambs	41	TF4006
Tholthorpe N York	55	SE4766
Thomas Town Warwks	28	SO0763
Thomastown Gramp	94	NJ5737
Thompson Norfk	42	TL9296
Thomshill Gramp	94	NJ2157
Thong Kent	14	TQ6770
Thongsleigh Devon	7	SS9011
Thoralby N York	61	SE0086
Thoresthorpe Lincs	51	TF4578
Thoresway Lincs	50	TF1696
Thorganby Lincs	51	TF2097
Thorganby N York	56	SE6841
Thorgill N York	62	SE7096
Thorington Suffk	33	TM4174
Thorington Street Suffk	25	TM0135
Thorlby N York	54	SD9653
Thorley Herts	31	TL4719
Thorley IOW	10	SZ3688
Thorley Street IOW	10	SZ3788
Thormanby N York	62	SE4974
Thornage Norfk	42	TG0536
Thornborough Bucks	30	SP7433
Thornborough N York	61	SE2979
Thornbury Avon	19	ST6490
Thornbury Devon	6	SS3908
Thornbury Devon	6	SS4008
Thornbury H & W	27	SO6159
Thornbury W York	55	SE1933
Thornby Cumb	67	NY2951
Thornby Nhants	39	SP6675
Thorncliff Staffs	48	SK0158
Thorncombe Street Surrey	12	TQ0042
Thorncott Green Beds	30	TL1547
Thorndon Suffk	33	TM1469
Thorndon Cross Devon	4	SX5293
Thorne S York	56	SE6813
Thorne Somset	8	ST6217
Thorne St. Margaret Somset	7	ST0920
Thorner W York	55	SE3740
Thornes Staffs	38	SK0703
Thorney Cambs	41	TF2804
Thorney Notts	50	SK8572
Thorney Somset	8	ST4222
Thorney Hill Hants	10	SZ2099
Thornfalcon Somset	8	ST2723
Thornford Dorset	9	ST6013
Thorngumbald Humb	57	TA2026
Thornham Norfk	42	TF7343
Thornham Magna Suffk	33	TM1071
Thornham Parva Suffk	33	TM1072
Thornhaugh Cambs	40	TF0600
Thornhill Cent	81	NN6600
Thornhill D & G	66	NX8795
Thornhill Derbys	48	SK1983
Thornhill Hants	10	SU4612
Thornhill W York	55	SE2418
Thornholme Humb	57	TA1163
Thornicombe Dorset	9	ST8703
Thornington Nthumb	77	NT8833
Thornley Dur	61	NZ1137
Thornley Dur	62	NZ3639
Thornliebank Strath	74	NS5459
Thorns Green Gt Man	47	SJ7984
Thornsett Derbys	48	SK0187
Thornthwaite Cumb	58	NY2225
Thornthwaite N York	56	SE5618

Place	Pg	Grid
Thornthwaite N York	55	SE1758
Thornton Bucks	30	SP7435
Thornton Cleve	62	NZ4713
Thornton Fife	83	NT2897
Thornton Humb	56	SE7545
Thornton Lancs	53	SD3342
Thornton Leics	39	SK4607
Thornton Lincs	51	TF2467
Thornton Nthumb	77	NT9547
Thornton Tays	88	NO3946
Thornton W York	55	SE0932
Thornton W York	55	SE1032
Thornton Curtis Humb	57	TA0017
Thornton Dale N York	63	SE8383
Thornton Heath Gt Lon	23	TQ3168
Thornton Hough Mersyd	46	SJ3081
Thornton Rust N York	61	SD9689
Thornton Steward N York	61	SE1787
Thornton Watlass N York	61	SE2385
Thornton le Moor Lincs	50	TF0496
Thornton-in-Craven N York	54	SD9048
Thornton-in-Lonsdale N York	60	SD6873
Thornton-le-Beans N York	62	SE3990
Thornton-le-Clay N York	62	SE6875
Thornton-le-Moor N York	62	SE3988
Thornton-le-Moors Ches	46	SJ4474
Thornton-le-Street N York	62	SE4186
Thorntonhall Strath	74	NS5955
Thorntonloch Loth	76	NT7574
Thornydkes Border	76	NT6148
Thornythwaite Cumb	59	NY3922
Thoroton Notts	50	SK7642
Thorp Arch W York	55	SE4346
Thorpe Derbys	48	SK1550
Thorpe Humb	56	SE9946
Thorpe N York	54	SE0161
Thorpe Notts	50	SK7649
Thorpe Surrey	22	TQ0168
Thorpe Abbotts Norfk	33	TM1979
Thorpe Acre Leics	39	SK5120
Thorpe Arnold Leics	40	SK7720
Thorpe Audlin W York	55	SE4715
Thorpe Bassett N York	63	SE8673
Thorpe Bay Essex	24	TQ9185
Thorpe Constantine Staffs	39	SK2508
Thorpe End Norfk	43	TG2811
Thorpe Green Essex	25	TM1623
Thorpe Green Lancs	54	SD5823
Thorpe Green Suffk	32	TL9354
Thorpe Hesley S York	49	SK3796
Thorpe Langton Leics	40	SP7492
Thorpe Lea Surrey	22	TQ0270
Thorpe Malsor Nhants	30	SP8378
Thorpe Mandeville Nhants	29	SP5344
Thorpe Market Norfk	43	TG2435
Thorpe Morieux Suffk	32	TL9453
Thorpe Perrow N York	61	SE2685
Thorpe Salvin S York	49	SK5281
Thorpe Satchville Leics	39	SK7311
Thorpe St. Andrew Norfk	43	TG2608
Thorpe St. Peter Lincs	51	TF4860
Thorpe Thewles Cleve	62	NZ4023
Thorpe Tilney Lincs	50	TF1257
Thorpe Underwood N York	55	SE4659
Thorpe Underwood Nhants	40	SP7880
Thorpe Waterville Nhants	40	TL0281
Thorpe Willoughby N York	56	SE5731
Thorpe by Water Leics	40	SP8996
Thorpe in Balne S York	56	SE5810
Thorpe in the Fallows Lincs	50	SK9180
Thorpe le Street Humb	56	SE8343
Thorpe on the Hill Lincs	50	SK9065
Thorpe on the Hill W York	55	SE3125
Thorpe-le-Soken Essex	25	TM1722
Thorpeness Suffk	33	TM4759
Thorrington Essex	25	TM0920
Thorverton Devon	7	SS9202
Thrandeston Suffk	33	TM1176
Thrapston Nhants	30	SP9978
Threapwood Ches	46	SJ4344
Threave Strath	73	NS3406
Threapwood Staffs	48	SK0342
Three Ashes H & W	27	SO5123
Three Bridges W Susx	12	TQ2837
Three Chimneys Kent	14	TQ8238
Three Clocks Powys	27	SO1737
Three Crosses W Glam	17	SS5794
Three Cups Corner E Susx	13	TQ6320
Three Hammers Cnwll	4	SX2387
Three Leg Cross E Susx	14	TQ6831
Three Mile Cross Berks	22	SU7167
Three Miletown Loth	75	NT0675
Three Oaks E Susx	14	TQ8314
Threekingham Lincs	40	TF0836
Threepwood Border	76	NT5143
Threlkeld Cumb	58	NY3225
Threshfield N York	54	SD9963
Thrigby Norfk	43	TG4612
Thringarth Dur	60	NY9322
Thringstone Leics	39	SK4217
Thrintoft N York	61	SE3193
Thriplow Cambs	31	TL4346
Throcking Herts	31	TL3330
Throckley T & W	69	NZ1566
Throckmorton H & W	28	SO9749
Throop Dorset	9	SY8292
Throop Dorset	9	SZ1294
Throphill Nthumb	69	NZ1386
Thropton Nthumb	68	NU0202
Throsk D & G	66	NX8784
Throwleigh Devon	5	SX6690
Throwley Forstal Kent	15	TQ9854
Thrumpton Notts	39	SK5131
Thrumster Highld	100	ND3345
Thrunscoe Humb	51	TA3001
Thrup Oxon	21	SU2998
Thrupp Gloucs	20	SO8603
Thrushesbush Essex	23	TL4909
Thrushgill Lancs	54	SD6462
Thrussington Leics	39	SK6515
Thruxton H & W	27	SO4334
Thruxton Hants	21	SU2845
Thrybergh S York	49	SK4695
Thulston Derbys	39	SK4030
Thundergarth Mains D & G	67	NY1780
Thundersley Essex	24	TQ7988
Thurcaston Leics	39	SK5610
Thurcroft S York	49	SK4988
Thurdistoft Highld	100	ND2167
Thurgarton Norfk	43	TG1835
Thurgarton Notts	49	SK6949
Thurgoland S York	49	SE2801
Thurlaston Leics	39	SP5099
Thurlaston Warwks	39	SP4671
Thurlbear Somset	8	ST2621
Thurlby Lincs	40	TF0916
Thurlby Lincs	50	SK9061
Thurlby Lincs	51	TF4876
Thurlestone Devon	5	SX6742
Thurloxton Somset	8	ST2730
Thurlstone S York	49	SE2303
Thurlton Norfk	43	TM4198
Thurlwood Ches	47	SJ8057
Thurmaston Leics	39	SK6109
Thurnby Leics	39	SK6403
Thurne Norfk	43	TG4015
Thurnham Kent	14	TQ8057
Thurning Nhants	40	TL0883
Thurning Norfk	42	TG0829
Thurnscoe S York	49	SE4605
Thursby Cumb	67	NY3250
Thursden Lancs	54	SD9035
Thursford Norfk	42	TF9833
Thursley Surrey	11	SU9039
Thurso Highld	100	ND1168
Thurstaston Mersyd	46	SJ2484
Thurston Suffk	32	TL9365
Thurstonfield Cumb	67	NY3156
Thurstonland W York	55	SE1610
Thurton Norfk	43	TG3200
Thurvaston Derbys	39	SK2437
Thuxton Norfk	42	TG0307
Thwaite Suffk	33	TM1168
Thwaite N York	60	SD8998
Thwaite Head Cumb	58	NY3490
Thwaite St. Mary Norfk	43	TM3395

Thwing *Humb* ... 57 TA0570
Tibbermore *Tays* ... 82 NO0523
Tibbers *D & G* ... 66 NX8696
Tibberton *Gloucs* ... 28 SO7521
Tibberton *H & W* ... 28 SO9057
Tibberton *Shrops* ... 37 SJ6820
Tibbie Shiels Inn *Border* ... 75 NT2320
Tibenham *Norfk* ... 33 TM1389
Tibshelf *Derbys* ... 49 SK4361
Tibthorpe *Humb* ... 56 SE9855
Ticehurst *E Susx* ... 14 TQ6930
Tichborne *Hants* ... 11 SU5730
Tickencote *Leics* ... 40 SK9809
Tickhill *S York* ... 49 SK5993
Ticklerton *Shrops* ... 37 SO4891
Ticknall *Derbys* ... 39 SK3524
Tickton *Humb* ... 57 TA0641
Tidcombe *Wilts* ... 21 SU2858
Tidcombe *Wilts* ... 21 SU2858
Tiddington *Oxon* ... 29 SP6404
Tiddington *Warwks* ... 29 SP2255
Tideford *Cnwll* ... 4 SX3459
Tidenham *Gloucs* ... 19 ST5595
Tideswell *Derbys* ... 48 SK1575
Tidmarsh *Berks* ... 21 SU6374
Tidmington *Warwks* ... 29 SP2538
Tiers Cross *Dyfed* ... 16 SM9010
Tiffield *Nhants* ... 30 SP6951
Tifty *Gramp* ... 95 NJ7740
Tigerton *Tays* ... 89 NO5364
Tigharry *W Isls* ... 102 NF7171
Tighnabruaich *Strath* ... 71 NR9873
Tighnafiline *Highld* ... 91 NG8789
Tigley *Devon* ... 5 SX7560
Tilbrook *Cambs* ... 30 TL0769
Tilbury *Essex* ... 14 TQ6476
Tilbury Green *Essex* ... 32 TL7441
Tile Hill *W Mids* ... 39 SP2777
Tilehurst *Berks* ... 22 SU6673
Tilford *Surrey* ... 11 SU8743
Tilgate *W Susx* ... 12 TQ2735
Tilham Street *Somset* ... 82 ST5535
Tillicoultry *Cent* ... 25 NS9297
Tillingham *Essex* ... 25 TL9904
Tillington *H & W* ... 27 SO4644
Tillington *W Susx* ... 12 SU9621
Tillington Common *H & W* ... 27 SO4545
Tillybirloch *Gramp* ... 95 NJ6807
Tillycairn *Gramp* ... 89 NO4697
Tillyfourie *Gramp* ... 94 NJ6412
Tillygreig *Gramp* ... 95 NJ8823
Tillyrie *Tays* ... 82 NO1006
Tilmanstone *Kent* ... 15 TR3051
Tilney All Saints *Norfk* ... 41 TF5618
Tilney High End *Norfk* ... 41 TF5617
Tilney St. Lawrence *Norfk* ... 41 TF5414
Tilshead *Wilts* ... 20 SU0347
Tilstock *Shrops* ... 37 SJ5437
Tilston *Ches* ... 46 SJ4651
Tilstone Fearnall *Ches* ... 47 SJ5660
Tilsworth *Beds* ... 30 SP9724
Tilton on the Hill *Leics* ... 40 SK7405
Tiltups End *Gloucs* ... 20 ST8497
Timberland *Lincs* ... 50 TF1258
Timbersbrook *Ches* ... 48 SJ8962
Timberscombe *Somset* ... 7 SS9542
Timble *N York* ... 55 SE1753
Timpanheck *D & G* ... 67 NY3274
Timperley *Gt Man* ... 47 SJ7888
Timsbury *Avon* ... 20 ST6658
Timsbury *Hants* ... 10 SU3424
Timsgarry *W Isls* ... 102 NB0634
Timworth *Suffk* ... 32 TL8669
Timworth Green *Suffk* ... 32 TL8669
Tincleton *Dorset* ... 9 SY7690
Tindale *Cumb* ... 68 NY6259
Tindale Crescent *Dur* ... 61 NZ2027
Tingewick *Bucks* ... 29 SP6532
Tingley *W York* ... 55 SE2826
Tingrith *Beds* ... 30 TL0032
Tinhay *Devon* ... 4 SX3985
Tinhay *Devon* ... 4 SX3985
Tinkersley *Derbys* ... 49 SK2665
Tinsley *S York* ... 49 SK4090
Tinsley Green *W Susx* ... 12 TQ2839
Tintagel *Cnwll* ... 4 SX0588
Tintern Parva *Gwent* ... 19 SO5200
Tintinhull *Somset* ... 8 ST5019
Tintwistle *Derbys* ... 48 SK0297
Tinwald *D & G* ... 66 NY0081
Tinwell *Leics* ... 40 TF0006
Tipp's End *Norfk* ... 41 TL5095
Tippacott *Devon* ... 7 SS7646
Tipton Green *W Mids* ... 38 SO9492
Tipton St. John *Devon* ... 8 SY0991
Tiptree *Essex* ... 24 TL8816
Tiptree Heath *Essex* ... 24 TL8815
Tirabad *Powys* ... 26 SN8741
Tiretigan *Strath* ... 71 NR7262
Tirley *Gloucs* ... 28 SO8328
Tiroran *Strath* ... 79 NM4721
Tirphil *M Glam* ... 18 SO1303
Tirril *Cumb* ... 59 NY5026
Tisbury *Wilts* ... 9 ST9429
Tisman's Common *W Susx* ... 12 TQ0732
Tissington *Derbys* ... 48 SK1752
Titchberry *Devon* ... 6 SS2427
Titchfield *Hants* ... 11 SU5305
Titchmarsh *Nhants* ... 40 TL0279
Titchwell *Norfk* ... 42 TF7643
Tithby *Notts* ... 49 SK6936
Titmore End *Herts* ... 31 TL2027
Titsey *Surrey* ... 23 TQ4054
Tittensor *Staffs* ... 38 SJ8738
Tittleshall *Norfk* ... 42 TF8921
Titton *H & W* ... 28 SO8270
Tiverton *Ches* ... 47 SJ5560
Tiverton *Devon* ... 59 SS9512
Tivetshall St. Margaret *Norfk* ... 33 TM1787
Tivetshall St. Mary *Norfk* ... 33 TM1686
Tivington *Somset* ... 7 SS9345
Tixall *Staffs* ... 38 SJ9722
Tixover *Leics* ... 40 SK9700
Toab *Shet* ... 103 HU3811
Toadhole *Derbys* ... 49 SK3957
Toadmoor *Derbys* ... 49 SK3450
Tobermory *Strath* ... 79 NM5055
Toberonochy *Strath* ... 79 NM7408
Tobson *W Isls* ... 102 NB1438
Tocher *Gramp* ... 95 NJ6932
Tochieneal *Gramp* ... 94 NJ5165
Tockenham *Wilts* ... 20 SU0379
Tocketts *Cleve* ... 62 NZ6117
Tockington *Avon* ... 19 ST6086
Tockwith *N York* ... 55 SE4652
Todber *Dorset* ... 9 ST7920
Todburn *Nthumb* ... 69 NZ1195
Toddington *Beds* ... 30 TL0128
Toddington *Gloucs* ... 28 SP0343
Todds Green *Herts* ... 31 TL2126
Todenham *Gloucs* ... 29 SP2436
Todhills *Cumb* ... 67 NY3663
Todhills *Tays* ... 83 NO4239
Todmorden *W York* ... 54 SD9324
Todwick *S York* ... 49 SK4984
Toft *Cambs* ... 31 TL3655
Toft *Ches* ... 47 SJ7676
Toft *Lincs* ... 40 TF0617
Toft *Shet* ... 103 HU4376
Toft *Warwks* ... 29 SP4870
Toft Hill *Dur* ... 61 NZ1428
Toft Monks *Norfk* ... 33 TM4295
Toft next Newton *Lincs* ... 50 TF0488
Toftrees *Norfk* ... 42 TF8927
Tofts *Highld* ... 100 ND3668
Toftwood *Norfk* ... 42 TF9911
Togston *Nthumb* ... 69 NU2402
Tokavaig *Highld* ... 84 NG6011
Tokers Green *Oxon* ... 22 SU7077
Toll Bar *S York* ... 55 SE5507
Tolland *Somset* ... 8 ST1032
Tolland Royal *Wilts* ... 9 SY1232
Toller Fratrum *Dorset* ... 8 SY5797
Toller Porcorum *Dorset* ... 8 SY5697
Toller Whelme *Dorset* ... 8 ST5101
Tollerton *N York* ... 55 SE5164
Tollerton *Notts* ... 39 SK6134
Tollesbury *Essex* ... 25 TL9510

Tolleshunt D'Arcy *Essex* ... 25 TL9312
Tolleshunt Knight *Essex* ... 24 TL9114
Tolleshunt Major *Essex* ... 24 TL9011
Tolpuddle *Dorset* ... 9 SY7994
Tolsta *W Isls* ... 102 NB5349
Tolstachaolais *W Isls* ... 102 NB1938
Tolver *Cnwll* ... 2 SW4332
Tolworth *Gt Lon* ... 23 TQ1966
Tomakrock *Tays* ... 82 NN8821
Tomatin *Highld* ... 93 NH8028
Tomchrasky *Highld* ... 92 NH3512
Tomdoun *Highld* ... 86 NH1501
Tomich *Highld* ... 92 NH3127
Tomich *Highld* ... 93 NH6348
Tomich *Highld* ... 93 NH6971
Tomich *Highld* ... 97 NC6005
Tomintoul *Gramp* ... 88 NO1490
Tomintoul *Gramp* ... 94 NJ1618
Tomlow *Warwks* ... 29 SP4663
Tomnacross *Highld* ... 92 NH5141
Tomnavoulin *Gramp* ... 94 NJ2026
Tondu *M Glam* ... 18 SS8984
Tonedale *Somset* ... 8 ST1221
Tonfanau *Gwynd* ... 34 SH5604
Tong *Kent* ... 14 TQ9556
Tong *Shrops* ... 37 SJ7907
Tong *W York* ... 55 SE2230
Tong Norton *Shrops* ... 37 SJ7908
Tong Street *W York* ... 48 SE1901
Tonge *Leics* ... 39 SK4123
Tongham *Surrey* ... 22 SU8849
Tongland *D & G* ... 65 NX6954
Tongue *Highld* ... 99 NC5957
Tongwynlais *S Glam* ... 18 ST1382
Tonmawr *W Glam* ... 18 SS8096
Tonna *W Glam* ... 18 SS7798
Tonwell *Herts* ... 31 TL3316
Tonypandy *M Glam* ... 18 SS9991
Toot Baldon *Oxon* ... 21 SP5600
Toot Hill *Essex* ... 23 TL5102
Toot Hill *Hants* ... 10 SU3718
Toothill *Wilts* ... 20 SU1283
Tooting *Gt Lon* ... 23 TQ2771
Tooting Bec *Gt Lon* ... 23 TQ2872
Topcliffe *N York* ... 62 SE4076
Topcroft Street *Norfk* ... 33 TM2692
Toppesfield *Essex* ... 24 TL7437
Toprow *Norfk* ... 43 TM1698
Topsham *Devon* ... 5 SX9788
Toravaig *Highld* ... 90 NG4944
Torbay *Devon* ... 5 SX8962
Torbeg *Strath* ... 72 NR8929
Torboll *Highld* ... 97 NH7599
Torbreck *Highld* ... 94 NH8440
Torbryan *Devon* ... 5 SX8266
Torcastle *Highld* ... 86 NH1378
Torcross *Devon* ... 5 SX8242
Tore *Highld* ... 92 NH6052
Torhousemuir *D & G* ... 64 NX3957
Torksey *Lincs* ... 50 SK8378
Torlum *W Isls* ... 102 NF7850
Tormarton *Avon* ... 20 ST7678
Tormitchell *Strath* ... 64 NX2394
Tormore *Strath* ... 72 NR8932
Tornagrain *Highld* ... 93 NH7649
Tornaveen *Gramp* ... 89 NJ6106
Torness *Highld* ... 92 NH5826
Torosay Castle *Strath* ... 79 NM7235
Torpenhow *Cumb* ... 58 NY2039
Torphichen *Loth* ... 75 NS9772
Torphins *Gramp* ... 89 NJ6202
Torpoint *Cnwll* ... 4 SX4355
Torquay *Devon* ... 5 SX9164
Torquhan *Border* ... 76 NT4447
Torr *Devon* ... 4 SX5751
Torran *Highld* ... 90 NG5949
Torrance *Strath* ... 74 NS6174
Torranyard *Strath* ... 73 NS3544
Torre *Somset* ... 7 ST0439
Torridon *Highld* ... 91 NG8055
Torridon House *Highld* ... 91 NG8657
Torrin *Highld* ... 84 NG5720
Torrisdale *Highld* ... 99 NC6761
Torrisdale Square *Strath* ... 72 NR7936
Torrish *Highld* ... 97 NC9718
Torrisholme *Lancs* ... 53 SD4563
Torroble *Highld* ... 97 NC5904
Torrobull *Highld* ... 89 NJ9405
Torryburn *Fife* ... 82 NT0386
Tortan *H & W* ... 38 SO8472
Torteval *Guern* ... 101 SV0000
Torthorwald *D & G* ... 66 NY0378
Tortington *W Susx* ... 12 TQ0005
Tortworth *Avon* ... 20 ST7093
Torver *Cumb* ... 58 SD2894
Torwood *Cent* ... 82 NS8384
Torworth *Notts* ... 49 SK6586
Toscaig *Highld* ... 85 NG7138
Toseland *Cambs* ... 31 TL2362
Tosside *Lancs* ... 54 SD7656
Tostock *Suffk* ... 32 TL9663
Totaig *Highld* ... 90 NG2050
Tote *Highld* ... 90 NG4149
Tote Hill *W Susx* ... 11 SU8624
Totegan *Highld* ... 99 NC8268
Totland *IOW* ... 10 SZ3286
Totley *S York* ... 49 SK3079
Totnes *Devon* ... 5 SX8060
Totronald *Strath* ... 78 NM1656
Totscore *Highld* ... 90 NG3866
Tottenham *Gt Lon* ... 23 TQ3390
Tottenhill *Norfk* ... 42 TF6411
Totteridge *Gt Lon* ... 23 TQ2494
Totternhoe *Beds* ... 30 SP9821
Tottington *Gt Man* ... 54 SD7712
Totton *Hants* ... 10 SU3513
Touchen End *Berks* ... 22 SU8776
Toulton *Somset* ... 8 ST1931
Toulvaddie *Highld* ... 97 NH8880
Toux *Gramp* ... 94 NJ5458
Tovil *Kent* ... 14 TQ7554
Toward *Strath* ... 73 NS1367
Toward Quay *Strath* ... 73 NS1168
Towcester *Nhants* ... 30 SP6948
Towednack *Cnwll* ... 2 SW4838
Towersey *Oxon* ... 22 SP7305
Towie *Gramp* ... 94 NJ4412
Town End *Cambs* ... 41 TL4195
Town End *Cumb* ... 59 SD4484
Town End *Cumb* ... 67 NY3687
Town Head *N York* ... 55 SE1648
Town Kelloe *Dur* ... 62 NZ3637
Town Littleworth *E Susx* ... 13 TQ4111
Town Street *Suffk* ... 32 TL7786
Town Yetholm *Border* ... 76 NT8127
Towngate *Lincs* ... 40 TF1310
Townhead *Cumb* ... 58 NY0736
Townhead *D & G* ... 65 NX6946
Townhead *S York* ... 48 SE1602
Townhead of Greenlaw *D & G* ... 65 NX7465
Townhill *Loth* ... 82 NT1089
Townsend *Somset* ... 19 ST3714
Townshend *Cnwll* ... 2 SW5932
Towthorpe *Humb* ... 56 SE9062
Towthorpe *N York* ... 56 SE6258
Towthorpe *N York* ... 56 SE6258
Towton *N York* ... 55 SE4839
Toy's Hill *Kent* ... 13 TQ4751
Toynton All Saints *Lincs* ... 51 TF3963
Trabboch *Strath* ... 73 NS4321
Trabbochburn *Strath* ... 73 NS4621
Tracewell *Somset* ... 7 ST0720
Tradespark *Highld* ... 93 NH8656
Traethsaith *Dyfed* ... 36 SN2751
Trafford Park *Gt Man* ... 47 SJ7896
Trallong *Powys* ... 26 SN9629
Tranent *Loth* ... 76 NT4072
Trantelbeg *Highld* ... 99 NC8952
Trantlemore *Highld* ... 99 NC8953
Trapp *Dyfed* ... 26 SN6519
Traquair *Border* ... 75 NT3334
Traveller's Rest *Devon* ... 6 SS6027

Trawden *Lancs* ... 54 SD9138
Trawsfynydd *Gwynd* ... 45 SH7035
Tre-Vaughan *Dyfed* ... 17 SN4021
Tre-gagle *Gwent* ... 27 SO5208
Tre-groes *Dyfed* ... 17 SN4044
Trealaw *M Glam* ... 18 SS9992
Trealaw *M Glam* ... 18 ST0092
Treales *Lancs* ... 53 SD4332
Trearddur Bay *Gwynd* ... 44 SH2478
Treaslane *Highld* ... 90 NG3953
Trebanos *W Glam* ... 18 SN7103
Trebarwith *Cnwll* ... 4 SX0586
Trebetherick *Cnwll* ... 3 SW9378
Treborough *Somset* ... 7 SK9630
Treburick *Cnwll* ... 3 SW8972
Treburley *Cnwll* ... 4 SX3477
Tredaule *Cnwll* ... 4 SX2381
Tredavoe *Cnwll* ... 2 SW4527
Treddiog *Dyfed* ... 16 SM8927
Tredegar *Gwent* ... 26 SO1408
Tredington *Gloucs* ... 28 SO9029
Tredington *Warwks* ... 29 SP2543
Tredinnick *Cnwll* ... 3 SW9270
Tredogan *S Glam* ... 18 ST0668
Tredomen *Powys* ... 26 SO1331
Tredunnock *Gwent* ... 19 ST3794
Tredustan *Powys* ... 26 SO1431
Treen *Cnwll* ... 2 SW3923
Treeton *S York* ... 49 SK4387
Trefasser *Dyfed* ... 16 SM8938
Trefdraeth *Gwynd* ... 44 SH4070
Trefeglwys *Powys* ... 35 SN9690
Treffgarne *Dyfed* ... 16 SM9523
Treffgarne Owen *Dyfed* ... 16 SM8625
Treffynnon *Dyfed* ... 16 SM8428
Trefilan *Dyfed* ... 34 SN5457
Trefnant *Clwyd* ... 45 SJ0570
Trefonen *Shrops* ... 36 SJ2526
Trefor *Gwynd* ... 44 SH3779
Treforest *M Glam* ... 18 ST0888
Tregadillett *Cnwll* ... 4 SX3083
Tregare *Gwent* ... 27 SO4110
Tregarne *Cnwll* ... 2 SW7822
Tregaron *Dyfed* ... 26 SN6859
Tregarth *Gwynd* ... 44 SH6067
Tregeare *Cnwll* ... 4 SW8750
Tregeiriog *Clwyd* ... 36 SJ1733
Tregele *Gwynd* ... 44 SH3592
Tregenna *Cnwll* ... 3 SX0973
Tregeseal *Cnwll* ... 2 SW3832
Tregew *Cnwll* ... 2 SW8034
Tregidden *Cnwll* ... 2 SW7523
Treglemais *Dyfed* ... 16 SM8229
Tregole *Cnwll* ... 6 SX1998
Tregonce *Cnwll* ... 3 SW9373
Tregonetha *Cnwll* ... 3 SW9563
Tregony *Cnwll* ... 3 SW9244
Tregoss *Cnwll* ... 3 SW9656
Tregowris *Cnwll* ... 2 SW7523
Tregoyd *Powys* ... 27 SO1937
Tregunnon *Cnwll* ... 4 SX2283
Tregurrian *Cnwll* ... 3 SW8465
Tregustick *Cnwll* ... 3 SW9966
Tregynon *Powys* ... 36 SO1099
Trehafod *M Glam* ... 18 ST0490
Trehan *Cnwll* ... 4 SX4058
Treharris *M Glam* ... 18 ST0896
Treherbert *M Glam* ... 18 SS9773
Treherbert *Dyfed* ... 26 SN6536
Treheveras *Cnwll* ... 2 SW8146
Trehunist *Cnwll* ... 4 SX3163
Trekenner *Cnwll* ... 4 SX3478
Trelawnyd *Clwyd* ... 46 SJ0879
Treleague *Cnwll* ... 2 SW7822
Treleaver *Cnwll* ... 2 SW7516
Trelech *Dyfed* ... 17 SN2830
Treleddyd-fawr *Dyfed* ... 16 SM7528
Trelew *Cnwll* ... 2 SW8540
Trelewis *M Glam* ... 18 ST1096
Treligga *Cnwll* ... 4 SX0584
Trelights *Cnwll* ... 3 SW9979
Trelill *Cnwll* ... 3 SX0478
Trelleck *Gwent* ... 27 SO5005
Trelminoe *M Glam* ... 3 SJ3181
Trelogan *Clwyd* ... 46 SJ1180
Trelow *Cnwll* ... 3 SW9269
Treluggan *Cnwll* ... 3 SW8838
Tremadog *Gwynd* ... 44 SH5640
Tremail *Cnwll* ... 4 SX1686
Tremain *Dyfed* ... 17 SN2348
Tremaine *Cnwll* ... 4 SX2388
Tremains *Cnwll* ... 4 SX2388
Trematon *Cnwll* ... 4 SX3959
Tremeirchion *Clwyd* ... 46 SJ0773
Tremore *Cnwll* ... 3 SX0165
Trenance *Cnwll* ... 3 SW6718
Trenance *Cnwll* ... 3 SW8567
Trenance *Cnwll* ... 3 SW9270
Trench *Shrops* ... 37 SJ6913
Trencreek *Cnwll* ... 2 SW8260
Trencreek *Cnwll* ... 6 SX1896
Trendeal *Cnwll* ... 3 SW8952
Trenear *Cnwll* ... 2 SW6831
Treneglos *Cnwll* ... 4 SX2088
Trent *Dorset* ... 9 ST5918
Trent *Lincs* ... 50 SK8381
Trentham *Staffs* ... 38 SJ8641
Trentishoe *Devon* ... 18 SS6448
Treoes *S Glam* ... 18 SS9478
Treorchy *M Glam* ... 18 SS9597
Trequite *Cnwll* ... 3 SX0277
Trerhyngyll *S Glam* ... 18 ST0077
Trerulefoot *Cnwll* ... 4 SX3359
Tresawle *Cnwll* ... 3 SW8946
Trescowe *Cnwll* ... 2 SW5731
Tresham *Avon* ... 20 ST7991
Treshnish *Cnwll* ... 3 SW8646
Treskinnick Cross *Cnwll* ... 6 SX2098
Tresmeer *Cnwll* ... 4 SX2387
Tresparrett *Cnwll* ... 4 SX1491
Tressait *Tays* ... 87 NN8160
Tresta *Shet* ... 103 HU3651
Tresta *Shet* ... 103 HU6190
Treswell *Notts* ... 50 SK7779
Treswithian *Cnwll* ... 2 SW6241
Trethevey *Cnwll* ... 4 SX0789
Trethurgy *Cnwll* ... 3 SX0355
Tretio *Dyfed* ... 16 SM7828
Tretire *H & W* ... 27 SO5123
Tretower *Powys* ... 27 SO1821
Treuddyn *Clwyd* ... 46 SJ2557
Trevague *Cnwll* ... 4 SX2379
Trevalga *Cnwll* ... 4 SX0890
Trevalyn *Clwyd* ... 46 SJ3856
Trevanson *Cnwll* ... 3 SW9672
Trevarrack *Cnwll* ... 2 SW4831
Trevarren *Cnwll* ... 3 SW9160
Trevarrian *Cnwll* ... 3 SW8566
Trevarrick *Cnwll* ... 3 SW9843
Trevaughan *Dyfed* ... 17 SN1915
Treveal *Cnwll* ... 2 SW7858
Treveighan *Cnwll* ... 3 SX0779
Trevellas *Cnwll* ... 2 SW7452
Trevelmond *Cnwll* ... 3 SX2063
Treverbyn *Cnwll* ... 3 SX0157
Treverva *Cnwll* ... 2 SW7531
Trevescan *Cnwll* ... 2 SW3524
Trevethin *Gwent* ... 19 SO2802
Trevilledor *Cnwll* ... 3 SW8967
Trevine *Dyfed* ... 16 SM8432
Treviscoe *Cnwll* ... 3 SW9456
Trevithal *Cnwll* ... 2 SW4626
Trevone *Cnwll* ... 3 SW8975
Trevor *Gwynd* ... 44 SH3746
Trevorgans *Cnwll* ... 2 SW4025
Trevose *Cnwll* ... 3 SW8675
Trewalder *Cnwll* ... 3 SX0782
Trewarlett *M Glam* ... 4 SX0886
Trewarmett *Cnwll* ... 4 SX0582
Treween *Cnwll* ... 4 SX2282
Trewen *Cnwll* ... 3 SX0577
Trewennack *Cnwll* ... 2 SW6828
Trewetha *Cnwll* ... 3 SX0080
Trewidland *Cnwll* ... 4 SX2560
Trewint *Cnwll* ... 4 SX1080
Trewint *Cnwll* ... 4 SX2180
Trewoodloe *M Glam* ... 4 SX3271
Trewoon *Cnwll* ... 3 SW9952

Treyford *W Susx* ... 11 SU8218
Triangle *Gloucs* ... 19 SO5401
Triangle *W York* ... 55 SE0422
Trickett's Cross *Dorset* ... 10 SU0801
Triermain *Cumb* ... 67 NY5967
Trimdon *Dur* ... 62 NZ3634
Trimdon Colliery *Dur* ... 62 NZ3635
Trimdon Grange *Dur* ... 62 NZ3634
Trimingham *Norfk* ... 43 TG2738
Trimley *Suffk* ... 25 TM2737
Trimley Heath *Suffk* ... 25 TM2738
Trimsaran *Dyfed* ... 17 SN4504
Trimstone *Devon* ... 6 SS5043
Trinafour *Tays* ... 87 NN7264
Tring *Herts* ... 22 SP9911
Trinity *Jersey* ... 101 SV0000
Trinity *Tays* ... 89 NO6061
Trinity Gask *Tays* ... 75 NS9618
Triscombe *Somset* ... 7 ST2537
Triscombe *Somset* ... 8 ST1535
Trislaig *Highld* ... 86 NN0874
Trispen *Cnwll* ... 3 SW8450
Tritlington *Nthumb* ... 69 NZ2092
Trochry *Tays* ... 82 NN9741
Trodigal *Strath* ... 72 NR6420
Troedrhiwfuwch *M Glam* ... 26 SO1204
Troedyraur *Dyfed* ... 17 SN3245
Troedyrhiw *M Glam* ... 26 SO0630
Troedyrhiw *M Glam* ... 18 SO0702
Trois Bois *Jersey* ... 101 SV0000
Troon *Cnwll* ... 2 SW6638
Troon *Strath* ... 73 NS3230
Troqhain *D & G* ... 65 NX6879
Trossachs Hotel *Cent* ... 81 NN5107
Troston *Suffk* ... 32 TL8972
Trottiscliffe *Kent* ... 14 TQ6460
Trotton *W Susx* ... 11 SU8322
Troughend *Nthumb* ... 68 NY8692
Troutbeck *Cumb* ... 59 NY4002
Troutbeck *Cumb* ... 59 NY4000
Troutbeck Bridge *Cumb* ... 59 NY4002
Trow Green *Gloucs* ... 27 SO5706
Troway *Derbys* ... 49 SK3879
Trowbridge *Wilts* ... 20 ST8557
Trowle Common *Wilts* ... 20 ST8358
Trowse Newton *Norfk* ... 43 TG2406
Troy *W York* ... 55 SE2438
Trudoxhill *Somset* ... 20 ST7443
Trull *Somset* ... 8 ST2122
Trumfleet *S York* ... 56 SE6012
Trumisgarry *W Isls* ... 102 NF8674
Trumpan *Highld* ... 90 NG2261
Trumpet *H & W* ... 27 SO6539
Trumpington *Cambs* ... 31 TL4454
Trunch *Norfk* ... 43 TG2834
Truro *Cnwll* ... 2 SW8244
Trusham *Devon* ... 5 SX8582
Trusley *Derbys* ... 39 SK2535
Trysull *Staffs* ... 38 SO8594
Tubney *Oxon* ... 21 SU4398
Tuckhill *Shrops* ... 37 SO7888
Tuckingmill *Cnwll* ... 2 SW6540
Tuckingmill *Wilts* ... 9 ST9329
Tuckton *Dorset* ... 10 SZ1492
Tucoyse *Cnwll* ... 3 SW9466
Tuddenham *Suffk* ... 33 TM1948
Tuddenham *Suffk* ... 32 TL7371
Tudhoe *Dur* ... 61 NZ2535
Tudweiloig *Gwynd* ... 44 SH2336
Tuffley *Gloucs* ... 28 SO8316
Tufton *Dyfed* ... 16 SN0428
Tufton *Hants* ... 21 SU4546
Tugby *Leics* ... 40 SK7601
Tugford *Shrops* ... 37 SO5587
Tughall *Nthumb* ... 77 NU2126
Tullibody *Cent* ... 82 NS8595
Tullich *Highld* ... 92 NH6328
Tullich *Highld* ... 88 NH8876
Tullich *Strath* ... 80 NN0815
Tullich Muir *Highld* ... 97 NH7273
Tulliemet *Tays* ... 88 NO0052
Tulloch *Cent* ... 81 NN5120
Tulloch *Gramp* ... 89 NO7671
Tulloch *Gramp* ... 95 NJ4731
Tulloch Station *Highld* ... 86 NN3580
Tullochgorm *Strath* ... 71 NR9695
Tullybeagles Lodge *Tays* ... 82 NO0136
Tullynessle *Gramp* ... 94 NJ5519
Tumble *Dyfed* ... 17 SN5411
Tumby *Lincs* ... 51 TF2359
Tumby Woodside *Lincs* ... 51 TF2757
Tummel Bridge *Tays* ... 87 NN7659
Tunstall *Humb* ... 57 TA3031
Tunstall *Kent* ... 14 TQ8961
Tunstall *Lancs* ... 59 SD6073
Tunstall *N York* ... 61 SE2195
Tunstall *Norfk* ... 43 TG4108
Tunstall *Suffk* ... 37 SJ7727
Tunstall *Staffs* ... 47 SJ8551
Tunstall *T & W* ... 33 TM3655
Tunstead *Derbys* ... 69 NZ3953
Tunstead *Derbys* ... 48 SK1175
Tunstead *Norfk* ... 43 TG3022
Tunstead Milton *Derbys* ... 48 SK0280
Tunworth *Hants* ... 22 SU6748
Tur Langton *Leics* ... 40 SP7194
Turgis Green *Hants* ... 22 SU6959
Turin *Tays* ... 89 NO5352
Turkdean *Gloucs* ... 28 SP1017
Turleigh *Wilts* ... 20 ST8060
Turnastone *H & W* ... 27 SO3536
Turnberry *Strath* ... 73 NS2005
Turnchapel *Devon* ... 4 SX4952
Turnditch *Derbys* ... 49 SK2944
Turner's Green *E Susx* ... 13 TQ6218
Turner's Hill *W Susx* ... 12 TQ3435
Turners Puddle *Dorset* ... 9 SY8394
Turnworth *Dorset* ... 9 ST8107
Turriff *Gramp* ... 95 NJ7250
Turton Bottoms *Gt Man* ... 54 SD7315
Turvey *Beds* ... 30 SP9452
Turville *Bucks* ... 22 SU7691
Turweston *Bucks* ... 29 SP6037
Tushielaw *Border* ... 75 NT3018
Tushingham cum Grindley *Ches* ... 46 SJ5246
Tutbury *Staffs* ... 39 SK2128
Tutnall *Ches* ... 19 ST5495
Tuttington *Norfk* ... 43 TG2227
Tutwell *M Glam* ... 4 SX3876
Tuxford *Notts* ... 50 SK7471
Twatt *Ork* ... 103 HY2624
Twatt *Shet* ... 103 HU3253
Twechar *Strath* ... 74 NS6975
Tweedmouth *Nthumb* ... 77 NT9952
Tweedsmuir *Border* ... 75 NT1024
Twelve Oaks *E Susx* ... 14 TQ6820
Twemlow Green *Ches* ... 47 SJ7868
Twenty *Lincs* ... 40 TF1520
Twickenham *Gt Lon* ... 23 TQ1673
Twigworth *Gloucs* ... 28 SO8422
Twineham *W Susx* ... 12 TQ2519
Twinhoe *Avon* ... 20 ST7359
Twinstead *Essex* ... 24 TL8636
Twitchen *Devon* ... 7 SS7830
Twitham Kent ... 15 TR2556
Two Bridges *Devon* ... 5 SX6075
Two Dales *Derbys* ... 49 SX2762
Two Mile Oak Cross *Devon* ... 5 SX8487
Twycross *Leics* ... 39 SK3305
Twyford *Berks* ... 22 SU7976
Twyford *Bucks* ... 30 SP6626
Twyford *Derbys* ... 39 SK3228
Twyford *Hants* ... 10 SU4824
Twyford *Leics* ... 40 SK7210
Twyford *Norfk* ... 42 TG0124
Twyford Common *H & W* ... 27 SO5035
Twynholm *D & G* ... 65 NX6654
Twyning *Gloucs* ... 28 SO8936
Twyning Green *Gloucs* ... 28 SO9036
Twynllanan *Dyfed* ... 26 SN7524
Twynmynydd *Dyfed* ... 26 SN6614
Twywell *Nhants* ... 30 SP9578
Ty Rhiw *M Glam* ... 18 ST1283
Ty-nant *Clwyd* ... 36 SJ0243
Ty-n-dwr *Clwyd* ... 36 SJ2244
Ty-n-y-bryn *M Glam* ... 18 SS0087
Ty-n-y-groes *Gwynd* ... 45 SH7771
Ty-nant *Clwyd* ... 45 SH9845
Tycroes *Dyfed* ... 27 SN6010
Tycrwyn *Powys* ... 36 SJ1018

Tydd Gote *Lincs* ... 41 TF4518
Tydd St. Giles *Cambs* ... 41 TF4216
Tydd St. Mary *Lincs* ... 41 TF4418
Tye Green *Essex* ... 24 TL5424
Tye Green *Essex* ... 24 TL5515
Tyldesley *Gt Man* ... 47 SD6802
Tyler Hill *Kent* ... 15 TR1461
Tylorstown *M Glam* ... 18 ST0095
Tyn-y-graig *Powys* ... 26 SO0149
Tyn-y-nant *M Glam* ... 18 ST0685
Tynant *M Glam* ... 18 ST0684
Tyndrum *Cent* ... 80 NN3330
Tynemouth *T & W* ... 69 NZ3669
Tynewydd *M Glam* ... 18 SS9399
Tyninghame *Loth* ... 83 NT6179
Tynron *D & G* ... 66 NX8093
Tyntesfield *Avon* ... 19 ST5071
Tynygongl *Gwynd* ... 44 SH5182
Tynygraig *Dyfed* ... 35 SN6969
Tyringham *Bucks* ... 30 SP8546
Tythecott *Devon* ... 6 SS4117
Tythegston *M Glam* ... 18 SS8578
Tytherington *Avon* ... 20 ST6788
Tytherington *Ches* ... 48 SJ9175
Tytherington *Somset* ... 20 ST7744
Tytherington *Wilts* ... 20 ST9140
Tytherleigh *Devon* ... 8 ST3203
Tywardreath *Cnwll* ... 3 SX0854
Tywyn *Gwynd* ... 44 SH5790
Tywyn *Gwynd* ... 45 SH7978

U

Uachdar *W Isls* ... 102 NF7955
Ubbeston Green *Suffk* ... 33 TM3272
Ubley *Avon* ... 19 ST5257
Uckerby *N York* ... 61 NZ2402
Uckfield *E Susx* ... 13 TQ4721
Uckinghall *H & W* ... 28 SO8637
Uckington *Gloucs* ... 28 SO9224
Uckington *Shrops* ... 37 SJ5709
Uddingston *Strath* ... 74 NS6960
Uddington *Strath* ... 74 NS8633
Udimore *E Susx* ... 14 TQ8719
Udny Green *Gramp* ... 95 NJ8726
Uffcolme *Devon* ... 7 ST0620
Uffington *Oxon* ... 21 SU3089
Uffington *Shrops* ... 37 SJ5314
Ufford *Cambs* ... 40 TF0904
Ufton *Warwks* ... 29 SP3762
Ufton Nervet *Berks* ... 21 SU6367
Ugadale *Strath* ... 72 NR7828
Ugborough *Devon* ... 5 SX6755
Uggeshall *Suffk* ... 33 TM4480
Ugglebarnby *N York* ... 63 NZ8807
Ughill *Derbys* ... 48 SK2590
Ugley *Essex* ... 31 TL5228
Ugley Green *Essex* ... 31 TL5227
Ugthorpe *N York* ... 63 NZ7911
Uig *Highld* ... 90 NG1952
Uig *Highld* ... 90 NG3763
Uig *Strath* ... 78 NM1754
Uig *W Isls* ... 102 NB0534
Uigshader *Highld* ... 90 NG4346
Uisken *Strath* ... 78 NM3919
Ulbster *Highld* ... 100 ND3241
Ulcat Row *Cumb* ... 59 NY4022
Ulceby *Humb* ... 57 TA1014
Ulceby *Lincs* ... 51 TF4272
Ulceby Skitter *Humb* ... 57 TA1014
Ulcombe *Kent* ... 14 TQ8448
Uldale *Cumb* ... 58 NY2437
Uley *Gloucs* ... 20 ST7898
Ulgham *Nthumb* ... 69 NZ2392
Ullapool *Highld* ... 96 NH1294
Ullenhall *Warwks* ... 28 SP1267
Ulleskelf *N York* ... 55 SE5139
Ullesthorpe *Leics* ... 39 SP5087
Ulley *S York* ... 49 SK4687
Ullingswick *H & W* ... 27 SO5950
Ullinish *Highld* ... 84 NG3237
Ullock *Cumb* ... 58 NY0724
Ulpha *Cumb* ... 58 SD1993
Ulpha *Cumb* ... 59 SD3581
Ulrome *Humb* ... 57 TA1656
Ulsta *Shet* ... 103 HU4680
Ulverley Green *W Mids* ... 38 SP1381
Ulverston *Cumb* ... 58 SD2878
Umachan *Highld* ... 90 NG6150
Umberleigh *Devon* ... 6 SS6023
Under Burnmouth *D & G* ... 67 NY4783
Under River *Kent* ... 13 TQ5552
Underbarrow *Cumb* ... 59 SD4692
Undercliffe *W York* ... 55 SE1834
Underdale *Shrops* ... 37 SJ5013
Underwood *Gwent* ... 19 ST3888
Underwood *Gwent* ... 19 ST3486
Undy *Gwent* ... 19 ST4386
Union Mills *IOM* ... 52 SC3578
Unstone *Derbys* ... 49 SK3777
Unthank *Cumb* ... 68 NY6050
Up Cerne *Dorset* ... 9 ST6502
Up Exe *Devon* ... 7 SS9302
Up Holland *Lancs* ... 46 SD5105
Up Marden *W Susx* ... 11 SU7914
Up Mudford *Somset* ... 8 ST5718
Up Nately *Hants* ... 22 SU6951
Up Somborne *Hants* ... 10 SU3932
Up Sydling *Dorset* ... 9 ST6201
Upavon *Wilts* ... 20 SU1354
Upchurch *Kent* ... 14 TQ8467
Upcott *Devon* ... 6 SS5739
Upcott *Devon* ... 7 SS7529
Upcott *Somset* ... 7 SS9025
Upgate *Norfk* ... 43 TG1418
Uphall *Dorset* ... 8 ST5502
Uphall *Loth* ... 75 NT0671
Upham *Hants* ... 11 SU5320
Upham *H & W* ... 27 SO3963
Uphampton *H & W* ... 28 SO8364
Uphill *Avon* ... 19 ST3158
Uplawmoor *Strath* ... 73 NS4355
Upleadon *Gloucs* ... 28 SO7427
Upleatham *Cleve* ... 62 NZ6319
Uplees *Kent* ... 15 TR0004
Uplowman *Devon* ... 7 ST0115
Uplyme *Devon* ... 8 SY3293
Upminster *Gt Lon* ... 24 TQ5686
Upottery *Devon* ... 8 ST2007
Upparthong *W York* ... 55 SE1208
Uppat House *Highld* ... 97 NC8702
Upper Affcot *Shrops* ... 36 SO4486
Upper Ardchronie *Highld* ... 97 NH6188
Upper Arley *H & W* ... 37 SO7680
Upper Arncott *Oxon* ... 29 SP6017
Upper Basildon *Berks* ... 21 SU5976
Upper Batley *W York* ... 55 SE2325
Upper Beeding *W Susx* ... 12 TQ1910
Upper Benefield *Nhants* ... 40 SP9789
Upper Bentley *H & W* ... 28 SO9966
Upper Bighouse *Highld* ... 99 NC8857
Upper Boat *M Glam* ... 18 ST1087
Upper Boddington *Nhants* ... 29 SP4853
Upper Brailes *Warwks* ... 29 SP3040
Upper Breakish *Highld* ... 85 NG6823
Upper Broadheath *H & W* ... 28 SO8056
Upper Broughton *Notts* ... 39 SK6826
Upper Bucklebury *Berks* ... 21 SU5468
Upper Burgate *Hants* ... 10 SU1516
Upper Cairnie *Tays* ... 72 NS0319
Upper Cairn *D & G* ... 66 NS6912
Upper Caldecote *Beds* ... 31 TL1645
Upper Canada *Avon* ... 19 ST3658
Upper Chapel *Powys* ... 26 SO0040
Upper Cheddon *Somset* ... 8 ST2328
Upper Chickgrove *Wilts* ... 9 ST9730
Upper Chute *Wilts* ... 21 SU2953
Upper Chute *Wilts* ... 21 SU2953
Upper Clapton *Gt Lon* ... 23 TQ3487

Upper Clatford *Hants* ... 21 SU3543
Upper Clynnog *Gwynd* ... 44 SH4746
Upper Coberley *Gloucs* ... 28 SO9815
Upper Cokeham *W Susx* ... 12 TQ1705
Upper Cound *Shrops* ... 37 SJ5505
Upper Cudworth *S York* ... 55 SE3908
Upper Cumberworth *W York* ... 55 SE2008
Upper Cumberworth *W York* ... 55 SE2108
Upper Cwmtwrch *Powys* ... 26 SN7611
Upper Dallachy *Gramp* ... 94 NJ3662
Upper Deal *Kent* ... 15 TR3651
Upper Dean *Beds* ... 30 TL0467
Upper Dicker *E Susx* ... 13 TQ5509
Upper Dovercourt *Essex* ... 25 TM2331
Upper Drumbane *Cent* ... 81 NN6606
Upper Dunsforth *N York* ... 55 SE4463
Upper Eashing *Surrey* ... 12 SU9543
Upper Egleton *H & W* ... 27 SO6345
Upper Elkstone *Staffs* ... 48 SK0559
Upper Ellastone *Staffs* ... 48 SK1143
Upper Elmers End *Gt Lon* ... 23 TQ3667
Upper End *Derbys* ... 48 SK0876
Upper Enham *Hants* ... 21 SU3649
Upper Ethrie *Highld* ... 93 NH7662
Upper Farmcote *Shrops* ... 37 SO7792
Upper Farringdon *Hants* ... 11 SU7135
Upper Framilode *Gloucs* ... 28 SO7510
Upper Froyle *Hants* ... 11 SU7545
Upper Godney *Somset* ... 19 ST4842
Upper Gravenhurst *Beds* ... 30 TL1136
Upper Green *Essex* ... 24 TL5935
Upper Hackney *Derbys* ... 49 SK2961
Upper Hale *Surrey* ... 22 SU8449
Upper Halliford *Surrey* ... 22 TQ0968
Upper Hambleton *Leics* ... 40 SK9007
Upper Harbledown *Kent* ... 15 TR1158
Upper Hatherley *Gloucs* ... 28 SO9221
Upper Hatton *Staffs* ... 38 SJ8337
Upper Hayton *Shrops* ... 37 SO5281
Upper Heaton *W York* ... 55 SE1719
Upper Helmsley *N York* ... 56 SE6956
Upper Hergest *H & W* ... 27 SO2654
Upper Heyford *Nhants* ... 30 SP6659
Upper Hill *H & W* ... 27 SO4753
Upper Hopton *W York* ... 55 SE1918
Upper Howsell *H & W* ... 28 SO7748
Upper Hulme *Staffs* ... 48 SK0160
Upper Inglesham *Wilts* ... 21 SU2096
Upper Keith *Loth* ... 76 NT4562
Upper Killay *W Glam* ... 17 SS5892
Upper Kinchrackine *Strath* ... 80 NN1627
Upper Lambourn *Berks* ... 21 SU3180
Upper Langford *Avon* ... 19 ST4659
Upper Langwith *Derbys* ... 49 SK5169
Upper Largo *Fife* ... 83 NO4203
Upper Leigh *Staffs* ... 48 SK0136
Upper Lochton *Gramp* ... 89 NO6997
Upper Longdon *Staffs* ... 38 SK0614
Upper Lybster *Highld* ... 100 ND2537
Upper Lydbrook *Gloucs* ... 27 SO6015
Upper Lye *H & W* ... 27 SO3965
Upper Milton *H & W* ... 37 SO8072
Upper Minety *Wilts* ... 20 SU0091
Upper Moor *H & W* ... 28 SO9747
Upper Mulben *Gramp* ... 94 NJ3551
Upper Nesbet *Border* ... 76 NT6727
Upper Netchwood *Shrops* ... 37 SO6192
Upper Nobut *Staffs* ... 38 SK0435
Upper Norwood *W Susx* ... 11 SU9317
Upper Ollach *Highld* ... 84 NG5137
Upper Padley *Derbys* ... 48 SK2478
Upper Pond Street *Essex* ... 31 TL4536
Upper Poppleton *N York* ... 56 SE5554
Upper Pulley *Shrops* ... 37 SJ4808
Upper Quinton *Warwks* ... 29 SP1846
Upper Ratley *Hants* ... 10 SU3223
Upper Rochford *H & W* ... 27 SO6367
Upper Ruscoe *D & G* ... 65 NX5661
Upper Sapey *H & W* ... 28 SO6863
Upper Shelton *Beds* ... 30 SP9843
Upper Sheringham *Norfk* ... 43 TG1441
Upper Shuckburgh *Warwks* ... 29 SP4961
Upper Slaughter *Gloucs* ... 28 SP1523
Upper Soudley *Gloucs* ... 27 SO6510
Upper Spond *H & W* ... 27 SO3163
Upper Standen *Kent* ... 15 TR2240
Upper Stepford *D & G* ... 66 NX8681
Upper Stoke *Norfk* ... 43 TG2502
Upper Stondon *Beds* ... 30 TL1535
Upper Stowe *Nhants* ... 29 SP6456
Upper Street *Hants* ... 10 SU1418
Upper Street *Norfk* ... 43 TG3217
Upper Street *Norfk* ... 43 TG3617
Upper Street *Suffk* ... 32 TL7851
Upper Street *Suffk* ... 33 TM1051
Upper Street *Suffk* ... 25 TM1434
Upper Sundon *Beds* ... 30 TL0427
Upper Swell *Gloucs* ... 29 SP1726
Upper Tankersley *S York* ... 49 SK3399
Upper Tasburgh *Norfk* ... 43 TM2095
Upper Tean *Staffs* ... 48 SK0139
Upper Town *Avon* ... 19 ST5265
Upper Town *Derbys* ... 48 SK2462
Upper Town *H & W* ... 27 SO5848
Upper Town *Suffk* ... 32 TL9267
Upper Tysoe *Warwks* ... 29 SP3343
Upper Ufford *Suffk* ... 33 TM2953
Upper Victoria *Tays* ... 83 NO5336
Upper Wardington *Oxon* ... 29 SP4945
Upper Weedon *Nhants* ... 29 SP6158
Upper Wellingham *E Susx* ... 13 TQ4313
Upper Weston *Avon* ... 20 ST7266
Upper Weybread *Suffk* ... 33 TM2379
Upper Whiston *S York* ... 49 SK4588
Upper Wield *Hants* ... 11 SU6238
Upper Winchendon *Bucks* ... 30 SP7414
Upper Witton *W Mids* ... 38 SP0892
Upper Woodford *Wilts* ... 10 SU1237
Upper Wootton *Hants* ... 21 SU5854
Upperby *Cumb* ... 67 NY4153
Upperglen *Highld* ... 90 NG3151
Uppermill *Gt Man* ... 54 SD9905
Upperthorpe *Derbys* ... 49 SK4580
Upperton *W Susx* ... 12 SU9522
Uppertown *Highld* ... 100 ND3576
Upperup *Gloucs* ... 20 SU0396
Upperwood *Derbys* ... 49 SK2957
Uppincott *Devon* ... 7 SS9106
Uppingham *Leics* ... 40 SP8699
Uppington *Dorset* ... 10 SU0106
Uppington *Shrops* ... 37 SJ5909
Upsall *N York* ... 62 SE4586
Upsettlington *Border* ... 77 NT8446
Upshire *Essex* ... 23 TL4100
Upstreet *Kent* ... 15 TR2263
Upton *Berks* ... 22 SU9779
Upton *Bucks* ... 22 SP7711
Upton *Cambs* ... 40 TF1000
Upton *Cambs* ... 31 TL1778
Upton *Cnwll* ... 4 SX2772
Upton *Devon* ... 5 SX7042
Upton *Devon* ... 7 ST0902
Upton *Devon* ... 8 ST1002
Upton *Dorset* ... 9 SY7483
Upton *Dorset* ... 9 SY9893
Upton *Hants* ... 21 SU3555
Upton *Hants* ... 10 SU3717
Upton *Leics* ... 39 SP3699
Upton *Lincs* ... 50 SK8686
Upton *Mersyd* ... 46 SJ2788
Upton *Norfk* ... 43 TG3912
Upton *Notts* ... 50 SK7354
Upton *Notts* ... 31 TL2826
Upton *Oxon* ... 21 SU5186
Upton *Somset* ... 7 SS9928
Upton *Somset* ... 8 ST4526
Upton *W York* ... 55 SE4713
Upton Bishop *H & W* ... 27 SO6527
Upton Cheyney *Avon* ... 20 ST6970
Upton Cressett *Shrops* ... 37 SO6592
Upton Crews *H & W* ... 27 SO6527
Upton Cross *Cnwll* ... 4 SX2872
Upton Grey *Hants* ... 22 SU6948
Upton Heath *Ches* ... 46 SJ4169
Upton Hellions *Devon* ... 7 SS8303
Upton Lovell *Wilts* ... 20 ST9440
Upton Magna *Shrops* ... 37 SJ5512
Upton Noble *Somset* ... 20 ST7139
Upton Pyne *Devon* ... 7 SX9197

Upton Scudamore *Wilts* ... 20 ST8647
Upton Snodsbury *H & W* ... 28 SO9454
Upton St. Leonards *Gloucs* ... 28 SO8615
Upton Warren *H & W* ... 28 SO9367
Upton upon Severn *H & W* ... 28 SO8540
Upwaltham *W Susx* ... 12 SU9413
Upwell *Norfk* ... 41 TF5002
Upwey *Dorset* ... 9 SY6684
Upwick Green *Herts* ... 31 TL4524
Upwood *Cambs* ... 41 TL2582
Urchany *Highld* ... 93 NH8849
Urchfont *Wilts* ... 20 SU0356
Urlay Nook *Cleve* ... 62 NZ3816
Urmston *Gt Man* ... 47 SJ7694
Urquhart *Gramp* ... 94 NJ2862
Urra *N York* ... 62 NZ5601
Urray *Highld* ... 92 NH5052
Ushaw Moor *Dur* ... 61 NZ2242
Usk *Gwent* ... 19 SO3700
Usselby *Lincs* ... 50 TF0993
Usworth *T & W* ... 69 NZ3058
Utley *W York* ... 55 SE0543
Uton *Devon* ... 7 SX8298
Utterby *Lincs* ... 51 TF3093
Uttoxeter *Staffs* ... 38 SK0933
Uxbridge *Gt Lon* ... 22 TQ0584
Uyeasound *Shet* ... 103 HP5901
Uzmaston *Dyfed* ... 16 SM9714

V

Vale *Guern* ... 101 SV0000
Valley End *Surrey* ... 22 SU9564
Valtos *Highld* ... 90 NG5163
Valtos *W Isls* ... 102 NB0936
Vange *Essex* ... 24 TQ7187
Vardre *W Glam* ... 18 SN6902
Vatsetter *Shet* ... 103 HU5389
Vatten *Highld* ... 90 NG2843
Vaynor *M Glam* ... 26 SO0410
Velindre *Dyfed* ... 16 SN1039
Velindre *Dyfed* ... 17 SN3538
Velindre *Powys* ... 27 SO1536
Venn *Cnwll* ... 3 SX2608
Venn *Devon* ... 5 SX6550
Venn Ottery *Devon* ... 5 SY0791
Venngreen *Devon* ... 6 SS3711
Ventnor *IOW* ... 11 SZ5677
Venton *Devon* ... 5 SX5856
Vernham Dean *Hants* ... 21 SU3456
Verwig *Dyfed* ... 17 SN1849
Verwood *Dorset* ... 10 SU0908
Veryan *Cnwll* ... 3 SW9139
Vicarage *Devon* ... 8 SY2088
Vickerstown *Cumb* ... 53 SD1868
Victoria *Cnwll* ... 3 SW9861
Victoria *S York* ... 55 SE1605
Vidlin *Shet* ... 103 HU4765
Viewfield *Gramp* ... 94 NJ2864
Viewpark *Strath* ... 74 NS7061
Villavin *Devon* ... 6 SS5816
Ville la Bas *Jersey* ... 101 SV0000
Villiage *Guern* ... 101 SV0000
Vine's Cross *E Susx* ... 13 TQ5917
Virginia Water *Surrey* ... 12 TQ0007
Virginstow *Devon* ... 4 SX3792
Vobster *Somset* ... 20 ST7048
Voe *Shet* ... 103 HU4063
Vowchurch *H & W* ... 27 SO3636

W

Wackerfield *Dur* ... 61 NZ1522
Wacton *Norfk* ... 33 TM1791
Wadborough *H & W* ... 28 SO9047
Waddesdon *Bucks* ... 30 SP7416
Waddeton *Devon* ... 5 SX8756
Waddingham *Lincs* ... 50 SK9896
Waddington *Lancs* ... 54 SD7343
Waddington *Lincs* ... 50 SK9764
Waddon *Dorset* ... 9 SY6185
Wadebridge *Cnwll* ... 3 SW9972
Wadeford *Somset* ... 8 ST3110
Wadenhoe *Nhants* ... 40 TL0183
Wadesmill *Herts* ... 31 TL3517
Wadworth *S York* ... 49 SK5697
Waen *Clwyd* ... 45 SJ0062
Waen *Powys* ... 36 SJ2320
Wainfleet All Saints *Lincs* ... 51 TF4958
Wainhouse Corner *Cnwll* ... 6 SX1895
Wainscott *Kent* ... 14 TQ7470
Wainstalls *W York* ... 55 SE0428
Waitby *Cumb* ... 60 NY7508
Waithe *Lincs* ... 51 TA2800
Wake Green *W Mids* ... 38 SP0882
Wakefield *W York* ... 55 SE3320
Wakerley *Nhants* ... 40 SP8599
Wakes Colne *Essex* ... 24 TL8928
Walberswick *Suffk* ... 33 TM4974
Walberton *W Susx* ... 12 SU9706
Walbutt *D & G* ... 65 NX7468
Walcombe *Somset* ... 19 ST5546
Walcot *Lincs* ... 40 TF0635
Walcot *Lincs* ... 40 TF1356
Walcot *Shrops* ... 37 SJ5912
Walcot *Wilts* ... 20 SU1684
Walcote *Leics* ... 39 SP5783
Walcot Green *Norfk* ... 33 TM1280
Walcott *Lincs* ... 51 TF1257
Walden Stubbs *N York* ... 56 SE5516
Walderslade *Kent* ... 14 TQ7663
Walderton *W Susx* ... 11 SU7910
Walditch *Dorset* ... 8 SY4892
Waldley *Derbys* ... 48 SK1237
Waldridge *Dur* ... 69 NZ2549
Waldron *E Susx* ... 13 TQ5419
Wales *S York* ... 49 SK4882
Wales *Somset* ... 8 ST5525
Walesby *Lincs* ... 50 TF1392
Walesby *Notts* ... 49 SK6870
Walford *H & W* ... 27 SO5820
Walford *H & W* ... 36 SO3872
Walford *Staffs* ... 37 SJ8134
Walford Heath *Shrops* ... 36 SJ4519
Walgherton *Ches* ... 47 SJ6949
Walgrave *Nhants* ... 30 SP8071
Walhampton *Hants* ... 10 SZ3395
Walk Mill *Lancs* ... 54 SD8729
Walkden *Gt Man* ... 47 SD7303
Walker *T & W* ... 69 NZ2964
Walker's Green *H & W* ... 27 SO5247
Walkerburn *Border* ... 76 NT3637
Walkeringham *Notts* ... 50 SK7692
Walkern *Herts* ... 31 TL2826
Walkford *Dorset* ... 10 NO2301
Walkhampton *Devon* ... 4 SX5369
Walkington *Humb* ... 56 SE9937
Walkley *S York* ... 49 SK3388
Walkwood *H & W* ... 28 SP0364
Wall *Border* ... 76 NT4623
Wall *Nthumb* ... 68 NY9168
Wall *Staffs* ... 38 SK0906
Wall End *Cumb* ... 67 NY2383
Wallacetown *D & G* ... 64 NX8487
Wallacetown *Strath* ... 73 NS2703
Wallacetown *Strath* ... 73 NS4010
Wallands Park *E Susx* ... 13 TQ4010
Wallasey *Mersyd* ... 46 SJ2992
Waller's Green *H & W* ... 28 SO6738
Wallfield *Fife* ... 82 NO1909

Wallhead *Cumb* ... 67 NY4661
Wallington *Oxon* ... 21 SU6089
Wallington *Gt Lon* ... 23 TQ2864
Wallington *Hants* ... 11 SU5806
Wallington *Herts* ... 31 TL2933
Wallington Heath *W Mids* ... 38 SJ9902
Wallisdown *Dorset* ... 10 SZ0694
Walliswood *W Susx* ... 12 TQ1238
Walls *Shet* ... 103 HU2449
Wallsend *T & W* ... 69 NZ2966
Wallyford *Loth* ... 76 NT3671
Walmer *Kent* ... 15 TR3750
Walmer Bridge *Lancs* ... 53 SD4824
Walmley Ash *W Mids* ... 38 SP1392
Walpole *Somset* ... 19 ST3041
Walpole *Suffk* ... 33 TM3674
Walpole Cross Keys *Norfk* ... 41 TF5119
Walpole Highway *Norfk* ... 41 TF5113
Walpole St. Andrew *Norfk* ... 41 TF5017
Walpole St. Peter *Norfk* ... 41 TF5016
Walrow *Somset* ... 19 ST3347
Walsall *W Mids* ... 38 SP0198
Walsden *W York* ... 54 SD9321
Walsham le Willows *Suffk* ... 32 TM0071
Walshaw *W York* ... 54 SD9731
Walshford *N York* ... 55 SE4153
Walsoken *Norfk* ... 41 TF4710
Walston *Strath* ... 75 NT0577
Walsworth *Herts* ... 31 TL1930
Walterston *S Glam* ... 18 ST0771
Waltham *Humb* ... 57 TA2503
Waltham *Kent* ... 15 TR1048
Waltham Abbey *Essex* ... 23 TL3800
Waltham Chase *Hants* ... 11 SU5615
Waltham Cross *Herts* ... 23 TL3600
Waltham St. Lawrence *Berks* ... 22 SU8276
Waltham on the Wolds *Leics* ... 40 SK8024
Walthamstow *Gt Lon* ... 23 TQ3688
Walton *Bucks* ... 30 SP8936
Walton *Cumb* ... 67 NY5264
Walton *Derbys* ... 49 SK3568
Walton *Leics* ... 39 SP5987
Walton *Powys* ... 27 SO2559
Walton *Shrops* ... 37 SJ5818
Walton *Staffs* ... 38 SJ8528
Walton *Staffs* ... 38 SJ8933
Walton *Suffk* ... 25 TM2935
Walton *W Susx* ... 11 SU8104
Walton *W York* ... 55 SE4447
Walton Cardiff *Gloucs* ... 28 SO9032
Walton East *Dyfed* ... 16 SN0223
Walton Elm *Dorset* ... 9 ST7717
Walton Lower Street *Suffk* ... 25 TM2834
Walton Park *Avon* ... 19 ST4172
Walton West *Dyfed* ... 16 SM8613
Walton on the Hill *Surrey* ... 23 TQ2255
Walton on the Naze *Essex* ... 25 TM2622
Walton on the Wolds *Leics* ... 39 SK5919
Walton-in-Gordano *Avon* ... 19 ST4273
Walton-on-Thames *Surrey* ... 22 TQ1066
Walton-on-Trent *Derbys* ... 39 SK2118
Walton-on-the-Hill *Staffs* ... 38 SJ9520
Walwen *Clwyd* ... 46 SJ1771
Walworth *Dur* ... 61 NZ2318
Walwyn's Castle *Dyfed* ... 16 SM8711
Wambrook *Somset* ... 8 ST2907
Wamphray *D & G* ... 67 NY1295
Wanborough *Surrey* ... 22 SU9348
Wanborough *Wilts* ... 21 SU2082
Wandel *Strath* ... 75 NS9427
Wangford *Suffk* ... 33 TM4679
Wanlip *Leics* ... 39 SK5910
Wanlockhead *D & G* ... 66 NS8712
Wannock *E Susx* ... 13 TQ5703
Wansford *Cambs* ... 40 TL0799
Wansford *Humb* ... 57 TA0656
Wanshurst Green *Kent* ... 14 TQ7645
Wanstead *Gt Lon* ... 23 TQ4088
Wanstrow *Somset* ... 20 ST7141
Wanswell *Gloucs* ... 20 SO6801
Wantage *Oxon* ... 21 SU3988
Wapley *Avon* ... 20 ST7179
Wappenbury *Warwks* ... 29 SP3769
Wappenham *Nhants* ... 29 SP6245
Warbister *Ork* ... 103 HY3933
Warbleton *E Susx* ... 13 TQ6018
Warborough *Oxon* ... 21 SU5993
Warbourne Ford *Devon* ... 5 SX7162
Warboys *Cambs* ... 41 TL3080
Warbreck *Lancs* ... 53 SD3238
Warbstow *Cnwll* ... 4 SX2090
Warcop *Cumb* ... 60 NY7415
Ward Green *Suffk* ... 32 TM0564
Warden *Nthumb* ... 68 NY9166
Wardington *Oxon* ... 29 SP4946
Wardle *Ches* ... 47 SJ6057
Wardle *Gt Man* ... 54 SD9116
Wardley *Leics* ... 40 SK8300
Wardlow *Derbys* ... 48 SK1874
Wardy Hill *Cambs* ... 41 TL4782
Ware *Herts* ... 31 TL3514
Wareham *Dorset* ... 9 SY9287
Warehorne *Kent* ... 15 TQ9832
Warenford *Nthumb* ... 77 NU1328
Wareside *Herts* ... 31 TL3915
Waresley *Cambs* ... 31 TL2454
Warfield *Berks* ... 22 SU8872
Warfleet *Devon* ... 5 SX8750
Wargrave *Berks* ... 22 SU7978
Warham All Saints *Norfk* ... 42 TF9441
Warham St. Mary *Norfk* ... 42 TF9441
Wark *Nthumb* ... 68 NY8576
Wark *Nthumb* ... 77 NT8238
Warkleigh *Devon* ... 7 SS6422
Warkton *Nhants* ... 40 SP8979
Warkworth *Nhants* ... 29 SP4840
Warkworth *Nthumb* ... 77 NU2406
Warlaby *N York* ... 62 SE3591
Warleggan *Cnwll* ... 3 SX1569
Warlingham *Surrey* ... 23 TQ3658
Warmanbie *D & G* ... 67 NY1968
Warmfield *W York* ... 55 SE3720
Warmingham *Ches* ... 47 SJ7161
Warmington *Nhants* ... 40 TL0791
Warmington *Warwks* ... 29 SP4147
Warminster *Wilts* ... 20 ST8644
Warmley *Avon* ... 20 ST6673
Warmsworth *S York* ... 49 SE5400
Warmwell *Dorset* ... 9 SY7585
Warnford *Hants* ... 11 SU6223
Warnham *W Susx* ... 12 TQ1533
Warnham Court *W Susx* ... 12 TQ0307
Warningcamp *W Susx* ... 12 TQ0307
Warninglid *W Susx* ... 12 TQ2526
Warren *Ches* ... 47 SJ8870
Warren *Dyfed* ... 16 SR9397
Warren Row *Berks* ... 22 SU8180
Warren Street *Kent* ... 14 TQ9253
Warrenby *Cleve* ... 69 NZ5755
Warrenhill *Strath* ... 75 NS9439
Warrington *Bucks* ... 30 SP8955
Warrington *Ches* ... 47 SJ6088
Warriston *Loth* ... 75 NT2575
Warsash *Hants* ... 10 SU4906
Warslow *Staffs* ... 48 SK0858
Warsop *Notts* ... 49 SK5667
Warsop Vale *Notts* ... 56 SE5467
Warter *Humb* ... 56 SE8750
Warthermaske *N York* ... 61 SE2078
Warthill *N York* ... 56 SE6755
Wartling *E Susx* ... 13 TQ6509
Wartnaby *Leics* ... 40 SK7123
Warton *Lancs* ... 53 SD4128
Warton *Lancs* ... 53 SD4972
Warton *Nthumb* ... 68 NU0003
Warton *Warwks* ... 39 SK2803
Warwick *Cumb* ... 67 NY4656
Warwick *Warwks* ... 29 SP2865
Warwick Bridge *Cumb* ... 67 NY4657
Warwicksland *Cumb* ... 67 NY4477
Wasdale Head *Cumb* ... 58 NY1808
Wash *Devon* ... 5 SX7765
Washbourne *Devon* ... 5 SX7954
Washbrook *Somset* ... 19 ST4150
Washbrook *Suffk* ... 33 TM1142
Washfield *Devon* ... 7 SS9315
Washfold *N York* ... 61 NZ0502
Washford *Somset* ... 7 ST0441
Washford Pyne *Devon* ... 7 SS8111
Washingborough *Lincs* ... 50 TF0170

Washington Whatley

Washington *T & W* 69 NZ2956
Washington *W Susx* 12 TQ1212
Wasperton *Warwks* 29 SP2659
Wass *N York* 62 SE5579
Watchet *Somset* 7 ST0743
Watchfield *Oxon* 21 SU2490
Water *Devon* 5 SX7580
Water Eaton *Oxon* 29 SP5112
Water End *Beds* 30 TL1151
Water End *Essex* 31 TL5840
Water End *Herts* 22 TL0310
Water End *Humb* 56 SE7938
Water Fryston *W York* 55 SE4626
Water Newton *Cambs* 40 TL1097
Water Orton *Warwks* 38 SP1791
Water Stratford *Bucks* 29 SP6534
Waterbeach *Cambs* 31 TL4965
Waterbeach *W Susx* 11 SU8908
Waterbeck *D & G* 67 NY2477
Watercombe *Dorset* 9 SY7585
Waterend *Cumb* 58 NY1222
Waterfall *Staffs* 48 SK0851
Waterfoot *Strath* 74 NS5655
Waterford *Herts* 31 TL3114
Watergate *Cnwll* 3 SX1181
Waterhead *Cumb* 59 NY3804
Waterhead *Strath* 73 NS5411
Waterheads *Border* 75 NT2451
Waterhouses *Staffs* 48 SK0850
Wateringbury *Kent* 14 TQ6853
Waterloo *Dorset* 9 SZ0194
Waterloo *Dyfed* 16 SM9803
Waterloo *Highld* 85 NG6623
Waterloo *Mersyd* 46 SJ3298
Waterloo *Strath* 74 NS8054
Waterloo *Tays* 82 NO0537
Waterlooville *Hants* 11 SU6809
Watermillock *Cumb* 59 NY4422
Waterperry *Oxon* 29 SP6206
Waterrow *Somset* 7 ST0525
Waters Upton *Shrops* 37 SJ6319
Watersfield *W Susx* 12 TQ0115
Waterside *Cumb* 67 NY2445
Waterside *Lancs* 54 SD7123
Waterside *Strath* 73 NS4308
Waterside *Strath* 73 NS4843
Waterside *Strath* 74 NS6773
Waterside *Surrey* 13 TQ3945
Waterstock *Oxon* 29 SP6305
Waterston *Dyfed* 16 SM9306
Watford *Herts* 22 TQ1196
Watford *Nhants* 29 SP6069
Wath *N York* 55 SE1467
Wath *N York* 62 SE3276
Wath Upon Dearne *S York* 49 SE4300
Watlington *Norfk* 41 TF6211
Watlington *Oxon* 22 SU6894
Watten *Highld* 100 ND2454
Wattisfield *Suffk* 32 TM0074
Wattisham *Suffk* 32 TM0151
Watton *Dorset* 8 SY4592
Watton *Humb* 56 TA0150
Watton *Norfk* 42 TF9100
Watton Green *Norfk* 42 TF9301
Watton Green *Norfk* 42 TF9301
Watton-at-Stone *Herts* 31 TL3019
Wattsville *Gwent* 19 ST2091
Wauldby *Humb* 56 SE9629
Waulkmill *Gramp* 89 NO6492
Waunarlwydd *W Glam* 17 SS6095
Waunfawr *Dyfed* 34 SN6081
Waunfawr *Gwynd* 44 SH5259
Waunlwyd *Gwent* 27 SO1807
Wavendon *Bucks* 30 SP9037
Waverbridge *Cumb* 67 NY2249
Waverton *Ches* 46 SJ4663
Waverton *Cumb* 67 NY2247
Wawne *Humb* 57 TA0936
Waxham *Norfk* 43 TG4426
Way Village *Devon* 7 SS8810
Wayford *Somset* 8 ST4006
Waytown *Devon* 6 SS3622
Waytown *Dorset* 8 SY4698
Weacombe *Somset* 18 ST1140
Weald *Oxon* 21 SP3002
Wealdstone *Gt Lon* 22 TQ1589
Wear Head *Dur* 60 NY8539
Weardley *W York* 55 SE2944
Weare Giffard *Devon* 6 SS4721
Wearne *Somset* 8 ST4228
Weasdale *Cumb* 60 NY6904
Weasenham All Saints *Norfk* 42 TF8421
Weasenham St. Peter *Norfk* 42 TF8522
Weasle *Gt Man* 47 SJ8098
Weaverham *Ches* 47 SJ6174
Weaverthorpe *N York* 56 SE9670
Webheath *H & W* 28 SP0266
Wedderlairs *Gramp* 95 NJ8532
Wedding Hall Fold *N York* 54 SD9446
Weddington *Warwks* 39 SP3693
Wedhampton *Wilts* 20 SU0557
Wedmore *Somset* 19 ST4347
Wednesbury *W Mids* 38 SO9895
Weecar *Notts* 50 SK8267
Weedon *Bucks* 30 SP8118
Weedon Lois *Nhants* 29 SP6046
Weeford *Staffs* 38 SK1404
Week *Devon* 6 SS5726
Week *Somset* 7 SS9133
Week St. Mary *Cnwll* 6 SX2397
Weeke *Hants* 10 SU4631
Weekley *Nhants* 40 SP8881
Weel *Humb* 56 TA0039
Weeley *Essex* 25 TM1422
Weeley Heath *Essex* 25 TM1520
Weem *Tays* 87 NN8449
Weethley Hamlet *Warwks* 28 SP0555
Weeting *Norfk* 32 TL7788
Weeton *Humb* 51 TA3600
Weeton *Lancs* 53 SD3834
Weeton *W York* 55 SE2846
Weetwood *W York* 55 SE2737
Weir *Lancs* 54 SD8625
Weir Quay *Devon* 4 SX4365
Weirbrook *Shrops* 36 SJ3524
Welborne *Norfk* 42 TG0610
Welbourn *Lincs* 50 SK9654
Welburn *N York* 56 SE7168
Welbury *N York* 62 NZ3902
Welby *Lincs* 40 SK9738
Welcombe *Devon* 6 SS2218
Welford *Nhants* 39 SP6480
Welford-on-Avon *Warwks* 28 SP1442
Welham *Leics* 40 SP7692
Welham *Notts* 50 SK7382
Welham Green *Herts* 23 TL2305
Well *Hants* 22 SU7646
Well *Lincs* 51 TF4473
Well *N York* 61 SE2681
Well Head *Herts* 31 TL1727
Well Town *Devon* 18 SS9050
Welland *H & W* 28 SO7940
Wellbank *Tays* 83 NO4737
Wellesbourne Mountford *Warwks* 29 SP2855
Wellfield *Dur* 62 NZ4137
Welling *Gt Lon* 23 TQ4575
Wellingborough *Nhants* 30 SP8968
Wellingham *Norfk* 42 TF8722
Wellingore *Lincs* 50 SK9856
Wellington *Cumb* 58 NY0704
Wellington *H & W* 27 SO4948
Wellington *Shrops* 37 SJ6511
Wellington *Somset* 8 ST1320
Wellington Heath *H & W* 28 SO7140
Wellow *Avon* 20 ST7358
Wellow *IOW* 10 SZ3887
Wellow *Notts* 49 SK6666
Wells *Somset* 19 ST5445
Wells Green *Ches* 47 SJ6853
Wells of Ythan *Gramp* 94 NJ6338
Wells-Next-The-Sea *Norfk* 42 TF9143
Wellstye Green *Essex* 24 TL6318
Welltree *Tays* 75 NS9622
Wellwood *Fife* 82 NT0988
Welney *Norfk* 41 TL5294
Welsh End *Shrops* 37 SJ5035
Welsh Frankton *Shrops* 36 SJ3633
Welsh Newton *H & W* 27 SO4918
Welsh St. Donats *S Glam* 18 ST0276
Welshampton *Shrops* 36 SJ4335
Welshpool *Powys* 36 SJ2207
Welton *Cumb* 67 NY3544
Welton *Humb* 56 SE9527
Welton *Lincs* 50 TF0079
Welton *Nhants* 29 SP5865
Welton le Marsh *Lincs* 51 TF4768
Welton le Wold *Lincs* 51 TF2787
Welwick *Humb* 57 TA3421
Welwyn *Herts* 31 TL2316
Welwyn Garden City *Herts* 31 TL2312
Wem *Shrops* 37 SJ5129
Wembdon *Somset* 19 ST2837
Wembley *Gt Lon* 23 TQ1885
Wembury *Devon* 4 SX5148
Wemyss Bay *Strath* 73 NS1969
Wendens Ambo *Essex* 31 TL5136
Wendlebury *Oxon* 29 SP5519
Wendling *Norfk* 42 TF9312
Wendover *Bucks* 22 SP8607
Wendron *Cnwll* 2 SW6731
Wendy *Cambs* 31 TL3247
Wenhaston *Suffk* 33 TM4275
Wennington *Cambs* 41 TL2379
Wennington *Lancs* 54 SD6169
Wensley *Derbys* 49 SK2661
Wensley *N York* 61 SE0989
Wentbridge *W York* 55 SE4817
Wentnor *Shrops* 36 SO3892
Wentworth *Cambs* 31 TL4878
Wentworth *S York* 49 SK3898
Wenvoe *S Glam* 18 ST1272
Weobley *H & W* 27 SO4051
Weobley Marsh *H & W* 27 SO4151
Wepham *W Susx* 12 TQ0408
Wereham *Norfk* 42 TF6801
Wergs *Staffs* 38 SJ8701
Wernrheolydd *Gwent* 27 SO3913
Werrington *Cambs* 40 TF1603
Werrington *Cnwll* 4 SX3287
Wervin *Ches* 46 SJ4271
Wesham *Lancs* 53 SD4133
Wessington *Derbys* 49 SK3757
West Acre *Norfk* 42 TF7715
West Alvington *Devon* 5 SX7243
West Anstey *Devon* 7 SS8527
West Appleton *N York* 61 SE2294
West Ashling *W Susx* 11 SU8107
West Ashton *Wilts* 20 ST8755
West Auckland *Dur* 61 NZ1826
West Ayton *N York* 63 SE9884
West Bagborough *Somset* 8 ST1633
West Bank *Ches* 46 SJ5184
West Barkwith *Lincs* 50 TF1580
West Barnby *N York* 63 NZ8112
West Barns *Loth* 83 NT6578
West Barsham *Norfk* 42 TF9033
West Bay *Dorset* 8 SY4690
West Beckham *Norfk* 43 TG1439
West Bedfont *Surrey* 22 TQ0674
West Bergholt *Essex* 25 TL9527
West Bexington *Dorset* 8 SY5386
West Bilney *Norfk* 42 TF7115
West Blatchington *E Susx* 12 TQ2706
West Boldon *T & W* 69 NZ3443
West Bourton *Dorset* 9 ST7629
West Bowling *W York* 55 SE1630
West Brabourne *Kent* 15 TR0742
West Bradenham *Norfk* 42 TF9208
West Bradford *Lancs* 54 SD7444
West Bradley *Somset* 19 ST5536
West Bretton *W York* 55 SE2813
West Bridgford *Notts* 49 SK5837
West Bromwich *W Mids* 38 SP0091
West Buckland *Devon* 7 SS6531
West Buckland *Somset* 8 ST1720
West Burnside *Gramp* 89 NO7070
West Burton *N York* 61 SE0186
West Burton *W Susx* 12 TQ0014
West Butsfiel *Dur* 68 NZ0945
West Butterwick *Humb* 56 SE8305
West Cairngaan *D & G* 64 NX1232
West Caistor *Norfk* 43 TG5111
West Calder *Loth* 75 NT0163
West Camel *Somset* 8 ST5724
West Chaldon *Dorset* 9 SY7783
West Challow *Oxon* 21 SU3688
West Charleton *Devon* 5 SX7542
West Chelborough *Dorset* 8 ST5405
West Chevington *Nthumb* 69 NZ2297
West Chiltington *W Susx* 12 TQ0918
West Chinnock *Somset* 8 ST4613
West Chisenbury *Wilts* 20 SU1352
West Clandon *Surrey* 12 TQ0452
West Cliffe *Kent* 15 TR3444
West Coker *Somset* 8 ST5113
West Compton *Dorset* 8 SY5694
West Compton *Somset* 19 ST5942
West Cottingwith *N York* 56 SE6942
West Cowick *Humb* 56 SE6521
West Craigneuk *Strath* 74 NS7765
West Cross *W Glam* 17 SS6189
West Curthwaite *Cumb* 67 NY3249
West Dean *Hants* 10 SU2526
West Dean *W Susx* 11 SU8512
West Dean *Wilts* 10 SU2526
West Deeping *Lincs* 40 TF1008
West Derby *Mersyd* 46 SJ3993
West Dereham *Norfk* 41 TF6500
West Down *Devon* 6 SS5142
West Drayton *Gt Lon* 22 TQ0679
West Drayton *Notts* 49 SK7074
West Dunnet *Highld* 100 ND2171
West Ella *Humb* 56 TA0029
West End *Avon* 19 ST4569
West End *Beds* 30 SP9853
West End *Berks* 22 SU8275
West End *Cambs* 31 TL3168
West End *Cumb* 67 NY3258
West End *Gwent* 19 ST2195
West End *Gwent* 19 ST2294
West End *Hants* 10 SU4614
West End *Herts* 23 TL2608
West End *Herts* 23 TL3306
West End *Humb* 56 SE9131
West End *Humb* 57 TA1830
West End *Humb* 57 TA2627
West End *N York* 55 SE5140
West End *Norfk* 42 TF9109
West End *Norfk* 43 TG5011
West End *Oxon* 21 SU5886
West End *Somset* 9 ST6735
West End *Surrey* 22 TQ1364
West End *Surrey* 22 SU9461
West End *Wilts* 9 ST9123
West End *Wilts* 9 ST9824
West End Green *Hants* 22 SU6661
West Farleigh *Kent* 14 TQ7152
West Farndon *Nhants* 29 SP5251
West Felton *Shrops* 36 SJ3425
West Firle *E Susx* 13 TQ4707
West Garforth *W York* 55 SE3833
West Garty *Highld* 97 NC9912
West Geirnish *W Isls* 102 NF7741
West Grafton *Wilts* 21 SU2460
West Green *Hants* 22 SU7456
West Grimstead *Wilts* 10 SU2026
West Grinstead *W Susx* 12 TQ1720
West Haddlesey *N York* 56 SE5626
West Haddon *Nhants* 39 SP6371
West Hagbourne *Oxon* 21 SU5187
West Hagley *H & W* 38 SO9080
West Hallam *Derbys* 49 SK4341
West Halton *Humb* 56 SE9020
West Ham *Gt Lon* 23 TQ3983
West Handley *Derbys* 49 SK3977
West Hanney *Oxon* 21 SU4092
West Hanningfield *Essex* 13 TQ7300
West Harnham *Wilts* 10 SU1229
West Harting *W Susx* 11 SU7821
West Hatch *Somset* 8 ST2820
West Hatch *Wilts* 9 ST9228
West Heath *W Mids* 38 SP0277
West Helmsdale *Highld* 97 ND0115
West Hendred *Oxon* 21 SU4488
West Heslerton *N York* 63 SE9175
West Hewish *Avon* 19 ST3964
West Hill *Devon* 7 SY0694
West Hoathly *W Susx* 12 TQ3632
West Holme *Dorset* 9 SY8885
West Horrington *Somset* 19 ST5747
West Horsley *Surrey* 12 TQ0752
West Hougham *Kent* 15 TR2640
West Howe *Dorset* 10 SZ0595
West Howetown *Somset* 7 SS9135
West Huntspill *Somset* 19 ST3044
West Hythe *Kent* 15 TR1234
West Ilsley *Berks* 21 SU4782
West Itchenor *W Susx* 11 SU7900
West Kennet *Wilts* 20 SU1168
West Kilbride *Strath* 73 NS2048
West Kingsdown *Kent* 14 TQ5763
West Kington *Wilts* 20 ST8077
West Kirby *Mersyd* 46 SJ2186
West Knapton *N York* 63 SE8775
West Knighton *Dorset* 9 SY7387
West Knoyle *Wilts* 9 ST8532
West Lambrook *Somset* 8 ST4118
West Langdon *Kent* 15 TR3247
West Langwell *Highld* 97 NC6909
West Laroch *Highld* 86 NN0758
West Lavington *W Susx* 11 SU8920
West Lavington *Wilts* 20 SU0052
West Layton *N York* 61 NZ1410
West Leake *Notts* 39 SK5226
West Leigh *Devon* 5 SX7557
West Leigh *Devon* 7 SS6805
West Leigh *Somset* 8 ST1231
West Lexham *Norfk* 42 TF8417
West Lilling *N York* 56 SE6465
West Linton *Border* 75 NT1551
West Littleton *Avon* 20 ST7675
West Lockinge *Oxon* 21 SU4187
West Luccombe *Somset* 7 SS8946
West Lulworth *Dorset* 9 SY8280
West Lutton *N York* 56 SE9369
West Lydford *Somset* 8 ST5632
West Lyng *Somset* 8 ST3228
West Lynn *Norfk* 41 TF6120
West Malling *Kent* 14 TQ6857
West Malvern *H & W* 28 SO7646
West Marden *W Susx* 11 SU7713
West Markham *Notts* 49 SK7272
West Marsh *Humb* 57 TA2509
West Marton *N York* 54 SD8950
West Melta *S York* 49 SE4001
West Meon *Hants* 11 SU6424
West Meon Hut *Hants* 11 SU6526
West Mersea *Essex* 25 TM0112
West Milton *Dorset* 8 SY5096
West Minster *Kent* 14 TQ9073
West Monkton *Somset* 8 ST2528
West Moors *Dorset* 10 SU0802
West Morden *Dorset* 9 SY9095
West Mudford *Somset* 8 ST5620
West Ness *N York* 62 SE6879
West Newton *Humb* 57 TA2037
West Newton *Norfk* 42 TF6928
West Newton *Somset* 8 ST2829
West Norwood *Gt Lon* 23 TQ3171
West Ogwell *Devon* 5 SX8170
West Orchard *Dorset* 9 ST8216
West Overton *Wilts* 20 SU1267
West Parley *Dorset* 10 SZ0997
West Peckham *Kent* 13 TQ6452
West Pelton *Dur* 69 NZ2352
West Pennard *Somset* 19 ST5438
West Pentire *Cnwll* 2 SW7760
West Perry *Cambs* 30 TL1466
West Porlock *Somset* 18 SS8797
West Preston *W Susx* 12 TQ0502
West Pulham *Dorset* 9 ST7008
West Putford *Devon* 6 SS3616
West Quantoxhead *Somset* 18 ST1142
West Raddon *Devon* 7 SS8902
West Rainton *T & W* 69 NZ3246
West Rasen *Lincs* 50 TF0589
West Raynham *Norfk* 42 TF8725
West Rounton *N York* 62 NZ4103
West Row *Suffk* 32 TL6775
West Rudham *Norfk* 42 TF8128
West Runton *Norfk* 43 TG1842
West Safford *Dorset* 9 SY7289
West Saltoun *Loth* 76 NT4667
West Sandford *Devon* 7 SS8102
West Sandwick *Shet* 103 HU4588
West Scrafton *N York* 61 SE0783
West Somerton *Norfk* 43 TG4720
West Stoke *W Susx* 11 SU8308
West Stonesdale *N York* 60 NY8802
West Stour *Dorset* 9 ST7822
West Stourmouth *Kent* 15 TR2562
West Stow *Suffk* 32 TL8171
West Stowell *Wilts* 20 SU1362
West Street *Kent* 14 TQ7376
West Street *Suffk* 32 TL9871
West Tanfield *N York* 61 SE2678
West Taphouse *Cnwll* 3 SX1463
West Tarbert *Strath* 71 NR8467
West Tarring *W Susx* 12 TQ1203
West Thorney *W Susx* 11 SU7602
West Thorpe *Notts* 39 SK6225
West Thurrock *Essex* 24 TQ5877
West Tisted *Hants* 11 SU6529
West Torrington *Lincs* 50 TF1381
West Town *Avon* 19 ST4868
West Town *Devon* 6 SS3221
West Town *Hants* 11 SZ7099
West Town *Somset* 20 ST7041
West Tytherley *Hants* 10 SU2730
West Tytherley *Hants* 10 SU2730
West Tytherton *Wilts* 20 ST9474
West Walton *Norfk* 41 TF4713
West Walton Highway *Norfk* 41 TF4913
West Weetwood *Nthumb* 77 NU0029
West Wellow *Hants* 10 SU2818
West Wellow *Hants* 10 SU2918
West Wembury *Devon* 4 SX5249
West Wemyss *Fife* 83 NT3294
West Wick *Avon* 19 ST3762
West Wickham *Cambs* 31 TL6149
West Wickham *Gt Lon* 23 TQ3766
West Williamston *Dyfed* 16 SN0305
West Winch *Norfk* 41 TF6316
West Winterslow *Wilts* 10 SU2232
West Wittering *W Susx* 11 SZ7898
West Witton *N York* 61 SE0588
West Woodburn *Nthumb* 68 NY8986
West Woodhay *Berks* 21 SU3962
West Wordham *Hants* 11 SU7437
West Worthing *W Susx* 12 TQ1302
West Wratting *Essex* 31 TL6052
West Yoke *Kent* 14 TQ5965
West Youlstone *Cnwll* 6 SS2615
West melbury *Dorset* 9 ST8720
Westbere *Kent* 15 TR1961
Westborough *Lincs* 50 SK8544
Westbourne *W Susx* 11 SU7507
Westbrook *Berks* 21 SU4272
Westbrook *Kent* 15 TR3470
Westbury *Bucks* 29 SP6235
Westbury *Shrops* 36 SJ3509
Westbury *Wilts* 20 ST8751
Westbury Leigh *Wilts* 20 ST8649
Westbury on Severn *Gloucs* 28 SO7114
Westbury-on trym *Avon* 19 ST5877
Westbury-on-Trym *Avon* 19 ST5777
Westbury-sub-Mendip *Somset* 19 ST5049
Westby *Lancs* 53 SD3831
Westcliff-on-Sea *Essex* 24 TQ8686
Westcombe *Somset* 20 ST6739
Westcote *Gloucs* 29 SP2120
Westcott *Bucks* 30 SP7117
Westcott *Devon* 7 ST0204
Westcott *Surrey* 12 TQ1448
Westcott Barton *Oxon* 29 SP4325
Westcourt *Wilts* 21 SU2261
Westdean *E Susx* 13 TV5299
Westdowns *Cnwll* 3 SX0582
Wester Causewayend *Loth* 75 NT0861
Wester Drumashie *Highld* 92 NH6032
Wester Ellister *Strath* 70 NR2053
Wester Essenside *Border* 76 NT4320
Wester Ochiltree *Loth* 75 NT0374
Wester Pitkierie *Fife* 83 NO5505
Wester Rarichie *Highld* 97 NH8374
Westerdale *Highld* 100 ND1251
Westerdale *N York* 62 NZ6605
Westerfield *Suffk* 33 TM1747
Westergate *W Susx* 11 SU9305
Westerham *Kent* 23 TQ4454
Westerhope *T & W* 69 NZ1966
Westerland *Devon* 5 SX8662
Westerleigh *Avon* 20 ST6979
Westerloch *Highld* 100 ND3258
Westerton *Tays* 89 NO6754
Westfield *Loth* 75 NS9472
Westfield *Norfk* 42 TF9909
Westfields of Rattray *Tays* 88 NO1846
Westford *Somset* 8 ST1120
Westgate *Dur* 60 NY9038
Westgate *Humb* 56 SE7707
Westgate *Norfk* 42 TF9740
Westgate on Sea *Kent* 15 TR3270
Westhall *Gramp* 95 NJ6826
Westhall *Suffk* 33 TM4280
Westham *Dorset* 9 SY6579
Westham *E Susx* 13 TQ6404
Westham *Somset* 19 ST4046
Westhampnett *W Susx* 11 SU8806
Westhay *Somset* 19 ST4342
Westhide *H & W* 27 SO5843
Westhill *Gramp* 95 NJ8307
Westholme *Somset* 19 ST5642
Westhope *H & W* 27 SO4651
Westhope *Shrops* 37 SO4786
Westhorpe *Lincs* 41 TF2231
Westhorpe *Suffk* 32 TM0568
Westhoughton *Gt Man* 47 SD6506
Westhouse *N York* 60 SD6673
Westhouses *Derbys* 49 SK4257
Westhumble *Surrey* 12 TQ1651
Westlake *Devon* 5 SX6253
Westleigh *Devon* 6 SS4728
Westleigh *Devon* 7 ST0517
Westleton *Suffk* 33 TM4469
Westley *Suffk* 32 TL8264
Westley Heights *Essex* 24 TQ6887
Westley Waterless *Cambs* 31 TL6156
Westlington *Bucks* 22 SP7610
Westlinton *Cumb* 67 NY3964
Westmarsh *Kent* 15 TR2761
Westmeston *E Susx* 12 TQ3313
Westmill *Herts* 31 TL3627
Westmoor *T & W* 69 NZ2670
Westmuir *Tays* 88 NO3652
Westnewton *Cumb* 67 NY1344
Westoe *T & W* 69 NZ3765
Weston *Avon* 20 ST7366
Weston *Berks* 21 SU3973
Weston *Ches* 47 SJ7252
Weston *Devon* 8 ST1500
Weston *Devon* 8 SY1688
Weston *Dorset* 9 SY6871
Weston *Hants* 11 SU7221
Weston *Herts* 31 TL2530
Weston *Lincs* 41 TF2925
Weston *Nhants* 29 SP5846
Weston *Notts* 50 SK7767
Weston *Shrops* 36 SO3373
Weston *Shrops* 37 SJ5629
Weston *Shrops* 36 SJ2927
Weston *Staffs* 38 SJ9727
Weston *W York* 55 SE1747
Weston Beggard *H & W* 27 SO5841
Weston Colley *Hants* 10 SU5039
Weston Colville *Cambs* 31 TL6153
Weston Corbett *Hants* 22 SU6846
Weston Coyney *Staffs* 48 SJ9343
Weston Favel *Nhants* 30 SP7962
Weston Favell *Nhants* 30 SP7962
Weston Green *Cambs* 32 TL6252
Weston Heath *Shrops* 37 SJ7713
Weston Jones *Staffs* 37 SJ7624
Weston Longville *Norfk* 43 TG1115
Weston Lullingfields *Shrops* 36 SJ4224
Weston Patrick *Hants* 22 SU6946
Weston Rhyn *Shrops* 36 SJ2835
Weston Subedge *Gloucs* 28 SP1240
Weston Turville *Bucks* 22 SP8510
Weston Underwood *Bucks* 30 SP8650
Weston Underwood *Derbys* 49 SK2942
Weston by Welland *Nhants* 40 SP7791
Weston under Penyard *H & W* 27 SO6322
Weston under Wetherley *Warwks* 29 SP3669
Weston-Super-Mare *Avon* 19 ST3261
Weston-in-Gordano *Avon* 19 ST4474
Weston-on-Trent *Derbys* 39 SK4028
Weston-on-the-Green *Oxon* 29 SP5318
Weston-under-Lizard *Staffs* 37 SJ8010
Westonbirt *Gloucs* 20 ST8589
Westoning *Beds* 30 TL0332
Westonzoyland *Somset* 8 ST3534
Westow *N York* 56 SE7565
Westport *Somset* 8 ST3820
Westport *Strath* 72 NR6526
Westquarter *Cent* 82 NS9178
Westra *S Glam* 18 ST1471
Westridge Green *Berks* 21 SU5679
Westrigg *Loth* 74 NS9067
Westrop *Wilts* 21 SU1992
Westruther *Border* 76 NT6349
Westry *Cambs* 41 TL3998
Westward *Cumb* 67 NY2744
Westward Ho *Devon* 6 SS4329
Westwell *Kent* 15 TQ9847
Westwell *Oxon* 29 SP2210
Westwell Leacon *Kent* 14 TQ9547
Westwick *Cambs* 31 TL4265
Westwood *Devon* 7 SY0199
Westwood *Kent* 15 TR3667
Westwood *Wilts* 20 ST8059
Westwoodside *Humb* 50 SE7400
Wetham Green *Kent* 14 TQ8467
Wetheral *Cumb* 67 NY4654
Wetherby *W York* 55 SE4048
Wetherden *Suffk* 32 TM0062
Wetheringsett *Suffk* 33 TM1266
Wethersfield *Essex* 24 TL7131
Wetherup Street *Suffk* 33 TM1464
Wetley Rocks *Staffs* 48 SJ9649
Wettenhall *Ches* 47 SJ6261
Wetton *Staffs* 48 SK1055
Wetwang *Humb* 56 SE9358
Wetwood *Staffs* 37 SJ7733
Wexcombe *Wilts* 21 SU2658
Wexcombe *Wilts* 21 SU2758
Weybourne *Norfk* 43 TG1143
Weybread *Suffk* 33 TM2480
Weybread Street *Suffk* 33 TM2479
Weybridge *Surrey* 22 TQ0764
Weycroft *Devon* 21 SU3099
Weydale *Highld* 100 ND1564
Weyhill *Hants* 21 SU3146
Weymouth *Dorset* 9 SY6778
Whaddon *Bucks* 30 SP8034
Whaddon *Cambs* 31 TL3546
Whaddon *Gloucs* 28 SO8313
Whaddon *Wilts* 20 ST8861
Whaddon *Wilts* 10 SU1926
Whaley *Derbys* 49 SK5171
Whaley Bridge *Derbys* 48 SK0180
Whaley Thorns *Notts* 55 SE5271
Whaligoe *Highld* 100 ND3140
Whalley *Lancs* 54 SD7336
Whalton *Nthumb* 69 NZ1281
Wham *N York* 54 SD7762
Whaplode *Lincs* 41 TF3224
Whaplode Drove *Lincs* 41 TF3113
Wharf *Warwks* 29 SP4352
Wharfe *N York* 54 SD7869
Wharles *Lancs* 53 SD4435
Wharley End *Beds* 30 SP9342
Wharncliffe Side *S York* 49 SK2995
Wharram le Street *N York* 56 SE8665
Wharton *H & W* 27 SO5055
Whasset *Cumb* 59 SD5181
Whaston *N York* 61 NZ1506
Whatcote *Warwks* 29 SP2944
Whateley *Warwks* 39 SP2299
Whatfield *Suffk* 32 TM0246
Whatley *Somset* 8 ST3607
Whatley *Somset* 20 ST7347

Whatlington *E Susx*	14	TQ7618
Whatsole Street *Kent*	15	TR1144
Whatton *Notts*	40	SK7439
Whauphill *D & G*	64	NX4049
Wheal Rose *Cnwll*	2	SW7244
Wheatacre *Norfk*	43	TM4694
Wheathampstead *Herts*	31	TL1714
Wheathill *Shrops*	37	SO6282
Wheatley *Hants*	11	SU7840
Wheatley *Oxon*	29	SP5905
Wheatley Hill *Dur*	62	NZ3738
Wheatley Hills *S York*	56	SE5905
Wheaton Aston *Staffs*	38	SJ8512
Wheddon Cross *Somset*	7	SS9238
Wheelock *Ches*	47	SJ7559
Wheelock Heath *Ches*	47	SJ7457
Wheelton *Lancs*	54	SD6021
Wheldale *W York*	55	SE4426
Wheldrake *N York*	56	SE6844
Whelpley Hill *Bucks*	22	TL0004
Whelpo *Cumb*	67	NY3149
Whemstead *Herts*	31	TL3121
Whenby *N York*	56	SE6369
Whepstead *Suffk*	32	TL8358
Wherstead *Suffk*	33	TM1540
Wherwell *Hants*	21	SU3941
Wheston *Derbys*	48	SK1376
Whetsted *Kent*	13	TQ6546
Whetstone *Leics*	39	SP5597
Whicham *Cumb*	58	SD1382
Whichford *Warwks*	29	SP3134
Whickham *T & W*	69	NZ2061
Whiddon Down *Devon*	5	SX6992
Whight's Corner *Suffk*	33	TM1242
Whigstreet *Tays*	89	NO4844
Whilton *Nhants*	29	SP6364
Whim *Border*	75	NT2153
Whimble *Devon*	6	SS3403
Whimple *Devon*	7	SY0497
Whimpwell Green *Norfk*	43	TG3829
Whinburgh *Norfk*	42	TG0009
Whinnie Liggate *D & G*	65	NX7152
Whipcott *Devon*	7	ST0718
Whippingham *IOW*	11	SZ5193
Whipsnade *Beds*	22	TL0108
Whipton *Devon*	5	SX9493
Whisby *Lincs*	50	SK9067
Whissendine *Leics*	40	SK8214
Whistley Green *Berks*	22	SU7974
Whiston *Mersyd*	46	SJ4791
Whiston *Nhants*	30	SP8460
Whiston *S York*	49	SK4490
Whiston *Staffs*	38	SJ8914
Whiston *Staffs*	48	SK0347
Whitbeck *Cumb*	58	SD1184
Whitbourne *H & W*	28	SO7156
Whitburn *Loth*	75	NS9464
Whitburn *T & W*	69	NZ4062
Whitby *N York*	63	NZ8910
Whitchurch *Avon*	19	ST6167
Whitchurch *Bucks*	30	SP8020
Whitchurch *Devon*	4	SX4972
Whitchurch *Dyfed*	16	SM8025
Whitchurch *H & W*	27	SO5417
Whitchurch *Hants*	21	SU4648
Whitchurch *Oxon*	21	SU6377
Whitchurch *S Glam*	19	ST1579
Whitchurch *Shrops*	37	SJ5441
Whitchurch Canonicorum *Dorset*	8	SY3995
Whitchurch Hill *Oxon*	21	SU6378
Whitcombe *Dorset*	9	SY7188
Whitcot *Shrops*	36	SO3791
Whitcott Keysett *Shrops*	36	SO2782
White Chapel *Lancs*	53	SD5541
White Colne *Essex*	24	TL8830
White Coppice *Lancs*	54	SD6119
White Cross *Cnwll*	2	SW6821
White End *H & W*	28	SO7834
White Kirkley *Dur*	68	NZ0255
White Lackington *Dorset*	9	SY7198
White Ladies Aston *H & W*	28	SO9252
White Notley *Essex*	24	TL7818
White Pit *Lincs*	51	TF3777
White Roding *Essex*	24	TL5613
White Stake *Lancs*	53	SD5125
White Stone *H & W*	27	SO5642
White Stone Cross *Devon*	5	SX8993
White Waltham *Berks*	22	SU8577
White-le-Head *Dur*	69	NZ1754
Whiteacre Heath *Warwks*	39	SP2292
Whiteash Green *Essex*	24	TL7931
Whitebridge *Highld*	92	NH4815
Whitebrook *Gwent*	27	SO5306
Whitecairns *Gramp*	95	NJ9218
Whitechapel *Gt Lon*	23	TQ3381
Whitecraig *Loth*	75	NT3470
Whitecroft *Gloucs*	27	SO6106
Whiteface *Highld*	97	NH7088
Whitefarland *Strath*	72	NR8642
Whitefield *Gt Man*	47	SD8006
Whiteford *Gramp*	95	NJ7126
Whitegate *Ches*	47	SJ6269
Whitehall *Ork*	103	HY6528
Whitehaven *Cumb*	58	NX9718
Whitehill *Hants*	11	SU7934
Whitehill *Kent*	15	TR0950
Whitehills *Gramp*	94	NJ6565
Whitehouse *Gramp*	94	NJ6114
Whitehouse *Strath*	71	NR8161
Whitekirk *Loth*	83	NT5981
Whitelackington *Somset*	8	ST3815
Whiteley Bank *IOW*	11	SZ5581
Whiteley Village *Surrey*	22	TQ0962
Whitemire *Gramp*	93	NH9854
Whitemoor *Cnwll*	3	SW9757
Whitemoor *Derbys*	49	SK3648
Whitemoor *Notts*	49	SK5442
Whitenap *Hants*	10	SU3721
Whiteparish *Wilts*	10	SU2423
Whiterashes *Gramp*	95	NJ8523
Whiterow *Gramp*	93	NJ0257
Whiterow *Highld*	100	ND3648
Whiteshill *Gloucs*	28	SO8407
Whitesmith *E Susx*	13	TQ5214
Whitestaunton *Somset*	8	ST2810
Whitestreet Green *Suffk*	32	TL9739
Whiteway *Avon*	20	ST7263
Whitewell *Lancs*	54	SD6646
Whitewell-on-the-Hill *N York*	56	SE7265
Whitfield *Avon*	20	ST6791
Whitfield *Kent*	15	TR3045
Whitfield *Nhants*	29	SP6039
Whitfield *Nthumb*	68	NY7758
Whitford *Clwyd*	46	SJ1478
Whitford *Devon*	8	SY2595
Whitgift *Humb*	56	SE8022
Whitgift *Humb*	56	SE8122
Whitgreave *Staffs*	38	SJ8928
Whithorn *D & G*	64	NX4440
Whiting Bay *Strath*	72	NS0425
Whitington *Norfk*	42	TL7199
Whitland *Dyfed*	17	SN1916
Whitlaw *Border*	67	NT5012
Whitletts *Strath*	73	NS3623
Whitley *Berks*	22	SU7270
Whitley *Ches*	47	SJ6178
Whitley *N York*	56	SE5620
Whitley *S York*	49	SK3494
Whitley *Wilts*	20	ST8866
Whitley Bay *T & W*	69	NZ3572
Whitley Chapel *Nthumb*	68	NY9357
Whitley Lower *W York*	55	SE2217
Whitlieburn *Strath*	73	NS2163
Whitminster *Gloucs*	28	SO7708
Whitmore *Staffs*	37	SJ8041
Whitnage *Devon*	7	ST0215
Whitnash *Warwks*	29	SP3263
Whitney *H & W*	27	SO2647
Whitney *H & W*	27	SO2747
Whitrigglees *Cumb*	67	NY2457
Whitsbury *Hants*	10	SU1218
Whitsome *Border*	77	NT8650
Whitson *Gwent*	19	ST3883
Whitstable *Kent*	15	TR1066
Whitstone *Cnwll*	6	SX2698
Whittingham *Nthumb*	68	NU0612
Whittingslow *Shrops*	36	SO4388
Whittington *Derbys*	49	SK3773
Whittington *Derbys*	49	SK3875
Whittington *Gloucs*	28	SP0120
Whittington *H & W*	28	SO8752
Whittington *Lancs*	59	SD5976
Whittington *Shrops*	36	SJ3231
Whittington *Staffs*	38	SO8682
Whittington *Staffs*	38	SK1508
Whittington *Warwks*	39	SP2999
Whittle-le-Woods *Lancs*	54	SD5821
Whittlebury *Nhants*	30	SP6943
Whittlesey *Cambs*	41	TL2697
Whittlesford *Cambs*	31	TL4748
Whitton *Cleve*	62	NZ3921
Whitton *Humb*	56	SE9024
Whitton *Powys*	27	SO2767
Whitton *Shrops*	37	SO5772
Whittonstall *Nthumb*	68	NZ0757
Whitway *Hants*	21	SU4559
Whitwell *Derbys*	49	SK5276
Whitwell *Herts*	31	TL1820
Whitwell *IOW*	11	SZ5277
Whitwell *Leics*	40	SK9208
Whitwell *N York*	61	SE2899
Whitwell Street *Norfk*	43	TG1022
Whitwick *Leics*	39	SK4316
Whitwood *W York*	55	SE4124
Whitworth *Lancs*	54	SD8818
Whixall *Shrops*	37	SJ5134
Whixley *N York*	55	SE4458
Whorlton *Dur*	61	NZ1014
Whorlton *N York*	62	NZ4802
Whyle *H & W*	27	SO5561
Whyteleafe *Surrey*	23	TQ3358
Wibdon *Gloucs*	19	ST5797
Wibtoft *Warwks*	39	SP4887
Wichenford *H & W*	28	SO7860
Wichling *Kent*	14	TQ9256
Wick *Avon*	20	ST7072
Wick *Devon*	8	ST1604
Wick *Dorset*	10	SZ1591
Wick *H & W*	28	SO9645
Wick *Highld*	100	ND3650
Wick *M Glam*	18	SS9272
Wick *Somset*	8	ST4027
Wick *W Susx*	12	TQ0203
Wick Rissington *Gloucs*	29	SP1821
Wick St. Lawrence *Avon*	19	ST3665
Wicken *Cambs*	31	TL5770
Wicken *Nhants*	30	SP7439
Wicken Bonhunt *Essex*	31	TL4933
Wickenby *Lincs*	50	TF0882
Wicker Street Green *Suffk*	32	TL9742
Wickersley *S York*	49	SK4791
Wickford *Essex*	24	TQ7593
Wickham *Berks*	21	SU3971
Wickham *Hants*	11	SU5711
Wickham Bishops *Essex*	24	TL8412
Wickham Green *Berks*	21	SU4072
Wickham Green *Suffk*	33	TM0969
Wickham Market *Suffk*	33	TM3055
Wickham Skeith *Suffk*	33	TM0969
Wickham St. Paul *Essex*	24	TL8336
Wickham Street *Suffk*	32	TM0869
Wickhambreaux *Kent*	15	TR2158
Wickhambrook *Suffk*	32	TL7554
Wickhamford *H & W*	28	SP0641
Wickhampton *Norfk*	43	TG4205
Wicklewood *Norfk*	42	TG0702
Wickmere *Norfk*	43	TG1733
Wickwar *Avon*	20	ST7288
Widdington *Essex*	31	TL5331
Widdop *Lancs*	54	SD9333
Widdrington *T & W*	69	NZ2595
Wide Open *T & W*	69	NZ2372
Widecombe in the Moor *Devon*	5	SX7176
Widemouth Bay *Cnwll*	6	SS2002
Widford *Essex*	24	TL6905
Widford *Herts*	31	TL4116
Widmer End *Bucks*	22	SU8796
Widmerpool *Notts*	39	SK6327
Widmore *Gt Lon*	23	TQ4268
Widnes *Ches*	46	SJ5184
Widworthy *Devon*	6	SX2199
Wigan *Gt Man*	47	SD5805
Wigborough *Somset*	8	ST4415
Wiggaton *Devon*	8	SY1093
Wiggenhall St. Germans *Norfk*	41	TF5914
Wiggenhall St. Mary Magdalan *Norfk*	41	TF5911
Wiggenhall St. Mary the Virgin *Norfk*	41	TF5814
Wiggens Green *Essex*	32	TL6642
Wigginton *Herts*	22	SP9310
Wigginton *N York*	56	SE5958
Wigginton *Oxon*	29	SP3833
Wigginton *Staffs*	39	SK2106
Wigglesworth *N York*	54	SD8157
Wiggold *Gloucs*	28	SP0404
Wiggonby *Cumb*	67	NY2953
Wigham *Devon*	7	SS7508
Wighill *N York*	55	SE4746
Wighton *Norfk*	42	TF9439
Wigley *Hants*	10	SU3217
Wigmore *H & W*	27	SO4169
Wigsley *Notts*	50	SK8570
Wigsthorpe *Nhants*	40	TL0482
Wigston *Leics*	39	SP6199
Wigston Parva *Leics*	39	SP4689
Wigthorpe *Notts*	49	SK5983
Wigtoft *Lincs*	41	TF2636
Wigton *Cumb*	67	NY2548
Wigtown *D & G*	64	NX4355
Wike *W York*	55	SE3342
Wilbarston *Nhants*	40	SP8188
Wilberfoss *Humb*	56	SE7350
Wilburton *Cambs*	41	TL4785
Wilby *Nhants*	30	SP8666
Wilby *Norfk*	32	TM0389
Wilby *Suffk*	33	TM2472
Wilcot *Wilts*	20	SU1360
Wilday Green *Derbys*	48	SK2274
Wildboarclough *Ches*	48	SJ9868
Wilden *Beds*	30	TL0955
Wilden *H & W*	38	SO8272
Wildmanbridge *Strath*	74	NS8253
Wildmoor *H & W*	38	SO9575
Wildsworth *Lincs*	50	SK8097
Wilkesley *Ches*	37	SJ6241
Wilkhaven *Highld*	97	NH9486
Wilkieston *Fife*	75	NT1268
Willand *Devon*	7	ST0310
Willaston *Ches*	46	SJ3377
Willaston *Ches*	47	SJ6752
Willcott *Shrops*	36	SJ3718
Willen *Bucks*	30	SP8741
Willenhall *W Mids*	38	SO9698
Willenhall *W Mids*	39	SP3676
Willerby *Humb*	56	TA0230
Willerby *N York*	63	TA0079
Willersey *Gloucs*	28	SP1039
Willersley *H & W*	27	SO3147
Willesborough *Kent*	15	TR0441
Willesborough Lees *Kent*	15	TR0342
Willesden *Gt Lon*	23	TQ2284
Willesley *Wilts*	20	ST8588
Willett *Somset*	8	ST1033
Willey *Shrops*	37	SO6799
Willey *Warwks*	39	SP4984
Willey Green *Surrey*	22	SU9351
Williamscot *Oxon*	29	SP4745
Willian *Herts*	31	TL2230
Willingale *Essex*	24	TL5907
Willingdon *E Susx*	13	TQ5902
Willingham *Cambs*	31	TL4070
Willingham *Lincs*	50	SK8784
Willingham Green *Cambs*	32	TL6254
Willington *Beds*	30	TL1150
Willington *Derbys*	39	SK2928
Willington *Dur*	61	NZ1935
Willington *Kent*	14	TQ7853
Willington *Warwks*	29	SP2638
Willington Corner *Ches*	46	SJ5366
Willington Quay *T & W*	69	NZ3167
Willitoft *Humb*	56	SE7434
Williton *Somset*	7	ST0740
Willoughby *Lincs*	51	TF4771
Willoughby *Warwks*	29	SP5167
Willoughby Waterleys *Leics*	39	SP5792
Willoughby-on-the-Wolds *Notts*	39	SK6325
Willoughton *Lincs*	50	SK9293
Willows Green *Essex*	24	TL7219
Willtown *Somset*	8	ST3924
Wilmcote *Warwks*	28	SP1658
Wilmington *Devon*	8	SY2199
Wilmington *E Susx*	13	TQ5404
Wilmington *Kent*	23	TQ5371
Wilmslow *Ches*	47	SJ8481
Wilnecote *Staffs*	39	SK2201
Wilsden *W York*	55	SE0936
Wilsford *Lincs*	50	TF0042
Wilsford *Wilts*	20	SU1057
Wilsford *Wilts*	10	SU1339
Wilshaw *W York*	55	SE1109
Wilsill *N York*	55	SE1864
Wilsley Green *Kent*	14	TQ7737
Wilson *Leics*	39	SK4024
Wilsontown *Strath*	75	NS9455
Wilstead *Beds*	30	TL0643
Wilsthorpe *Lincs*	40	TF0913
Wilstone *Herts*	30	SP9014
Wilton *Cleve*	62	NZ5819
Wilton *Cleve*	62	NZ5819
Wilton *Cumb*	58	NY0411
Wilton *H & W*	27	SO5824
Wilton *N York*	63	SE8582
Wilton *Wilts*	10	SU0931
Wilton *Wilts*	21	SU2661
Wilton Dean *Border*	67	NT4914
Wimbish *Essex*	24	TL5936
Wimbish Green *Essex*	24	TL6035
Wimbledon *Gt Lon*	23	TQ2370
Wimblington *Cambs*	41	TL4192
Wimborne Minster *Dorset*	9	SZ0199
Wimborne St. Giles *Dorset*	9	SU0212
Wimbotsham *Norfk*	41	TF6205
Wimpstone *Warwks*	29	SP2148
Wincanton *Somset*	9	ST7128
Winchburgh *Loth*	75	NT0974
Winchcombe *Gloucs*	28	SP0228
Winchelsea *E Susx*	14	TQ9017
Winchelsea Beach *E Susx*	14	TQ9115
Winchester *Hants*	10	SU4829
Winchet Hill *Kent*	14	TQ7340
Winchfield *Hants*	22	SU7654
Winchmore Hill *Bucks*	22	SU9395
Winchmore Hill *Gt Lon*	23	TQ3194
Wincle *Ches*	48	SJ9666
Wincobank *S York*	49	SK3891
Windermere *Cumb*	59	SD4198
Winderton *Warwks*	29	SP3240
Windhill *Highld*	92	NH5348
Windlesham *Surrey*	22	SU9264
Windmill *Cnwll*	3	SW8975
Windmill Hill *E Susx*	13	TQ6412
Windmill Hill *Somset*	8	ST3116
Windrush *Gloucs*	29	SP1913
Windsole *Gramp*	94	NJ5560
Windsor *Berks*	22	SU9576
Windsor Green *Suffk*	32	TL8954
Windsoredge *Gloucs*	20	ST8499
Windy Arbour *Warwks*	39	SP2971
Windygates *Fife*	83	NO3500
Wineham *W Susx*	12	TQ2320
Winestead *Humb*	57	TA2924
Winewall *Lancs*	54	SD9139
Winfarthing *Norfk*	33	TM1085
Winford *Avon*	19	ST5465
Winford *IOW*	11	SZ5684
Winford Terrace *Avon*	19	ST5568
Winforton *H & W*	27	SO2946
Winfrith Newburgh *Dorset*	9	SY8084
Wing *Bucks*	30	SP8822
Wing *Leics*	40	SK8903
Wingate *Dur*	62	NZ4037
Wingerworth *Derbys*	49	SK3867
Wingfield *Beds*	30	SP9926
Wingfield *Beds*	30	TL0026
Wingfield *Wilts*	20	ST8256
Wingham *Kent*	15	TR2457
Wingmore *Kent*	15	TR1846
Wingrave *Bucks*	30	SP8719
Winkburn *Notts*	49	SK7158
Winkfield *Berks*	22	SU9072
Winkfield Row *Berks*	22	SU8971
Winkhill *Staffs*	48	SK0651
Winkleigh *Devon*	7	SS6308
Winksley *N York*	55	SE2571
Winlaton *T & W*	69	NZ1762
Winless *Highld*	100	ND3054
Winllan *Powys*	36	SJ2222
Winmarleigh *Lancs*	53	SD4747
Winnall *Hants*	10	SU4929
Winnall Common *H & W*	27	SO4534
Winnersh *Berks*	22	SU7870
Winnington *Ches*	47	SJ6474
Winscombe *Avon*	19	ST4157
Winsford *Ches*	47	SJ6566
Winsford *Somset*	7	SS9034
Winsh-wen *W Glam*	18	SS6896
Winsham *Devon*	6	SS5038
Winsham *Somset*	8	ST3706
Winshill *Staffs*	39	SK2623
Winskill *Cumb*	67	NY5745
Winslade *Hants*	21	SU6548
Winsley *N York*	55	SE2461
Winsley *Wilts*	20	ST7960
Winslow *Bucks*	30	SP7627
Winson *Gloucs*	28	SP0908
Winster *Cumb*	59	SD4193
Winster *Derbys*	48	SK2460
Winston *Dur*	61	NZ1416
Winston *Suffk*	33	TM1861
Winstone *Gloucs*	28	SO9609
Winswell *Devon*	6	SS4913
Winterborne Came *Dorset*	9	SY7088
Winterborne Clenston *Dorset*	9	ST8302
Winterborne Herringston *Dorset*	9	SY6887
Winterborne Houghton *Dorset*	9	ST8104
Winterborne Kingston *Dorset*	9	SY8697
Winterborne Monkton *Dorset*	9	SY6787
Winterborne Stickland *Dorset*	9	ST8304
Winterborne Whitechurch *Dorset*	9	ST8300
Winterborne Zelston *Dorset*	9	SY8997
Winterbourne *Avon*	19	ST6580
Winterbourne *Berks*	21	SU4572
Winterbourne Abbas *Dorset*	9	SY6190
Winterbourne Bassett *Wilts*	20	SU0974
Winterbourne Dauntsey *Wilts*	10	SU1734
Winterbourne Earls *Wilts*	10	SU1633
Winterbourne Gunner *Wilts*	10	SU1735
Winterbourne Monkton *Wilts*	20	SU0971
Winterbourne Steepleton *Dorset*	9	SY6289
Winterbourne Stoke *Wilts*	20	SU0740
Winterburn *N York*	54	SD9358
Winteringham *Humb*	56	SE9222
Winterley *Ches*	47	SJ7457
Winterslow *Wilts*	10	SU2232
Winterton *Humb*	56	SE9218
Winterton-on-Sea *Norfk*	43	TG4919
Winthorpe *Notts*	50	SK8156
Winton *Cumb*	60	NY7810
Winton *Dorset*	10	SZ0894
Winton *E Susx*	13	TQ5103
Wintringham *N York*	63	SE8873
Winwick *Cambs*	40	TL1080
Winwick *Ches*	47	SJ6092
Winwick *Nhants*	39	SP6273
Wirksworth *Derbys*	49	SK2854
Wirswall *Ches*	47	SJ5444
Wisbech *Cambs*	41	TF4609
Wisbech St. Mary *Cambs*	41	TF4208
Wisborough Green *W Susx*	12	TQ0525
Wiseton *Notts*	49	SK7189
Wishanger *Gloucs*	28	SO9009
Wishaw *Strath*	74	NS7955
Wishaw *Warwks*	38	SP1794
Wisley *Surrey*	22	TQ0659
Wispington *Lincs*	51	TF2071
Wissett *Suffk*	33	TM3679
Wissington *Suffk*	25	TL9533
Wistanstow *Shrops*	36	SO4385
Wistanswick *Shrops*	37	SJ6629
Wisterfield *Ches*	47	SJ8271
Wiston *Dyfed*	16	SN0218
Wiston *Strath*	75	NS9532
Wiston *W Susx*	12	TQ1512
Wistow *Cambs*	41	TL2781
Wistow *N York*	56	SE5835
Wiswell *Lancs*	54	SD7437
Witcham *Cambs*	41	TL4680
Witchampton *Dorset*	9	ST9806
Witchford *Cambs*	31	TL5078
Witcombe *Somset*	8	ST4721
Withacott *Devon*	6	SS4315
Witham *Essex*	24	TL8214
Witham Friary *Somset*	20	ST7440
Witham on the Hill *Lincs*	40	TF0516
Withcall *Lincs*	51	TF2883
Withdean *E Susx*	12	TQ0007
Witherenden Hill *E Susx*	13	TQ6426
Witheridge *Devon*	7	SS8014
Witherley *Leics*	39	SP3297
Withern *Lincs*	51	TF4282
Withernsea *Humb*	57	TA3427
Withernwick *Humb*	57	TA1940
Withersdale Street *Suffk*	33	TM2681
Withersfield *Essex*	32	TL6448
Witherslack *Cumb*	59	SD4384
Witherslack Hall *Cumb*	59	SD4386
Withiel *Cnwll*	3	SW9965
Withiel Florey *Somset*	7	SS9832
Withies *H & W*	27	SO5642
Withington *Ches*	47	SJ8169
Withington *Gloucs*	28	SP0315
Withington *Gt Man*	47	SJ8593
Withington *H & W*	27	SO5543
Withington *H & W*	27	SO5643
Withington *Shrops*	37	SJ5713
Withington *Staffs*	38	SK0335
Withleigh *Devon*	7	SS9012
Withybed Green *H & W*	38	SP0172
Withybrook *Warwks*	39	SP4384
Withycombe *Somset*	7	ST0141
Withyham *E Susx*	13	TQ4935
Withypool *Devon*	7	SS8435
Witley *Surrey*	12	SU9439
Witnesham *Suffk*	33	TM1751
Witney *Oxon*	29	SP3509
Wittering *Cambs*	40	TF0502
Wittersham *Kent*	14	TQ8927
Witton *H & W*	28	SO8962
Witton *Norfk*	43	TG3009
Witton *Norfk*	43	TG3331
Witton Gilbert *Dur*	69	NZ2345
Witton Park *Dur*	61	NZ1730
Witton le Wear *Dur*	61	NZ1431
Wivelrod *Hants*	11	SU6738
Wivelsfield *E Susx*	12	TQ3420
Wivelsfield Green *E Susx*	12	TQ3520
Wivelsfield Station *W Susx*	12	TQ3220
Wivenhoe *Essex*	25	TM0322
Wiveton *Norfk*	42	TG0443
Wix *Essex*	25	TM1628
Wixford *Warwks*	28	SP0854
Wixhill *Shrops*	37	SJ5628
Wixoe *Essex*	32	TL7143
Woburn *Beds*	30	SP9433
Woburn Sands *Bucks*	30	SP9235
Woking *Surrey*	22	TQ0058
Wokingham *Berks*	22	SU8168
Wold Newton *Humb*	51	TF2496
Wold Newton *Humb*	63	TA0473
Woldingham *Surrey*	23	TQ3755
Wolf Hills *Nthumb*	68	NY7259
Wolf's Castle *Dyfed*	16	SM9526
Wolfclyde *Strath*	75	NT0236
Wolferton *Norfk*	42	TF6528
Wolfhill *Tays*	82	NO1533
Wolfsdale *Dyfed*	16	SM9321
Woll *Gramp*	94	NJ4622
Wollaston *Nhants*	30	SP9062
Wollaston *Shrops*	36	SJ3212
Wollaton *Notts*	49	SK5239
Wollerton *Shrops*	37	SJ6230
Wollescote *W Mids*	38	SO9283
Wolseley *Staffs*	38	SK0220
Wolston *Warwks*	39	SP4175
Wolvercote *Oxon*	29	SP5009
Wolverhampton *W Mids*	38	SO9198
Wolverley *H & W*	38	SO8279
Wolverton *Bucks*	30	SP8141
Wolverton *Hants*	21	SU5558
Wolverton *Wilts*	9	ST7831
Wolverton Common *Hants*	21	SU5659
Wolvesnewton *Gwent*	19	ST4599
Wolvey *Warwks*	39	SP4387
Wolvey Heath *Warwks*	39	SP4388
Wolviston *Cleve*	62	NZ4525
Wombleton *N York*	62	SE6683
Wombourne *Staffs*	38	SO8793
Wombwell *S York*	49	SE3902
Womenswold *Kent*	15	TR2250
Womersley *N York*	56	SE5319
Wonersh *Surrey*	12	TQ0145
Wonford *Devon*	5	SX9391
Wonston *Hants*	10	SU4739
Wooburn Green *Bucks*	22	SU9188
Wood Bevington *Warwks*	28	SP0554
Wood Dalling *Norfk*	43	TG0927
Wood Eaton *Staffs*	38	SJ8417
Wood End *Beds*	30	TL0046
Wood End *Gt Lon*	22	TQ1385
Wood End *Herts*	31	TL3225
Wood End *W Mids*	38	SJ9401
Wood End *Warwks*	38	SP1171
Wood Enderby *Lincs*	51	TF2764
Wood Green *Gt Lon*	23	TQ3090
Wood Hayes *W Mids*	38	SJ9401
Wood Norton *Norfk*	42	TG0127
Wood Row *W York*	55	SE3826
Wood Street *Norfk*	43	TG3722
Wood Street *Surrey*	12	SU9551
Wood Top *Lancs*	53	SD5644
Wood Walton *Cambs*	41	TL2180
Wood's Corner *E Susx*	14	TQ6619
Wood's Green *E Susx*	13	TQ6333
Woodacott Cross *Devon*	6	SS3807
Woodall *S York*	49	SK4880
Woodbastwick *Norfk*	43	TG3315
Woodborough *Notts*	49	SK6347
Woodbridge *Devon*	6	SX1895
Woodbridge *Suffk*	33	TM2749
Woodbury *Devon*	3	SX0087
Woodbury *Devon*	5	SY0087
Woodbury Salterton *Devon*	5	SY0189
Woodchester *Gloucs*	20	SO8302
Woodchurch *Kent*	14	TQ9434
Woodcombe *Somset*	7	SS9546
Woodcote *Oxon*	21	SU6482
Woodcote *Shrops*	37	SJ7715
Woodcroft *Gloucs*	19	ST5495
Woodditton *Cambs*	32	TL6559
Woodeaton *Oxon*	29	SP5312
Woodend *Cumb*	58	SD1696
Woodend *Highld*	79	NM7861
Woodend *Loth*	75	NS9269
Woodend *Nhants*	29	SP6149
Woodend *W Susx*	11	SU8108
Woodend Green *Essex*	24	TL5528
Woodford *Gloucs*	20	ST6996
Woodford *Gt Lon*	23	TQ4092
Woodford *Gt Man*	47	SJ8882
Woodford *Nhants*	30	SP9676
Woodford Bridge *Gt Lon*	23	TQ4291
Woodford Halse *Nhants*	29	SP5452
Woodford Wells *Gt Lon*	23	TQ4093
Woodgate *Devon*	8	ST1015
Woodgate *H & W*	28	SO9666
Woodgate *Norfk*	42	TG0216
Woodgate *W Susx*	11	SU9304
Woodgreen *Hants*	10	SU1717
Woodgreen *Oxon*	29	SP3610
Woodhall *N York*	61	SD9790
Woodhall Hill *W York*	55	SE1935
Woodhall Spa *Lincs*	50	TF1962
Woodham *Bucks*	30	SP7018
Woodham *Lincs*	51	TF2367
Woodham Ferrers *Essex*	24	TQ7999
Woodham Mortimer *Essex*	24	TL8104
Woodham Walter *Essex*	24	TL8107
Woodhaven *Fife*	83	NO4126
Woodhead *Gramp*	95	NJ7938
Woodhill *Shrops*	37	SO7384
Woodhill *Somset*	8	ST3527

Woodhorn Zouch

Woodhorn *Nthumb* 69 NZ2988
Woodhouse *Leics* 39 SK5315
Woodhouse *S York* 49 SK4284
Woodhouse *W York* 55 SE2932
Woodhouse *W York* 55 SE3821
Woodhouse Eaves *Leics* 39 SK5214
Woodhouselee *Fife* 75 NT2364
Woodhouses *Staffs* 38 SK0809
Woodhouses *Staffs* 38 SK1519
Woodhurst *Cambs* 31 TL3176
Woodingdean *E Susx* 12 TQ3505
Woodkirk *W York* 55 SE2725
Woodland *Devon* 5 SX6250
Woodland *Devon* 5 SX7968
Woodland *Dur* 61 NZ0726
Woodland *Gramp* 95 NJ8723
Woodland *Kent* 15 TR1441
Woodland *Strath* 64 NX1795
Woodland Street *Somset* 19 ST5437
Woodlands *Dorset* 10 SU0508
Woodlands *Gramp* 89 NO7895
Woodlands *Hants* 10 SU3211
Woodlands *N York* 55 SE3255
Woodlands *S York* 56 SE5308
Woodlands Park *Berks* 22 SU8678
Woodlands St. Mary *Berks* 21 SU3375
Woodlands St. Mary *Berks* 21 SU3375
Woodleigh *Devon* 5 SX7348
Woodley *Berks* 22 SU7773
Woodley *Gt Man* 48 SJ9492
Woodlords *Strath* 75 NT0056
Woodmancote *Gloucs* 28 SO9727
Woodmancote *Gloucs* 28 SP0008
Woodmancote *Gloucs* 20 ST7697
Woodmancote *W Susx* 11 SU7707
Woodmancott *Hants* 21 SU5642
Woodmansey *Humb* 57 TA0538
Woodmansgreen *W Susx* 11 SU8627
Woodmansterne *Surrey* 23 TQ2759
Woodmanton *Devon* 3 SX0185
Woodmill *Staffs* 38 SK1321
Woodminton *Wilts* 9 SU0122
Woodnesborough *Kent* 15 TR3157
Woodnewton *Nhants* 40 TL0394
Woodplumpton *Lancs* 53 SD5034
Woodrising *Norfk* 42 TF9803
Woodrow *H & W* 38 SO8875
Woodseaves *Staffs* 37 SJ7925
Woodsend *Wilts* 21 SU2275
Woodsetts *S York* 49 SK5483
Woodsford *Dorset* 9 SY7690
Woodside *Berks* 22 SU9371
Woodside *D & G* 66 NY0475
Woodside *Dyfed* 16 SN1406
Woodside *Fife* 83 NO4207
Woodside *Gt Lon* 23 TQ3467
Woodside *Tays* 82 NO2037
Woodstock *Oxon* 29 SP4416
Woodston *Cambs* 40 TL1897
Woodton *Norfk* 43 TM2994
Woodtown *Devon* 6 SS4123
Woodtown *Devon* 6 SS4926
Woodvale *Mersyd* 53 SD3011
Woodville *Derbys* 39 SK3119
Woofferton *Shrops* 27 SO5268
Wookey *Somset* 19 ST5145
Wool *Dorset* 9 SY8486
Woolacombe *Devon* 6 SS4643
Woolage Green *Kent* 15 TR2349
Woolage Village *Kent* 12 TQ2250
Woolaston Common *Gloucs* 19 SO5801
Woolavington *Somset* 19 ST3441
Woolbeding *W Susx* 11 SU8722
Woolbrook *Devon* 4 SX1289
Woolcotts *Somset* 7 SS9731
Wooler *Nthumb* 77 NT9928
Wooley Bridge *Derbys* 48 SK0195
Woolfardisworthy *Devon* 6 SS3321
Woolfardisworthy *Devon* 7 SS8208
Woolfold *Gt Man* 54 SD7812
Woolhampton *Berks* 21 SU5766
Woolhope *H & W* 27 SO6135
Woolland *Dorset* 9 ST7707
Woollaton *Devon* 6 SS4712
Woolley *Avon* 20 ST7468
Woolley *Cambs* 30 TL1474
Woolley *Cnwll* 3 SX2516
Woolley *W York* 55 SE3113
Woolmer Green *Herts* 31 TL2518
Woolmere Green *H & W* 28 SO9663
Woolmerston *Somset* 8 ST2533
Woolminstone *Somset* 8 ST4008
Woolpack Inn *Cumb* 58 NY1901
Woolpit *Suffk* 32 TL9762
Woolscott *Warwks* 29 SP4968
Woolsgrove *Devon* 7 SS7902
Woolstaston *Shrops* 36 SO4598
Woolsthorpe *Lincs* 40 SK8333
Woolsthorpe *Lincs* 40 SK9224
Woolston *Hants* 10 SU4410
Woolston *Shrops* 36 SO4287
Woolston *Shrops* 36 SJ3224
Woolston *Somset* 18 ST1139
Woolston *Somset* 9 ST6528
Woolston Green *Devon* 5 SX7765
Woolstone *Bucks* 30 SP8738
Woolstone *Gloucs* 28 SO9530
Woolstone *Oxon* 21 SU2987
Woolton *Mersyd* 46 SJ4286
Woolton Hill *Hants* 21 SU4261
Woolvers Hill *Avon* 19 ST3860
Woolverstone *Suffk* 25 TM1838
Woolverton *Somset* 20 ST7853
Woolwich *Gt Lon* 23 TQ4478
Woonton *H & W* 27 SO3552
Woonton *H & W* 27 SO5562
Woore *Shrops* 37 SJ7342
Wootten Green *Suffk* 33 TM2373
Wootton *H & W* 27 SO3252
Wootton *Humb* 57 TA0815
Wootton *IOW* 11 SZ5492
Wootton *Kent* 15 TR2246
Wootton *Nhants* 30 SP7656
Wootton *Oxon* 29 SP4319
Wootton *Staffs* 48 SK1045
Wootton Bassett *Wilts* 20 SU0782
Wootton Bridge *IOW* 11 SZ5492
Wootton Courtenay *Somset* 7 SS9343
Wootton Fitzpaine *Dorset* 8 SY3695
Wootton Rivers *Wilts* 21 SU1963
Wootton St. Lawrence *Hants* 21 SU5953
Wootton Wawen *Warwks* 28 SP1563
Worcester *H & W* 28 SO8555
Worcester Park *Gt Lon* 23 TQ2165
Wordsley *W Mids* 38 SO8987
Worfield *Shrops* 37 SO7596
Workington *Cumb* 58 NX9928
Worksop *Notts* 49 SK5879
Worlaby *Humb* 56 TA0113
World's End *Berks* 21 SU4876
Worlds End *W Susx* 12 TQ3220
Worle *Avon* 19 ST3563
Worleston *Ches* 47 SJ6556
Worlingham *Suffk* 33 TM4489
Worlington *Devon* 7 SS7713
Worlington *Suffk* 32 TL6973
Worlingworth *Suffk* 33 TM2368
Wormald Green *N York* 55 SE3065
Wormbridge *H & W* 27 SO4230
Wormegay *Norfk* 42 TF6611
Wormelow Tump *H & W* 27 SO4930
Wormhill *Derbys* 48 SK1274
Wormingford *Essex* 25 TL9332
Worminghall *Bucks* 29 SP6308
Wormington *Gloucs* 28 SP0336
Worminster *Somset* 19 ST5742
Wormiston *Border* 75 NT2345
Wormit *Fife* 83 NO3926
Wormleighton *Warwks* 29 SP4453
Wormley *Herts* 23 TL3605
Wormley *Surrey* 12 SU9438
Wormshill *Kent* 14 TQ8857
Wormsley *H & W* 27 SO4247
Worplesdon *Surrey* 12 SU9753
Worrall *S York* 49 SK3092
Worsbrough *S York* 55 SE3503
Worsbrough Bridge *S York* 55 SE3403
Worsbrough Dale *S York* 49 SE3402
Worsley *Gt Man* 47 SD7500
Worstead *Norfk* 43 TG3026
Worsthorne *Lancs* 54 SD8732
Worston *Devon* 5 SX5952
Worston *Lancs* 54 SD7742
Worth *Kent* 15 TR3356
Worth *Somset* 19 ST5145
Worth *W Susx* 12 TQ3036
Worth Abbey *Surrey* 12 TQ3134
Worth Matravers *Dorset* 9 SY9777
Wortham *Suffk* 32 TM0877
Worthen *Shrops* 36 SJ3204
Worthenbury *Clwyd* 46 SJ4246
Worthing *Norfk* 42 TF9919
Worthing *W Susx* 12 TQ1402
Worthington *Leics* 39 SK4020
Wortley *W York* 55 SE2732
Worton *N York* 61 SD9589
Worton *Wilts* 20 ST9757
Wortwell *Norfk* 33 TM2784
Wotter *Devon* 4 SX5562
Wotton *Surrey* 12 TQ1247
Wotton Under Edge *Gloucs* 20 ST7593
Wotton Underwood *Bucks* 30 SP6816
Woughton on the Green *Bucks* 30 SP8737
Wouldham *Kent* 14 TQ7164
Woundale *Shrops* 37 SO7793
Wrabness *Essex* 25 TM1731
Wrafton *Devon* 6 SS4935
Wragby *Lincs* 50 TF1378
Wrangaton *Devon* 5 SX6757
Wrangbrook *W York* 55 SE4013
Wrangle *Lincs* 51 TF4250
Wrangway *Somset* 8 ST1217
Wrantage *Somset* 8 ST3022
Wrawby *Humb* 56 TA0108
Wraxall *Avon* 19 ST4871
Wraxall *Somset* 19 ST6036
Wray *Lancs* 54 SD6067
Wray Castle *Cumb* 59 NY3730
Wraysbury *Berks* 22 TQ0074
Wrayton *Lancs* 54 SD6172
Wrea Green *Lancs* 53 SD3931
Wreaks End *Cumb* 67 NY2186
Wreay *Cumb* 59 NY4424
Wreay *Cumb* 67 NY4348
Wrecclesham *Surrey* 22 SU8245
Wrekenton *T & W* 69 NZ2758
Wrelton *N York* 63 SE7686
Wrenbury *Ches* 47 SJ5947
Wreningham *Norfk* 43 TM1699
Wrentham *Suffk* 33 TM4982
Wrentnall *Shrops* 36 SJ4203
Wressing *Devon* 7 ST0508
Wressle *Humb* 56 SE7031
Wressle *Humb* 56 SE9709
Wrestlingworth *Beds* 31 TL2547
Wretton *Norfk* 42 TF6900
Wrexham *Clwyd* 46 SJ3350
Wribbenhall *H & W* 37 SO7975
Wright's Green *Essex* 31 TL5017
Wrinehill *Staffs* 47 SJ7547
Wrington *Avon* 19 ST4762
Writhlington *Somset* 20 ST7054
Wrockwardine *Shrops* 37 SJ6212
Wroot *Humb* 56 SE7103
Wrose *W York* 55 SE1636
Wrotham *Kent* 14 TQ6159
Wrottesley *Staffs* 38 SJ8201
Wroughton *Wilts* 20 SU1480
Wroxall *IOW* 11 SZ5579
Wroxall *Warwks* 39 SP2271
Wroxeter *Shrops* 37 SJ5608
Wroxham *Norfk* 43 TG3017
Wroxton *Oxon* 29 SP4141
Wyaston *Derbys* 48 SK1842
Wyatt's Green *Essex* 24 TQ5999
Wyberton *Lincs* 51 TF3240
Wyboston *Beds* 31 TL1656
Wybunbury *Ches* 47 SJ6949
Wych *Dorset* 8 SY4791
Wychbold *H & W* 28 SO9266
Wychnor *Staffs* 38 SK1716
Wyck *Hants* 11 SU7539
Wycliffe *Dur* 61 NZ1114
Wycoller *Lancs* 54 SD9339
Wycomb *Leics* 40 SK7724
Wycombe Marsh *Bucks* 22 SU8892
Wyddial *Herts* 31 TL3731
Wye *Kent* 15 TR0546
Wyesham *Gwent* 27 SO5111
Wyke *Devon* 6 SX2996
Wyke *Dorset* 9 ST7926
Wyke *Surrey* 22 SU9251
Wyke *W York* 55 SE1526
Wyke Champflower *Somset* 9 ST6634
Wyke Regis *Dorset* 9 SY6677
Wyke The *Shrops* 37 SJ7306
Wykeham *N York* 63 SE9683
Wyken *Shrops* 37 SO7695
Wyken *W Mids* 39 SP3680
Wykey *Shrops* 36 SJ3925
Wylam *Nthumb* 69 NZ1164
Wylde Green *W Mids* 38 SP1294
Wyllie *Gwent* 19 ST1794
Wylye *Wilts* 20 SU0037
Wymeswold *Leics* 39 SK6023
Wymington *Beds* 30 SP9564
Wymondham *Leics* 40 SK8518
Wymondham *Norfk* 43 TG1101
Wyndham *M Glam* 18 SS9392
Wynford Eagle *Dorset* 9 SY5895
Wyre Piddle *H & W* 28 SO9647
Wysall *Notts* 39 SK6027
Wyson *H & W* 27 SO5267
Wythall *H & W* 38 SP0774
Wytham *Oxon* 29 SP4708
Wythenshawe *Gt Man* 47 SJ8386
Wyton *Cambs* 31 TL2772
Wyton *Humb* 57 TA1733
Wyverstone *Suffk* 32 TM0468
Wyverstone Street *Suffk* 32 TM0367
Wyvis Lodge *Highld* 96 NH4873

Y

Y-Rhiw *Gwynd* 44 SH2227
Y-Ffrith *Clwyd* 45 SJ0483
Yaddlethorpe *Humb* 56 SE8806
Yafforth *N York* 62 SE3494
Yalberton *Devon* 5 SX8658
Yalding *Kent* 14 TQ7050
Yalverton *Devon* 4 SX5267
Yanworth *Gloucs* 28 SP0713
Yapham *Humb* 56 SE7851
Yapton *W Susx* 12 SU9703
Yarborough *Avon* 19 ST3858
Yarburgh *Lincs* 51 TF3493
Yarcombe *Devon* 8 ST2408
Yard *Devon* 7 SS7721
Yarde *Somset* 7 ST0538
Yardley *W Mids* 38 SP1386
Yardley Gobion *Nhants* 30 SP7644
Yardley Hastings *Nhants* 30 SP8656
Yardley Wood *W Mids* 38 SP1080
Yarkhill *H & W* 27 SO6042
Yarlet *Staffs* 38 SJ9129
Yarley *Somset* 19 ST5045
Yarlington *Somset* 9 ST6529
Yarm *Cleve* 62 NZ4111
Yarmouth *IOW* 10 SZ3589
Yarnbrook *Wilts* 20 ST8654
Yarnfield *Staffs* 38 SJ8632
Yarnscombe *Devon* 6 SS5523
Yarnton *Oxon* 29 SP4712
Yarpole *H & W* 27 SO4664
Yarrow *Border* 75 NT3528
Yarrow *Somset* 19 ST3747
Yarrowford *Border* 76 NT4030
Yarwell *Nhants* 40 TL0797
Yate *Avon* 20 ST7082
Yateley *Hants* 22 SU8260
Yatesbury *Wilts* 20 SU0671
Yattendon *Berks* 21 SU5574
Yatton *Avon* 19 ST4365
Yatton *H & W* 27 SO6330
Yatton *H & W* 27 SO4367
Yatton Keynell *Wilts* 20 ST8676
Yaverland *IOW* 11 SZ6185
Yaxham *Norfk* 42 TG0010
Yaxley *Cambs* 40 TL1892
Yaxley *Suffk* 33 TM1274
Yazor *H & W* 27 SO4046
Yeading *Gt Lon* 22 TQ1182
Yeadon *W York* 55 SE2040
Yealand Conyers *Lancs* 59 SD5074
Yealand Redmayne *Lancs* 59 SD4975
Yealand Stores *Lancs* 59 SD5075
Yealmpton *Devon* 4 SX5751
Yearby *Cleve* 62 NZ5921
Yearngill *Cumb* 67 NY1343
Yearsley *N York* 62 SE5874
Yeaton *Shrops* 36 SJ4319
Yeaveley *Derbys* 48 SK1840
Yedingham *N York* 63 SE8979
Yelford *Oxon* 29 SP3504
Yelland *Devon* 6 SS4932
Yelling *Cambs* 31 TL2662
Yelvertoft *Nhants* 39 SP5975
Yelvertoft *Nhants* 39 SP6075
Yelverton *Norfk* 43 TG2902
Yenston *Somset* 9 ST7120
Yeoford *Devon* 7 SX7898
Yeolmbridge *Cnwll* 4 SX3187
Yeovil *Somset* 8 ST5515
Yeovil Marsh *Somset* 8 ST5418
Yeovilton *Somset* 8 ST5422
Yesnaby *Ork* 103 HY2215
Yetminster *Dorset* 9 ST5910
Yettington *Devon* 5 SY0585
Yetts O'Muckhart *Cent* 82 NO0001
Yew Green *Warwks* 29 SP2367
Yews Green *W York* 55 SE1030
Yielden *Beds* 30 TL0167
Yieldshields *Strath* 74 NS8750
Yiewsley *Gt Lon* 22 TQ0680
Ynysboeth *M Glam* 18 ST0695
Ynysddu *Gwent* 19 ST1792
Ynyshir *M Glam* 18 ST0292
Ynyslas *Dyfed* 35 SN6293
Ynyswen *M Glam* 18 SS9597
Ynysybwl *M Glam* 18 ST0594
Yockleton *Shrops* 36 SJ3910
Yokefleet *Humb* 56 SE8124
Yoker *Strath* 74 NS5169
Yonder Bognie *Gramp* 94 NJ6046
Yondertown *Devon* 5 SX5958
York *N York* 56 SE6052
York Town *Hants* 22 SU8660
Yorkletts *Kent* 15 TR0963
Yorkley *Gloucs* 27 SO6307
Youlgreave *Derbys* 48 SK2164
Youlthorpe *Humb* 56 SE7655
Youlton *N York* 55 SE4963
Young's End *Essex* 24 TL7419
Youngsbury *Herts* 31 TL3618
Yoxall *Staffs* 38 SK1418
Yoxford *Suffk* 33 TM3968
Ysbyty Ifan *Gwynd* 45 SH8448
Ysbyty Ystwyth *Dyfed* 35 SN7371
Ysceifiog *Clwyd* 46 SJ1571
Ystalyfera *W Glam* 26 SN7708
Ystrad *M Glam* 18 SS9895
Ystrad Aeron *Dyfed* 34 SN5256
Ystrad Meurig *Dyfed* 35 SN7067
Ystrad Mynach *M Glam* 18 ST1494
Ystradfellte *Powys* 26 SN9313
Ystradgynlais *Powys* 26 SN7910
Ystradowen *Dyfed* 26 SN7512
Ystradowen *S Glam* 18 ST0177
Ythsie *Gramp* 95 NJ8830

Z

Zeal Monachorum *Devon* 7 SS7104
Zeals *Wilts* 9 ST7731
Zelah *Cnwll* 2 SW8151
Zennor *Cnwll* 2 SW4538
Zouch *Notts* 39 SK5023

Local radio

EXPLANATION
The first number (1) in red or blue corresponds to the location number on the map of the radio station.
This is followed by name of radio station (RADIO SCOTLAND) in bold capital letters. This, in turn, is followed by FM MHz frequencies (92.5–94.7) then MW KHz/metres frequencies (810/370).
The same order of information is used for all other transmitters.

SCOTLAND
BBC
1 RADIO SCOTLAND 92·5–94·7 810/370. North-west Scotland 97·7–99·3 810/370

IBA
2 MORAY FIRTH RADIO Inverness 97·4 1107/271
3 NORTHSOUND RADIO Aberdeen 96·9 1035/290
4 RADIO CLYDE Glasgow 102·5 1152/261
5 RADIO FORTH Edinburgh 97·3 1548/194
6 RADIO TAY Dundee, Perth 102·8 1161/258
7 WEST SOUND Ayr 96·7 1035/290. Girvan 97·5 1035/290

THE NORTH
BBC
8 GREATER MANCHESTER RADIO 95·1 1458/206
9 RADIO CLEVELAND 95·0 1548/194. Whitby 95·8 1548/194
10 RADIO CUMBRIA North Cumbria 95·6 756/397. Whitehaven 95·6 1458/206
11 RADIO FURNESS South Cumbria 96·1 837/358. Kendal 95·2 837/358. Windermere 104·2 837/358
12 RADIO HUMBERSIDE 95·9 1485/202
13 RADIO LANCASHIRE 95·5 855/351. Lancaster 104·5 1557/193. South Lancashire 103·9 855/351
14 RADIO LEEDS 92·4 774/388. Ilkley, Otley 95·3 774/388
15 RADIO MERSEYSIDE 95·8 1485/202
16 RADIO NEWCASTLE 95·4 1458/206. N.E. Northumberland 96·0 1458/206. Newcastle & Gateshead 104·4 1458/206
17 RADIO SHEFFIELD 104·1 1035/290. Sheffield 88·6 1035/290
18 RADIO YORK 103·7 666/450. Scarborough 95·5 1260/238. Central N. Yorks 104·3 666/450

IBA
19 METRO RADIO Tyne & Wear 97·1 1152/261
20 PENNINE RADIO Bradford 97·5 1278/235. Huddersfield/ Halifax 102·5 1530/196
21 PICCADILLY RADIO Manchester 103·0 1152/261
22 RADIO AIRE Leeds 96·3 828/362
23 RADIO CITY Liverpool 96·7 1548/194
24 RADIO HALLAM Sheffield 97·4 1548/194. Rotherham 96·1 1548/194. Doncaster 103·4 990/303. Barnsley 102·9 1305/230
25 RED ROSE RADIO Blackpool & Preston 97·4 999/301

26 TFM RADIO Stockton-on-Tees 96·6 1170/257
27 VIKING RADIO Humberside 96·9 1161/258

WALES
BBC
28 RADIO WALES 882/340. Llandrindod Wells/Builth Wells area 1125/267. Radio Cymru (Welsh Language Service) 92·5–94·5 South Wales 96·8

IBA
29 MARCHER SOUND Wrexham & Deeside 103·4 1260/238
30 RED DRAGON RADIO Cardiff 103·2 1359/221. Newport 97·4 1305/230
31 SWANSEA SOUND 96·4 1170/257

THE MIDLANDS
BBC
32 RADIO CAMBRIDGESHIRE 96·0 1026/292. Peterborough & N. Cambs 95·7 1449/207
33 RADIO DERBY 104·5 1116/269. Derby 94·2 1116/269. Bakewell & Matlock 95·3
34 RADIO HEREFORD & WORCESTER Hereford 94·7 819/336. Worcester 104·0 738/407
35 RADIO LEICESTER 95·1 837/358
36 RADIO LINCOLNSHIRE 94·9 1368/219
37 RADIO NORFOLK East Norfolk 95·1 855/351. West Norfolk 104·4 873/344
38 RADIO NORTHAMPTON 104·2 1107/271. Corby 103·6 1107/271
39 RADIO NOTTINGHAM 103·8 1521/197. Central Notts. 95·5 1584/189
40 RADIO SHROPSHIRE 96·0 1584/189. Ludlow 95·0 1584/189
41 RADIO STOKE-ON-TRENT 94·6 1503/200
42 RADIO W.M. (WEST MIDLANDS) 95·6 1458/206. Wolverhampton 95·6 828/362

IBA
43 BEACON RADIO Wolverhampton 97·2 990/303. Shrewsbury & Telford 103·1 990/303
44 BRMB RADIO Birmingham 96·4 1152/261
45 HEREWARD RADIO Peterborough 102·7 1332/225
46 LEICESTER SOUND 103·2 1260/238
47 MERCIA SOUND Coventry 97·0 1359/220
48 RADIO BROADLAND Gt Yarmouth & Norwich 102·4 1152/260
49 RADIO ORWELL Ipswich 97·1 1170/257
50 RADIO TRENT Nottingham 96·2 999/301. Derby 102·8 945/317
51 RADIO WYVERN Hereford 97·6 954/314. Worcester 102·8 1530/196
52 SAXON RADIO Bury St Edmunds 96·4 1251/240
53 SIGNAL RADIO Stoke-on-Trent 102·6 1170/257

THE SOUTH WEST
BBC
54 BBC WILTSHIRE SOUND Swindon 103·6 1368/219. Salisbury 103·5 North Wilts 104·3 1332
55 RADIO BRISTOL 95·5 1548/194. Bristol 94·9 1548/194. Bath 104·6 1548/194. Central Somerset 95·5 1323/227
56 RADIO CORNWALL East Cornwall 95·2 657/457. West Cornwall 103·9 630/476. Isles of Scilly 96·0 630/476
57 RADIO DEVON Exeter & Devon 95·8 990/303. Torbay 103·4 1458/206. Plymouth 103·4 855/351. Barnstaple 94·8 801/375. North Devon 103·4 801/375. Okehamptom 96·0 801/375
58 RADIO GLOUCESTER 104·7 603/498. Stroud 95·0

IBA
59 DEVONAIR RADIO Exeter 97·0 666/450. Torbay 96·4 954/314
60 GREAT WEST RADIO Bath 103·0 Bristol 96·3 1260/238. Marlborough 96·5 Swindon 97·2 1161/258. West Wilts 102·2 936/321
61 PLYMOUTH SOUND Plymouth 97·0 1152/261. Tavistock 96·6
62 SEVERN SOUND Cheltenham & Gloucester 102·4 774/388. Stroud 103·0
63 2CR (TWO COUNTIES RADIO) Bournemouth 97·2 828/362

THE SOUTH EAST
BBC
64 BBC RADIO ESSEX 103·5 765/392. N. E. Essex 103·5 729/412. S.E. Essex 95·3 1530/196
65 GREATER LONDON RADIO 94·9 1458/206
66 RADIO BEDFORDSHIRE 95·5 630/476. Bedford 95·5 1161/258. Luton & Dunstable 103·8 630/476
67 RADIO KENT 96·7 1035/290. Tunbridge Wells 96·7 1602/187. East Kent 104·2 774/388
68 RADIO OXFORD 95·2 1485/202
69 RADIO SOLENT 96·1 999/300. Bournemouth 96·1 1359/221
70 RADIO SUSSEX Brighton & Worthing 95·3 1485/202. East Sussex & part of West Sussex 104·5 1161/258. Reigate, Crawley & Horsham 104·0 1368/219. Newhaven FM Frequency to be announced

IBA
71 CAPITAL RADIO London 95·8 1548/194
72 CHILTERN RADIO Bedford 96·9 792/378. Luton 97·6 828/362. Northampton 96·6 1557/193
73 COUNTY SOUND Guildford 96·4 1476/203
74 ESSEX RADIO Chelmsford 102·6 1359/220. Southend 96·3 1431/210
75 INVICTA RADIO Maidstone/ Medway 103·1 1242/242. Dover 97·0 603/497. Thanet 95·9 603/497. Canterbury 102·8 603/497. Ashford 96·1 603/497
76 LBC London 97·3 1152/261
77 OCEAN SOUND Southampton 103·2 1557/193. Portsmouth 97·5 1170/257
78 RADIO MERCURY Crawley/ Reigate 102·7 1521/197. Horsham 97·5
79 RADIO 210 Thames Valley, Reading & N. Hants 97·0 1431/210. Basingstoke, Andover 102·9 1431/210. Winchester 96·7
80 SOUTHERN SOUND Brighton 103·5 1323/227